Perspectives of Jesus
in the Writings of Paul

Perspectives of Jesus in the Writings of Paul

A Historical Examination of Shared Core Commitments with a View to Determining the Extent of Paul's Dependence on Jesus

Gerry Schoberg

James Clarke & Co

James Clarke & Co
P.O. Box 60
Cambridge
CB1 2NT

www.jamesclarke.co
publishing@jamesclarke.co

ISBN: 978 0 227 17405 0

British Library Cataloguing in Publication Data
A record is available from the British Library

First published by James Clarke & Co, 2014

Published by arrangement
with Pickwick Publications

Revised Standard Version of the Bible, Apocrypha, copyright 1957; The
Third and Fourth Books of the Maccabees and Psalm 151, copyright 1977
by the Division of Christian Education of the National Council of the
Churches of Christ in the United States of America.
Used by permission. All rights reserved.

Contents

Preface

It has been said that there are two kinds of people in the world: those who divide the world into two kinds of people, and those who don't! Underlying this study is the question of whether there are two kinds of Christians in the world—those who follow Jesus, and those who follow Paul—or whether in fact there ought to be just one, and what that one might look like if Paul were to be understood as a promoter of the movement founded by Jesus.

The importance of this question was impressed upon me in the early 2000s when I was involved in the discussions and debates in the Diocese of New Westminster as to whether to approve of a rite for the blessing of same-sex couples. The issue was complicated, with a number of agendas being pursued. But to some extent it seemed to me that there were genuine believers on both sides, with one group fully convinced that they were following the authoritative example of their Lord, and with the other group fully convinced that they were following the authoritative teaching of the Apostle Paul; and the result was the two could not agree. Clearly it raised the question whether one or the other was wrong. But beyond that, it also raised the question whether Jesus and Paul themselves would have been on the same page, so to speak. Does the New Testament give us a unified vision of the Christian movement, or are there (at least) two major strands to it—strands which may not always be reconcilable?

In addition to this particular experience, it has long seemed to me a useful exercise to try to trace the lines of development from the early days of the life of Jesus, when his followers remembered and re-told the things he said and did, to the many more theologically reflective statements made by those same followers, and by people like Paul, about the significance of Jesus, speaking of him as "Lord" and "Son of God," and affirming that his death was "for our sins." How did the followers of Jesus draw such insightful conclusions about him? We are, unfortunately, hampered by having a very incomplete account of the early church, making such inquiry difficult. And yet, I consider the effort worthwhile because I find myself ever confronted with the same kind of question: How am I to make theological sense of the many details I experience from day to day? If we could show that Jesus and Paul were on the same page, then perhaps we might gain some insight as to how to go about answering this question.

The issues I mention above will not reappear in the pages that follow. The critical question of the relationship between Jesus and Paul has been well established in New Testament studies now for over 150 years and it needs to be addressed with all the tools of historical criticism that scholarship has developed. But it may be helpful for the reader to recognize from the beginning some of the issues that such a study as this could have a bearing on.

Acknowledgments

While the work of scholarship is largely a solitary endeavor, scholars typically owe much to those who have gone before and who have challenged and supported them. This is certainly true of myself.

The present work is a slightly revised doctoral dissertation that I submitted to the University of Bristol, and I owe many thanks to my supervisor, Prof. John Nolland, for his insightful critiques and helpful suggestions at many points along the way. His clarity in relation to the issues and breadth of knowledge have proven to be invaluable resources. I also acknowledge the helpful contributions of my examiners, Profs. David Wenham and Markus Bockmuehl, whose perceptive questions have helped to sharpen the argument.

I give thanks to the staff and students at Trinity College, Bristol, who have assisted me in various ways. Special thanks must go to Su Brown for her professional and gracious service in the library. I also note with appreciation the suggestions made by fellow students in the post-graduate seminar.

I am happy to acknowledge the assistance given by Katja Benyon, Riad Klassen, and Ann Zlindra in helping with translation issues, and by Cindy Aalders in proof-reading the text.

I owe a great deal to those who have supported and encouraged me emotionally and spiritually in what has proven to be an enjoyable but challenging project. I think particularly of the many friends at St. Aldhelm's Church in Bedminster, Bristol, and especially of my wife, Merry Carol, who has been a constant companion along this road.

Abbreviations

I have followed the recommendations of the Society of Biblical Literature for all abbreviations.[1] Abbreviations I have used that are not included in the *SBL Handbook of Style* are the following:

AYB	Anchor Yale Bible
BAFCS	The Book of Acts in Its First Century Setting
BNP	Brill's New Pauly: Encyclopedia of the Ancient World
BRS	Biblical Resource Series
BSL	Biblical Studies Library
CTHP	Cambridge Texts in the History of Philosophy
DSSR	The Dead Sea Scrolls Reader
EDSS	Encyclopedia of the Dead Sea Scrolls
FSC	Faith and Scholarship Colloquies
GAP	Guides to Apocrypha and Pseudepigrapha
HeyM	Heythrop Monographs
LBS	Library of Biblical Studies
LDSS	The Literature of the Dead Sea Scrolls
MBP	Mellen Biblical Press
NGS	New Gospel Studies
NSBT	New Studies in Biblical Theology
NTC	New Testament Commentary
PTMS	Princeton Theological Monograph Series
SCJ	Studies in Christianity and Judaism
SJSHRZ	Studien zu den jüdischen Schriften aus hellenistisch-römischer Zeit
SNTS	Studiorum Novi Testamenti Societas
SNTW	Studies of the New Testament and Its World
TSA	Themes in Social Anthropology
TZTh	Tübinger Zeitschrift für Theologie
UJT	Understanding Jesus Today
YJS	Yale Judaica Series

1. Alexander et al., eds., *SBL Handbook of Style*.

Translations of Ancient Sources

Unless otherwise indicated, I have used the following English translations for ancient texts:

Old Testament, New Testament, and Apocrypha: The Revised Standard Version of the Bible: Old Testament (1952); New Testament (2nd ed., 1971); Apocrypha (1957); 3 Maccabees, 4 Maccabees, and Psalm 151 (1977). [RSV]

Pseudepigrapha: *The Old Testament Pseudepigrapha*, ed. James H. Charlesworth, 2 vols. (Garden City, NY: Doubleday, 1983–1985). [*OTP*]

Dead Sea Scrolls: *The Dead Sea Scrolls: Study Edition*, ed. Florentino García Martínez and Eibert J. C. Tigchelaar, 2 vols. (Leiden/New York/Köln: Brill, 1997). [*DSSSE*]

Targums: The Aramaic Bible series (Edinburgh: T & T Clark). [ArBib]

Mishnah: *The Mishnah: A New Translation*, ed. Jacob Neusner (New Haven, CT/London, Eng.: Yale University Press, 1988).

Tosefta: *The Tosefta: Translated from the Hebrew with a New Introduction*, trans. Jacob Neusner, 2 vols. (Peabody, MA: Hendrickson, 2002).

Palestinian Talmud: *The Talmud of the Land of Israel*, ed. Jacob Neusner, trans. Jacob Neusner et al., 35 vols. (Chicago/London: University of Chicago Press, 1982–1994).

Babylonian Talmud: *The Babylonian Talmud*, ed. Isidore Epstein, 18 vols. (London: Soncino, 1978).

Classical writers (including Josephus, Philo, Clement of Alexandria, and Eusebius): The Loeb Classical Library series (Cambridge, MA: Harvard University Press/London: Heinemann). [LCL]

Early Christian writings: The Ancient Christian Writers series (New York: Newman) [ACW], and the Ante-Nicene Fathers series (Grand Rapids, MI: Eerdmans). [ANF]

1

Introduction

IMAGINE A HYPOTHETICAL MEETING BETWEEN PAUL AND THE AU-
thors of the four Gospels. Would they agree on the significance of the
life of Jesus? Granted, each of the Gospel writers had access to different
traditions about Jesus, and each one shaped the story of Jesus so as to
highlight certain aspects of his life. But, at the end of the day, it is clear
that they each thought that what Jesus said and did was important.
Did Paul?

The question arises because Paul and Jesus sound so very different from each other. To some extent this is understandable: Jesus ministered primarily in rural Galilee among Aramaic-speaking peasants,
whereas Paul related to Greek-speaking residents of major Greco-
Roman cities. Also, Paul saw great importance in something that was
still in the future for Jesus—namely, Jesus' own death and resurrection.
But even taking these factors into account, we wonder why Paul makes
so little explicit reference to Jesus' words or deeds. Based on his letters, he certainly does not appear on the surface to see himself as a
typical disciple of a Jewish rabbi who is committed to spreading his
master's teaching. The apparent difference between Jesus and Paul has
led many—at both scholarly and popular levels—to question whether
these two men in fact shared the same faith.

In what follows I intend to address this question by arguing that,
even though Paul rarely cites Jesus, he was profoundly shaped by
Jesus. That is to say, Paul shared certain core convictions with Jesus
that distinguished both of them from their Jewish and Greco-Roman
milieux. The argument will be essentially historical in nature. I am not
interested in showing the role each person plays within a consistent
theological framework, but rather with examining Jesus and Paul as

historical people, and seeing to what extent it is reasonable to believe that the latter was dependent on the former.

In this chapter I will do three things: survey how the relationship between Jesus and Paul has been explained since the middle of the nineteenth century, set forth how I intend to move the debate forward, and explain how I view the New Testament writings as source documents for historical investigation.

Literature Review

A number of useful surveys of the Jesus-Paul debate are available.[1] My purpose here is to identify the salient issues in the debate, and to describe some of the more recent developments.

A Radical Break between Jesus and Paul

The critical question of Paul's relationship to Jesus began in the nineteenth century with the rise of historical criticism.[2] F. C. Baur—known for his division of early Christianity into Pauline and Petrine parties[3]—laid the foundations for the debate by arguing that whereas Jesus challenged people with the moral demands of the kingdom of God, Paul focused on the person of Jesus himself and on his achievement on the cross for the sake of humanity.[4] A wide-ranging debate, however, was not triggered until 1894 when Hans Hinrich Wendt

---

1. The most useful surveys are Furnish, "Jesus-Paul Debate," 17–50; Dungan, *Sayings of Jesus*, xvii–xxix; Barclay, "Jesus and Paul," 492–503; Fraser, *Jesus and Paul*, 11–32; and Simmons, *Theology of Inclusion*, 8–33. Other surveys can be found in Keegan, "Paul," 450–84; and Riesner, "Paulus," 347–65.

2. Setting the stage from the previous century was H. S. Reimarus, who distinguished between "what the apostles present in their writings from what Jesus himself actually said and taught during his lifetime" (cited in Kümmel, *New Testament*, 89). Also significant, as an indicator of opinion outside the theological community, is F. Nietzsche, who disliked Paul for inventing his own gospel: "The life, example, teachings, death, meaning, and rights of the whole evangel—nothing was left after this hatred-inspired counterfeiter realized what he and he alone could use. *Not* reality, *not* the historical truth! . . . Basically, he had no use whatsoever for the life of the redeemer" (Nietzsche, *The Anti-Christ*, 38–39).

3. Baur, "Christuspartei," 61–206.

4. Baur, *Vorlesungen*, 123–24; see translated excerpts in Kümmel, *New Testament*, 142.

argued that Paul had taken Jesus' message of piety based on the father-hood of God and had transformed it, according to his own Pharisaic presuppositions, into a universal religion that emphasized a distinctive means of salvation. And in suggesting that Jesus' message was the more powerful of the two, Wendt implied that the church ought to go back past Paul to Jesus.[5] William Wrede added fuel to the fire by arguing that in moving from the religion of Jesus, which called people to yield their whole selves to God, to the theology of Paul, which stressed the importance of believing in the acts of God—"the incarnation, death, and resurrection of a celestial being"—Paul became "the second founder of Christianity."[6] Wilhelm Heitmüller, observing that even if Paul cites some sayings of Jesus, he does not cite them *as* sayings of Jesus, suggested that the difference between Jesus and Paul was due to the latter's involvement in the Hellenistic Christian community that had distanced itself somewhat from the Palestinian community.[7] This prepared the way for Wilhelm Bousset and others in the history of religions school to explore other ways in which Paul may have been shaped by Hellenism, with particular attention being given to mystery religions, from which, Bousset argued, Paul derived his view of a mystical union with Christ.[8] Finally, Albert Schweitzer suggested that Paul's mysticism came not from mystery religions but from Jewish apocalyptic: when Paul saw that Jesus' expectation for the kingdom had failed to materialize, he reinterpreted that expectation so that believers would now enter into a mystical relationship with Christ and thereby enter into an entirely new reality.[9]

Responses to the Radical Perspective

In response to these views, those who have defended a line of continuity between Jesus and Paul have done so in one of three ways.

5. Wendt, "Lehre des Paulus," 1–78.

6. Wrede, *Paul*, 163, 179. For a contemporary expression of a similar view, see Crossan, *Birth of Christianity*, 407–17, who, in discussing the development of the traditions of the early church, speaks of the sayings of the historical Jesus forming what he calls a "Life Tradition," whereas the preaching of Paul that focuses on Jesus' death and resurrection forms a "Death Tradition."

7. Heitmüller, "Problem," 321–22, 330.

8. Bousset, *Kyrios Christos*.

9. Schweitzer, *Mysticism*, 98–99, 109–14, 141, 269–72, 334.

Continuity with Development

The first kind of response has been to argue that the difference in Paul is not a diversion from the teaching of Jesus, but rather a development of it. The person most often associated with this view is Adolf von Harnack who argued that in freeing Christianity from Judaism, and transforming Jesus' message of the fatherhood of God into a universal religion, Paul showed that he "was the one who understood the Master and continued his work."[10] Johannes Weiss further argued that Paul's dependence on Jesus is evident in the transformation that he experienced: his new understanding of the Messiah came as a result of reflection, not on his Jewish heritage, but on "the human personality of Jesus."[11] Paul's experience of the grace of God, his perception of the fatherhood of God, and his understanding of Christian ethics, are all inspired by the earthly Jesus.[12] Arnold Meyer gave expression to a view that would become standard within liberal Protestant theology: the central point of Paul's gospel—that Christ died for our sins—stems from Jesus not because this is what Jesus preached, but because it is an interpretation of Jesus' death in light of the forgiving love that characterized his life; that is to say, Paul's gospel was in keeping with "the Spirit of Jesus."[13] Thus, Meyer could say, on the one hand, that "[o]ur religion in its essence is derived from Christ" while, on the other, that Paul "though not the sole founder was still the principal founder of that form of Christianity which alone proved capable of subduing the wide world to Christ."[14]

Consistent in Theology

The second way in which scholars sought to defend Paul's dependence on Jesus was to look for a line of continuity in their theology.

Following the lead of Heitmüller, Rudolf Bultmann assumed that Paul was shaped by the Hellenistic wing of the church and consequently was not influenced, either directly or indirectly, by the histori-

---

10. Harnack, *What Is Christianity?* 176.

11. Weiss, *Paul and Jesus*, 31.

12. Ibid., 92–96, 118.

13. Meyer, *Jesus or Paul?* 103.

14. Ibid., 28.

cal Jesus.[15] According to Bultmann, the importance of Jesus lay not in his teaching of new ideas about God, in a new morality, in his example of living, or in his achievements, but rather in his call for people to make a decision for God. And through his preaching of the cross Paul evoked this same encounter with God by challenging people to submit themselves to God.[16] But even if the details of Jesus' life were not important to Paul, Bultmann still found a number of commonalities between the two: an eschatology of the two ages; an emphasis on love, with a focus on one's intentions rather than merely on outward actions; the identification of the ultimate sin being that of boasting; the call to live sacrificially, to give up what one has for the sake of the kingdom, to live "as though not";[17] and a view of God's grace that is freely available to all, but that at the same time must not be taken for granted.[18]

Werner Kümmel tried to give a balanced assessment of both similarities and differences: (i) both Jesus and Paul speak of God's graciousness and his judgment; (ii) both declare that the era of the law has come to an end, although Paul goes further in stating that the purpose of the law was to promote sin; (iii) while Paul grounds his message of salvation not in Jesus' call to repentance or in his fellowship with sinners, but rather in his death and resurrection, the core of both of their messages is "that God has done the utmost to save men from perdition"; (iv) while there are significant differences in Christology, the differences are reduced when we see that Paul's christological categories express "the conviction that God himself achieves his eschatological salvation in Jesus Christ," which is essentially the same as Jesus' claim "that God's eschatological kingdom became reality in [his own] teaching and working"; (v) the practices of baptism and the Lord's Supper connect the participants with "the salvation event initiated by Jesus"; (vi) with regard to the church, the idea of being incorporated into the body of Christ meant for Paul "participation in God's eschatological saving work that is begun in Christ"; (vii) Paul does see humanity "as farther removed from God than does Jesus," but this does not result in

15. Bultmann, "Significance," 220–23.

16. Ibid., 235–46. Both Fuchs, *Zur Frage*, and Jüngel, *Paulus und Jesus*, develop this view further by describing the preaching of both Jesus and Paul as a "speech-event" (*Sprachereignis*) in which people encounter the gracious invitation of God.

17. 1 Cor 7:29–31.

18. Bultmann, "Jesus and Paul," 183–201.

a conflict between the respective cores of Jesus' and Paul's messages; and (viii) the one fundamental difference is that whereas Jesus understood himself as both messenger and agent of the kingdom of God, Paul saw himself only as messenger and as servant of his Lord—hence his focus on Christology rather than on the kingdom of God.[19]

EVIDENCE OF THE JESUS TRADITION IN PAUL

The third form of response to the arguments of Baur and Wrede came in the form of attempts to detect evidence of the Jesus tradition in Paul's letters. The name most associated with this project is Alfred Resch who claimed to have identified 925 allusions in Paul's letters to sayings of Jesus.[20] For most, however, Resch's compilation was an example of "parallelomania,"[21] and did not persuade many who doubted Paul's dependence on Jesus to begin with.

Recent Developments

With the advent, in the 1970s, of renewed confidence in historical Jesus studies,[22] together with the emergence of new perspectives on Paul,[23] investigation of the relationship between Jesus and Paul received some fresh impetus. Some indications of this renewed interest include: a 1984 Festschrift for Francis Wright Beare entitled *From Jesus to Paul*;[24] a series of seminars under the title "Paulus und Jesus" held at

19. Kümmel, *Theology*, 244–54, citations from pp. 251, 252, and 253.

20. Resch, *Der Paulinismus*. In addition, Resch claimed another 133 allusions in Ephesians, 100 in the Pastoral Epistles, and 64 in the Pauline speeches of Acts.

21. Although Sandmel, "Parallelomania," 1–13, does not specifically refer to Resch, his warning against making exaggerated and uncritical claims with regard to verbal parallels in early Jewish and Christian literature is appropriate here.

22. See the account of the development of historical Jesus studies in, for example, Wright, *Jesus*, 3–124.

23. Two perspectives in particular ought to be mentioned here: (i) the shift from interpreting Paul primarily in Hellenistic terms, to seeing him against a Jewish background (see below, pp. 231); and (ii) the watershed work of Sanders—*Paul and Palestinian Judaism* (1977)—which argues that the Judaism of the first century was not a legalistic system devoid of grace, and that therefore Paul's gospel of grace and his critique of the law (assuming he did not misunderstand Judaism) needed to be reassessed.

24. Richardson and Hurd, eds., *From Jesus to Paul*.

the annual meetings of the Studiorum Novi Testamenti Societas from 1984–1988,[25] followed shortly thereafter by a volume of essays edited by Alexander Wedderburn that sought to describe the current state of scholarship on the Jesus-Paul question;[26] a 1990 collection of several previously-published articles by James Dunn that, taken together, argue for a connection between Jesus and Paul based on the Jewish law;[27] a popular level book by Victor Paul Furnish discussing the issues involved;[28] a substantial volume by David Wenham, published in 1995, exploring both verbal and thematic connections;[29] a colloquium held at Truett Theological Seminary in 2004 at which six scholars explored new ways to relate Paul to Jesus;[30] and several doctoral dissertations— of particular note are those by David Dungan,[31] Biörn Fjärstedt,[32] Michael Thompson,[33] William Simmons,[34] and Maureen Yeung[35]—in addition to numerous journal articles.

The dissertations by Dungan and Fjärstedt in the 1970s, both focusing on 1 Corinthians, led to a renewed interest in finding echoes of the Jesus tradition in Paul. In the subsequent two decades, several articles and books were written arguing for or against specific verbal links between Paul and Jesus, sometimes with suggestions of blocks of tradition with which Paul may have been familiar. Those participating in this debate can generally be classified into one of three groups— minimalists, moderates, and maximalists—depending on how much Jesus tradition they thought could be found in Paul. For example:

25. The topics covered were: Fundamental Problems in the Relationship of Paul to the Jesus Tradition (1984); Law and the Will of God in Paul and Jesus (1985); The Material Correspondence between Jesus and Paul in Proclamation and Practice (1986); Imitation of Christ and Pauline Christology (1987); and History, Historicity and the Historical Jesus in the Christology of Paul (1988); see Wedderburn, "Preface," *Paul and Jesus*, 7.

26. Wedderburn, ed., *Paul and Jesus*.

27. Dunn, *Jesus, Paul, and the Law*. Some of these papers were presented at the SNTS *Paulus und Jesus* seminars.

28. Furnish, *Jesus*.

29. Wenham, *Paul*.

30. Still, ed., *Jesus and Paul Reconnected*.

31. Dungan, *Sayings of Jesus*.

32. Fjärstedt, *Synoptic Tradition*.

33. Thompson, *Clothed with Christ*.

34. Simmons, "Jesus and Paul"; revised and published as *Theology of Inclusion*.

35. Yeung, *Faith in Jesus and Paul*.

(i) Nikolaus Walter,[36] Frans Neirynck,[37] and Christopher Tuckett[38] each challenge the legitimacy of specific claims that Paul was influenced by the Jesus tradition; (ii) Dale Allison,[39] James Dunn,[40] and Victor Paul Furnish[41] accept a limited number of Pauline allusions to Jesus; and (iii) Seyoon Kim,[42] Michael Thompson,[43] and David Wenham[44] all argue that there are extensive examples of echoes of Jesus' sayings in Paul's writings.

A parallel line of inquiry has focused on Paul's knowledge of the story of Jesus' life. Furnish acknowledges a very limited list of details that Paul knew about Jesus,[45] whereas Wenham is more optimistic in finding evidence that Paul was familiar with numerous aspects of Jesus' life.[46]

Alongside this renewed interest in Paul's knowledge of the Jesus tradition, attempts have been made to find other kinds of connections between Jesus and Paul. First, some have emphasized the *significance* of the story of Jesus. Larry Hurtado, for example, argues that in the hymn in Phil 2:5–11, Paul portrays Jesus as an example to follow: the words δοῦλος, ταπεινόω, and ὑπήκοος, used to describe Jesus in verses 7–8, recall Paul's description both of himself and of the Christian life, and recall a key theme in the story of Jesus.[47] Christian Wolff argues that Paul saw his own experience of deprivation, his renunciation of marriage, his humble service, and his suffering persecution, as concrete examples in which he imitated the life of Jesus.[48] And Alexander Wedderburn suggests that the story of Jesus was for Paul a myth that functioned on a theoretical level in developing an other-worldly per-

---

36. Walter, "Paul," 51–80.

37. Neirynck, "Paul," 265–321.

38. Tuckett, "Paul," 376–81; idem., "Synoptic Tradition," 160–82.

39. Allison, "Pauline Epistles," 1–32.

40. Dunn, "Jesus Tradition in Paul," 155–78.

41. Furnish, *Jesus according to Paul*, 40–65.

42. Kim, "Jesus," 474–92.

43. Thompson, *Clothed with Christ*.

44. Wenham, *Paul*.

45. Furnish, *Jesus according to Paul*, 19–39.

46. Wenham, *Paul*, chap. 8; idem., "Story of Jesus," 297–311.

47. Hurtado, "Jesus' Death," 413–33.

48. Wolff, "Humility," 145–60.

spective of Jesus—"Christ had to be like this to do what he did; he needed to be amongst other things a universal representative of all humanity, and so his nature was described in such terms as would set out this all-inclusive role"—and on a practical level in instructing believers on how to live.[49]

Second, some scholars have drawn *missiological* connections between Jesus and Paul. Seán Freyne suggests that Jesus and Paul shared a similar vision with regard to the restoration of Israel that focused on national geographic expansion rather than on the setting up of religious or social boundaries designed to separate the people of God from outsiders.[50] Other studies have developed along similar lines, focusing on the role of the Hellenists in shaping Paul's perspective and in possibly serving as a bridge between him and Jesus. Charles Scobie argues that Paul's sense of the present being the time of fulfillment of the prophetic hope for the ingathering of the nations goes back to elements in Jesus' ministry and is developed by the missional activity of the Hellenists.[51] Building on the view of Heikki Räisänen that the Hellenists had accommodated Gentile converts by not requiring circumcision,[52] Wedderburn and William Simmons propose that justification for this circumcision-free gospel Paul promoted so strongly was found in Jesus' practice of welcoming outcasts: "what Paul stated systematically, Jesus had already lived, in his attitudes and in his activities."[53] And John Barclay reflects on this same situation and suggests that Jesus and Paul share a radical understanding of the grace of God: "Both enact and express a paradigm of God's grace that is simultaneously welcoming to the lost outsider and deeply challenging to the insider."[54]

Third, attempts have been made to find connections between Jesus and Paul by using *sociological* categories. Dunn makes the point that, from a sociological perspective, the early church would have

---

49. Wedderburn, "Paul and the Story of Jesus," 161–89, citation from p. 187.

50. Freyne, "Jesus-Paul Debate," 143–63.

51. Scobie, "Jesus or Paul," 47–60.

52. Räisänen, "The 'Hellenists,'" 149–202; an earlier draft of this article was presented at the Jesus and Paul Seminar of the SNTS meeting in Trondheim in 1985. Cf. Dunn, "Mark 2.1–3.6," 10–36.

53. Wedderburn, "Similarity and Continuity," 117–43, citation from p. 131; cf. Simmons, *Theology of Inclusion*.

54. Barclay, "Caustic Grace," 1–17.

needed traditions in order to form its own identity and to distinguish itself from other movements.[55] Bruce Longenecker has suggested there may be continuity in terms of caring for the poor.[56] And Scott Bartchy argues that both Jesus and Paul challenge values associated with patriarchy: they reject patriarchal authority and domination; they create communities based on sibling-like kinship rather than on blood relations; and they redefine honor and power, placing the emphasis on service rather than on competition.[57]

Assessment

This survey is by no means complete, but it does give a sense of the shape the debate has taken and of some more recent lines of development. Although first written forty-five years ago, Furnish's assessment of the Jesus-Paul debate is still worth repeating.[58] He suggested that three firm conclusions could be drawn from the research at that time, each of which leads to further questions. First, Paul reveals relatively little of the life and teachings of Jesus. Why is this? Second, the attempt to identify parallels between Paul and the Gospels will not solve the problem of the relationship between Paul and Jesus. However, we can still ask whether there are "material correspondences"[59] that can be detected between Jesus and Paul. And third, attention needs to be given to the broader context of the development of early Christianity and not be limited only to the two figures of Paul and Jesus. How did the various Jewish and Greco-Roman milieux shape the messages of Jesus and Paul? And finally, Furnish notes that a fundamental question will always be, "what accounts for the distinctive features of Paul's gospel?"[60]

---

55. Dunn, *Theology*, 185–89; cf. Scroggs, "Earliest Christian Communities," 1–23, who argues that the early church functioned as a religious sect, and who shows how several of the Jesus traditions would have addressed specific issues concerning the life and identity of the sect.

56. Longenecker, "Good News," 37–65.

57. Bartchy, "Father," 35–47; idem., "Patriarchy," 68–78; cf. Bauckham, "Kingdom," 1–26.

58. Furnish, "Debate," 43–47; originally published in *BJRL* 47 (1964–65): 342–81.

59. Ibid., 46.

60. Ibid., 47–50, citation from p. 47.

Regarding his first conclusion, due to the lack of evidence, we may never be able to speak with confidence as to why Paul does not refer to the Jesus tradition in his letters.[61] It is doubtful that the reason Paul does not cite Jesus is simply because he did not witness the life of Jesus firsthand, since he does explicitly cite Jesus on a few occasions,[62] and on another occasion it seems he would have cited him if he had known a relevant saying.[63] It is significant to note, however, as Michael Thompson has shown, that Paul is no exception in regard to utilizing few citations of Jesus when compared with other New Testament writers and the Apostolic Fathers.[64] Regarding Furnish's second conclusion, I would agree that many of the parallels proposed are speculative and subjective; however, I would not agree that the effort to find verbal echoes of the Jesus tradition in Paul's writings has been fruitless. Indeed, it would be difficult to argue that Paul was fundamentally shaped by Jesus if we could not find *any* evidence in Paul of Jesus' sayings. Furthermore, some of the more recent proposals noted above to find theological, missiological, and sociological links between Jesus and Paul are significant in demonstrating Paul's dependence on Jesus. Regarding the third conclusion, some progress has been made since the mid-1960s concerning the development of the early church and the respective contexts in which to understand Jesus and Paul, and this will become evident in the following study.

A Way Forward

General Considerations

In order to move the Jesus-Paul debate forward, I suggest three things are needed. First, appreciation must be given to the profound developments in both historical Jesus and Pauline studies since Furnish wrote his assessment. A renaissance in historical Jesus research began about 1980 that has been characterized by a much more optimistic view of the possibility of speaking confidently of what Jesus said and did

---

61. Although, I will make some proposals in the Conclusions (see below, pp. 337–38).

62. 1 Cor 7:10–11; 9:14; cf. 11:23–25.

63. 1 Cor 7:25.

64. Thompson, *Clothed with Christ*, 37–63; cf. Riesner, "Paulus," 356–59.

than had characterized scholarship earlier in the twentieth century. Scholars are now intent on understanding Jesus' aims: How did he view his own ministry? What was he attempting to achieve? And, most significantly, how are we to understand him within his Jewish context? Similarly, Pauline scholars have become much more interested in Paul's Jewishness and his continuing concern for Israel. For example, in his widely influential book, *Paul and Palestinian Judaism*, E. P. Sanders has argued, contrary to much scholarly and popular opinion, that the Judaism of the first century was not a legalistic system devoid of grace, and thus Paul's gospel of grace and his critique of the law either seriously misunderstand Judaism or they need to be radically reassessed. While some aspects of this "New Perspective" on Paul may be open to challenge, overall it represents a significant advance in Pauline studies. Taking account of these two developments will certainly open up new possibilities for the Jesus-Paul debate than were available prior to the last quarter of the twentieth century.

Second, the focus of attention needs to be on matters that were for Jesus and Paul of fundamental importance. This would address one of the frequent criticisms of many attempts to find connections between Jesus and Paul—namely, that they focus on peripheral matters, or at least on matters that seem not to be integrally related to the heart of each person's mission and mindset. Thompson, for example, argues that there are several references to the Jesus tradition in Rom 12–15 and so he concludes that "dominical teachings significantly influenced Paul."[65] He finds one probable allusion—"nothing is unclean in itself"[66]—in addition to numerous probable echoes: the injunction to "Bless those who persecute you,"[67] the fulfilling of the law by means of love,[68] the prohibition against judging,[69] the identification of the kingdom of God with righteousness, peace, and joy as opposed to food and drink,[70] the warning against placing a stumbling block in the way of a brother,[71] the admonition to render to everyone what they are due,[72]

---

65. Thompson, *Clothed with Christ*, 238.

66. Rom 14:14; cf. Mark 7:15; Matt 15:11.

67. Rom 12:14; cf. Matt 5:44//Luke 6:28.

68. Rom 13:8–10; cf. Mark 12:28–34//Matt 22:34–40.

69. Rom 14:13a; cf. Matt 7:1//Luke 6:37a.

70. Rom 14:17; cf. Luke 14:12–24//Matt 22:1–10 and Matt 12:28//Luke 11:20.

71. Rom 14:13b; cf. Matt 18:6//Mark 9:42//Luke 17:2.

72. Rom 13:7; cf. Mark 12:17//Matt 22:21//Luke 20:25.

the forbidding of retaliation,[73] the exhortation to genuine love,[74] and the eschatological perspective.[75] While these are all very important teachings, they are generally paraenetic in nature and, I would argue, they do not encapsulate the distinctive core convictions of either Jesus or Paul. What leaves skeptics unconvinced of Paul's dependence on Jesus is that the heart of Paul's gospel and the heart of his mission do not seem to derive from the heart of Jesus' ministry. Attention, therefore, needs to focus on matters that were of fundamental importance for Jesus and Paul.

And third, while many topics could be investigated to try to find lines of connection between Jesus and Paul, I suggest it is important to engage those scholars who currently do not think Paul was dependent on Jesus, and to keep them at the table, as it were, for as long as possible.[76] To this end, I suggest for strategic reasons, that we step very carefully when dealing with certain contentious issues—particularly issues where scholars have entrenched positions on what can be reliably ascribed to Jesus. For example, in comparing Paul's letters to the Gospels, it is conceivable how connections between Jesus and Paul could be found around issues such as, say, the significance of Jesus' death, his identity, and eschatology. However, while such issues are certainly very important, the scholarly fault lines that run through the debates concerning them are such that it is doubtful whether any progress in the Jesus-Paul problem would be made if they were the focus of attention. At least if we deal with such issues, we will need to be well aware of where the contentious matters lie. Some may complain that this step is in tension with the second point I made above, and to some extent it may be. The tension will need to be faced, however, if we want to address issues that were central to both Jesus and Paul *and* to have our discussion engage those who seriously disagree.

---

73. Rom 12:17–19; cf. similar emphasis in the Sermon on the Mount/Plain.

74. Rom 12:9; cf. Jesus' warnings against hypocrisy.

75. Rom 13:11–12; cf. Matt 16:1–4; Luke 12:56; 19:41–44; Mark 13:33.

76. In 1994 Dunn, "Jesus tradition," 155, commented: "The largest consensus still maintains that Paul knew or cared little about the ministry of Jesus apart from his death and resurrection."

Specific Shape of the Argument

I intend to make the case that Paul was fundamentally shaped by certain perspectives that Jesus expressed in his ministry. This would fall into the quest for what Furnish called "material correspondences" between Jesus and Paul.[77] I will not necessarily be looking for common sayings, but for a common mindset[78]—that is, for issues on which Jesus and Paul shared a core commitment, even though they may have expressed their commitments differently.

In order to determine what issues might be appropriate for such investigation, I note, as a starting point, the three images that Richard Hays has proposed as being central to the New Testament[79]—community, cross, and new creation[80]—and that, he argues, express the fundamental story to which its writers bear witness, a story that he describes as follows:

> The God of Israel, the creator of the world, has acted (astoundingly) to rescue a lost and broken world through the death and resurrection of Jesus; the full scope of that rescue is not yet apparent, but God has created a community of witnesses to this good news, the church. While awaiting the grand conclusion of the story, the church, empowered by the Holy Spirit, is called to reenact the loving obedience of Jesus Christ and thus to serve as a sign of God's redemptive purposes for the world.[81]

Hays proposes these three as better images than, say, love or liberation, in that they are more widespread in the New Testament

---

77. See above, p. 10.

78. By "mindset" I mean the particular set of beliefs and aims of a person. Wright, *New Testament*, 110, helpfully defines mindset as "the individual subset of, or variant on, the worldview held by the society or societies to which the individual belongs," and he further describes worldview as consisting of a combination of, and interaction among, stories, praxis, symbols, and answers to questions that would be fundamental in any society—specifically, the questions "who are we, where are we, what is wrong, and what is the solution?" (122–26). And in his *Jesus and the Victory of God*, 467–72, Wright adds a fifth question in light of the Jewish context: What time is it? Cf. Walsh and Middleton, *Transforming Vision*, 31–39.

79. It should be noted that Hays's survey of the New Testament literature does not include Colossians, 2 Thessalonians, Hebrews, James, 1 or 2 Peter, or Jude.

80. Hays, *Moral Vision*.

81. Ibid., 193.

and concrete, and thus are less susceptible to misuse.[82] "Community" speaks of God's purpose in redeeming and forming a covenant relationship with a corporate body as opposed to focusing only on individuals; "cross" points to the climax of Jesus' life and provides the paradigm for discipleship; and "new creation" expresses the power of the resurrection that has broken into this world and provides both a taste of the age to come and hope for full redemption. That these three images are widespread in the New Testament suggests that (i) they expressed matters that were of fundamental importance to early Christians; and

---

82. Ibid., 200–204. Burridge, *Imitating Jesus*, challenges Hays on this point and argues that love should be the focus of New Testament ethics. Rather than taking a canonical approach, as Hays does, Burridge begins with the historical Jesus and his double command to love God and neighbor, expressed both in Jesus' words and actions, and then traces this theme in Paul, the Gospels, and Acts. He contends that it is better to use love as a focus than community, cross, and new creation because "references to 'love' are many times more frequent," and he suggests that Hays derives his three images primarily from Paul "and then applies them briefly to the rest of the New Testament" (ibid., 54). While I would certainly not want to question the importance of love in the New Testament, I do not think Burridge has done justice to Hays's proposal. Burridge's comment that the three images come primarily from Paul is not an accurate assessment of Hays's survey where he demonstrates how community, cross, and new creation appear throughout the New Testament (Hays, *Moral Vision*, 60–157). But further, Hays argues (i) that the vocabulary of love is not prominent in Mark, Acts, Hebrews, or Revelation, suggesting that the "motif [of love] cannot serve as the common denominator for New Testament ethics" (ibid., 202); (ii) that love is more abstract than community, cross, and new creation, meaning that what is meant by love is brought into sharper focus by these latter three images; and (iii) that the importance of the previous point can be seen in popular discourse today where love "has lost its power of discrimination, having become a cover for all manner of vapid self-indulgence" (ibid.). Thus, the issue is not about the *importance* of love as a moral imperative, but about the *usefulness* of love as an image for synthesizing New Testament material and for conveying clearly the distinctive message of that material. I think Hays is right that the images of community, cross, and new creation do this better than love. And, although Hays uses a canonical approach, I hope to demonstrate that his images can usefully be employed in a historical analysis as well.

Cranfield, "Response," 171–72, agrees with Hays's images but suggests he should have also included the images of creation and of Jesus' lordship. While one can see how these additions may be important for theological discussions, I suspect they would not be helpful for historical ones: it would be difficult to show from what little Jesus and Paul say about creation that they held a view in common that was distinct from the views of other Jews; and with regard to Jesus' lordship, it is very controversial when trying to distinguish between Jesus' own view and the views of his followers after the resurrection.

(ii) they arose very early in the life of the church, before Christians began to disperse, perhaps even going back to Jesus himself.

But these three images are still too broad to be covered adequately in a study of this scope. Furthermore, in the previous section I noted that I wanted to choose topics carefully so as to avoid, as much as possible, major fault lines in scholarship. Thus, if we think of Hays's images as lenses through which we see central aspects of the early Christian movement, I intend to narrow the focus in each case by selecting only part of the field of vision. In particular: with regard to community, I will look at the *kind* of people Jesus and Paul associated with, and will draw a connection between Jesus' practice of having table fellowship with tax collectors and sinners and Paul's mission to the Gentiles. With the image of the cross, I will focus on ways in which both Jesus and Paul expressed the irony that dying leads to life. And with regard to the image of new creation, I will consider how Jesus and Paul thought of the time in which they lived as, to some extent, a realization of the hopes of Israel. In each case I will argue that Paul is dependent on Jesus. That these issues were for Jesus matters of core commitment is indicated by his perseverance in expressing them even in the face of opposition. That they were central also to Paul's mindset seems obvious enough: Paul sees himself as apostle to the Gentiles, he places significant emphasis on the cross, and his eschatological perspective shapes much of his teaching. I make no claim that these topics are all that could be discussed under the rubrics of community, cross, and new creation, or that there are not other profitable approaches; I only claim that these three topics were important to Jesus and Paul. And, with the apparent independence of these topics, it may strengthen the overall argument by pursuing three lines of inquiry instead of just one, in case one or two lines fail to convince.

In order to make such an argument, three things need to be established in each case: (i) the authenticity and significance of specific sayings or acts; (ii) a family resemblance between Jesus and Paul;[83] and

---

83. I recognize that "family resemblance" is a somewhat slippery term involving subjective evaluation. While some will find a resemblance between A, B, and C in Jesus and a, b, and c in Paul, others will not (see, for example, the debate between Allison, "Pauline Epistles," 1–32; and Neirynck, "Paul," 265–321, on Paul's use of the Jesus tradition). Subjectivity, however, cannot be avoided; it is the nature of historical investigation. But other aspects of my argument will seek to lessen the uncertainty in the subjective assessment.

(iii) a plausible explanation that shows why Jesus is the most likely source for Paul. Regarding the third point, depending on the evidence available, the emphasis may be on tracing the historical connection between Jesus and Paul, or on ruling out the possibility of other influences on Paul. My general procedure, therefore, will be, for each of the images, to establish the authenticity of the relevant aspect of Jesus' ministry, and then follow this with an argument that shows that a corresponding aspect in Paul likely derives from Jesus.

Use of Ancient Sources

Since I am developing a historical argument, a word on my use of source material is in order. Where I have used translations, I have generally followed widely accepted and available editions.[84] Since readers may not be familiar with ancient non-biblical sources, I have provided in Appendix A a brief description of each writing cited, together with its approximate date. Naturally, the study will draw heavily from the New Testament, and so a comment on this material is warranted.

With regard to Jesus, while we have no primary sources, we do have numerous ancient secondary sources—several accounts of the life of Jesus known as gospels, a few references elsewhere in the New Testament, plus a smattering of references in Jewish and pagan literature.[85] There is widespread agreement that the four canonical Gospels are the best source of historical information about Jesus, and within those Gospels other sources have been identified, the most important of which is Q—identified as the non-Markan material that Matthew and Luke have in common.[86] I share the majority view that the two-document hypothesis is the best solution to the source-critical problem of the Synoptic Gospels. For a number of reasons, however, I think caution needs to be exercised in building theories on Q. First, we need to realize that, while acknowledged by a large majority to be the best solution to the Synoptic Problem, the two-documentary hypothesis

84. See above p. xi.

85. For a full discussion of the sources, see Meier, *Marginal Jew*, 1:41–166; Charlesworth and Evans, "Jesus in the Agrapha," 479–533; and Evans, "Jesus in Non-Christian Sources," 443–78.

86. For convenience, the remainders of Matthew and Luke, after Mark and Q have been accounted for, are frequently referred to as M and L respectively. Some scholars also believe there was a signs source used by John.

is in fact not without its problems: for example, there are texts where Matthew and Luke agree with each other against Mark.[87] Second, while we may infer with some confidence that a document existed in the early church containing the material we have defined above as Q— consisting primarily of some of Jesus' sayings, but also including some narrative material,[88] one healing account,[89] and a few parables[90]—we may *not* infer with confidence what this document did *not* contain or that it existed in only one form. Based on both Matthew's and Luke's selective treatment of Mark,[91] we ought to assume that they treated Q in the same way,[92] and that therefore there was likely some material in the document Q that we do not know about. And third, while we may reasonably infer that if such a document existed, it would have been valued by a community of Christians, it does *not* follow that even if we knew the full contents of Q we could conclude that these Christians did not value anything that was not in Q—such as Jesus' death and resurrection.[93] Needless to say, I find the attempts to identify stages of development in Q—an original wisdom layer supplemented later by a prophetic and apocalyptic layer[94]—even more speculative.[95]

87. For a detailed discussion of the problems and the various solutions offered see Sanders and Davies, *Synoptic Gospels*, 67–119.

88. Jesus' temptation (Matt 4:1–11//Luke 4:1–13).

89. Healing the centurion's slave (Matt 7:28a; 8:5–10, 13//Luke 7:1–10).

90. Parables of the mustard seed and leaven (Matt 13:31–33//Luke 13:18–21), of the great banquet (Matt 22:2–10//Luke 14:16–24), of the lost sheep (Matt 18:12–14// Luke 15:4–7), and of the talents/pounds (Matt 25:14–20//Luke 19:12–27).

91. According to Sanders and Davies, *Synoptic Gospels*, 53, Matthew included about 90 percent of Mark while Luke included just over 50 percent.

92. Evans, "Authenticating," 6–10, illustrates the problem well by imagining a scenario in which we had only Matthew, Luke, and Q and tried to determine the contents of Mark. He notes that the resultant reconstruction would differ from our Gospel of Mark in a number of ways, one of the most significant being with regard to Mark's Christology: we would lack Mark's opening verse and the centurion's confession at the cross (Mark 15:39), and Jesus' affirmative and provoking response to the High Priest's question—"Are you the Christ, the Son of the Blessed?" (Mark 14:61)—would be somewhat muted.

93. Hurtado, "Jesus' Death," 416 n. 7, argues, based on the assumption that both Matthew and Luke used Q extensively, that Q circulated widely and that neither Matthew nor Luke had significant theological concerns with its content.

94. As, for example, in Kloppenborg, *Formation of Q*, and in Mack, *Lost Gospel*.

95. For example, see Horsley, "*Logoi Prophētōn*, 195–209, who argues that Q is better understood as being fundamentally prophetic in character.

Recently debate has also focused on whether the *Gospel of Thomas* represents another source for some of Jesus' sayings.[96] John Dominic Crossan, for example, is representative of those who take *Thomas* to be a collection of Jesus' sayings that pre-dates the canonical Gospels (Crossan places the earliest edition in the 50s CE), giving us a very early (and thus presumably more accurate) portrayal of Jesus.[97] Others, however, argue that *Thomas* is dependent on the canonical Gospels and therefore much later in origin. James Charlesworth and Craig Evans, for example, note that *Thomas* contains both (i) material that is distinctive to Matthew, Luke, and John, and (ii) redactional material from Matthew and Luke.[98] Furthermore, the earliest complete text of the *Gospel of Thomas*, which is part of the Nag Hammadi Library and has been dated ca. 400, clearly displays gnostic tendencies.[99] No doubt the debate will continue.[100] Caution, therefore, seems to be called for when using *Thomas* to establish sayings of Jesus, realizing that (i) it may, in some instances, contain a tradition independent to what we find in the Gospels, while in others it may be dependent on the canonical Gospels; and (ii) that the principal text we have has its own theological tendency. Thus, texts will need to be treated on a case by case basis.

Having identified the sources, however, it is noted that the Gospels do not always agree with each other, and so it is supposed that the Jesus tradition was shaped to some extent by the needs and perspectives of the early church, whether in the process of oral transmission (form criticism) or in the final composition of the Gospels themselves (redaction criticism). Consequently, so it is argued, the Gospels must be read critically in order to look beyond the Jesus of the early church and to discover the "real" Jesus of Nazareth. To this

96. For a survey of the debate, see Fallon and Cameron, "Gospel of Thomas," 4195–4251.

97. Crossan, *Historical Jesus*, 427–28; see also Hedrick, "Thomas," 39–56; Patterson, "Thomas," 86–88.

98. Charlesworth and Evans, "Jesus in the Agrapha," 496–503. See also Meier, *Marginal Jew*, 1:123–39; Snodgrass, "Thomas," 19–38; Tuckett, "Thomas," 132–57.

99. Compare, for example, the opening words of the Nag Hammadi text—"These are the secret words"—with those from the earlier POx 654—"These are the words." See Blatz, "Introduction," 111–14.

100. Arguing in favor of *Thomas* being dependent on the Gospels are Tuckett, "Thomas," 132–57; and Snodgrass, "Thomas," 19–38; arguing for *Thomas'* independence are Hedrick, "Thomas," 39–56; and Patterson, "Thomas," 86–88.

end, scholars have developed a series of criteria in order to identify historically authentic elements within the Gospels. Gerd Theissen and Dagmar Winter have offered a helpful critique and reformulation of these criteria that avoids many of the problems in earlier formulations.[101] They propose a set of criteria that have in view a historically plausible portrayal of Jesus. Their criteria are divided into two sets: the first asks what we can plausibly infer about Jesus based on what we know of the historical effects of his life (or, perhaps better put, based on what we know that followed). Here they employ (i) the criterion of dissimilarity to the tendencies in the early church (or, as they put it, "opposition to traditional bias"),[102] and (ii) the criterion of coherence of independent sources (the sources being different documents or different forms or genres). Thus, a piece of tradition is more likely to be authentic if Christians repeated it even though it was in tension with Christian beliefs or practices, or if it appears in multiple sources or genres. The second set of criteria asks what we can plausibly infer about Jesus based on the fact that he was a first-century Jew and on what we know of first-century Palestine. Here the authors speak both of (i) the criterion of contextual appropriateness (the extent to which a specific Jesus tradition is explicable within a Jewish context) and (ii) the criterion of contextual distinctiveness (those aspects of Jesus that distinguished him from others but that are still explicable within a Jewish framework). Thus, a piece of tradition is more likely to be authentic if it is both explicable within and distinctive from the first-century Jewish context.

While Theissen and Winter's formulation is helpful, it should be noted that all such criteria are better suited for establishing authenticity than inauthenticity. That is, if an element in a Gospel fails the authenticity tests, then the criteria actually have no comment whatsoever on the historicity of that element. This point, as obvious as it may seem, has not always been recognized in historical Jesus research. While it may be true that a piece of tradition that stands in tension with the early church is more likely to be authentic than not, the converse does not necessarily follow: it does not follow that a tradition that is not in tension with the early church is not likely to be authentic. It is

---

101. Theissen and Winter, *Quest*.

102. See Holmén, "Double Dissimilarity," 47–80, for a critique of the criterion of dissimilarity with regard to first-century Judaism.

quite possible, for example, for the early church to have been shaped by something that Jesus said that, through the accidents of history, we happen to have recorded in only one Gospel. Claims of inauthenticity, I suggest, are based on prior judgments—judgments about the shape of Second Temple Judaism or of early Christianity; about what kinds of events are possible; about the theological purposes, and thus historical reliability, of the authors; and about the transmission process of the Jesus tradition in the early church. And often underlying all of this is an epistemology stemming from the Enlightenment that focuses on the knowledge of the individual, as opposed to the community, and that stresses the importance of the individual being able to verify all claims to knowledge him- or herself, and that therefore minimizes the role of testimony—trusting what someone else says.[103]

With regard to the theological perspective of the author, and the supposed influence this might have on his shaping of the tradition, we should note that in fact there is no "historical Jesus" devoid of someone's perspective. There are facts of Jesus' life that historians may study—words that Jesus said, things that he did—but any collection of those facts involves selection by a historian, and any statement about the significance of those facts involves an act of interpretation. Thus, any presentation of Jesus requires subjective judgment. This does not in itself discredit any particular portrayal of Jesus, canonical or otherwise; rather it removes the myth of historical neutrality and objectivity: a historical portrayal is someone stating an opinion based on selected evidence. All portrayals of Jesus will be guided to some extent or another by the motivations of the author.[104]

With regard to the question of the transmission process of the Jesus tradition, form criticism has had a dominant influence in shaping scholarly opinion about the historical value of the Gospels. In particular, form critics postulate a lengthy oral transmission process in

---

103. See Bauckham, *Eyewitnesses*, 476; cf. Provan, "Knowing," 229–66.

104. It could be argued, for example, that the motivations of certain members of the Jesus Seminar to counter the influence of Christian fundamentalism in the United States, or to promote certain political or social issues, or to address the role of their nation as a world empire, might influence how they portray Jesus. In some cases their motivations might lead to new and valid insights, whereas in others they may create blinders. Thus, realizing that the writer of history has motivations does not for that reason invalidate his or her work; this is the nature of history. Understanding those motivations will, however, assist us in evaluating the work as history.

which the Jesus tradition was shaped by the needs of the early church, a church that had more interest in Jesus as the risen and reigning Lord than in Jesus as a historical person, with the result that the canonical Gospels are often viewed as a distortion of the historical Jesus. Thus, the prejudice seems to be that unless traditions can be shown to be authentic, they are probably not.

Richard Bauckham, however, has challenged this central tenet of form criticism, arguing that the Gospels are closer to eyewitness testimony than to oral tradition shaped by transmission through anonymous communities.[105] This fundamentally changes one's approach to the Gospels for it implies that the transmission of the Jesus tradition was formally controlled by specific people—that is, teachers—who personally remembered the events and by those who had been entrusted with this testimony.[106] Consequently, the general attitude that the Gospels are not authentic until proven otherwise is unjustified. This does not, however, imply a return to a naive reading of the Gospels. All testimony must be critically assessed, for witnesses can forget some details and exaggerate or elaborate on others; they can either filter out or emphasize some aspects of an event because of their own perspective or because of the changed situation in which they now find themselves; they can confuse or harmonize similar events; and they can at times imagine they remember things that did not in fact happen.[107] The differences among the Gospels, for example, must still be explained. Bauckham draws on Paul Ricoeur's view of critical realism with regard to the use of testimony in history where "there is a

---

105. Bauckham, *Eyewitnesses*. Important for Bauckham's argument is the distinction made by Vansina, *Oral Tradition*, between oral history and oral tradition, namely that the former has to do with the testimony of witnesses whereas the latter involves tradition older than the current generation. Bauckham argues that in the latter part of the first century, the Jesus tradition was still oral history because some eyewitnesses would still be living (important evidence for this is the presence of archaisms in the Gospels), and that the error of form critics is that they assumed too easily that the transmission of Jesus tradition had long been subject to the dynamics of oral tradition before the Evangelists received it. For critical interaction with Bauckham, see the articles in *JSHJ* 6, 2 (2008).

106. Bauckham, *Eyewitnesses*, chap. 10–13, devotes considerable attention to defending a plausible scenario in which the transmission of tradition within the early church would have been controlled by specific eyewitnesses and teachers.

107. See ibid., chap. 13, for a discussion of the nature of eyewitness testimony.

dialectic of trust and critical assessment."[108] With regard to the Gospel differences, Bauckham offers five possible explanations: (i) Jesus re-used, adapted, and developed his own material in different settings; (ii) the translation from Aramaic to Greek involved some flexibil-ity; (iii) oral performance normally produces variation, particularly with regard to details considered to be of secondary importance; (iv) modifications were made in order to interpret the tradition in light of the post-Easter situation;[109] and (v) the Evangelists adapted material in order to integrate the Jesus tradition into their Gospel narratives.[110] Thus, there is still a place for critical assessment. However, in addition to the authenticity criteria outlined above we might add the follow-ing: unless there are good reasons for judging otherwise, if an ancient witness demonstrates the signs of reliability—internal consistency and consistency with other testimony—then it ought to be given the benefit of the doubt even in cases where the other criteria cannot be applied.[111]

The ultimate test, however, for all judgments of authenticity will be the creation of a historical hypothesis that makes sense of the vari-ous pieces of evidence. Like a scientist drawing a best-fit curve through a number of data points and then hypothesizing, in light of this data and other knowledge she has, on the relationship between the various

108. Ibid., 490.

109. On this point Bauckham writes: "Such changes, it should be noted, are en-tirely compatible with word-for-word memorization of, for example, aphorisms of Jesus, since the changes would be made quite deliberately to a known form of exact words. Such changes are also quite compatible with a formal process of transmission, since it would be authorized tradents who, from their own familiarity with the tradi-tion, would be competent to make such changes" (ibid., 286).

110. Bauckham, *Eyewitnesses*, 286; Allison, *Historical Christ*, 61.

111. See also Marrou, "Conditions," 103–30, who writes: "[The historian] cer-tainly should not confront the witnesses of the past with an attitude that is surly, fussy, or peevish, like some unpleasant policeman for whom anyone summoned to court is suspect, *a priori*, and regarded as guilty until there is proof to the contrary. . . . [Historical understanding] presupposes the existence of a broad basis of fraternal communion between the subject and the object, between historian and document. . . . How can we understand unless we have that attitude of mind which makes us connatural with others? It is this that enables us to feel their passions and re-conceive their ideas in the very light in which they were experienced—in short, it permits us to commune with them. Even the word 'sympathy' is insufficient in this respect. Between the historian and his object a friendship must be formed, or how else can the historian understand?" (pp. 103–4). Cf. Reiser, "Eschatology," 218–26.

elements under consideration, so also the historian must make sense of the evidence by creating a best-fit story. And the more explanatory power the hypothesis has, the more convincing it will be.[112]

With regard to Paul, we have both primary and secondary sources. Of the thirteen letters in the New Testament that bear his name, seven are widely considered to be authentic—Romans, 1 and 2 Corinthians, Galatians, Philippians, 1 Thessalonians, and Philemon—and these will serve as our primary source of information about Paul. However, there is a strong, albeit minority, opinion that Colossians, 2 Thessalonians, and/or Ephesians may also be authentic, and if not authentic, at least faithful in representing the views of Paul. Consequently, while it may not be wise to develop arguments based solely on material in these three letters, it would also be wise not to make claims about Paul that are radically at variance with them. The other three letters in the New Testament bearing Paul's name—1 and 2 Timothy and Titus—are widely considered not to have been written by Paul, and to have arisen from a significantly different situation; consequently, we will treat them as secondary sources for understanding Paul's thoughts and aims.

The book of Acts is also a secondary source for information about Paul. In principle, since Acts was written as a continuation of the third Gospel, it should be treated in similar fashion to how the Gospels are treated with regard to its historicity (see above). Thus, although we do not have parallel accounts to use for comparison purposes, as we do with the Gospels, we ought to imagine Luke to be using his sources and drafting his narrative of early Christianity in much the same way that he did for the life of Jesus. Scholarly debate on the historical character of Acts has, of course, ranged widely over the past two hundred years. Those following in the tradition of F. C. Baur—especially M. Dibelius, E. Haenchen, P. Vielhauer, and H. Conzelmann—have been skeptical of the historical value of Acts, arguing, for example, that Luke's theological or pastoral concerns were more important to him than historical accuracy. On the other hand, those following in the tradition of J. B. Lightfoot—especially W. M. Ramsay, F. F. Bruce, A. N. Sherwin-White, C. J. Hemer, and M. Hengel—have argued, based on the agreement between Acts and other sources concerning numerous

112. For further discussion on the process of critical realism, see Meyer, "Lonergan's 'Breakthrough," 147–56; Wright, New Testament, 32–46. Allison, Historical Christ, also makes an important contribution, arguing that historical fictions may still contain historical truth.

historical details, that theological and historical purposes are not necessarily at odds with each other.[113]

While not trying to settle this debate here, I note two issues that
will be important for the use of Acts. The first has to do with its reliability with regard to its portrayal of Paul. Haenchen, for example,
has argued that due to Luke's theological purposes, his portrayal of
Paul is significantly different from what we find in his letters and can
therefore not be trusted. He notes several points of contrast: Paul and
Luke are both interested in the Gentile mission, but they differ on the
justification of the gospel for the Gentiles; miracles play a more important role for Paul in Acts than they do in his letters; Paul seems to
be more adept as an orator in Acts than he admits to himself; Paul insists that he is an apostle, whereas Luke seems to limit this term to the
original Twelve; and there is a difference in the reasons Paul and Luke
give for the Jewish opposition to Paul's preaching, with Paul focusing
on matters around the law and Luke emphasizing the offense caused
by proclaiming that Jesus had been raised from the dead.[114] Lightfoot,
on the other hand, draws attention to numerous details in Acts that
can be confirmed historically. In particular, he notes Luke's accuracy
with regard to the titles of Roman provincial governors—whether
a proconsul (ἀνθύπατος), a propraetor (ἀντιστράτηγος) or a legate
(πρεσβυτής)—and this at a time when the form of administration in
the provinces frequently changed.[115] The point is, that if Luke was accurate in these details, which seem fairly inconsequential, we ought
to conclude that he both had access to and highly valued accurate information. As a practical way forward, then, I propose that evidence
needs to be assessed on a case by case basis, giving Luke the benefit
of the doubt unless there is reason to question his portrayal. Joseph
Fitzmyer, in my opinion, expresses a fair judgment when he writes:

> [W]e have to admit that the Lucan story in Acts is a good ex-
> ample of a Hellenistic historical monograph. . . . That desig-
> nation does not guarantee, of course, the historicity of every
> Lucan statement or episode, but it reveals that what is recount-
> ed in Acts is substantially more trustworthy from a historical
> point of view than not. To admit that, however, does not ab-

---

113. For details of the debate, see Gasque, *History*.

114. Haenchen, *Acts*, 112–16.

115. Lightfoot, "Discoveries," 291–302.

solve one of the obligation of checking the historical value of every episode.[116]

The second issue involving the book of Acts concerns the historicity of its speeches. Early in the twentieth century, Martin Dibelius questioned their historical value.[117] But, while it is wise to consider seriously Luke's own contribution when reading the speeches he records, on the argument that ancient historians took significant license in such situations, complete historical skepticism is not justified. In this regard, Thucydides' explanation, in writing about the Peloponnesian War, is worth repeating:

> As to the speeches that were made by different men, either when they were about to begin the war or when they were already engaged therein, it has been difficult to recall with strict accuracy the words actually spoken, both for me as regards that which I myself heard, and for those who from various other sources have brought me reports. Therefore the speeches are given in the language in which, as it seemed to me, the several speakers would express, on the subjects under consideration, the sentiments most befitting the occasion, though at the same time I have adhered as closely as possible to the general sense of what was actually said. But as to the facts of the occurrences of the war, I have thought it my duty to give them, not as ascertained from any chance informant nor as seemed to me probable, but only after investigating with the greatest possible accuracy each detail, in the case both of the events in which I myself participated and of those regarding which I got my information from others.[118]

Thucydides' goal was to be as accurate as possible in recording the words of speeches and historical details, but he also felt at liberty to be creative in constructing speeches that gave the same sense as what was said, probably in summary form. Thus, the practice of ancient historians lay somewhere between literal dictation, on the one hand, and invention, on the other.[119] This suggests that it is inappropriate,

116. Fitzmyer, *Acts*, 127; see also Barrett, *Acts*, 2:xl–xli.

117. Dibelius, "Speeches," 138–85; see further, Hill, *Hellenists and Hebrews*, 51–52.

118. Thucydides 1.22.1–2 (Foster, LCL). For further discussion of the purpose and method of ancient historians in recording speeches, see Gempf, "Public Speaking," 259–303.

119. See further, Glasson, "Speeches," 165.

without specific argument, to suggest that Luke's speeches do not provide historically reliable information. Each speech will need to be considered on a case by case basis; but there is good reason to assume that if Luke shows himself to be generally reliable elsewhere, he should be given the benefit of the doubt in specific cases.

Conclusion

Having situated my approach within the context of the Jesus-Paul debate and explained the method by which I intend to proceed, and having indicated my general approach to the ancient sources, we are now ready to turn to the evidence to see to what extent we can demonstrate corresponding areas of core commitment between Jesus and Paul.

2

Jesus' Table Fellowship with Tax Collectors and Sinners

THE PURPOSE OF THIS CHAPTER IS TO DESCRIBE THE PLACE OF THE "tax collectors and sinners" in the story of Jesus and how his welcome of such people formed a distinctive trait of his ministry. This particular focus is significant because, since he associated with such people even in the face of considerable criticism from others, it is reasonable to believe that we are dealing here with a core commitment of Jesus. In the following chapter we will trace how this commitment may have reached Paul and how it may have been expressed by him.

Historicity

There is widespread agreement that Jesus associated with "sinners." E. P. Sanders writes: "the promise of salvation to sinners is the undeniably distinctive characteristic of Jesus' message."[1] Marcus Borg calls his table fellowship with sinners "one of the most striking features of Jesus' ministry."[2] N. T. Wright states that "[t]here is a more or less universal consensus among scholars . . . that Jesus offered a welcome to, and shared meals with, 'sinners.'"[3]

Richard Horsley, however, has mounted a challenge to this view. He argues, first, that the phrase "tax collectors and sinners" occurs only three times in the Gospels and that none of these provides historically reliable information: (i) Luke 15:1 is widely regarded as redactional; (ii) Mark 2:15–16 is widely regarded as a construction of the early

1. Sanders, *Jesus and Judaism*, 174.
2. Borg, *Jesus: A New Vision*, 101; cf. 131–33; idem., *Conflict*, 93–109.
3. Wright, *Jesus*, 264.

church; and (iii) Matt 11:19//Luke 7:34 is an accusation against Jesus that need not be true.[4] Second, he argues that the Lukan texts that speak of the kingdom being offered especially to "sinners" are probably redactional in light of Luke's interest in repentance: (a) while the parables of Luke 15 may be authentic, the interpretation that speaks of there being joy over "one sinner who repents"[5] is a Lukan addition;[6] (b) similarly, in the parable of the Pharisee and the tax collector,[7] the authenticity of the latter's breast-beating humility is suspect in light of Luke's thematic intent; and (c) the account of Jesus and Zacchaeus "is clearly secondary."[8] Third, Jesus' saying—"I came not to call the righteous, but sinners"—appears from its language ("I came . . .") to have been created by Christians, and may have been so created in order to defend Jesus' actions in light of accusations that he associated with the wrong kind of people.[9] And so Horsely concludes that there is "no evidence that 'sinners,' in the sense of 'despised outcasts' or simply of 'the wicked,' constituted an important element among Jesus' following."[10]

As a general comment in response, it should be noted that proof that something is redactional does not in itself say anything one way or another about its historicity. An editorial comment may sometimes be accurate. It is true, for example, that Luke has a special interest in repentance.[11] Both Mark and Q, however, share a similar interest, albeit not to the same extent as in Luke.[12] Thus, even if Luke did embellish the parable of the Pharisee and the tax collector by describing the latter with stereotypical language of a penitent person, this does not mean that Jesus did not tell such a parable. Furthermore, the theme of repentance in the Gospels is far broader than redactional material, as Bruce Chilton comments: "Repentance, a turning back to what alone has value, is a necessary and inescapable aspect of entering the

4. Horsley, *Violence*, 217.

5. Luke 15:7, 10.

6. Cf. Matt 18:10–14.

7. Luke 18:9–14.

8. Horsley, *Violence*, 217–18, citation from p. 218.

9. Ibid., 218.

10. Ibid., 223.

11. See, e.g., Luke 5:32 (cf. Mark 2:17); 13:3, 5; 15:7, 10; 16:30; 17:3 (cf. Matt 18:15), 4 (cf. Matt 18:21–22); 24:47. The theme of repentance is continued in Acts.

12. Mark 1:4, 15; 6:12 (oddly not in the Lukan par.); Matt 3:8//Luke 3:8; Matt 11:21//Luke 10:13; Matt 12:41//Luke 11:32.

Kingdom; it is implicit within much of Jesus' discourse, and need not be named to be operative."[13]

The other aspects of Horsely's argument can be addressed in connection with an examination of the authenticity of Jesus' association with tax collectors.[14] William Walker gives six reasons why he thinks this was not an authentic aspect of the historical Jesus. First, he notes that there is no mention of tax collectors in the Gospel of John.[15] This is noteworthy, but is not sufficient in itself to contest the historicity of Jesus' association with tax collectors. Such association is attested in multiple sources—Mark, Q, and L;[16] it also appears in various forms— a controversy story,[17] a pronouncement story,[18] words of criticism,[19] and a summary statement.[20] Furthermore, Jesus speaks of tax collectors on other occasions,[21] and the theme of eating with disreputable people is well attested in the Gospels.[22] Finally, if Jesus' contact with tax collectors had been restricted to Galilee, then perhaps John, who focuses attention much more on Jesus' activity in Jerusalem, Judea, and Samaria,[23] either did not have access to traditions involving tax collectors or did not think them relevant for his purpose.

13. Chilton, "Repentance," 4.

14. With regard to tax collectors, Horsley, *Violence*, 212, is concerned to address two views often expressed in scholarship: (i) that if Jesus associated with tax collectors, who were in league with the Romans, then Jesus could not be understood to be in support of the Zealots; and (ii) Jesus' association with tax collectors, who had for all intents and purposes become Gentiles, was the main cause that led to his death.

15. Walker, "Tax Collectors," 224.

16. Mark 2:13–17 par.; Matt 11:19//Luke 7:34; Luke 15:1–2; 19:1–10.

17. Mark 2:13–17 par.

18. Luke 19:1–10.

19. Matt 11:19//Luke 7:34.

20. Luke 15:1–2.

21. Matt 21:31; Luke 7:29; 18:10–14.

22. Luke 7:36–50; 14:12–14; Matt 8:11–12//Luke 13:28–29; Matt 22:1–13//Luke 14:15–24, cf. *Gos. Thom.* 64.

23. The only pre-resurrection scenes expressly set in Galilee in John's Gospel are: the calling of Philip and Nathaniel (1:43–51); the wedding at Cana (2:1–11); the healing of an official's son (4:43–54); and the feeding of the five thousand, walking on water, and aftermath (6:1–71).

Second, Walker cites certain Synoptic sayings showing that Jesus had a negative view of tax collectors.[24] In two texts, one from Q and the other from M, tax collectors are paired with Gentiles:

> For if you love those who love you, what reward have you? Do not even the tax collectors do the same? And if you salute only your brethren, what more are you doing than others? Do not even the Gentiles do the same? (Matt 5:46–47; par. in Luke 6:32–34[25])

> If he refuses to listen to them, tell it to the church; and if he refuses to listen even to the church, let him be to you as a Gentile and a tax collector. (Matt 18:17)

Elsewhere, they are associated with extortioners, the unjust, adulterers, and harlots, and contrasted with the righteous.[26] What this amounts to is a negative stereotype for tax collectors that Jesus apparently shared. This does not, however, necessarily mean that Jesus did not associate with such people, only that he did not condone their behavior. An expectation of repentance, which we do find in the tradition,[27] would be consistent with Jesus' willingness to associate with such people but not to condone their behavior.

Third, Walker warns that accusations from Jesus' opponents that he associated with tax collectors may not be trustworthy sources of historical information.[28] Of primary concern here is the following Q text:

> For John came neither eating nor drinking, and they say, "He has a demon"; the Son of man came eating and drinking, and

24. Walker, "Tax Collectors," 224–29.

25. Most take Matthew's "tax collectors" and "Gentiles" to be more authentic than Luke's "sinners": see Davies and Allison, *Matthew*, 1:557–58; Luz, *Matthew 1–7*, 345; Fitzmyer, *Luke*, 1:640; Bovon, *Luke* 1:1–9:50, 237; Michel, "τελώνης," 103 n. 146.

26. Luke 18:11; Matt 21:31–32; Mark 2:17 par.

27. The clearest example of the repentance of a tax collector is that of Zacchaeus (Luke 19:8); but mention could also be made of Jesus' parables in Luke 15, each of which emphasizes repentance (Luke 15:7, 10, 18–21) and is set in the context of criticism of Jesus for associating with tax collectors; and although "to repentance" in Luke 5:32 is clearly redactional, it does show that in Luke's opinion Jesus called on tax collectors to repent. Also significant here is the positive response of tax collectors to the preaching of John the Baptist who called on people to repent (Luke 3:12; 7:29; Matt 21:32).

28. Walker, "Tax Collectors," 230–31.

they say, "Behold, a glutton and a drunkard, a friend of tax
collectors and sinners!" (Matt 11:18–19; par. in Luke 7:33–34;
cf. Luke 15:2)

Since Jesus presumably did not agree with the charge that John had
a demon, then perhaps he also did not agree with the charge against
himself that he was a glutton and a friend of tax collectors. But the
comparison between the two charges is not quite that straightforward.
Walker himself makes the point that "[i]t is not at all uncommon for
charges against individuals to be exaggerated."[29] Thus, the options in
evaluating an accusation for historical content are not limited to only
true or false; it may also be an exaggeration of something similar in
kind but different in extent. So, while Jesus may not have agreed with
the deduction that John had a demon, he may very well have agreed
with his accusers regarding John's behavior—namely, that he was a
radical preacher living in the desert and was an eccentric in terms of
his clothing and diet.[30] Similarly, it is quite plausible that Jesus would
have agreed with his accusers regarding their observation of his own
behavior—namely that he ate and drank (i.e., he was not an ascetic
like John[31])—but not regarding their deduction that he was a glutton
and a drunkard.[32] In similar fashion, he would agree that he associated in some way with tax collectors and sinners, but not that he was
their friend, if by friend it was meant that he was not critical of their
behavior. John Nolland writes:

> Whereas John's asceticism was interpreted as and exaggerated
> into self-abuse, Jesus' positive engagement with unsavoury
> people allowed his enjoyment of food and drink in a com-
> munal context and his celebratory posture to be interpreted as
> and exaggerated into gross excess.[33]

29. Ibid., 231.

30. The historical plausibility of such a charge is defended by Nolland, *Matthew*,
463–64; Davies and Allison, *Matthew*, 2:263.

31. Nolland, *Matthew*, 463.

32. Wright, *Jesus*, 440, suggests that behind this criticism was the insinuation that
Jesus was a "rebellious son" who, according to Deut 21:20–21, ought to be stoned to
death.

33. Nolland, *Matthew*, 464.

Thus, Walker's caution, while valid to an extent, does not warrant the conclusion that Jesus did not associate with tax collectors and sinners at all.

Fourth, Walker argues that the historicity of the scenes where Jesus eats with tax collectors is questionable.[34] In particular, he follows Bultmann who argues (i) that the account of Jesus eating dinner at Levi's house is artificial and therefore probably a creation of the early church; and (ii) that the story of Zacchaeus is in fact an extended version of Levi's conversion and therefore is not an independent witness to Jesus' association with tax collectors.[35] The former reads as follows:

> He went out again beside the sea; and all the crowd gathered about him, and he taught them. And as he passed on, he saw Levi the son of Alphaeus sitting at the tax office, and he said to him, "Follow me." And he rose and followed him.
>
> And as he sat at table in his house, many tax collectors and sinners were sitting with Jesus and his disciples; for there were many who followed him. And the scribes of the Pharisees, when they saw that he was eating with sinners and tax collectors, said to his disciples, "Why does he eat with tax collectors and sinners?" And when Jesus heard it, he said to them, "Those who are well have no need of a physician, but those who are sick; I came not to call the righteous, but sinners." (Mark 2:13–17; par. in Matt 9:9–13//Luke 5:27–32)

Numerous aspects of this account are commonly identified as evidence of non-historicity, the most significant of these being: (a) the unlikely appearance of the scribes of the Pharisees at a dinner with tax collectors; (b) the "I came" + infinitive construction of v. 17b that many take to indicate a post-resurrection perspective;[36] and (c) the existence of contemporary parallels for v. 17a ("Those who are well . . .").[37] Walker

---

34. Walker, "Tax Collectors," 231.

35. Bultmann, *History*, 33–34, 47–48.

36. Note the similar language in some clearly post-resurrection compositions: Luke 9:55 (longer reading); 1 Tim 1:15.

37. Similar adages involving an analogy between a physician attending to the sick and associating with disreputable people appear to have been common: Diogenes, *Ep.* 38.4: "I did not dine with everyone, but only with those in need of therapy" (Malherbe); Lucian, *Demon.* 7: "though [Demonax] assailed sins, he forgave sinners, thinking that one should pattern after doctors, who heal sicknesses but feel no anger at the sick" (Harmon, LCL); Dio Chrysostom, *Virt.* 8.5: "just as the good physician should go and offer his services where the sick are most numerous, so . . . the man of wisdom should take up his abode where fools are thickest in order to convict them of

suggests the account was composed by early Christians who combined a saying attributed to Jesus ("Those who are well . . .") with the charge from Jesus' critics that he eats with tax collectors and sinners.[38]

However, aspects (a) and (b) may simply be the result of a redactor summarizing an event, admittedly from a post-resurrection perspective, while (c) has no bearing on the historicity of the event, unless we are to assume that Jesus was unable to say anything that anyone else had ever said![39] But in addition to this, it is difficult to imagine why early Christians would create an incident of Jesus eating with tax collectors and sinners simply based on an unfriendly accusation that he did so. Is it likely that they would have believed such an accusation unless they had independent verification of it? I suspect not. The account would seem to be an admission on the part of Christians that at least on some occasions Jesus did dine with tax collectors. So, even if we cannot verify the historicity of all the details of this specific account, it is likely that the account reflects that to some extent Jesus did have table fellowship with tax collectors and sinners.

Regarding the story of Zacchaeus,[40] Walker admits that the addition of the name "Zacchaeus" is somewhat problematic for his view, but suggests that Luke may have chosen it because (i) he needed a different name from "Levi" to make it look like a separate incident from that in Luke 5:27–32; and (ii) the name, meaning "righteous one"

---

their folly and reprove them" (Cohoon, LCL); Plutarch, *Apoph. lac.* 230F: "physicians, too, are wont to spend their time, not among the healthy, but where the sick are" (Babbitt, LCL); Diogenes Laertius, *Vit. phil.* 2.70: "In answer to one who remarked that he always saw philosophers at rich men's doors, he said, 'So, too, physicians are in attendance on those who are sick, but no one for that reason would prefer being sick to being a physician'" (Hicks, LCL). Cf. Diogenes Laertius, *Vit. phil.* 6.6: "physicians are in attendance on their patients without getting the fever themselves" (Hicks, LCL); *Vit. phil.* 6.36: "If you had been ill and had purchased a doctor, would you then, instead of obeying him, have said 'Backward the streams flow to their founts'?" (Hicks, LCL). Also, Taylor, *Mark*, 207, is probably correct to conclude that "the comparison is so natural that there is no need to suggest borrowing"—at least not borrowing from a specific source.

38. Walker, "Tax Collectors," 232. The Jesus Seminar rated the occasion of Jesus eating with tax collectors and sinners and the critical question raised against him both as red, the involvement of the Pharisees as pink, and the role of the disciples and Jesus' response as black; see Funk and the Jesus Seminar, *Acts of Jesus*, 28–31.

39. Davies and Allison, *Matthew*, 2:103, argue that the saying would fit well historically into the life of Jesus; cf. Marcus, *Mark 1–8*, 228.

40. Luke 19:1–10.

or "pure one," may have been chosen for its irony in belonging to a tax collector. But in fact the appearance of the name is not the only problem for Walker's view. The description of Zacchaeus being short and climbing a tree—specifically, a sycamore tree—are details that sound much more like personal reminiscence than literary creation.[41] If the name Zacchaeus was chosen because it had a particular significance, what was the significance of these other details? Furthermore, it is not clear why Luke, who tends to avoid doublets, would have thought it necessary to create this account when he already had the Levi account. I will not deny that some redactional activity has taken place in the Zacchaeus account,[42] but it seems more likely on balance to be based on a historical recollection than to be an expansion and transformation of the earlier incident.[43]

Fifth, Walker argues that the tradition is inconsistent in identifying one of the Twelve as a tax collector, suggesting that we cannot with confidence rely on it.[44] He notes that each of the Synoptic Gospels and Acts mention a Matthew as one of Jesus' disciples, but only the first Gospel identifies him as a tax collector.[45] Commentators generally agree that this identification is dependent on Matt 9:9 where Jesus calls a tax collector named Matthew to follow him—although Mark and Luke call this person Levi. As a consequence, Matt 10:3 cannot be used as independent evidence that Jesus associated with tax collectors.

Walker is probably correct in drawing this conclusion. However, the likelihood of Matthew, one of the Twelve, being a tax collector is dependent on the reason the writer of the first Gospel used this name instead of Levi in Matt 9:9. Davies and Allison outline various possibilities here: (i) one of Jesus' disciples had two Semitic names, Levi and Matthew, the latter possibly given to him by Jesus, just as he gave a second name to Simon; (ii) the writer believed that anyone called in such a fashion by Jesus must be one of the Twelve and, seeing that Levi did not belong to this group, he substituted one of the other names; (iii) the writer knew of a disciple named Matthew who was a tax collector but, since he had no account of this person's call, chose to adapt Mark's

41. Such is the view of Bauckham, *Eyewitnesses*, 55.

42. See Fitzmyer, *Luke*, 2:1218–22.

43. Nolland, *Luke*, 3:904; Marshall, *Luke*, 695.

44. Walker, "Tax Collectors," 234–37.

45. Matt 10:3; cf. Mark 3:18; Luke 6:15; Acts 1:13.

account of the call of Levi; (iv) the name Ματθαῖος was chosen because of its similarity in sound to μαθητής that appears three times in Matt 9:10–13; (v) the writer wanted to give information about the assumed author of the Gospel; or (vi) the writer wanted to include in the story someone named Matthew who was known to his readers.[46] Positions (i), (iii) and (vi) would favor one of the Twelve being a tax collector because they each assume the writer or his audience had independent knowledge of this person; if one of the other views is correct, we could not, based on this evidence, say with confidence that one of Jesus' disciples was a tax collector.

And sixth, Walker proposes that the appearance of τελῶναι in the tradition may be due to a confusion over the similar sounding Aramaic word, מְלָרִי, that can be translated as "sporters, night demons or urchins"—Walker suggests a contemporary equivalent might be "playboys."[47] While we must admit this to be a possibility, it seems very unlikely: this is not a typical mistake that translators make.

In the end, Walker suggests that the accounts that indicate that Jesus did associate with tax collectors and sinners may have been created by the early church for one of three possible reasons: (i) to respond to the accusations against Jesus that he was a friend of such people; (ii) to justify early Christian outreach to "sinners" (presumably he means Gentiles); or (iii) to create polemic apologetic against Jews—either against Pharisees in particular in light of the church's struggle with Pharisaism, or against Jews in general in light of the church's attempt to show itself more attractive to a Roman audience. I have already commented that (i) seems very unlikely.[48] Concerning option (ii), one wonders why the early church would have included tax collectors in the stories they created if they had wanted to justify their outreach to Gentiles; had Christians felt the liberty radically to rewrite the tradition, presumably they could have depicted Jesus as more welcoming and concerned about Gentiles themselves.[49] Regarding (iii), Dunn argues that the tradition in Mark 2 predates 70 CE, and so predates the

46. Davies and Allison, *Matthew*, 2:98–99.

47. Walker, "Tax Collectors," 231.

48. See above, p. 34.

49. Luke demonstrates an interest in Gentiles (see esp. Luke 2:32; 3:6; 7:1–10; 24:47), but the emphasis is hardly what we would expect in light of the significance of the mission to the Gentiles in the early church, had Luke felt he had the liberty to shape the tradition to the extent of creating new material.

rise of Pharisaic dominance over Judaism.[50] Furthermore, it is not clear that showing Jesus associating with tax collectors and sinners—against the complaints of Jews of his day who were presumably concerned that he was behaving immorally—would have been the most effective way for Christians to endear themselves to Gentiles in the Greco-Roman world. It would probably not impress many, for example, who were attracted to Judaism in part for its high moral standards, from among whom Christians recruited numerous converts.[51]

It appears, then, that the simplest explanation of all the texts is that, although Jesus spoke of tax collectors in a stereotypically negative way, using them as a standard above which his followers must reach, and as a way of shaming some Jews, he did associate with such people.

The Identity of Tax Collectors and Sinners: Major Views

But precisely what kind of people were tax collectors and sinners? It will be important to establish with some confidence the identity of the tax collectors and sinners with whom Jesus associated, and the reason this association caused such offense. To begin with we will consider the views of three scholars: Norman Perrin, Joachim Jeremias, and E. P. Sanders.

Norman Perrin

Perrin proposes that the means of forgiveness within Judaism were of "limited effectiveness" and that Jews in Jesus' day longed for "ultimate forgiveness" by God.[52] This is the context, according to Perrin, in which to understand Jesus offering forgiveness—a more complete forgiveness than what was available in Judaism. But to clarify this offer, he proposes three categories of sinners: (i) Jews who occasionally sin but who can turn to God in repentance and find forgiveness;

50. Dunn, "Pharisees," 69–71; for a summary, see the discussion under "The Gospels" in the Appendix B below.

51. See Acts 10:2, 22; 13:16, 26, 43; 16:14; 17:4, 17; 18:7.

52. Perrin, *Rediscovering*, 91. Perrin identifies the following means of forgiveness: "Temple sacrifice, the Day of Atonement ritual, ritual cleansing, works of supererogation, especially almsgiving, repentance, suffering, and, under certain circumstances, death" (ibid.).

(ii) Gentiles for whom most Jews thought forgiveness was impossible; and (iii) "Jews who made themselves as Gentiles"—that is, Jews who engaged in certain occupations that in the eyes of most Jews were so disreputable that the practitioners forfeited their rights as Jews and became essentially "Gentile sinners."[53] The "occupations" in view here are listed in several rabbinic texts, and one of these lists includes tax collectors.[54] Perrin notes that such people were denied certain rights as citizens, such as being a witness.[55] Furthermore, he suggests, tax collectors were also hated for being quislings, since "they collected taxes from their fellow Jews on behalf of hated Gentiles."[56] This is why we often find tax collectors mentioned alongside other stereotypical disreputable people—robbers, prostitutes, extortioners, adulterers, Gentiles, or more generally, sinners—both in the New Testament[57] and in rabbinic literature.[58] Such people, Perrin concludes, "were widely regarded as beyond hope of penitence or forgiveness."[59]

Perrin goes on to argue that Jesus' association with such people, particularly in his regular practice of receiving them in table fellowship and offering them forgiveness, was the offense that led to his death. Perrin supports this with the following arguments: (i) the two accusations that Jesus was "a glutton and a drunkard" and "a friend of tax collectors and sinners"[60] are best understood as two aspects of one offense rather than as two different offenses, as would be expected if the issue was one of table fellowship with outcasts;[61] (ii) the universalism expressed in Jesus' anticipation of the messianic banquet—"many will

---

53. Ibid., 93–94.

54. *b. Sanh.* 25b. For a discussion of the various rabbinic lists, see Jeremias, *Jerusalem*, 301–12.

55. Perrin, *Rediscovering*, 93.

56. Ibid.

57. Matt 11:19//Luke 7:34; Matt 18:17; 21:31–32; Mark 2:15–16 par.; Luke 15:1; 18:11; 19:7.

58. *m. Tehar.* 7:6; *m. B. Qam.* 10:2; *m. Ned.* 3:4; *b. Šebu.* 39a; *Der. Er. Rab.* 2.

59. Perrin, *Rediscovering*, 94.

60. Matt 11:19//Luke 7:34.

61. Perrin, *Rediscovering*, 105–6, thinks it unlikely that the first accusation would have been based on Jesus' failure to practice fasting as others did, or that this would have been a cause of such offense that some would want to kill him. He further argues that the prominence of communal meals in early Christianity is best explained if meals played a central role in Jesus' ministry (104).

come from east and west"[62]—is best understood as arising out of Jesus' fellowship with outcasts;[63] and (iii) the gravity of the offense implicit in Jesus' parables of the prodigal son, the lost sheep, and the lost coin[64] is best explained in light of Jesus' fellowship with outcasts.[65] Perrin does not claim that all of Jesus' followers were penitent tax collectors and sinners; these are simply the extreme examples in whom God's radical forgiveness is displayed.[66] But by welcoming such outcasts into table fellowship, and suggesting that this was an expression of the kingdom of God, Jesus deeply offended those who emphasized the importance of maintaining Jewish distinctiveness, particularly in the face of foreign influence.

Joachim Jeremias

Jeremias understands the situation somewhat differently. He argues that the people who gathered around Jesus were those whom he called "the poor" but whom his opponents called "sinners." Jeremias points to the occasion when, after summarizing his ministry to some disciples of John the Baptist, Jesus says, "And blessed is he who takes no offence at me," implying that some people were in fact taking offense at him.[67] But why? Jeremias suggests that no one would have been offended by the healings he mentions; therefore, it must be the fact that "the poor have the good news preached to them" that causes offense.[68] These were, according to the prophets, "the oppressed who cannot defend themselves, the desperate, the hopeless";[69] but, according to rabbinic literature, they were known as the עַמְמֵי הָאָרֶץ ("people of the land")[70] whom the rabbis often looked down on because of their ignorance of both Torah and the teaching of the sages, their lack of

62. Matt 8:11//Luke 13:29.

63. Perrin, *Rediscovering*, 106.

64. Luke 15.

65. Perrin, *Rediscovering*, 107.

66. Ibid.

67. Matt 11:6//Luke 7:23. For discussion of authenticity of this text, see below, pp. 267–68.

68. Jeremias, *Theology*, 109.

69. Ibid., 113.

70. The singular form is עַם הָאָרֶץ.

piety, and their failure to observe rabbinic standards concerning tith-ing and purity.[71] Jeremias suggests that the Pharisees in Jesus' day were critical of the masses for these reasons and believed that the common people were sinners and thus separated from salvation: these people "did not observe the demands of religious laws as they did, and in contrast to [them] the Pharisees considered themselves to be the true Israel."[72] And so they criticized Jesus for associating with such sinners.[73] Tax collectors belong to this group, not because they have made them-selves to be Gentiles,[74] but simply because theirs is one of the despised occupations mentioned in rabbinic literature, despised because they were believed to lead to dishonesty.[75] As such, tax collectors "are the typical ἁμαρτωλοί in the gospels."[76] Jeremias concludes:

> Jesus' following consisted predominantly of the disreputable, the ʿammē hā-ʾāreṣ, the uneducated, the ignorant, whose reli-gious ignorance and moral behaviour stood in the way of their access to salvation, according to the convictions of the time.[77]

Jesus' offense, then, from Jeremias's perspective, was that he wel-comed those who failed to live up to the standards of the Pharisees, and declared that they were forgiven and welcomed by God.

E. P. Sanders

Sanders strongly disputes the claims of both Jeremias and Perrin. Regarding Jeremias's views he argues first that the "sinners" are not the עַמֵּי הָאָרֶץ, the common people from the perspective of the Pharisees, but rather they were the wicked, "those who sinned wilfully and hei-

---

71. See, e.g., John 7:49; m. Demai 2:2; m. Ṭehar. 8:1, 3; b. Soṭah 25a; b. Ber. 47b; b. Pesaḥ 49b; b. Ned. 20a. See further Str-B 2:494–519. Sandmel, Judaism, 166–67, suggests, based on the scorn which the sages had toward them, that the עַמֵּי הָאָרֶץ "were rural illiterates, ordinary peasants, whose illiteracy impeded a scrupulous fidel-ity to the religious requirements." Cf. Danby, Mishnah, 793.

72. Jeremias, Jerusalem, 259.

73. Mark 2:17; Luke 7:37, 39; 15:2; 19:7.

74. Donahue, "Tax Collectors," 40, 42, refers to some private correspondence from Jeremias to Perrin (11 September 1967) in which he directly challenges this point.

75. Jeremias, Jerusalem, 303–12.

76. Jeremias, Theology, 110.

77. Ibid., 112.

nously and who did not repent."[78] Sanders claims that ἁμαρτωλοί is a translation of רְשָׁעִים (or its Aramaic equivalent) that "is virtually a technical term" for "the wicked"—people who effectively renounced the covenant, that would include such people as tax collectors, not only because they were engaged in a despised profession but because they collaborated with the Romans.[79] But nowhere in Jewish literature are the עַמְמֵי הָאָרֶץ, or ordinary people, referred to as "the wicked."[80]

Second, Sanders argues that the offense Jesus caused did not have to do with purity. In rabbinic literature, it was the חֲבֵרִים—who according to Sanders overlapped with but were not identical to the Pharisees[81]—who took it upon themselves to apply in their everyday lives certain purity laws that pertained only to priests in the temple, and in this way set themselves apart from the עַמְמֵי הָאָרֶץ.[82] But there is no evidence that the חֲבֵרִים saw themselves as "the righteous" and everyone else as cut off from Israel.[83] In any case, as lay people, neither the חֲבֵרִים nor the Pharisees had the authority or the power to exclude anyone from the covenant even if they wanted to.[84]

Regarding the position of Perrin, Sanders maintains that Jesus' offense did not consist merely in offering forgiveness to people. He argues that (i) there is no evidence that Jews thought the means of forgiveness they had were inadequate; and (ii) it is not the case that certain Jews were beyond forgiveness: he suggests that (a) anyone who repented could always find forgiveness; (b) had tax collectors and sinners actually wanted forgiveness, all they had to do was to talk to a

---

78. Sanders, *Jesus and Judaism*, 177. Sanders (386 n. 16) refers to his *Paul and Palestinian Judaism* where he discusses "the wicked" in Jewish literature.

79. Ibid., 177–78.

80. Ibid., 179–80.

81. Ibid., 187–88.

82. This is not to say that other Jews, including the עַמְמֵי הָאָרֶץ, did not observe purity laws at all—only that the חֲבֵרִים were more scrupulous. See Westerholm, *Jesus and Scribal Authority*, 65–66.

83. Sanders, *Jesus and Judaism*, 180–82. Sanders argues against identifying the חֲבֵרִים with the Pharisees and vice versa, although he admits there may have been an overlap between the two before 70, and that after 70 the rabbis accepted the two main points of the חֲבֵרִים—strict tithing and priestly purity for the laity. Regarding Pharisees, however, all we know for sure is that they were a party "defined by its zeal for the knowledge of the law, belief in the resurrection, and acceptance of the tradition of the elders" (188).

84. Ibid., 192–98.

priest; (c) Jesus may have been able to admit sinners to *his* community, but he was not a gate-keeper of the Jewish institutions; (d) repentance was not prominent in Jesus' preaching; and (e) no one would have been offended if Jesus had led wicked people to repent.[85] Rather, according to Sanders, Jesus' offense lay in offering the wicked "inclusion in the kingdom not only *while they were still sinners* but also *without* requiring repentance as normally understood, and therefore he could have been accused of being a friend of people who indefinitely *remained* sinners."[86]

Assessment

The main achievement of Sanders' contribution to this discussion has been to correct something of a caricature of Second Temple Judaism. In particular, we ought not to think that Jews thought their religion had an ineffective means of forgiveness, or that a particular group within Judaism—the חֲבֵרִים or Pharisees—had the power to exclude from the covenant anyone who did not live up to *their* standards. Still open for discussion, however, are a number of questions relating to the specific nature of Jesus' offense, which in turn relate to the specific identity and character of tax collectors and sinners and to the concerns of the Pharisees.

There is unfortunately at present much disagreement regarding the Pharisees. I argue in Appendix B below that they were a group of Jews committed to the law and certain oral traditions, and were especially known for their emphasis on regulations concerning food, ritual purity, Sabbath-keeping, and festival observance. Furthermore, from time to time they enjoyed a position of influence, and would exploit that when they could to shape the life of the nation according to their values.[87] If this is at all close to the truth, it should not be surprising that the Pharisees would oppose Jesus, particularly if he was a popular figure[88] and, in their view, was leading people astray.[89] Whatever criti-

---

85. Ibid., 200–204.

86. Ibid., 204–8, citation from p. 206, emphasis original.

87. See below, Appendix B.

88. On Jesus' popularity, see below, p. 258 n. 100.

89. See Stanton, "Jesus of Nazareth," 164–80, who argues that is it plausible that Jesus' opponents thought of him in terms of the "misleading prophet" of Deut 13 who

cisms the Pharisees had about the common people, it is quite plausible that they saw Jesus to be making matters worse, and thus needed to be opposed.

Jesus probably offended the Pharisees in a number of ways: according to the Gospels, he often spoke critically of them,[90] and they took offense at him speaking words of forgiveness,[91] healing on the Sabbath,[92] and telling parables against them.[93] Perrin is probably correct to identify a key point of offense as being Jesus' table fellowship. In the ancient world, table fellowship was a means of defining social boundaries. Dennis Smith writes: "the banquet functioned as the primary way in which various social groups exemplified and solidified their group identity."[94] In Judaism, food laws had always served to define the boundary between Jews and Gentiles. But table fellowship was not simply about eating the right kind of food; it also involved eating with the right kind of people. Jerome Neyrey writes:

> commensality or its absence should be interpreted in terms of group membership: "Likes eat with likes." Hence the meals of Judeans indicate either their distinctive group affiliation, if eaten with other Judeans, or their separation, if commensality was refused. Moreover, food functioned as a metaphor for the word of God. Hence concern for doctrinal and ethnic purity

leads people astray, and who therefore ought to be killed. Such a perspective may be implied in some Gospel texts (Matt 27:63 ("that imposter"); Mark 11:18 ("the chief priests . . . feared him, because all the multitude was astonished at his teaching"); Luke 23:2 ("we found this man perverting our nation"), 5 ("He stirs up the people"), 14 ("as one who was perverting the people"); John 7:12 ("he is leading the people astray"), 32 ("The Pharisees heard the crowd thus muttering about him, and the chief priests and Pharisees sent officers to arrest him"), 47 ("Are you led astray, you also")). In the so-called *Testimonium Flavianum*, Josephus writes: "πολλὺς μὲν Ἰουδαίους, πολλοὺς δὲ καὶ τοῦ Ἑλληνικοῦ ἐπηγάγετο" (*Ant.* 18.63), which could be translated, "He led astray many Jews and many Greeks" (BDAG notes that the verb used here, ἐπάγω, is usually used in connection with bringing on something bad). In his debate with Trypho, Justin Martyr notes that many Jews thought of Jesus as "a magician and a deceiver of God's people" (*Dial.* 69.7). And the Talmud states that Jesus "practised sorcery and enticed Israel and led Israel astray," and makes specific reference to Deut 13:8–9 to justify his execution (*b. Sanh.* 43a; cf. 107b).

90. Matt 5:20; Matt 15:1–9//Mark 7:1–13; Matt 16:1–4//Mark 8:11–13//Luke 12:54–56; Matt 19:3–9//Mark 10:2–9; Matt 23:1–36; Luke 11:37–54; 16:14–15.

91. Matt 9:2–3//Mark 2:5–7//Luke 5:20–21; Luke 7:36–50.

92. See below, pp. 257–59.

93. Matt 21:33–46//Mark 12:1–12//Luke 20:9–19; Luke 18:9–14.

94. Smith, "Table Fellowship," 303.

are replicated in the dietary and commensality practices of the Judeans.[95]

Thus, Jesus' offense is that he welcomed into fellowship the wrong kind of people. And again, if Jesus had a popular following and was considered by many to be a prophet, then there would be good reason for the Pharisees to be upset with him.

Sanders is certainly correct to argue that Jesus' offense in connection with eating with tax collectors and sinners consisted of more than associating with the common people of whom the Pharisees, on Jeremias's view, disapproved; but he is almost certainly incorrect to locate that offense in Jesus' failure to require repentance. Bruce Chilton effectively argues that repentance is too deeply imbedded in Jesus' teaching to be set aside as secondary.[96] Sanders accepts as authentic only three passages that show that Jesus called for people to repent;[97] other references he argues reflect a post-resurrection perspective.[98] Chilton, however, counters that (i) even if some texts emphasizing repentance are Christian creations, such an emphasis among Jesus' followers is best explained if the call to repentance originated with Jesus; (ii) several parables emphasize the importance of giving up all for the sake of the kingdom, implying a reorientation of life similar to repentance;[99] (iii) two of Jesus' sayings indicate that entering the kingdom is a challenge—like a camel going through the eye of a needle or a person becoming a child again[100]—as is repentance; and (iv) the theme of debt remission in the Lord's Prayer and in some of Jesus' parables is indicative of a concern for repentance.[101]

95. Neyrey, "Meals," 170; here Neyrey is building on the work, done from an anthropological perspective, of Feeley-Harnik, Lord's Table.

96. Chilton, "Repentance," 1–18.

97. Matt 11:21–24//Luke 10:13–15; Matt 12:38–42//Luke 11:29–32; Luke 13:1–5.

98. Sanders, Jesus and Judaism, 109, takes Mark 1:15 par. to reflect the preaching of the church, the parables of the lost sheep and coin (Luke 15:4–7, 8–10) to be focused on God's action rather than human repentance, and other references to be redactional or late (Mark 6:12; Luke 5:32; 16:30).

99. Matt 13:44–46; Matt 22:1–10//Luke 14:15–24; Matt 22:11–14.

100. Matt 10:24//Mark 10:25//Luke 18:25; Matt 18:3//Mark 10:15//Luke 18:17; cf. John 3:3–4.

101. Matt 6:12//Luke 11:4; Matt 18:23–35; Luke 7:40–43; 16:1–9. Chilton, "Repentance," 9–10, challenges Sanders' identification of ἁμαρτωλοί with רְשָׁעִים, argues that the Aramaic root חובא, meaning "sinner" or "debtor," provides a better parallel, and notes that this "is the natural counterpart of ἁμαρτωλός in the Septuagint"

The Identity of Tax Collectors and Sinners: Examining the Sources

We turn now to look in more detail at what can be said about the identity of the tax collectors and sinners.

Tax Collectors

The method of tax collection varied in the Roman empire depending on the kind of tax in question, on the administration in power in a particular region, and on the period of history. Broadly speaking, there were two kinds of Roman taxes: (i) direct taxes (κῆσος), consisting of the land tax (the *tributum agri*) that was a tax on produce, and the head tax (the *tributum capitis*) that was a tax on people; and (ii) indirect taxes (τέλος), which consisted of tolls and customs duties. The Greek word τελώνης denoted a collector of indirect taxes.[102]

The most popular means of tax collection in the Roman empire was a tax farming system. Rulers would grant the authority to collect taxes to the highest bidder who would typically pay the calculated annual tax in advance and then collect the taxes plus his own commissions from the people. In the time of the Republic, a wealthy group from the equestrian class known as "publicans" (the *societas publicanorum*) controlled the tax collection. With little government oversight and with the support of the military, publicans were often free to inflate their own costs, thereby effectively practicing extortion, with the people having little recourse.[103] In the 40s BCE, however, Julius Caesar began to reform the tax system: in 44 he removed the publicans from Palestine and gave responsibility for tax collection to Hycranus and his officials.[104]

---

(10). Thus, he argues that a common Aramaic word lies behind both ἁμαρτωλός and ὀφειλέτης.

102. In order to make the distinction clear, some prefer to use a different term for the translation of τελώνης, such as "toll collector." I have chosen to stay with the more generic term "tax collector" because of its widespread usage and the fact that the τελῶναι collected both tolls and customs, but with a clear understanding that it is the collection of indirect taxes that is in view.

103. Plutarch, *Luc.* 20.1, speaks of the cities of Asia as having been "plundered and reduced to slavery by the tax-gatherers and money-lenders" (Perrin, LCL); cf. *Luc.* 7.6.

104. Josephus, *Ant.* 14.200–201. See Michel, "τελώνης," 94, for a summary of the tax reforms from Julius Caesar to the second century CE.

We can assume, however, that tax collectors were never well-liked. Even at the best of times, people typically fail to draw the connection between tax revenues and the benefits they provide. So, it is no surprise that we have records of complaints against high taxes: Josephus accuses Herod of being harsh on his subjects because of the great expense of his many projects;[105] Tacitus reports that in 17 CE people in Syria and Judea appealed for tax relief because of financial hardship.[106] But Otto Michel comments that the τελῶναι in particular were generally feared and despised throughout the Roman world because of their shady methods.[107] Due to the complexity of the tax system and the authority of tax collectors to determine the value of goods, they were often suspected of charging unfair rates. John the Baptist's charge to tax collectors that they collect no more than what has been appointed, and Zacchaeus' pledge to repay those he had defrauded, reflect this reality.[108] Thus, tax collectors were generally despised for dishonesty and greed,[109] and so were considered disreputable.[110]

105. Josephus, *Ant.* 16.154; *J.W.* 1.524; 2.84–87.

106. Tacitus, *Ann.* 2.42. See further, Jeremias, *Jerusalem*, 124–26.

107. Michel, "τελώνης," 99.

108. Luke 3:12–13; 19:8. The Talmud refers to tax collectors whose rates could not be checked: *b. Ned.* 28a; *b. B. Qam.* 113a.

109. See further, Cicero, *Off.* 1.150: "those means of livelihood are rejected as undesirable which incur people's ill-will, as those of tax-gatherers and usurers" (Miller, LCL); Herodas 6.64: "for every door now-a-days shudders at the tax-gatherers" (Headlam and Knox); Lucian, *Men.* 11–12: the narrator describes the post-mortem judgment of "adulterers, procurers, tax-gatherers, toadies, informers, and all that crowd of people who create such confusion in life"—condemned because in life they were known for their "pride of wealth and place" (Harmon, LCL); Plutarch, *An ignis* 12 [958D]: "Man has been granted but a little time to live and . . . sleep, like a tax-collector, takes away half of that" (Helmbold, LCL); *y. Ned.* 3:4: tax collectors are included alongside murderers and robbers.

110. Dio Chrysostom, 1 *Serv. lib.* 14.14: "things . . . regarded as base and unseemly by mankind . . . , for example, collecting taxes, or keeping a brothel" (Cohoon, LCL); Theophrastus, *Char.* 6.5: "He [the shameless man] is apt to keep an inn or run a brothel or be a tax collector, and he rejects no disgraceful occupation" (Rusten, Cunningham & Knox, LCL); Dionysius of Halicarnassus, *Amm.* 12.36: in trying to defend himself, a tax collector acknowledges the general opinion that tax collecting is shameful—"If it is not shameful for you to sell the taxes, it is not shameful for us to buy them" (Usher, LCL); Lucian, *Pseudol.* 30: "It can be overlooked . . . if a man in the pinch of hunger . . . shamelessly asks for gifts—begs, in fact—and steals and plies the trade of publican" (Harmon, LCL); Plutarch, *Apoph. lac.* 236B: "Another [Spartan] . . . saw that the Athenians were hawking salt fish and dainties, collecting taxes, keeping public brothels, and following other unseemly pursuits" (Babbitt, LCL); Plutarch,

Rabbinic literature expresses a similar dislike for tax collectors. Here a distinction is made between collectors of direct taxes (גַּבָּאִין) and collectors of indirect taxes (מוֹכְסִין).[111] According to the rabbis, repentance for tax collectors (both kinds) was difficult;[112] this was because according to Jewish law theft required restitution, but tax collectors had cheated so many people that simply remembering every instance was virtually impossible.[113] In various texts, tax collectors are associated with other disreputable people: thieves, extortioners, murderers.[114] One text associates them with dice players, usurers, pigeon trainers, sabbatical year traders, robbers, herdsmen—those who because of dishonesty are disqualified from being a witness.[115] Interestingly, however, the same text goes on to record the opinion of Rabbi Judah that the גַּבָּאִין *are* in general eligible to be witnesses (unless they are known to tax exorbitantly), and then to tell of the father of Rabbi Zera, a גַּבָּאִי, who showed himself to be honorable by warning people to hide when the tax officer came to town so that they might avoid paying heavy taxes. Significantly, however, it is the גַּבָּאִין who were considered by some to be worthy, not the מוֹכְסִין.

Some have argued that in addition to the above, Jews would have disliked Jewish tax collectors because of their association with Gentiles—that is, (i) they represented the enemy and would have been viewed by fellow Jews as traitors, and (ii) they may have been consid-

---

An seni 19 [794A]: "the old man in public life who undertakes subordinate services, such as the farming of taxes and the supervision of harbours and of the market-place . . . seems to me, my friend, a pitiable and unenviable object, and to some people, perhaps, a burdensome and vulgar one" (Fowler, LCL); cf. Plutarch, *Vit. aere al.* 5 [829C].

111. Perrin, *Rediscovering*, 93 n. 1, makes no distinction between the different kinds of tax collection, suggesting that "[i]n Jewish eyes they were all tarred with the same brush and our sources do not distinguish them systematically from one another." It seems likely that Jews (like most people) would have disliked all collectors of taxes, but the assertion that they did not distinguish between collectors of direct and indirect taxes, disliking them for different reasons, would need to be demonstrated. The evidence that follows suggests otherwise.

112. *b. B. Qam.* 94b.

113. Michel, "τελώνης," 103.

114. *m. Ṭehar.* 7:6; *m. B. Qam.* 10:2; *m. Ned.* 3:4; *b. Šebu.* 39a; *Der. Er. Rab.* 2.

115. *b. Sanh.* 24b–25b. In could be that tax collectors were excluded from other roles as well; the specific focus on eligibility for being a witness here probably reflects the general concern of the Sanhedrin tractate for matters relating to the law court. See also the discussion in Donahue, "Tax Collectors," 51–52.

ered to be impure.[116] Unfortunately, not all the evidence we have is consistent, which probably reflects nothing more than that there was a range of opinion among Jews at the time.

During Jesus' ministry tax collection in Galilee was under the authority of Herod Antipas—direct taxes were collected by Jewish councils and indirect taxes by tax farmers—whereas in Judea it would have been directly under Roman oversight.[117] Technically, therefore, tax collectors in Galilee would have been agents of a Jewish administration—government officials in the case of direct taxes, and tax farmers employed by the government in the case of indirect taxes—whereas in Judea collectors would have dealt directly with Roman overlords. It is more likely to be the case, therefore, that tax collectors in Judea would have been viewed as representatives of a foreign power than would those in Galilee,[118] but it is difficult to say how much this distinction would have meant to the Jewish public. Donahue thinks the difference would have been significant,[119] but Farmer disagrees arguing that most Galileans would have seen Antipas as nothing more than a client ruler of the Romans.[120] Although Jewish authorities were involved in the collection of taxes,[121] many Jews resented it. We recall that the revolt in response to the Roman census of 6 CE (which was necessary for tax purposes) was led by a Galilean named Judas,[122] and that it was his descendants who led the revolutionaries known as Sicarii later in the 60s, suggesting that Judas' cause did not die with him.[123] This is not to say that all Galileans shared Judas' view, but no doubt some did; certainly the fact that Antipas was a Jew made no difference to Judas. It is probably safe to say that the attitude of individual Jews towards tax collectors mirrored their attitude towards Romans in general—that to

116. See above, p. 39–40.

117. Donahue, "Tax Collectors," 45.

118. It may be significant, for example, that when Jesus was challenged in Jerusalem about paying the Roman head tax, the issue in question is not the amount but the lawfulness of paying taxes at all to the Romans (Mark 12:13–17).

119. Donahue, "Tax Collectors," 45–46.

120. Farmer, "Tax Collectors," 171 n. 1.

121. Josephus, *J.W.* 2.403–5, records Agrippa's complaint against the Jews for failing to pay tribute to Rome, after which the Jewish authorities collected what was lacking and paid it.

122. Josephus, *Ant.* 18.4–10; cf. *J.W.* 2.118.

123. Josephus, *J.W.* 7.253–54, 324.

the extent that they saw Romans as their oppressors they would have seen tax collectors as quislings. But Michel suggests that this would be more the case for collectors of direct taxes; those who collected indirect taxes were also disliked, but more for their dishonesty than their collusion with the enemy.[124]

Were tax collectors considered to be unclean? It seems quite plausible that someone whose employment brought them into contact with all kinds of people, including Gentiles, and who needed to inspect people's baggage or belongings would often be in a state of uncleanness. The evidence usually presented to support this, however, is not as clear as is often assumed. In the context of his argument that tax collectors had made themselves to be like Gentiles, Perrin, for example, argues that according to the rabbis they were deemed to be unclean.[125] According to *m. Ṭehar* 7:6, if a tax collector entered a house, everything in the house became unclean; thus, presumably the tax collector himself was considered unclean—that is, he was in the same state as a Gentile.[126] The situation, however, is not quite that simple.

124. Michel, "τελώνης," 102–3. Gibson, "HOI TELŌNAI," 429–33, argues that the link between tax collectors and prostitutes in Matt 21:31–32 was based on their both being known to collaborate with the Romans. The evidence he presents in support of prostitutes collaborating with the Romans, however, is not convincing: (i) Josephus, *Ant.* 19.356–57, tells of an incident in which Roman soldiers erected and abused some statues of the late Agrippa's daughters on the roofs of some brothels; (ii) *b. Šabb.* 33b complains that everything the Romans built in Palestine was for themselves: "they built market-places, to set harlots in them; . . . bridges, to levy tolls for them"; and (iii) *b. ʿAbod. Zar.* 18a tells of the Romans punishing a rabbi and his family, which involved consigning the daughter to a brothel because on one occasion she "took particular care of her step" in the presence of some Roman men who were eying her. These texts, however, tell very little, if anything, about *why* respectable Jews, like the Pharisees, would have objected to prostitutes. Now, it is almost certainly true that Jewish prostitutes would have had more business among Romans than among Jews, since most of the Roman men in Palestine would have been soldiers (unmarried or there without their wives), would have been wealthier than the average Jew, and would have had fewer moral scruples about engaging the services of a prostitute than would most Jews have had. This does not, however, entail that the *main* cause of offense of prostitutes was that they were collaborating with the Romans, as if the Jewish reprehension would have been any less had they plied their trade only among Jews. Surely those Jews who disapproved of prostitutes did so because of their immorality, not because they were being immoral with the wrong people.

125. Perrin, *Rediscovering*, 94; see also Borg, *Conflict*, 98–100.

126. Note that uncleanness by itself did not put a Jew into the same state as a Gentile. Non-priestly Jews contracted uncleanness for all sorts of reasons, but this

First, it should be noted that the word used in the Mishnah text is גַּבָּאִין, not מוֹכְסִין; hence, the τελῶναι are not in view here.[127] And second, b. Ḥag. 26a suggests that the uncleanness caused in a situation where a tax collector entered a house was due to the presence of an accompanying Gentile.[128] Another text (m. Kel. 15:4), possibly relating to those who collected customs duties, states that the exciseman's staff is unclean due to the fact that he uses it to poke around in the packs of travellers. It is significant, however, that the uncleanness relates to the staff and not to the person; and it is possibly significant that the word for exciseman—בַּלָּשִׁין—is not the usual word for collectors of indirect taxes—מוֹכְסִין.[129] Consequently, while it is quite possible that tax collectors were often suspected of uncleanness, explicit evidence is lacking.[130]

Interestingly, we also have accounts of some tax collectors who were considered to be exemplary Jews. Josephus tells of a tax collector named John who, along with other Jewish leaders, tried to intercede on behalf of the Jews in Caesarea in a case where they were being obstructed in accessing their synagogue.[131] Also, the Talmud tells of a tax collector, Bar Maayan, who was so respected that when he died work in the city had to stop because so many were attending his funeral.[132] But, anticipating our discussion below about the general opinion of tax

---

did not place them outside the covenant. Perrin's argument must assume that tax collectors had so flaunted Torah, specifically the holiness code, that they had essentially abandoned the covenant and thus become like Gentiles.

127. Clearly, collectors of tolls and customs duties would not have had occasion to enter a house in the performance of their duties.

128. b. Ḥag. 26a tries to solve an apparent contradiction between m. Ṭehar. 7:6 and m. Ḥag. 3:6 regarding whether tax collectors should be believed when they say they did not touch anything in the house. The Gemara suggests that where a tax collector is not to be believed is when a Gentile—presumably his superior—accompanied him, for it can be assumed that the latter would have insisted that the tax collector make a thorough search. See Maccoby, "Tax-Collectors," 60–61.

129. For a discussion on each of these rabbinic texts, see Donahue, "Tax Collectors," 50–51.

130. See also Maccoby, "Tax-Collectors," 60–63, who draws on the anthropological work of Mary Douglas to argue that in contrast to other societies governed by purity regulations "the Jewish laws never use purity to demarcate societal divisions" (61). The other rabbinic texts cited by Michel, "τελώνης," 101, do not lead to the conclusion that tax collectors were considered to be unclean.

131. Josephus, J.W. 2.284–88.

132. y. Ḥag. 2:2 (V.C).

collectors throughout the Mediterranean world, these should probably to be taken as exceptions to the rule. While there could certainly be exemplary representatives of the profession, the profession itself had a stereotypical reputation of being disreputable.

Sinners

The word ἁμαρτωλός is found primarily in Jewish and Christian writings. According to Karl Rengstorf, ἁμαρτωλός (together with its cognates) is extremely rare in Hellenistic literature.[133] Where it does occur, it can refer to immorality, foolishness, or ungodliness.

In the Septuagint ἁμαρτωλός occurs 145 times.[134] Of the ninety-four times that it appears in a text translated from Hebrew, it is used to translate five different Hebrew roots:[135] חטא ("sinner"),[136] חנף ("profane person"),[137] חרש ("a plougher," used figuratively of one who oppresses),[138] רע ("an evil person"),[139] and רשע ("a wicked person")[140]— the last representing more than 75 percent of the cases. Also, several Greek words are associated with ἁμαρτωλός in the Septuagint, either by simple conjunction or by poetic parallelism. From their usage, the following words would appear to overlap in meaning with ἁμαρτωλός: ἀσεβής ("godless, impious"),[141] ἄδικος ("unjust"),[142] πονηρός ("wicked, evil-doer"),[143] ὑπερήφανος ("arrogant, proud"),[144] ἄνομος ("lawless"),[145]

---

133. Rengstorf, "ἁμαρτωλός," 317. Neale, *None but the Sinners*, 75 n. 2, confirms that the word occurs only five times in classical Greek.

134. The following analysis is based on Hatch and Redpath, *Concordance to the Septuagint*.

135. Note that there are three texts where ἁμαρτωλός appears without a specific corresponding word in Hebrew.

136. חטא (three times), חטא (eleven times), and חטאה (one time).

137. חנף (one time).

138. חרש (one time).

139. רע (one time).

140. רשע (seventy-one times) and רשע (two times).

141. Pss 1:1, 5; 57(58):10; Prov 11:31; Sir 12:6. Cf. Prov 11:9; 15:8; Ezek 33:11 where one version of the LXX reads ἁμαρτωλός and another reads ἀσεβής.

142. Pss 9:24(10:3); 70(71):4; 139(140):4; cf. Pss 27(28):3; 100(101):8.

143. Gen 13:13; Ps 9:36(10:15); cf. Ps 7:9.

144. Sir 23:8; cf. 35:11.

145. Pss 72(73):3; 103(104):35; Isa 1:28, 31; cf. Pss 70(71):4 (παρανομοῦντος); 91(92):7; 118(119):119 (παραβαίνοντας); 128(129):3.

λοιμός ("troublesome"),[146] δόλιος ("deceitful, treacherous"),[147] and κακοποιός ("evil-doer").[148] Several other words are used in contrast to ἁμαρτωλός: δίκαιος ("upright, just, righteous"),[149] εὐσεβής ("devout, godly, pious, reverent"),[150] πραΰς ("humble, meek"),[151] πτωχός ("poor"), and πένης ("poor"),[152] together with the phrases ἐλπίζοντα ἐπὶ κύριον ("the one who hopes in the Lord")[153] and τοὺς ἀγαπῶντας [κύριον] ("those who love [the Lord]").[154]

Furthermore, based on usage in the Septuagint, we could say the following about the ἁμαρτωλός: in contrast to the righteous, sinners forsake God's law;[155] they are characterized as being boastful, proud,[156] deceptive,[157] ungracious,[158] hypocritical,[159] troublemakers,[160] and not open to correction;[161] they are malevolent towards others,[162] hence the psalmist often prays for deliverance from sinners[163] and for their judgment,[164] and thus it is fitting to speak of enemies at war, or the

146. Ps 1:1.

147. Ps 108(109):2.

148. Prov 24:19.

149. Pss 1:5; 36(37):12, 17, 21, 32; 67(68):2–3; 74(75):10; 124(125):3; 140(141):5; Prov 11:31; 12:13; cf. Ps 33(34):21.

150. Sir 13:17; 36(33):14.

151. Ps 146(147):6.

152. Pss 36(37):14; 81(82):4.

153. Ps 31(32):10; cf. Ps 36(37):40.

154. Ps 144(145):20.

155. Pss 1:1–2, 5; 118(119):53, 155; cf. Ps 72(73):3.

156. Pss 9:24–25(10:3–4); 93(94):3.

157. Ps 27(28):3; Sir 5:9; 6:1.

158. Ps 36(37):21.

159. Ps 49(50):16–17.

160. Sir 3:27; 28:9.

161. Sir 35:17.

162. Sinners plot against the poor (Ps 36(37):14), the righteous (Pss 10(11):3; 36(37):12, 32), and guests (Wis 19:13), and are often depicted as the enemies of the psalmist (Pss 3:7; 7:9; 10:3(11:2); 38(39):1; 54(55):3; 108(109):2; 118(119):61, 95, 110); cf. Gen 13:13; Jer 5:26; Sir 11:32; 36(33):14 (LXX).

163. Pss 3:7; 7:9; 35(36):11; 70(71):4; 81(82):4; 139(140):4, 8; 140(141):5; cf. Ps 96(97):10.

164. Pss 9:16–17; 9:36(10:15); 67(68):2; 103(104):35; 138(139):19. In other places the psalmist speaks confidently of the judgment of sinners: Pss 10(11):7; 36(37):10, 17, 20, 34; 57(58):10; 74(75):8; 91(92):7; 93(94):13; 111(112):10; 140(141):10; 144(145):20; 145(146):9; 146(147):6; cf. Isa 1:28, 31; 13:9; Amos 9:10; Sir 12:6; 16:13; 27:30.

ungodly nations, as sinners;[165] indeed God delivers the righteous and
judges sinners;[166] and thus sinners are destined to perish,[167] sometimes
to suffer from their own schemes;[168] and yet God's openness to teach
sinners would suggest the possibility that they could change.[169]

It is significant, however, that in most cases it is virtually impossible to identify a historical or sociological referent to the "sinners"
in the Septuagint. The writers may originally have had specific sinners in view,[170] but the descriptions they give tend to be so general
that specific identification is not possible. For much of the literature,
however, especially the Psalms, this simply makes it easier to adapt
for later readers. The point is, then, that the "sinners" are by definition
those who oppose the "righteous" and their identity depends on the
perspective of those who consider themselves to be "righteous." David
Neale concludes:

> the words 'righteous' and 'sinner' are defined primarily in ideological terms. . . . Just as the 'righteous' represent those who
> do God's will, the 'sinners' are those who represent a whole
> complex of behaviour that is opposed to God and his ways.
> . . . The condemnation of the 'sinner' represents, more than
> anything else, an ideological point of view based on a conception of absolute right and wrong.[171]
>
> The term 'sinners' is merely a symbol for the enemies of
> God, the representatives of the condemned, the identification of whom makes possible the self-identification of the
> 'righteous'.[172]

165. 1 Sam 15:18; Ps 9:17; Tob 13:6; 1 Macc 2:48; cf. *Jub.* 23.23–24; *Pss. Sol.* 1.1;
2.1–2.

166. Pss 10(11):7; 27(28):3; 36(37):10, 17, 20, 34, 40; 57(58):10; 67(68):2; 74(75):8,
10; 90(91):8; 91(92):7; 93(94):13; 96(97):10; 105(106):18; 124(125):3; 128(129):4;
144(145):20; 145(146):9; 146(147):6; Isa 1:28; 13:9; 14:5; Amos 9:10; Sir 5:6; 12:6.

167. Pss 36(37):20, 34; 91(92):7; 93(94):13; Sir 21:10; cf. Ps 118(119):155.

168. Pss 9:16; 140(141):10; Prov 12:13; 13:21 (ἁμαρτάνοντας).

169. Ps 24(25):8 (ἁμαρτάνοντας); Ezek 33:8, 11, 19; Tob 13:6.

170. Two texts where the identity of the sinners is explicit are Ps 105(106):18
where Dathan and Abiram are called ἁμαρτωλοί, and Isa 14:5 where the king of
Babylon is named an ἁμαρτωλός.

171. Neale, *None but the Sinners*, 95.

172. Ibid., 97.

Where there is more than one group who consider themselves to be righteous, their respective identification of sinners may differ. James Dunn argues that this was the situation in Second Temple Judaism. Factions developed, each with its own understanding of righteousness, each with its own view of how God's people ought to live in light of the present political and cultural realities—whether these be foreign rulers with a program of Hellenization, Hasmonean rulers behaving like foreigners, a non-Zadokite priesthood controlling the temple, or whatever.[173] From the perspective of one faction, then, sinners were those outside the group—those who were not righteous according to the group's understanding of righteousness, and particularly those whom the faction viewed as a threat in some way. In general, Gentiles could always be referred to as sinners[174] because they did not have the law and they threatened Jewish identity by imposing their rule and culture. But other Israelites could also be referred to as sinners. For example: from the perspective of the Maccabees, those renegade Jews who served the Syrians in their Hellenizing of Palestine were sinners.[175] The writer of 1 Enoch typically speaks of sinners as the wicked, those who became wealthy at the expense of the righteous and who will therefore suffer judgment;[176] but in one text he distinguishes between the righteous and the sinners on the basis of observance of the 364-day calendar, which was an issue among Jews.[177] Those who lived at Qumran thought other Jews to be wicked because they did not obey the law according to the community's own interpretation.[178] And the *Psalms of Solomon* speak of the contrast between the righteous and sinners,[179] but three psalms in particular specifically identify as sinners the Hasmonean rulers who were deposed when Pompey captured Jerusalem.[180] Dunn concludes that

173. Dunn, "Pharisees," 73–77.

174. Ps 9:17; *Jub.* 23.23–24; *Pss. Sol.* 1.1; 2.1–2; Matt 5:47//Luke 6:33; Gal 2:15.

175. 1 Macc 1:34; 2:44, 48; cf. 1:11–15.

176. *1 En.* 1.1, 9; 22.9–13; 91.10; 95.3; 97, esp. vv. 7–8; 98.2–3, 6, 10–16; 100.7–9; 102.3, 9; 103.5–6, 11; 104.5–7.

177. *1 En.* 82.4–7; cf. 5.4 where the writer criticizes some of his readers for not obeying "the commandments of the Lord." The same issue appears in *Jub.* 6.32–38 where although the word "sinners" is not used, the sense is similar.

178. CD IV,7–8; VI,17–20; 1QS V,7–11; 1QpHab II,1–9.

179. *Pss. Sol.* 4.8; 13.1–12; 15.1–13.

180. *Pss. Sol.* 2.3–17; 8.12–13; 17.5–9; cf. 4.1–8 where the psalmist criticizes those

no period of ancient Judaism was so riven with factional dispute as the time of Jesus. Nor should we regard those labelled 'sinners' simply as 'apostates'—those who in the eyes of all Jews had abandoned the covenant. That they had done so is certainly the view of the various authors; but that is simply to underline the factional character of these documents. From the perspective of those with a narrower definition of what covenant righteousness required it was natural to accuse those who disagreed with that definition of having abandoned the covenant.[181]

The usage of ἁμαρτωλός in the Gospels confirms this view. Generally, sinners are those, in contrast to the righteous, who behave immorally and are therefore subject to judgment.[182] But the perspective is essentially factional. Gentiles can be spoken of as sinners, but it is Jews who do so.[183] Jesus refers to tax collectors and the people who will put him to death as sinners,[184] whereas Pharisees speak of Jesus as a sinner.[185]

Consequently, the righteous are advised to avoid sinners because sinners pose a threat to them. This is implicit in many of the texts that speak of sinners. Some texts explicitly counsel against fellowship with sinners;[186] but the underlying assumption of the many texts, particularly in the Psalms, that speak of the character of sinners, that depict their opposition to the righteous, and that call for or speak of their destruction, is that the righteous ought to have nothing to do with them. The threats posed by sinners, although not often made explicit, could be of various kinds: they could be physical or military threats;[187] they could be economic in nature—the wicked rich taking advantage of the

---

"sitting in the council of the devout" (v. 1) which Wright, "Psalms of Solomon," 655, takes to be the Sanhedrin in Jerusalem.

181. Dunn, "Pharisees," 76.

182. Matt 9:13//Mark 2:17//Luke 5:32; Luke 13:2; 18:13; cf. Rom 3:7; 1 Tim 1:9.

183. Matt 5:47//Luke 6:33; cf. Gal 2:15.

184. Matt 5:46//Luke 6:32; Matt 26:45//Mark 14:41; cf. Heb 12:3.

185. John 9:16, 24, 31. We will examine the significance of Paul's usage later, but for now we just note a development: Paul speaks of himself as a sinner in the context of all humanity being sinners—all those whom Christ came to save (Rom 3:7; 5:8, 19; Gal 2:17; cf. 1 Tim 1:15; Luke 18:13).

186. Ps 1:1; Sir 7:16; 13:17; cf. 12:4, 7.

187. 1 Sam 15:18.

righteous poor;[188] they could involve an attack against one's reputation;[189] or the threats could be religious in the sense of people behaving in a way that opposed the ideal of how the righteous understood Israelites should live as the people of God.

One other significant point arising from the above survey: prior to the New Testament, people did not refer to themselves as a "sinner" or as being "sinful," using ἁμαρτωλός either as a noun or as an adjective. There are numerous examples of humility and penitence in Jewish literature: one might confess to have sinned or to belong to a sinful nation: the psalmist acknowledges his sin, confesses that he has no peace because of his sins, speaks of having been conceived in sin, prays for God to be merciful to him because of his sin (using the noun ἁμαρτία);[190] Daniel confesses on behalf of the nation that has sinned (using the verb ἁμαρτάνειν);[191] Tobit calls on Israel, "a nation of sinners [ἁμαρτωλός]," to repent.[192] And indeed the sacrificial system assumes that people sin. But the word ἁμαρτωλός seems to have been reserved for the enemy, the person outside the covenant, the one who deserves judgment.[193]

The Identity of Tax Collectors and Sinners: A Non-Literal Perspective

Dennis Smith and Kathleen Corley both suggest that the phrase "tax collectors and sinners" ought to be understood not in a literal sense, but symbolically as a term of slander. Smith's focus, in *From Symposium to Eucharist*,[194] is on the Greco-Roman banquet tradition itself as the proper context within which to understand the significance of meals in the New Testament. With regard to the Gospels, he argues that all

188. Pss 36(37):14; 81(82):2, 4; cf. Ps 72(73):12; Prov 23:17; 24:19; Sir 9:11.

189. Pss 38(39):1; 108(109):2.

190. Pss 24(25):11; 31(32):5; 37(38):3; 50(51):5; cf. *Pss. Sol.* 17.5.

191. Dan 9:4–19, esp. vv. 5, 8, 15; cf. Ezra 9:6.

192. Tob 13:6; cf. Isa 1:4; Amos 9:8, 10.

193. One exception to this rule might be *T. Ab.* 9.3 where Abraham confesses before Michael to being a sinner. We should note, however, that shortly after this a voice from heaven comments that "Abraham has not sinned and he has no mercy on sinners" (*T. Ab.* 10.14).

194. For a summary of his argument in relation to the Gospel material, see his earlier article, "Historical Jesus," 466–86.

of the scenes involving Jesus eating with people are literary fictions created by early Christians who borrowed the Greco-Roman banquet motif in order "to characterize and idealize Jesus as a hero" and thereby to define the social boundaries of the Christian community.[195] He suggests that underlying this motif may be Jesus' practice of "preaching toward a critique of the norms of social stratification in his society," but that in fact the phrase "tax collectors and sinners" is simply a generic term of slander rather than a literal designation.[196]

Corley's main argument in *Private Women, Public Meals* is that the attitudes towards women reflected in the New Testament—both liberating perspectives and conservative reactions—were not unique to Christianity, but were a reflection of developments in the wider Greco-Roman culture. She notes that during the late Republican and early Imperial eras, attitudes towards women—particularly, Roman attitudes—were changing, and one place this could be seen was in public meals or banquets.[197] Traditionally, in ancient Greece, public meals held in someone's home were solely for men: the guests would typically recline on couches, first for the meal (δεῖπνον), and then for the "drinking-party" (συμπόσιον) during which there would be drinking, conversation, and entertainment.[198] The only women present at such an affair would be slaves employed for the service and entertainment of the men—typically, table servants, flute players, dancers, and prostitutes or courtesans.[199] Respectable women would eat in women's quarters lest they be thought to be disreputable.[200] While the Romans

195. Smith, *Symposium*, chap. 8, citation from p. 237.

196. Ibid., 235.

197. Corley, *Private Women*, xv–xvii. Corley, ibid., 12, also mentions other ways in which the roles of particularly aristocratic women were becoming more public: using "their wealth to build public buildings and temples, participate in city offices, and act as patrons. . . . Although traditionally the respectable Roman matron was to limit herself to running her husband's estate or other domestic tasks such as spinning wool, but in the imperial period many matrons became active in Roman society, religion, philosophy, and politics." Smith, *Symposium*, 43, notes a similar movement in Greek culture as well.

198. Smith, *Symposium*, chap. 2.

199. Corley, *Private Women*, 25–28.

200. Ibid., 11–15. Corley identifies four classes of women in the Greco-Roman world: (i) aristocratic women: those born free into families of considerable wealth and social standing; (ii) freedwomen: those born into slavery but who earned enough to purchase their freedom; (iii) free women: those born free but not into an aristocratic

adopted most aspects of the Greek public meal, one innovation they brought was to allow women to accompany their husbands and often to recline with them, although they typically left after the meal and before the entertainment.[201] This development was, however, opposed by social conservatives who so associated women at public meals with slaves and prostitutes that they believed a respectable woman brought disrepute on herself and threatened fundamental social values simply by attending such a function. Consequently, it would have been thought appropriate by some to slander such a woman by calling her a "prostitute."[202]

Significantly for our purpose, Corley also notes that tax collectors often appear in ancient literature in connection with prostitutes. Although prostitutes under Roman law were not taxed prior to the reign of Gaius Caligula (37–41 CE), they were still required to be licensed and registered in order to practice their trade, and lists of registered prostitutes were kept by tax collectors, sometimes called πορνοτελῶναι.[203] Furthermore, tax collectors were clearly held in disrepute. We have seen above that they were assumed to be dishonest.[204] But in addition to that, they are frequently associated with others who engage in shameful activities, particularly activities involving

---

family; and (iv) slaves: those owned by a master. Furthermore, prostitutes were often slaves, and brothels were often owned by freedwomen who continued in their former trade by teaching others.

201. Ibid., 28–31.

202. Ibid. Corley does not have direct evidence for this type of slander used in this kind of situation, but she does show that (i) women at public meals were associated with prostitutes, (ii) there was criticism of respectable women who were thought to be behaving inappropriately for women, such as living immodestly, discussing philosophy and literature, drinking, or crossing too far into the public arena—which was reserved for men—such as attending public meals, and (iii) the word "prostitute" was used to slander respectable women who, for example, belonged to rival philosophical schools (42–66). For example, she cites Cicero who described married women at public meals using language typically reserved for prostitutes (42–43).

203. Julius Pollux, *Onom.* 7.202.2; 9.29.7; cf. Aeschines, *Tim.* 117–20: "every single year the senate farms out the tax on prostitutes, and that the men who buy this tax do not guess, but know precisely, who they are that follow this profession" (Adams, LCL).

204. See above, p. 46 nn. 109–10.

sexual impropriety—adulterers, procurers, and keepers of brothels.[205] Consequently, "tax collector" itself could be used as a term of slander.[206]

When Corley comes to the Synoptic material, she finds a connection between tax collectors, prostitutes, and sinners, on the one hand, and the Greco-Roman banquet imagery, on the other. Following Dunn, she takes "sinners" to be a term often connoting sexual impropriety, but typically used to slander those outside a particular sect.[207] Thus, she writes:

> such language functioned as rhetorical slander, and did not identify actual tax-collectors, sinners, or prostitutes within a particular group or characterize that group's actual behavior at meals. The force of "tax-collectors and sinners" is therefore connotative rather than denotative and merely characterizes Jesus or his followers as opponents.[208]

So, for example, Corley follows those who take the account of Jesus eating at Levi's house[209] to be a Markan creation that reflects the conflicts between Christians and Jews in the early church.[210] However, she takes the criticism that Jesus ate with tax collectors and sinners to be historically authentic, but to be understood not literally but rather as a slanderous attack against his supposedly inappropriate association with women at meals.[211] As in the Roman context, so also here, Jesus is criticized for holding parties that supposedly brought disrepute on the women in attendance.

Corley finds a number of other texts that support this reading. First, Matt 21:31–32 specifically associates prostitutes together with tax collectors in a saying designed to shame Jesus' opponents by stat-

---

205. Dio Chrysostom, 4 *Regn.* 4.98; 1 *Serv. lib.* 14.14; Lucian, *Men.* 11; Plutarch, *Apoph. lac.* 65 [236B]; Theophrastus, *Char.* 6.5; see the texts cited in the next footnote and above, p. 46 n. 110; see further, references in Corley, *Private Women*, 40 n. 77.

206. Dio Chrysostom, 4 *Regn.* 4.98: "is it not plain to see that many who are called kings are only traders, tax-gatherers, and keepers of brothels?" (Cohoon, LCL); Aristophanes, *Eq.* 248: "Hit him, hit the scoundrel, the harrier of the horse troops, the tax farmer, the chasm and Charybdis of rapacity, the scoundrel, the scoundrel!" (Henderson, LCL).

207. Corley, *Private Women*, 91–92.

208. Ibid., 92–93.

209. Mark 2:14–17.

210. See, for example, Mack, *Myth of Innocence*; Smith, *Symposium*, 228–30.

211. Corley, *Private Women*, 93.

ing that disreputable people are entering the kingdom ahead of them; and in light of this, the "sinners" in Matthew's version of Jesus' meal with tax collectors[212] ought to be understood to include the so-called "prostitutes"—women slandered for eating with Jesus.[213] Second, the Q text that contains the accusation that Jesus was "a glutton and a drunkard, a friend of tax collectors and sinners,"[214] contains a number of features that are reminiscent of the banquet setting:[215] the mention of a flute player recalls one of the roles of female slaves who entertained at dinner parties;[216] the mention of gluttony and drunkenness recalls the excess of many Roman banquets;[217] and the mention of friendship recalls their fundamental purpose.[218]

Third, Luke's account of the woman who anointed Jesus explicitly depicts him associating with a sinful woman in the context of a meal.[219] Corley suggests that Luke's description of her as γυνὴ ἥτις ἦν ἐν τῇ πόλει ἁμαρτωλός probably implies that she was known to be a prostitute, and that this is probably what Simon meant in calling her a "sinner."[220] Corley then follows interpreters who identify this woman as one of those who had been baptized by John and who had experienced forgiveness at that time, making this foot-washing/anointing incident a re-dramatization of the earlier occasion, mentioned by Luke just prior to this incident, in which "all the people and the tax collectors" who were baptized by John are contrasted with the Pharisees who reject God.[221] Thus, Jesus should be seen here as welcoming a forgiven sinner rather than a practicing prostitute.[222] But the point still is that he

212. Matt 9:9–13.

213. Corley, *Private Women*, 152.

214. Matt 11:16–19//Luke 7:31–34.

215. Corley, *Private Women*, 153–54.

216. Smith, *Symposium*, 35, notes that "[A] flute girl seems to be the most consistent feature of entertainment at a symposium, being included in virtually every pictorial representation of a symposium and mentioned in nearly every description."

217. Ibid., 36–38.

218. Smith, "Historical Jesus," 478.

219. Luke 7:36–50. Corley, *Private Women*, 122–23, takes the various Gospel accounts involving a woman anointing Jesus to be variations of one original story (cf. Matt 26:6–13; Mark 14:3–9; John 12:1–8).

220. Ibid., 124, and see her references in n. 89.

221. Luke 7:29–30.

222. In support of this view, Corley, *Private Women*, 125–26, notes that (i) it

related favorably with a woman associated with prostitution, thereby bringing into question more generally the appropriateness of women associating with him. And fourth, Luke 8:1–3 specifically mentions women who followed Jesus, and in particular some who were women of means, for they helped to support Jesus' ministry financially, and at least one of whom was married—precisely the kind of people in a Roman context who would be criticized for attending public meals.

There is much in the works of both Smith and Corley that is open to challenge—in particular, their uncritical acceptance of the view that Q and the *Gospel of Thomas* represent the earliest form of Christianity and of the view that the Gospels reflect far more the life of the early church and the views of the authors as opposed to the sayings and actions of Jesus himself.[223] Having said that, however, the evidence that Corley points to strongly suggests that the accusation levelled against Jesus for his associating with tax collectors and sinners is, at least in part, to be understood as (i) a slanderous charge that he associated with all kinds of disreputable people, and (ii) a charge that he was bringing disrepute on the women in his company. I suspect, however, that it is going too far to understand the criticism of associating with tax collectors in particular entirely in a non-literal manner. If the problem were simply that Jesus had inappropriate associations with women at meals, would the criticism have included reference to tax collectors? I think not. Reference to tax collectors is explicable only if in fact Jesus did associate with such people. The Synoptic texts that Corely cites do indicate that Jesus associated with women, and Matt 11:16–19//Luke 7:31–34 may connote a banquet setting, but it is difficult to believe that the specific mention of tax collectors would have entered the tradition if Jesus never associated with any actual tax collectors.[224] If that had been the case, then presumably his critics would have found the designation "sinners" by itself to be sufficient to describe the people around

corresponds with the parable (vv. 41–42) which implies that love is the response to forgiveness, and (ii) the perfect tense of ἀφέωνται suggests that her sins had been forgiven prior to this encounter.

223. Much of Smith's social background and literary analysis is highly insightful; however, his argument in support of the use of the banquet motif and against the historical authenticity of the Gospel scenes has been challenged by Blomberg, *Contagious Holiness*.

224. Since Capernaum was a customs depot for collecting duties on goods imported from the Decapolis (Michel, "τελώνης," 98), it is quite possible that Jesus would have encountered some tax collectors.

Jesus. But knowing that "tax collector" was also a term of slander helps to understand why such a specific occupation is mentioned alongside the more general reference to "sinners." Such a view first helps to explain why there is a particular interest in tax collectors in the Gospels, and second provides the criticism that we might have expected given Jesus' frequent dealings with women.

Conclusions

We are now in a position to draw some conclusions regarding Jesus' associations, at least in so far as they are indicated by the reference to tax collectors and sinners. The following seems to be the most likely reading of all the evidence.

First, it is likely that Jesus held at least as high moral standards as did the Pharisees, and would have disapproved, for example, of the dishonesty and cheating for which tax collectors were known, and of the sexual activity for which prostitutes were known.

Second, it seems clear that on at least one occasion Jesus ate with some tax collectors, one of whom was named Levi who became in some sense a follower of Jesus. It is possible that Levi literally followed Jesus for some time, and it is possible that one of Jesus' closest disciples had previously been a tax collector; but we cannot affirm either of these with any confidence. The evidence does not require Jesus to have had a special concern for tax collectors in comparison with other kinds of people.

Third, this association with at least one tax collector gained Jesus the reputation, particularly among the Pharisees, that he associated with disreputable people. For example, his associations with some women were also brought into question. Such associations concerned people like the Pharisees because, based on their understanding of the law and their traditions, they believed it was important to recognize the wickedness of such people and to respond by maintaining strict social boundaries that excluded them from fellowship. Failure to do so would threaten the moral fabric of Israel and hence Israel's relationship with God. Furthermore, it is plausible that because they saw Jesus to be a popular figure, they were concerned that he was leading many people astray.

Fourth, the Pharisees expressed their concern by criticizing, and probably exaggerating, Jesus' associations, making him out to be a "friend" of disreputable people. And, to express this criticism, they used stereotypical language: the term "tax collectors" was fitting because Jesus at least once ate with a tax collector, and because this was a classic figure of disrepute throughout the Mediterranean world; added to this was the term "sinners" that was the classical term for wicked people in the Jewish context.

3

Paul's Welcome of the Gentiles

THE PURPOSE OF THIS CHAPTER IS TO TRACE A LINE OF CONNECTION
from Jesus' welcome of tax collectors and sinners to Paul's understanding of the gospel for the Gentiles. In order to accomplish this, we will
need to consider the nature of Paul's conversion—in particular, the extent to which his change in perspective was due to divine revelation or
to his involvement in the church. This will necessitate a focus specifically on the church in Antioch and the role of the so-called "Hellenists"
there, which in turn will require an understanding of these Hellenists
beginning from their time in Jerusalem and the persecution they faced
there. In brief, then, we will focus on how the Hellenists served as a
link between Jesus and Paul by their modeling of Jesus' practice of
table fellowship in their own welcome of Gentiles. I will argue that this
context was formative for Paul's understanding of the gospel and of his
own commission as apostle to the Gentiles.

A Theology of Inclusion

We have the advantage that this ground has been substantially covered
by William Simmons in his *A Theology of Inclusion in Jesus and Paul*.
Since I intend to follow the main lines of Simmons's argument, I will
begin with a summary of his account of the development of the early
church and then move on to specific issues that I think need further
attention.

Summary of Simmons's Argument

Simmons argues that the connection between Jesus and Paul lies in a
common understanding of God reflected, in Jesus' case, in his table

fellowship and, in Paul's case, in his acceptance of Gentiles without requiring them to become Jews. Paul came to his view by means of both his Damascus road experience and his association with the Hellenist believers who were following the example of Jesus.

Simmons's argument begins with the "Hellenists," identified by Luke as a group within the early church in Jerusalem, in contrast to the "Hebrews."[1] The Hellenists, he argues, were not Gentiles,[2] but rather Greek-speaking Jews from the Diaspora who had become Christians.[3] Thus, this distinction within the early church is a reflection, more generally, of the composition of the Jewish community in Jerusalem.[4] Greek-speaking Jews living in Jerusalem would have needed their own synagogue in order to have services in their own language.[5]

A debate arises over whether the difference between the Hellenists and the Hebrews in the Jerusalem church was based on anything more than language.[6] That there was a fundamental distinction is suggested, Simmons thinks, by the fact that a separate leadership group was appointed for the former.[7] Luke explains that the reason for this was to attend to the distribution of funds for widows, but his description of

---

1. For a survey of the issues involved in the identification of the Hellenists, see Windisch, "Ἕλλην," 504–16.

2. Simmons, *Theology of Inclusion*, 94, adds further reasons for taking the Hellenists in Acts 6 as Greek-speaking Jews rather than as Gentiles: (i) it would require a radical rewriting of Acts to allow for Gentile converts at this early date; (ii) Nicolaus is identified as a proselyte (Acts 6:5), implying that he was a circumcised Gentile convert to Judaism, and suggesting that the other six Hellenist leaders were not—had they been Gentiles (and thus not circumcised) then we would have expected the internal dispute over circumcision to have arisen much earlier than it did; and (iii) it would be difficult to understand why, when they were scattered (Acts 11:19), these Hellenists initially preached only to Jews, if they themselves were Gentiles.

3. Ibid., 94–95; cf. Hengel, "Jesus and Paul," 4–16; Bruce, *History*, 217–18; Dunn, *Unity and Diversity*, 268–69; Räisänen, "Hellenists," 149.

4. The reference to the synagogue of the Freedmen in Acts 6:9, consisting of Jews from Cyrene, Alexandria, Cilicia, and Asia, is evidence of Diaspora Jews living in Jerusalem; see Barrett, *Acts*, 323–35.

5. Acts 6:9. See Hengel, "Jesus and Paul," 14.

6. For a survey of the scholarly discussion of the Hellenists, see Hill, *Hellenists and Hebrews*, 5–17. Hill (ibid., 22–24) himself argues that there was no difference other than language between the two groups.

7. Acts 6:3–6.

specific members of this leadership group (e.g., Stephen, Philip) suggests that these Christians had a distinctive vision for ministry.[8]

Simmons accepts, however, that this distinctive vision did not arise out of a general ideological or theological perspective that characterized all Diaspora Jews.[9] Jews living in Gentile cities represented a variety of views, some tending towards a rigorous and literal reading of the Torah and others towards allegorical or spiritual interpretations.[10] Simmons does, however, find a distinction between the Hellenists and the Hebrews, beyond that of language, in the Hellenists' experience of associating with Gentiles.[11] This is not to say that all Hellenists agreed on what were, and what were not, appropriate ways of associating with Gentiles, but they would all have been shaped to some extent or other—more than the Hebrews would have been—by their needing to find a way to live as Jews within a Gentile environment.

Simmons then hypothesizes that very early in the Christian movement, while still living in Jerusalem, the Hellenists began to accept Gentiles into their fellowship without requiring circumcision.[12] The reason they did this, he suggests, was not due to their supposed spiritualizing tendency, but rather because (i) they were following Jesus' example of having table fellowship with marginalized people, and (ii) they had a sympathy for God-fearers—with whom they would have associated in synagogues, both in Jerusalem and elsewhere—who would have been marginalized by being excluded from the Court of Israel in the temple.[13] Thus, Simmons argues:

> this radical practice of the Hellenists was not primarily due to a rejection of the law and the temple *per se*. Rather, just as Jesus' extraordinary emphasis upon the availability of God's

8. Acts 6:8–8:40.

9. Here Simmons reflects the view recently argued by Hill, *Hellenists and Hebrews*, 3: "The diversity of first-century Judaism challenges the notion that the earliest church was divided into ideological groups called Hellenists and Hebrews"; cf. pp. 1–4, 21, 24, 49.

10. Simmons, *Theology of Inclusion*, 96–98. Thus, Simmons, ibid., 99, 116–17, rejects the view of Räisänen, "Hellenists," 190–91, who argues that all Hellenists tended to spiritualize Jewish laws.

11. Simmons, *Theology of Inclusion*, 98–99; cf. Wedderburn, "Similarity and Continuity," 122–24; Segal, *Paul the Convert*, 92.

12. Simmons, *Theology of Inclusion*, 105.

13. Ibid., 100–101; the latter reason is drawn from Esler, *Community and Gospel*, 155.

grace and mercy to the undeserving tended to undermine the central importance of these institutions, the theology of the Hellenists did the same.[14]

This explains, Simmons suggests, why it was the Hellenists in particular who were chased out of Jerusalem. In Luke's account of the early church, it is the speech of Stephen—a Hellenist—that leads to his own martyrdom and to the expulsion of the Hellenists from Jerusalem.[15] The point of this speech, according to Simmons, was not to reject the law or the temple, as is often assumed,[16] but rather to argue that God's presence could not be limited to the temple.[17] And, if God is not limited to the temple, then Gentiles can have access to God apart from the temple. Simmons writes:

> Stephen's point is that an improper understanding of the temple stems from an improper understanding of God. God cannot be confined by any boundaries, no matter how ancient and sacred they may be. The worship of God is not 'location specific,' nor can it be used to enhance the national identity of the Jews to the exclusion of all other people.[18]

According to Luke, this triggered a "great persecution" against the church in Jerusalem that resulted in all "except the apostles" being scattered.[19] Simmons takes this to be a persecution aimed particularly at the Hellenists, with "the apostles" in Acts 8:1 being a synecdoche for the whole Hebrew wing of the church.[20] He acknowledges that the Hebrews were persecuted too,[21] but he suggests that this was a "qualitatively different" persecution in comparison to that directed at the Hellenists.[22] The conditions were such that the Hellenists in particular could no longer live in Jerusalem.

14. Simmons, *Theology of Inclusion*, 102.

15. Acts 7:54—8:1.

16. Simmons, *Theology of Inclusion*, 108–9.

17. Ibid., 110–14.

18. Ibid., 113–14.

19. Acts 8:1.

20. Simmons, *Theology of Inclusion*, 105; cf. Conzelmann, *Acts*, 61; Marshall, *Acts*, 160.

21. Acts 4:1–18; 5:18–40. Hill, *Hellenists and Hebrews*, 32–40, argues that the persecution in Jerusalem was in common against all the Christians, Hebrews and Hellenists, and that it was due to their proclamation of a crucified Messiah.

22. Simmons, *Theology of Inclusion*, 104–5, citation from p. 104.

Apart from the activities of Philip,[23] the next development in the account of the Hellenists is the reference to their mission in Antioch that was now consciously directed towards Gentiles—probably God-fearers who were associated with the synagogue(s). Simmons thinks that the success of this mission is best explained by the Hellenists not insisting on the same requirements as what Jews insisted on for proselyte conversion—most especially, circumcision.[24] And, as he argued earlier, the motivation behind this was not a spiritualizing of the law, but rather the example of Jesus. But now there is a new dimension: now the Hellenists themselves were marginalized, and so their ability to empathize with and welcome marginalized God-fearers was all the stronger.[25]

The waiving of circumcision, Simmons argues, was the reason for the persecution of Christians, not only from Jews in Jerusalem but also from Paul.[26] But Simmons argues that the issue was not merely one of maintaining religious rites, but rather of confusing the distinction between God's people and pagans. This is what was behind Paul's description of his pre-Christian self as being zealous for the traditions:[27] the word "zeal" was commonly used in the Old Testament and in Jewish literature of people who demonstrated "total devotion to maintaining the exclusive identity of Israel."[28] And the importance of maintaining the distinction between God's people and pagans was that it preserved the proper understanding of God. Simmons writes:

> [Paul] perceived that the Hellenists were advocating an understanding of God that virtually obliterated the distinction between Jews and Gentiles. In so doing, the Hellenists struck at the very core of Israel's *raison d'être* at a very troubled time in her history. So from Paul's perspective, the problem with the Jesus movement was not simply a matter of doctrine or interpretation. Rather the god represented therein was a foreign

---

23. Luke describes Philip in connection with a mission to Samaria (Acts 8:5–24), an encounter with a proselyte or God-fearer from Ethiopia (Acts 8:26–39), and a preaching tour through (presumably) Jewish towns (Acts 8:40).

24. Simmons, *Theology of Inclusion*, 115.

25. Ibid., 116.

26. Ibid., 119–22. Note that years later Paul himself said that the waiving of circumcision led to persecution (Gal 5:11; 6:12).

27. Gal 1:14; Phil 3:5–6.

28. Simmons, *Theology of Inclusion*, 121.

god; one that ignored the traditional categories of righteousness, holiness, the condemnation of sinners and the affirmation of Israel as the distinct, unadulterated people of God.[29]

Simmons stresses the importance of the fact that as a result of his Damascus road experience, Paul joined and promoted the group that he had been persecuting. Thus, if his conversion could be described as an experience of God's grace, it was God's grace as understood by the Hellenists. He writes:

> [Paul] experienced what the outcasts and sinners experienced when they sat at table with Jesus. He experienced what the Hellenists were so attracted to and what the Gentiles experienced via the Hellenists. In the midst of his violent persecution of the church and his absolute rejection of the theology that motivated the Hellenists to receive Gentiles, Paul experienced the *unmitigated grace of God.* . . . His experience conveyed a God who unconditionally offered his acceptance and one who, in his love, provided the basis for reconciliation irrespective of the moral condition of the recipient.[30]

This inclusive understanding of God's grace becomes the foundation for Paul's understanding of the gospel.[31] He preaches a gospel that does not require physical circumcision;[32] a gospel that speaks of God reaching out to the ungodly, sinners, and enemies[33]—that, because of his own persecution of the church, included Paul himself;[34] a gospel that can be exemplified by God saving both Abraham—an uncircumcised Gentile—and David—an ungodly Israelite.[35] Thus, Paul "now understands that in light of the paradigm of Jesus and his own personal experience, God's covenantal faithfulness cannot be restricted to the Jews."[36]

---

29. Ibid., 120.

30. Simmons, *Theology of Inclusion*, 125.

31. Ibid., 125–34.

32. Gal 2:3; 5:2–3, 6, 11; Rom 2:25–29; Phil 3:3.

33. Rom 5:6, 8, 10.

34. 1 Cor 15:8–9; Gal 1:13; Phil 3:6.

35. Rom 4:1–12.

36. Simmons, *Theology of Inclusion*, 130–31.

Critique

There is much in Simmons's argument with which I concur. First, he has demonstrated a family resemblance between Jesus' manner of table fellowship and Paul's gospel where Gentiles are welcomed without needing to be circumcised. The symbolic significance of the terms "tax collector" and "sinner," which we saw in the previous chapter, would have allowed and facilitated a re-application of Jesus' example of inclusive table fellowship in a new context.[37] And, given the common Jewish identification of Gentiles as sinners, which we also find in Paul's writings,[38] it is certainly plausible that a re-application of Jesus' example could have been made with Gentiles in view. Furthermore, I would add, in light of our conclusion from the previous chapter that no one ever identified themselves as a sinner,[39] that Paul's inclusion of himself in that category as he reflects on his pre-Christian state—"while we were yet sinners"[40]—and possibly also the post-Pauline description of him as being "the foremost of sinners,"[41] may suggest a conscious reflection on Paul's part in identifying himself with those whom Jesus welcomed.[42] Second, Simmons has, correctly in my view, identified the Hellenists as key players in the link between Jesus and Paul—those Greek-speaking Jews who had come to live in Jerusalem and who had subsequently become Christians.[43] And third, he has rightly focused

37. See above, p. 61.

38. Gal 2:15.

39. See above, p. 56.

40. Rom 5:8.

41. Even though 1 Tim 1:15 was probably not authored by Paul, it is difficult to imagine someone who wrote in Paul's name ascribing such a statement to him if this did not in fact reflect Paul's own perspective.

42. Note also the admissions of Peter—"Depart from me, for I am a sinful man [ἀνὴρ ἁμαρτωλός], O Lord" (Luke 5:8)—and of the tax collector in the temple—"God, be merciful to me a sinner [τῷ ἁμαρτωλῷ]" (Luke 18:13). While there is no specific evidence linking these traditions to Paul, it is certainly possible that he was aware of them and that they shaped his own self-understanding.

43. Some care needs to be taken regarding the word "Hellenists." According to Metzger, *Textual Commentary*, 340–42, the word Ἑλληνιστής derives from ἑλληνίζειν, and therefore denotes simply one who uses Greek language or customs; further questions of ethnic or religious identity would need to be determined by the context. This helps to make sense of the different ways in which Luke uses the word Ἑλληνιστάς: in Acts 6:1 the Hellenists are Greek-speaking Jewish Christians who stand in contrast to Hebrew/Aramaic-speaking Jewish Christians; in Acts 9:29 they are Greek-speaking

on the influence the Antioch church would have had on Paul, being a church comprised of Hellenists and Gentile converts.

Two issues, however, require further attention. To begin with, if we can assume that Paul, in becoming a follower of Jesus, adopted the views of those whom he had formerly persecuted, we need to be clear about the reason for the opposition against them. While Simmons's hypothesis that the Hellenists did not require circumcision for Gentile converts would explain the Jewish opposition, the success of the Gentile mission in Antioch, and Paul's circumcision-free gospel, it also creates a number of problems. First, there is no a priori reason why Jewish Christians would think that Gentile converts should not be circumcised. Throughout the Greco-Roman world, there was a spectrum of degrees of interest and commitment shown by some Gentiles to Judaism, ranging from admiration of certain aspects of the faith, to extending benefits to Jews, to participating in certain Jewish rituals, to committing oneself to the God of the Jews, to associating with a Jewish community, to complete conversion.[44] Proselyte conversion, however, virtually always required circumcision;[45] furthermore, if an exception

---

non-Christian Jews who debate with Paul; and in Acts 11:20 they are Greek-speaking Gentiles with whom the gospel is being shared by those Christian "Hellenists" who fled from Jerusalem. As a matter of convention, unless otherwise clearly indicated, by "Hellenists" I will mean the Greek-speaking Jewish Christians identified in Acts 6:1.

Regarding the text critical issue in Acts 11:20, most interpreters have favored Ἕλληνας over Ἑλληνιστάς largely on the grounds that the context demands that the people in question be Gentiles; see Hengel, "Jesus and Paul," 8; Barrett, *Acts*, 1:550–51; Bruce, *Acts of the Apostles*, 272; Haenchen, *Acts*, 365 n. 5; Conzelmann, *Acts*, 87. Metzger, however, argues textually for Ἑλληνιστάς (with a certainty ranking of "C") but with the understanding given above; see now Pervo, *Acts*, 291.

44. See Cohen, "Crossing the Boundary," 13–33.

45. While there is some evidence that some Jews may not have insisted on circumcision for proselytes, there appear to have been few who did, and fewer still who would have been considered by most to be still within the covenant. (i) The books of Maccabees tell of the pressure from Syrian officials for Jews to adopt Hellenistic customs, including abandoning the practice of circumcision, which some did willingly by reversing the marks of their own circumcision (1 Macc 1:15; cf. 1 Cor 7:18), while others no doubt did reluctantly by not circumcising their sons (1 Macc 2:46; cf. 1 Macc 1:60–61; 2 Macc 6:10; 4 Macc 4:25). The praise the authors give to those who continued to practice circumcision, even under threat of torture, suggests that they considered those who abandoned the practice to have abandoned the covenant. (ii) Philo was known for his allegorical interpretations of Scripture, and he reflected on the symbolic significance of circumcision (*Spec.* 1.8–9; *QG* 3.47–82) and spoke of the importance of circumcision of the heart (*Spec.* 1.305); yet he also clearly maintained the importance of physical circumcision (*Migr.* 89, 92–93; al-

to this rule were ever made, we would not expect it to come from Jews who had chosen to live in Jerusalem. There would need to be very good reason, therefore, to justify the waiving of circumcision in the case of Christian conversion of Gentiles. Second, had circumcision been consciously waived as early as Simmons suspects—in the early days in Jerusalem—then it is remarkable that the Jerusalem Council,[46] which addressed the issue of circumcision for Gentiles, was not held until some fifteen to twenty years later.[47] And third, in Galatians Paul insists that the gospel he preaches came to him not from a human source, but "through a revelation of Jesus Christ."[48] And while it can certainly be argued that there were some things that Paul learned from other Christians, it is difficult to accept that the waiving of circumcision for Gentiles was one of them: if he had learned this from others, his argument in Galatians would be seriously weakened. In combating the

---

though, note the curious comment in *QE* 2.2: "the sojourner is one who circumcises not his uncircumcision but his desires and sensual pleasures and the other passions of the soul" (Marcus, LCL)). (iii) Josephus tells of a certain King Izates who, wanting to convert to Judaism and assuming this implied undergoing circumcision, was counseled by a Jewish merchant named Ananias not to become circumcised because of the likely revolt of his subjects. Ananais told him: "The king could . . . worship God without being circumcised if indeed he had fully decided to be a devoted adherent of Judaism for it was this that counted more than circumcision. . . . [F]urthermore, . . . God Himself would pardon him if, constrained thus by necessity and by fear of his subjects, he failed to perform this rite" (Feldman, LCL). Some time later, however, a Galilean Jew named Eleazar (a man with "a reputation for being extremely strict when it came to the ancestral laws" (43)) convinced Izates that circumcision was not an option for converts (*Ant.* 20.34–48, citation from 41). The point of the story seems to be that while there may be some Jews who think that circumcision may be waived under certain conditions, this was not the opinion of Palestinian Jews, even for converts in the Diaspora, even under exceptional circumstances.

For debate on whether these and other rabbinic texts demonstrate a Jewish openness to the possibility of foregoing circumcision in some cases of Gentile conversion, see McEleney, "Conversion," 328–33, who argues that there was, and Nolland, "Uncircumcised Proselytes?," 173–94, who argues there was not. See also Borgen, "Early Church," 55–78.

46. I am assuming that the Jerusalem Council of Acts 15:1–21 is essentially historical, and that it corresponds with Paul's meeting with the apostles mentioned in Gal 2:1–10. If either of these assumptions is incorrect, the historical description would change somewhat, but I do not believe it would invalidate my argument. See Barrett, *Acts*, 2:xxxvi–xlii, 709–11; Fitzmyer, *Acts*, 137–38, 540; Betz, *Galatians*, 81–83.

47. Most scholars place Jesus' death in the year 30, or possibly 33, and the Jerusalem Council in the year 48 or 49; see Brown, *Introduction*, xxxviii–xxxix; Donfried, "Chronology," 1016; Kümmel, *Introduction*, 255.

48. Gal 1:12.

view that Gentile converts needed to be circumcised, which is much of Paul's focus in Galatians, it is difficult to explain why Paul would so insist that his gospel came by revelation and not from other Christians, if in fact it could be easily shown that the waiving of circumcision had been accepted prior to his conversion. Thus, we need to consider again the reasons for Jewish opposition of Christians and, in particular, why the Hellenist Christians seem to have faced a more severe persecution than the Hebrew wing of the early church.

The second issue arising from Simmons's argument concerns Paul's conversion and the extent to which the change he underwent was due to divine revelation versus integration into the Christian community at Antioch. If it was due to the latter, then we may have a historical connection between Paul and the early Christian community in Jerusalem and, by extension, to Jesus; if, however, it was due entirely to the former, then the question arises (invoking Ocham's Razor) of whether any reference to the early church, and hence to the life of Jesus, is necessary to explain Paul's new commitment and theology.[49] Simmons makes the argument that, in his conversion, Paul would likely have adopted the views of those whom he had been persecuting. While I think this is a fair assumption, I also think this argument needs to be expanded.

To these two issues we now turn.

The Persecution of Early Christians and the Role of the "Hellenists"

General Considerations

INITIAL ASSUMPTIONS

I take it that from the very beginning of the Christian movement, Jews opposed Christians.[50] As evidence that gives some credence to Luke's

49. The suggestion that the risen Jesus could have informed Paul of some of the Jesus tradition by special revelation—during, for example, his Damascus road experience—will always appear to many as special pleading.

50. Although the term "Christian" eventually came to denote members of a distinct religion, and so is somewhat anachronistic prior to that development, I use the term merely to denote followers of Jesus, without making any assumptions of their relationship to or distinctiveness from Judaism.

account in Acts, we have Paul's own testimony to having once been a persecutor of the church[51] and then later to having been persecuted as a Christian by Jews;[52] we know that later in the first century there was a parting of the ways between Jews and Christians, and the tensions that led to this are evident elsewhere in the New Testament;[53] and, of course, since Jesus had been persecuted, it would be natural for us to expect his followers to be persecuted too.[54] I make two assumptions about the nature of the opposition that the Christians faced. First, the reasons for opposing Christians would certainly have been related to the reasons for opposing Jesus, although new grounds for opposition may have arisen given new situations.[55] And second, as in cases of strong opposition, the issues Jews would have raised against Christians probably tended to multiply and to be exaggerated. Thus, while there may have been specific reasons why Jews were offended by Christians, in a situation where the offense actually leads to violence, as it did in Jerusalem, we can expect that some accusations may have been an exaggeration of the actual case. Consequently, one needs to take care to see through the polemic while trying to identify actual historical causes.

Jewish Sensitivities in the Early 30s

The first step in understanding Jewish opposition towards Christians in Jerusalem is to appreciate the context. During Pilate's procuratorship, Jewish sensitivities over matters relating to the law and the temple sometimes led to radical action. Jesus' execution is a good example, but Josephus and Philo record others. When Roman soldiers entered Jerusalem bearing the image of the emperor on their standards,

---

51. 1 Cor 15:9; Gal 1:13, 23; Phil 3:6.

52. Rom 15:30–31; 2 Cor 11:24–26; Gal 5:11; 1 Thess 2:13–16; cf. 1 Cor 4:12; 2 Cor 4:9; 12:10.

53. Matt 10:17–18//Mark 13:9//Luke 21:12; Luke 12:11; Rev 2:9; 3:9.

54. See Matt 10:24–25; John 7:13; 9:22; 12:42–43; 16:2–3; 19:38; 20:19.

55. Clearly not all Jews were opposed to Christians: rather, there was a spectrum of response ranging from opposition to toleration to acceptance. For an evaluation of the evidence of each response given in Acts, see Setzer, *Jewish Responses*, 46–82. She concludes that although "some interest and tolerance toward Christians never totally died out," throughout the account in Acts, "there are more unfavorable Jewish reactions to Christians than favorable ones" (79).

many Jews appealed to Pilate for their removal on the grounds that they were an infringement of the second commandment; and when Pilate threatened them with death, Josephus writes that "they, casting themselves prostrate and baring their throats, declared that they had gladly welcomed death rather than make bold to transgress the wise provisions of the laws."[56] Again, when Pilate placed some votive shields in Herod's palace in Jerusalem, a number of Jews, thinking that these violated their ancient traditions, appealed to Tiberius to have them removed.[57] And again, when Pilate took money from the temple treasury to pay for a new aqueduct, some Jews objected, on the grounds that that money was sacred and should not be used for such purposes, and expressed their displeasure by forming a mob around him and hurling insults at him when he visited Jerusalem.[58]

If we look beyond the time of Pilate we find evidence of a consistent and widespread willingness among Judean Jews, throughout the Seleucid and Roman periods, not only to suffer for their law but also to fight for it.[59] The accounts of the Maccabees demonstrate both the willingness of Jews to die rather than transgress laws that distinguished them from Gentiles, and the readiness of many to take up arms to defend their law and the temple.[60] Similarly, Philo describes Jews as "preferring to die in defense of their national institutions," and explains that "there are thousands who have their eyes upon [God] full of zeal for the laws";[61] and Josephus writes with reference to the war with Rome: "when pressure is put upon us to alter our statutes, then we deliberately fight, even against tremendous odds, and hold out under reverses to the last extremity."[62] This passion to protect that

---

56. Josephus, *Ant.* 18.55–59, citation from 18.59 (Feldman, LCL); cf. *J.W.* 2.169–74.

57. Philo, *Legat.* 299–306.

58. Josephus, *Ant.* 18.60–62; *J.W.* 2.175–77.

59. Farmer, *Maccabees*, 60–68.

60. On the willingness of Jews to die for their laws: 1 Macc 1:62–63; 2 Macc 6:18–20, 27–28; 7:1–42; 4 Macc 4:23–26, 5–18; on the willingness of Jews to fight for their laws and the temple: 1 Macc 2:23–27, 42–48, 50, 67–68; 3:20–21, 43, 58–59; 13:3–6; 14:29; 2 Macc 2:19–22; 8:21; 10:1; 13:14; 15:17; 3 Macc 1:23.

61. Philo, *Legat.* 215 (Colson, LCL); *Spec.* 2.253 (Colson, LCL); cf. *Legat.* 208.

62. Josephus, *Ag. Ap.* 2.272 (Thackeray, LCL); cf. 2.292; *Ant.* 17.149–63, 213–18.

which lay at the heart of Second Temple Judaism eventually led to the outbreak of the Jewish War in 66.[63]

Clearly, we would not expect Jews in the Diaspora to behave the same way; Jews living among Gentiles did not have the same issues regarding the application of the law as did those living in the Holy Land. The question arises, however: How far did the Holy Land extend? And hence, how far from Jerusalem might Jewish sensitivities be expressed? Markus Bockmuehl has presented various pieces of evidence to suggest that some Jews considered the land of Israel to extend, ideally, as far north as Antioch.[64] He notes, for example, Old Testament and Qumran descriptions of the land extending to the Taurus Mountains and the River Euphrates; Hasmonean battles in Antioch and in Ituraea where people were permitted to remain "in the land" only if they obeyed the Jewish laws; Roman authority given to Herod the Great to exercise influence in Syria; Palestinian Targums that speak of Antioch on the border of Israel; some rabbinic sources that identify the northern border at Amanah, a mountain possibly located to the northwest of Antioch; and a debate, towards the end of the first century, recorded in the Mishnah that resulted in Syria no longer being regarded as lying within the land of Israel.[65] Bockmuehl notes that while such a vision would have been politically unrealistic, it still may have shaped Jewish sensitivities, particularly regarding the activities of the Jewish communities in cities like Damascus and Antioch. He writes:

> At a time of heightened messianic expectations for the restoration of the Holy City and the Land, it is not unreasonable to suspect that the utopian dimensions of the biblical promises would once again come alive in the hopes of observant Jews.
>
> . . .
>
> Quite plausibly, therefore, many first-century Palestinian Jews regarded Antioch as the gateway from the Exile to the Holy Land, and thus fraught with a considerable symbolic significance. For religious Jews concerned about the redemption of the Twelve Tribes, Antioch's status as a large metropolis inside the biblical Promised Land might well carry special halakhic sensitivities.[66]

63. For details of the growth of this Jewish fervor during Paul's lifetime, see Dunn, "Incident at Antioch," 133–36; Hengel, *Zealots*, 337–58.

64. Bockmuehl, *Jewish Law*, 61–70.

65. See Bockmuehl's footnotes for references.

66. Bockmuehl, *Jewish Law*, 70.

CHRISTIANITY AS A JEWISH SECT

Another aspect of the setting of the Jewish opposition is that, probably throughout Paul's lifetime, the Christian movement was considered by Jewish authorities to lie within their jurisdiction. Although Paul is quite critical of his Jewish past, he continues to consider himself a member of the Jewish community: he speaks of himself as an Israelite,[67] and he refers to Jews as his own people and his brothers.[68] But more to the point, when Paul says that five times he received thirty-nine lashes from Jews[69]—a reference to an official form of synagogue discipline— he shows that from the Jewish perspective, Christians at the time of Paul were still considered to be under Jewish authority.[70] This reality is reflected in the fact that Christians shared the same legal status as Jews, being considered a Jewish sect.[71]

But, it also needs to be noted, notwithstanding what has been said above, that Second Temple Jews tolerated a significant degree of diversity among themselves. Why, then, the persecution of Christians? Terence Donaldson has helpfully suggested that the solution may require a sociological as well as a theological answer:

> Judaism did not engage thought police to ferret out those hold-
> ing theological opinions deviating from the norm. In fact, . . .
> first-century Judaism was characterized by a considerable de-
> gree of tolerance towards parties, sects, and movements with
> diverse viewpoints. In the case of early Christianity, however,

67. Rom 11:1; 2 Cor 11:22; cf. Acts 22:3.

68. Rom 9:3; 2 Cor 11:26. On early Christians understanding themselves as part of the Jewish faith, see Dunn, *Unity and Diversity*, 237–39. On the confusion often raised by the use of the terms "Judaism" and "Christianity," see Dunn, "Paul's Conversion," 77–79.

69. 2 Cor 11:24. For a discussion of Jewish forms of disciplinary action, see Hultgren, "Persecutions," 104.

70. See further Thrall, *2 Corinthians*, 2:737–38. Paul's reference to having been stoned (2 Cor 11:25) also indicates Jewish opposition, but if he is thinking of the incident in Lystra (Acts 14:19), it is more likely a mob action rather than an official sentence that is in view.

71. That Christians were included in the expulsion of Jews from Rome (Acts 18:2; cf. Suetonius, *Claud.* 25.4), and that Roman officials treated Jewish complaints against Christians as an internal matter (Acts 18:12–17), suggest that the Roman authorities did not distinguish between them. The first evidence of a distinction being made from a Roman perspective occurs in 64 when Nero blamed the Christians for the fire of Rome.

> Jewish communities perceived the Christian movement, in its actions and its attitudes towards the symbols and institutions defining Jewish social identity, as exceeding the limits of tolerance and threatening social cohesion; their response was to take . . . action to preserve social boundaries and protect ethnic solidarity.[72]

I propose, at a general level, a relatively simple explanation for the Jewish persecution of Christians: (i) Christians were substantially heretical with regard to some matters that Jews in Jerusalem thought to be very important, and (ii) they were successful in drawing converts. Both of these are necessary to explain the Jewish opposition, but neither is sufficient in and of itself. As F. F. Bruce succinctly put it, this was "a malignant growth that called for drastic surgery."[73] This helps to explain the Jewish persecution of Christians: they thought Christians were seriously wrong, and they were concerned that the spread of this movement would threaten the spiritual health of Jerusalem and of Jewish communities elsewhere.

Specific Considerations

We now move to examine specific suggestions regarding the nature of the offense that incited Jewish opposition towards Christians.

Proclamation of a Crucified Messiah

According to Luke, the authorities in Jerusalem opposed the apostles and tried to stop them from preaching in the name of Jesus.[74] Although Luke does not specify what the cause of offense was, we can be fairly certain that they objected to the Christians' claims about Jesus—that God had raised him from the dead and that he was the Messiah.[75] If either of these had been true, this would mean that the authorities were responsible for opposing God's servant sent to liberate his people—

72. Donaldson, "Zealot and Convert," 670.

73. Bruce, *Paul*, 71.

74. Acts 4:13–18; 5:17–40. Jesus had previously warned of official opposition (Matt 10:17//Mark 13:9//Luke 21:12; Luke 12:11); cf. Setzer, *Jewish Responses*, 36–38.

75. See Setzer, "Christological Claims," 315–28.

essentially, that is, for opposing God's salvation. Furthermore, while the former would seem highly unlikely, the latter would have sounded ludicrous: the very fact that Jesus had been crucified must have seemed proof enough, even at first to some of Jesus' own followers, that he was not the Messiah.[76]

Numerous scholars have argued that prior to his conversion, Paul took this view.[77] Presumably Paul the persecutor agreed with the assessment of the Jewish authorities that Jesus ought to have been put to death, perhaps basing his assessment on information he received from other Pharisees.[78] The appearance of a group proclaiming that God had raised a convicted criminal from the dead and that he was

76. For what was probably a typical Jewish reaction to the Christians' claim that the Messiah had been crucified, see Trypho's comments in Justin, *Dial.* 32.1: "These and such like Scriptures [referring to Dan 7], sir, compel us to wait for Him who, as Son of man, receives from the Ancient of days the everlasting kingdom. But this so-called Christ of yours was dishonourable and inglorious, so much so that the last curse contained in the law of God fell on him, for he was crucified" (ANF); 89.1–2: "Be assured that all our nation waits for Christ; and we admit that all the Scriptures which you have quoted refer to Him. . . . But whether Christ should be so shamefully crucified, this we are in doubt about. For whosoever is crucified is said in the law to be accursed, so that I am exceedingly incredulous on this point" (ANF); 90.1: "[P]rove to us whether He must be crucified and die so disgracefully and so dishonourably by the death cursed in the law. For we cannot bring ourselves even to think of this" (ANF).

77. See, for example, Hultgren, "Persecutions," 99–102.

78. Against many claims to the contrary, we can be almost certain that in order to be an effective persecutor of the Christians, Paul would have had to have known about Jesus, knowledge which he could have gained from his fellow Pharisees or from his interactions with Christians. From Paul's letters we know that he, as an apostle, often had to deal with people who disagreed with him—or deal with those who were influenced by people who disagreed with him—and that while he may have had authority to impose a solution in specific situations (1 Cor 4:21; 2 Cor 10:2–6; 13:1–3, 10), he regularly engaged in reasoned argument. In 2 Cor 10:5–6 he writes: "We destroy arguments and every proud obstacle to the knowledge of God, and take every thought captive to obey Christ, being ready to punish every disobedience, when your obedience is complete." Apart from the reference to Christ here, there is no reason to think that Paul prior to his conversion would have conducted his opposition to Christians in a different manner; in fact, if we replaced "Christ" with "Torah" in 2 Cor 10:5, these verses could very easily express Paul's pre-Christian modus operandi. But if he engaged in argument with these Christians, then he must have had a significant amount of information about them; and since early Christians remembered and interpreted the deeds and sayings of Jesus, and made various claims about him—about who he was, about the significance of his death, and that he had been raised from the dead—Paul must have had a significant amount of knowledge about Jesus, otherwise he could not have held his ground in an argument.

Israel's Messiah would obviously not have been welcome. Perhaps Paul had his own pre-Christian perspective in mind when he described the message of the cross as the power of God even though it appears weak, as the wisdom of God although it appears foolish, and therefore as "a stumbling block to Jews."[79] Philippe Menoud writes:

> Jesus could not be the Messiah. To Saul, as to every Jew, a Messiah crucified was a stumbling-block, a contradiction in terms. The Messiah, according to the common expectation, was to appear suddenly in power and glory to put an end to the present age and to establish the kingdom of God. Well, Jesus had been condemned not only by the highest authorities of Judaism, but even by God himself who had permitted him to suffer the most ignominious death and to fall under this sentence of the law: "Cursed be every one who hangs on a tree" (Deut. 21:23, quoted Gal. 3:13).[80]

While it seems safe to assume that Jews would have been offended, from the beginning, at the claim that Jesus was the Messiah, many have further argued, as does Menoud, that Jews,[81] and Paul in particular,[82] concluded that simply because Jesus had been crucified—that is, hung on a tree—he was, according to Deut 21:22–23, cursed of God.[83] The text reads:

> And if a man has committed a crime punishable by death and he is put to death, and you hang him on a tree, his body shall not remain all night upon the tree, but you shall bury him the same day, for a hanged man is accursed by God; you shall not defile your land which the LORD your God gives you for an inheritance. (Deut 21:22–23)

79. 1 Cor 1:18–25. See below, p. 133–34, for a comment on whether Paul would have used Deut 21:23 to justify his opposition to Christians.

80. Menoud, "Revelation and Tradition," 133; cf. Wood, "Conversion of Paul," 278; Longenecker, "Realized Hope," 23.

81. See the comments of Trypho above, p. 79 n. 76.

82. See Gal 3:13.

83. Menoud, "Revelation and Tradition," 133; Wood, "Conversion of Paul," 278; Bruce, History, 240–41; idem., "Curse of the Law," 32; Hengel, Crucifixion, 84–85; idem., Atonement, 43–44; idem., "'Christos' in Paul," 71; Betz, Galatians, 152 n. 136; Beker, Paul the Apostle, 182; Kim, Origin of Paul's Gospel, 46–47; Dietzfelbinger, Berufung, 36–37; Johnson, Writings, 108–9, 137, 246, 309; Sänger, "Verflucht," 279–85; Longenecker, "Realized Hope," 24; Hurtado, Lord Jesus Christ, 77, 94, 188.

We must be cautious, however, of a too facile reading of this text as though Jews concluded that a crucifixion would necessarily entail that the victim had been cursed of God. Such a view is difficult to maintain in light of the variety of ways Jews actually interpreted this text. Kelli O'Brien notes the following:[84] (i) although some Jewish texts understand the hanging on the tree in Deut 21 to be the means of execution,[85] both the Masoretic Text and the Septuagint see the hanging as a public display of a person already executed by other means; (ii) the phrase קִלְלַת אֱלֹהִים (lit. "curse of God") in verse 23 is grammatically ambiguous and appears to have been read by some as (a) an objective genitive, meaning either that the criminal was hanged because he cursed God,[86] or that the hanging of a person on a tree is itself an affront to

84. O'Brien, "Curse of the Law," 55–76; many of the following ancient references are from her article. Cf. Tuckett, "Deuteronomy 21:23," 345–50.

85. 11QTemple LXIV,7–13: "If a man passes on information against his people or betrays his people to a foreign nation, or does evil against his people, you shall hang him on a tree and he will die. . . . And their corpse shall not spend the night on the tree; instead you shall bury them that day because those hanged on a tree are cursed by God and man; thus you shall not defile the land which I give you for inheritance"; apparently also the Nahum Pesher, commenting on Nah 2:13 (Heb.), 4QpNah (=4Q169) I,6–8: "Its interpretation concerns the Angry Lion [who filled his cave with a mass of corpses, carrying out rev]enge against those looking for easy interpretations, who hanged living men [from the tree, committing an atrocity which had not been committed] in Israel since ancient times, for it is [hor]rible for the one hanged alive from the tree." For discussion of these texts, see Fitzmyer, "Crucifixion," 493–513. Note also the Peshitta: "And if any man has committed a sin worthy of death, and he is crucified on a tree, and thus put to death; His body shall not remain all night upon the tree" (Lamsa). O'Brien, "Curse of the Law," 64, notes that the words used in these texts for execution in Hebrew (תלה) and in Aramaic (צלב) can refer either to crucifixion or hanging; for the sake of argument, she assumes they refer to crucifixion.

86. Symmachus: "he was hanged because of blasphemy of God" (my translation); *Tg. Onq.* Deut 21:23: "he was impaled for having sinned before the Lord" (Grossfeld, ArBib); Peshitta: "he who shall revile God shall be crucified" (Lamsa); *m. Sanh.* 6:4: "*he that is hanged is a curse against God*; as if to say: Why was this one hanged? Because be [*sic*] blessed [footnote reads: "Euphemism for 'cursed'"] the Name, and the Name of Heaven was found profaned" (emphasis original, indicating citation of Scripture); *Sipre Deut* §221: "*For he that is hanged is a curse unto God* (21:23): That is to say, why was he hanged? Because he cursed God, thus profaning the Name of heaven"; *b. Sanh.* 45b citing the view of R. Eliezer: "Just as the blasphemer . . . is executed by stoning, so all who are stoned [must be subsequently hanged]"; cf. Josephus, *Ant.* 4.202: "Let him that blasphemeth God be stoned, then hung for a day, and buried ignominiously and in obscurity" (Thackeray, LCL). For a full discussion of the texts noted here and in the following two footnotes, see Bernstein, "כי קללת אלהים תלוי (Deut. 21:23)," 19–45.

God,[87] and by others as (b) a subjective genitive, meaning that God curses those hanged on a tree;[88] (iii) of the numerous ancient Jewish texts that refer to crucifixion,[89] only one associates it with a curse,[90] suggesting there was not an automatic connection in Jewish thinking between crucifixion and curse;[91] (iv) in light of the fact that the execution in view in 11QTemple LXIV,13—the only ancient Jewish text that takes both "curse of God" in Deut 21:23 as a subjective genitive and the hanging on a tree as a form of execution—was punishment for treason, it would be conceivable that the Deuteronomy text could be applied to Jesus if the title "King of the Jews" was interpreted as treason against Rome, but there is no evidence that anyone had charged him with committing treason against Israel; (v) while it is always possible that Deut 21:23 did play a role in Jewish anti-Christian polemics,[92] the number of references or allusions to this text in the New Testament[93] may have arisen not from Jewish polemics but from an early Christian testimonium that sought to explain why Jesus was buried so quickly;[94]

87. *b. Sanh.* 46b and *t. Sanh.* 9:7 which record R. Meir's parable of people being offended at the execution of the king's twin implying that it is a disgrace to hang someone made in the image of God; cf. *Tg. Ps.-J.* Deut 21:23: "it is a disgrace before the Lord to hang a man, unless his guilt caused it" (Clarke, ArBib).

88. Gal 3:13: "Cursed be every one who hangs on a tree"; Deut 21:23 (LXX): "everyone who is hanged on a tree has been cursed by God"; 11QTemple LXIV,13: "those hanged on a tree are cursed by God and man." Somewhat ambiguous is *Tg. Neof.* Deut 21:23: "every one who is hanged is accursed before the Lord" (McNamara, ArBib); cf. Trypho's comments recorded by Justin, cited above, p. 79 n. 76.

89. See Philo, *Prov.* 2.24–25; *Post.* 61; *Somn.* 2.213; *Flacc.* 72, 83; Josephus, *Ant.* 11.261, 266–68 (referring to Haman's crucifixion without mention of a curse, even though we might have expected one); 12.255–56; 13.380–81; 17.295; 18.64 (probably); 19.94; 20.129; *J.W.* 1.97, 113; 2.75, 253, 306–8; 3.321; 5.289, 449–51; *T. Mos.* 6.9; 8.1; *Tg. Ruth* 1:17; *Tg. Num* 25:4 (mention of execution "in broad daylight," but no mention of a curse); 4QpNah I,6–8.

90. 11QTemple LXIV,13.

91. Presumably some of the 800 Pharisees crucified by Alexander Jannaeus (Josephus, *Ant.* 13.380–81; *J.W.* 1.97,113), some of the 2000 revolutionaries crucified by Varus (Josephus, *Ant.* 17.295; *J.W.* 2.75), some of the 3600 (including women and children) crucified by Florus (Josephus, *J.W.* 2.306–8), and some of those crucified leading up to the Jewish War (Josephus, *J.W.* 5.289, 449–51), were thought by many of their compatriots to have died as righteous martyrs and not as accursed reprobates.

92. See Dunn, *Theology*, 209; Dietzfelbinger, *Berufung*, 36–37.

93. See Acts 5:30; 10:39; 13:29; 1 Pet 2:24; the concern in John 19:31 over not allowing Jesus to remain on the cross over the Sabbath may also have arisen from Deut 21:23.

94. Here O'Brien, "Curse of the Law," 72, cites Wilcox, "Upon the Tree," 85–99.

and (vi) later Christian references to Deut 21:23 either do not refer to the curse[95] or appear to be dependent on Gal 3:13.[96]

Thus, while it is probably true that the claim that Jesus—as one who had been opposed by the Jewish leadership and crucified by the Romans—was Israel's Messiah would have been offensive to many Jews, Deut 21:23 could not by itself have been the basis of this offense, even if it was used polemically against Christians. Furthermore, it could not be concluded that Christians were necessarily disregarding the law by claiming that God's Messiah had been crucified. Other ways of reading Deut 21:23 were available.

DEVOTION TO JESUS

Taking this one step further, it is quite possible for Jews to have been opposed to Christians, not only because of their messianic claims, but also for their devotion to Jesus. Larry Hurtado has demonstrated that early Christians were united in their high regard for Jesus, a regard that went beyond any Jewish figure, including the Messiah. Hurtado summarizes:

> By the divine action registered in raising Jesus from death into eschatological and glorious life, he has been declared to be God's "Son" and "holy servant." Indicative of Jesus' exalted status, his name has been made powerfully efficacious. Healing and other miracles can be worked through faith in his name. Indeed, it is now requisite to "call upon" him/his name, and this appears to have become the distinguishing feature of cultic practice at an astonishingly early point in Judean circles (so early that we cannot see clearly a time when the practice was not operative among them).[97]

This, he suggests, is "what mainly prompted opposition from other Jews."[98] On this view, then, Jews were offended by what appeared to be almost a blasphemous devotion to Jesus; not even the Messiah should be accorded such reverence.

---

95. Justin, *Dial.* 10.3; 38.1.

96. Justin, *Dial.* 32.1; 89.2; 90.1; Tertullian, *Adv. Jud.* 10.1, appears to be dependent on Justin. See O'Brien, "Curse of the Law," 59–63.

97. Hurtado, *Lord Jesus Christ*, 215.

98. Ibid., 213; cf. O'Brien, "Curse of the Law," 74–75.

An Unlikely Group

Consistent with the previous proposal is the suggestion made by Martin Dibelius that the offense of the early Christians lay in the claims that it was *they* who knew something about God's salvation and that God's Messiah had appeared specifically to *them*—a collection of people from the margins of Judean and Galilean society.[99] Who were they to make such claims, implying that they knew more than the priests and Pharisees? It is plausible that the leaders of Jerusalem were offended at the populist nature of the Christian movement, since it tended to leave them out and possibly undermine their authority in the eyes of many.

Reasons for the Persecution of the Hellenist Christians in Jerusalem

The above suggestions help to explain the general opposition to the Christian movement. They are not mutually exclusive; indeed, they could all be true, and some Jews may have been more offended for one reason than for another. According to Luke, however, it was the Hellenists in particular who experienced the most severe persecution: Stephen, a leader of the Hellenists, is killed for his views, and this sparked a "great persecution" that forced all Christians "except the apostles" to leave Jerusalem,[100] and some of these we learn went as far as Phoenicia, Cyprus, and Antioch.[101] If this was a persecution that targeted only the Hellenists, as Simmons suggests,[102] then perhaps the real instigators were the non-Christian Hellenists who were upset with the disturbance being caused by the Christian Hellenists. Two factors, however, suggest that Hebrew/Aramaic-speaking Christians may have been included in this persecution as well: (i) the use of "the apostles" in Acts 8:1 to denote the Hebrew wing of the church is somewhat puzzling since Luke has already used "Hebrews" for this purpose; and (ii) some of those who were scattered initially went, according to the same text, throughout Judea.[103] The existence of a church later in

---

99. Dibelius, *Paul*, 51–52; cf. Donaldson, "Zealot and Convert," 678–79; Davies, *Invitation*, 261; Gaventa, *Darkness to Light*, 39.

100. Acts 7:57—8:3.

101. Acts 11:19.

102. Cf. Hengel, "Jesus and Paul," 13.

103. See Hurtado, 211–12; cf. Barrett, *Acts*, 1:391.

Jerusalem, however, suggests that the scattered Hebrews were able to return once the furor had died down.[104] Either way, while the above suggestions may explain the general opposition towards Christians in Jerusalem, they do not explain why the Hellenists in particular received the more severe opposition: it was the ministry of Stephen and his martyrdom that sparked the persecution, and it appears these Hellenists were not able to return to Jerusalem. A number of suggestions have been made to address this more specific issue of opposition.

CHARISMATIC ACTIVITY

Martin Hengel suggests that the Hellenists offended Jewish authorities by their charismatic activity—miracles, wisdom, inspired speech, and Stephen's heavenly vision. He writes:

> The 'Hellenistic' missionaries evidently understood themselves as the bearers of special 'wisdom', through the eschatological inspiration of the Spirit. This new freedom of the spirit and the wisdom revealed by God is the only explanation for the offence caused by Stephen and his colleagues.[105]

It is possible that Jews were offended by this type of activity—offended by the claim that God's Spirit was at work in this group of ordinary people, in the same way that they may have been offended by the claim that the Messiah had appeared to such people.[106] Heikki Räisänen, however, notes that this does not explain the persecution directed specifically at the Hellenist community, since Spirit-inspired activity was also known in the Hebrew community[107]—for example, when they were meeting together on the Day of Pentecost and afterwards,[108] in Peter's defense before the Jerusalem authorities,[109] in

---

104. See Acts 9:26–27; 11:2, 22; 12:12; 15:4.

105. Hengel, "Jesus and Paul," 19.

106. Recall the proposal of Dibelius above, p. 84.

107. Räisänen, "The Hellenists," 172–74. Although Räisänen also argues that the portrayal of the Hellenists (Stephen, in particular) as Spirit-inspired is due to Lukan redaction, it is illegitimate to conclude simply on that basis that the portrayal is unhistorical.

108. Acts 2:1–13; 4:31.

109. Acts 4:5–12.

his vision and encounter with Cornelius,[110] and in Agabus' prophesying.[111] Nevertheless, it will be important to keep in mind this charismatic quality of early Christianity in what follows, because it suggests that early Christian behavior derives not only from a reflection on the teaching and example of Jesus or on the theological implications of his death and resurrection, but also from their experience of God working among them.

CRITICISM AGAINST THE LAW?

According to Luke, there were some men from the synagogue of the Freedmen in Jerusalem who accused Stephen of making blasphemous statements regarding the law and the temple.[112] Regarding the law: he utters "blasphemous words against Moses," he speaks "against . . . the law," and he says that Jesus "will change the customs which Moses delivered to us"; regarding the temple: he uses "blasphemous words against . . . God,"[113] he speaks "against this holy place," and he says that Jesus "will destroy this place." The comment that these Jews "set up false witnesses" to testify against Stephen[114] implies that Luke himself thinks these charges could not be substantiated; but the fact that these charges were made in the first place suggests we ought to inquire about what the Hellenists were doing that led to the charge that central aspects of the Jewish faith were under attack.[115] We need to determine to what extent these charges are valid and exactly what it was that the Hellenists were saying that was causing offense.

With regard to the charges concerning the law, Christian Dietzfelbinger argues that the Hellenists, represented by Stephen and in contrast to the Hebrews, were following a law-critical perspective which came from Jesus. He writes:

---

110. Acts 10.

111. Acts 11:28; 21:10.

112. Acts 6:9–14. For similar charges made against Paul, see Acts 21:28; 25:8.

113. Given the context, it seems reasonable to take blasphemy against God as a reference to criticism of the temple as first suggested by Loisy, *Acts des Apotres*, 309.

114. Acts 6:13.

115. For a discussion of the charges brought against Stephen, see Wedderburn, *History*, 47–49.

> While the community of the 'Hebrews', which was led by the circle of Twelve, consciously approved of the framework of Jewish tradition for their own thinking and actions, similarly those in Stephen's group who had consciously pushed to the forefront elements of the law-critical Jesus tradition (Mark 7:15; 10:5f; Matt 5:21–48; in addition Mark 14:58) had also put particular weight on the accounts of the law-critical actions of Jesus (Mark 2:15ff; 2:23ff; 3:1ff; also Matt 11:19), and, as Acts 6:11ff shows, translated them into proclamation.[116]

If Dietzfelbinger is correct in supposing that the persecution of the Hellenists was due to their view of the law, then we must suppose, in light of the general tolerance Jews exhibited towards one another that we noted above,[117] that the Hellenists' view must have involved a fundamental criticism of the law, and not just a different halakhah. Indeed, Dietzfelbinger describes the Hellenists as a group "who were oriented in fundamental distance to the law."[118]

But if so, what is the evidence for such a fundamental criticism? Beginning with the account of Stephen we are confronted with some difficult historical problems, the most important being the historicity of both Stephen's trial and his speech. These two are interrelated: (i) the stoning of Stephen was more likely the action of an angry mob than the sentence of the Sanhedrin, since it is not likely the Sanhedrin had such authority and since such official action would almost certainly have had serious repercussions from the Romans; and yet (ii) it is difficult to imagine Stephen's speech, which does not directly answer the accusations brought against him, and which is longest of the speeches in Acts, being delivered before an angry mob. Thus, if Stephen's speech is authentic, it only makes sense for it to have been delivered before the Sanhedrin; yet his speech seems unconnected to the accusations and the Sanhedrin is unlikely to have executed him. Commentators assess these problems variously.[119] To examine these historical problems fully, however, would take us too far from our topic. Instead, I will assume, for the sake of argument, that Luke believed that Stephen's speech accurately reflected perspectives of Stephen and the Hellenist communi-

---

116. Dietzfelbinger, *Berufung*, 19 (my translation).

117. See above, p. 77–78.

118. Dietzfelbinger, *Berufung*, 29 (my translation).

119. For various options taken, see Barrett, *Acts*, 1:318–22; Haenchen, *Acts*, 272–74; Hill, *Hellenists and Hebrews*, 53–67; Pervo, *Acts*, 174–80.

ty.[120] With this assumption in place we can examine the speech to see if there are any grounds for the accusations raised—first with regard to the law, and in the following section with regard to the temple.

In Stephen's speech, there are in fact no grounds for the accusation that he was critical of the law. Granted, the speech is something of a puzzle: rather than defending himself—by denying the charges, accepting the charges, or nuancing his statements that may have given rise to the charges—he instead develops a counter-charge against his accusers. First, he shows himself to be orthodox with regard to the law: he notes that Abraham was given the "covenant of circumcision" and a promise, the time of which drew near with the raising up of Moses whom God made "ruler and deliverer," and through whom God gave "salvation" and "living oracles" to his people.[121] And second, he charges his accusers of having not kept the law.[122] Indeed, the thrust of the speech, couched in a historical survey of the nation, is a counter-charge that identifies Stephen's accusers with rebellious Israelites from the past: like the patriarchs who sold Joseph into slavery, like the Israelites in Egypt who rejected Moses' leadership and who committed idolatry in the wilderness, like those who thought they could contain Yahweh within a temple,[123] and like their forbearers who killed the prophets, so too Stephen's accusers are insensitive to and stand opposed to God.[124] But, in the end, there is nothing here to suggest that the Hellenists were critical of the law.

We should, however, also consider the possibility, as Dietzfelbinger proposes, that the Hellenists were transmitting a law-critical perspective that they received from Jesus, even if there is no other evidence in Acts other than the charge brought against Stephen. But in this case, it

120. Barrett, *Acts*, 1:339, comments: "The speech of Acts 7, which can hardly have been spoken by Stephen in the circumstances described, recovers great historical value as a document of that sector of Judaism from which Stephen and his colleagues are said to have come"; Fitzmyer, *Acts*, 365, comments: "It is . . . likely that Luke has passed on to us an inherited form of Stephen's speech, into which he has introduced modifications. . . . In its present form it is certainly a Lucan composition, but it builds on inherited tradition, possibly Antiochene."

121. Acts 7:8, 17, 25, 35, 38.

122. Acts 7:53.

123. It may be that Stephen's description of the temple as χειροποίητος may have incited some since this was a word commonly used in Jewish condemnation of idolatry (see Dunn, *Unity and Diversity*, 271).

124. Acts 7:9, 25–29, 39–43, 51–53.

is not at all obvious that Jesus was in fact critical of the law. The texts that Dietzfelbinger cites do not clearly support his position. While Mark draws the conclusion from the hand-washing incident that Jesus "declared all foods clean," Jesus' saying itself about defilement being due not to what goes into a person but to what comes out from within, was probably intended to stress the importance of the whole person with regard to purity, rather than to make a comment on food laws.[125] Jesus' challenge to live by a higher standard or by the fundamental principles inherent within the law, such as his rejection of Moses' provision for divorce and his so-called antitheses in the Sermon on the Mount, are not criticisms of the law per se (note that with regard to his teaching on divorce, the creation story is also part of Torah).[126] It may be true that by having table fellowship with tax collectors and sinners, and by healing on the Sabbath, Jesus caused offense, and that his critics accused him of either breaking the law or at least of failing to safeguard the law. I note, however, that in the previous chapter we did not find evidence that Jesus was flaunting the law by eating with marginalized and disreputable people; indeed, the emphasis on repentance in Jesus' teaching speaks against this.[127] Also, in a following chapter I will argue that Jesus' practice of healing on the Sabbath was not primarily intended to change Sabbath law, even though this may have led to a new understanding of Sabbath as the Christian mission began to engage Gentiles.[128] Finally, we note that Jesus was apparently never arrested for breaking the law.[129] In his own study of Jesus' attitude to the law, Sanders concludes that "nothing which Jesus said or did which bore on the law led his disciples after his death to disregard it."[130]

It is true that one of the Jewish criticisms of Christians—especially those associated later with the Gentile mission—was that they did not keep the law.[131] Paul's waiving of circumcision and his failure to insist on keeping food laws would be good examples of legitimate grounds

125. Mark 7:14–23. Dunn, "Jesus and Ritual Purity, 37–60; Guelich, *Mark 1–8:26*, 374–76; Collins, *Mark*, 353–56. See also below, p. 262 n. 121.

126. Mark 10:5–6; Matt 5:21–48.

127. See above, p. 44.

128. See below, pp. 254–63.

129. With regard to Jesus' saying, "let the dead bury the dead" (Matt 8:22//Luke 9:62), which has sometimes been taken as contrary to the fifth commandment, see below, p. 169 n. 193.

130. Sanders, *Jesus and Judaism*, 245–69, citation from p. 268.

131. Acts 18:13; 21:27–28; 23:29; Justin, *Dial.* 10.1; Origen, *Cels.* 2.1–4; 5.33.

for such Jewish criticism (even though Luke's depiction of Paul later in Acts shows him—at least while among Jews—to be law-observant[132]). And it is understandable, in the case of a messianic movement, why questions might arise, whether from those within the movement or from outsiders, concerning the relationship between the teaching and authority of the acclaimed Messiah and the traditional locus of authority—in this case, Torah and the Jewish leaders. However, it does not appear that, from the beginning, a criticism of the law per se was fundamental to the Christian movement. Jesus appears to have raised moral standards, and he appears to have called attention to the "weightier matters of the law";[133] furthermore, he may have pushed the boundaries of what was considered appropriate behavior for a pious Jew by having fellowship with tax collectors and sinners or by healing on the Sabbath. For these reasons it may be that some Jews thought Christians were law-breakers from the beginning, and that this was the cause of the offense; however, the evidence does not support the claim that an overthrow of the law was part of the Christian agenda.[134]

CRITICISM AGAINST THE TEMPLE

We turn now to the accusation that Stephen—and by implication, the Hellenists—spoke against the temple. In this case, it does appear that part of Stephen's speech could have caused offense: while agreeing that Solomon did build a house for God, he goes on to assert, "Yet the Most High does not dwell in houses made with hands," and he cites an Isaianic prophecy in support.[135] It is not clear, however, what the specific object of his criticism was. It is doubtful that he thought there never should have been a temple, since Solomon himself also acknowledged that God cannot be contained within a human structure.[136] Furthermore, presumably the "tent of witness," of which Stephen seems to approve, would have been subject to the same criticism.[137]

132. Acts 20:16; 21:21–26; see Nolland, "Luke's Readers," 131–32.

133. Matt 23:23; cf. Luke 11:42.

134. Räisänen, "The Hellenists," 163, comments: "the Hellenists are unlikely candidates as transmitters of law-critical Jesus tradition apart from the love command which, in itself, need not imply any criticisms of the law at all."

135. Acts 7:47–50; Isa 66:1–2.

136. 1 Kgs 8:27.

137. The obvious difference between the tent and the temple is one of mobility; however, there is nothing in the text to suggest Stephen is focusing on this.

Although it is possible that Stephen thought something fundamentally needed to change with regard to the temple in light of the death and resurrection of Jesus the Messiah, another possibility is that Stephen was making an implicit criticism of the temple authorities: just as they were not keeping the law, so there was something improper about their administration of the temple. Or, perhaps the implicit criticism was directed more specifically at the authorities' opposition of the Christian movement: Stephen's comment that God cannot be contained within the temple could very well have been intended, and heard, as a message that control of the temple does not imply control of God; God can work, and indeed he is at work, apart from the temple authorities. These are all possibilities; unfortunately, Stephen's speech itself does not give us any more clarity than this.

We may be able to take a step further by considering that (i) Stephen's opponents may have been repeating the accusations with regard to the temple that had been brought against Jesus: "We heard him say, 'I will destroy this temple that is made with hands, and in three days I will build another, not made with hands'";[138] and (ii) Stephen and the Hellenists may have inherited Jesus' own critical view of the temple. Either or both of these could be true. We will need to examine evidence from the Gospels to know exactly what was Jesus' view of the temple and what was the nature of the criticism brought against him.

Each of the Synoptics records Jesus' prediction of the destruction of the temple,[139] and all four Gospels tell the account of Jesus overturning tables in the temple area.[140] Sanders has famously argued that the temple incident was not a criticism of the religious leaders or of the operation of the temple, but rather a prediction and a symbolic act that pointed to the pending destruction of the temple that was necessary so that the eschatological temple could take its place.[141] Key to his argument is a denial of the authenticity of (i) the scriptural citations in the temple incident—"Is it not written, 'My house shall be called

---

138. Mark 14:58 (par. Matt 26:61); cf. Matt 27:40//Mark 15:29. In John's account, Jesus challenges his accusers: "Destroy this temple, and in three days I will raise it up" (John 2:19).

139. Matt 24:2//Mark 13:2//Luke 21:5–6.

140. Matt 21:12–13//Mark 11:15–17//Luke 19:45–46//John 2:13–17.

141. Sanders, *Jesus and Judaism*, 61–76. This is in keeping more generally with Sanders' critique of the stereotypical way he sees Christian scholars assessing Judaism as a corrupt religion.

a house of prayer for all the nations'? But you have made it a den of robbers"[142]—and of (ii) a number of sayings that could be construed as being critical of the temple: (a) according to Mark, Jesus praised a scribe who ranked love of God and neighbor as being more important than sacrifices;[143] and, (b) according to Matthew, Jesus cited from Hosea—"I desire mercy, and not sacrifice"—to defend his practice of eating with sinners and of plucking grain on the Sabbath.[144] Thus, Sanders argues that although Jesus intended to signify by his action the imminent destruction of the temple in order to make way for the eschatological temple, Mark reinterpreted that action and made it into a critique of the injustice or impiety of the temple authorities.[145]

There is an important aspect of Sanders' argument with which I concur: Jesus had in view a new temple that would replace Herod's. While the part of the rumor that attributed to Jesus a threat to destroy the temple ("We heard him say, 'I will destroy this temple . . . ,'" "You who would destroy the temple . . .") is probably best understood as a hostile exaggeration intended to support a charge of blasphemy brought against him—that is, Jesus predicted the destruction of the temple but did not threaten to destroy it[146]—the best explanation for the phrase "and I will rebuild it in three days" is that it is authentic.[147] Why else would unsympathetic people have attributed such a saying to Jesus? Furthermore, there are indications that Jesus supported the function of the temple per se and expected it to continue. Although the Jesus Seminar assigned a gray ranking to the saying regarding leaving one's gift at the altar in order to be first reconciled with one's brother,[148] they acknowledged the antiquity of the tradition in light of the reference to the temple, and confessed that "on balance, these words echo something Jesus may have said."[149] Also, the Seminar ranked as black

---

142. Mark 11:17; par. in Matt 21:13//Luke 19:46; citations from Isa 56:7; Jer 7:11.

143. Mark 12:28–34.

144. Matt 9:13; 12:7. See Sanders, *Jesus and Judaism*, 66–67.

145. Ibid., 75.

146. Apart from *Gos. Thom.* 71, there is no indication in the Gospel tradition that Jesus thought he would destroy the temple. Collins, *Mark*, 701, suggests that the passive verbs in Mark 13:2 probably indicate that Jesus thought that God would destroy the temple.

147. See above, 91 n. 138.

148. Matt 5:23–24.

149. Funk et al., *Five Gospels*, 142.

Jesus' instruction to a cleansed leper not to tell anyone but to go to a priest and to offer the gift for a sacrifice that would have been made at the temple.[150] But they did this because of the presence of the Markan motif of the messianic secret;[151] it is difficult, however, to imagine why a Christian would create such a saying if indeed Jesus had thought the function of the temple was coming to an end. These two sayings suggest Jesus saw the function of the temple per se as valid. In addition, Jesus' own teaching and healing in the temple court[152] would seem odd if he had thought the temple itself was not only doomed to destruction, but was now no longer relevant. And finally, the continuing practice of his disciples of attending the temple after Jesus' death suggests that they certainly believed that this place had ongoing significance.[153] All of this is difficult to explain if Jesus had proclaimed that the temple would be abolished or replaced by a spiritual temple.

In fact, in light of Jewish expectation for a new temple in the age to come,[154] Jesus' saying that he would rebuild the temple may have been an implicit messianic claim.[155] Be that as it may, the description of the present temple as having been χειροποίητον ("made with hands") would certainly have caused offense, given the association of this word with idolatry.[156] The description of the temple that Jesus would build as being ἀχειροποίητον ("made without hands") means that the new temple would be built by divine, rather than human, agency.[157] (We should be cautious, however, with regard to assessing the authenticity of ἀχειροποίητον in Mark 14:58, given that it appears only here in the

---

150. Matt 8:4//Mark 1:44//Luke 5:14; cf. Lev 14:10ff.

151. Funk et al., *Five Gospels*, 43.

152. Luke 19:47; Matt 21:23//(Mark 11:27)//Luke 20:1; Mark 12:35; Luke 21:37–38; Matt 26:55//Mark 14:49//Luke 22:53; John 7:14, 28; 8:2, 20; 18:20; Matt 21:14.

153. Acts 2:42, 46; 3:1; 5:12, 19–21, 42. Note also Jesus' parable of the Pharisee and the tax collector where Jesus assumes that the temple is an appropriate place for prayer (Luke 18:10).

154. See Sanders, *Jesus and Judaism*, 77–90.

155. Zech 6:12; *Tg. Zech* 6:12: "Behold, the man whose name is Anointed will be revealed, and he shall be raised up, and shall build the temple of the Lord" (Cathcart & Gordon, ArBib); *Tg. Isa* 53:5: "And he [i.e., Messiah; cf. 52:13] will build the sanctuary which was profaned for our sins" (Chilton, ArBib).

156. LXX of Lev 26:1; Isa 2:18; 10:11; 19:1; Dan 5:4, 23; 6:28.

157. Evans, *Mark 8:27—16:20*, 445–46; Collins, *Mark*, 702–3; Hooker, *Mark*, 358–59.

Gospel accounts and that on the lips of hostile witnesses.[158]) But, in the end, Jesus still has a standing temple in view.

The main thrust of Sanders' argument, however—that Jesus' temple action was intended as a prediction of destruction rather than as a criticism of the authorities—is open to challenge. Craig Evans, in my view, has effectively done this.[159] He argues, first, that it is unlikely, in light of the pending or recent destruction of the temple, that Mark would have been embarrassed by a prediction of Jesus that the temple would fall; and even if he was, and sought to redact the tradition in order to distance Jesus from this view, it is puzzling why he left Jesus' clear prediction in Mark 13:2 unchanged.[160] Surely an explicit prediction of the destruction of the temple would have been just as offensive to Jews as an act symbolizing destruction.[161] Second, in light of the strong anti-temple motif in Mark—in addition to Jesus' prediction, the accusation at his trial, and the mocking at his crucifixion, we note the bracketing of the temple incident with Jesus' cursing of the barren fig tree,[162] the allusion in the parable of the vineyard to Isaiah's song of the vineyard that came to be understood as a prediction of the destruction of the first temple,[163] and the tear in the veil of the temple at Jesus' death[164]—Evans thinks it unlikely that Mark would have reinterpreted an incident that clearly spoke of the destruction of the temple and changed it into a criticism of the temple authorities.[165] Third, although John's tradition of the temple incident is clearly independent of the Synoptic tradition, it is significant that he too interprets the event as a "cleansing."[166] And fourth, there is evidence elsewhere in the Gospels

158. The Jesus Seminar ranks the saying as gray (Funk et al., *Five Gospels*, 121).

159. Evans, "Jesus' Action," 237–70.

160. Ibid., 238–39.

161. Evans notes the punishment inflicted on Jesus ben Ananias for preaching against the temple just before its destruction (Josephus, J.W. 6.300–304).

162. Mark 11:12–14, 20–25.

163. Mark 12:1–12. Evans cites the following: *Tg. Isa.* 5:2, 5: "and I built my sanctuary in their midst, and I even gave my altar to atone for their sins. . . . And now I will tell you what I am about to do to my people. I will take up my Shekhinah from them . . . ; I will break down the place of their sanctuaries . . ." (Chilton, *ArBib*); *t. Meʿil.* 1:16: commenting on Isa 5:2: "'He built a watchtower'—this is the *Hekhal*. 'He hewed out a wine vat in it'—this is the altar" (Neusner); cf. *t. Sukkah* 3:15.

164. Mark 15:38.

165. Evans, "Jesus' Action," 239–42.

166. John 2:13–22, esp. v. 16; see Evans, "Jesus' Action," 242–43.

that Jesus was critical of the priesthood,[167] and there is evidence outside the New Testament of corruption associated with the temple during the first century.[168]

I take it, therefore, that while Jesus assumed a functioning temple, he was critical of the temple establishment and, perhaps connected

---

167. The challenge of Jesus' authority regarding the temple incident suggests animosity between Jesus and the temple authorities (Mark 11:27–33); the parable of the vineyard is clearly critical of religious leaders (Mark 12:1–12); if Fitzmyer is correct in taking the widow's mite incident as originally being a lament against the religious establishment, this could be understood as a criticism of the wealth of the temple (Mark 12:41–44); the presence of the servant of the high priest at Jesus' arrest suggests that the high priest was taking personal interest in silencing Jesus (Mark 14:47); in light of Josephus' statement (*Ant.* 18.118) that John the Baptist was popular with the people, it is likely that his criticism was directed primarily at the religious establishment (Matt 3:7//Luke 3:7–9); and, if the passion predictions are taken to be authentic, the specific mention of the chief priests there indicate enmity between Jesus and the priesthood (Mark 8:31; 10:33 par.).

168. Evans, "Jesus' Action," 256–64. Note also the following criticisms and predictions concerning the temple and the priesthood: the temple sacrifices have no value (Isa 1:11); priests are corrupt (Isa 28:7; 29:9–10); the temple will be destroyed because of the corruption of the leaders (Mic 3:9–12); steadfast love and knowledge of God are to be preferred over sacrifices (Hos 6:6); criticism of priests (Hos 4:4–6; 6:9; 9:15); priests and rulers are charged with crimes and the temple is threatened with destruction (Jer 7:1–34; 26:6, 9; cf. 2:8; 6:13; 8:10; 14:18; 23:11, 33–34; 32:31–32; 34:19); criticism of the priests (Ezek 22:26); looking forward to a new, cleansed, purified, and holy temple (Ezek 40–43); Jerusalem was destroyed because of the sins of the prophets and the priests (Lam 4:13); criticism against priests (Zeph 3:4); looking forward to a time of ritual purity in the temple (Zech 14:20–21); the temple is corrupt (Mal 1:6–14; 2:1–11), so the Lord will come to purify it (Mal 3:1–4); criticism of priests (*Jub.* 23.21; probably the Hasmonean high priesthood originally, but could have been reapplied in later centuries); prediction that in the end-time priests will be corrupt and impure (*T. Levi* 14.1–6; 17.11; see 14.2 where a Christian copyist applied this to Jesus); the second temple was polluted (*1 En.* 89.73); the priests have failed the Israelites (*1 En.* 89–90); the Messiah will purge Jerusalem of corrupt officials (*Pss. Sol.* 17–18); criticism of the priesthood (*T. Mos.* 5.3—6.1).

Evans (ibid., 250–56) adds a fifth point: while some Jewish literature does look forward to the replacement of the present temple with a new one (*1 En.* 90.28–30; *Jub.* 1.17; 11QTemple XXIX,8–18; *Sib. Or.* 5.435; *2 Bar.* 4.3), "[t]here are no texts that predict the appearance of a messianic figure who first destroys (or predicts the destruction of) the temple and then rebuilds it" (ibid., 250), and there are many texts that are either critical of priests or that look forward to a purified temple, thereby making the expectation for a new temple just one motif among many in light of which Jesus' temple incident could be interpreted. However, if the promise to rebuild the temple is authentic for Jesus, as seems likely, it would suggest that Jesus did, along with other Jews, expect the temple to be replaced.

with this, he predicted the destruction and rebuilding of the temple. But he did not promote the temple's abolition.

Returning to Stephen and the Hellenists, it is possible that they remembered Jesus' criticism of the temple and expressed it in some way. Stephen's description of the temple as being χειροποίητον may reflect this,[169] although with the authenticity of this word in Mark 14:58 being uncertain, it is impossible to be sure. In any case, it is not yet clear why the Hellenists in particular, in contrast to the Hebrews who continued to attend the temple, would have emphasized this aspect of Jesus' teaching: we recall that originally the Hellenists had probably been drawn to Jerusalem precisely because they highly valued the temple. Alternatively, it is possible that Stephen's accusers were offended by something that he and the Hellenists were saying or doing and that this caused them to recall the charge that had been brought against Jesus.

I think it unlikely that at this early date the Hellenists had developed the idea that a spiritual temple would replace the physical one and that this was the point of contention. Paul speaks of a spiritual temple,[170] but he was working at a distance from the Jerusalem temple with people who had no hope of ever gaining access to it.[171] Furthermore, there is little evidence, with a good claim to authenticity, that Jesus was moving in this direction.[172] And while it is true that some Dead Sea Scrolls

169. Acts 7:48; cf. v. 41 where Stephen describes the idolatrous calf in the wilderness as "the works of their hands."

170. Temple language is used with reference to the community of believers: 1 Cor 3:16; 2 Cor 6:16; cf. Eph 2:21; Heb 13:15. Temple language is also used with reference to the individual believer: Rom 12:1; 1 Cor 6:19; 2 Cor 5:1.

171. Also, if we can trust Luke's account of Paul's final visit to Jerusalem, Paul apparently did not see a contradiction between speaking of believers as the temple of God and attending the temple in Jerusalem (Acts 21:26).

172. Some Gospel texts could be interpreted as suggesting a spiritual understanding of the temple: e.g., Jesus' citation of Ps 118:22–23 implying that he was the new cornerstone (Mark 12:10–11); Jesus' saying that true worshippers will worship not in Jerusalem or on Mt. Gerizim, but "in spirit and truth" (John 4:21–24); John's interpretation of Jesus' saying—"Destroy this temple and in three days I will rebuild it"—with reference to Jesus' death and resurrection (John 2:21–22). However, it is difficult to establish the authenticity of the first two (the Jesus Seminar ranks them both as black), and the third text sounds very much like a post-Easter reflection on the temple incident. Also, even if the authenticity of Matt 12:6 ("something greater than the temple is here") could be established, this text does not suggest a spiritual temple, but rather is simply a claim that Jesus is more important than the temple.

texts use temple language with reference to the Qumran community,[173] other texts show that hope for a restored temple in Jerusalem was still very much in view.[174]

Two other hypotheses, however, have been offered to try to explain what the Hellenists may have been doing in connection with the temple that ignited such fierce reaction from the synagogue. The first of these comes from Dietrich-Alex Koch who argues that the Hellenists interpreted the death of Jesus as an atoning sacrifice, from which they may have concluded that the temple sacrificial system was no longer relevant, and if so that therefore a substantial portion of the law was no longer relevant.[175] He bases his argument on the assumption that Rom 3:25–26a represents a pre-Pauline tradition that derived from the Hellenist community.[176] The consequence of this is that the Hellenists would have spoken of Jesus' death as a ἱλαστήριον, an atoning sacrifice,[177] offered by God to deal with sin. Koch explains:

> Against the background of the Hellenistic use of ἱλαστήριον for an object of placation, especially for a monument, it is a metaphorical use, referring no more to a real monument. . . , but to a formerly human, now heavenly being. And as God himself has put him forward as ἱλαστήριον this term no longer means a gift to God, but a means of atonement comprising above all the remission of "the sins previously committed" (Rom 3:25c). Thus, in the pre-Pauline tradition of Rom 3:25–26a, the Hellenistic concept of ἱλαστήριον is adapted in a characteristically Jewish

173. 1QS VIII,5–8; IX,3–5.

174. 11QTemple II–XIII, XXX–XLVII; 1 QM II,3; VII,11–12; cf. *1 En.* 90.28–29.

175. Koch, "Crossing the Border," 306–7.

176. Dunn, *Romans*, 1:163–64, gives as evidence for Rom 3:25–26a being a pre-Pauline tradition the appearance of several non-Pauline words: προτίθημι ("put forward"; elsewhere only in Rom 1:13, but with a different sense), ἱλαστήριον ("sacrifice of atonement"; *hap. leg.*), ἔνδειξις ("evidence"; elsewhere only in 2 Cor 8:24), πάρεσις ("overlooking"; *hap. leg.*), προγίνομαι ("happen previously"; *hap. leg.*), ἁμάρτημα ("sin"; elsewhere only in 1 Cor 6:18), and ἀνοχή ("forbearance"; elsewhere only in Rom 2:4). Also in support are Reumann, "Gospel," 433–43; Fitzmyer, *Romans*, 342–43; Bultmann, *Theology*, 1:46. Some of these argue that the traditional material begins with v. 24, but this is more disputed and is not necessary for Koch's thesis. Opposed is Cranfield, *Romans*, 1:200–201 n. 1, who thinks that in light of the centrality of these verses in Paul's argument, it is more likely that this is Paul's independent formulation. But the distinctive vocabulary in these verses argues in favor of pre-Pauline tradition.

177. For a summary of the issues involved in the interpretation of ἱλαστήριον in Rom 3:25, see Koch, "Crossing the Border," 300–303; Dunn, *Theology*, 213–15.

way. And in the Jewish context of the ἡμέρα τοῦ ἱλασμοῦ there is a clear antithetic relation of Christ as ἱλαστήριον: Christ's death is an expiatory act beyond all cultic connotations, thus replacing the temple rituals of expiation.[178]

Oddly enough, Koch does not mention 1 Cor 15:3, where Paul clearly states that the tradition he received interpreted Jesus' death as having been "for our sins." This would seem to strengthen Koch's argument since the phrase probably implies some kind of atonement.[179] Furthermore, if we accept that Rom 3:25–26a is traditional material, all we can say for certain is that it is *pre-Romans* in origin; but if 1 Cor 15:3 is *pre-Pauline*, which seems likely,[180] then it is more plausible that an atonement term like ἱλαστήριον could have been used with reference to Jesus' death prior to Paul's conversion.

Knowing that early Christians would have had to have given some explanation of Jesus' death in light of the apparent contradiction it posed for most Jews with regard to their messianic expectations, Koch further suggests that the Hellenists in Jerusalem could conceivably have arrived at such a view based on (i) their Diaspora experience where worship in the synagogue focused on prayer, hymns, and reading of Scripture, and not on sacrifice;[181] (ii) the longstanding prophetic tradition of criticism of the temple cult;[182] and (iii) the belief that the death of martyrs could benefit the nation.[183] And, we could

178. Koch, "Crossing the Border," 303.

179. Conzelmann, *1 Corinthians*, 255; Thiselton, *1 Corinthians*, 1191; Barrett, *1 Corinthians*, 338.

180. Jeremias, *Eucharistic Words*, 129–30, gives evidence why 1 Cor 15:3–5 is not only non-Pauline, but originating in a Jewish-Christian milieu, perhaps originally composed in Aramaic; cf. Fee, 1 *Corinthians*, 718: "it is generally agreed that in vv. 3–5 Paul is repeating a very early creedal formulation that was common to the entire church."

181. Note two comments in this regard from the Diaspora: *Let. Aris.* 234: "'What is the highest form of glory?' The reply was, 'Honoring God. This is not done with gifts or sacrifices, but with purity of heart and of devout disposition'" (Charlesworth, *OTP*); Philo, *Spec.* 1.272: "though the worshippers bring nothing else, in bringing themselves they offer the best of sacrifices, the full and truly perfect oblation of noble living, as they honour with hymns and thanksgivings their Benefactor and Saviour, God" (Colson, LCL).

182. 1 Sam 15:22 (cf. Mark 12:33); Hos 6:6 (cited in Matt 9:13 and 12:7); Amos 4:4–5; 5:21–24; Mic 6:6–8 (cf. Matt 23:23); Isa 1:10–17 (cf. v. 15 with Matt 6:7); Jer 6:20; 7:3–4, 21–23; Pss 40:6; 50:8–15; 51:16–17.

183. It is possible that belief in the atoning significance of Jesus' death originated directly from Jesus himself. Jewish literature, particularly the books of the Maccabees,

probably add to this (iv) Jesus' own prediction of the destruction of the temple.[184] Thus, Christians may have reasoned: in light of the imminent destruction of the temple, Jesus' death as a righteous martyr can be understood not only as being for the benefit of the nation, but also as a sacrifice of atonement—in particular, as a sacrifice to end all sacrifices. We can easily see how such an interpretation of Jesus' death would be considered by Jews to have been critical of the temple,

---

contain numerous accounts of martyrs whose deaths were thought to have benefited others: (i) *T. Mos.* 9.4–7 tells the story of a Jewish father, Taxo, and his seven sons who were prepared to die voluntarily rather than break the law, with the understanding that afterwards, their "blood will be avenged before the Lord" (Priest, *OTP*); (ii) 1 Macc 6:44 tells of a warrior named Eleazar who died while slaying the king's elephant: "So he gave his life to save his people and to win for himself an everlasting name"; (iii) 2 Macc 7:37–38 concludes the account of the martyrdom of the seven brothers: "I, like my brothers, give up body and life for the laws of our fathers, appealing to God to show mercy soon to our nation and . . . to bring to an end the wrath of the Almighty which has justly fallen on our whole nation"; (iv) 4 Macc 17:21–22 reflects on the value of martyrdoms: "the homeland [was] purified—they having become, as it were, a ransom for the sin of our nation. And through the blood of those devout ones and their death as an expiation [ἱλαστήριον], divine Providence preserved Israel that previously had been afflicted"; and (v) 4 Macc 18:4 continues the reflection: "Because of them the nation gained peace, and by reviving observance of the law in the homeland they ravaged the enemy."

The text of 4 Macc 17:21–22 is particularly interesting since it speaks of the martyrs' deaths as a ἱλαστήριον. 4 Maccabees, however, is difficult to date with certainty (for an overview and assessment of various proposals, see deSilva, *4 Maccabees*, 14–18). Anderson, "Maccabees," 453, comments that "[w]hereas the major part of the work deals with the brave endurance unto death of the famous Maccabean martyrs, it is in fact a philosophical discourse on how and why such amazing courage was possible, and as such it could have been written almost any time in the last century B.C.E. until the reign of Hadrian in the early 2d century C.E." Bickermann, "Date of Fourth Maccabees," 277–81, however, argues more precisely for a date between 20 and 54 CE based on (i) the use of the non-Hellenistic words θρησκεία (4 Macc 5:7, 12; "religion") and νομικός (4 Macc 5:4; "about law") that are not commonly used until the reign of Augustus (30 BCE–14 CE), and (ii) the change in the designation of Apollonius from "governor of Coele-Syria and Phoenicia" in 2 Macc 3:5 to "governor of Syria, Phoenicia and Cilicia" in 4 Macc 4:2—presumably an attempt to modernize the narration in light of current political realities. Bickermann argues that Syria, Phoenicia, and Cilicia were under one Roman jurisdiction only from about 19 to 54 CE; van Henten, "Datierung und Herkunft," 140–42, however, has extended this limit by showing that part of Cilicia remained within this region of Roman jurisdiction until 72 CE. Thus, while it is possible that a text speaking of the death of martyrs as a ἱλαστήριον was current in the earliest stage of the church, it is certainly true that at this time the death of martyrs could be thought of as being beneficial for others.

184. Matt 24:12//Mark 13:1–2//Luke 21:5–6; Matt 26:60–61//Mark 14:57–58; Matt 27:40//Mark 15:29.

and therefore also of the law, and hence deeply offensive, and would therefore explain the persecution against the Hellenists.

While Koch's scenario is possible, I think it is not likely. Unfortunately, his proposal suffers from the fact that we know very little of early Christians' attitude toward the temple and the cult. But we do know, as we saw above, that although Jesus was critical of the temple, he did see its function as being valid. Also, the Jewish texts that speak of the consequent benefit of the deaths of the martyrs do not suggest that for that reason the sacrificial system of the temple was inadequate or obsolete. Furthermore, caution needs to be exercised when drawing conclusions about the perspective of the Hellenists based on the fact that they had been Diaspora Jews. Some Diaspora Jews may not have valued the temple, but others, particularly those who had chosen to live in Jerusalem, probably valued it very highly. Consequently, even if Koch is dealing with views to which Christians eventually came, it is not clear why the Hellenists in particular would have developed such views, and why they would have done so while still living in Jerusalem.

The second hypothesis to be considered regarding criticism over the temple comes from Alexander Wedderburn. He argues that the Hellenists may have proposed that the Gentile Christians, whom they had welcomed into their fellowship, were entitled to have full access to the temple just like any Jew.[185] This could certainly have elicited the charge of blasphemy against the temple from other Jews. Interestingly, this is the same charge that was brought against Paul on his last visit to Jerusalem;[186] Wedderburn suggests that Jews were suspicious of Paul because they believed that the Hellenist wing of Christianity, which Paul represented, wanted to see Gentiles admitted to the temple. Furthermore, Wedderburn argues that the quotation of Isa 56:7 in Mark 11:17—"My house shall be called a house of prayer for all the nations"—even if not an authentic word of Jesus, is an application of Scripture that could well have been made by the Hellenists.[187] In this view, the Hellenists would, like the Hebrews, have seen themselves as being loyal to the temple, even if they were calling for a fundamental change in its operation.

185. Wedderburn, *History*, 54–55.
186. Acts 21:28.
187. Wedderburn, "Similarity and Continuity," 127–28.

I think Wedderburn's proposal is plausible, with some aspects being more probable than others; even though specific evidence may be lacking, it does offer a hypothetical cause for a known effect—namely, the criticism and the persecution directed against the Hellenists—and does so where other explanations of this effect have been shown to be problematic. I shall discuss presently the likelihood that Gentiles may have been included in the fellowship of Hellenist Christians in Jerusalem. If this had been happening, however, it is possible to see how this could have served as grounds for the charges raised against the Hellenists with regard to the temple and, for that matter, with regard to the law. If the Hellenists were including Gentiles in their fellowship in a way that seemed inappropriate to other Jews, this could—when added to the other reasons for Jewish criticism of Christians discussed above (proclamation of a crucified Messiah, devotion to Jesus)—have led to further concern among Jews about what these Hellenists were intending. And interestingly, such suspicion and criticism could have arisen even if the Hellenists were not, as Wedderburn suggests, explicitly proposing that Gentiles should be granted access to the temple. The Jews could have reasoned as follows: If these Hellenists, in addition to their claim that a crucified man was the Messiah and had been exalted to heaven, were violating such a fundamental principle of maintaining Jewish identity by accepting Gentiles into their fellowship, surely they had distanced themselves from the central foci of Jewish identity, namely the temple and Torah. Hence the criticism brought against Stephen. But all of this depends on the likelihood of the presence of Gentiles in the fellowship of Hellenist Christians in Jerusalem, to which we must now turn.

ASSOCIATING WITH GENTILES

If Simmons's description of the Hellenists is correct—namely that they were distinguished from the Hebrews by being Greek-speaking and by their associations with Gentiles—then it seems intrinsically plausible that the point of offense that sparked persecution against them in particular had something to do with how they related to Gentiles. Sensitivities over such matters, from both Christian and non-Christian Jews in Jerusalem, are expressed later: specifically, complaints against Peter regarding the Cornelius incident, the delegation James sent to

Antioch to address table fellowship, and charges against Paul that he brought a Gentile into the temple.[188]

Simmons had suggested that the point of offense concerning the Hellenists was that they had accepted Gentiles into their fellowship without requiring circumcision; I, however, found that to be problematic.[189] I suggest a better hypothesis would be to suppose that the Hellenists in Jerusalem did welcome Gentiles into their fellowship, but that the point of offense was over table fellowship rather than circumcision. Wedderburn has proposed a similar argument. He suggests that they, in their desire to follow Jesus in his openness to sinners, may have expressed openness to Gentiles on the understanding that, from the Jewish perspective, Gentiles were clearly sinners.[190] And while the Hebrew Christian community may have also valued this tradition, we would expect the Hellenists to be the first to apply it to their relationships with Gentiles, since they spoke a Gentile language and had once lived in a Gentile context.[191] Further support for making this connection could be found in the few examples of Jesus' openness to or concern for Gentiles themselves.[192] Wedderburn does not suggest that the Hellenists actually engaged in a mission to the Gentiles while in Jerusalem, but only that they welcomed those who inquired about joining their fellowship.[193] Furthermore, he does not argue that in doing so the Hellenists were expressing criticism of the law, but only that they saw inclusion of the Gentiles as a high enough priority that they

188. Acts 11:2–3; Gal 2:11–13; Acts 21:27–29.

189. See above, pp. 71–73.

190. Wedderburn, *History*, 49–55. Note especially Gal 2:15.

191. Wedderburn, "Similarity and Continuity," 123–24. It is difficult to say how much the fact that the Hellenists had once lived in the Diaspora would have led them to be more accommodating to Gentiles. Presumably for some it would; there is evidence that in some ways Diaspora Jews were strongly influenced by the Greco-Roman culture. However, the fact that the Hellenists had chosen to live in Jerusalem, the heart of Judaism, would suggest that these Diaspora Jews tended to be more conservative. In any case, we can at least say that the Hellenists would have been *more* used to interacting with Gentiles than the Hebrews would have been.

192. Note, for example, Jesus' encounter with the Syrophoenician woman (Matt 15:21–18//Mark 7:24–30), his healing of the centurion's servant in Capernaum (Matt 8:5–13//Luke 7:1–10), and Mark's "for all the nations" added to the end of Jesus' statement that the temple should be a place of prayer (Mark 11:17). See further, Schnabel, "Mission to the Gentiles," 37–58.

193. Wedderburn, *History*, 51.

were willing to make certain accommodations that, they believed, were in accordance with God's will.[194] Although there is no direct evidence that Gentiles were included in the Hellenist community in Jerusalem,[195] the plausibility of such a hypothesis can be raised by considering the following.

Apart from Roman officials and soldiers, Gentiles, who might have been sympathetic to the Christian movement, could be found in Jerusalem either as pilgrims visiting during one of the annual feasts, or as slaves working in Jewish households.[196] Gentiles from either group could have been brought into the Hellenist community without there having been a dedicated mission to them: visiting Gentiles may have wanted to investigate this new community that others were talking about, or they may have sought out Jewish friends they had met on previous pilgrimages who, they now discover, had joined a new sect; and Gentile slaves could have been incorporated on the understanding that the conversion of the head of a house often entailed the conversion of the whole household,[197] including slaves.[198] That there was an openness to welcoming outsiders like Gentiles may be indicated by Philip's mission to Samaria—that is, to people estranged from Jews—and by his encounter with the Ethiopian eunuch—that is, with a Gentile pilgrim to Jerusalem.[199]

194. Wedderburn, "Similarity and Continuity," 121–22.

195. We can only speculate as to why Luke, who has a keen interest in the Gentile mission, would not have mentioned the presence of Gentiles in the Jerusalem church had there been any. One plausible explanation is that from his perspective, writing in the latter part of the first century, the most significant accounts of the beginning of the Gentile mission were the preaching of Philip, Peter's meeting with Cornelius, and Paul's missionary journeys. The presence of a few Gentiles (perhaps slaves) in the Hellenists' meetings might not have been judged to be that significant by Luke (had he known about it), whereas such association may have caused great offence to the non-Christian Jews in Jerusalem at the time. It may have served Luke's purpose more to describe specific incidents involving the leaders of the Christian movement, whereas the association of the Hellenists with Gentiles in Jerusalem may have seemed to Luke not as clear an incident for his purpose.

196. See Jeremias, *Jerusalem*, chap. 16.

197. 1 Cor 1:16; 16:15–16; Acts 16:15, 31–34; 18:8; cf. Acts 10:1–2, 44.

198. A conversion of the head of the house may have often involved the conversion of most or all within the household, but the example of Philemon would indicate that this was not always the case. See Barrett, *Acts*, 1:501; Cohen, "Crossing the Boundary," 24–25; Delling, "Taufe von 'Häusern,'" 288–310, esp. 302; Meeks, *First Urban Christians*, 30.

199. Acts 8:4–39.

The issue that would necessarily have arisen over a Christian community welcoming Gentiles would be that of table fellowship. Wedderburn suggests that the presence of Gentiles at the celebration of the Lord's Supper would naturally have raised issues of food and purity.[200] I suggest that the practice of holding communal meals—the so-called agape feast[201]—would have raised even greater concern. Luke's description of the Jerusalem Christians—"day by day . . . breaking bread in their homes, they partook of food with glad and generous hearts"—indicates that meal celebration was prominent in the early church.[202] Although Esler has argued that Jews would never eat meals together with Gentiles,[203] Sanders has shown that in fact there was among first-century Jews a range of opinion on this matter.[204] While there is evidence that some Jews, as a matter of principle, would not eat with Gentiles,[205] other Jews did so eat since, as long as the food was not impure and had been properly tithed,[206] there was no legal hindrance to dining with Gentiles.[207] It is true that Gentiles themselves

200. Wedderburn, *History*, 52. Regarding Jews not eating with Gentiles, see Esler, *Community and Gospel*, 76–86.

201. Communal meals are mentioned elsewhere in the New Testament (1 Cor 11:21; 2 Pet 2:13; Jude 12) and in second-century writers (*Diogn.* 5; Pliny, *Ep.*, 10.96; Ignatius, *Smyrn.* 8.2; Tertullian, *Apol.* 39.16–18).

202. Acts 2:46. See Barrett, *Acts*, 170–71.

203. Esler, *Community and Gospel*, 76–86.

204. Sanders, "Jewish Association," 176–80; cf. Tomson, *Paul and the Jewish Law*, 230–36.

205. *Jub.* 22.16: "Separate yourself from the gentiles, and do not eat with them, and do not perform deeds like theirs. And do not become associates of theirs. Because their deeds are defiled, and all of their ways are contaminated, and despicable, and abominable" (Wintermute, *OTP*); *Jos. Asen.* 7.1: "And Joseph entered the house of Pentephres and sat upon the throne. And they washed his feet and set a table before him by itself, because Joseph never ate with the Egyptians, for this was an abomination to him" (Burchard, *OTP*).

206. Sanders, "Jewish Association," 176–77, notes that the problem that prevents table fellowship in most of the texts that Esler cites has to do with the appropriateness of the food and not with Gentile association per se (see Dan 1:3–17; 2 Macc 7:1–2; 3 Macc 3:4, 7; Jdt 10:5; 12:17–19; Add Esth 14:17 (LXX 4:17x); Tob 1:11).

207. *Let. Aris.* 180–81, which introduces the seven-day banquet in which the Jewish translators dined with the Egyptian king (vv. 182–294): "'It will therefore be my wish to dine with you this day. Everything of which you partake,' [the king] said, 'will be served in compliance with your habits; it will be served to me as well as to you.' They expressed their pleasure and the king ordered . . . the preparations for the banquet to be made" (Shutt, *OTP*); *m. 'Abod. Zar.* 5:5: "[If an Israelite] was eating

were considered to be impure, but then so were most Jews most of the time; purity was important for entering the temple, eating Passover, and eating the second tithe, but it was not required for eating regular meals.[208]

But the Jewish concern over table fellowship was not simply a legal one; the larger issue was that of holiness, of being separate. Enshrined in the Torah,[209] and given fresh impetus after the return from exile,[210] was the importance of being a separate people. Sanders notes that it was by keeping themselves distinct that Jews avoided idolatry and maintained their devotion to the one true God.[211] Indeed, both Gentile and Jewish writers testify to this.[212] And maintaining the boundaries of

---

with [a gentile] at the same time. . . ." For other ways in which Jews associated with Gentiles, see Sanders, "Jewish Association," 179–80.

208. Ibid., 175. According to the law, foreigners residing in Israel were obligated to observe Sabbath (Exod 20:10; 23:12; Deut 5:14), the laws of cleanliness (Lev 18:26), and the law forbidding blasphemy (Lev 24:16), and to fast on the Day of Atonement (Lev 16:29); and they were permitted to participate in sacrifices (Lev 17:8–13; 22:18; Num 15:14–15) and in the festivals (Deut 16:14), including Passover if they were circumcised (Exod 12:48–49). Josephus tells of the openness of Judaism to Gentiles: *Ag. Ap.* 2.210: "To all who desire to come and live under the same laws with us, [Moses] gives a gracious welcome, holding that it is not family ties alone which constitute relationship, but agreement in the principles of conduct. On the other hand, it was not his pleasure that casual visitors should be admitted to the intimacies of our daily life"; *Ag. Ap.* 2.261: "We. . . , while we have no desire to emulate the customs of others, yet gladly welcome any who wish to share our own" (Thackeray, LCL).

209. Exod 23:31–33; 34:11–16; Deut 7:1–6.

210. Ezra 9:1–15; 10:10–11; Neh 9:2; 10:28–31; 13:3.

211. Sanders, "Jewish Association," 180–85; he cites evidence.

212. Diodorus, *Bib. hist.* 34/35.1.2: when the Jews settled around Jerusalem, they "made their hatred of mankind into a tradition, and . . . introduced utterly outlandish laws: not to break bread with any other race, nor to show them any good will at all" (Walton, LCL); 40.3: "The sacrifices that [Moses] established differ from those of other nations, as does their way of living, for as a result of their own expulsion from Egypt he introduced an unsocial and intolerant mode of life" (Walton, LCL); Josephus, *Ag. Ap.* 2.148, 258, cites Apollonius Molon as accusing the Jews of being "misanthropes" and of "declining to associate with those who have chosen to adopt a different mode of life" (Thackeray, LCL); Pompeius Trogus: after being driven out of Egypt because of an infection, the Israelites "took care . . . to have no communication with strangers; a rule which, from having been adopted on that particular occasion, gradually became a religious institution" (Stern, ed., *Greek and Latin Authors*, 1:338); Tacitus, *Hist.* 5.5: "the Jews are extremely loyal to one another, and always ready to show compassion, but toward every other people they feel only hate and enmity. They sit apart at meals and they sleep apart. . . . They adopted circumcision to distinguish themselves from other peoples by this difference" (Moore, LCL); Philostratus, *Vit.*

table fellowship was one way this separateness was achieved. Writing from an anthropological perspective, Gillian Feeley-Harnik argues that during the first century CE, "food, articulated in terms of who eats what with whom under which circumstances, had long been one of the most important languages in which Jews conceived and conducted social relations among human beings and between human beings and God."[213] Their concern was not only the legal stipulations regarding purity and food, but rather more fundamentally their distinctiveness as the people of God and, as a consequence, the holiness of God himself.[214] Commenting on the confrontation in Antioch that Paul records,[215] Sanders concludes that the issue was a concern over too much association with Gentiles—there was "a worry about the results of fraternization."[216] If so, we would expect the response to association with Gentiles in Jerusalem to be even stronger, as we hear expressed by Peter: "You yourselves know how unlawful it is for a Jew to associate with or to visit any one of another nation."[217] I suggest this is what was behind the persecution of the Hellenists.

Apoll. 5.33.4: "The Jews cut themselves off long ago, not only from the Romans, but from all mankind, since people who have devised an unsociable way of life, with no meals, libations, prayers, or sacrifices in common with other men, have moved further away from us than Ausa, Bactria, and the Indians beyond that" (Jones, LCL); *Let. Aris.* 139–42: "[Moses] . . . surrounded us with unbroken palisades and iron walls to prevent our mixing with any of the other peoples in any matter, being thus kept pure in body and soul, preserved from false beliefs, and worshipping the only God omnipotent over all creation" (Shutt, *OTP*); Philo, *Mos.* 1.278: "in virtue of the distinction of their peculiar customs they do not mix with others to depart from the ways of their fathers" (Colson, LCL); Josephus, *Ag. Ap.* 2.209: "[Moses] took the best of all possible measures . . . to secure our own customs from corruption" (Thackeray, LCL).

213. Feeley-Harnik, *Lord's Table*, 72. For a more general discussion of food as a language or code that relates to social relationships, see Douglas, "Deciphering a Meal," 249–75.

214. That offense could be caused without breaking the law is evident in the case of Jesus. That he was not arrested until the very end suggests that he did not break the law (at least not obviously), and yet he deeply offended some Jews.

215. Gal 2:11–14.

216. Sanders, "Jewish Association," 186.

217. Acts 10:28.

Assessment

We noted above that it was intrinsically likely that the opposition to Christians in Jerusalem was both diverse and a mixture of genuine and spurious complaint, and our analysis has borne that out. It is quite possible that opposition was motivated by Christian claims that Jesus, a man who had been crucified, was the Messiah; by their devotion to Jesus; and perhaps by the fact that the Christians themselves were not from the higher classes of society. But we found that these reasons failed to explain why the Hellenist community in particular was the target of the more severe persecution such that they had to flee Jerusalem permanently. Regarding the charge brought against Stephen, that he spoke against the law, we found no supporting evidence for this either in Stephen's speech or in the ministry of Jesus. However, we must admit (i) that in Jewish minds, particularly Jews living in Jerusalem, Torah encompassed so much of life that it would not be surprising if a complaint between Jews—in this case, non-Christian Jews and Christian Jews—referred to Torah in some way; and (ii) some Jews who were familiar with Jesus' ministry—for example, his fellowship with disreputable people or his activity on the Sabbath—may have developed the impression that he was disregarding Torah, even if this was not Jesus' intention. In this case the charge would be spurious, but understandable. Regarding the charge that Stephen spoke against the temple, we found that there probably were grounds for this, although it was difficult to be certain about what the precise point of contention with the Hellenists was. If we assume that Stephen's speech accurately reflects the views of the Hellenists, then it does appear that the Hellenists in some way criticized the temple. Since Stephen criticizes his accusers of failing to keep the law, it is plausible that his criticism of the temple was a reflection of Jesus' criticism concerning the temple establishment, probably with some form of corruption or abuse in view. However, it is not clear why the Hellenists in particular, more so than the Hebrews, would have been transmitters of Jesus' criticism of the temple.

The proposal that the Hellenists were welcoming Gentiles into their fellowship, although lacking any direct evidence, does have a number of factors in its favor: (i) there is an intrinsic plausibility that the Hellenist community, rather than the Hebrews, would have associated with Gentiles; (ii) such association would explain why the

Hellenists faced a more severe persecution than the Hebrews; and (iii) it is plausible that a welcoming of Gentiles could have been modeled after Jesus' welcome of tax collectors and sinners. The suggestion that the point of contention with other Jews was one of table fellowship seems more likely than Simmons's proposal that Hellenists, at this early date, had already waived the requirement of circumcision for Gentile converts. And finally, Wedderburn's proposal, that the Hellenists had actually been suggesting that these Gentile believers should be permitted access to the temple, links the proposal that the Hellenists associated with Gentiles with the charge that they spoke against the temple, but without further evidence it must remain as only a possibility.

Paul's Conversion and the Role of the "Hellenists"

The second substantial issue requiring more investigation than what Simmons gives is that of Paul's conversion.[218] In particular, we need

218. In speaking of Paul's conversion I am thinking not only of how he changed on the Damascus road, but rather of the change in direction his life took as a result of the Damascus road experience—a change that may have taken some time to flesh out.

There is debate over whether to speak of Paul's Damascus road experience as a "conversion" or a "call." The issue was first raised by Stendahl, "Paul among Jews," 1–77, who argued that Paul speaks of his encounter en route to Damascus more like a commission to service than like a change of religions. While it is true that the word conversion sometimes carries connotations that are inappropriate in Paul's case (e.g., Paul did not begin to worship a new God, nor did he change his Scriptures; he apparently was neither dissatisfied nor frustrated as a Pharisee (Phil 3:6); he does not use the standard conversion terminology—ἐπιστρέφω/ἐπιστροφή, μετανοέω/μετάνοια—with reference to himself), it is certainly true that he underwent a profound change in his life. Gaventa, *Darkness to Light*, 9–12, proposes a new set of categories: (i) "conversion" involves a complete rejection of one's past and a radical change in one's perspective (e.g., when a person changes allegiance from, say, a right wing political party to a left wing one); (ii) "alternation" [sic] is where the past is not rejected, but where new commitments grow out of the past (e.g., when a woman becomes a mother); and (iii) "transformation" refers to a change in which the past is not rejected but rather re-interpreted in light of a radically new perspective (e.g., when Copernicus suggests that the sun, rather than the earth, should be considered the center of the solar system). I would argue, however, that each of these categories, in different ways, would be appropriate for Paul. Consequently, I will continue to use the word conversion with reference to Paul, but with the realization that this involved a new call to service, and with a broad understanding of how Paul changed. Below (pp. 118–35) I shall argue that it is important to distinguish between Paul's Damascus road experience—regardless of whether it is described as a conversion or a calling—and his understanding of the *significance* of that experience, particularly in light of how his understanding may have developed in the ensuing years.

to see whether it is reasonable to believe that Paul was shaped by the Hellenists' practice of welcoming Gentiles, which in turn was inspired by the example of Jesus welcoming tax collectors and sinners. It is clear that the church Paul joined in Antioch accepted Gentiles into fellowship; if such acceptance by members of the Hellenist wing of the church originated in Jerusalem (as I have argued above), then it is possible that this was at the root of Paul's pre-Christian persecution of the church and was an important issue in his own conversion. Of key importance here will be the question of the ways in which Paul's change in perspectives and commitments was due to divine revelation versus integration within a Christian community.

Paul the Zealot

In order to understand Paul's conversion, we need first to understand why he persecuted Christians.[219] Luke connects his campaign against Christians with the persecution of the Hellenists in Jerusalem,[220] and while there is some debate over whether Paul was actively involved in Jerusalem,[221] the fact that it was the Hellenists that Paul would have encountered elsewhere suggests that it is likely that he took offense for the same reasons that Jews in Jerusalem did.

On two occasions when Paul refers to his persecution of the church, he describes his action as an expression of zeal—zeal "for the traditions of my fathers."[222] By so doing Paul places himself within a

219. Dibelius, *Paul*, 50–51.

220. Acts 7:58; 8:1, 3; 9:1; 26:10–11.

221. Luke places him in Jerusalem (Acts 7:58; 8:1), and we might expect a Pharisee to be involved in the affairs of Judea; however, Paul himself notes that three years after his conversion he was "still not known by sight to the churches of Christ in Judea" (Gal 1:22). Haenchen, *Acts*, 297–98, thinks that Paul's persecuting activity was limited to the area around Damascus; Hultgren, "Persecutions," 105–7, argues that Paul means only that these Christians in Judea had not seen him since his conversion, but this does not seem to be the most natural way of understanding ἀγνοούμενος τῷ προσώπῳ; Dunn, *Galatians*, 81, suggests that the problem can be solved if we assume that Paul's involvement in the Jerusalem persecution was limited to the Hellenists, and that the Hellenists fled to Greek-speaking areas outside of Judea (implying that some of the Hebrews were scattered throughout Judea and Samaria (Acts 8:1)); Bruce, *Galatians*, 104, thinks it is possible that Paul played a supervisory role in the Jerusalem persecution so that the Christians would not have known him personally, but it seems questionable that a person in such a role would have been called a νεανίας (Acts 7:58).

222. Gal 1:14; Phil 3:6; cf. Acts 22:3–4; 1 Tim 1:12–13.

tradition in Second Temple Judaism in which some Jews were ready to use whatever means was necessary to oppose those, Gentile or Jew, who by breaking the law were compromising the purity of the community of Israel.[223] The exemplars of this tradition were: (i) Phinehas, who slew with his spear a fellow Israelite, Zimri, and the Midianite woman whom he had brought into his tent, and by so doing made atonement for Israel;[224] (ii) Simeon and Levi, who avenged their sister's honor by slaughtering the Shechemites;[225] (iii) Elijah, presumably for his defeat of the prophets of Baal on Mount Carmel and his slaying of 450 of them in the aftermath;[226] and (iv) Jehu, who slaughtered the Baal worshippers and destroyed their place of worship.[227]

The more recent and most vivid expression of such zeal stems from the Maccabean revolt, which began when Mattathias killed first the Jew in the village of Modein who came forward to offer pagan sacrifice on the altar, and second the Syrian officer who was compelling Jews to do so. The writer of 1 Maccabees describes him as having "burned with zeal for the law, as Phinehas did against Zimri," and then rallying people for revolt: "Let every one who is zealous for the law and supports the covenant come out with me!"[228] In surveying the many

---

223. See Hengel, *Zealots*, 146–228; Rhoads, "Zealots," 1043–54; Donaldson, "Zealot and Convert," 672–74; Dunn, "Paul and Justification," 88–90; Farmer, *Maccabees*, 60–69; but on the use of the term "Zealot" to designate a party that did not appear prior to 66 CE, see Borg, "Currency of the Term 'Zealot,'" 504–12.

224. Num 25:6–13; Ps 106:30–31; Sir 45:23–24; 1 Macc 2:26, 51, 54; 4 Macc 18:12; *L.A.B.* 47.1.

225. Gen 34:25–29; Jdt 9:2–4; *Jub.* 30.17–19; *T. Levi* 6.3.

226. 1 Kgs 18:36–40; 19:10–18; Sir 48:1–3; 1 Macc 2:58.

227. 2 Kgs 10:16–27; *2 Bar.* 66.5.

228. 1 Macc 2:26–27; cf. 2:50; 2 Macc 4:2; 4 Macc 18:12; Josephus, *Ant.* 12.271. See also *T. Ash.* 4.1–5 where those who "live by zeal for the Lord" are called "righteous" because they "destroy the wicked"—that is, they destroy those who are "two-faced," who uphold the law in some ways, but break it in others (Kee, *OTP*).

Dunn also notes that this expression of zeal towards God was essentially the mirror of God's zeal towards Israel, as expressed, for example, in the reason for the commandment prohibiting idolatry: "for I the LORD your God am a jealous [LXX: ζηλωτής] God" (Exod 20:5; cf. Exod 34:14; Deut 4:24; 5:9; 6:15; Josh 24:19; Ezek 39:25; Joel 2:18; Nah 1:2; Zech 1:14; 8:2). Dunn, "Justification by Faith," 88, writes: "God's 'zeal' was expressed in his choice of Israel to be his own, and the conclusion drawn was that Israel should maintain the exclusiveness of its devotion to Yahweh and the distinctiveness of its religion in the face of other nations and religions round about."

acts of zeal mentioned in Second Temple literature, David Rhoads writes:

> Those zealous for the Law would not only personally endure imprisonment, beatings, and death rather than transgress the Law . . . , such zealots might also maim, kill, or destroy the property of others who disobeyed the Law. They would "root out" transgressors in order to turn back God's wrath because transgressors defiled Israel (*Jub.* 41:25). The literature identifies numerous offenses against which people might take zealous action.[229]

The issues of law that particularly rose to the surface during the Maccabean revolt related to proper worship, the keeping of Sabbath and other festivals, circumcision, and food.[230] These were the kinds of issues over which zealous Jews fought to defend their people's identity, often in the face of severe opposition.[231]

In one of the contexts where Paul describes his former life in terms of zeal, he speaks of having "advanced in Judaism" beyond many of his fellow Jews.[232] Commenting on this, Dunn makes the point that here Paul is not simply referring to his previous religion, but to the cause for which he previously fought. Based on the few occurrences of the word "Judaism" prior to Paul,[233] Dunn concludes that this word "denotes the national religion of the people of Judea, under attack from their Syrian overlords, and becomes a rallying point for the resistance to the Syrians and for maintenance of national identity as the covenant people of the Lord."[234] Moreover, Dunn notes that depending on what aspects of Jewish expression the Syrians were trying to suppress or to force Jews to compromise on, the resistance tended to focus on those aspects and to turn them into issues of Jewish identity.[235] Thus, "'Judaism' defined itself by its separation from the wider world

---

229. Rhoads, "Zealots," 6:1044. See also the discussion of Jewish sensitivities above, pp. 74–76.

230. 1 Macc 1:15, 39, 41–50, 60–63; 2:23–26, 45–48; 2 Macc 1:19–22; 6:1–11, 18–31; Josephus, *Ant.* 12.255–56.

231. In addition to the Maccabean texts above, see *T. Mos.* 8.1.

232. Gal 1:13.

233. 2 Macc 2:21; 8:1; 14:38; 4 Macc 4:26.

234. Dunn, "Paul's Conversion," 86.

235. Ibid., 86–87.

and understood the function of the Torah, in part at least, as reinforcing and protecting that separateness."[236]

Paul's persecution of the Christians, therefore, stemmed from a zeal for God, expressed in terms of zeal for the law, and followed the examples of scriptural and Maccabean heroes who used whatever means were necessary, against offending Jew or Gentile, in order to ensure the distinctiveness of Israel. Given this background, anything that was thought to threaten the distinctiveness of Israel would likely have caused offense and could have been grounds for persecution. The hypothesis developed above that the Hellenists were known for having table fellowship with Gentiles is consistent with this understanding of Paul's zealous persecution of the church. And if the Hellenists' welcome of Gentiles began in Jerusalem, then perhaps they were doing this—or, at least, were thought to be doing this—in Damascus as well, giving Paul every justification for trying to abolish their fellowship there.[237] This calls for a closer look at the Hellenists in Syria.

The Hellenists in Syria

According to Luke, the Hellenists who fled from Jerusalem went as far as Phoenicia, Cyprus, and Antioch. All of them shared their gospel with other Jews, but those who went to Antioch engaged in a mission that included Gentiles.[238] It seems reasonable to suppose that many of the Gentiles in view here were those who had already shown their interest in the Jewish religion by attaching themselves to a synagogue. According to Josephus, there was a large number of Jews in Antioch who "were constantly attracting to their religious ceremonies multitudes of Greeks, and these they had in some measure incorporated with themselves."[239] The phrase "in some measure" probably suggests that there was a range of levels of commitment represented by these interested Gentiles, some being circumcised proselytes, others uncircumcised but sympathetic adherents—Luke's so-called "God-fearers."[240]

---

236. Ibid., 87.

237. For a survey of proposals that seek to explain Paul's persecution of Christians, see Donaldson, "Zealot and Convert," 674–80.

238. See above, p. 70 n. 43.

239. Josephus, *J.W.* 7.45 (Thackeray, LCL).

240. On God-fearers in the synagogues, see Segal, *Paul the Convert*, 93–96;

Prior to this, Luke tells of Paul going to Damascus to arrest Christians there (presumably their leaders).[241] Apparently, some of those who fled Jerusalem had settled there, which is not surprising since Damascus was a major city en route to Antioch. Furthermore, Josephus also mentions that there were many Jews in Damascus, and it is reasonable to suppose that they enjoyed similar relations with Gentiles as did the Jews in Antioch.[242] Luke's general statement that those who fled from Jerusalem sought to convert others,[243] and the appearance of a Jewish resident of Damascus who had joined the Christian movement—Ananias[244]—suggest that those who led the persecution in Jerusalem might have had good reason to fear trouble in other cities like Damascus. Not only was Damascus within the boundaries of the idealized land of Israel,[245] suggesting that some Jews may have seen it not simply as a foreign city but as one in which certain standards must be maintained where possible; but if it was thought that the Christian

---

Crossan and Reed, *In Search of Paul*, 23–26, 35–38; Barrett, *Acts*, 1:499–501; Dunn, "Incident at Antioch," 144–48.

241. Acts 9:1–2. Luke records the account of Paul's conversion three times (Acts 9:1–9; 22:4–11; 26:9–18), and although there are differences among Luke's accounts and indications that they may be crafted to suit Luke's theological purposes, there are good reasons to accept a historical core here: both Luke and Paul describe the latter's experience in visionary terms (Luke in terms of Paul seeing a great light and hearing Jesus' voice (Acts 9:3–6; 22:6–10; 26:13–18), and Paul in terms of having seen the risen Lord (1 Cor 9:1; 15:8) and of God revealing his Son to him (Gal 1:16)); as a result he experienced a radical change from being a zealous persecutor of the church to being an apostle to the Gentiles (Gal 1:13–16; 1 Cor 15:9–10); and the location of Damascus seems to be confirmed by Paul saying that he "returned to Damascus" after immediately going to Arabia (Gal 1:17), and by his account of escaping from Damascus through a window in the city wall (2 Cor 11:32–33)—assuming that Luke has collapsed his account and has simply ignored Paul's trip to Arabia (Acts 9:23–25; in fact Luke's explanation that Paul was being persued by Jews rather than, as Paul says, by the governor under King Aretas, may indicate a limitation of his knowledge of the events immediately following Paul's conversion).

242. Josephus, *J. W.* 2.559–561; 7.368.

243. Acts 8:4; 11:19.

244. That Ananias was a Christian is clear from his initial resistance to meeting Paul (Acts 9:13–14) and from his words to Paul (9:17); that he was a Jew is clear from his name (the same as the name of the high priest (23:2; 24:1) and of one of Daniel's three friends (Dan 1:6 (LXX)) and from Luke's description of him as "a devout man according to the law" (22:12); and that he was a resident of Damascus seems to be implied by Luke's comment that he was "well spoken of by all the Jews who lived there" (22:12).

245. See above, pp. 76.

movement was gaining Gentile converts, particularly those associated with the synagogue—which Jerusalem Jews would have reason to do if the issue concerning the Hellenists had been their association with Gentiles—some Jews may have been concerned about the future of the synagogue. Crossan and Reed note that the attachment of Gentiles to synagogues outside of Palestine brought the benefit of both economic assistance and political protection to the Jewish community, and they argue that the conversion of such people under Paul the apostle's ministry was a primary reason for Jewish opposition against him.[246] It is plausible, therefore, that this was an additional reason for Paul's journey to Damascus.

Simmons suggests that the Hellenists waived the requirement of circumcision for Gentile converts, and that this explains not only the persecution against them but also the success of the Gentile mission in Antioch.[247] I admit that such a policy would have been attractive to God-fearers who were attracted to the monotheism and moral standards of Judaism but who were repulsed by the idea of circumcision.[248] But such a hypothesis is not required to explain the success of the Gentile mission. While some may question whether Luke has not downplayed some of the struggles and exaggerated the successes of the early Christian movement, it is clear that the movement grew among both Jews and Gentiles, and that it was characterized by genuine signs of new life. Luke portrays the Christian movement as a movement

246. Crossan and Reed, *In Search of Paul*, 36–40. In addition, Hengel, "Stance of the Apostle Paul," 82, writes: "in the synagogues of the Syrian cities, not only did the sympathizers from the Greek-speaking upper class strengthen the social and political standing of the synagogue community, one could see in them the harbinger of the coming messianic kingdom, since Syria as far as the Euphrates and Taurus was regarded as a portion of it: it had once already belonged to the Great Empire of David."

247. Acts 11:21.

248. On pagan dislike of the practice of circumcision, see esp. Josephus, *Ag. Ap.* 2.137: "He denounces us for sacrificing domestic animals and for not eating pork, and he derides the practice of circumcision" (LCL, Thackeray); Philo, *Spec.* 1.2: "Now the practice which is thus ridiculed, namely the circumcision of the genital organs . . ." (LCL, Colson); Strabo, *Geogr.* 16.4.9: "And then . . . to the Creophagi, of whom the males have their sexual glands mutilated and the women are excised in the Jewish fashion" (LCL, Jones); Tacitus, *Hist.* 5.5.1–2: "the other customs of the Jews are base and abominable, and owe their persistence to their depravity. . . . They sit apart at meals, and they sleep apart. . . . They adopted circumcision to distinguish themselves from other peoples" (LCL, Jackson). Hence the practice of some Jews to remove the marks of their circumcision (1 Macc 1:43–49).

of the Holy Spirit: believers were filled with the Spirit,[249] they spoke with boldness by means of the Spirit,[250] they had a sense of being guided by the Spirit,[251] and they understood this as a fulfillment of prophecy;[252] furthermore, people were being healed,[253] impostors were being exposed,[254] and threats to the movement were being overcome;[255] in a word, these were exciting times.[256] Paul concurs with Luke by describing the role of the Spirit as being fundamental to the Christian movement:[257] he speaks of the experience of the Spirit at people's conversion,[258] and the work of the Spirit in Christians generally,[259] expressing to them God's love,[260] and confirming their intimate connection with God.[261] With an ethos of heightened excitement over the sense that God was truly at work in a new way in this community, it is not difficult to see why others would be attracted to it, especially those who already shared Jewish values, whether Jew or Gentile.

Within such a community, how might the Hellenists have thought about issues such as circumcision, food laws, and the like with regard to Gentile converts?[262] It is difficult to say with certainty, but one suspects

249. Acts 2:4, 38; 8:17; 9:17; 10:44–47; 11:15; 13:9; 15:8; 19:6.

250. Acts 2:4; 4:8, 31; 6:10.

251. Acts 8:29; 10:19; 11:12, 28; 13:2, 4; 16:6–7; 20:22–23; 21:11.

252. Acts 1:5, 8; 2:17–18.

253. Acts 3:1–10; 5:15–16; 8:6–7; 9:18, 33–34, 36–41; 14:8–11; 19:11–12; 20:9–12; 28:3–6, 8–9.

254. Acts 5:1–11; 8:18–24.

255. Acts 5:19–24; 12:6–11; 13:8–11; 16:25–34; 27:21–26, 44.

256. Note the various references to joy in Acts: 5:41; 8:8, 39; 13:52; 15:3, 31; 16:34.

257. See Fee, "Paul's Conversion," 166–83.

258. Gal 3:1–5. It is not obvious what evidence of the Spirit Paul had in mind in this context, but it may have included the miracles referred to in verse 5 (cf. 1 Cor 12:4–11; 14:26–33a; 2 Cor 12:12).

259. Gal 3:14; Rom 5:1–5; 8:15–16.

260. Rom 5:5.

261. Rom 8:16.

262. The two issues of circumcision and food in particular seem to have been closely related both in Galatians, where Peter broke fellowship with Gentiles for fear of the circumcision party (Gal 2:11–14), and in Acts, where Luke combines these issues in his account of Peter and Cornelius (Acts 11:1–18). Dunn, "Works of the Law," 217, makes the observation that from the Gentile perspective, circumcision and food laws were "two of the clearest distinguishing marks of the Jewish race." For ancient texts referring to Jews as circumcised, see Josephus, *Ant.* 13.319; *Ag. Ap.* 2.137; Strabo, *Geogr.* 16.2.37; 16.4.9; 17.2.5; Horace, *Sat.* 1.9.69–70; Persius, *Sat.* 5.184; Petronius,

that as the movement grew there would have been a range of opinion. Presumably some would have thought of the Gentiles in their presence as analogous to the Gentiles in the synagogue—those who had been circumcised were full converts (proselytes), others were converts in process (God-fearers). Other Hellenists, however, no doubt impressed by the evidence that uncircumcised Gentile believers were experiencing the same spiritual blessings as other believers, would have begun to question—along the lines of Peter in connection with Cornelius, and along the lines of Paul and Barnabas in connection with their Gentile mission—as many did at the Jerusalem Council, whether circumcision in particular should be required for such Christians.[263] Perhaps some emphasized more the importance of the circumcision of the heart that we hear of in Stephen's speech[264] and in other Jewish circles,[265] drawing on an important Old Testament image,[266] and perhaps following the spiritualizing tendency of some Jews that Philo complains about.[267]

Satyr. 102.14; *Frag.* 37; Martial, *Epigram.* 7.30, 35; Tacitus, *Hist.* 5.5.1–2; Juvenal, *Sat.* 14.104; Suetonius, *Dom.* 12.2. For references to the distinctiveness of Jewish dietary laws (esp. their refusal to eat pork), see Diodorus, *Bib. hist.* 34–35; Josephus, *Ag. Ap.* 2.137; Erotianus *Voc. Hip.*; Arrian, *Epict. diss.* 1.22.4; Plutarch, *Quaest. conv.* 4.5.1–3 [669E–671C]; Tacitus, *Hist.* 4.1–3; Juvenal, *Sat.* 6.156–60; Sextus Empiricus, *Pyr.* 3.223.

263. Acts 15:1–29. Also in Paul's account of the Council (Gal 2:1–10) we find the exercise of discernment based on the testimony of another (vv. 7, 9). Paul does not say what it was that convinced the leaders that his gospel was genuine, but it is quite possible that it was, as in Acts, the recognition that it brought about genuine conversion among Gentiles.

264. Acts 7:51.

265. Philo, *Migr.* 89–93; *Spec.* 1.305; 1QpHab XI,13 (cf. 1QS V,5–6).

266. Lev 26:41; Deut 10:16; 30:6; Jer 4:4; 6:10; 9:25–26; Ezek 44:7, 9.

267. Philo, *Migr.* 89–93: "There are some who, regarding laws in their literal sense in the light of symbols of matters belonging to the intellect, are overpunctilious about the latter, while treating the former with easy-going neglect." Specifically he has in mind those who, because they understand the "inner meaning" of Sabbath, festivals, and circumcision, have thought this to be sufficient reason to forgo their literal observance. His argument against this is: "we should look on all these outward observances as resembling the body, and their inner meanings as resembling the soul. It follows that, exactly as we have to take thought for the body, because it is the abode of the soul, so we must pay heed to the letter of the laws" (Colson & Whitaker, LCL). Räisänen, "Paul's Conversion," 14–15, suggests other ways in which the Hellenists may have spiritualized the law, which are reflected in Paul's writings, including the teaching that: (i) keeping the commandments is more important than circumcision or uncircumcision (1 Cor 7:19); (ii) the law is summed up in the command to love (Gal 5:14; Rom 13:8ff); (iii) Christians are God's temple (1 Cor 3:16; 6:19; 2 Cor 6:16);

Paul too picks up this theme, but he clearly sets it against the need for physical circumcision.[268]

Presumably a similar range of opinion existed with regard to the application of other Jewish distinguishing marks such as food laws. At some point Christians interpreted Jesus' saying in Mark 7:15 to mean that "he declared all foods clean."[269] In light of Paul's echo of Jesus' saying—"nothing is unclean in itself"[270]—and the similar application he draws with regard to eating food,[271] it is tempting to think that he learned this line of interpretation from the church that he eventually joined.[272] But as long as the Gentile converts were few in comparison to the Jewish Christians, the question probably did not have to come to a head.[273]

My proposal then is that the church that Paul joined in Antioch welcomed Gentiles, following the example of Jesus welcoming tax collectors and sinners. It is not necessary to posit that the church had come to a particular position concerning Gentile observance of laws dealing with circumcision and food. In the midst of the general excitement of the early Christian movement, it is reasonable to think that the church represented a range of opinions on these matters. It would have been Paul, then, who took the next step to say that uncircumcised Gentile believers were full members of the community as they were, and to articulate the theological rationale for such a view.[274] This hypothesis helps to explain why it was Paul, rather than the Hellenists, who came to be known as the arch-enemy of Jewish Christianity.[275]

(iv) Christians should be a living sacrifice (Rom 12:1); and (v) Gentiles do by nature what God requires (Rom 2:15).

268. Rom 2:29; Phil 3:3.

269. Mark 7:19. On how early Christians may have arrived at such a conclusion, see below, p. 262 n. 121.

270. Rom 14:14.

271. Rom 14:15–21.

272. See Thompson, *Clothed with Christ*, chap. 12; Wenham, *Paul*, 93–94; Furnish, *Jesus according to Paul*, 55–58; Dunn, "Jesus Tradition in Paul," 162–63; opposed is Räisänen, "The Hellenists," 163–64.

273. Dunn, "New Perspective: Whence, What and Whither?" 38; idem., *Partings of the Ways*, 124–27.

274. Best, "Revelation to Evangelize," 30, tentatively suggests a similar view.

275. Dunn, "Light to the Gentiles," 92.

The Development of Paul's Understanding of the Gospel for the Gentiles

With this historical setting in view, what can we say about Paul's conversion and the development of his understanding of his mission to the Gentiles? Here I will argue that while Paul certainly understood his Damascus road experience in terms of God's call for him to be apostle to the Gentiles, it was only as he was involved in a mission to the Gentiles at the church in Antioch that he developed his own distinctive understanding of the gospel with regard to Gentiles. If this is true, then it seems quite plausible that Paul's gospel could have been shaped by the Hellenists who were in turn following the example of Jesus in welcoming sinners. We will begin by looking at the early years of Paul's Christian ministry and then at how Paul's thought is dependent on tradition and revelation.

Paul's Early Years as a Christian

Paul claims that the purpose behind the revelation he received on the Damascus road was, as he says, so "that I might preach [Christ] among the Gentiles."[276] It is important to remember, however, that he wrote these words perhaps twenty years after his Damascus road experience, and so we must take into account the benefit of hindsight for his appreciation of the significance of that event. It may very well be, as Wedderburn comments, that Paul's testimony here "may simply mean that this was God's ultimate purpose in revealing his Son to Paul, a purpose of which Paul only gradually became aware."[277]

Luke's account of Paul's early years appears to confirm this. If we assume that the visit to Jerusalem that Paul records in Gal 2 is the same as that in Acts 15, and that the fourteen years Paul mentions in Gal 2:1 includes the three years he mentions in Gal 1:18, then there are fourteen years between Acts 9 and Acts 15.[278] Within this time Luke tells

276. Gal 1:16; cf. Rom 16:25–26. Elsewhere Paul speaks of being an apostle to the Gentiles (Rom 1:5; 11:13; 15:15–16), and twice connects his apostleship with the fact that he had seen the risen Lord (1 Cor 9:1; 15:8–9). See also the "mystery-motif" in Paul, which has to do with salvation being offered to the Gentiles (Rom 11:25; 16:25–26; cf. Col 1:26–27; Eph 3:2–9).

277. Wedderburn, *History*, 85.

278. Making other assumptions could easily lengthen this time: If Gal 2 relates

us that Paul preached to Jews in the Damascus synagogues,[279] that he argued with Hellenists in Jerusalem,[280] that he went to Tarsus in Cilicia where he may have planted some churches,[281] that Barnabas brought him from Tarsus to Antioch where a Gentile mission was already underway and where Paul ministered as a prophet/teacher for a year,[282] that he accompanied Barnabas on a famine-relief mission to Judea,[283] and that Barnabas and Paul went on a mission to Cyprus, Pisidia, and southern Galatia during which a number of Gentiles became Christians.[284] If we generously assign a year for this latter mission,[285] then, taking into account the year Paul spent in Antioch, there were at least twelve years between Paul's Damascus road experience and the first time we hear of him having contact with a Gentile mission. This is somewhat surprising if indeed Paul had a clear understanding of his call to be apostle to the Gentiles, and of his gospel for the Gentiles, directly from his conversion experience. Given that Luke is quite interested in the Gentile mission, and given that Luke seems to know something about Paul's early years, it is curious that he makes no specific mention of him being involved in a Gentile mission for at least the first twelve years of his Christian life. For example, he knows that Paul went to Cilicia, but he makes no comment about him preaching to Gentiles there.[286] In addition, it is curious that we have no Pauline correspondence from this period. Paul's own explanation of the gospel

---

to an earlier visit to Jerusalem—as is suggested by those who defend the Southern Galatian hypothesis with regard to the book of Galatians—or if Paul's fourteen years are subsequent to his three years, then this time would be lengthened and my argument would be even stronger.

279. Acts 9:20–22. In addition to this, Paul adds that immediately after his conversion he went to Arabia for some time and returned to Damascus (Gal 1:17), which was presumably the occasion on which he was pursued by King Aretas of Nabatea (2 Cor 11:32).

280. Acts 9:29.

281. Acts 9:30; note the prior existence of churches in Cilicia mentioned in Acts 15:41.

282. Acts 11:20–26; 13:1.

283. Acts 11:27–30; 12:25.

284. Acts 13–14.

285. It is difficult to know how long this mission took, but Luke's account does not depict Barnabas and Paul staying in any one place very long.

286. Acts 9:30; 15:41.

as being "to the Jew first and also to the Greek,"[287] and his testimony that "[t]o the Jews I became as a Jew, in order to win Jews,"[288] would be consistent with him having engaged in a Jewish ministry prior to a Gentile one.[289]

Furthermore, Luke gives various explanations of how Paul came to understand the significance of his conversion vis-à-vis his commission to preach to the Gentiles. In Luke's own account of Paul's conversion, God tells Ananias that Paul will preach to the Gentiles, but Ananias does not mention this to Paul;[290] in Paul's defense before the people of Jerusalem, he notes that Ananias said to him, "you will be a witness for him to all men of what you have seen and heard";[291] and in Paul's defense before King Agrippa, he tells of how he received the commission to preach to the Gentiles directly from Jesus.[292] However, given that these latter two defenses come towards the end of Paul's ministry, we need again to consider the possibility that, with the advantage of hindsight, Paul or Luke is simplifying what was in fact a more complex historical process. As evidence of this greater complexity, we note the account Luke gives, in connection with Paul's first defense, of how he received the specific commission to preach to the Gentiles sometime after his conversion while he was in a trance in the Jerusalem temple.[293]

In fact, there is nothing in Paul's letters or in Acts that implies he began a mission to Gentiles as soon as he was converted. Thus, it is reasonable to think that Paul came to appreciate his commission as apostle to the Gentiles only after he came into contact with the church in Antioch, a church that had already begun a Gentile mission.

Revelation and Tradition in Paul

The issue regarding how Paul may have been shaped in his understanding of the gospel for the Gentiles can be addressed by exploring

---

287. Rom 1:16; cf. Rom 2:9–10.

288. 1 Cor 9:20. The use of the aorist, ἐγενόμην, throughout 9:20–22 suggests that Paul is speaking of previous ways of behaving rather than current ones.

289. See further, Watson, *Paul*, 28–31.

290. Acts 9:15–17.

291. Acts 22:15.

292. Acts 26:15–18.

293. Acts 22:17–21.

the relationship between revelation and tradition in his letters. The question of how to reconcile Paul's claim to revelation with the evidence that he received and used tradition has received a great deal of attention,[294] but rarely from a perspective that takes into account the historical context of the early church, vis-à-vis Gentile believers, and of his own conversion. Regarding Paul's revelation at his conversion, he speaks of having seen Jesus Christ[295] and of having received his

294. Numerous explanations have been offered which seek to avoid the conclusion, particularly with reference to Gal 1:11–12 and 1 Cor 15:3–8, that Paul is contradicting himself (as argued, for example, by Sanders, "'Autobiographical' Statements," 335–43). Now widely discounted is the view that tradition refers to the historical facts of the gospel, whereas revelation refers to their significance. Specifically, we note that the tradition "Christ died for our sins" (1 Cor 15:3) contains both fact and significance. Fridrichsen, "Apostle," 11, has suggested that Paul shared with the other apostles the same gospel "since the basic substance of his gospel was the very same *parádosis* concerning Christ's death and resurrection," but that his gospel also "contained an interpretation of Christ's death and resurrection which was essential to the Gentiles." Paul's insistence, however, on there being only one gospel (Gal 1:6–9), his mention that he and the other apostles preached the same message (1 Cor 15:11), and his criticism of Peter for acting inappropriately (Gal 2:12), all make it difficult to see Paul having a fundamentally different gospel for the Gentiles (see further, Fung, "Revelation and Tradition," 34–37; Chamblin, "Revelation and Tradition," 2–4). Cullmann, "Tradition," 63–75, has argued that since Paul refers to both Jesus of Nazareth and the heavenly Christ as κύριος, both tradition—which ultimately began with Jesus—and revelation can be said to have come from the Lord, and hence there is no conflict between them. But, even if Cullmann is correct, this does not explain what Paul was rejecting in Gal 1:11–12 (see further Fung, "Revelation and Tradition," 37–38). More promising is the attempt of some to distinguish between a revelatory core and traditional aspects of the gospel. Ladd, "Revelation and Tradition," 223–30, defines the core as the central claim "that Jesus was the resurrected and exalted Messiah" (230). Baird, "Kerygma," 181–91, distinguishes between "the form" and the "essential dynamic nature" of the gospel (90), the former which he knew by tradition, the latter by revelation (cf. Kim, *Origin*, 67–70). Similarly, Winger, "Tradition," 65–86, draws a distinction between the information contained in the message—that is, tradition—and the announcement of the gospel that comes with the power of God—that is, revelation (see Gal 3:1–5; 1 Cor 1:18; Rom 1:16; 1 Thess 2:13). He writes: "Whatever the language of preaching, that language is not itself the gospel, and handing on this language is not the same as delivering the gospel" (78). Thus the revelation that Paul speaks of in Gal 1:11–12 is similar to the experience of the Spirit among Galatian believers that he points to in Gal 3:1–5 (85–86).

295. Gal 1:12, 16; cf. 1 Cor 9:1; 15:8; Acts 9:17; 26:16. The genitive Ἰησοῦ Χριστοῦ at the end of Gal 1:12 could, by itself, be either objective or subjective, but in vv. 15–16 he implies that it was God who did the revealing, and that the content of the revelation was his Son (taking ἐν ἐμοί, along with the following ἐν τοῖς ἔθνεσιν, to be dative of indirect object)—so most commentators: see Martyn, *Galatians*, 144; Betz, *Galatians*, 63. Longenecker, *Galatians*, 23–24, argues for subjective genitive based on 1:1, but in light of 1:16 the objective genitive is to be preferred.

gospel;[296] but it is difficult to draw specific conclusions from these texts concerning the specific content of that revelation. I suggest we can, however, move forward by observing how Paul speaks of revelation and tradition, and then by examining his view of the law as a specific instance of how revelation and tradition shaped his understanding of the gospel for the Gentiles.

Revelation

Let us consider briefly Paul's claim to have received revelation. Both he and Luke describe his Damascus road experience in terms of an encounter with the resurrected Jesus.[297] In his letter to the Galatians, Paul insists that he received his gospel by revelation and that it was not handed on from other people.[298] He makes this statement presumably because his opponents, who were trying to convince Gentile believers that they needed to be circumcised, were saying, among other things, that he was subordinate to the authorities in Jerusalem, and that these authorities were saying that Gentile Christians must be circumcised. This is why Paul recounts his meeting with the apostles in Jerusalem when he explained his gospel and they affirmed him and agreed to cooperate by not interfering in his ministry, and why he mentions that the so-called "false brethren" were not able to compel Titus to be circumcised.[299] But prior to that he insists that he received the gospel directly by revelation and not by human tradition, with the implication being that the validity of his gospel is not subject to any human authority. He writes:

> For I would have you know, brethren, that the gospel which
> was preached by me is not man's gospel. For I did not receive it

296. Gal 1:11. See the discussion of the role of the Spirit above (pp. 114–15) regarding the personal nature of this revelation.

297. 1 Cor 9:1; 15:8; Gal 1:15–16; Acts 9:3–5; 22:6–8; 26:12–15. Presumably, when Paul claims to have seen "Jesus our Lord" (1 Cor 9:1) he is referring to his Damascus road experience (see Fee, 1 *Corinthians*, 395) and, he has in view, regardless of the nature of the revelation, the man who previously lived in Galilee—otherwise it would be difficult to explain the use of the name "Jesus."

298. Gal 1:11–12. Elsewhere Paul speaks of having received revelation: Rom 16:25; 1 Cor 2:10; 2 Cor 12:1, 7; Gal 2:2; cf. Eph 3:3, 5.

299. Gal 2:1–10.

> from man, nor was I taught it, but it came through a revelation
> of Jesus Christ. (Gal 1:11–12)

And furthermore, he goes on to insist that (i) it was at least three years
before he ever went up to Jerusalem, and even then it was only for fifteen days and he saw only Peter and James; and (ii) when the churches
in Judea heard of his ministry, they glorified God.[300] Therefore, the
opponents' argument is shown to be unfounded.

Tradition

Turning to the issue of Paul's dependence on tradition, scholars generally agree that in a number of places Paul reflects sayings or beliefs
that he has inherited from Christians before him. First, there are
two instances where Paul specifically states that he "received" and
"delivered"[301] material pertaining to Jesus, both of which contain an
interpretation of Jesus' death: (i) 1 Cor 11:23–26 speaks of his death
enacting a new covenant,[302] and (ii) 1 Cor 15:3–5 says that "Christ
died for our sins." Furthermore, in 1 Cor 11:2 Paul speaks of having
delivered "traditions" to his readers.[303]

Second, commentators are generally agreed that there are other
passages where, although Paul does not use the technical terminology
for transmitting tradition, the vocabulary and/or structure of his writing suggests he may be borrowing material from elsewhere. Some of
the more likely of these passages are: (i) Rom 1:3–4 where Paul notes
several things about Jesus: he is the subject of the gospel, he was a

---

300. Gal 1:15–24. Since Paul's argument depends so much on the veracity of his
historical account, and since several details of his account could have been easily
checked, we have reason to believe that Paul is being careful with his facts here—
hence, Paul's oath in 1:20.

301. The terms παραλαμβάνω and παραδίδωμι, which correspond in Hebrew
to קִבֵּל מִן and מָסַר לְ respectively, are technical terms relating to the receiving and
passing on of tradition. Note especially, *m. 'Abot* 1:1: "Moses *received* Torah at Sinai
and *handed it on* to Joshua, Joshua to elders, and elders to prophets. And prophets
handed it on to the men of the great assembly" (emphasis added); cf. *m. Pe'ah* 2:6. See
Conzelmann, *1 Corinthians*, 195–96; Barrett, *1 Corinthians*, 1:264.

302. The technical language of tradition in the context strongly suggests that "I
received from the Lord" (1 Cor 11:23) has in view the reception of tradition rather
than direct reception from the risen Lord. See Cullmann, "Tradition," 63–66; Barrett,
1 Corinthians, 265–66.

303. Cf. 2 Thess 2:15.

descendant of David, and his divine sonship was made clear by his resurrection;[304] (ii) Rom 3:25–26a, as we have seen above,[305] where Paul speaks of Jesus' death being an atoning sacrifice that brings redemption and by which God graciously reveals his righteousness to those who respond with faith; and (iii) Gal 3:26–28 where Paul cites what appears to have been a baptismal liturgy that emphasizes the equality of all followers of Jesus—Jew and Gentile, slave and free, male and female.[306]

Third, there are a number of phrases or concepts in Paul's letters that seem to reflect early Christian formulae—confessional statements or possibly liturgical responses.[307] In particular, on the basis of their frequency of occurrence and regularity of expression, Dunn draws attention to texts that speak of: (i) God raising Jesus from the dead;[308] (ii) Christ having died for us;[309] (iii) Christ having been handed over

304. For reasons for taking Rom 1:3–4 to contain pre-Pauline tradition, see Dunn, *Romans*, 1:5; Cranfield, *Romans*, 1:57–58.

305. See above, p. 97 n. 176.

306. In support of Gal 3:26–28 containing pre-Pauline tradition are: Betz, *Galatians*, 181–85; Martyn, *Galatians*, 378–80; Longenecker, *Galatians*, 151. Casting some doubt is Dunn, *Galatians*, 201, who thinks it unlikely that liturgies like this developed at an early stage. It is possible that both could be correct—that the material is non-Pauline, but does not go back to the earliest days of the Christian movement.

Some would also include 1 Thess 1:9–10 and Phil 2:6–11 as being pre-Pauline, the latter widely considered to be an early Christian hymn. It is not as clear in these cases, however, that the material was not authored by Paul.

307. Dunn, *Theology*, 174–75. For details see Kramer, *Christ*, 19–44; Neufeld, *Christian Confessions*, 42–68.

308. Rom 4:24–25: "[God who] raised from the dead Jesus our Lord, who was . . . raised for our justification"; 7:4: "to him who has been raised from the dead"; 8:11: "the Spirit of him who raised Jesus from the dead"; 10:9: "believe in your heart that God raised him from the dead"; 1 Cor 6:14: "God raised the Lord"; 15:4: "he was raised on the third day"; 15:12: "if Christ is preached as raised from the dead"; 15:20: "Christ has been raised from the dead"; 2 Cor 4:14: "he who raised the Lord Jesus"; Gal 1:1: "God the Father, who raised him from the dead"; 1 Thess 1:10: "whom he [God] raised from the dead." Cf. Col 2:12: "God, who raised him from the dead"; Eph 1:20: "when he raised him from the dead"; 2 Tim 2:8: "Jesus Christ, risen from the dead"; 1 Pet 1:21 "God, who raised him from the dead"; Acts 3:15: "whom God raised from the dead"; 4:10: "whom God raised from the dead"; 5:30: "God of our fathers raised Jesus"; 10:40: "God raised him on the third day"; 13:30: "God raised him from the dead"; 13:37: "he whom God raised up."

309. Rom 5:6: "Christ died for the ungodly"; 5:8: "Christ died for us"; 14:15: "one for whom Christ died"; 1 Cor 8:11: "the brother for whom Christ died"; 15:3: "Christ died for our sins"; 2 Cor 5:14–15: "one has died for all. . . . And he died for all . . . for him who for their sake died"; 1 Thess 5:10: "Christ, who died for us."

for us;[310] (iv) both the death and resurrection of Christ;[311] and (v) the lordship of Jesus Christ.[312] Dunn admits the possibility that these may simply be characteristic Pauline expressions, but he gives two reasons why they probably reflect pre-Pauline formulae: (a) the first churches would have needed such summary statements in their preaching, teaching, and worship; and (b) the regularity of the expressions and the appearance of some of them outside of Paul's writings suggests "a commonality of faith and of expression of that faith."[313]

Fourth, Paul's inclusion of a transliterated Aramaic prayer in 1 Cor 16:22—μαραναθα—best translated as "Our Lord, come," probably suggests that he inherited from the early church an eschatological perspective.[314] Similar prayers have been noted in Rev 22:20 and *Did.* 10.6. Some have argued for setting this prayer in a eucharistic context, making it an entreaty for the divine presence in worship.[315] But Thiselton, building on the works of Moule and Eriksson, has argued convincingly that the prayer should be understood eschatologically, particularly in light of (i) the adjoining curse placed on those who do not love the Lord, for which μαραναθα, understood eschatologi-

310. παραδίδωμι texts (note the verbs in italics): Rom 4:25: "who was *put to death* for our trespasses"; 8:32: "he who . . . *gave* him *up* for us all"; 1 Cor 11:23: "on the night that he *was betrayed*"; Gal 2:20 "who loved me and *gave* himself for me"; cf. Eph 5:2: "Christ loved us and *gave* himself *up* for us"; 5:25: "Christ loved the church and *gave* himself *up* for her." Note also δίδωμι texts: Gal 1:4: "who *gave* himself for our sins"; cf. 1 Tim 2:6: "who *gave* himself as a ransom for all"; Titus 2:14: "who *gave* himself for us."

311. Rom 4:25: who was put to death for our trespasses and raised for our justification"; 8:34: "Is it Christ Jesus, who died, yes, who was raised from the dead"; 14:9: "Christ died and lived again"; 1 Cor 15:3–4: "Christ died for our sins. . . , that he was raised on the third day"; 2 Cor 5:15: "live . . . for him who for their sake died and was raised"; 13:4: "he was crucified in weakness, but lives by the power of God"; 1 Thess 4:14: "Jesus died and rose again."

312. Rom 10:9: "Jesus is Lord"; 1 Cor 8:6: "for us there is . . . one Lord, Jesus Christ"; 12:3: "Jesus is Lord"; 2 Cor 4:5: "we preach . . . Jesus Christ as Lord"; Phil 2:11: "Jesus Christ is Lord." Cf. Col 2:6: "you received Christ Jesus the Lord"; Eph 4:5: "There is . . . one Lord"; Acts 2:36: "God made him both Lord and Christ, this Jesus"; 10:36: "Jesus Christ (he is Lord of all)"; John 20:28: "My Lord and my God."

313. Dunn, *Theology*, 175–76, citation from p. 176.

314. There is a slight difference in the textual tradition: some MSS (B², D²) read μαρὰν ἀθά, meaning "Our Lord has come," but better supported (p⁴⁶, ℵ, A, B*, C, D*) is μαράνα θά, which translates as "Our Lord, come."

315. Lietzmann, *Mass and Lord's Supper*, 186; Cullmann, *Early Christian Worship*, 13–14; Robinson, "Liturgical Sequence," 38–41; Conzelmann, *1 Corinthians*, 300–301.

cally, would naturally serve as a sanction, and (ii) the command to "Be watchful" in v. 13 which recalls the theme of eschatology in the letter.[316]

And fifth, there are various pieces of Jesus tradition that Paul would have received from the Hellenists and from the apostles, concerning which there is of course great debate.[317]

All of this suggests that Paul inherited a variety of concepts from other Christians that included at least the following affirmations: (i) Jesus' death was an atoning sacrifice for us and was instrumental in establishing a new covenant; (ii) God raised Jesus from the dead; (iii) the gospel is about Jesus who is Son of God and Lord; (iv) Jesus is coming; and (v) there is equality among Christians.

It may be objected that while we may be able to argue that all of the items mentioned above are *non*-Pauline in origin, we cannot with equal certainly claim that they are all *pre*-Pauline, that is, pre-dating Paul's conversion. This may be the case, for example, for Rom 1:3–4 and Gal 3:26–28—texts created by someone other than Paul, but created after his conversion. But even still, Paul's use of such material does still demonstrate his dependence on Christian tradition, and this is significant. It shows that not all of the content of his gospel came via revelation without connection to the practice and convictions of other Christians.

PAUL'S VIEW OF THE LAW AS AN EXAMPLE OF REVELATION AND TRADITION

As an example of the roles of revelation and tradition in Paul's thought, we will consider his view of the law—a subject on which Paul gives us a significant amount of information. As a Christian, Paul made some fundamental changes in his thinking, and none was more radical than his view of the law. It would be instructive to know to what extent this new perspective was due to revelation and to what extent it was due to the tradition of the early church.

We begin by noting that Paul says some very critical things about the law.[318] Numerous times he makes the point that justification can

---

316. Thiselton, *1 Corinthians*, 1348–50; cf. Moule, "Context of Maranatha," 307–10; Eriksson, "Maranatha," 279–98; Fee, *1 Corinthians*, 838.

317. See above, pp. 6–10.

318. See esp. Räisänen, *Paul and the Law*, 199–202.

be attained only by faith and not by means of the law,[319] and so he sets faith in contrast to the law;[320] in fact he states that the law served both to define sin[321] and to increase it,[322] and rather than bringing life[323] it was co-opted by the power of sin to bring death;[324] but Christians have died to the law[325] and are no longer under it but are under grace,[326] for "Christ is the end of the law."[327] And then in one place he speaks of the law as bifurcated: there is the law of God, in which he rejoices, and the law of sin, from which Christians have been set free.[328] On two specific issues, Paul argues against Gentile believers obeying the law of circumcision,[329] and he subordinates the importance of food laws to the greater concern for love.[330] Clearly, Paul would not have said these things prior to becoming a Christian. Indeed, these statements would be shocking and offensive to most Jews who looked to the law with delight[331] as evidence of God's grace and as a path to life.[332] So, did this constitute a rejection of the law for Paul?

319. Gal 2:21; 5:4; or more commonly, by means of the "works of the law": Rom 3:28; Gal 2:16, 21; 3:10–11; although see Rom 2:13.

320. See also Rom 4:13; 10:4; Gal 3:12, 23–24.

321. Rom 3:20; 5:13; 7:7.

322. Rom 5:20; 7:5, 8–9.

323. Rom 8:3; Gal 3:21.

324. Rom 7:8–9; Cor 15:56.

325. Rom 7:4, 6; Gal 2:19.

326. Rom 6:14; Gal 5:18; cf. 1 Cor 9:21.

327. Rom 10:4. τέλος here has been understood variously as fulfilment, goal or termination, and sometimes as combinations of these. For a discussion see Cranfield, *Romans*, 2:516–20, who decides in favor of goal, and Dunn, *Romans*, 1:596–98, who opts for termination.

328. Rom 7:23, 25; 8:2. On νόμος throughout Rom 7:21–8:8 referring consistently to Torah, see Dunn, *Romans*, 1:392; Wright, *Climax of the Covenant*, 199; Barrett, *Romans*, 139–40. Cranfield, *Romans*, 1:361–87, suggests that the references to νόμος throughout Rom 7 and 8 are to Torah, except the following: Rom 7:21 ("I find it to be a νόμος"), 23 ("another νόμος"), 23, 25 ("the νόμος of sin"), and 8:2 ("the νόμος of sin and death") refer to the power that sin exercises over people; the νόμος of the Spirit (8:2) then is the power that the Spirit exercises over believers. As others have noted, however, it seems odd and confusing that Paul would use a key word in his argument in such different ways.

329. Gal 5:2.

330. Rom 14.

331. E.g., Ps 119.

332. E.g., Deut 4:5–8; 30:15.

Here we need to be careful: What would a rejection of the law mean? Paul seems not to have rejected law per se—that is, the articulation of moral imperatives—for he still prescribes and forbids specific actions for Christians.[333] And some of this ethic still comes from the Jewish law: if he praises the Thessalonians for turning to God from idols, it is unlikely he thought the second commandment was now optional;[334] if he includes murder and covetousness in a list of consequences of human rebellion, it is unlikely he thought the sixth or tenth commandments had been abrogated.[335] In fact, it is important to point out, in light of the critical statements above, that Paul also makes some very positive statements about the law: he speaks of the law being holy, just, good,[336] spiritual,[337] something to uphold[338] and delight in,[339] something that ought to be fulfilled[340] and that can be fulfilled through love;[341] and he states: "For neither circumcision counts for anything nor uncircumcision, but keeping the commandments of God,"[342] which admittedly is somewhat puzzling since circumcision was one of God's commandments.[343]

Clearly, Paul's view of the law is complex and characterized by tension. Kim describes it in terms of dialectic;[344] Räisänen speaks of

---

333. See, for example, Rom 12:1–15:6; 1 Cor 5:1–2, 9–13; 6:1–11; 10:14; Gal 5:13–6:2; Phil 2:1–4; 1 Thess 4:1–12.

334. 1 Thess 1:9.

335. Rom 1:29.

336. Rom 7:12, 16.

337. Rom 7:14.

338. Rom 3:31.

339. Rom 7:22.

340. Rom 8:4.

341. Rom 13:8, 10; Gal 5:14.

342. 1 Cor 7:19.

343. For discussion on the role of Torah in Paul's ethics, see further Rosner, *Paul, Scripture, and Ethics*, who argues that Paul's instructions to the Corinthian church is informed by Torah, even in places where he does not cite a scriptural text; and Tomson, *Paul and the Jewish Law*, who demonstrates the constructive role of Jewish halakha in Paul's teaching, focusing primarily on 1 Corinthians, but also including Gal 2 and Rom 14–15.

344. Kim, *Origin*, 356: "I believe that Paul made both negative and positive affirmations about the law in his letters because in his mind they were not mutually contradictory . . . but they were resolved satisfactorily in a necessary dialectic."

it as outright contradiction.[345] Either way, I suggest that Paul's view of the law resembles views that develop over time and through much struggle, rather than views that become apparent in a moment.[346] This suggests that in order to understand his view of the law, we need to take into account not only his Damascus road experience, but also his experience over the years between then and when he wrote his letters.

Can we be more specific about what Paul rejected with regard to the law? In Phil 3 Paul draws a contrast between his present and former life in terms of a change with regard to the law.[347] Here he warns his readers of those who insist on circumcision for Gentile converts.[348] After claiming that Christians are the "true circumcision," he then asserts that he no longer places any value on the privileges that were his by virtue of the fact that he had been born a Jew (circumcised, an Israelite, a Benjaminite, a Hebrew) or due to his personal achievements (a Pharisee, a zealot, blameless regarding the law).[349] He writes:

> But whatever gain I had, I counted as loss for the sake of Christ. Indeed I count everything as loss because of the surpassing worth of knowing Christ Jesus my Lord. For his sake I have suffered the loss of all things, and count them as refuse, in order that I may gain Christ and be found in him, not having a righteousness of my own, based on law, but that which is through faith in Christ, the righteousness from God that depends on faith. (Phil 3:7–9)

---

345. Räisänen, "Paul's Call Experience," 17–21.

346. Räisänen (ibid., 19) writes: "Even if Paul's thought on the law is viewed in terms of 'dialectic', it still seems to me too complex to have originated all at once."

347. See also Gal 2:19–21 where again Paul implies that his conversion involved a change with regard to the law. For a survey of views on how Paul developed a law-critical perspective, see Donaldson, "Zealot and Convert," 658–68; Räisänen, *Paul and the Law*, 229–63.

348. Phil 3:2; cf. Gal 5:2–3; 6:12–15.

349. Phil 3:5–6. See O'Brien, "Was Paul Converted?," 372–73; Hawthorne and Martin, *Philippians*, 184–87. Paul's claim to be "a Hebrew born of Hebrews" could probably go in either category. I take it that he is claiming here more than simply being born a Jew, but to have been brought up by parents who spoke the sacred language, and probably also to have had close connections with the Hebrew/Aramaic-speaking Jews of Jerusalem (recall Luke's category of "Hebrews" in Acts 6:1), which, together with him being a Pharisee, would tend to support Luke's comment that Paul studied under the famous rabbi, Gamaliel I, in Jerusalem (Acts 22:3), although we still might wonder why Paul did not mention this in Phil 3.

What does this mean? Räisänen's view is that Paul is here abandoning the covenant, even if he would not want to admit it.[350] Indeed Paul would not want to admit that, in light of what he says elsewhere of his own identity as an Israelite,[351] of his continuing commitment to the Scriptures,[352] or of his arguments regarding Christians inheriting the promise of Abraham.[353] And, given the context of Phil 3, I do not think we need to settle for such a radical conclusion as what Räisänen offers. The context is determined by the presence of some who insist upon circumcision, and who, according to Paul, place their "confidence in the flesh."[354] Specifically, what Paul means by this is adhering to a value system—a system that he once shared and excelled in—that places great weight on the qualities he lists in verses 5–6.[355] Thus, what Paul is rejecting here is a value system that defined godliness in terms of privilege and achievement, and he is exchanging this for "knowing Christ Jesus my Lord." He expresses this again when he speaks of rejecting "a righteousness of my own, based on law" in favor of "righteousness from God that depends on faith."[356] What he has lost in exchange for gaining Christ are his achievements that gave him standing in the Jewish community and, so he thought, in the presence of God. What he does not say, however, is that the Jewish traditions themselves are of no value; only that righteousness must be based on faith. Bockmuehl suggests that what is at issue is "*the way* the Torah is seen to function in the light of Christ."[357]

Furthermore, it is probably reading too much into the text to say that Paul is here rejecting Judaism as a legalistic system wherein people's salvation is dependent on how well they keep the law. This view of Second Temple Judaism has been strongly challenged by

350. Räisänen, "Paul's Conversion," 410; he sees something similar going on in Rom 9–11.

351. See above, p. 77.

352. Rom 1:2; 4:3; 9:17; 10:11; 11:2; 15:4; 1 Cor 15:3–4; Gal 3:8, 22; 4:30; and his numerous citations and allusions to scriptural texts.

353. Rom 4:13–16; 15:8–9; Gal 3:15–29.

354. Implied by Paul in Phil 3:3.

355. Gal 1:14 would suggest that the value system also fostered competitiveness: "I advanced in Judaism beyond many of my own age among my people, so extremely zealous was I for the traditions of my fathers."

356. Phil 3:9; see Fee, *Philippians*, 315–16.

357. Bockmuehl, *Philippians*, 213.

Sanders,[358] and although his own proposal of a Judaism characterized by "covenantal nomism"[359] has been rightly criticized for neglecting differences within Judaism and for placing too much emphasis, in some streams of Judaism, on the covenant side and not enough on the nomism side,[360] his recognition that grace and covenant are important

358. Sanders, *Paul and Palestinian Judaism*.

359. Sanders (ibid., 422) describes covenant nomism in the following way: "(1) God has chosen Israel and (2) given the law. The law implies both (3) God's promise to maintain the election and (4) the requirement to obey. (5) God rewards obedience and punishes transgression. (6) The law provides for means of atonement, and atonement results in (7) maintenance or re-establishment of the covenantal relationship. (8) All those who are maintained in the covenant by obedience, atonement and God's mercy belong to the group which will be saved. . . . [Thus it follows that] election and ultimately salvation are considered to be by God's mercy rather than human achievement."

360. See now the articles in Carson et al., eds., *Complexities of Second Temple Judaism*, which examine Second Temple Jewish literature, to see how appropriate "covenant nomism" is to describe Jewish faith. Note the following comments: Craig Evans on Scripture-based stories in the Pseudepigrapha: "as these Scripture-based stories stand, their understanding of election, sin, and redemption is largely consistent with what we find in early Christianity. . . . However, elements are present in some of the writings . . . that still reflect a works-righteousness understanding of justification. . . . This is not to say that the authors of these writings did not view God as gracious and forgiving; they did. There is no indication, however, that they believed that people could gain God's acceptance apart from obedience to the law" (72); Peter Enns on expansions of Scriptures: "it might be less confusing to say that *election* is by grace but *salvation* is by obedience" (98); Philip Davies on didactic stories: "all of these narratives make it clear that it was as a member of the Jewish people that each individual had to relate to God, and that equally the fate of that people depended on the allegiance, resourcefulness, reliability, and honor of every single member" (131); Paul Spilsbury on Josephus: the relationship between God and Israel can be aptly called "'patronal nomism' . . . [by which is meant] an exchange relationship in which people enjoy the blessings of God's patronage to the extent that they display gratitude in the practice of their lives for the divine benefaction which is God's law" (259). It should be noted, however, that some of the writers arrive at conclusions not far from Sanders: Robert Kugler on the testaments: "These . . . works offer qualified support to the notion that covenantal nomism was pervasive in Jewish literature" (213); Donald Gowan on wisdom literature: "The law of God plays a major role. . . , but as a theme rather than as a set of statutes to be expounded. It is God's gift to Israel, making it clear what God wants of his people. There is no suggestion that works of the law are expected to prove anything to God, or that God counts up merits" (239); Markus Bockmuehl on the *Rule of the Community* (1QS): "the Qumran community had a strongly covenantal understanding of the salvation of Israel as centered in its own covenant community. Membership in the covenant of God was characterized both by a sustained individual voluntarism and by an all-embracing doctrine of divine predestination. The community combined a strong sense of the sinfulness of all humanity with a belief in divine grace to the believer as the only means of salvation" (413).

aspects of Judaism is valid. In any case, regardless of how one evalu-
ates the relative roles of grace and works within Judaism, Dunn has
raised the point that the same question can be raised for Paul. No one
questions that Paul proclaimed a gospel of salvation based on God's
grace;[361] and yet, at the same time he stresses the importance of right
living. Dunn writes:

> Obedience is also required of believers (Rom. 1.5; 6.16, 19;
> 15.18 . . .). The OT's insistence that one could not be righteous
> before God without acting righteously towards the neighbour
> (e.g. Deut. 24.10–22; Ezek. 18.5–9) remains true for the fol-
> lowers of Jesus (e.g. . . . . Rom. 14.1–15.7). Paul expected his
> converts to 'lead a life worthy of God' (1 Thess. 2.12); he looked
> for 'the harvest or fruit of righteousness' in their lives (2 Cor.
> 9.9–10; Phil. 1.11). Paul . . . looks for 'fulfilment' of the law (. . .
> Rom. 8.4), for believers to produce 'good works' (. . . 2 Cor. 9.8;
> . . .). In speaking of the love which fulfils the law Paul evident-
> ly had very specific conduct in mind (Rom. 12.9–13.10; Gal.
> 5.13–15). 'Keeping' the requirements of the law continued to
> be important for Paul (Rom. 2.26–27; 1 Cor. 7.19). Final judg-
> ment will be 'according to works' (. . . Rom. 2.6–11; 1 Cor. 3.8;
> 2 Cor. 5:10 . . .). Imagery of reward for achievement or good
> deeds (works) is not lacking (. . . 1 Cor. 3.14; 9:24–25; Phil.
> 3.14 . . .). Salvation (eternal life) is in some degree conditional
> on faithfulness (. . . Rom. 8.13; 1 Cor. 15.2; Gal. 6.8 . . .).[362]

The point, therefore, is that the contrast between Paul and Judaism
is not as simple as a black-and-white contrast between grace and legal-
ism. I am not suggesting there was no difference between Paul and the
Judaism of his day, but the differences need to be carefully assessed
and nuanced in order to do justice to both.[363] Both saw the importance

361. Rom 3:24; 4:16; 5:2, 6–8, 15–21; 6:14; 8:3–4; 11:5–6; 1 Cor 1:26–31; 2 Cor
1:9–10; 4:6; Gal 2:19–21; cf. Eph 2:5, 8.

362. Dunn, "New Perspective," 75–76; cf. Räisänen, "Paul's Conversion," 412.

363. I would suggest, in the same way, that describing the new means of salvation
that Paul discovered at his conversion as "Christ" rather than as "the law" may confuse
as much as it explains, even if such language can be found in Paul (Rom 7:4; 10:4; Gal
2:16, 19–21; 3:13; Phil 3:9). "Law" refers to the need for Jews to keep God's commands
in order to maintain their covenant relationship; "Christ" refers to Jesus' death which
is understood to have been a sacrifice of atonement making salvation available to all
those who come to God in faith. However, we must not forget that "law" also spoke of
atonement (otherwise, why the sacrifices that dealt with sin?), and "Christ" also implied a particular way of living (thus the otherwise surprising phrase, "law of Christ"
(1 Cor 9:21; Gal 6:2), not to mention all of Paul's moral instruction). Again, I am not

of grace—for Jews grace was demonstrated in God's election and in his giving of the law, whereas Paul discovered a new dimension of grace in Jesus Christ;[364] and both had respect for the law—for Jews obedience was essential for maintaining the covenant, whereas Paul held a more complex view of the law, both promoting it and criticizing it. The relevance of this for my argument is that we need to avoid thinking of Paul's conversion as a simplistic and absolute change from law to grace; the situation is more complex than that.

I have critiqued above the argument that a Jew like Paul would have concluded that Jesus was cursed of God simply on the basis of Deut 21:23.[365] But even if Paul had so reasoned, it is not clear that a reversal in his opinion of Jesus would have entailed a reversal of his opinion of the law, as though he would have argued along the following lines: since Jesus was crucified, he, according to the law, was cursed of God; but if in fact Jesus is the Messiah, the Lord, the Son of God, then the law must be wrong. Christopher Tuckett demonstrates that other options were available:[366] Paul could have, for example, reasoned that Jesus' death involved a miscarriage of justice, or that the application of the law in the charge against him was incorrect, or that since he had been executed by Romans, the law had nothing to do with his death, or that "curse of God" in Deut 21:23 should be understood as an objective rather than subjective genitive. It is too much to expect that a Pharisee like Paul, one who was zealous for the law, would have determined that the whole law was fundamentally flawed simply on the basis of the interpretation of one text,[367] and Dunn makes the point that Paul in fact never does develop this line of argument.[368] In any case, it appears that the Hebrew Christians living in Jerusalem did not

---

suggesting that Paul did not receive a fundamentally new understanding of salvation at his conversion, but I am saying that care needs to be taken so as not to skew either Second Temple Judaism or the thought of Paul.

364. For an attempt to connect Paul with Jesus based on his experience of grace, see Barclay, "Caustic Grace," 1–17.

365. See above, pp. 80–83.

366. See again Tuckett, "Deut 21:23," 345–50; cf. Sanders, *Paul, the Law, and the Jewish People*, 25–26; Räisänen, *Paul and the Law*, 249–51.

367. Consider a contemporary analogy: I doubt that many Christians who have become convinced of the appropriateness of women exercising leadership in the church conclude, solely on the basis of 1 Cor 14:35, that therefore Paul or the New Testament ought to be discarded.

368. Dunn, "Light to the Gentiles," 92–93.

have a problem with remaining faithful to the law in light of the fact of Jesus' crucifixion.[369]

I suggest that a more confident path to take that leads to Paul reassessing the role of the law, and one that is historically plausible, is to understand his rejection of the value system spoken of in Phil 3 as a rejection of zeal for the law. That is to say, at his conversion Paul understood that what he was doing was wrong, that his pursuit of zeal for the law was not an appropriate expression of zeal for God. What did this mean practically? Certainly Paul the apostle would have continued to think of himself as a zealot for God—that is, as one passionately committed to serving the God of his ancestors. But there is clearly an aspect of his former zeal which he separates himself from— the zeal that led him to persecute the church,[370] the zeal of his own countrymen which he describes as "unenlightened."[371] Furthermore, as we have seen above, zeal for the law had to do with doing whatever was necessary in order to ensure that Jews kept the law and thereby maintained Israel's distinctiveness.[372] From his letters we know that Paul was particularly concerned with the issues of circumcision and food. It seems plausible, therefore, that this is the contribution that

369. I suggest that Paul's reference to Deut 21:23 in Gal 3:13 is probably best understood as part of a rabbinic argument in which, through the common mention of the word "curse," this text is brought together with Deut 27:26 in an attempt to show that by his death Jesus had freed people from the curse which the law had threatened. In Gal 3:10–14 Paul is employing *a* view of crucifixion that was held by *some* Jews of his time (see above, p. 81 n. 85), and presumably he found this to be useful for making a Christian argument. In this difficult text, Paul is using a rabbinic form of argument (known as *Gezera šawa*) which finds a common catchword in two scriptural texts and draws a conclusion from them (see Bruce, *Galatians*, 30). His argument runs as follows: (i) there is a curse hovering over those who live by the law (Deut 27:26)—that is, it is not that the Jews are cursed simply because they try to live by the law, but rather that they face the threat of a curse (i.e., exile) if they disregard the law; (ii) Jesus became a curse when he was hanged on the cross/tree (Deut 21:23); therefore, (iii) assuming Jesus died in some sense as a substitute for his people, and assuming that by his resurrection he was victorious over the enemy, Jesus set people free from the curse of the law. See Fitzmyer, "Crucifixion," 510–12. Dunn, "Light to the Gentiles," 99–100, takes this one step further: by being crucified and hence cursed, Christ was put out of the covenant, that is, in the same place as Gentile sinners; but by vindicating Christ, God has shown that he is in favor of the sinner outside the covenant, that is, in favor of Gentiles.

370. Phil 3:6.

371. Rom 10:2.

372. See above, pp. 109–12.

Paul brought into the Antioch church—that Gentiles did not need to be circumcised or to keep Jewish food laws, and that this view was consistent with Scripture. And given the description of this church above, it seems reasonable that many there would have welcomed such a message, Barnabas being a prime example.[373]

The hypothesis I have developed, therefore, shows how Paul's view of the law, and also his understanding of himself as apostle to the Gentiles, were matters of divine revelation but, at the same time, were integrally connected to his experience as a Christian. And since his struggle with the law was fundamentally connected to his mission to the Gentiles, it seems likely that his year in the church in Antioch, where Christians who had formerly belonged to the church in Jerusalem (the Hellenists and Barnabas) were leading a mission to the Gentiles, must have been a formative time for him in this regard. I noted above that it is likely that Paul was responsible for arguing that circumcision should not be required for Gentile converts;[374] it is quite plausible, however, that this was worked out in the context of a Gentile mission. In this way we see revelation and tradition working together—that is, Paul's Damascus road experience being worked out in the context of his involvement in the life of the church in Antioch with its welcome of Gentiles.

Conclusions

In the end, I do share the view of Simmons that the Hellenists served as a link between Jesus and Paul, modeling Jesus' welcome of tax collectors and sinners by their own practice of welcoming Gentiles. I differ, however, in my understanding of the dynamics at work within the Hellenist community. Contrary to Simmons, I argue that the particular offense they caused—in addition to a number of other offenses that Jews took towards all Christians—was not the waiving of circumcision, but rather their association with Gentiles, their failure (in the eyes of other Jews) to maintain the proper distinctions between Jew and Gentile, particularly concerning issues of table fellowship. I suggest that the Hellenists were essentially law abiding, although I allow that some may have begun to entertain the possibility of accommodating

373. Acts 9:27; 11:25; 13:1; 15:12; although recall Gal 2:13.

374. See above, pp. 71–73.

Gentile believers by spiritualizing some laws. And I go further than Simmons in arguing that Paul's conversion needs to be understood not only as a result of divine revelation, but also as a consequence of his integration into the church of Antioch—a church that had already been engaged in a mission to Gentiles. This historical conditioning of Paul's understanding of the gospel and of his own commission to the Gentiles is crucial for seeing the Hellenists as a causal link between Jesus and Paul. Failure to appreciate Paul in this way risks making his conversion/call into a theological singularity point in which case he would lack any vital connection to the early church and, by extension, to Jesus of Nazareth.

4

Jesus' Challenge to Share His Fate

THE PURPOSE OF THIS CHAPTER IS TO EXPLORE WAYS IN WHICH JESUS challenged people to follow him—in particular, to see how his disciples would, in some way, share in Jesus' own fate. In the following chapter, we will then relate these to what Paul says about believers participating in the death of Jesus. The sayings of Jesus that we need to consider—for example, "Take up your cross and follow me," "Whoever seeks to save his life will lose it; and whoever loses his life will save it," "The cup that I dink, you will drink"—express the irony that life is to be found by means of death. But these are more than simply proverbial maxims, for they are sayings that are part of the call to follow Jesus who himself would die for the cause for which he was working. We need to begin, therefore, with an appreciation of how the threat of death marked Jesus' life.

Jesus' Anticipation of His Own Death

While there is considerable debate over what significance Jesus saw in his death on the cross, the evidence is fairly convincing that Jesus would have anticipated his own death.

The Passion Predictions

In each of the Gospels Jesus predicts his own death—somewhat cryptically in John,[1] but explicitly in the Synoptics.[2] If we could assume the

---

1. See John 2:19–22; 3:14; 6:51; 8:28; 10:11, 15, 17–18; 12:7, 32–33; cf. also the ironic statements in John 11:16, 50.

2. Matt 16:21//Mark 8:31//Luke 9:22; Matt 17:22–23//Mark 9:31//Luke 9:44; Matt 20:18–19//Mark 10:33–34//Luke 18:31–33; cf. Matt 9:15//Mark 2:20//Luke 5:33; Luke 13:33.

authenticity of these predictions, my argument that Jesus anticipated his own death would be all the stronger. Their authenticity, however, is often strongly contested for various reasons.[3] Rudolf Bultmann notes that "the predictions of the passion and resurrection . . . have long been recognized as secondary constructions of the Church."[4] Although there are many who defend their authenticity,[5] for strategic reasons I will not base my argument on them, but will instead focus on less contentious evidence.

A Context of Violence

Setting aside the passion predictions, there is evidence that Jesus lived in a context where violence and executions were common. At a general level, a number of Jesus' parables reflect a context of violence.[6] More specifically, however, Roman rule in Palestine often involved lethal action against movements perceived to be revolutionary.[7] Josephus records numerous accounts of such action around the time of Jesus. Prior to becoming king in 37 BCE, Herod killed many of a group of revolutionaries, including their leader, Hezekiah, in order to win fa-

---

3. Nolland, *Luke*, 2:459–64, notes the following difficulties regarding the historicity of Luke 9:22 par.: (i) the more general problems involving "Son of man" sayings; (ii) the absence of any predictions in Q (not a serious challenge since "Q is an incomplete rendering of the Jesus tradition" [461]); (iii) the apparent incompatibility between Son of man sayings involving death and resurrection and those involving parousia and glory; (iv) the seemingly inappropriate response of the disciples to what appears to be a straightforward prediction of Jesus' death, however unexpected and unwanted it may have been (e.g., incomprehension [Mark 9:10, 32], arguing over which of them would be the greatest [Mark 9:33–34], and James and John requesting to sit on Jesus' right and left [Mark 10:35–37]); (v) the prediction of resurrection following death; (vi) syntactical difficulties and unevenness in Mark 8:31 and 9:31; and (vii) specific terms used in Mark 10:34 (esp. "mock," "spit," and "flog") which look suspiciously like borrowings from the passion narrative itself (Mark 15:15, 19, 20, 31). Nolland's own view is that while it is difficult to assign specific prediction sayings to Jesus with any confidence, there are other indications in the Gospels which indicate that he anticipated his own death and subsequent vindication.

4. Bultmann, *History*, 152; cf. Wrede, *Messianic Secret*, 91.

5. Balla, "What Did Jesus Think," 242–49; Evans, "Did Jesus Predict," 82–97, although Evans locates the passion predictions within Jesus' last week in Jerusalem; Davies and Allison, *Matthew*, 2:654–55; Jeremias, *New Testament Theology*, 277–86; Schweizer, *Mark*, 171; Cranfield, *Mark*, 266–67; Taylor, *Formation*, 150.

6. Matt 21:33–39//Mark 12:1–7//Luke 20:9–15; Matt 22:5–6; Luke 10:30–37.

7. See Wright, *New Testament*, 170–81.

vor with Rome.[8] Towards the end of his life, Herod killed—some by
burning alive—a group of about forty young men, together with two
rabbis, Judas and Matthias, who had incited them to remove a large
golden eagle that Herod had erected over the gate of the temple.[9] In 4
BCE during the interim between Herod's death and the appointment
of his son, Archelaus, as successor in Judea, a number of disturbances
broke out: Archelaus killed about three thousand Jews who, at the time
of Passover, caused a disturbance over the memory of the slaying of
Matthias and his followers;[10] a Roman army defeated the followers of
a certain Simon—a former slave of Herod who had declared himself
to be king and had burned and plundered several Roman buildings—
and beheaded Simon himself;[11] a shepherd named Athronges formed a
band of rebels, declared himself king, and made raids against Romans
and Jews who collaborated with Rome, but in the end was captured by
Archelaus;[12] and Judas (the son of the Hezekiah mentioned above) and
his followers plundered the Roman palace in Sepphoris, which brought
Varus, the Roman general over Syria, in pursuit, finally defeating them
in Jerusalem where he crucified two thousand of them.[13] In reaction
to the Roman census and taxation in 6 CE, Judas "the Galilean" led
a revolt and, according to Luke, was killed.[14] Some time later Judas'
sons, James and Simon, were crucified under the procurator, Tiberius
Alexander, presumably for more revolutionary activity.[15] Also, according to Luke, Pilate killed some Galilean Jews while they were offering
sacrifice, presumably because they opposed him in some way.[16]

Similar action against revolutionary movements continued, ultimately leading to the Jewish War.[17] Two incidents in particular show
that the Romans would take preemptive measures if they perceived a

8. Josephus, *Ant.* 14.158–60, 420–30; cf. Schürer, *History*, 1:275.

9. Josephus, *Ant.* 17.149–67; *J.W.* 1.648–55.

10. Josephus, *Ant.* 17.206–18; *J.W.* 2.1–13.

11. Josephus, *Ant.* 17.273–77; *J.W.* 2.57–59.

12. Josephus, *Ant.* 17.278–84; *J.W.* 2.60–65.

13. Josephus, *Ant.* 17.271–72, 286–98; *J.W.* 2.56, 66–79.

14. Josephus, *Ant.* 18.4–10, 23–25; *J.W.* 2.118; Acts 5:37.

15. Josephus, *Ant.* 20.102.

16. Luke 13:1.

17. See, e.g., executions under Cumanus (Josephus, *J.W.* 2.241–42; *Ant.* 20.129),
Felix (*J.W.* 2.253; *Ant.* 20.161), and Florus (*J.W.* 2.306–8).

movement to be dangerous: in the mid-40s a prophet named Theudas promised to lead his followers up to the Jordan River and to divide the waters so they could pass through; Fadus, however, attacked, killing many and beheading Theudas.[18] And an unnamed Egyptian Jew led a large group from the wilderness up the Mount of Olives, but they were met by the Roman army before they came to Jerusalem and were routed and dispersed.[19] Clearly Jesus lived in a political climate where activity that threatened Roman order would not be tolerated. Thus, to the extent that Jesus was perceived by Romans to be a threat to their rule, or simply to their effort to keep the peace, his life was in jeopardy.

The Death of John the Baptist

But perhaps what would have convinced Jesus more than anything that his life could be at risk was the execution of his close associate, John the Baptist. According to the Synoptics, Herod Antipas had John arrested because he spoke out against Antipas' marriage to his second wife, Herodias,[20] but according to Josephus, Antipas wanted to silence John in order to prevent a possible rebellion.[21] Robert Webb proposes a scenario where both could be correct:[22] according to Josephus, Antipas' first marriage was to the daughter of Aretas IV, king of Nabatea, and the divorce was considered an insult by the Nabateans and eventually led to war.[23] Now if John was preaching in Perea, east of the Jordan, he would have been in Antipas' territory but possibly near to the Nabatean border; and if he was preaching a message that challenged the legitimacy of Antipas' second marriage, then, even if motivated solely by a concern for Jewish piety, he could easily have created a volatile situation.[24] Consequently, Antipas had him arrested and executed.[25]

18. Josephus, *Ant.* 20.97–99. Luke places this incident prior to Judas the Galilean (Acts 5:36).

19. Josephus, *J.W.* 2.261–63; cf. Acts 21:38.

20. Matt 14:3–4//Mark 6:17–18//Luke 3:19–20.

21. Josephus, *Ant.* 18.118.

22. Webb, "John the Baptist," 208–9.

23. Josephus, *Ant.* 18.109–20.

24. Josephus, *Ant.* 18.113, also mentions that Antipas and Aretas had a border dispute.

25. Mark gives the impression that Antipas was somewhat sympathetic towards

According to the Synoptics, when Antipas heard about what Jesus was doing, he wondered whether John the Baptist had been raised from the dead.[26] This suggests that no matter how much Jesus wanted to distinguish himself from John, to someone like Antipas the two were similar as were the political problems they presented. If Antipas knew that Jesus had formerly been working together with John,[27] this would have been reason enough for him to oppose Jesus. Knowledge of this would no doubt have given Jesus pause: not only was he being noticed by the tetrarch of Galilee, but he was being likened to someone that the tetrarch had recently executed. In fact, not only does Luke make it clear that Antipas wanted to kill Jesus, but he records Jesus' intention to leave the area because, as he says, "it cannot be that a prophet should perish away from Jerusalem."[28] And immediately following this, Luke appends the Q-saying where Jesus laments over Jerusalem for "killing the prophets and stoning those who are sent to you."[29] Here Jesus clearly sets himself within the tradition of the persecuted prophets[30]—a tradition, beginning in the Old Testament and becoming well-established in Second Temple Judaism, in which true prophets become martyrs in the context of a disobedient Israel.[31]

Opposition to Jesus

Further evidence for the view that Jesus would have been aware of the possibility that he could be killed for what he was doing is found in the various conflicts he faced. According to the Gospels, Jesus faced opposition from various Jewish groups: while in Galilee his opponents were

---

John and that he killed him only because of a promise he had made to his stepdaughter of which Herodias took advantage (Mark 6:20–28). However authentic this account may be, Antipas was certainly not sympathetic enough toward John to release him from prison.

26. Matt 14:1–2//Mark 6:14–16//Luke 9:7–9.

27. See Webb, "John the Baptist," 211–29.

28. Luke 13:31, 33. While Bultmann, *History*, 35, 364, takes v. 32b to be secondary, he thinks the rest of the scene is historical.

29. Matt 23:37//Luke 13:34.

30. Matt 5:12//Luke 6:23; Matt 23:29–31//Luke 11:47–48; Matt 23:34–35//Luke 11:49–51.

31. For the tradition that prophets were killed in Jerusalem, see Fitzmyer, *Luke*, 2:1032; Jackson and Lake, eds., *Beginnings of Christianity*, 4:82; Davies and Allison, *Matthew*, 1:465–66.

principally Pharisees[32] and sometimes scribes,[33] whereas in Jerusalem, while these two groups are also mentioned, it was the chief priests[34] and elders[35] who took the leading role. While there is some debate over the respective roles and identities of these groups, particularly of the Pharisees, it is clear that the conflict between Jesus and various Jewish groups is well attested, occurring in all the Gospel traditions (Mark, Q, M, L, John, and *Gospel of Thomas*) and in various kinds of traditions (e.g., indictments of Jesus, conflict stories, parables).

In Mark we read of Pharisees and/or scribes confronting Jesus regarding his practice of table fellowship with sinners,[36] breaking the Sabbath law,[37] not keeping the traditions of the elders by washing hands before eating,[38] forgiving sins,[39] and his interpretation of the law;[40]

32. On the Pharisees, see Appendix B below.

33. Saldarini, "Scribes," 1012–16, describes the scribes as "bureaucrats and experts on Jewish life. They could have been low-level officials and judges both in Jerusalem and in the towns and villages of the country" (1015). In the Gospels they appear as "teachers of the law" (Luke 5:17, 21; cf. Matt 23:2), respected authorities with whom Jesus' teaching is contrasted (Mark 1:22; Matt 7:28–29; Matt 17:10//Mark 9:11), and close associates of the chief priests and elders in Jerusalem. For a more general discussion of scribes, see Meier, *Marginal Jew*, 3:549–60.

34. Davies and Allison, *Matthew*, 1:239–40, describe the chief priests as a collective group which included "the current high priest and his predecessors, the captain of the temple, the heads of the weekly courses, the directors of the daily courses, the temple overseers, and the temple treasurers." Their central concern was for the temple and all that went on there, but given the paramount importance of the temple for all Jews, they were concerned with all aspects of Jewish life, particularly in Jerusalem and Judea. See also Jeremias, *Jerusalem*, 160–81.

35. Jeremias, *Jerusalem*, 222–24, describes the elders as the lay nobility, the heads of the leading families of Jerusalem who exercised a collective rule together with the chief priests. It is probably this group that Luke describes as "the principal men of the city" (Luke 19:47), and it is possible that Joseph of Arimathea belonged to this group (Mark 15:43//Luke 23:50–51).

36. Mark 2:16 (scribes of the Pharisees), par. in Matt 9:11 (Pharisees)//Luke 5:30 (Pharisees and their scribes); cf. Luke 15:1–2 (Pharisees and scribes).

37. Mark 2:24 (Pharisees), par. in Matt 12:2 (Pharisees)//Luke 6:2 (Pharisees); cf. Luke 14:1–5 (lawyers and Pharisees).

38. Mark 7:1–5 (Pharisees and scribes), par. in Matt 15:1–2 (Pharisees and scribes); cf. Luke 11:37–38 (Pharisee). That it was in fact Jesus' disciples who were observed not washing their hands rather than Jesus himself is probably immaterial; the question comes to Jesus because he is responsible for his disciples and thus he defends their practice.

39. Mark 2:6–7 (scribes), par. in Matt 9:3 (scribes)//Luke 5:21 (scribes and Pharisees).

40. Mark 10:2 (Pharisees), par. in Matt 19:3 (Pharisees).

they also challenged him to perform a miraculous sign in order to test him.[41] According to Mark it was scribes who accused Jesus of casting out demons by means of Beelzebul.[42] Q and the *Gospel of Thomas* include numerous criticisms directed at the Pharisees and scribes for hypocrisy.[43] Luke also includes a parable where Jesus praises the piety of a tax collector over that of a Pharisee.[44] Mark tells of Jesus warning his disciples about the "leaven of the Pharisees," and at the same time he mentions the "leaven of Herod";[45] the combination of these two may be a reflection of the Pharisees, while in Galilee, conspiring with the Herodians[46] in order to do away with Jesus.[47]

41. Mark 8:11 (Pharisees), par. in Matt 16:1 (Pharisees and Sadducees); cf. Matt 12:38 (scribes and Pharisees).

42. Mark 3:22, par. in Matt 12:24 (Pharisees)//Luke 11:15 (unidentified); cf. Matt 9:34.

43. Matt 23:23//Luke 11:42; Matt 23:25–26//Luke 11:39–41; Matt 23:27//Luke 11:44; Matt 23:29//Luke 11:47; *Gos. Thom.* 39; 102. Each of the Matthean criticisms is directed to scribes and Pharisees, whereas Luke and *Thomas* mention only the Pharisees (the last two Lukan references do not mention Pharisees, but in the context of Luke 11 it is clear that the Pharisees are in view).

44. Luke 18:9–14.

45. Mark 8:15, par. in Matt 16:6 (Pharisees and Sadducees)//Luke 12:1 (Pharisees).

46. Little is known about the Herodians (Ἡρῳδιανοί). Josephus (*J.W.* 1.319) mentions a group with a similar name (Ἡρῳδεῖοί) who were supporters of Herod the Great (Meier, *Marginal Jew*, 3:561, thinks that Mark's spelling may be based on a Latin form, *Herodiani*, in the same way that we find Καισαριανοί for the Latin *Caesariani* (various supporters of Caesar) and Χριστιανοί for *Christiani*). But Herod was known not to have had good relations with the Pharisees (Josephus, *J.W.* 1.571; *Ant.* 17.41–47), and so Mark's reference to the Pharisees conspiring with the Herodians (Mark 3:6) is somewhat puzzling. If Mark's Herodians were supporters of Herod Antipas (which is probably what Mark expected his readers to assume), then something must have changed in their relationship with Antipas since the time of his father. That is certainly possible: if the Pharisees' and Antipas' opposition to Jesus was stronger than their qualms with each other, it would be reasonable for them to conspire together against Jesus—politics often making strange bed-fellows. Such cooperation might reflect a move toward the improved relations we can observe in subsequent generations between Herod's descendants and the Pharisees (or their successors, the rabbis): Herod's grandsons, Agrippa I and II (who were more ethnically Jewish than was Herod) were eager to pursue Jewish concerns (see Acts 12:2–3; Josephus, *Ant.* 19.331; 20.139; *m. Soṭah* 7:8). However, Rowley, "Herodians," 14–27, argues that the Herodians were not officials associated with Herod's rules, but rather "men of standing and influence, whose outlook was . . . [one of] friendliness to the Herodian rule, and consequently to the Roman rule on which it rested" (p. 27). See further Marcus, *Mark 1–8*, 249–50; and Meier, *Marginal Jew*, 3:560–65.

47. Mark 3:6, par. in Matt 12:14 (Pharisees)//Luke 6:11 (Pharisees and scribes, cf. v. 7).

When the action moves to Jerusalem the temple authorities—chief priests, scribes, and elders—take the lead in opposing Jesus,[48] although each of the Gospels (with the exception of Luke) continues to mention the Pharisees. According to Mark the Pharisees, still colluding with the Herodians, try to trap Jesus with a question about paying taxes to Caesar;[49] according to Matthew the Pharisees also confront Jesus with a question about the greatest commandment, and they appear with the chief priests to request a guard be placed at Jesus' tomb;[50] and according to John the Pharisees play a leading role throughout in opposing Jesus and in conspiring against him.[51]

While the exact identity of which group is involved in each scene is not always clear,[52] what is clear is that Jesus faced significant opposition from his fellow Jews.[53] Furthermore, there is evidence that while he was in Galilee some of his opponents were conspiring to have him arrested by Antipas which, as far as Jesus would have known, could have ended in his death. Almost certainly Jesus would not have thought that by leaving Antipas' territory and going to Jerusalem he would be escaping danger. If his words and actions caused offense in Galilee, how much more so in Jerusalem! And in fact his actions in the Jerusalem temple—both overturning the tables[54] and teaching openly,[55] including telling a parable that implied the current Jewish leadership

---

48. See, e.g., Mark 11:18; 11:27; 14:1, 43, 53, par.

49. Mark 12:13, par. in Matt 22:15–16 (Pharisees and Herodians)//Luke 20:20 (spies).

50. Matt 27:62.

51. John 7:32, 45–52; 9:13–34; 11:47–53, 57; 18:3.

52. The confusion among the Gospels with regard to the precise identity of Jesus' opponents may be due, to some extent, to the fact that the categories are not all of the same kind: Pharisees were people committed to a particular piety; scribes and chief priests were people with specific occupations; and elders were hereditary heads of leading families in Jerusalem. Thus, the groups were not mutually exclusive: scribes, for example, could be Pharisees if they so chose. It may also be that, with this lack of clear boundaries, the Gospel writers felt the freedom to change the names in order to develop their own particular perspective.

53. Wright, *Jesus*, 439–42, argues that the motive behind the opposition was that Jesus was perceived to be a deceiver, leading people astray, as warned against in Deut 13. Indications of this are found in Justin Martyr (*Dial.* 69.7) and the Talmud (*b. Sanh.* 43a; 107b). See above, p. 42 n. 89.

54. Mark 11:12–19 par.

55. Mark 11:27; 12:35; 14:49 par.

would be judged and replaced[56]—suggest that he was in no way avoiding confrontation with the temple authorities. In fact, such actions raise the question whether he was actually provoking confrontation in Jerusalem with those who were responsible for protecting the temple and for ensuring its proper operation.[57] It is at least plausible to suggest that, if Jesus believed he would likely be killed for what he was doing, he may have chosen Jerusalem as the place where he wanted to die.[58] It is also plausible to suppose that Jesus would have reflected on the significance of his pending death with regard to his mission.[59] It is possible, for example, that he saw himself in the tradition of those Israelites who suffered or were martyred for just causes[60]—the prophets who were killed for their preaching,[61] the righteous who were oppressed by the wicked,[62] the Maccabean martyrs whose death was thought to be beneficial for the nation[63] and whom God would raise again to life.[64] Be that as it may, we cannot conclude that Jesus simply had a death wish. His central focus with regard to the proclamation of the kingdom of God is consistent throughout his ministry; the decision to put him to death was made in reaction to what he said and did.

56. Mark 12:1–12 par.

57. Note esp. the severe reaction to Jesus ben Ananias in 62 CE for prophesying the destruction of the temple (Josephus, *J.W.* 6.300–304).

58. Of the Gospel writers, Luke seems to make the most of the necessity for Jesus to die in Jerusalem (Luke 9:31, 51; 13:33–34; 18:31; cf. Matt 16:21).

59. John portrays Jesus as being aware of the necessity and significance of his own death from early in his ministry (John 2:19–22; 3:14; 8:28; 10:11, 15, 17; 12:24). The Synoptics are more restrained in this regard, but some significant sayings occur (Mark 10:45; 12:1–12 par.; 14:22–25 par.).

60. From a variety of perspectives, see Wright, *Jesus*, 579–84; Jonge, "Jesus' Death," 142–51; Downing, "Jesus and Martyrdom," 279–93; Freyne, "Jesus the Martyr," 48–59; O'Neill, "Did Jesus Teach," 9–27.

61. On persecution of the prophets in the Jesus tradition, see Matt 5:11–12//Luke 6:22–23; Matt 23:29–36//Luke 11:47–51; Matt 23:37//Luke 13:34; Acts 7:52. On the identity of Jesus as a prophet, see Matt 13:57//Mark 6:4//Luke 4:24 (cf. John 4:44); Mark 6:15//Luke 9:8; Matt 16:14//Mark 8:28//Luke 9:19; Matt 21:11; 21:46; Luke 7:16, 39; 13:33; 24:19; John 4:19; 6:14; 7:40; 9:17.

62. For examples from the Psalms, note where the psalmist prays for rescue from death (see below, p. 150 n. 90), and where he describes the activity of sinners (see above, pp. 52–53). One clear reference to this tradition is in Mark 15:34 par., citing Ps 22:2; for other possible allusions, see Pesch, *Markusevangelium*, 2:13–15.

63. 2 Macc 6:12–17; 7:37–38; 4 Macc 6:27–29; 9:23–24; 17:20–22; 18:3–4.

64. 2 Macc 7:9, 11, 14, 22–23, 29, 36.

It is disputed, however, whether the Jewish leaders in Jerusalem had the authority to execute someone. John suggests they did not and that this was the reason the chief priests had to bring Jesus to Pilate if they wanted him executed.[65] There is historical evidence to support this: according to Josephus, in 6 CE when Coponius was installed as the first Roman procurator in Judea, he was granted full authority, including the right to inflict capital punishment.[66] Sherwin-White argues that the Romans closely guarded the authority for capital punishment since, particularly in a place like Judea where there was strong anti-Roman sentiment, such power could be used against friends of Rome.[67] There are, however, indications that the Jewish authorities may have been authorized to execute those who committed certain crimes: there was an inscription in the Jerusalem temple that forbade any non-Jew, on pain of death, to enter the holy place[68] and, according to Josephus, Titus acknowledged that the Romans had granted the Jews the authority to execute anyone who transgressed this directive.[69] Furthermore, there are indications that, whether authorized or not, Jews did put people to death from time to time: note specifically the stonings of Stephen[70] and of James the brother of Jesus,[71] the proposed stoning of an adulterous woman brought to Jesus,[72] and Luke's account

65. John 18:31.

66. Josephus, *J.W.* 2.117.

67. Sherwin-White, *Roman Society*, 35–43. He notes specifically the withdrawing of capital authority in Cyrene.

68. See the temple inscription in Barrett, ed., *New Testament Background*, 50; cf. Josephus, *J.W.* 5.193–94.

69. Josephus, *J.W.* 6.124–26. According to Acts, Paul was accused of bringing a Gentile into the temple (Acts 21:28–29), and his appeal to Caesar seems to be based on a suspicion that he would be killed (one way or another) if he went to Jerusalem to be tried (Acts 25:9–11).

70. Acts 7:58.

71. Josephus, *Ant.* 20.197–200.

72. The account in John 8:1–11 makes best sense if the woman's accusers were in fact prepared to stone her. On a textual basis this account must be judged not to be original to the Gospel of John. Many, however, conclude that it bears the marks of an authentic account (whether or not actually authentic itself) which was incorporated into the Gospel at an early date (note that one manuscript places the same incident at the end of Luke 21); see Brown, *John*, 1:335; Schnackenburg, *John*, 2:170. It seems unlikely that the story would have survived if it had been mistaken about such a basic matter as whether or not Jews would have stoned someone for such an offense.

of Paul voting in favor of the death penalty for Christians.[73] We do not know whether the authority granted to Jews to execute extended beyond the one specific temple crime, but it is clear that people could be killed for other offenses.[74] But even if, for whatever reason, Jews could not put someone to death, it was well known that the high priest was appointed by the Roman procurator and presumably he could engineer some political maneuvering in order to have someone executed if he really wanted to—thus, the account in the Gospels of Jesus being arrested by Jewish authorities and handed over to Roman authorities for execution is not at all implausible. It seems reasonable that Jesus, upon coming to Jerusalem, must have considered the likelihood that he would be put to death there.

Jesus' Anticipation of Crucifixion?

Could Jesus have anticipated that he would be crucified? This also seems possible but less certain.[75] First, he would have had to assume that the Jewish authorities would choose not to kill him themselves but would instead conspire with Pilate to have him killed; and second, he would have had to assume that Pilate would agree to execute him and to do so by means of crucifixion.[76] In hindsight the sequence of events

73. Acts 26:10. Regardless of how one judges the historicity of Paul's involvement in such an action, this would be an odd thing for Luke to say if it was known that the Jewish leadership never made such judgments.

74. Naturally, Jews showed special sensitivity in connection with the temple. According to Acts, Peter and John are arrested for teaching in the temple area (Acts 4–5), Stephen is stoned supposedly for speaking against the temple (Acts 6:13; 7:48–50) and Paul's life is endangered because he is accused of bringing a Gentile into the temple (see above, p. 146 n. 69). It is understandable, then, why attention would be given in Jesus' trial to charges that he spoke against the temple (Mark 14:55–59; 15:29–30 par.).

75. Interestingly, only in Matthew's version of the passion predictions does Jesus state that he would die on a Roman cross (Matt 20:19). In one of the Markan predictions he mentions that he would be handed over to Gentiles, flogged and then killed (Mark 10:33–34 par.), but this does not necessarily imply crucifixion since the Romans also executed criminals by beheading and by burning (for the Roman practice of crucifixion, see O'Collins, "Crucifixion," 1207–10; and Hengel, *Crucifixion*, 33–38, 46–50). The Johannine predictions often speak of Jesus being lifted up (John 3:14; 8:28; 12:32–33), which on the one hand is a reference to his glorification, but on the other hand could ironically suggest death by crucifixion.

76. We do not know whether Pilate executed by means of beheading or burning, but we do know that these other methods were used in Palestine (see above, pp. 138–40).

makes historical sense: Jesus offended the Jewish authorities and posed a threat to the extent that they decided he should be killed; because of the number of people in Jerusalem for Passover, many of whom appeared to be sympathetic towards Jesus, the authorities agreed that they would act quickly and secretly so as to avoid a riot;[77] they found a way to persuade Pilate to have him crucified. But how much of this could have been anticipated, in a volatile context like Jerusalem at Passover, is difficult to say. Clearly, at the Last Supper Jesus is aware that his death is imminent; however, even here he gives no indication of how he will die.[78] We need, however, to admit the limitation of our knowledge at this point: if Jesus was insightful enough, perhaps he was able to read the political dynamics far better than we can and could anticipate reasonably well how the chief priests and Pilate would react.

It is difficult, however, but perhaps not impossible, to imagine anyone *wanting* to be crucified given the horrific suffering it involved[79]—although, incredible people are known to do incredible things. It is true that early Christians saw theological significance not only in Jesus' death but also in the *manner* of his death: for example, Paul's argument involving the foolishness of the cross would not have the same forcefulness had Jesus been executed in a more humane fashion;[80] he argues that "Christ redeemed us from the curse of the law" on the basis of the law pronouncing anyone hanging on a tree to be cursed;[81] he describes the extent of Christ's humility and obedience by referring to his willingness to die—"even death on a cross";[82] and several New Testament writers draw significance from the fact that Jesus not only died but that he suffered: Paul speaks about sharing in Jesus' sufferings,[83] Hebrews sees Jesus' suffering as an essential element

---

77. Mark 11:18; 12:12; 14:1–2.

78. Mark 14:18–25 par.

79. Josephus, *J.W.* 7.203, referred to crucifixion as "the most wretched of deaths" and, *J.W.* 5.451, described how "soldiers out of rage and hatred amused themselves by nailing their prisoners in different postures" (Thackeray, LCL); Cicero, *Verr.* 2.5.165, described it as "that cruel and disgusting penalty" (Greenwood, LCL)); and Seneca, *Ep.* 101.10–14, advised suicide as a way to escape the horrors of crucifixion. See also Hengel, *Crucifixion*, 22–32.

80. 1 Cor 1:18; cf. his emphasis on preaching Christ crucified in 1 Cor 1:23; 2:1–2; Gal 3:1.

81. Gal 3:13; cf. Deut 21:23.

82. Phil 2:8.

83. Rom 8:17; 2 Cor 1:5; Phil 3:10; cf. Col 1:24.

in salvation,[84] and 1 Peter draws on the example of Jesus in enduring suffering.[85] Some of this is probably implicit in the Gospels, judging from the extensive description each of them gives of Jesus' death—far more attention than any other ancient writer gave to a crucifixion.[86] However, apart from the occasional reference to Scripture being fulfilled in a particular way,[87] it is not clear from the Gospels why, if Jesus had to die, he had to die *in this way*. The Gospels seem to be concerned to portray Jesus' innocence and his character throughout this ordeal; however it is not clear that their perspective would have been significantly different had Jesus been, say, stoned or beheaded. It may be that if Jesus believed he was going to die in Jerusalem then to do so publicly as a martyr might have brought more attention to his cause, and crucifixion was the most public form of execution; or it may be that Jesus foresaw the significance his death would have for his followers as a supreme example of persevering in the face of hardship, and crucifixion provided a better opportunity to do that than other forms of execution would have. But crucifixion had such a negative stigma attached to it[88] that such a death might actually risk his being discredited. It seems that the only way he could have wanted to be crucified is if he truly believed that God would somehow vindicate him.

---

84. Heb 2:9–10.

85. 1 Pet 2:21–23; 4:1, 13; cf. Heb 12:1–2.

86. Hengel, *Crucifixion*, 25.

87. See, e.g., John 19:34–37.

88. Evidence for the negative stigma associated with crucifixion is widespread. Paul speaks of the foolishness of the cross which is "a stumbling block to Jews and folly to Gentiles" (1 Cor 1:23). Justin's defense against the charge that Christianity is nonsense reflects the public opinion of the day: "For they proclaim our madness to consist in this, that we give to a crucified man a place second to the unchangeable and eternal God, the Creator of all" (*1 Apol.* 13 (ANF)). The Alexamanos Graffito (ca. 200 CE), discovered on Palatine Hill in Rome, which depicts a man worshipping a figure on a cross having the head of an ass, is an anti-Christian parody that demonstrates the contempt people had for crucified criminals and the apparent absurdity of the Christians' veneration of a crucified man. And the relative sparseness of the mention of crucifixion in Roman writers, in comparison to the prevalence of its occurrence in the empire, is indicative of the fact that "the Roman world was largely unanimous that crucifixion was a horrific, disgusting business" (Hengel, *Crucifixion*, 37). For further examples see ibid., 1–10.

More could be said about how Jesus may have understood the significance of his own death.[89] For our purposes, however, with regard to the sayings of Jesus to be considered below, it is enough to establish that violence—especially crucifixion—was part of the context in which he lived and that he must have anticipated the possibility of his own death.

Conceptual Background for Jesus' "Dying in Order to Find Life" Sayings

Before examining Jesus' sayings themselves that have to do with dying in order to find life, I will explore the possibility of Jesus drawing on ideas from the Old Testament or from Hellenism—specifically the concept of noble death.

The Old Testament

There is not a great deal of Old Testament background for the image of dying in order to gain life. The psalmist often prays for God to rescue his life from danger; on occasion he speaks of God saving him from the brink of death.[90] Israel's experience of exile could be likened to a death, and her release to a gaining of new life. In the context of warning Israel of the curses that would ensue if she did not keep the covenant with Yahweh, the book of Deuteronomy likens God's punishment for disobedience, which includes exile, to death;[91] hence the choice at the time of covenant renewal is between life and death.[92] Ezekiel's vision of a valley of dry bones coming to life portrays Israel's exile as a kind of death and her restoration as a coming to life again.[93] Also, if the servant in the fourth Servant Song of Isaiah was understood in the original context to be Israel,[94] then exile would both be likened to

89. See above, p. 145.

90. E.g., Pss 9:13; 16:10; 18:4–6; 23:4; 30:3; 49:15; 56:13; 68:20; 86:13; 103:4; 116:8.

91. Deut 28:15–68, esp. vv. 22, 26, 45, 61, 63.

92. Deut 30:15–20.

93. Ezek 37:1–14. See Allen, *Ezekiel 20–48*, 187–88; Greenberg, *Ezekiel 21–37*, 747–49.

94. See Isa 41:8–9; 43:10; 44:1–2, 21; 45:4; 48:20; 49:3. The identification of the servant in Second Isaiah is complicated by the fact that while these texts speak col-

death[95] and be seen to be beneficial for the nation in that it atoned for sin.[96] Thus, there is in the Old Testament the image of God rescuing his people from death, of God's people (metaphorically) going through death and being brought to life again, and of this death having been beneficial to the people. However, there is no instance where people are enjoined to experience death so that they might gain life. Apart from the consequence of old age, death in the Old Testament, real or metaphorical, is always a tragedy or a punishment.

The Concept of Noble Death

David Seeley has argued that the concept of noble death, popular in the Greco-Roman world, and particularly in the Cynic-Stoic circles, is the proper background against which to read Jesus' "taking up one's cross" saying in Matt 10:38//Luke 14:27.[97]

The ideal of dying willingly for the sake of others or for important causes was highly valued in both Greek and Roman societies.[98] As early as Homer we find evidence that the Greeks praised those who died heroically in battle: Achilles, for example, speaks of his pending death in battle as a means of gaining imperishable renown.[99] Xenophon observes that in war, those who are anxious to save their lives are typically the ones to die, whereas those who accept the inevitability of death and who "strive to meet death nobly" are more likely to live a long life.[100] Numerous plays of Euripides portray people who willingly sacrifice

---

lectively of Israel as Yahweh's servant, one text in particular seems to have in view an individual who has a ministry to Israel (Isa 49:5–6); in other texts the identification of the servant is ambiguous. See further Reventlow, "Basic Issues," 23–38; and Clements, "Isaiah 53," 39–54.

95. Isa 53:8–9.

96. Isa 53:4–5, 10–12; cf. 40:2.

97. Seeley, "Jesus' Death," 222–34.

98. See van Henten and Avemarie, *Martyrdom*, 9–23; Droge and Tabor, *Noble Death*, 17–51.

99. Homer, *Il.* 9.410–16; cf. 22:303–5: Hector's last wish: "Not without a struggle let me die, nor ingloriously, but having done some great deed for men yet to be born to hear" (Murray & Wyatt, LCL); Herodotus, *Hist.* 1.30: Tellus, an Athenian, is praised for having "crowned his life with a most glorious death" when "he attacked and routed the enemy" (Godley, LCL).

100. Xenophon, *Anab.*, 3.1.43 (Brownson, LCL).

themselves in order to appease the gods or a spirit and thereby win a victory or save someone from peril.[101] Funeral orations were composed praising soldiers who died in battle: Demosthenes, for example, honors those who died at the Battle of Chaeronaea (338 BCE):

> For, since they scorned the love of life that is inborn in all men and chose rather to die nobly than to live and look upon Greece in misfortune, how can they have failed to leave behind them a record of valour surpassing all power of words to express?[102]

In the philosophical tradition, the noble death par excellence was that of Socrates—someone who lived consistently in the pursuit of virtue and in obedience to the gods and, when condemned by others, willingly accepted the consequence of death rather than altering his convictions.[103] For this reason the Stoic philosopher Epictetus depicts Socrates as the ideal philosopher in part because of how he died: "he is saved by death, and not by flight";[104] and so the memory of Socrates' death becomes as important as the memory of his deeds and words.[105] He also points to Diogenes, the proto-Cynic, as a model of freedom, for he refused to be attached to anything—property, friends, family, even his own body—and so in the end he died "cheerfully."[106] Aristotle describes the virtuous person as one who, if necessary, would lay down

---

101. Euripides, *Iph. aul.* 1368–1401: Iphigeneia, the commander's daughter, agrees to sacrifice her life to the goddess Artemis in order to ensure victory over the Trojans; *Phoen.* 913–14, 930–59: Menoeceus is sacrificed in order to appease the gods and to save his home town of Thebes; *Hec.* 38–41, 367–78, 448–49, 484–582: Polyxena appeases the spirit of Achilles by being sacrificed following the fall of Troy; *Alcestis*: a play about a wife who agrees to sacrifice her own life in the place of her husband.

102. Demosthenes, *Epitaph.* 60.1. For other examples, see Thucydides 2.34–46: Pericles' speech regarding the victims of the war; Plato, *Menex.*: Socrates' account of a funeral oration by Aspasia; Hyperides, *Speech* 6: Hyperides' funeral oration for those who died in the Lamian war (322 BCE).

103. See Plato's record of his defense in *Apol.* 28A–30B; cf. *Phaed.* 58E–59A.

104. Epictetus, *Diatr.* 4.1.165 (Oldfather, LCL); cf. idem., 1.9.25: Socrates compared remaining true to one's calling to the soldier willing to die rather than desert his post; idem., 4.1.161: Socrates chose to preserve his honor; idem., 4.1.168–69: "[I]f we were useful to men by living, should we not have done much more good to men by dying when we ought, and as we ought? And now that Socrates is dead the memory of him is no less useful to men, nay, is perhaps even more useful, than what he did or said while he still lived" (Oldfather, LCL).

105. Epictetus, *Diatr.* 4.1.168–69.

106. Ibid., 4.1.151–54.

his life for his friends and country, thereby gaining nobility.[107] And Philostratus affirms that "for the wise it is more proper to die on behalf of their beliefs."[108]

Roman writers also admired the example of Socrates: Tacitus likens the deaths of Seneca and of Thrasea Paetus to that of Socrates.[109] Seneca highlights the example of Socrates, along with many others, to encourage his readers that death is not to be feared;[110] he also comments that stories of noble deaths were a popular topic for school curriculum.[111] In the context of battle, the Romans practiced what they called the *devotio*—a commitment made by a commander or soldier in which he dedicated himself and/or the army of the enemy to the gods of the underworld. Livy, for example, in describing a battle between Rome and the Latins (340 BCE), tells of how one of the commanders, Decius Mus, when seeing that the battle was not going well, performed a ceremonial rite of dedication and then charged at the enemy in a suicide mission.[112] According to Livy, his death served as an atonement for the gods[113] who then granted Rome the victory. Interestingly, Decius' son met a similar fate.[114] Van Henten and Avemarie comment: "The *devotio* . . . was a self-sacrifice that brought atonement in the form of compensation to the gods, and a substitute death at the same time, since one died instead of many."[115]

Similar sayings do appear in the Jewish tradition, but not until well after Jesus: one comes from the Babylonian Talmud: "What shall a man do to live? They replied: Let him mortify himself. What should a man do to kill himself? They replied: Let him keep himself alive."[116]

107. Aristotle, *Eth. Nic.* 9.8.9 [1169A].

108. Philostratus, *Vit. Apoll.* 7.14.2 (Jones, LCL).

109. Tacitus, *Ann.* 15.60–64; 16.34–35.

110. Seneca, *Ep.* 24.

111. Seneca, *Ep.* 24.6.

112. Livy 8.9.1–14.

113. Livy 8.9.9–10: he charged into the enemy "as though sent from heaven to expiate all anger of the gods, and to turn aside destruction from his people and bring it on their adversaries" (Foster, LCL); cf. Statius, *Theb.* 10.799.

114. Livy 10.28.12–18.

115. Van Henten and Avemarie, *Martyrdom*, 20–21.

116. *b. Tamid* 32a. On this Nolland, *Matthew*, 443, comments: "In the context of the piety represented, mortifying oneself is likely to mean study and hard work, and possibly self-deprivation; keeping oneself alive is likely to connote self-indulgence, but also possibly survival by means of apostasy."

Another comes from Syriac Menander who speaks of the reward for those who fight nobly and die in battle: "Do not fall back in battle; for whosoever does not fall back in battle and gives himself unto death, shall immediately find life and a good name and he shall be praised."[117]

What is the likelihood that Jesus came into contact with the noble death tradition in Galilee? While we know that Hellenism was widespread even among Jews, and that there were Gentiles living in Galilee (Sepphoris, Tiberias), it is difficult to tell the extent of this influence in the rural areas in which Jesus moved. Although the point is debated, that Jesus was in touch with some Hellenistic traditions seems to be suggested by the similarity between him and the Cynics.[118] With regard to Jesus' sayings that connect discipleship with death, it cannot be denied that there is some similarity with the noble death tradition which was generally popular throughout the Hellenistic world, and expressed by Cynics, and it is at least possible that Jesus came into contact with proponents of this view. We should bear in mind, however, that admitting a possible influence on Jesus is not the same as categorizing him: similarity does not entail identity. Jesus may have borrowed some Cynic ideas or sayings, but there is plenty of evidence to show that he was thoroughly Jewish in orientation. By attending synagogue[119] and showing respect for the law[120] and the authority[121] of Moses, even in the detail of wearing a cloak with the Jewish tassels,[122]

---

117. *Syr. Men.* 315–19 (Baarda, *OTP*).

118. The literature here is extensive. Principal proponents in favor of there being Cynic influence on Jesus are: Crossan, *Historical Jesus*, esp. 421–22; idem., "Open Healing," 16–18; Mack, *Myth of Innocence*, 67–74; idem., *Lost Gospel*, esp. 114–21; idem., "Cynic-Like Jesus," 25–36; Downing, *Christ and the Cynics*; idem., *Cynics and Christian Origins*; idem., "Cynics and Early Christianity," 281–304; idem., "Deeper Reflections," 97–104; idem., "Jewish Cynic Jesus," 184–214; cf. Seeley, "Cynics Revisited," 704–12. For critical assessments of this view, see: Betz, "Jesus and the Cynics," 453–75; Horsley, "Itinerant Cynic," 68–97; Eddy, "Jesus as Diogenes," 449–69; Aune, "Jesus and Cynics," 176–92; Tuckett, "Cynic Q," 349–76.

119. Mark 1:21//Luke 4:31; Mark 1:23//Luke 4:33; Matt 4:23//Mark 1:39//Luke 4:44; Matt 9:35; Matt 12:9//Mark 3:1//Luke 6:6; Matt 13:54//Mark 6:2//Luke 4:16. Luke 4:15; 13:10; John 6:59.

120. Matt 5:17–18//Luke 16:17; Matt 7:12; Matt 8:4//Mark 1:44//Luke 5:14; Mark 7:10; Matt 22:35–40//Mark 8:28–34//Luke 10:25–28; Matt 23:23.

121. Matt 23:2.

122. Matt 9:20//Luke 8:44; Matt 14:36//Mark 6:56.

he is hardly playing the role of a Cynic who shows disdain for social conventions.

Jesus' Sayings about Dying in Order to Find Life

We turn now to the sayings of Jesus themselves which connect his death with discipleship. Jesus' anticipation that he would be killed, as I have argued above, provides the historical context for these sayings, and they become more credible as sayings of Jesus if he is aware of the dangers ahead; and the Hellenistic tradition of the noble death provides a conceptual background from which Jesus could have drawn in developing his own teaching.

Take Up Your Cross

Q, Mark, and the *Gospel of Thomas* each have sayings about taking up one's cross and following Jesus:

> Q: He who does not take his cross and follow me is not worthy of me. (Matt 10:38)
>
> Whoever does not bear his own cross and come after me, cannot be my disciple. (Luke 14:27)
>
> Mark: If anyone would come after me, let him deny himself and take up his cross and follow me. (Mark 8:34,[123] par. in Matt 16:24//Luke 9:23[124])
>
> Thomas: And (he who does not) hate his brothers and sisters and take up his cross like me, will not be worthy of me. (*Gos. Thom.* 55:2)

The Q version of this saying has clearly been modified by Matthew and/or Luke. John Meier argues that Matthew's ending—"is not worthy of me"—is an assimilation to the preceding verse (Matt 10:37), and suggests the Q saying read as follows: "Whoever does not take [or: carry] his cross and come after [i.e., follow] me cannot be my disciple."[125]

---

123. Modified from the RSV.

124. Both Matthew and Luke make some minor vocabulary changes; the most substantial is Luke's addition of "daily" following "cross." Note that the reference to taking up the/your cross in some MSS of Mark 10:21 (e.g., A, W, Byz.) is best explained as a scribal gloss.

125. Meier, *Marginal Jew*, 3:66.

While the Markan version is clearly similar to Q with the common image of taking up one's cross and following Jesus, it is also dissimilar in its positive perspective ("If anyone would . . . let him . . ." over against "Whoever does not . . . cannot be . . ."), structure (A¹–B¹–B²–A²),[126] and vocabulary ("deny himself," "follow"), implying that Mark and Q are independent of each other. If the saying is authentic, this could be an instance where Jesus himself gave more than one version on different occasions. The addition of "like me" in the *Gospel of Thomas* version is probably a later Christian attempt to make reference to Jesus carrying a cross; in addition, the reference to hating one's siblings could have arisen from reflection on the previous few verses in Matthew's account that speak of animosity within the family.

The authenticity of the saying of followers needing to take up their cross is supported by multiple attestation and by the shocking nature of the image: the thought that Jesus would have used an image as horrific and shameful as crucifixion to describe what would be required of those who wanted to follow him would have shocked Jesus' hearers; however, he was known to use some shocking images.[127] But the very mention of the cross, a central image throughout early Christianity, is seen by many to argue against authenticity. The Jesus Seminar concludes:

> The admonition to take up one's cross appeals to the fate of Jesus as the standard of commitment. It probably reflects a time when the Christian community was exposed to the pressures of persecution. There is no evidence that the cross served as a symbol of radical self-denial outside the context of the crucifixion of Jesus or prior to that event.[128]

This reflects a valid question: Is it not too coincidental to claim that Jesus made a "take up your cross" saying without knowing that he would eventually be crucified?

Four arguments, however, can be raised in response: (i) although in the Markan context it is almost certainly implied that Jesus too

---

126.   A¹: If any man would come after me   B¹: let him deny himself
B²: take up his cross   A²: follow me

127.   Note, for example, the image of people making themselves eunuchs for the kingdom (Matt 19:12).

128.   Funk et al., *Five Gospels*, 78–79. The Jesus Seminar ranked all of the "take up your cross" sayings as black (ibid., 78–79, 174–75, 208, 313, 353).

is bearing a cross, the focus in this saying is entirely on his followers bearing their own crosses. Had this been a Christian creation we
might have expected something like "take up *my* cross," the addition
of "like me" in *Thomas*, or at least a clearer distinction between the
significance of Jesus' cross/death and that of the disciples. (ii) The
image of crucifixion was both widespread and graphic—indeed the
most graphic form of execution of the day—making it the most suit-
able image to use in a saying intended to alert would-be followers to
the costs of discipleship.[129] (iii) Although there are no contemporary
Semitic texts that speak of carrying a cross,[130] Martin Hengel notes
some Roman and Greek sayings where cross is used metaphorically:[131]
(a) in advising his students against provoking someone in a legal dispute, Epictetus says, "if you wish to be crucified, wait, and the cross
will come";[132] (b) Seneca likens personal desires to "crosses into which
each one of you drives his own nails";[133] (c) Philo speaks of the human
condition of people who are enslaved to the desires of their bodies
as having souls that "depend on and hang from lifeless things, for,
like men crucified and nailed to a tree, they are affixed to perishable
materials till they die,"[134] and he likens the mind devoid of art to "a
headless corpse . . . nailed like the crucified to the tree of helpless and
poverty-stricken indiscipline."[135] And (iv) anticipating the discussion
to come, the idea that following Jesus would involve a sacrifice of one's
life coheres with other sayings of Jesus. Thus, while on the one hand
it may be somewhat coincidental that Jesus would make such a cross

129. On the graphic nature of crucifixion, see Hengel, *Crucifixion*, 22–32. He
writes: "crucifixion was a punishment in which the caprice and sadism of the execu-
tioners were given full rein" (25); cf. Josephus, *J.W.* 5.449–51.

130. Cf. a similar image in *Gen. Rab.* 56.3 (on Gen. 22:6) which speaks of Isaac
carrying the wood for the sacrifice of himself as "one who carries his stake [of execu-
tion] on his shoulder." It is debated whether Jewish reflection on the significance of
the sacrifice of Isaac—commonly referred to as the Aqedah—pre-dated the rise of
Christianity or whether it developed (at least in part) in response to the destruction of
the temple and the emergence of Christian views of atonement. On the former view,
see Daly, "Sacrifice of Isaac," 45–75; on the latter view, see Davies and Chilton, "The
Aqedah," 514–46.

131. Hengel, *Crucifixion*, 66–68.

132. Epictetus, *Diatr.* 2.2.20 (Oldfather, LCL).

133. Seneca, *Dial. 7, Vita beata* 19.3, translation by Hengel, *Crucifixion*, 67.

134. Philo, *Post.* 61 (Colson & Whitaker, LCL).

135. Philo, *Somn.* 2.213 (Colson & Whitaker, LCL).

saying and then be crucified himself (assuming he was not able to fore-see the manner of his own death), on the other there is good reason to believe he could have used the image of the cross to depict the high demand of discipleship.

But what would Jesus have meant by taking up one's cross? The image derives from the Roman custom of requiring condemned pris-oners to carry their own crosses (or more accurately, the cross-beam) to the place of crucifixion.[136] Johannes Schneider surveys the range of meanings commentators have proposed:[137] (i) Jesus was using an existing idiom, perhaps coined by Zealots, in order to challenge his followers to prepare themselves for opposition from the Romans; (ii) Jesus foresaw his own fate and was challenging his followers to commit themselves to the extent that they would follow him to death; (iii) the original saying had to do with taking up a yoke[138]—that is, the wooden frame used to harness working animals together, which was used as a metaphor for service and obedience[139]—which was then changed af-ter the crucifixion with the substitution of the word "cross"; (iv) Jesus spoke metaphorically, likening the self-denial required for discipleship to a man condemned to death; and (v) Jesus spoke symbolically of a cultic marking for protection of those dedicated to God similar to the "ת"—the last letter of the Hebrew alphabet, written in Hebrew as an "X" at the time, and in Greek as a "T"—in one of Ezekiel's visions which protected those who wore it on their foreheads from judgment.[140] Davies and Allison add one more alternative: (vi) Jesus spoke ana-logically with reference to Isaac who bore wood for his own sacrifice, implying that his own followers must offer themselves as a sacrifice.[141]

While nuances may differ, several of these proposals are similar in essence: all of them imply a challenge to commitment. Some of them

136. Plutarch, *Sera* 9 [554B]: "every criminal who goes to execution must carry his own cross on his back" (de Lacy & Einarson, LCL).

137. Schneider, "σταυρός," 578–79; see his references to commentators in his footnotes.

138. See Matt 11:29.

139. See Fitzmyer, *Luke*, 1:785–86. Note that the rabbis often spoke of taking up the yoke of the law or the yoke of the kingdom. See Davies and Allison, *Matthew*, 2:289, esp. n. 241.

140. Ezek 9:4–6; cf. *Pss. Sol.* 15.8–10; Rev 7:2–3; 14:1; *Odes Sol.* 8.13.

141. Davies and Allison, *Matthew*, 2:223.

have in view the possibility of literal death for Jesus' followers—(i), (ii), and possibly (vi)—while others view taking up the cross metaphorically as referring to following Jesus' teaching (iii) or living sacrificially (iv), which could conceivably lead to death (vi). Proposal (v) seems unlikely since it does not cohere with anything else Jesus said or did. Proposal (iii) seems to be an attempt to avoid any reference to a cross by Jesus, but in light of our discussion above showing the possibility of Jesus' anticipation of his own death and of the prevalence of the image of crucifixion in Palestine, such a move is not necessary. Thus it is plausible that Jesus used an image of death—cross—to describe what would be required of his followers. Deciding whether Jesus had in view literal or metaphorical death is difficult without further information. It is certainly possible that he could have meant both.

Losing and Finding Life

Both Q and Mark also have sayings about losing life and finding/saving life, and John has a similar saying framed in terms of loving and hating life:

> Q: He who finds his life will lose it, and he who loses his life for my sake will find it. (Matt 10:39)

> Whoever seeks to gain his life will lose it, but whoever loses his life will preserve it. (Luke 17:33)

> Mark: For whoever would save his life will lose it; and whoever loses his life for my sake and the gospel's will save it. (Mark 8:35, par. in Matt 16:25//Luke 9:24[142])

> John: He who loves his life loses it, and he who hates his life in this world will keep it for eternal life. (John 12:25)

Here we have four versions of a similar aphorism about the paradox between holding on to life which leads to losing it and losing life which leads to finding it. Meier argues that the Markan and Q forms are probably independent of each other[143] but that they both could have

---

142. Both Matthew and Luke omit "and the gospel's," and Matthew has "find" instead of the second "save."

143. His argument for independence is: (i) Luke, who avoids doublets, has already used the saying, found in Mark, at Luke 9:24; (ii) both Matthew and Luke treat this saying in similar fashion (although Meier does not specify how: perhaps he has in

derived from a common Aramaic source, with a translation such as: "Whoever seeks to save his life will lose it; and whoever loses his life will save it."[144] The Jesus Seminar considered the Lukan version of the Q saying to be close to authentic.[145] The Johannine version is clearly similar, but also distinct enough to conclude it is independent of both Mark and Q.[146] After removing what appear to be redactional additions by John, Meier suggests the following as the original: "The one who loves his life will lose it, and the one who hates his life will keep it."[147] That we have an authentic saying of Jesus seems clear enough: it is multiply attested, its aphoristic form is similar to the form of other sayings of Jesus,[148] and its paradoxical juxtaposition of values is similar to the reversal of fortunes we see, for example, in Jesus' beatitudes.[149]

---

mind that both Matthew and Luke replaced Mark's "save" with different verbs but kept Mark's "lose" in both cases); and (iii) although Matthew and Luke place this saying in different contexts, they both place it within a body of Q material—Matthew at the end of his missionary discourse (Matt 10:5–42) and Luke imbedded in the discourse concerning the day of the Son of man (Luke 17:22–37); Meier, *Marginal Jew*, 3:58–59.

144. Ibid., 3:61. Meier argues that (i) Mark's "for my sake and the gospel's" is redactional on the basis that "gospel" is distinctively Markan and both the Lukan and the Johannine forms lack any qualification in the second half of the aphorism; (ii) the different verbs in Mark 8:35 and Luke 17:33 could be alternate translations from a common Aramaic source; and (iii) Matthew's "for my sake," his use of participles, and his substitution of "find" in the place of "save" or "preserve," are all redactional.

145. Funk et al., *Five Gospels*, 366–67, gave Luke 17:33 a pink ranking, which is close to Meier's proposed original.

146. In addition to the distinctive vocabulary in the Johannine version (the verbs "loves," "hates" and "keeps," and the phrases "in this world" and "for eternal life"), although John 12:25 has an antithetical structure, it does not have the chiastic structure evident particularly in Mark and Matthew. On hating one's life, see Luke 14:26: "If any one comes to me and does not hate his own father and mother . . . and even his own life, he cannot be my disciple" (cf. Matt 10:37). See further, Brown, *John*, 1:473–74.

147. Meier, *Marginal Jew*, 3:63. The Jesus Seminar ranked John 12:25 as gray, but the voting was strongly polarized. Those who voted in favor of authenticity argued (i) John 12:25 is similar to Luke 17:33 which was already ranked as pink; (ii) the aphoristic form of the saying is typical of Jesus and removable from its Johannine context; and (iii) the saying lacks any distinctively Christian theme. Others, however, argued that the love/hate contrast was typical Johannine language (Funk et al., *Five Gospels*, 442). Significantly, however, Jesus uses the love/hate contrast in Matt 6:24//Luke 16:13 ("either he will hate the one and love the other"), a saying which the Seminar ranked as pink (ibid., 151).

148. See Jeremias, *Theology*, 30–31.

149. See Luke 6:20–26.

This again appears to be an instance of an authentic saying that Jesus himself may have given in different forms.

Commenting on the Markan text, but equally applicable to the others, France insists that the possibility of literal loss of life is in view, but then he goes on:

> To extend this sense to the loss of privilege, advantage, reputation, comfort, and the like may be legitimate in principle, but only so long as this primary and more radical sense is not set aside. To cling to the things of this life, the things which humanity naturally values most, is the way to forfeit *true* life; clinging to life itself is the ultimate example of this concern, and is set in contrast with the acceptance of death (for the right reason) as the way to real life.[150]

This makes perfect sense if we understand that Jesus not only understood himself to be standing in the tradition of the persecuted prophet, but that he invited his followers to do the same.[151] By following the persecuted prophet one could also expect to face persecution, and hence, in some sense, a loss of life. But Jesus' point is that this vocation of proclaiming the kingdom and living by kingdom values is indeed the path to true life.[152] Thus, this saying has a similar meaning to the "take up your cross" saying, except that here "dying" is stated explicitly as a means to a benefit.

The Grain of Wheat

The fourth Gospel records a parabolic saying about a seed dying in order to grow:

> Truly, truly, I say to you, unless a grain of wheat falls into the earth and dies, it remains alone; but if it dies, it bears much fruit. (John 12:24)

There are Synoptic parables that liken the kingdom of God to seeds being sown and bringing forth fruit: the seed sown on different kinds

---

150. France, *Mark*, 340–41, emphasis original.

151. Matt 5:12//Luke 6:23.

152. Matt 6:25–33.

of ground,[153] the seed which grows secretly,[154] and the grain of mustard seed growing into a large bush.[155] But this is the only instance where the death of the seed is highlighted. Brown suggests that the mention of the seed bearing "much fruit" (πολὺν καρπόν) here is an allusion to the fruitfulness of the great tree in Nebuchadnezzar's dream in Dan 4,[156] to which, interestingly, the parable of the mustard seed also seems to allude with its image of the nesting birds.[157] This commonality, together with the common mention of the word "grain" (κόκκος), and the fact that Jesus told parables involving seeds, argues in favor of authenticity.[158]

The image of a grain of wheat dying and coming to life is often used in rabbinic literature with reference to the eschatological resurrection. Schnackenburg writes:

> It was an argument *a minori ad maius*: if the grain of wheat, which is laid naked in the ground, grows up again in however many changes of clothing, how much more will that be true of the just, who are buried in their garments (and will one day rise again in them).[159]

In the context of John's Gospel, the parable is clearly being applied to Jesus as he approaches his death: Jesus is the grain of wheat that will die in order to bear much fruit. While some of Jesus' parables have only one specific referent in view (particularly parables based on a narrative), we might expect in this case, where the parable is based on a natural process, that it would be appropriate to find application beyond the specific instance of Jesus' death, even if we did so metaphorically rather than literally. That John took this saying to be applicable to Jesus' followers is implied by verse 25 which speaks of losing and keeping life.

153. Matt 13:1–9//Mark 4:1–9//Luke 8:4–8.

154. Mark 4:26–29.

155. Matt 13:31–32//Mark 4:30–32//Luke 13:18–19.

156. The LXX of Dan 4:9 (MT 4:12) reads ὁ καρπὸς αὐτοῦ πολύς.

157. Brown, *John*, 1:472.

158. The Jesus Seminar ranked this text as gray, although the opinions were strongly divided. Tipping the balance in favor of inauthenticity was the appearance of the image of a sown seed being transformed into a resurrected body in 1 Cor 15:36–37, a text which was written prior to John. Of course this begs the question regarding Paul's source.

159. Schnackenburg, *John*, 2:383; cf. *b. Sanh.* 90b.

Sharing Jesus' Cup

In one other saying that alludes to death, Jesus implies that his disciples will suffer the same fate as he. In response to the request from James and John[160] that they be granted to sit on either side of him in his glory, Jesus says:

> You do not know what you are asking. Are you able to drink the cup that I drink, or to be baptized with the baptism with which I am baptized?

And in response to their affirmative reply, Jesus says:

> The cup that I drink you will drink; and with the baptism with which I am baptized, you will be baptized; but to sit at my right hand or at my left is not mine to grant, but it is for those for whom it has been prepared. (Mark 10:38–40, par. in Matt 20:22–23)[161]

In the Old Testament one's cup referred to one's lot in life, whether it be blessed[162] or cursed.[163] Very often the cup was used as a symbol for God's activity: he gives people the cup of salvation[164] or the cup of wrath or judgment.[165] And so one's lot was a direct reflection of the

160. Matthew has their mother making the request.

161. The Matthean text mentions drinking the cup but lacks any reference to baptism.

162. Pss 16:5: "The LORD is my chosen portion and my cup; thou holdest my lot"; 23:5: "my cup overflows."

163. Ps 11:6: "a scorching wind shall be the portion of their cup." Two Aramaic targums (*Tg. Neof.* Gen 40:23; *Tg. Neof.* Deut 32:1) use the idiom of tasting the "cup of death" simply as a way of speaking of one's death. One text from the Pseudepigrapha (*Mart. Ascen. Isa.* 5.13) in which Isaiah is about to be killed reads: "for me alone the Lord has mixed this cup" (Knibb, *OTP*). Cf. *T. Ab.* 1.3; 16.11.

164. Ps 116:13: "cup of salvation"; Jer 16:7: "cup of consolation."

165. Ps 75:8: all the wicked shall drain the draught the LORD pours from his cup; Isa 51:17: "the cup of his wrath," cf. v. 22; Jer 25:15: "the cup of the wine of wrath"; 49:12: even those who did not deserve punishment drank from the LORD's cup; 51:7: "Babylon was a golden cup in the LORD's hand"; Lam 4:21: Edom will also have to drink from the cup; Ezek 23:31–33: the cup is a symbol of judgment brought on Samaria and about to come on Jerusalem; Hab 2:16: "the cup in the LORD's right hand will come around to you, and shame will come upon your glory"; Zech 12:2: Jerusalem is to become "a cup of reeling"; cf. *Pss. Sol.* 8.14: "God . . . gave them a cup of undiluted wine to make them drunk" (Wright, *OTP*); Rev 14:10: "the cup of his anger"; 16:19. 1QpHab XI,10–15: "The cup of YHWH's right hand will turn against you and disgrace come upon your glory. . . . [T]he cup of [Go]d's anger will consume him." See further, Goppelt, "ποτήριον," 148–58.

cup handed to them by God.[166] The reference to baptism in this saying, however, does not seem to have any precedent outside the Gospels. Although used predominantly in the New Testament of a water rite, the word βαπτίζω can refer to being engulfed in an adverse situation,[167] and here we recall John the Baptist's use of it in connection with judgment.[168] In itself, the baptism saying does not appear to add anything that the cup saying did not already contain. They both speak of James and John sharing in what Jesus was about to go through.

The most significant difference in the Matthean text is the lack of any reference to baptism. Davies and Allison suggest that Matthew omitted this because he may have found it to be redundant (the baptism saying meaning essentially the same thing as the cup saying), obscure (what does being baptized with a baptism mean?) or misleading (perhaps by suggesting a sacramental interpretation of cup and baptism).[169] Koester, however, argues that the reference to baptism was not in Matthew's version of Mark, but was added later, "most likely a homiletic reference to the Christian sacraments, eucharist (drinking the cup) and baptism";[170] the language was presumably borrowed from the source of Luke 12:50. The coincidence between the Markan version of Jesus' saying and the Christian sacraments of the Lord's Supper and baptism suggests that Koester may be correct here. In favor of the authenticity of the cup saying, however, Casey argues that it is unlikely that the early church would have created such a saying that did

---

166. See further, *Mart. Ascen. Isa.* 5.13: "for me alone the Lord has mixed the cup" (Knibb, *OTP*); *Mart. Pol.* 14.2: "I bless you for making me worthy of this day and hour, that I may receive a share among the number of the martyrs in the cup of your Christ" (Ehrman, LCL). Rabbinic writings use the image of the cup to speak of one's lot in the age to come, whether reward or punishment (*Midr. Ps.* 75.4; *Sipre Deut* §324 (on Deut 32:34); *b. Ḥul* 92a). Note also Plautus, *Cas.* 933: "And then . . . I took to my heels and made for the door . . . so that the old man might have a dose from the same cup as myself" (Nixon, LCL).

167. Isa 21:4 (LXX): "lawlessness overwhelms me [ἡ ἀνομία με βαπτίζει]" (my translation); Josephus, *J.W.* 4.137: "it was just this circumstance [the actions of the Zealots] which . . . eventually wrecked the city [ὕστερον ἐβάπτισεν τὴν πόλιν]" (Thackeray, LCL); Plutarch, *Galb.* 21.2: "immersed [βεβαπτισμένον] in debts" (Perrin, LCL); Diodorus, *Bib. hist.* 1.73.6: "they do not swamp [βαπτίζουσι] the private citizens by taxation" (Oldfather, LCL).

168. Matt 3:10–11//Luke 3:9, 16.

169. Davies and Allison, *Matthew*, 3:89.

170. Koester, *Ancient Christian Gospels*, 277–79.

not support their belief in "the uniqueness of [Jesus'] atoning death."[171] The cup saying, as it stands, is explicable without reference to the Lord's Supper, even if when read in retrospect it does have sacramental overtones; it is a statement that emphasizes the disciples' need for commitment to and solidarity with Jesus, without any sense of there being a unique significance to Jesus' death. This sounds more like a statement from Jesus than from the early church. Finally, Bultmann's suggestion that verses 38–39 are "a manifest *vaticinium ex eventu*"[172] created in light of James' martyrdom[173] founders on the fact that there is no early evidence of John being martyred,[174] nor is there any mention here of a reward for martyrdom that might have been expected from a Christian source.[175]

Jesus' question, "Are you able. . . ?" implies that drinking this cup involves a challenge of some kind. That Jesus understood this cup to entail death for himself is confirmed by his prayer in Gethsemane for God "to remove this cup from me."[176] Furthermore, Jesus' saying shows that he expected that his followers would somehow share in his experience, and this is confirmed by his sharing the "cup of his blood" at the Last Supper, giving the cup to his disciples just as God had given the cup to him.[177]

Metaphorical Expressions of Dying

We find, therefore, in Q, Mark, and John, Jesus using language of dying to describe the life of discipleship: followers must carry their own cross, lose their life in order to find it, die in order to bear fruit, and drink from the cup Jesus drinks from. In addition, Davies and Allison note that the first three of these sayings have been brought together in Mark (8:34–35), John (12:24–25), and possibly Q (Matt 10:38–39)—three independent sources—implying that the combination of them must

171. Casey, *Aramaic Sources*, 206.

172. Bultmann, *History*, 24.

173. Acts 12:2.

174. Casey, *Aramaic Sources*, 206.

175. See Evans, *Mark 8:27—16:20*, 117.

176. Matt 26:39//Mark 14:36//Luke 22:42. This saying has a good claim to authenticity in light of the embarrassment it could have caused early Christians. Cf. John 18:11.

177. Matt 26:27–28//Mark 14:23–24//Luke 22:20.

have occurred very early, perhaps even going back to Jesus.[178] Thus, it would appear to be justifiable to interpret these sayings in light of each other: for example, taking up one's cross is similar to losing one's life in order to find it.

But can we be any more specific regarding the concrete expression of those who took up their cross or lost their life in order to find it? First, is the death Jesus had in view literal or metaphorical? One can certainly imagine the leader of a movement telling his followers that they need to be prepared to lay down their lives for the cause. This seems plausible for Jesus: if he believed it likely that he would be killed as a consequence of his ministry, presumably he would have considered the possibility that his followers who were assisting him would meet the same fate, and therefore would have required a level of commitment commensurate with that reality. That is not to say that Jesus believed they would all be killed; some may be, but all would need to count the cost before signing on.

This is consistent with Jesus' predictions that his followers would face opposition and persecution. In a Q beatitude Jesus calls his followers blessed when they face persecution.[179] When commissioning his disciples for mission Jesus says that he is sending them out as sheep before wolves[180] and indicates that some people would not accept their message.[181] On another occasion he challenges his disciples to make public the things they have learned from him in secret, and not to fear those who could kill them[182]—an odd exhortation if there would be no serious opposition. Also, Jesus indicates that opposition would arise from within his followers' own families.[183] And finally, in his dis-

178. Davies and Allison, *Matthew*, 2:223.

179. Matt 5:11–12//Luke 6:22–23. Although the Jesus Seminar ranked this saying as gray, the members also agreed that "some earlier form of [this] beatitude . . . may go back to Jesus" (Funk et al., *Five Gospels*, 290).

180. Matt 10:16//Luke 10:3.

181. Matt 10:14//Mark 6:11//Luke 9:5; Luke 10:10–12.

182. Matt 10:27–28//Luke 12:3–4; cf. *Gos. Thom.* 33:1. The Jesus Seminar ranked this saying as black on the basis that persecution occurred in the early church but not during Jesus' ministry (Funk et al., *Five Gospels*, 336). But our historical argument given above suggests that opposition was certainly part of Jesus' experience, and persecution would easily have been seen on the horizon.

183. Matt 10:34–36//Luke 12:51–53. The Jesus Seminar doubted the authenticity of this saying (ranked as black and gray respectively) because (i) it contrasts with Jesus' preaching elsewhere of unqualified love (e.g., Matt 5:43–48), (ii) here Jesus re-

course on the Mount of Olives, Jesus predicts severe persecution for his followers.[184]

It is probable, however, that Jesus also intended a metaphorical understanding of taking up the cross or of losing one's life. The fact that we have four different sayings that speak of his followers dying, and that each saying is not univocal—for example, "you need to be prepared to die for the cause"—but rather is somewhat cryptic in that they could be understood either literally or metaphorically—"take up your cross," "lose your life," "a seed in the ground must die," "you will drink the cup that I drink"—suggests that Jesus was trying to communicate a truth that could come to expression in different ways in different people's lives. Some would be martyred for their faith, others not; but all would be called on, in some way, to lose their life in order to find it.

In various ways the Gospel writers give some indication of how they saw this "loss of life" expressed in the lives of Jesus' followers. Luke suggests a metaphorical understanding of taking up the cross by adding the word "daily,"[185] suggesting that Jesus had in view the nature of discipleship and not simply its end. In a number of ways Jesus indicates that following him would involve personal sacrifice. He told two parables that teach that the kingdom of God demands total commitment: the kingdom is like a hidden treasure or a precious pearl such that when someone finds it they sell all that they have in order

---

fers to himself in the first person which presumably he did not do, and (iii) it alludes to Scripture (Mic 7:5–6) which, in their opinion, is something early Christians could do but not Jesus (ibid., 173–74, 342–43). Regarding (i), it is difficult to understand why the early church would have created such a saying; regarding (ii) without any further information, this seems to be based on a questionable assumption that Jesus did not see himself as having a significant role or place in the message of the kingdom; and regarding (iii) one wonders why a Jew presumably brought up in the synagogue and involved in a ministry for the restoration of Israel would not be able to reflect on Scripture, or whether the most likely explanation for early Christian reflection on Scripture is that Christians were following their leader's example!

184. Matt 10:17–22 + 24:9–14//Mark 13:9–13//Luke 21:12–19. The Jesus Seminar ranked this material as black since these sayings "all reflect detailed knowledge of events that took place—or ideas that were current—*after* Jesus' death" (ibid., 110; emphasis original). Perhaps so. And yet, there is nothing inherently unlikely in the hypothesis that if Jesus believed his own end was near, he would have warned his followers of coming persecution.

185. Luke 9:23.

to attain it.[186] Elsewhere Jesus makes it clear that the sacrifice could involve personal possessions.[187] He emphasizes the incompatibility of serving both God and mammon:[188] his followers must demonstrate exclusive commitment to God and avoid the competing demands of the pursuit of possessions.[189] Mark tells of a man who had kept all the commands of the law since his youth, but whom Jesus challenged to sell his possessions, give to the poor, and come follow him.[190]

In addition, the Gospel writers' arrangement of material around the various sayings concerning "dying" suggests other ways the sacrifice could be expressed. For example, the editor of Q juxtaposed Jesus' saying about taking up one's cross with a saying about the need for followers to place higher priority on Jesus than on one's own family.[191] Matthew emphasized this connection further by adding, in the same context, another Q saying regarding the effect of Jesus' ministry in causing family strife.[192] This coheres with two other sayings that imply that those who followed Jesus by traveling with him (as opposed to sympathizers who stayed at home) often had to sacrifice family relationships in light of the pressing demands of the kingdom: (i) to one

186. Matt 13:44, 45–46; cf. *Gos. Thom.* 76, 109. The Jesus Seminar ranks both of these parables as pink (Funk et al., *Five Gospels*, 196–97). Cf. Luke 9:62; Matt 6:33.

187. Hengel, *Charismatic Leader*, 18–34, notes that the requirement to give up possessions was commonplace for followers of charismatic prophets leading people into holy war, apocalyptic prophets, and Greek philosophers, but interestingly not for students of rabbis.

188. Matt 6:24//Luke 16:13; cf. *Gos. Thom.* 47. The Greek μαμωνᾶς appears to be a loan word from Aramaic denoting one's possessions (see Hauck, "μαμωνᾶς," 388–90). The Jesus Seminar ranks this saying as pink (Funk et al, *Five Gospels*, 151).

189. Several similar sayings can be found in both Jewish and Hellenistic texts; see Nolland, *Matthew*, 304–5 n. 388.

190. Mark 10:17–22 par. The major reason the Jesus Seminar ranked the saying in Mark 10:21 as gray was the promise of a reward ("treasure in heaven") which the members thought was a post-Easter adaptation. The earlier part of the saying regarding selling everything "seemed to many Fellows to be consonant with [Jesus'] teaching about wealth" (Funk et al., *Five Gospels*, 91). The connection between renouncing possession and taking up one's cross has often been made in the history of the church; see Davies and Allison, *Matthew*, 3:49 n. 70.

191. Matt 10:37–38//Luke 14:26–27; cf. *Gos. Thom.* 55:1–2. The Jesus Seminar gave Luke 14:26 a pink ranking (Funk et al., *Five Gospels*, 353). Hengel, *Charismatic Leader*, 13, suggests the background for this and other sayings regarding family relationships lies in texts that speak of family turmoil as a sign of judgment prior to the end of this age (Mic 7:6; Zech 13:3; *1 En.* 99.5; 100.1–2; *Jub.* 23.16; *2 Bar.* 70.6).

192. Matt 10:34–36, par. in Luke 12:51–53; cf. Mark 13:12 par.

would-be follower who asked if he could first bury his father, Jesus said, "Let the dead bury the dead";[193] and (ii) on another occasion Peter remarks, "we have left everything and followed you,"[194] to which Jesus responds with a word of assurance that those who have left their houses and families for his sake will be compensated.[195]

Another form of sacrifice suggested by the Gospels concerns the quest for honor. We recall that in the context of the "drinking the cup" saying, James and John were requesting positions of privilege and power in the kingdom.[196] Mark concludes this account with Jesus' say-

---

193. Matt 8:22//Luke 9:60 (cf. 1 Kgs 19:19–21). The Jesus Seminar ranked this saying as pink (Funk et al., *Five Gospels*, 160–61, 316–17). This saying has been the subject of much discussion due to its apparent disregard for traditional Jewish piety based on the fifth commandment: "Honour your father and your mother" (Exod 20:12//Deut 5:16; see Hengel, *Charismatic Leader*, 3–15; Sanders, *Jesus and Judaism*, 252–55). Davies and Allison, *Matthew*, 2:56–57, survey various attempts to avoid this conclusion: (i) the Aramaic saying has been mistranslated or the Greek text has been corrupted (perhaps Jesus meant to let the burial society bury the dead); (ii) the idiom has been misunderstood (the would-be follower meant that his father was aged and needed care until he died); (iii) there were extenuating circumstances not mentioned in the text (e.g., perhaps there were other family members who could attend to the father); and (iv) the saying was proverbial without any literal application. Davies and Allison, however, argue that the saying should be taken at face value, as shocking as it may be, but liken it to God's instructions (a) to Jeremiah to be celibate and to refrain from both celebrating and mourning (Jer 16:1–9), and (b) to Ezekiel not to mourn for the dead (Ezek 24:15–18): "When the hour of crisis comes, God communicates through a dramatic and unforgettable flouting of custom" (ibid., 2:57). Bockmuehl, *Jewish Law*, 34–48, tentatively proposes another line of interpretation: that Jesus' saying should be understood in light of the radical nature of Nazirite vows (which were popular in first-century Palestine), implying that Jesus' "message and lifestyle . . . shared with the Nazirite way of life a comprehensive vision of holiness (note Num 6.5, 8) and purity as constituted by God. . . . In this context, Jesus' challenge to a prospective disciple to 'let the dead bury their own dead' would indeed raise eyebrows. But it is by no means necessary or even plausible to see it as a significant attack on the Torah, or even as deliberately requiring disobedience to it (so Hengel, Sanders). Instead, the notion of a special religious duty transcending even basic family obligations is one that would have been culturally familiar to Jesus' audience" (46–47).

194. Mark 10:28 par.

195. Matt 19:29//Mark 10:29–30//Luke 18:29–30. Although the Jesus Seminar ranked this saying as gray, the members admitted that "the saying could be attributed to Jesus" if one were to eliminate "for my sake and for the gospel" (Mark 10:29) and "with persecutions, and in the age to come eternal life" (Mark 10:30) (Funk et al., *Five Gospels*, 93). That is, they agreed that Jesus promised compensation for those who left houses and families.

196. Matt 20:21–23//Mark 10:37–40.

ing about service being the appropriate path to greatness, which stands in contrast to the exercise of authority commonly seen in the world:

> You know that those who are supposed to rule over the Gentiles lord it over them, and their great men exercise authority over them. But it shall not be so among you; but whoever would be great among you must be your servant, and whoever would be first among you must be slave of all. (Mark 10:42–44, par. in Matt 20:25–27//Luke 22:25–26)[197]

Matthew includes this saying in the same context as Mark, but Luke includes it in the context of a dispute among all the disciples about which of them was the greatest, which occurred immediately after the institution of the Lord's Supper,[198] again underlining the connection between death and service as the means to greatness.

Finally, a saying about the last becoming first and the first last appears several times in the Gospels. Matthew concludes his parable of the workers in the vineyard with it;[199] Luke places it in a context where Jesus says that some who expect to be welcomed in the kingdom will be left out and will be replaced by people from the east, west, north, and south.[200] But Mark's placements are significant for our purpose: in one case he places it immediately following the saying about those who forfeit house and family being compensated—which we have already seen to be an example of "cross-bearing"—and immediately before Jesus' third passion prediction.[201] And in a second case he places it in the context of the disciples arguing who would be the greatest, which followed immediately after Jesus' second passion prediction.[202] And immediately after this text he gives the account of Jesus taking

197. Although the Jesus Seminar ranked this saying as gray, the members conceded: "The sayings in Mark 10:42–44 and their parallels vaguely reflect something Jesus might have said: those who aspire to greatness must become servants, and those who want to be 'number one' must become slaves. Yet these sayings are so intimately bound up with the leadership struggles that ensued in the Christian communities that it is impossible to divorce the saying from the later situation. As a consequence, the Fellows decided to designate the complex as gray to indicate that the words echo Jesus' teaching, but with a strong Markan accent" (Funk et al., *Five Gospels*, 95).

198. Luke 22:14–30.

199. Matt 20:16. The Jesus Seminar ranks this saying as pink (Funk et al., *Five Gospels*, 224).

200. Luke 13:30.

201. Mark 10:31; cf. Matt 19:30.

202. Mark 9:35.

a child and saying "Whoever receives one such child in my name receives me."[203] Luke records Jesus' teaching about choosing a lowly seat at a banquet rather than the seat of honor, and this concludes with the saying, "For every one who exalts himself will be humbled, and he who humbles himself will be exalted."[204] This leads naturally into the parable of the great dinner,[205] but immediately following that is the account with Jesus' saying about the need to carry one's cross.[206]

Admittedly, while we may be able to demonstrate that much of this material is authentic, we are not able to trace the arrangement of the material back to Jesus. Thus, the various concrete expressions given above of losing one's life in order to find it are from the Gospel writers. It may be that they were faithfully reflecting the view of Jesus, but it is difficult to demonstrate this with the criteria for authenticity that we have.

Conclusions

We have seen that it is likely that Jesus anticipated his own death, although it is less certain, but possible, that he anticipated that he would be crucified. In light of this it is also likely that Jesus considered the possibility that some of his followers would also be killed because of their association with him, and that Jesus told people that they would need to accept this possibility if they wanted to follow him. But more than this, Jesus used death as a metaphor that spoke of a sacrificial life required by all his followers. The Gospels suggest three kinds of sacrifices followers made: possessions, family, and honor. The overall impression is that Jesus' followers had to be willing to sever all ties with that which provided security and status in order to commit themselves wholly to his mission. Finally, Jesus intimated that his followers would, in some sense, share in his own fate—taking up their cross and following him, drinking from his cup—which could be understood either literally or metaphorically.

203. Mark 9:37.
204. Luke 14:11.
205. Luke 14:15–24.
206. Luke 14:27.

5

Paul's Participationist Language

THE PURPOSE OF THIS CHAPTER IS TO SEE WHETHER OR NOT IT IS reasonable to understand Paul to be dependent on the perspective of Jesus expressed in the sayings we argued to be authentic in the previous chapter. We will focus particularly on Paul's participationist language with regard to the death of Jesus. And our strategy will be to note family resemblances between this aspect of Paul's language and Jesus' sayings, and to examine other possible sources for Paul's language in order to find the best explanation for it.

Paul's Language about the Death of Jesus

Christ's Death "for Us"

Paul would have welcomed the epithet "theologian of the cross." He speaks of the significance of Jesus' death frequently and affirms more than any other writer in the New Testament (outside the Gospels) that his death was by crucifixion.[1] Clearly, by focusing on the cross we are dealing with an issue that was for Paul of fundamental importance.

Paul does not focus on the historical causes of Jesus' death. In some places he speaks of Jesus voluntarily offering himself;[2] elsewhere he describes Jesus' death in terms of God offering his Son[3] and sees in it the supreme evidence of God's love for people,[4] for ultimately, according to Paul, Jesus died for the sake of others: using the preposition

---

1. See Murphy-O'Connor, "Even Death on a Cross," 21–29.
2. Gal 1:4; 2:20; Phil 2:5–8.
3. Rom 8:3; Gal 4:4–5.
4. Rom 5:8; 8:32.

ὑπέρ, he states that Christ died "for me,"[5] "for you,"[6] "for us,"[7] "for our sins,"[8] "for the ungodly,"[9] "for many,"[10] and "for all."[11]

In the end it may be somewhat artificial to separate Jesus' death from his resurrection in Paul's thought. Together this one event of victory over death is the basis for Paul's assurance of God's final victory over all death[12] and for his conviction that God is now offering life to those who currently live under the sentence of death.[13] Indeed, he can speak simply of salvation being "in Christ" in contexts where only his death or both his death and resurrection are in view.[14]

And yet, there is still clearly an emphasis in Paul's writings on Jesus' death. Rather than losing sight of Jesus' death in the wake of his resurrection, which might have been understandable, Paul continues to speak of Christ as the crucified one: he describes his own mission in terms of preaching "Christ crucified"[15] and proclaiming "the word of the cross,"[16] he boasts in the cross,[17] and he describes the Lord's Supper as a proclamation of "the Lord's death."[18] Clearly Jesus' death has not been lost sight of in the light of his resurrection. At first sight this seems quite curious for someone who celebrates the resurrection and sees in it the dawning of the new age.

---

5. Gal 2:20.

6. 1 Cor 11:24; cf. 1 Cor 1:13.

7. Rom 5:8; 8:32; 2 Cor 5:21; Gal 3:13; 1 Thess 5:10; cf. Eph 5:2; Titus 2:14.

8. Gal 1:4; 1 Cor 15:3; cf. Rom 4:25.

9. Rom 5:6; cf. vv. 8, 10.

10. Rom 5:15.

11. Rom 5:18; 2 Cor 5:14–15; cf. 1 Tim 2:6.

12. 1 Cor 15:21, 26, 54–55.

13. Rom 5:17, 21; 6:23; 8:2.

14. Only death: Rom 3:24–25; 1 Cor 1:18, 26–30; Gal 3:13–14. Death and resurrection: Rom 6:3–11, 23.

15. 1 Cor 1:23; 2:2; Gal 3:1. As is generally recognized, the perfect tense of the participle, ἐσταυρωμένος, in these texts suggests that the state of being crucified is, for Christ, something that persists and is not simply descriptive of a past event; see Burton, *Galatians*, 145; Longenecker, *Galatians*, 101; Orr and Walther, 1 *Corinthians*, 156.

16. 1 Cor 1:18.

17. Gal 6:14.

18. 1 Cor 11:26.

In order to explore the significance of Jesus' death, Paul speaks of a variety of ways by which God achieved salvation by means of the cross: justification, whereby God rectified what had gone wrong;[19] redemption, by which God set people free from slavery;[20] reconciliation, in which God restored broken relationships;[21] victory, in which God defeated the powers that were opposed to him;[22] and sacrifice of atonement, by which God forgave people's sins.[23] Furthermore, he compares and contrasts Jesus' act of obedience—presumably meaning his decision to follow God's will even though it led to his death—with Adam's act of disobedience, arguing that whereas the consequence of the latter was death, the consequence of the former was life.[24] And finally, Paul says that the purpose behind Jesus' death and resurrection was so that he "might be Lord both of the dead and of the living."[25]

Paul received at least some of this material as tradition from the early church. He says so explicitly, for example, when he writes: "I delivered to you as of first importance what I also received, that Christ died for our sins."[26] And, as we noted earlier, Paul appears to reflect traditional views regarding the significance of Jesus' death elsewhere as well.[27]

Our Death with Christ

Paul makes other references to Jesus' death, however, that do not focus on what Christ has done "for us," but rather on how believers participate with Christ in his death. If the former perspective considers Jesus' death objectively (*extra nos*), the latter appears to be quite

19. Rom 3:24, 26, 28, 30; 4:5, 25; 5:1, 9, 18; 6:7; 8:30, 33; 1 Cor 6:11; Gal 2:16; 3:8, 24.

20. Rom 3:24; 8:23; 1 Cor 1:30; cf. Eph 1:7; Col 1:14.

21. 2 Cor 5:18–19.

22. Gal 4:3; cf. Eph 1:20–23; Col 1:13.

23. Paul speaks of Christ dying "for our sins" (1 Cor 15:3; Gal 1:4; cf. Rom 4:25), of God sending his Son περὶ ἁμαρτίας (Rom 8:3) and of God viewing Jesus' death as a ἱλαστήριον (Rom 3:25), all of which suggest Jesus' death was a sacrifice that dealt with the problem of human sins.

24. Rom 5:12–21; 1 Cor 15:21–22.

25. Rom 14:9; cf. Rom 1:4.

26. 1 Cor 15:3.

27. See above, pp. 123–26.

subjective in its depiction of believers being involved in the event. The source of this participatory language is not obvious from what Paul says: Was it also part of the tradition from the early church? Was it from the Hellenistic wing of the church? Did Paul adapt something from the Jewish tradition? Or, did Paul borrow concepts from outside the Jewish or Christian traditions? Through a process of elimination, I intend to show that it is reasonable to believe that in his participatory language Paul was, to some extent, expressing a perspective that Jesus articulated in sayings such as those we identified in the previous chapter.

The following is a survey, with little commentary, of this participatory language. We note first some texts where Paul speaks of sharing in Jesus' death in some way in connection with his own hardships:

> We are afflicted in every way, but not crushed; perplexed, but not driven to despair; persecuted, but not forsaken; struck down, but not destroyed; always carrying in the body the death of Jesus, so that the life of Jesus may also be manifested in our bodies. For while we live we are always being given up to death for Jesus' sake, so that the life of Jesus may be manifested in our mortal flesh. So death is at work in us, but life in you. (2 Cor 4:8–12)

> For he was crucified in weakness, but lives by the power of God. For we are weak in him, but in dealing with you we shall live with him by the power of God. (2 Cor 13:4)

> I bear on my body the marks of Jesus. (Gal 6:17)

Paul broadens this theme of sharing in Jesus' death to all believers by describing baptism in terms of being buried with Jesus in his death and the Lord's Supper in terms of a fellowship in his death:

> Do you not know that all of us who have been baptized into Christ Jesus were baptized into his death? We were buried therefore with him by baptism into death, so that as Christ was raised from the dead by the glory of the Father, we too might walk in newness of life.
>
> For if we have been united with him in a death like his, we shall certainly be united with him in a resurrection like his. We know that our old self was crucified with him so that the sinful body might be destroyed, and we might no longer be enslaved to sin. (Rom 6:3–6)

> The cup of blessing which we bless, is it not a participation [κοινωνία] in the blood of Christ? The bread which we break, is it not a participation [κοινωνία] in the body of Christ? . . . You cannot drink the cup of the Lord and the cup of demons. You cannot partake of the table of the Lord and the table of demons. (1 Cor 10:16, 21)

Important to note here is that Paul is not saying that at one time we were dead and now, through Christ, we are alive,[28] but rather that we have shared in Jesus' death and this somehow is supposed to lead to a new way of life:

> I have been crucified with Christ; it is no longer I who live, but Christ who lives in me; and the life I now live in the flesh I live by faith in the Son of God, who loved me and gave himself for me. (Gal 2:20[29])

Furthermore, Paul speaks of himself or of believers as having died to something in particular with the result of a new way of life being open to them:

> Likewise, my brethren, you have died to the law through the body of Christ, so that you may belong to another, to him who has been raised from the dead in order that we may bear fruit for God. (Rom 7:4)

> For I through the law died to the law, that I might live to God. (Gal 2:19)

> But the fruit of the Spirit is love. . . . And those who belong to Christ Jesus have crucified the flesh with its passions and desires. (Gal 5:23–24)

> But far be it from me to glory except in the cross of our Lord Jesus Christ, by which the world has been crucified to me, and I to the world. (Gal 6:14)

Here it would appear that dying to the law, the flesh, and the world is something that all believers have done by virtue of being believers. However, Paul can also use similar language to enjoin his readers to put something to death in their lives:

---

28. As we find, for example, in Eph 2:1–3; Col 2:13.

29. The hardships in view here need to be inferred from Paul's account of the Antioch incident that he gives a few verses earlier (Gal 2:11–14).

> . . . for if you live according to the flesh you will die, but if by
> the Spirit you put to death the deeds of the body you will live.
> (Rom 8:13)

> So you also must consider yourselves dead to sin and alive to
> God in Christ Jesus. (Rom 6:11)

Following a different line of thought, in one place Paul implies that
Jesus' death resulted in the death of everyone:

> . . . we are convinced that one has died for all; therefore all have
> died. (2 Cor 5:14)

And in another place he speaks of his own goal in life in terms of a
sharing in both Jesus' death and his resurrection:

> For his sake I have suffered the loss of all things . . . in order
> that I may gain Christ. . . ; that I may know him and the power
> of his resurrection, and may share his sufferings, becoming
> like him in his death, that if possible I may attain the resurrec-
> tion from the dead. (Phil 3:8–11)

In summary we note the following: (i) Paul identifies with Jesus
in his death in the sense that he considers himself to have died with
him; and (ii) while this identification appears to be a primary focus of
baptism and of the Lord's Supper, (iii) it is also a continuous identification that comes to expression in the course of Paul's ministry.

The question is, Why does Paul speak of participating in the death
of Jesus in this way? This does not seem to follow from the language
of Christ having died "for us." Indeed, the image here is not that of
Christ dying for people, but of people dying with Christ. Furthermore,
we might have expected that Paul's belief in Jesus' resurrection would
have led him to emphasize images of life and triumph. And while he
does stress that believers should be victorious,[30] this does not lead him
to forget the death of Jesus or to deny his own hardships. Indeed, while
death may be the last enemy to be defeated,[31] Jesus' death is for Paul a
seminal and formative image for the Christian life. Why is this?

There is a related question that needs to be carefully distinguished:
What does Paul *mean* by "dying with Christ?" Our primary interest
is why Paul uses the metaphor—what sources may have influenced

30. See, e.g., Rom 8:31–39; Gal 5:16–26; Phil 3:12–16.
31. 1 Cor 15:26.

him; but it may be helpful to know the range of opinion on what Paul meant by the metaphor. Language can be adapted from one context to another with a consequent change in meaning, but how much that meaning changes is not always obvious; therefore, knowing the range of possible meanings may help to identify possible sources.

The Meaning of Paul's "Dying with Christ" Language

The Believer's Relationship with Jesus Christ

Before looking at the meaning of Paul's "dying with Christ" sayings, let us first set these sayings within a broader context of how Paul conceives of the believer's relationship with Christ.

First, we note generally how Paul speaks of believers being "with Christ." In the context of speaking of believers having died with Christ (Rom 6) he expresses the hope of being raised with him[32] and of living with him,[33] a hope that corresponds to the hope expressed elsewhere of being with the Lord forever.[34] This hope also includes being conformed (σύμμορφος) to the image of Christ,[35] sharing an inheritance with (συγκληρονόμος) Christ, and being glorified together with (συνδοξάζω) Christ—the latter predicated on believers first suffering with (συμπάσχω) Christ.[36]

---

32. In Rom 6 Paul speaks of believers sharing with Christ in his resurrection as something in the future (1 Cor 15:22–23; Phil 3:10–11; cf. 2 Tim 2:11). Although both Ephesians and Colossians speak of believers as already having been raised with Christ (Eph 2:5–6; Col 2:12–13; 3:1), the difference may not be all that substantial. Paul clearly believed that (i) the present was a kind of in-between time, bounded in the past by the resurrection of Jesus and in the future by the general resurrection; and (ii) in this in-between time a new way of life was possible for those who had faith in Jesus Christ. In order to explain how it is that this new life was possible now, Paul spoke of believers' identification with Christ. But an ambiguity arises in doing this: should believers be depicted to have already been identified with Christ in his resurrection, as an explanation of how new life is possible now, or should this sharing in resurrection be expressed as a hope for the future physical resurrection? There is a difference in how the imagery is used in Ephesians and Colossians, perhaps indicating the contribution of a different writer, but the reality that the imagery points to still appears to be Pauline.

33. Rom 6:5, 8.

34. Phil 1:23; 1 Thess 4:14, 17; 5:10; cf. Col 3:4.

35. Rom 8:29; Phil 3:21.

36. Rom 8:17, 29.

Second, in addition to the participatory language, Paul speaks of Christ as something like a sphere into which believers are incorporated. Believers are part of the "body of Christ" and have different functions in the same way that members of a human body have different functions.[37] But the most distinctive way Paul expresses this idea of incorporation is by saying that believers are "in Christ" (ἐν Χριστῷ)[38] or, less frequently, "in the Lord" (ἐν κυρίῳ);[39] in one place he contrasts being "in Christ" with being "in Adam" (ἐν τῷ Ἀδάμ).[40] Furthermore, he speaks of various aspects of salvation being made available to believers "in Christ,"[41] and of new values that pertain to those who are "in Christ."[42]

And third, the relationship between Christ and believers is expressed by Paul speaking of Christ as being presently active among believers. He speaks of believers enjoying various aspects of God's salvation made available "through Christ" (διὰ Χριστοῦ),[43] although admittedly Paul may have had in view here the effects of Jesus' death and resurrection rather than the effects of his ongoing activity. But the latter is clearly in view when he speaks of Christ indwelling believers[44] or when he aligns the work of Christ with that of the Spirit.[45]

37. Rom 12:3–8; 1 Cor 12:12–27; cf. Eph 1:22–23; 3:6; 4:4, 11–16; 5:23, 30; Col 1:18, 24; 2:19; 3:15.

38. Rom 6:11; 8:1; 12:5; 16:3, 7, 9, 10; 1 Cor 1:2, 30; 4:10; 15:18; 2 Cor 5:17; 12:2; Gal 1:22; 2:4; 3:26, 28; Phil 1:1; 2:1; 4:7, 21; 1 Thess 1:1, 14; 4:16; Phlm 23; cf. Col 1:2, 4; 2 Thess 1:1.

39. Rom 16:2, 8, 11, 12 (twice), 13, 22; 1 Cor 4:17; 16:19; Phlm 16; cf. Eph 4:1; Col 4:7.

40. 1 Cor 15:22.

41. Believers experience redemption (Rom 3:24), eternal life (Rom 6:23), freedom, due to "the law of the Spirit of life" (Rom 8:2), the love of God (Rom 8:39), the grace of God (1 Cor 1:4), a fresh vision of God (2 Cor 3:14), justification (Gal 2:17), the blessing of Abraham (Gal 3:14), and in the future they will experience resurrected life (1 Cor 15:22).

42. Paul stresses the importance of faith working through love (Gal 5:6), and giving thanks in all circumstances (1 Thess 5:18).

43. Through Christ believers experience the gift of grace in order to live fully (Rom 5:17, 21), victory over death (1 Cor 15:57), consolation in the midst of suffering (2 Cor 1:5), God's reconciling action (2 Cor 5:18), the ability to perform loving deeds so that on the last day they are pure and blameless (Phil 1:9–11), and salvation (1 Thess 5:9).

44. Rom 8:10; 2 Cor 13:5; Gal 2:20; cf. Eph 3:17; Col 1:27.

45. Rom 8:9–10.

The Meaning of Paul's "Dying with Christ" Language

Within this context, then, of the believers' relationship to Jesus Christ, how is the "dying with Christ" language to be understood? The following is a survey of answers to this question, not all of them necessarily mutually exclusive of the others.

Deissmann & Schweitzer: A Mystical Perspective

At the beginning of the twentieth century, Adolf Deissmann argued that this language of "dying with Christ" reflected a mysticism in which Paul saw Christ, not as a historical person, but as a kind of energy that, like the air we breathe, dwells in people and pervades all of life. What was central for Paul was the "immediacy of contact" with God which he discovered not through reason but through inner experience.[46] And so Paul shares experiences with Christ:

> [S]ince he suffers in Christ, his sufferings are to him the 'sufferings of Christ,' or the 'afflictions of Christ.' It is not the old Paul who suffers, but the new Paul, who is a member of the Body of Christ, and who therefore mystically experiences all that that Body experienced and experiences: he 'suffers with Christ,' is 'crucified with Christ,' 'has died with Christ,' 'been buried,' 'raised up,' and 'lives with Christ.'[47]

Wilhelm Bousset concurs, arguing that for Paul Christ had become "the supraterrestrial power which supports and fills with its presence his whole life."[48] But it was Albert Schweitzer who was most influential in emphasizing Paul's mysticism. He argued that the corporateness of Christ was for Paul not a metaphor, but a reality.[49]

---

46. Deissmann, *Paul*, 136, 138, 140, 149, citation from p. 149.

47. Ibid., 182.

48. Bousset, *Kyrios Christos*, 153–55, citation from p. 154.

49. Schweitzer, *Mysticism*, 127: "The Mystical Body of Christ is thus for Paul not a pictorial expression, nor a conception that has arisen out of symbolical and ethical reflections, but an actual entity. Only so can it be explained that not only can Christ suffer for the Elect, but also the Elect for Christ and for one another. This reciprocity of relations is founded on the fact that the existences in question are physically interdependent in the same corporeity, and the one can pass over into the other"; cf. pp. 15–16.

> Grafted into the corporeity of Christ, [the baptized person]
> loses his creatively individual existence and his natural per-
> sonality. Henceforth he is only a form of manifestation of the
> personality of Jesus Christ, which dominates that corporeity.[50]

It is through baptism that believers enter this new reality, through a
sharing in Christ's death and resurrection.

> Paul's conception is, believers in mysterious fashion share the
> dying and rising again of Christ, and in this way are swept
> away out of their ordinary mode of existence, and form a spe-
> cial category of humanity.[51]

Thus, believers have died to their old life characterized by flesh and
sin, and have risen to a new life, a life which is driven by a supernatural
"life-power."[52]

BULTMANN: AN ECCLESIOLOGICAL/ESCHATOLOGICAL/ ETHICAL PERSPECTIVE

In contrast to any mystical interpretation of Paul, Bultmann argued
that salvation had more to do with a new existential understanding of
oneself than with inward experiences or transformations.[53] He writes:

> The union of believers into one *soma* with Christ now has its
> basis not in their sharing the same supernatural substance, but
> in the fact that in the word of proclamation Christ's death-
> and-resurrection becomes a possibility of existence in regard
> to which a decision must be made, and in the fact that faith
> seizes this possibility and appropriates it as the power that de-
> termines the existence of the man of faith.[54]

He understands the phrase "in Christ"—which he takes to be a borrowing from Gnosticism[55]—in three senses. First, it speaks of those
belonging to the church:

---

50. Ibid., 125.
51. Ibid., 96.
52. Ibid., 119, 127, citation from p. 119.
53. Bultmann, *Theology*, 1:268–69.
54. Ibid., 1:302.
55. Ibid., 1:310.

> To belong to the Christian Church is to be 'in Christ'. . . . 'In Christ,' far from being a formula for mystic union, is primarily an *ecclesiological* formula.[56]

Second, since the church is God's eschatological community, the phrase "in Christ" takes on an eschatological connotation as well. And third, to be "in Christ" means to be under Christ's lordship:

> [The phrase "in Christ"] denotes not, to be sure, an individual mystical relationship to Christ, but the fact that the individual actual life of the believer, living not out of himself but out of the divine deed of salvation, is determined by Christ.[57]

Thus, we have an ecclesiological/eschatological/ethical understanding of incorporation.

Bultmann acknowledges the participatory perspective in Paul, particularly in connection with baptism and the Lord's Supper, and suggests that such language was due to the influence of the mystery religions.[58] He writes:

> *Baptism imparts participation in the death and resurrection of Christ.* This interpretation undoubtedly originated in the Hellenistic Church, which understood this traditional initiation-sacrament on analogy with the initiation-sacraments of the mystery religions. The meaning of the latter is to impart to the initiates a share in the fate of the cult-deity who has suffered death and reawakened to life—such as Attis, Adonis, or Osiris.
>
> In Hellenistic Christianity the Lord's Supper, like baptism, is understood *as a sacrament in the sense of the mystery religions.* . . . [I]n the mysteries [the sacramental meal] . . . is communion with a once dead and risen deity, in whose fate the partaker receives a share.[59]

---

56. Ibid., 1.311, emphasis original.

57. Ibid., 1:328.

58. Ibid., 1:140–44, 148–52, 311–14.

59. Ibid., 1:140, 148, emphasis original.

Tannehill: A Cosmic Perspective

Robert Tannehill has offered another non-mystical understanding of Paul's "dying with Christ" language, a view which is perhaps best described as "cosmic" in that it involves a reorientation with regard to the powers that shape people's lives.

Tannehill sets Paul's language of "dying and rising with Christ"[60] within the context of his portrayal of the human predicament. As a σῶμα, a person "is determined by the world within which he stands. The individual becomes what he is through that which has power over him,"[61] and the world into which people are born is dominated by the powers of sin, death, and the law. The opportunity to be set free from this power has been made possible by God invading the world and setting up an alternative dominion in which he himself reigns. This was done by means of the death and resurrection of Jesus Christ, and people can transfer from one dominion to the other by dying and rising with Christ.[62] Thus, "dying with Christ means a change of lordship. It means dying to an old master and living to a new one."[63]

This "dying and rising," however, is not an imitation of Jesus' death and resurrection, as if believers we trying to repeat his death; nor is it a subjective experience or sacramental process (here he denies the mystical interpretation of Deissmann and Schweitzer).[64] That is, it is not something that takes place within believers at the time of their conversion or baptism, or in the context of their lives. Rather, the "dying and rising" that Paul has in mind is something that happened at the time of Jesus' own dying and rising. "The believers died with Christ because Christ's crucifixion meant the crucifixion of 'our old man' and the 'body of sin.' These are corporate entities."[65] And so, while baptism may mark the transfer from the dominion of sin to the dominion of

60. Tannehill, *Dying and Rising*, 10, argues that the motif "dying and rising with Christ" (Col 2) was older than the motif "dying with Christ" (Rom 6). Wedderburn, *Baptism and Resurrection*, 1–6, explains that the refutation of this assumption was a fundamental impetus behind his major work.

61. Tannehill, *Dying and Rising*, 72.

62. Ibid., 14–20, 70–71.

63. Ibid., 18; cf. p. 70: Paul uses the motif of "dying and rising with Christ" "to indicate the decisive transfer of the believers from the old to the new aeon which has taken place in the death of Christ as an inclusive event."

64. Ibid., 30, 70–71.

65. Ibid., 29; cf. p. 24.

God, and while faith may make this transfer effective, the "dying and rising" of believers that Paul associates with this act is something that happened in and at the time of Jesus' own death and resurrection.[66] It appears to follow from this that "dying and rising," according to Tannehill, is an act of liberation but not one of transformation; believers are ushered into a new dominion which has been established by Jesus' own "dying and rising" and in this way are free to live new lives.

This, however, is not the end of the story. While believers have been transferred to the dominion of God, they continue to live in the dominion of sin and are exposed to, but not fully determined by, the influence of its powers. "Therefore, the new existence which is based upon the past death with Christ takes on the form of a continuing dying with Christ,"[67] which comes to expression in ethical action[68] and in suffering.[69] Tannehill writes:

> It is because the decisive break with the old world must continually be maintained and affirmed that what happened to the

66. Tannehill (ibid., 41–42) writes: "Baptism, and the decision of faith which accompanies it, are decisive events in the life of the individual. The individual is baptized 'into Christ' and 'into his death,' that is, through baptism he enters the new dominion which is determined by Christ and his saving acts. . . . However, this does not mean that we can explain dying with Christ by referring to a special quality of the sacrament of baptism. The believer is baptized into Christ's death and released from the old dominion not because baptism repeats Christ's death or enables it to be present in some unique way, but because in baptism the destruction of the old world and founding of the new which the cross brings about reaches its goal in the life of the individual." And again on p. 126: "God's grace in the cross reaches its goal in faith, for in faith the destructive power of the cross manifests itself in the life of the individual. . . . Faith is the recognition of the grace which destroys man's boast. . . . Since man's boast is surrendered in faith, faith also means the realization in the life of the individual of the death of the old self who was enslaved to the dominion characterized by that boast."

67. Ibid., 127.

68. Rom 6; 8:10–13; Gal 5:24–25. Tannehill (ibid., 81–82) writes: "Thus the transfer from the old dominion to the new which takes place through dying with Christ will manifest itself in the actions of the believer. . . . To be sure, there is a continuing struggle against the powers of the old dominion. . . . [But, t]he believer is not left without protection against the powers of the old dominion, for a new power determines his life, a power by which he is able to 'put to death the deeds of the body' (Rom. 8:13). . . . The believer can only escape from [enslavement to the power of God] if the death and resurrection of Christ cease to determine his life, so that it can no longer be said that he has died with Christ."

69. Rom 8:17; 2 Cor 1:3–9; 4:7–14; 12:7–9; Phil 3:3–11. Tannehill (ibid., 84) writes: "Paul interprets his suffering in terms of participation in Christ's death and resurrection."

Christian in the death of Christ also determines the present structure of his life, so that dying with Christ is not only the basis of the new dominion but remains a present reality within it and leaves its imprint upon existence there.[70]

Unfortunately, it is not clear, in Tannehill's work, how it is that "dying with Christ" is both (i) something that happened when Christ died and thus is not to be understood subjectively or sacramentally, and (ii) something that itself (not just its effects) is a continuing reality for the believer.[71]

SANDERS: A REAL PARTICIPATION

E. P. Sanders takes up the issue of Paul's participatory language in the context of discussing Paul's soteriology, arguing that this language reflects Paul's understanding of salvation at a fundamental level: "All who believe in him . . . are at present considered to participate in Christ's body."[72] He argues from 1 Cor 6:13–18 and 10:14–22 that participation with Christ is not simply a matter of self-understanding,[73] but rather that it involves the believer in a real sharing that could be jeopardized by other incompatible spheres of activity, for example, spheres involving sexual immorality or idolatry. Paul's argument against engaging with a prostitute and against eating food offered to idols is not based

70. Ibid., 127.

71. The view of Karl Barth could also be mentioned in this connection. He argues that Christ is the representative of all people, because he took into himself "the *humanum*, the being and essence, the nature and kind, which is that of all men." And therefore, as such, all people were included in Christ's death and resurrection: "then and there, in the person of Christ taking our place, we were present, being crucified and dying with Him" (Barth, *Church Dogmatics*, 4.2:48, 295). This view, however, is part of a much larger theological construct, and space limitations prevent me from dealing with it adequately. Suffice it to say that (i) 2 Cor 5:14 notwithstanding, Paul does not appear to be a universalist (see Rom 11:17–24; 1 Cor 1:18; 2 Cor 11:15; Phil 3:18–20), a view that is often associated with Barth's position, and (ii) Paul does not appear to be influenced by Plato's views of ontology (the particulars participating in the ideal) as seems implicit in Barth's view.

72. Sanders, *Paul*, 463.

73. Sanders (ibid., 454) suggests that Bultmann's motive behind his emphasis on self-understanding and his rejection of anything mystical is due to his concern to make Paul understandable to modern people.

on a moral code, but on the incompatibility of such involvements for those who have been united with Christ.[74]

With regard to the significance of Jesus' death, Sanders argues that Paul inherited the view that it atones for sins, but his own distinctive contribution was that believers participate in Jesus' death. With reference to the "dying with Christ" passages,[75] Sanders writes:

> Paul, in thinking of the significance of Christ's death, was thinking more in terms of a *change of lordship* which guarantees future salvation than in terms of the expiation of past transgression.[76]

> [B]y *sharing* in Christ's death, one dies to the *power* of sin or to the old aeon, with the result that one *belongs to God*. The *transfer* is not only from uncleanness of idolatry and sexual immorality to cleanness and holiness, but from one lordship to another. The transfer takes place by *participation* in Christ's death.[77]

In the end, Sanders falls somewhere between Bultmann and Schweitzer. On the one hand, he agrees with Bultmann that Paul's view of salvation should not be understood in terms of magical transference or cosmological speculation.[78] But on the other hand, while agreeing that Paul's gospel may involve a new self-understanding that arises out of decisions made when confronted with the word of God's grace, he disagrees that Paul's gospel can be reduced to this. He writes:

> Being one body and one Spirit with Christ is not simply living out of a revised self-understanding, although that may also result. It seems to me best to understand Paul as saying what he meant and meaning what he said: Christians really are one body and Spirit with Christ.[79]

But Sanders confesses that he is unable to describe exactly what this means:

---

74. Ibid., 454–56.

75. Rom 6:3–11; 7:4; Gal 2:19–20; 5:24; 6:14; Phil 3:10–11.

76. Sanders, *Paul*, 466, emphasis original.

77. Ibid., 467–68, emphasis original.

78. Ibid., 522.

79. Ibid.

> We seem to lack a category of 'reality'—real participation in
> Christ, real possession of the Spirit—which lies between naïve
> cosmological speculation and belief in magical transference
> on the one hand and a revised self-understanding on the other.
> I must confess that I do not have a new category of perception
> to propose here.[80]

By speaking of a transfer of lordship, Sanders reflects one aspect
of Bultmann's perspective; but in arguing that the participation in
Christ had a reality that could be affected by acts of immorality or
idolatry, he shows support for Schweitzer.

HAYS: A NARRATIVE PERSPECTIVE

Richard Hays interprets Paul's participatory language within the
context of the narrative of God's salvation, a narrative that begins
with God's promise to Abraham, comes to a climax with the sending of Jesus and his death and resurrection, continues in the lives of
Jesus' followers during a time when new creation is breaking into the
world, and finally is resolved in the parousia of Jesus and the usher-
ing in of the age to come.[81] This narrative, Hays argues, "provides the
symbolic matrix within which Paul's theological reflection lives and
moves."[82] Furthermore, whenever "he confronts pastoral problems in
his churches, he responds to them by thinking through the situation
in the light of the story, plotting the community's place within the un-
folding narrative."[83]

Fundamental to the way this theological reflection takes place
is Paul's understanding of how believers participate together with
Jesus: "they are personally united with Jesus and thus mysteriously
transformed."[84] Regarding the relationship between the Messiah and
his people, Hays cites N. T. Wright: "they are 'in' him such that what is
true of him is true of them."[85] Hays goes on:

---

80. Ibid., 522–23.
81. Hays, "Crucified with Christ," 232–33.
82. Ibid., 231.
83. Ibid., 234.
84. Ibid., 239.
85. Hays (ibid.) citing Wright, "Putting Paul Together Again," 205.

> Paul thinks of the fate of God's people as bound up in the fate of Jesus. The logic of salvation is a logic of *participation* in the destiny of Jesus, the divinely sent protagonist of the gospel story. . . . The life of God's elect is prefigured and carried by the life, death, and resurrection of Jesus.[86]

The way in which this participation takes place, according to Hays, is by the exercise of πίστις, for πίστις is at the heart of Paul's understanding of Jesus' ministry: "as we respond in faith, we participate in an ongoing re-enactment of Christ's faithfulness."[87] Jesus' death and resurrection are cosmic events that vicariously include believers. But more than this, "because Jesus Christ is the prototype of the new humanity, those whom God calls are conformed to the pattern defined by him, and the characteristic mark of this pattern is precisely πίστις."[88]

Hays goes on, somewhat more speculatively, to suggest that the role of the gospel as story may provide the conceptual category that eluded Sanders in trying to describe how the participation with Christ actually works. He writes:

> One widely recognized property of story is its power to lead hearers into an experience of identification with the story's protagonist. Precisely for this reason, stories can function as vehicles for the creation of community, as many individuals find a common identity within a single story. In the case of a story which becomes foundational for the self-understanding of a community, the identification of community members with the protagonist may be so comprehensive that it can be spoken of as 'participation' in the protagonist's destiny. If Paul's gospel is the story of Jesus Christ, then we might participate in Christ in somewhat the same way that we participate in (or identify with) the protagonist of any story. We find that the story lays a claim upon us and draws us into its world; we recognize ourselves in the protagonist and feel that our own destinies are somehow figured in his story. . . . We find ourselves, in Via's phrase, "projected into the paradigm of the death and resurrection of Jesus."[89]

---

86. Hays, "Crucified with Christ," 240.

87. Hays, *Faith of Jesus Christ*, 211.

88. Ibid., 212.

89. Ibid., 214; the citation is taken from Via, *Kerygma and Comedy*, 66.

Finally, since the climax of the story of Jesus is his death and resurrection, this becomes the primary focus in the believers' participation. Thus, "[t]he community called to live 'in Christ' will necessarily live in a way that corresponds to the pattern of faith/obedience defined by Christ's death on the cross."[90] This is then what is meant by "dying with Christ."[91]

BRONDOS: AN ATONEMENTLESS PERSPECTIVE

David Brondos has recently offered a view of Jesus' participationist language which is both similar to and different from that of Bultmann. Like Bultmann he denies a mystical interpretation in favor of an ethical focus. But unlike Bultmann he portrays Paul as taking the Jesus of history seriously.

Brondos presents an atonementless interpretation of Jesus' death. Beginning with the perspective of Jesus and of the early Christians, Brondos maintains that Jesus, in his life, through his words and deeds, invited people to experience salvation. It so happened that his actions led to his death; but he died willingly for the cause he was committed to, and desired for others the same thing in his death as what he worked for in his life. In this sense his death was sacrificial.[92] Furthermore, since he died willingly, "his death would also be seen as an implicit petition to God that what he had lived and worked for might become a reality in spite of his death or *through* his death," and his resurrection was confirmation that "God had accepted Jesus' sacrifice, responding favorably to Jesus' petition on behalf of others."[93] Thus, Brondos writes:

> Seen from the context of this story, Jesus' death is salvific *not in itself* but *because of what preceded and followed it.* All that he did previous to his death, including his ministry on behalf

90. Hays, "Crucified with Christ," 240.

91. Hays (ibid., 241) also points to a number of texts where suffering is viewed as an expression of participation with Christ (1 Thess 1:6; 2:14–15; Phil 3:10–11).

92. Brondos, *Paul on the Cross*, 33–62.

93. Ibid., 43–44, emphasis original. Brondos's account is somewhat confused here: on the one hand he claims that Jesus' death was sacrificial in that he died for the cause that he lived for; but on the other hand, he argues that the sacrificial language used in the New Testament to interpret the significance of Jesus' death implies that Jesus' death was in some way effective in its appeal to God to bring salvation. The former seems to be the position he wants to hold throughout, but the latter implies that Jesus' death was salvific in some sense.

of others, his teaching in word and deed, and his preparation of disciples, laid the foundation necessary for what came later, and revealed God's will to people in a new way so that they might live according to that will under a new covenant. His death was the consequence of his unbending dedication to this work.[94]

Brondos then tries to show that Paul had the same understanding of Jesus' death. We need not trace each aspect of his argument here; what concerns us is how Brondos deals with Paul's "dying with Christ" language.[95] He argues that to die with Christ is to suffer for the same cause that Jesus suffered for.[96] Commenting on Rom 6, Brondos argues against seeing "dying with Christ" in terms of (i) a participation taking place within Christ as a corporate person,[97] (ii) a mysterious change, either in the world or in people, whereby the power of sin no longer rules over believers,[98] or (iii) a decision on God's part to view believers differently.[99] Rather, dying with Christ involves identifying oneself, through baptism, with Christ, meaning that one is committed, as Jesus was, to God's will and to resisting conformity to the present age. Brondos writes:

> This means that the idea in Rom 6:1–12 is not that believers have participated in a past *event* (Christ's crucifixion) or in a *person*, as if Christ were some type of incorporative figure. Rather, what they have come to share in is a *present condition* similar to that of the crucified and risen Christ, as a result of their having broken radically with sin together with their Lord in order to live to God. . . . [D]ying and being buried with Christ involve an *ethical decision and commitment* on the part of believers.[100]

While it is doubtful that Brondos's atonementless interpretation of Jesus' death is going to persuade many, his view is interesting for our

---

94. Ibid., 49–50, emphasis original.

95. It is debatable whether Brondos's view of Paul's participatory language stands or falls with his atonementless view of Jesus' death. The former speaks of "dying with Christ," whereas the latter focuses on the meaning of Christ dying for us.

96. Brondos, *Paul on the Cross*, 170–73.

97. Brondos cites Sanders, *Paul*, 506–7; Dunn, *Romans*, 1:327; Tannehill, *Dying and Rising*, 24, 29–30.

98. Brondos cites Ziesler, *Romans*, 162; Tannehill, *Dying and Rising*, 15.

99. Brondos cites Cranfield, *Romans*, 1:316.

100. Brondos, *Paul on the Cross*, 175, 179, emphasis original.

purpose because he draws a clear line of continuity between the historical Jesus and Paul: just as Jesus died for the cause that he lived for, believers are to die to their old lives so that they too can be committed to the same cause. This is the language of solidarity—the followers stand together with the leader.[101]

Summary

Paul's "dying with Christ" language is clearly metaphorical: he was not literally crucified with Christ and he does not literally carry around Jesus' corpse. But, to what does the metaphor refer? Clearly it has in view at least a change in a person's mindset which comes to expression in a new way of life. But is it limited to this (Bultmann, Brondos), or is there something more? Is the referent a metaphysical change? And if so, does it refer to an ontological change happening within people, by being transformed in some way (Schweitzer), or does it refer to a cosmic change in the world around them, namely that they find themselves in a new situation with regard to the power structures of the world (Tannehill)? Or, is it difficult to say precisely what the metaphysical change involved beyond speaking about becoming one body with Christ and coming under his lordship (Sanders) or about becoming actors in a new narrative (Hays)? It is not my purpose to answer these questions, but rather to set the stage for thinking about where the language comes from by becoming aware of the range of possibilities of the meaning of the language.

The Background of Paul's Participation Language

We now explore the various possible backgrounds against which we can best understand Paul's "dying with Christ" language. We shall look at his own experience, Christian and Jewish tradition that he may have inherited, and aspects of his Greco-Roman environment.

---

101. For a similar view to that of Brondos, see Borg and Crossan, *The First Paul,* 123–54.

Paul's Own Life Experience

EXPERIENCE OF SUFFERING

Did the hardships that Paul faced, and the sufferings of the Christian life in general, lead him to consider the death of Jesus as an image for the Christian life? Paul speaks of hardship and opposition on numerous occasions,[102] and in some instances he describes himself as on the brink of death.[103] In two places he actually describes his life in terms of dying:

> Why am I in peril every hour? I protest, brethren, by my pride in you which I have in Christ Jesus our Lord, I die every day! (1 Cor 15:30–31)

> We are treated as imposters, and yet are true; as unknown, and yet well known; as dying, and behold we live; as punished, and yet not killed. (2 Cor 4:8–9)

And in one place he cites Scripture to show that such experience is typical of the Christian life:

> Who shall separate us from the love of Christ? Shall tribulation, or distress, or persecution, or famine, or nakedness, or peril, or sword? As it is written, "For thy sake we are being killed all the day long; we are regarded as sheep to be slaughtered." (Rom 8:35–36)

Consequently, not only does Paul say that suffering is part of the Christian life,[104] but in his defense of his own ministry he actually boasts of his weaknesses.[105]

But then Paul takes a significant step. He interprets his hardships as a sharing in the death of Jesus: it is precisely as persecuted that he is "always carrying in the body the death of Jesus"; reflecting on the fact that Christ was crucified in weakness, he says that "we are weak in him"; in light of the Antioch incident he speaks of having been "cru-

---

102. Rom 8:35; 1 Cor 4:10–13; 2 Cor 4:8–9; 6:4–5, 8–10; 11:23–29; 12:10; Phil 4:12. For a discussion of Paul's tribulation lists, see Hodgson, "Tribulation Lists," 59–80.

103. 1 Cor 4:9; 2 Cor 1:8–9; 11:23; Phil 2:17.

104. Rom 5:3; 8:17–18; 2 Cor 1:3–7; Phil 1:29; 3:8; 1 Thess 1:6; 2:14; 3:3–4; cf. Col 1:24; 2 Thess 1:5; 2 Tim 1:8, 12; 2:3, 9; 3:11; 4:5.

105. 2 Cor 11:16–33; 12:6–10.

cified with Christ"; and he bears on his body "the marks of Jesus."[106] True, this is not the whole story, for Paul goes on to say that he lives by the power of God. But, our focus here is on his identification with the death of Jesus.

This is a creative move. As we noted in connection with Jesus and the cross, Jews had a well-established tradition of the persecuted faithful: prophets killed for their preaching, the righteous opposed by the wicked, martyrs who stood against Hellenistic intrusion.[107] It would have been understandable if Paul had thought of himself within these categories, and perhaps he did; but he created a new image for describing his experience—identification with the death of Jesus. Why did he do this?

Alastair Campbell has argued that the incorporative and participatory language in Paul derives from his own experience rather than vice versa. He writes:

> [W]hat Paul says about Adam and Christ as inclusive personalities is better seen as a theological picture drawn from the facts of Christian experience, rather than a truth by which Christian experience is to be interpreted and Christian behaviour shaped. Paul, I suggest, did not start with the idea of a corporate Christ and deduce from it that we could not or should not sin. Rather he started with the fact of Christian conversion, including the suffering and abuse to which it leads for the believer, and came to see the sufferings of Christians as part of the sufferings of Christ and the best guarantee of Christian holiness.[108]

When Paul says, "I through the law died to the law,"[109] he does not mean that (i) it was actually Christ who died through the law in that he bore the curse of the law, so that the believer can be said to die through the law because he died with Christ;[110] or (ii) since it was the role of the law to lead people to faith in Christ and thereby making itself obsolete (as explained more fully in Gal 3:19–25), the believer can be said to have died to the law through the law;[111] or (iii) it was Paul's fanatical

---

106. 2 Cor 4:10; 13:4; Gal 2:20; 6:17.

107. See above, p. 145.

108. Campbell, "Dying with Christ," 275.

109. Gal 2:19.

110. Campbell cites Bruce, *Galatians*, 143; cf. Tannehill, *Dying and Rising*, 59.

111. Campbell cites Betz, *Galatians*, 122; and Longenecker, *Galatians*, 91.

devotion to the law that brought him to a crisis in which faith in Christ replaced his commitment to the law.[112] Instead, Campbell argues that what Paul means by "dying to the law" was the social scorn, rejection, and opposition he experienced as a result of his commitment to Christ:

> It is costly and the cost is not paid only in self-denial, but in the loss of honour, friendship and good will, and with these the loss of one's social identity. Potentially it may mean the loss of life itself, and meanwhile the end of life as it has been known and enjoyed. In Paul's case, since his former manner of life in Judaism has naturally been dominated by the law, to be crucified with Christ was to die to the law.[113]

Campbell suggests that this death to the law could be said to have been "through the law" in the same way that Jesus died to the law and through the law. He explains, "Jesus was put to death as a lawbreaker by due process of law," thus setting Jesus and the law in opposition to each other; but when God raised Jesus from the dead, "the law itself was by this action totally discredited."[114] And so by identifying himself with Jesus, Paul placed himself in the same position vis-à-vis the law, making himself subject to official opposition from the guardians of the law.

Similarly, in discussing Rom 6:1–11, where Paul speaks of believers dying and rising again with Christ, the reality that the dying refers to is the rejection experienced by believers as a consequence of their new faith expressed in baptism.

> The reality that gives the first picture [i.e., that in Rom 6:1–11] its force is not the death of Jesus, considered as a representative figure with whom by faith they identify, but the fact that in identifying with Jesus they have incurred the wrath of their old associates, and experienced the world's hatred just as he did. It was baptism that made this true, not in some sacramental or quasi-magical sense, but because the baptism by which they expressed their faith in Christ also made that faith public among their friends and neighbours and exposed them to public shame.[115]

112. Campbell cites Ziesler, *Galatians*, 22; and Dunn, *Galatians*, 143.

113. Campbell, "Dying with Christ," 283.

114. Ibid.

115. Ibid., 285.

Campbell's social understanding of "dying to the law" and "dying with Christ" is worthy of consideration. His explanation of Paul dying to the law fits the context of Gal 2 where Paul has just described the Antioch incident where the issue of facing opposition from guardians of the law arose.[116] More problematic, however, is his explanation of the phrase "through the law." His argument tends to confuse guardians of the law with the law itself: it may be that the guardians of the law condemned Jesus as a lawbreaker, but this does not mean that Jesus understood himself to be against the law, or that early Christians understood him thus.[117] Also, Campbell's view would seem to leave little room for the positive statements Paul makes regarding the law.[118] His suggestion that dying with Christ in Rom 6 referred to the social ostracism that arises from a public declaration of faith unfortunately lacks any clear evidence; the nearest clear reference to believers facing social opposition may be Rom 8:35 and then again in 12:2. But it is not obvious that believers in Rome who did not know Paul would have known that their own social ostracism was the proper context in which to understand their dying with Christ when reading Rom 6.

Furthermore, it seems unlikely that Paul would have concluded, solely from his understanding of the Christian life as a life of suffering, that believers have died with Christ. When we look in particular at how Paul speaks of baptism and of the Lord's Supper, both of which he speaks of in terms of an identification with Christ in his death, we note that the suffering of believers is not the primary focus. We have already mentioned this in connection with the reference to baptism in Rom 6:3–4. Furthermore, there is nothing about the rite of baptism itself that would require a connection with suffering; baptism could also be understood as a cleansing from sin[119] and as an acknowledgement of Jesus' lordship.[120] Campbell's argument leaves unexplained why Paul would have described baptism as an identification with Christ in his death. With regard to the Lord's Supper, we might not have been surprised by a reference to believers' experience of suffering, since the

---

116. Gal 2:11–14.

117. See above, pp. 88–90.

118. See above, p. 128.

119. Acts 2:38; 22:16

120. This seems to be the implication of being baptized "in the name of Jesus Christ" (Acts 2:38; 8:16; 10:48; 19:5; cf. Rom 6:3; Matt 28:19).

origin of the meal was in the context of Jesus' great suffering. Yet, not only is there no explicit mention of the believers' suffering in the tradition of the Lord's Supper that Paul received,[121] but when he speaks of the Lord's Supper as a participation in the blood and body of Christ in 1 Cor 10:16, his focus is not on a connection between the suffering of believers and the suffering of Christ, but rather on the fact that participation with Christ is inconsistent with participation in idolatry. And this is all the more significant because it is precisely their refusal to join in the ritual ceremonies in the pagan temple that would result in these believers facing marginalization within their guild.[122] But Paul's focus in the Lord's Supper is not on the suffering—as we might have expected it to be—but rather on the fact that it is an act of participation. In both of these rites, therefore, which Paul understands in terms of an identification with Christ in his death, the focus is not on connecting the suffering of believers with that of Christ. It may be that the experience of opposition and suffering facilitated Paul's sense of dying with Christ, but this experience is not sufficient in itself to explain the "dying with Christ" language.

Mysticism

Reflecting on the view of Schweitzer and others that Paul's "in Christ" language should be understood mystically, we might ask to what extent Jewish mysticism and/or mystical experiences may have shaped Paul's thinking. A number of texts both in Paul's letters and in the book of Acts suggest that Paul had mystical experiences in one form or another.[123]

---

121. 1 Cor 11:23–26. The suffering mentioned in vv. 27–32 is due to the Corinthians' failure to "discern the body" rather than to social ostracism. Furthermore, the Lord's Supper could be understood as an act to remind believers of the cost of their salvation (Luke 22:19; 1 Cor 11:23–25) and to lead them to reflect on the implications this has for their lives (1 Cor 11:28–34; cf. 1 Cor 6:20; 7:23).

122. Note Paul's specific reference to the trials of believers in 1 Cor 10:13. This reflects the difficulty of the situation the Corinthian believers faced by their refusal to participate in the pagan temple rituals.

123. See Segal, *Paul the Convert*, 36–37. While the nature of the experiences may vary, we can mention the heavenly vision itself (2 Cor 12:2–4); the "abundance of revelations" (2 Cor 12:7); the threefold request for removal of the "thorn," which might suggest something more than petitionary prayer (2 Cor 12:8–9); Paul's description of his conversion experience as a "revelation" (Gal 1:12, 15–17); his admission that at

Studies in Jewish mysticism generally begin with *merkabah* mysticism, a movement characterized primarily by interpretations of and speculations on Ezek 1, with the focus of attention being on the glory of the throne-chariot in Ezekiel's vision (מֶרְכָּבָה being the Hebrew for "chariot").[124] The main source for the writings of this movement is the *hekhalot* literature, a collection of Jewish writings dealing with heavenly ascensions, the revelation of cosmological secrets, and a secret method for studying Torah; according to Gruenwald, these date from c.a. 200 to 700 CE.[125] References to *merkabah* mysticism can, however, also be found in other ancient Jewish literature, including apocalyptic, Gnostic, and rabbinic writings; significantly, one of these references (*1 Enoch* 14) places *merkabah* mysticism as early as the first century BCE.[126] Also significant is the appearance in the *Songs of the Sabbath Sacrifice* from Qumran of cosmic speculation like that found in the later *merkabah* writings—in particular, speculation surrounding God's throne-chariot.[127]

Similarities between *merkabah* mysticism and some aspects of apocalyptic literature[128] have been recognized; especially significant is the common motif of the heavenly ascent.[129] Michael Mach concludes his study of this issue in the following way:

---

times he is "beside ourselves," while at other times he is "in our right mind" (2 Cor 5:13); and Luke's description of Paul's conversion (Acts 9:3–9; 22:6–11; 26:12–18) and of various visions (Acts 16:9–10; 18:9–10; 22:17–21).

124. For an annotated bibliography on *merkabah* mysticism and *hekhalot* literature, see Karr, "*Merkabah* Mysticism, 3–14.

125. Gruenwald, *Apocalyptic*, vii. For an introduction to *hekhalot* literature, see idem, 98–133. For a list of the ancient works belonging to, or associated with, the *hekhalot* literature, together with references to English translations of the texts, see Karr, "*Merkabah* Mysticism," 15–30.

126. See further, Davila, "Heavenly Ascents," 461–85.

127. 4Q403 11–15; 4Q405 20–22,1–5; 4Q11 16–18,1–7; cf. lines 33–39 of the composite of Sabbath Song 7, and lines 21–26 of the composite of Sabbath Song 11 in Charlesworth and Newsom, eds., *Angelic Liturgy*, 166–67, 181; cf. Scholem, *Jewish Gnosticism*, 128.

128. On the occurrence of visionary or mystical experiences in apocalypticism, see Rowland, *Open Heaven*, 52–61, 78–123.

129. See Scholem, *Jewish Mysticism*, 40–79; Gruenwald, *Apocalyptic*, esp. 29–123; Mach, "Apocalypticism," 229–64; Rowland, *Open Heaven*, 271–348; Himmelfarb, *Ascent to Heaven*; Morray-Jones, "Paradise Revisited," 185.

> The apocalypses and the Hekhalot texts are linked by the belief
> that human visionaries have access to a transcendent reality.
> This reality was out of reach for the people of biblical times.
> The door to heaven was opened by the apocalypses. Whether
> they were directly known to the later mystics or not, the apoc-
> alyptic writings are, therefore, the necessary precondition for
> the Hekhalot type of mysticism.[130]

Thus, although the two kinds of literature and their respective movements can be easily distinguished, there are grounds for finding reference in each to similar mystical experiences. The significance of this
for our study is that it locates a Jewish mystical tradition squarely
within Second Temple Judaism, prior to Paul, which later finds expression in the *hekhalot* writings, implying at least the possibility that
the experiences like those of *merkabah* mysticism were known at the
time of Paul.

Morray-Jones notes that the rabbis were very cautious with regard to *merkabah* mysticism. Mystics were forbidden to share their
experiences except with the wise, and even then only to one at a time.[131]
The rabbis' impression of the *merkabah* was "of something mysterious and wonderful, but terrifyingly dangerous and forbidden."[132] As
an illustration of this, the rabbis told the story of the four scholars
who entered paradise, commonly known as the *pardes* story: three
looked in but met with disaster, and only one ascended and returned
in peace.[133] This account also appears in the *hekhalot* literature;[134] this
version too spoke of the dangers facing mystics, although it did not
have the same demand for secrecy that the rabbis had. Furthermore,
James Davila has argued that there are significant points of resemblance between the *pardes* story and the so-called Hymn of the Garden

---

130. Mach, "Apocalypticism," 261.

131. *m. Ḥag.* 2:1: "They do not expound upon . . . the Chariot [Ezek. 1] before one,
unless he was a sage and understands of his own knowledge"; cf. *t. Ḥag.* 2:1; *b. Ḥag.*
11b; 13a; 14b; Sir 3:21–23. For discussion see Morray-Jones, "Paradise Revisited,"
185–88.

132. Ibid., 183.

133. *t. Ḥag.* 2:3–4; *b. Ḥag.* 14b; *y. Ḥag.* 2:1 (VII.A); *Song Rab.* 1 (on Song of Songs
1:4). Note also Jacob's injury as a result of his angelic encounter (Gen 32:25).

134. *Hekhalot Zutarti* and *Merkabah Rabbah*; for texts, see Morray-Jones,
"Paradise Revisited," 196–98.

in the *Hodayot*,[135] which clearly implies a pre-Pauline dating for this line of thought within Jewish circles.[136]

Similarities between the *pardes* story and Paul's vision recorded in 2 Cor 12:2–4[137] have been drawn since the beginning of the twentieth century.[138] Morray-Jones has argued for three significant points of contact.[139] The most obvious one is the word "paradise"—פַּרְדֵּס in the Hebrew texts, and παράδεισος in Greek. Morray-Jones argues that "paradise," originally referring to the Garden of Eden,[140] was "a technical term for the Holy of Holies in the highest heaven, where the glory of God resides."[141] Most commonly this is located in the seventh heaven in Jewish sources,[142] but an older threefold model of heaven, with which Paul seems to be familiar,[143] also appears to have existed.[144]

135. 1QHᵃ XVI, 4–26.

136. Davila, "*Hoydayot* Hymnist," 457–78.

137. Although the visionary in Paul's account is technically anonymous—"a man in Christ"—and although it seems somewhat surprising that Paul would trumpet his own personal experience of glory in order to defend his apostleship, particularly in the context of his ironic argument that focuses on his ignominious experiences (2 Cor 11:23–33), most interpreters take Paul to be the visionary in question. This view is based on detailed exegesis of the passage: see esp. Thrall, *2 Corinthians*, 2:775–809; cf. Furnish, *2 Corinthians*, 542–45; Martin, *2 Corinthians*, 398–408; Baird, "Visions," 651–62; Forbes, "Comparison," 1–30. The principal reasons for identifying Paul as the visionary are: (i) the introduction of another person's experience would interrupt the sequence of thought (How would telling of someone else's experience help to defend his own apostleship?); and (ii) Paul immediately admits to having had "an abundance of revelations" (v. 7). The use of the third person may best be explained as an expression of the displacement Paul felt within himself (so Thrall, *2 Corinthians*, 781–82; Furnish, *2 Corinthians*, 543; Dunn, *Jesus and the Spirit*, 214–15), perhaps following the example of the pseudepigraphic practice of Jewish apocalypses (so Rowland, *Open Heaven*, 242–45; Segal, *Paul the Convert*, 58–59). However, we should probably also consider the possibility of Paul expressing a rabbinic-like reservation about the disclosing of mystical experiences.

138. See references in Morray-Jones, "Paradise Revisited," 177 n. 1.

139. Ibid., 177–217, 265–92.

140. LXX: Gen 2:8; 13:10; Ezek 28:13; 31:8. פַּרְדֵּס is a loan word from Persian and thus does not appear in the Hebrew Scriptures; see Jeremias, παράδεισος, 765–73.

141. Morray-Jones, "Paradise Revisited," 268; cf. pp. 202–7. See also *Jub.* 3.9–13; 8.19; *2 Bar.* 4.2–7; *Ques. Ezra* 1.19–21.

142. *Midr. Ps* 11:6; *4 Ezra* 7.92–99; *Apoc. Mos.* 35.2; *Apoc. Ab.* 19.4; *2 En.* 3–22 (rec. A); *Ascen. Isa.* 6–11.

143. 2 Cor 12:2.

144. Morray-Jones, "Paradise Revisited," 205; see *T. Levi* 2.6–10; 3.1–4; *Apoc. Mos.* 37.5; *2 En.* 8.1; 42.3(J); *y. Ḥag.* 2:1 (V.H). See further, Collins, "Seven Heavens," 59–93.

A second point of contact is Paul's reference to hearing things that cannot be uttered.[145] Following the account of the *pardes* story in *Hekhalot Zutarti* we read of R. Aqiba telling of his ascension to the *merkabah* where he heard the voice[146] "from beneath the throne of glory," which through a series of questions emphasized the difficulty in making a heavenly ascent:

> And what man is able
> To ascend on high?
> To ride the chariot-wheels?
>
> . . .
>
> To behold his splendor?
>
> . . .
>
> To be transformed into his glory?
> To utter praise?
> To combine letters?
> To behold what is on high?
> And to behold what is below?
>
> . . .
>
> And who is able to explain, and who is able to see?

And then the voice goes on to explore the mysteries of God, noting various perceptions of what God is like, and concluding that he cannot be described with words:

> His holy ones on high say: "We see (him) like the appearance of lightning!" His prophets say: "We see (him) in a dream-vision, like a man who sees visions in the night." . . . But our rabbis say: "He is, so to speak, like us, but he is greater than everything—and this is his glory, which is hidden from us." Moses says to them, to these and those: "Do not investigate with your words, but let him be praised in his place!" Therefore it is said: Blessed be the glory of the LORD from his place![147]

The third point of contact that Morray-Jones proposes has to do with Paul's "thorn in the flesh," suggesting that this has something to

145. 2 Cor 12:4. Although he describes this event as a "vision," his failure to mention what he saw could be due either to his attempt not to boast like his opponents, or to a stricture, like what we read in rabbinic literature, concerning the telling of *merkabah* experiences. For references, see above, p. 198 n. 131.

146. Literally, a קוֹל בַּת, which was the term the rabbis used to speak of a voice from heaven declaring God's judgment; see Betz, "φωνή," 288–90.

147. Cited in and translated by Morray-Jones, "Paradise Revisited," 278–80.

do with his vision.[148] Rather than joining the speculation concerning the nature of the thorn, Morray-Jones looks to its cause. Building on a view proposed by Robert Price,[149] he argues that the "messenger of Satan" that Paul mentions in v. 7 was in fact "an angelic opponent similar to the gatekeepers of the hekhalot tradition, who attack and punish those deemed unworthy to ascend to the merkabah."[150] Here we recall the *pardes* story in which three scholars met with disaster when they ascended to heaven; one of them, Morray-Jones observes, was "stricken" (נִפְגַע), which is the meaning of the word Paul uses of himself (κολαφίζω).[151]

Alan Segal goes a step further and argues that evidence of Paul's dependence on mysticism goes far beyond having an isolated vision; mystical experiences, he says, "form the basis of his theology."[152] He argues, for example, that Paul owes his understanding of the divinity of Christ to his mystical experiences which are understandable in terms of *merkabah* mysticism. Segal identifies three aspects of Jewish mysticism that play an important role here. The first is the depiction of God as a human figure. He traces this development back to the book of Exodus where Israel's guardian angel is said to bear the divine name, where God reveals his glory to Moses by showing him his back but not his face, and where God appears to Moses and the elders on Mount Sinai.[153] In similar fashion, both Ezekiel and Daniel have a vision of God in human form seated upon a throne.[154] Segal writes:

> Yahweh himself, the angel of God, and his Glory (כָּבוֹד) are melded together in a peculiar way, which suggested to its readers a deep secret about the ways God manifested himself to humanity.[155]

---

148. Ibid., 281–83. If this is true, it would provide another reason why Paul mentions his vision in a context where he is magnifying his weaknesses: he cannot speak of his thorn unless he first speaks of his vision.

149. Price, "Punished in Paradise," 33–40.

150. Morray-Jones, "Paradise Revisited," 282.

151. Ibid., 283.

152. Segal, *Paul the Convert*, 69; see also Tabor, *Things Unutterable*. Important in the following discussion is the image of glory in Jewish and Pauline literature, on which see Newman, *Paul's Glory-Christology*.

153. Exod 23:21; 24:1–2, 9–11; 33:18–23.

154. Ezek 1:26; Dan 7:9–14.

155. Segal, "Jewish Mysticism," 100.

Second, Segal notes Jewish sources that speak of the glory of Adam before he sinned,[156] which consequently also speak of God's human appearance in this way.[157] Of special significance here is Ezekiel's description of his vision as "the appearance of the likeness of the glory of the LORD."[158] Therefore, writes Segal, "God's Glory or *kavod* can be a technical term for God's human appearances."[159] And third, Segal notes that during the Hellenistic period a principal angel appears, under various names, who "is not only head of the heavenly hosts but sometimes participates in God's own being or divinity":[160] for example, we read of Iaoel who, God says, mediates "my ineffable name";[161] Melchizedek, who is identified as the "god" who presides over the heavenly council in Ps 82;[162] Metatron, who is called "Prince of Divine Presence" and who sits on a throne;[163] and Eremiel, who is mistaken for God.[164] Also appearing are unnamed beings, one whose name cannot be given,[165] and another known as the "Son of Man."[166]

Alongside this tradition of the Glory of God is the portrayal of certain people ascending into heaven and being transformed into angels.[167] Particularly significant are Adam, Abel, Jacob, Moses, and

---

156. *Apoc. Mos.* 21.2, 6; *T. Ab.* 11.8–9; CD III,20; 1QS IV,23; 4Q504 8 recto. See Morray-Jones, "Transformational Mysticism," 15–17.

157. Segal, "Jewish Mysticism," 99.

158. Ezek 1:28.

159. Segal, *Paul the Convert*, 41; cf. Morray-Jones, "Transformational Mysticism," 2–6; Newman, *Glory-Christology*, 83–104.

160. Segal, "Jewish Mysticism," 100–101, citation from p. 101.

161. *Apoc. Ab.* 10.3. Segal (ibid., 100) notes that "[t]he name Yahoel [i.e., Iaoel] illustrates one interpretation of carrying the divine name, since it is a combination of the tetragrammaton and a suffix denoting angelic stature."

162. 11Q13 (Melch) II,9–13.

163. *3 En.* 10.1.

164. *Apoc. Zeph.* 6.4–15.

165. *Mart. Ascen. Isa.* 7.2–4.

166. Dan 7:13–14; *1 En.* 46.1–5; 48.1–6; 62.13–16; 69.27–29; cf. *4 Ezra* 11–13 and *2 Bar.* 36–39 which, while not using the term "Son of Man," both build on the vision of Dan 7.

167. Segal, "Jewish Mysticism," 101–8. If we assume that angels can be identified as stars (see Job 38:7; Isa 14:12–13), then one of the earliest references to people being transformed into angels is Dan 12:3 where it is said that the wise (i.e., the teachers) will shine like the stars.

Enoch,[168] the last two being particularly important.[169] Segal draws attention to a work based on Exod 1–15 written by Ezekiel the Tragedian, which dates at least as far back as the second century BCE.[170] In it we read of Moses having a vision of a figure seated on God's throne who hands Moses his scepter, summons him to sit on the throne and places a diadem on his head. Following this, the stars submit to him.[171] Philo also speaks of Moses ascending to heaven and being made into a divinity.[172] Speculation regarding Enoch also pre-dates Paul, as is evident from the books of *1 Enoch* and *Jubilees*. In *1 Enoch* we read of Enoch ascending to heaven and of him having a vision in which believers are transformed into the likeness of the Messiah;[173] in *Jubilees* he ascends to heaven and resides in the Garden of Eden "in greatness and honor."[174] Other texts also express this idea of all the righteous being glorified: *2 Baruch* speaks of the angelic transformation of all believers and reflects the language of Dan 12:3 where we read of the future resurrection when people will be made to shine like the stars;[175] Morray-Jones also identifies several midrashim that speak of the righteous being made superior to the angels.[176]

Segal argues that this is the proper background against which to understand Paul's language about Jesus Christ. Of particular significance is how Paul speaks of glory in connection with Christ: while he does not explicitly call Christ the "Glory of God," he does speak of Christ as the "Lord of glory" and of his "body of glory";[177] he speaks of God making known the "riches of his glory";[178] and particularly sig-

---

168. For ancient sources and modern references see ibid., 101–4, and his supporting literature.

169. Morray-Jones, "Transformational Mysticism," 10–14.

170. Segal, "Jewish Mysticism," 102.

171. *Ezek. Trag.* 68–82.

172. Philo, *Mos.* 1.155–58; *QE* 1.29, 40; *Sacr.* 8–10.

173. *1 En.* 14; 90.37–39. In the section known as "The Similitudes of Enoch" (chs. 37–71), Enoch ascends to heaven and is overcome by its glory. He performs various messianic tasks and in the end he is transformed into the figure of the "Son of Man" (*1 En.* 70–71). On the dating of the Similitues, see below, p. 307 n. 156.

174. *Jub.* 4.23–26 (Wintermute, *OTP*).

175. *2 Bar.* 51.3, 5, 10; cf. *2 En.* 22.7–10; *Mart. Ascen. Isa.* 6–11.

176. Morray-Jones, "Transformational Mysticism," 17–18.

177. 1 Cor 2:8; Phil 3:21.

178. Rom 9:23; cf. Phil 4:19; Eph 1:18; 3:16; Col 1:27.

nificant, in a context where Christian conversion is in view, he speaks of "the light of the gospel of the glory of Christ, who is the likeness [εἰκών] of God."[179] In light of this language and the evidence pointing to his mystical experiences, Segal concludes that Paul, in his conversion, identified Jesus with the heavenly figure known in Jewish mysticism as the "image" and "glory of God."[180]

According to Segal, Paul's view of salvation was similarly shaped by his vision of Christ as the glory of God: like those who made heavenly ascents, believers will be transformed so as to share in the glory of God—that is, to share in Christ. Like Adam, people have lost the glory of God because of their sin.[181] But believers look forward to the transformation of their bodies at the resurrection into a body like Christ's,[182] and to sharing in the glory of God in his kingdom,[183] something that God always intended.[184] Indeed, this transformation already begins as believers behold the glory of the Lord.[185] Paul's most sustained discussion of the transformation of believers is 2 Cor 3:7–4:6 where he contrasts the glory available to believers with that of Moses. Segal writes:

> Paul's term, "the glory of the Lord" must be taken both as a reference to Christ and as a technical term for the Kabod (כבוד), the human form of God appearing in biblical visions. In 2 Cor. 3:18 Paul says that Christians behold the Glory of the Lord as in a mirror and are transformed into his image. For Paul, as for the earliest Jewish mystics, to be privileged enough to see the Kabod or Glory of God is a prologue to transformation into His image. Paul does not say that all Christians have made the journey literally but compares the experience of knowing Christ to being allowed into the intimate presence of the Lord. . . . It is very difficult not to read this passage in terms of Paul's later description of the ascension of the man to the third heaven and conclude that Paul's conversion experience also involved his identification of Jesus as the "image" and "glory of

---

179. 2 Cor 4:4; cf. Col 1:15; 1 Tim 1:11. In Phil 2:6 Paul describes Christ as being "in the form [μορφή] of God."

180. Segal, "Jewish Mysticism," 111–12.

181. Rom 3:23.

182. Phil 3:21; 1 Cor 15:43.

183. Rom 5:2; 8:18; 2 Cor 4:17; 1 Thess 2:14; cf. Col 1:27; 3:4; 2 Thess 2:14.

184. 1 Cor 2:7.

185. 2 Cor 3:18.

God," as the human figure in heaven, and thereafter as Christ, son, and savior.[186]

Segal, therefore, explains Paul's "in Christ" language in terms of "being united with Christ's heavenly vision."[187] And that this is made available to all believers through baptism is understandable, says Segal, in light of the ritual preparations, including immersion (the *tevilah*), required to purify those who wished to make a heavenly ascent.[188] But then he goes on to assert that "[t]he mystical experience of conversion is not only with the risen Christ but with the crucified Christ."[189] Thus,

> Dying and being resurrected along with Christ in baptism is the beginning of the process by which the believer gains the same image of God, his *eikōn*, which was made known to humanity when Jesus became the son of man.[190]

The reason for this identification with the crucified Christ and not only with the risen Christ, according to Segal, is because of the believers' "divided state": by the Spirit they are "in Christ," but they also still belong to "the world of the flesh."[191] And so Segal writes:

> Paul is convinced that being united with Christ's crucifixion means not immediate glorification but suffering for the believers in this interim period. The glorification follows on the final consummation.[192]

We are indebted to Segal and others for demonstrating the importance of mysticism for understanding Paul. He may be correct in finding the source of Paul's "in Christ" language in his mysticism and his understanding of glory. Furthermore, he is certainly correct in saying that Paul understood that believers are currently living in an interim period where their lives are marked by an identification with the death of Christ; hence, they continue to experience suffering and death, and will experience glorification only at the end with the parousia. The

---

186. Segal, "Jewish Mysticism," 111–12.

187. Segal, *Paul the Convert*, 64.

188. Ibid., 61–62, 64.

189. Ibid., 68.

190. Ibid., 64.

191. Ibid., 68.

192. Ibid. See Paul's references to believers suffering: Rom 5:3; 8:17–18; 2 Cor 1:16; 8:2; Phil 1:29–30; 1 Thess 1:6; 2:14; 3:3–4; cf. 2 Thess 1:4–7.

question, however, is *why* Paul believed that believers in the current age should be marked by an identification with the death of Christ. The mysticism perspective does not seem to explain Paul's "dying with Christ" language. Indeed, if mysticism is the "basis of his theology," as Segal claims, it is not clear why Paul should think in terms of dying with Christ at all. Why not preach a glory-based gospel which leads believers into a proleptic experience of their glorification with Christ? Indeed, if the vision of the glorified Christ was all determinative for Paul, why would he even be concerned about Jesus' death? Segal has suggested how Paul's "dying with Christ" language relates to his mystical perspective, but he has not demonstrated how this language could have derived from Jewish mysticism. I suspect the problem here stems from his claim that mysticism is the *basis* of Paul's theology: no doubt his mystical experiences profoundly shaped his understanding of the gospel; however, there may be more going on in Paul than what can be derived from mysticism alone.

Christian Tradition

Were there aspects of the early Christian tradition that may have led Paul to develop his participatory language?

Eschatological Hope of Being "with Christ"

Eduard Schweizer has argued that Paul's "dying with Christ" language is a development from the eschatological hope of being "with Christ."[193] Several times Paul speaks of life "with Christ" either after death[194] or at the parousia[195]—language that Schweizer thinks derives from imagery in the Old Testament and in Jewish texts that speak of the Lord coming with his saints.[196] He then notes that "the formula 'with Christ' occurs only in either apocalyptic or baptismal contexts."[197] He argues that baptism was understood broadly in the early church in terms of

---

193. Schweizer, "Dying and Rising," 1–14.

194. Phil 1:23.

195. 1 Thess 4:17; 2 Cor 13:4; Rom 6:8; cf. Col 3:4.

196. Schweizer, "Dying and Rising," 2; here Schweizer is building on the work of Dupont, *L'union avec le Christ.*

197. Ibid., 3.

admission to the kingdom of God, an admission that according to Paul would take place in the future when believers would be "with Christ." Other early Christians, however, convinced by their experience of the Spirit that the new age had already begun, understood baptism as admission to God's present kingdom. In response, Paul, still emphasizing the future hope of rising with Christ, described baptism in terms of a "dying with Christ," meaning that believers had died to sin.[198]

But is such a process likely to have occurred? The eschatological hope was expressed in terms of *being* with Christ, whereas the language Paul uses of believers' baptism focuses on *dying* with Christ. If Paul wanted to address the overenthusiasm of some believers who were insisting on the present reality of the kingdom to the exclusion of any future hope (and it appears that Paul did have to do this, for example, in Corinth); and if he wanted to do so by retaining the future hope of being with Christ at the parousia and, at the same time, emphasizing the importance of new life that began at baptism, he certainly did not need to speak of believers "dying with Christ." Probably the easiest thing to do would have been to talk about the presence of the Spirit of God, the way the Spirit transforms believers, and perhaps the relationship between Jesus and the Spirit—all of which he, in fact, does do. But the idea of "dying with Christ" seems unnecessary to meet this purpose. Furthermore, the idea of "dying with Christ" seems to be different enough from that of "being with Christ" that it is difficult to see how the former could have grown out of the latter.

DYING WITH CHRIST IN THE JESUS TRADITION

Ulrich Wilckens[199] has suggested that Paul's "dying with Christ" language developed from the Jesus tradition where discipleship was defined in terms of being with Jesus,[200] with Peter expressing the ultimate form of discipleship—a willingness to die with Jesus.[201] However, in light of the fact that Peter and the others deserted Jesus and that none

198. Ibid., 8.

199. Wilckens, *Römer*, 2:60–61.

200. Mark 3:14: "he appointed twelve, to be with him"; John 15:27: "you also are witnesses, because you have been with me from the beginning"; Matt 12:30 par.: "He who is not with me is against me, and he who does not gather with me scatters"; cf. Luke 8:1; 22:14, 56; Mark 14:67.

201. Matt 26:35//Mark 14:31; Luke 22:33; cf. John 11:16.

of them did in fact die with him, it is difficult to see why this "with Jesus" language would have led Paul to develop the concept of believers dying with Christ.[202]

Jewish Tradition

Numerous attempts have been made to find the source of Paul's "in Christ" and "with Christ" language in the Old Testament.

Corporate Personality

Regarding Paul's incorporative language, many have observed that the Old Testament often reflects some kind of identification of the members of a group with an individual. The classic evidence for this is: (i) the judgment against the whole house of Achan even though it was only Achan who was guilty;[203] (ii) the alternation in some of the psalms between singular and plural first person pronouns, perhaps indicating a fluid movement between the identity of the psalmist and that of the Israelites collectively;[204] and (iii) the ambiguity in the identity of Deutero-Isaiah's Servant, sometimes depicted as Israel but at other times as an individual.[205]

Early in the twentieth century, H. Wheeler Robinson tried to explain this phenomenon by arguing that the Israelites possessed a primitive mentality known as "corporate personality" in which people understood their identity not as individuals but as members of a group;[206] and numerous scholars claimed this as the source of Paul's "in Christ" language.[207] Robinson's view, however, has now been largely discredited,[208] due primarily to two critiques: J. R. Porter argued that

202. See Wedderburn, *Baptism and Resurrection*, 346.

203. Josh 7.

204. See, e.g., Pss 20:5–8; 36:7–11; 44:4–8; 60:9–12; 66:6–15 (note also here the identification with the Israelites in history); 106:4–6, 47; 123:1–2; 137:1–6.

205. While some of the servant-texts are ambiguous in that they could be read as referring either to the nation or to an individual, there are some that clearly identify the servant as Israel (Isa 41:8–9; 43:10; 44:1–2, 21; 45:4; 48:20; 49:3) and others where it seems that an individual within Israel is in view (Isa 49:5–6; 53:8, 11).

206. Robinson, *Doctrine of Man*, 4–34; idem., *Corporate Personality*, 1–35.

207. See, e.g., Whiteley, *Theology*, 45–46, and his revised opinion on p. 292.

208. Although, as Porter, "Two Myths," 292–99, laments, the concept continues to be appealed to in scholarship uncritically.

Israelite law "operated on the basis of the individual rather than the group, and was concerned to fix individual guilt and inflict individual punishment";[209] and J. W. Rogerson challenged the anthropological and psychological basis of Robinson's analysis.[210]

In an attempt to adapt the "corporate personality" idea without reliance on Robinson's theory, N. T. Wright has tried to locate the background for Paul's "in Christ" language in the ancient understanding of kingship where "the king and the people are bound together in such a way that what is true of the one is true in principle of the other."[211] Especially relevant for him are texts that speak of the people's kinship or identification with the king in terms of being "in the king" or "in David."[212] While Wright does not claim that Paul drew on such texts directly, he does maintain that these texts "suggest a matrix of ideas out of which a fresh incorporative usage could grow, namely, that of the king representing the people."[213]

Another way to look for the source of Paul's incorporative language is to focus on the phrase "in Adam." Dunn, for example, notes the double meaning of the name "Adam" in the Genesis narrative, denoting either the first human or a generic human being[214] and thus suggesting a representative role of this figure.[215] While Adam is not referred to frequently in the Old Testament, he is mentioned as the first human being[216] and as the typical sinner;[217] but Ezekiel shows that the Genesis story could be adapted to depict the downfall of other

209. Porter, "Legal Aspects," 379.

210. Rogerson, "A Re-Examination," 1-16; idem., *Anthropology*, 46–65.

211. Wright, "ΧΡΙΣΤΟΣ as 'Messiah,'" 46; cf. Rogerson, "Re-Examination," 14–15, who, although proposing that the term "corporate personality" no longer be used for the sake of clarity, agrees that there are corporate identity aspects in the Old Testament, such as the "I" of the Psalms and the hopes of the Israelites being centered in their king. His argument is that these features can be explained without recourse to Robinson's psychological theory.

212. 2 Sam 19:43; 20:1; 1 Kgs 12:16.

213. Wright, "Messiah," 46.

214. *HALOT*, s.v. אָדָם. Dunn, *Theology*, 82 n. 10, notes that the LXX reflects this dual perspective by translating אָדָם as ἄνθρωπος up to Gen 2:18 but as Ἀδάμ thereafter.

215. Ibid., 82–83. In addition, it is possible that the extraordinary ages of individuals particularly in Gen 1–11 could suggest to later readers, like Paul, that these narratives should be read in a more-than-historical sense.

216. Deut 4:32; 1 Chron 1:1.

217. Hos 6:7; Job 31:33.

historical figures,[218] suggesting that the story itself was understood in some sense as an archetype rather than simply as history. During Second Temple Judaism, reflection on Adam increased significantly, and Dunn shows that Paul was aware of some of this reflection.[219] A tension arises in this reflection between the consequence of Adam's sin on all his descendants and the moral responsibility of all people. In the Greek version of the *Life of Adam and Eve*, Adam complains that the action of his wife has led to "death gaining rule over all our race."[220] In *4 Ezra*, the seer laments over Adam's sin which, he says, caused the fall of all his descendants: "the fall was not yours alone, but ours also who are your descendants."[221] The angel, Uriel, qualifies Ezra's statement, however, by affirming that people will be judged according to their own actions.[222] And in *2 Baruch* we read that although Adam "brought death upon all who were not in his own time," individuals are responsible for their own moral decisions: "Adam is, therefore, not the cause, except only for himself, but each of us has become our own Adam."[223]

Unfortunately, none of these three texts can be dated with confidence prior to the time of Paul;[224] in fact the fall of Jerusalem in 70 CE plays an important role in the latter two. If we could assume that such ideas as these pre-dated Paul, it would be possible to see in them the source for Paul's depiction of Adam as a representative figure such that he could speak of people being "in Adam," and thus by extension of believers as being "in Christ." However, even if this were so, it would not help to explain Paul's participatory language. In Rom 5 where Paul contrasts Adam and Christ, he is very clear that Christ's act of obedience is something done apart from believers. Rather than sharing in

---

218. Ezek 28:11–15. Zimmerli, *Ezekiel*, 90–91; Cooke, *Ezekiel*, 315; Allen, *Ezekiel 20–48*, 94.

219. Dunn, *Theology*, 82–83.

220. *Apoc. Mos.* 14 (Johnson, *OTP*).

221. *4 Ezra* 7.118 (Metzger, *OTP*).

222. *4 Ezra* 7.127–29.

223. *2 Bar.* 54.15, 19 (Klijn, *OTP*).

224. Johnson, "Life of Adam and Eve," 251–52, dates the original Hebrew text of the *Life of Adam and Eve* between 200 BCE and 100 CE, "more probably toward the end of the first Christian century"; Metzger, "Fourth Book of Ezra," 520, dates *4 Ezra* to about 100 CE; and Klijn, "2 Baruch," 616–17, dates *2 Baruch* between 100 and 120 CE.

his act of obedience (i.e., his death), believers receive the free gift of grace that his act has made available.[225]

Wedderburn takes another approach: he suggests, building on the view of W. D. Davies,[226] that Paul's "with Christ" language arose from the sense of solidarity that Jews had with their ancestors, particularly with those who participated in the historical act of redemption from Egypt. This solidarity can be seen in the use of personal pronouns in, for example, certain Old Testament texts:[227]

> Hear this word that the LORD has spoken against *you*, O people of Israel, against the whole family which I brought up out of the land of Egypt. (Amos 3:1; emphasis added)

Similarly, the "present reality of a past event"[228] is evident in the Passover liturgy of the Mishnah:

> In every generation a person is duty-bound to regard himself as if he personally has gone forth from Egypt. . . . Therefore we are duty-bound to thank, praise, glorify, honor, exalt, extol, and bless him who did for our forefathers and for us all these miracles. He brought us forth from slavery to freedom.[229]

Wedderburn then suggests that Paul's "in Adam" language reflects a "physical solidarity" based on Adam being "literally the ancestor of the whole human race"[230]—or to use the language of Heb 7:5, all people were already in the loins of Adam. Paul's "in Christ" language would then also reflect a sense of solidarity, but based not on a physical connection but rather on the decision and action of God:

> If [Christ] is our representative it is . . . because, we claim, God has tied our destinies to that of this one individual. He represents us because, we believe, God chose him to do so. In him we see the pattern of what God willed humanity to be. In what happened to him, both in its fearfulness and in its expressible

---

225. Rom 5:15–17.

226. Davies, *Rabbinic Judaism*, 102–8.

227. We could also add Deut 26:5–9.

228. Davies, *Rabbinic Judaism*, 103 n. 1.

229. *m. Pesaḥ.* 10:5 (Neusner). Davies, *Rabbinic Judaism*, 102–3, also cites from the Passover Haggadah, which he thinks was arranged by Gamaliel II probably between 80 and 120 CE: "We were slaves to the Pharaoh in Egypt, and the Lord our God brought us forth from thence."

230. Wedderburn, *Baptism and Resurrection*, 355.

hopes, we see ourselves before God and in God's eyes, as our Creator sees us and chooses to regard us. We are thereby called and challenged to align ourselves with that pattern of God's working and choosing.[231]

In this way, Wedderburn draws a connection between Paul's incorporative and participatory language: both speak of solidarity with Christ. To be "in Christ" is to identify oneself with Christ as the truly human one; to "die with Christ" is to identify oneself with the act of salvation centered around Jesus' death and resurrection. Furthermore, Wedderburn thinks that Paul's readers would have understood this language not in terms of the gods of the mystery religions, but rather on the analogy of how their own rulers (whom they could refer to as σωτήρ[232]) played "a representative role upon which their destinies and well-being depended."[233]

This explanation of the origin of Paul's "dying with Christ" language is intriguing, since it juxtaposes two major acts of salvation—just as Jews felt solidarity with those involved in the exodus story, so Christians felt solidarity with Jesus in his death and resurrection. And yet, we need to raise a note of caution: Jewish solidarity was with those who were being saved, not with the one doing the saving. There is some evidence that Paul saw Jesus as the first saved one: he was the one whom God raised from the dead[234] so that he would be the "first-born of many brethren"[235] and so that believers might be heirs of salvation with him.[236] Consistent with this, Paul speaks of God as the author of salvation,[237] as the one who orchestrated the coming of Jesus, his death, and his resurrection.[238] And yet, apparently without any fear of contradiction, Paul more frequently depicts Jesus Christ as Savior:[239]

---

231. Ibid.

232. Foerster, "σῴζω," 1008, 1010–12; BDAG, s.v. σωτήρ.

233. Wedderburn, *Baptism and Resurrection*, 356.

234. Rom 4:24; 6:4; 8:11; 10:9; 1 Cor 6:14; 15:15; 2 Cor 4:14; Gal 1:1; 1 Thess 1:10; note also the implication of the passive voice in the following: Rom 6:9; 7:4; 8:34; 1 Cor 15:4, 20; 2 Cor 5:15.

235. Rom 8:29; cf. Col 1:18.

236. Rom 8:17.

237. See above, p. 172.

238. Rom 3:25; 5:8; 8:3, 32; 1 Cor 1:25–30; Gal 1:4; 4:4–5.

239. Phil 3:20 (Paul's only use of the world σωτήρ); cf. Eph 5:23.

salvation is made possible through Jesus Christ;[240] it is Jesus Christ who welcomes believers,[241] makes them alive,[242] lives in them,[243] works through them,[244] and intercedes for them;[245] and in ways that must have shocked many Jews who steadfastly held to their belief in one God, Paul speaks of Jesus as a Jew would speak only of God,[246] describing him as the "likeness of God" and the "form of God"[247] and freely calling him "Lord."[248] Furthermore, two of the texts where Paul uses participatory language clearly portray Christ as Savior, not as the first saved one: (i) Paul says that "all have died" because "one has died for all"[249]—precisely what he means by "all have died" is debated, but this is clearly participatory language, and the phrase "one has died for all" portrays Christ as Savior; and (ii) Paul uses participatory language in the context of the Lord's Supper—"The bread which we break, is it not a participation in the body of Christ?"[250]—a rite which he understood as a remembrance of Jesus giving up his life for others,[251] suggesting again the role of Savior. So, if this sense of solidarity did influence Paul in his participatory language, we must conclude that there was something else influencing him as well.

240. Rom 5:1, 2, 11, 21; 1 Cor 15:57; 2 Cor 1:5; 3:4, 14; 5:18; Phil 1:11; 1 Thess 4:14; 5:9.

241. Rom 15:7.

242. Rom 8:10.

243. Gal 2:20.

244. Rom 15:18; 2 Cor 13:3; Phil 1:11.

245. Rom 8:34.

246. 1 Cor 8:6: Phil 2:6–11.

247. 2 Cor 4:4; Phil 2:6.

248. Rom 1:4, 7; 4:24; 5:1, 11, 21; 6:23; 7:25; 8:39; 10:9; 13:14; 14:9; 15:6, 30; 16:18, 20; 1 Cor 1:2–3, 7–10; 2:8; 5:4; 6:11, 14; 8:6; 9:1, 5, 14; 11:23; 12:3; 15:31, 57; 16:23; 2 Cor 1:2–3, 14; 4:5, 14; 8:9; 11:31; 13:14; Gal 1:3; 6:14, 18; Phil 1:2; 2:11, 19; 3:8, 20; 4:23; 1 Thess 1:1, 3; 2:15, 19; 3:11,13; 4:1–2; 5:9, 23, 28; Phlm 3, 5, 25.

249. 2 Cor 5:14.

250. 1 Cor 10:16.

251. 1 Cor 11:24.

Tradition of the Martyrs

David Seeley has argued that the concept of "noble death" shaped Paul's understanding of Jesus' death.[252] He suggests that the noble death tradition influenced Paul not directly, but rather through the tradition of Jewish martyrs. In particular, he proposes that the Hellenistic Jewish writings of 2 and 4 Maccabees, particularly their accounts of the martyrdoms of Eleazar and of the seven brothers with their mother,[253] present a Jewish version of the noble death tradition which is characterized by four basic elements. First, the deaths of the martyrs are vicarious—vicarious in the sense that they benefit others by providing an example to follow.[254] And the example serves as a model in two senses: (i) by encouraging those who face persecution and death to remain faithful, and (ii) by encouraging all to remain faithful in life and to exhibit the same values of nobility, honor, and courage that the martyrs demonstrated.[255] According to the writer of 4 Maccabees, it is precisely by means of the martyrs and people who followed their example by remaining faithful to their tradition that victory was won over Antiochus.[256] Second, the martyrs display obedience: in particular, they resolve to obey the law in defiance of the de-

252. Seeley, *Noble Death*. For the Greco-Roman concept of noble death, see above, pp. 151–53.

253. 2 Macc 6:18—7:42; 4 Macc 6–18.

254. 2 Macc 6:19–20, 27–28, 31; 4 Macc 6:18–19, 22; 7:8–9. Note also how the martyrs provided examples to one another (4 Macc 9:23; 10:16; 12:16; 13:8–18) and how they looked to figures in their tradition as examples (4 Macc 9:6; 16:18–23; 18:11–19).

255. Seeley, *Noble Death*, 89–91. Note the numerous references to virtues of nobility in the accounts of the martyrs: γενναῖος, κτλ. ("noble," "illustrious"): 2 Macc 6:28, 31; 7:5, 11, 21; 8:16; 4 Macc 6:10; 7:8; 8:3; 11:12; 15:24, 30, 32; 16:16; 17:2–4; εὐγενής, κτλ. ("high-born," "noble-minded"): 4 Macc 6:5, 22, 30; 8:4; 9:13, 22, 24, 27; 10:3, 15; 12:14; 13:11; καλοκἀγαθία ("nobility of character," "excellence"): 4 Macc 1:10 (cf. v. 8, ἀνδραγαθία: "bravery," "manly virtue"); 11:22; 13:25; 15:9; εὔκλεια ("good repute, glory"): 2 Macc 6:19; ἀγαθός ("a high standard of worth"): 2 Macc 7:20; τιμή ("value," "honour"): 4 Macc 1:10; 11:6; 17:20; μεγαλόφρων, κτλ. ("high-minded," "generous"): 4 Macc 6:5, 24; 9:21; σώφρων ("self-controlled"): 4 Macc 7:23 (Alexandrinus); 15:10; θαρρέω ("be courageous"): 4 Macc 13:11; 17:4; ἀνδρεία ("manly"): 4 Macc 1:11; 17:23–24; ἀνδρεῖος ("manly," "courageous"): 4 Macc 7:23; 15:10, 30; 17:24; εὐψυχία, κτλ. ("good courage," "high spirit"): 2 Macc 7:20; 4 Macc 9:23, 26 (καρτεροψυχία); ἄξιος ("worthy"): 2 Macc 6:23, 24, 27; 7:20, 29; 4 Macc 7:6; 11:6.

256. 4 Macc 1:11; 9:30; 11:23–25; 18:3–5. Interestingly, 4 Maccabees makes no mention of the Maccabees.

mand of Antiochus that they eat pork and adopt the Greek way of life.[257] Third, the martyrdoms take place in a military context—namely, the offensive of Antiochus against the Judeans. And while not themselves participants in a military battle, the martyrs' struggle is described with military language.[258] And fourth, the martyrs overcome physical vulnerability. Not only does each of the martyrs endure torture,[259] but Eleazar overcomes the frailty of age,[260] and 4 Maccabees highlights the victory of reason over emotions.[261] Seeley then notes that the element of sacrifice is present[262] but argues that it plays a secondary role.[263]

Seeley then goes on to argue that these same four elements can be found in Paul. First, the vicarious nature of Jesus' death consists in it being an example for people to imitate. For Paul, however, the imitation is metaphorical, not literal. In baptism believers re-enact Jesus' death, and by identifying themselves with him in his death they metaphorically die to the power of sin.[264] Thus, Paul mythologizes the noble death pattern of the martyrs.[265] Seeley writes:

> The difference between Paul and *4 Maccabees* lies in Paul's my-thologization of the mimetic pattern. One would not say that a person literally following the example of a martyr 'dies with' the latter, for the martyr is already dead. Now, Christ's cruci-fixion was a past event when the first believer was baptized, yet Paul speaks of dying with Christ. Paul seems to think that Christ's death is not limited by the constraints of temporality in the way other people's deaths are. It is in some sense a myth-ic event. Furthermore, the believer does not literally, physically cease to function. . . . This fact suggests that, for Paul, 'death' is

257. 2 Macc 6:1, 23, 28; 7:2, 9, 11, 23, 30, 37; 4 Macc 6:18, 21, 27, 30; 9:1–2, 15; 11:5, 12; 13:9, 13, 15; 15:9; 16:16, 24. The accounts in 4 Maccabees also speak of al-legiance to the religion of the ancestors (4 Macc 6:22; 9:6–7, 24, 29–30; 11:20; 12:11; 13:12, 27; 15:3, 12, 14, 32; 16:13–14, 17; 17:17; 18:3).

258. 4 Macc 7:4; 9:23–24; 13:16; 16:14.

259. See, for example, 2 Macc 6:30; 7:12; 4 Macc 7:16.

260. 2 Macc 6:24–28; 4 Macc 7:13.

261. 4 Macc 1:1, 7–9, 13; 6:30–35; 7:1, 4, 13–14, 16; 8:1; 9:17; 10:19; 11:27; 13:1, 3, 5–7; 14:11; 15:1, 11, 23; 16:1, 4; 18:2.

262. 4 Macc 6:28–29; 17:21–22. We shall discuss Seeley's handling of 2 Macc 7:37–38 below.

263. Seeley, *Noble Death*, 97–98.

264. Rom 6:1–11.

265. Seeley, *Noble Death*, 99–102.

primarily a matter of being moved out of Sin's dominion. . . .
The enemy is mythic, not literal like Antiochus.[266]

Second, Paul notes that Jesus' death was an act of obedience;[267] similarly, obedience is required of those who would imitate Jesus.[268] Furthermore, Jesus' faithfulness, rather than the faith of believers, may be what is in view in the phrase διὰ πίστεως in Rom 3:25[269] and in Paul's phrase πίστεως Ἰησοῦ Χριστοῦ (or similar) in Rom 3:22, 26; Gal 2:16 (twice); 3:22; Phil 3:9.[270] It may also be that Paul's phrase "Christ did not please himself" implies obedience.[271] Third, Paul uses military metaphors[272] and thinks in terms of a battle between two aeons "with Jesus' death as the point at which one aeon gains ascendancy over the other."[273] Thus, "believers die to one aeon and are proleptically raised to another (Rom 6.4–5, 8, 11)."[274] Fourth, even though he was human and therefore subject to the limitations of the flesh (which are evident

266. Ibid., 101. Here Seeley builds on Sanders' view of participation.

267. Phil 2:8; Rom 5:18–19. Even if Phil 2:8 is traditional, Seeley, *Noble Death*, 103, argues that Paul's insertion of the phrase, "even death on a cross," shows that the point of Jesus' obedience was particularly important to him.

268. Rom 1:5; 6:16–17; 10:16; 15:18; 16:19, 26; 2 Cor 9:13; 10:5–6; Phil 2:12.

269. See Williams, *Jesus' Death*, 46–47, who argues that, from the structural parallelism indicated by the use of prepositions, in the same way that διὰ τὴν πάρεσιν and ἐν τῇ ἀνοχῇ τοῦ θεοῦ in Rom 3:25–26 both refer to actions of God, so διὰ [τῆς] πίστεως and ἐν τῷ αὐτοῦ αἵματι in Rom 3:25 could both refer to actions of Jesus.

270. Seeley, *Noble Death*, 106–7, deals only with Rom 3:22, but building on the analysis of Richard Hays, the same argument would apply to the other texts as well; see Hays, *Faith of Jesus Christ*, 119–62. Seeley also notes Williams' argument against taking the objective genitive and subjective genitive in these texts to be mutually exclusive; see Williams, *Jesus' Death*, 47–49. A useful orientation to the issues involved in the debate over whether πίστις Χριστοῦ should be rendered as subjective or as objective genitive are the two essays by Dunn and Hays included as appendices in the second edition to Hays, *Faith of Jesus Christ* (Dunn, "Once More," 249–71; Hays, "Πίστις," 272–97).

271. Rom 15:3. While it is true that Paul's point here, in showing that Christ was willing to bear with insults rather than to please himself, was to present him as a model for the believers in Rome (see Jewett, *Romans*, 879), the model is clearly one of obedience to something or someone other than himself (see Cranfield, *Romans*, 2:732: he "sought rather to please His Father and to please men εἰς τὸ ἀγαθὸν πρὸς οἰκοδομήν").

272. Rom 13:12; 2 Cor 6:7; 10:4–5; 1 Thess 5:8.

273. Seeley, *Noble Death*, 107. Paul can also refer to the conflict in non-military language (Gal 5:16–26; 1 Cor 10:14–22).

274. Ibid., 108.

in Rom 7:14–25), Jesus withstood the power of sin.[275] And, finally, while Seeley acknowledges Paul's use of sacrificial language, he argues that, as in the accounts of the martyrs, sacrifice is a secondary theme.[276] Thus, he concludes:

> Paul has rendered the process of re-enacting Christ's death so that, when the believer 'reads' his or her own life in terms of Christ's story, this is not merely an imaginative re-enactment, but one with the sort of objective effect that pertains to the literal re-enactment of a martyrs' death. When one copies a martyrs' death and dies obediently, one gains a victory over the evil tyrant whose compulsions have proved ineffective. When one 'dies with' Christ, even though one does not literally die, one gains liberation from and shares in a victory over the evil tyrant Sin.[277]

There are a number of problems with Seeley's argument. First, he uses the word "vicarious" in more than one sense, or speaks of different modes of vicariousness, and this causes some confusion. For example, he concludes from 2 Maccabees that the deaths of the seven brothers are not vicarious because they are not expiatory, while the death of Eleazar is vicarious because it is exemplary.[278] The word "vicarious" is properly used of people who act as a substitute or representative for others or who achieve something on behave of others; being an example for others to follow is something different.[279] Furthermore, since "vicarious" is a heavily used theological term, and since it can be used in more than one sense, I suggest clarity would be gained if specific adjectives were used with reference to the death of the martyrs, such as "exemplary," "inspiring," "expiatory," or "atoning," rather than using an ambiguous term like "vicarious."

Second, the category "military context" is probably too general to be useful in defining a noble death pattern. If the martyrs' deaths can be described as military (and it is questionable whether Greek or Roman writers would accept this, since the martyrs were non-combatants),

---

275. Ibid., 109–10; 2 Cor 5:21.

276. Ibid., 19–37.

277. Ibid., 148.

278. Ibid., 88–89.

279. See the *Oxford English Dictionary*, s.v. "vicarious."

then virtually any killing of Judeans in the era when Judea was ruled over by a non-Jewish power could be described as a military death.

Third, if it can be established that Paul does in fact draw on the tradition of the martyrs, then it could possibly be argued that Paul mythologizes the mimetic aspect of the martyrs' deaths by speaking of believers dying with Christ, meaning they are inspired by the example of his death. However, since these two motifs—dying with Christ and the example of literal martyrdom—are significantly different as they stand, one cannot use them as part of the argument to show that Paul in fact was drawing on the tradition of the martyrs. That argument needs to be established on other grounds.

Fourth, there is insufficient evidence to show that Paul thought of Jesus' death as a case of overcoming physical vulnerability. It may be correct to deduce from Paul's identification of Jesus as human being, and from his claim that "he knew no sin," that he must have thought that Jesus triumphed over physical hardships. But Paul does not explicitly assert this, which is significant since Paul's was aware that Jesus suffered a painful death.[280]

And fifth, unlike the accounts of the martyrs, Paul does not describe Jesus' death as being noble. Where the writers of 2 and 4 Maccabees intended to motivate their readers by portraying the noble virtues of the martyrs in how they died,[281] Paul focuses on the love of Jesus[282] and on the love of God who was instrumental in Jesus' death;[283] he never describes Jesus' death as being noble, honorable, or courageous. This is a notable difference between Paul's account of Jesus and the accounts of the martyrs or the classical accounts of noble deaths.

This being said, there are other aspects of the martyrs' deaths which Seeley does not explore but which we do find in Paul, in particular, aspects associated with the martyrs' expression of hope. First, the martyrs express the hope that they will live again beyond their death. In the more Hellenistic account of 4 Maccabees,[284] this hope is

280. In addition to numerous references to his crucifixion (see above, p. 172–73), see the references to Christ's sufferings in 2 Cor 1:5; Phil 3:10.

281. See above, p. 214 n. 255.

282. Rom 8:35; 2 Cor 5:14.

283. Rom 5:8; 8:31–35.

284. The most obvious evidence of the extent of Hellenization in 4 Maccabees is its emphasis throughout on the superiority of reason over emotions (see above p. 215 n. 262).

for immortality;[285] but in 2 Maccabees the hope is more specifically for bodily resurrection.[286] Similarly, Paul strongly believed in the resurrection of Jesus.[287]

Second, hope is expressed that the deaths of the martyrs would represent an end to God's wrath against his people, a defeat of oppressive forces, and the establishment of peace.[288] In 2 Maccabees, this is first indicated by the mother who cites from the Song of Moses: "And he will have compassion on his servants" (2 Macc 7:6, citing Deut 32:36). John Downing notes the importance of the context of this citation in Deuteronomy:[289] after depicting God's judgment on a rebellious nation, the Song goes on to speak of God's vindication of his people and the overthrow of her adversaries.[290] Similarly the last of the seven brothers says:

> But you, who have contrived all sorts of evil against the Hebrews, will certainly not escape the hands of God. For we are suffering because of our own sins. And if our living Lord is angry for a little while, to rebuke and discipline us, he will again be reconciled with his own servants. (2 Macc 7:31–33)

> I, like my brothers, give up body and life for the laws of our fathers, appealing to God to show mercy soon to our nation and by afflictions and plagues to make you confess that he alone is God, and through [ἐν] me and my brothers to bring to an end the wrath of the Almighty which has justly fallen on our whole nation. (2 Macc 7:37–38)

285. 4 Macc 7:3; 14:5; 16:13; 17:12; 18:23; cf. 9:8 (being with God), 22 (immortality of Abraham); 17:18 (gaining a life of eternal blessedness).

286. 2 Macc 7:9: "the King of the universe will raise us up to an everlasting renewal of life"; 7:11: "and from him [God] I hope to get them [my tongue and hands] back again"; 7:14: "One cannot but choose to die at the hands of men and to cherish the hope that God gives of being raised again by him. But for you [Antiochus] there will be no resurrection to life!"; 7:23: "the Creator of the world . . . will in his mercy give life and breath back to you again"; 7:29: "Accept death, so that in God's mercy I may get you back again with your brothers." See further Goldstein, *2 Maccabees*, 305–15; Nickelsburg, *Resurrection*, 119–38.

287. Rom 1:4; 4:24–25; 6:4–5, 9; 7:4; 8:11, 34; 10:9; 1 Cor 6:14; 15:12–23; 2 Cor 4:14; 5:15; Gal 1:1; Phil 3:10; 1 Thess 1:10.

288. 2 Macc 7:38; 4 Macc 6:28–29; 17:20–22; 18:3–5.

289. Downing, "Martyrdom," 281–82.

290. See Deut 32:36–43.

Seeley makes an effort to show that the deaths of the seven brothers and their mother (2 Macc 7) were not expiatory as is sometimes claimed. He notes that (i) two of the brothers declare that they are suffering because of their own sins, not because of the sins of others (7:18, 32); (ii) the martyrs' appeal to God's mercy appears to be no different than that of Judas and his guerrillas (7:37; 8:2–4); and (iii) the ἐν here in 7:38 should be understood locatively rather than instrumentally, meaning that the prayer is that their deaths themselves would be the end of God's wrath, not that their deaths would be the means by which God's wrath would end.[291] I suspect Seeley is correct here; the focus is on the ending of God's wrath, rather than on the reason why God would change his disposition. It is quite possible, however, that a Christian reader, like Paul, convinced of the instrumental value of Jesus' death, could have found an instrumental reading here as well.

Four texts in 4 Maccabees express this theme of the death of the martyrs marking the end of oppression in Judea:

> Be merciful to your people, and let our punishment suffice for them. Make my blood their purification, and take my life in exchange for theirs. (4 Macc 6:28–29)

> I call on the God of our fathers to be merciful to our nation; but on you he will take vengeance both in this present life and when you are dead. (4 Macc 12:17–18)

> These, then, who have been consecrated for the sake of God, are honored . . . by the fact that because of them our enemies did not rule over our nation, the tyrant was punished, and the homeland purified—they having become, as it were, a ransom for the sin of our nation. And through the blood of those devout ones and their death as an expiation [ἱλαστηρίον], divine Providence preserved Israel that previously had been afflicted. (4 Macc 17:20–22)

> Therefore those who gave over their bodies in suffering for the sake of religion were not only admired by men, but also were

---

291. Seeley, *Noble Death*, 87–89. On the third point, see Williams, *Jesus' Death*, 85–90, who argues that (i) it is incongruous that God would use an external instrument to withhold his wrath, and (ii) the prayer of Judas, summarized in 2 Macc 8:2–4, appeals to God to come to their aid on the basis of all kinds of hardships the Jews were experiencing—the many who were oppressed, the temple which had been profaned, Jerusalem which was being destroyed, and the many who had died—not only on the basis of the deaths of the seven brothers.

> deemed worthy to share in a divine inheritance. Because of
> them the nation gained peace, and by reviving observance of
> the law in the homeland they ravaged the enemy. The tyrant
> Antiochus was both punished on earth and is being chastised
> after his death. Since in no way whatever was he able to compel
> the Israelites to become pagans and to abandon their ancestral
> customs, he left Jerusalem and marched against the Persians.
> (4 Macc 18:3–5)

Even if the writing of 4 Maccabees did not pre-date Paul,[292] these texts
demonstrate that there was consistency, from the time of the writing
of 2 Maccabees (according to Goldstein, originating between 78 and
63 BCE[293]) to that of 4 Maccabees, in the view that the death of the
martyrs brought about God's salvation. In light of the uncertainty of
the dating of 4 Maccabees, it would be precarious to go further to try
to draw a connection between how that work describes the martyrs'
deaths in sacrificial language (blood bringing purification, ransom,
expiation) and the sacrificial language Paul uses in relation to Jesus'
death. But we can say with confidence that the deaths of the martyrs
were understood as the event which led to God's salvation. And similarly, Paul thought of Jesus' death as the means to escape God's wrath[294]
and to enjoy peace and salvation.[295]

In addition to these two additional aspects of the martyr accounts,
there are other aspects in Paul's writings that suggest his thinking is
shaped by the martyr tradition. First, as Stephen Patterson observes,
Paul, in his letter to the Philippians, speaks of himself as a possible
martyr. He writes from prison, not knowing whether he will live or
die, but he reflects the courage of the martyrs:

> it is my eager expectation and hope that I shall not be at all
> ashamed, but that with full courage now as always Christ will
> be honored in my body, whether by life or by death. For to me
> to live is Christ, and to die is gain. (Phil 1:20–21)

And in language reminiscent of the account of Eleazar,[296] Paul speaks
of the possibility of his own death in sacrificial terms:

292. See above, p. 99 n. 183.

293. Goldstein, *2 Maccabees*, 71–83.

294. Rom 5:9; 1 Thess 1:10; 5:9.

295. Rom 5:1; 1 Cor 1:18; 1 Thess 5:9; cf. Eph 2:14.

296. 4 Macc 6:29.

> Even if I am to be poured as a libation upon the sacrificial of-
> fering of your faith, I am glad and rejoice with you all. (Phil
> 2:17)

Furthermore, he encourages his readers that if, in the midst of suffering, they live a life "worthy of the gospel of Christ," not being "fright-
ened in anything by [their] opponents," this will be a portent of their
salvation and of their opponents' destruction.[297]

And second, as Larry Hurtado (and others) has demonstrated,
Paul presented Jesus' death as paradigmatic for the life of believers.[298] Jesus' death was the model to inspire believers to humility,[299]
generosity,[300] and concern for others.[301] In the context of describing
the change in character that should mark believers, Paul uses language
that suggests an adaptation of the example of Jesus' death: "those
who belong to Christ Jesus have *crucified* the flesh with its passions
and desires";[302] "We were buried therefore with him by baptism into
death, so that . . . we too might walk in newness of life";[303] "you have
died to the law through the body of Christ, so that you may belong to
another."[304] And finally, Paul describes the change that he personally
has experienced in terms of the world being crucified to him, and he to
the world,[305] and he confesses that for himself, Jesus' death and resurrection, in some sense, now define the orientation of his whole life.[306]

Consequently, while there are some clear differences between the
accounts of the martyrs' deaths and Paul's view of Jesus' death, there
are some distinct similarities, so much so that it is reasonable to suggest that such accounts shaped Paul's thinking to some extent.[307] The

297. Phil 1:27–30.

298. Hurtado, "Jesus' Death," 413–33.

299. Phil 2:5–11.

300. 2 Cor 8:9.

301. Rom 14:15; 1 Cor 8:11.

302. Gal 5:24, emphasis added; cf. Col 2:20–3:17.

303. Rom 6:4.

304. Rom 7:4.

305. Gal 6:14; cf. 2:19–20.

306. Phil 3:10.

307. It may also be that while Paul may have received from the early church an
understanding of Jesus' death as a martyr's death, the origin of this idea could be Jesus
himself; see Downing, "Martyrdom," 279–93; Patterson, "Consider Yourself Dead,"
161–87.

significance of this is that it lends credence to finding a connection in terms of the first element in Seeley's model—vicariousness, or better, imitation. As Seeley suggests, Paul has transformed this element by speaking of *dying with* Christ, rather than simply *following and being inspired by the example* of Christ. It is certainly possible to see Paul's "dying with Christ" language as a transformation of the mimetic language of the martyr accounts. Seeley writes:

> By inspiring others to follow their example, i.e. to re-enact it either imaginatively or literally, the martyrs defeat Antiochus. . . . Paul, too, affirms that the believer must replicate the model's death, dying with Jesus in obedience and thereby gaining release from Sin's rule. *4 Maccabees* and Paul share a concern with the imaginative re-enactment of an obedient death. The former affirms a relatively straightforward sort of identification. The latter presents a more mythic, mystical . . . sort of re-actualization. In each case, however, the basic pattern is the same.[308]

Or, at least the pattern is similar. What is not yet clear, however, is *why* Paul does this. Why not simply present Jesus' death as an example to inspire believers? The image of "dying with Christ" does not obviously follow from the example of the martyrs. We will need to explore further to see if we can better understand why Paul made the changes to the pattern that he did.

Hellenism

Because Paul lived in a Hellenistic world, it is appropriate to ask to what extent he was influenced by that world or, perhaps better, to what extent he shaped his message according to the forms of thought in that world.

Hellenistic Judaism

There is abundant evidence to show that some Second Temple Jews were influenced by Hellenism. Some, like the "renegades" of 1 Maccabees, thought that it would be better to abandon their Jewish distinctiveness in exchange for adopting the Greek way of living;[309] others, like Philo,

308. Seeley, *Noble Death*, 111.

309. 1 Macc 1:11–15.

thought they could express their faith through Hellenistic forms of thought. If Paul was influenced by Hellenism, it is more likely he was following the second path rather than the first. While not representative of Hellenistic Judaism as a whole, Philo was clearly a Hellenistic Jew and one whom we can explore as a possible source of Paul's "dying with Christ" language.

A number of sayings can be found among Greek philosophers that focus on the irony of dying and living. Plato, for example, records Socrates' citation of Euripides: "Who knoweth if to live is to be dead, And to be dead, to live?"[310] Socrates goes on to explain that the death in view here is the condition of being entombed in a physical body. Heraclitus expresses a similar sentiment: "both life and death exist both in our state of life and in our state of death; for when we live our souls are dead and buried within us, and when we die our souls revive and live."[311] The emphasis in Stoicism was similar, but was directed more at overcoming the limitations of the body. Epictetus writes: "Who then is a Stoic? . . . Show me a man who though sick is happy, though in danger is happy, though dying is happy, though condemned to exile is happy, though in disrepute is happy."[312] Cynics took the death of Socrates as a metaphor for how all of life should be lived—one must die to the influences of the body. A Cynic named Aeschines, writes the following in the context of describing Socrates:

> The philosopher does nothing other than to die, since he disdains the demands of the body and is not enslaved by the pleasures of the body; and this is nothing other than the separation of the soul from the body, and death is nothing other again than the separation of the soul from the body.[313]

These perspectives view the souls of people as entrapped in their physical bodies, and hence in a state like death as long as the bodies live; release from this predicament comes either through physical death or through a new orientation to life that seeks to overcome the limitations of the body.

---

310. Plato, *Gorg.* 492E (Lamb, LCL).

311. Paraphrased by Sextus Empiricus, *Pyr.* 3.230 (Bury, LCL).

312. Epictetus, *Diatr.* 2.19.23–24 (Oldfather, LCL); cf. 1.19.7–9; Seneca, *Tranq.* 5.4–5.

313. Cited in Malherbe, ed., *Cynic Epistles*, 257, 259.

Philo exhibits a Hellenistic anthropology in that he speaks of people as being composed of bodies and souls, with the soul being something immortal which, in a way analogous to Abraham, left its home in heaven and came to earth, a place of mortality and evil, and now lives "like an immigrant and sojourner in this mortal body."[314] Consistent with this, then, he speaks of death in two senses, one physical and the other moral:

> one that of the man in general, the other that of the soul in particular. The death of the man is the separation of the soul from the body, but the death of the soul is the decay of virtue and the bringing in of wickedness.[315]

Thus he describes wicked people as those who "are dead to true life and bear their body with them like a tomb that they may bury their unhappy soul in it."[316] In contrast, he describes the wise, in words similar to those of Plato,[317] as those who:

> study to die to the life in the body, that a higher existence immortal and incorporeal, in the presence of Him who is Himself immortal and uncreate [*sic*], may be their portion.[318]

314. Philo, *QG* 4.74 (Marcus, LCL); cf. *Her.* 239–40; *Cher.* 113–15.

315. Philo, *Leg.* 105 (Colson & Whitaker, LCL).

316. Philo, *QG* 1.70 (Marcus, LCL); cf. *Post.* 45; *Her.* 292.

317. Plato, *Phaed.* 64A: "those who pursue philosophy aright study nothing but dying and being dead"; 67E: "the true philosophers practise dying, and death is less terrible to them than to any other men. . . . They are in every way hostile to the body and they desire to have the soul apart by itself alone" (Fowler, LCL).

318. Philo, *Gig.* 14–15 (Colson & Whitaker, LCL); cf. *Migr.* 9: "Depart, therefore, out of the earthly matter that encompasses thee: escape, man, from the foul prison-house, thy body, with all thy might and main, and from the pleasures and lusts that act as its jailers (Colson & Whitaker, LCL); *Leg.* 3.42: "it is not possible that he whose abode is in the body and the mortal race should attain to being with God; this is possible only for him whom God rescues out of the prison" (Colson & Whitaker, LCL); *Ebr.* 101: "While [the mind] is cooped up in the city of the body and mortal life, it is cabined and cribbed and like a prisoner in the gaol declares roundly that it cannot even draw a breath of free air; but when it has gone out of this city, its thoughts and reflections are at liberty, like the hands and feet of the unbound prisoner, and it finds free scope and range for the employment of its active powers, so that the clamours of the passions are at once restrained" (Colson & Whitaker, LCL).

Consequently, he prays, "May my soul die to the life of the body that it may be reckoned among the souls of the just."[319] And in one place he cites Heraclitus in support:

> "We live," he says, "their death, and are dead to their life." He means that now, when we are living, the soul is dead and has been entombed in the body as in a sepulchre; whereas, should we die, the soul lives forthwith its own proper life, and is released from the body, the baneful corpse to which it was tied.[320]

And thus Philo's hope for the immortal soul is to leave the mortal body and return to its true source, "the incorporeal Logoi of the divine world," also known as angels.[321] Philo's thought here needs to be understood from the Hellenistic perspective of an anthropological dualism: the soul and the body are at odds with each other. True life—that is, the soul experiencing the life for which it was created—can be found only by the soul dying to the body which, it seems, will never happen completely until the body dies physically.

At first glance it might appear as though Paul reflects Philo's perspective, particularly in light of his dualism of flesh versus the spirit. Paul calls on believers to "put to death the deeds of the body" so that they can live κατὰ πνεῦμα rather than κατὰ σάρκα.[322] There are, however, good reasons to distinguish Paul's perspective from that of Philo.[323] First, while there may be some argument over which instances of πνεῦμα in Paul refer to the Spirit of God and which to the spirit of a person, he clearly sees both at work: believers have the Spirit of God dwelling in them, and hence their spirits are alive.[324] The point is that whereas Philo thought of the soul as foreign to the body and ultimately needing release from the body, Paul sees the spirit as something that comes to life while in the body through the work of the Spirit of God.

---

319. Philo, *Mos.* 1.279 (Colson, LCL); cf. *Det.* 49: "the wise man, when seeming to die to the corruptible life, is alive to the incorruptible; but the worthless man, while alive to the life of wickedness, is dead to the life happy [*sic*]" (Colson & Whitaker, LCL); Unidentified frg. from *QE* 1: " Ἐὰν δὲ ἀποθάνῃ μέν τις τὸν θνητὸν βίον, ζήσῃ δὲ ἀντιλαβὼν τὸν ἀθάνατον [If anyone dies to the mortal life, he will live enjoying the immortal]."

320. Philo, *Leg.* 1.108 (Colson & Whitaker, LCL).

321. Philo, *QG* 3.11 (Colson & Whitaker, LCL); cf. *Her.* 275–83.

322. Rom 8:4–14 (citation from v. 13); Gal 5:16–25; 6:8.

323. On Paul's anthropology, see Bultmann, *Theology*, 192–210.

324. Rom 8:9–10.

Second, Paul does not disparage human physicality to the extent that Philo does. On the one hand, when Paul speaks of flesh, he has in view the proclivity of people to sin: there are sinful passions and desires coming from the flesh which must be overcome,[325] for these desires are opposed to the desires of the Spirit[326] and ultimately lead to death,[327] making it impossible for those who indulge such desires to please God.[328] In the end Paul concludes that "nothing good dwells within . . . my flesh."[329] On the other hand, Paul insists that "in the flesh" is precisely where the believer is called to live: he speaks of "always being given up to death for Jesus' sake, so that the life of Jesus may be manifested *in our mortal flesh*."[330] And in defending himself to the church at Corinth, by means of distinguishing himself from some whom he calls "false apostles," he draws a careful distinction between living ἐν σαρκί and acting κατὰ σάρκα.[331] From this context we can conclude that acting κατὰ σάρκα—that is, acting as his opponents were acting—included boasting of accomplishments, abilities, and heritage.[332] While such a distinction cannot be maintained based solely on Paul's use of prepositions,[333] the distinction is made clearly enough to conclude that there is an appropriate way to live "in the flesh."

One can only guess at why Paul would have made such a distinction since he does not tell us explicitly, but it would make sense if it had to do with Paul's belief in the goodness of God's creation[334] and especially in the resurrection of the body. Although creation has been "subjected to futility," it will one day "be set free from its bondage to

---

325. Rom 7:5; 13:14; Gal 5:16, 19, 24; cf. Col 2:23.

326. Rom 8:7; Gal 5:17.

327. Rom 8:6, 13; Gal 6:8.

328. Rom 8:8.

329. Rom 7:18.

330. 2 Cor 4:11, emphasis added; cf. Gal 2:20.

331. 2 Cor 10:3.

332. Paul complains about his opponents because (i) they brought "another gospel" (11:3–4); (ii) they sought to authenticate themselves (10:12; 11:18); (iii) they took advantage of the Corinthians (11:20); (iv) they were probably boasting about their skill in Hellenistic rhetoric (10:10; 11:6); and (v) they boasted of their Jewish heritage (11:21–22). For further discussion on the identity of Paul's opponents at Corinth see Furnish, *2 Corinthians*, 48–54; Martin, *2 Corinthians*, 346–42.

333. See, e.g., Rom 8:8; Phil 3:3.

334. Rom 1:20.

decay" so that it can "obtain the glorious liberty of the children of God" which, Paul says, will involve "the redemption of our bodies."[335] Thus, the resurrection of the body is that aspect of the renewal of all creation that pertains specifically to humans.[336] This is not the language of one who longs for the soul's escape from the body, but rather of one who looks for the re-creation of the whole person. It is questionable, therefore, how much Paul would have borrowed from a Hellenistic perspective like that of Philo, regarding the experience of death in the midst of life or as the means to life, since he had such a significantly different anthropology and hence a different understanding of the human predicament.

Mystery Religions

The phrase "mystery religions," or "mysteries" (μυστήρια) as they were known in ancient times, is an umbrella term denoting a variety of religious cults in the Greco-Roman world, some known to exist well before the advent of Christianity, but few after the fourth century CE.[337] The term originally referred only to the mysteries of Eleusis but later came to be used of other cults that to some degree followed the Eleusian pattern. Most of the cults were organized around a central sanctuary and were in that sense local, although in some cases their influence was widespread; the mysteries of Dionysus and Orpheus were exceptions in that they had no central shrine. While the cults differed one from the other, they held in common the view that salvation required a special ritual process whereby one was initiated into the secret mysteries of the cult. This led to a distinction between public and private ceremonies, with only initiates being admitted to the latter. Kurt Rudolph summarizes:

> Mysteries, then, are special initiation ceremonies that are eso-
> teric in character and often connected with the yearly agri-
> cultural cycle. Usually they involve the destiny of the divine
> powers being venerated and the communication of religious
> wisdom that enables the initiates to conquer death. The mys-
> teries are part of the general religious life, but they are to a

335. Rom 8:20–23.

336. 1 Cor 15: 20–23, 35–50; 2 Cor 4:14.

337. Theodosius I decreed the closure of the Eleusian sanctuary in 392 CE, and three years later it was destroyed by Alaric's Christian Goths.

special degree separated from the public cult that is accessible to all, and on this account they are also called "secret cults."[338]

Difficulties plague the study of mystery religions. Our basic problem is that, by their very nature, the mysteries were kept secret. Initiates were required to take a vow of silence regarding the cult's secrets, violation of which could result in severe punishment.[339] As a result, there is limited literary evidence for the mysteries, particularly evidence that helps us to understand the secrets themselves; furthermore, much of the evidence we do have comes from Christian apologists who in writing to defend their own faith did not necessarily give an unbiased portrayal of the mystery religions.[340] And yet the situation is not hopeless. Wedderburn provides a balanced assessment of the extent to which our evidence informs us of the mysteries:

> Mostly the innermost experiences of the mysteries remain, in all probability, closed to us. And yet some explanation of their goals and aspirations, their beliefs and their claims, did filter through to the general public, was even deliberately proclaimed to that public, and impressed itself upon the consciousness of that age to such an extent that, from Plato onwards, other religious and philosophical movements copied their language and their claims, however much they filled their words with another content. That is indication enough of a fair level of knowledge of, and esteem for, the mysteries, whether they were admired or feared as rivals.[341]

Early in the twentieth century, Schweitzer argued that it was only from the second century CE that mystery religions began to appear and, therefore, they were irrelevant for the study of the New Testament.[342] Wedderburn, however, presents some reliable evidence to show that mystery religions were active during the first century: (i) some literary, epigraphic, and pictorial evidence for mystery religions in the first century CE does exist—not the abundance of evidence that we have, say, for the second century, but evidence that arguably

338. Rudolph, "Mystery Religions," 6327.

339. See Bornkamm, "μυστήριον," 806–8; Wedderburn, *Baptism and Resurrection*, 91; Burkert, *Homo Necans*, 251–52.

340. Wedderburn, *Baptism and Resurrection*, 91.

341. Ibid., 98; cf. Wiens, "Mystery Concepts," 1249–51.

342. Schweitzer, *Paul and His Interpreters*, 181–236, esp. 191–92.

does suggest a widespread popularity of the mysteries;[343] (ii) there are two literary works that speak of mystery religions during the first century—Plutarch's *Isis and Orisis*, and Heraclitus' *Homeric Allegories*;[344] (iii) Eusebius speaks of two first-century figures, Cornutus and Chaeremon, who appear to have been involved in mystery religions;[345] and (iv) Plato, Plutarch, and Philo all use mystery religion language.[346]

Similarities between the New Testament and mystery religions have long been observed. The common use not only of the key word μυστήριον, but also of related words such as φωτισμός, παλιγγενεσία, ἐπιφάνεια, πλήρωμα, ἐμβατεύειν, ἁγνεία, εὐσέβεια, and τελετή, led early Christian apologists to conclude that pagan writers were borrowing from the New Testament.[347] Beginning in the late nineteenth century, the history of religions school argued for the converse, namely, that it was Paul who had borrowed from the mystery religions. Furthermore, it was understood that mystery religions had at their core a myth about a dying and rising god, and that initiation had to do with sharing in the destiny of this deity. This, so it was argued, is what gave shape to Paul's theology.[348] One of the most influential representatives of this school, Wilhelm Bousset, writes:

> The myth of the suffering, dying, and rising god was extraordinarily widely distributed in the Hellenistic religious life, strongly conditioned by the Orient. Above all it belongs to the characteristic features of almost all the so-called mystery religions.[349]

This myth of the dying and rising god was then expressed in the various cultic rites which in turn served as the means for devotees to identify with and share in the experience of the deity. Bousset continues:

---

343. Wedderburn, *Baptism and Resurrection*, 99–113.

344. Ibid., 130–36.

345. Ibid., 136. See Eusebius, *Hist. eccl.* 6.19.8 (LCL, Oulton).

346. Ibid., 149–58.

347. See Justin, 1 *Apol.* 66.4; *Dial.* 70.1; 78.6; Tertullian, *Praescr.* 40; Firmicus Maternus, *Err. prof. rel.* 22.

348. For a detailed survey of the research, see Wagner, *Pauline Baptism*, 7–57; for a review and evaluation, see Simon, "Religionsgeschichtliche Schule," 135–44; for a review of research up to 1980, see Wiens, "Mystery Concepts," 1252–79.

349. Bousset, *Kyrios Christos*, 188.

> This myth of the dying and suffering god . . . takes a generally anthropological and practically paraenetic turn. The god with his fate in victory and defeat becomes the type for the destiny of the pious. *What occurs here is not a once-for-all fact of the past; it happens ever anew. . . .*
>
> Already in the cultus of the god who dies and awakens to new life the way is paved for this *unio mystica* of the believers with the god. For this is the evident meaning of the cultic celebrations of all the dying and again rising vegetation deities, that the participant in the cult actively and imitatively takes part in the destiny of the god in frenzied grief and exuberant joy.[350]

And this then becomes a primary source for Paul's thinking:

> One will not be able to avoid the impression that here is given the spiritual atmosphere within which the Pauline dying-with-Christ and rising-with-Christ is located. . . .
>
> And the main idea is the same. The pious person experiences in mystical fellowship the same thing which the divine hero previously and fundamentally has experienced in exemplary power.[351]

This view, however, has now fallen out of favor and there are few today who would support it without substantial modification, if at all. This is due both to thorough criticism and to a general change of direction in Pauline studies. Regarding the latter, thanks especially to the work of Albert Schweitzer,[352] W. D. Davies,[353] and H. J. Schoeps,[354] and thanks to the discovery of the Dead Sea Scrolls,[355] current scholarship tends to be more confident than at the beginning of the twentieth century in finding the appropriate categories of thought for understanding Paul within Judaism and the Old Testament rather than in Hellenism.[356]

Regarding the criticism of the history of religions perspective, Marcel Simon notes, "One of the major mistakes of the school was . . . to construct a kind of inclusive mystery religion which in actual

---

350. Ibid., 191–92, emphasis original.

351. Ibid., 193–94.

352. Schweitzer, *Mysticism.*

353. Davies, *Paul and Rabbinic Judaism.*

354. Schoeps, *Paul.*

355. See, e.g., Murphy-O'Connor, ed., *Paul and Qumran.*

356. Simon, "Religionsgeschichtliche Schule," 137.

fact never existed."[357] That is, there was a tendency to treat all mystery religions as expressions of a common set of beliefs, without significant variance from place to place or from time to time. Thus, evidence from different religions and from different centuries was used to construct a kind of pan-Greco-Roman mystery religion that never actually existed.

Furthermore, many have argued that even if Paul did draw on terminology from the mystery religions, his meaning is radically different.[358] But others have maintained that even linguistic dependence is questionable: Harry Kennedy argued that Paul's vocabulary is understandable in light of the Old Testament, without reference to mysteries;[359] and Arthur Nock demonstrated that conclusions drawn on the coincidence of vocabulary in the New Testament and mystery religions are too simplistic if the respective usage of the words in question is not also compared—indeed, he argues, just as significant is the non-occurrence in the New Testament of numerous words commonly used in mystery religion contexts.[360] This suggests that it is unlikely that Paul borrowed directly from the mysteries. Wedderburn takes this a step further and argues that if there are points of contact between Paul and mystery religions, it is unlikely that Paul would have inherited mystery perspectives from the Hellenistic wing of the church since (i) most of the converts prior to Paul, including the Gentile believers, had previously belonged to the synagogue,[361] and (ii) it is unlikely that there were many converts from the mystery religions in light of the high financial commitment often required for initiation.[362] He goes on to suggest that any similarities are probably due to Paul sharing in knowledge commonly available in the Hellenistic world,[363] or to his adopting some mystery language from Hellenistic Judaism.[364] Regarding the latter, Wedderburn notes, for example, the way Philo

357. Ibid., 142; cf. Wedderburn, *Baptism and Resurrection*, 139–48.

358. See those cited in Wagner, *Pauline Baptism*, 43–57.

359. Kennedy, *Mystery-Religions*, 115–98.

360. Nock, "Vocabulary," 132–34; cf. Wedderburn, *Baptism and Resurrection*, 159.

361. Wedderburn, *Baptism and Resurrection*, 160–61.

362. Ibid., 158.

363. Ibid., 158–59.

364. Ibid., 158–60.

who, although strongly critical of mystery religions, "was quite prepared to present Judaism in terms appropriate to a mystery-religion."[365]

The similarity between Paul and mystery religions with regard to the "dying and rising god" motif has also been challenged.[366] Günter Wagner has argued, focusing especially on Rom 6, that the mystery religions do not inform Paul's understanding of baptism.[367] Wedderburn examines the various mystery religions and concludes that Paul's language of "dying with Christ" did not come from them.[368] His conclusions are important for our study:[369] (i) in both Paul and the mystery religions, hope is placed in the power of the deity or deities for salvation; (ii) in both Paul and some mystery religions, the rescue of a deity who died is seen as a prototype for what will happen to devotees;[370] (iii) both Paul and the mystery religions connect an anticipation of future salvation with the initiation ritual; but (iv) unlike the mystery religions, Paul's understanding of salvation arises not from ritual—baptism was "no re-enactment of Christ's death and resurrection or ritual representation of the initiate's death and resurrection on the analogy of Christ's"[371]—but from (a) his conviction that in his death Christ represented all humanity thereby freeing people from slavery to sin, and (b) his experience of the Spirit as the power of the age to come. He writes:

> the ritual of baptism plays its part in this experience, it is true, but not by portraying before Christians' eyes Christ crucified and risen, but by reminding them that they had already been caught up in, involved in, Christ's past death and resurrection, in that God had addressed his word of condemnation and of restoration and restitution to them too, as represented by the eschatological Adam, Christ.[372]

365. Ibid., 153–58, citation from p. 154.

366. For the debate over the existence of the "dying and rising gods" motif in oriental religions, see Mettinger, *Riddle of Resurrection*, 15–39; Smith, "Dying and Rising Gods," 2535–40.

367. Wagner, *Pauline Baptism*; cf. Pelser, "Formulas," 117–24.

368. Wedderburn, *Baptism and Resurrection*, 296–359.

369. Ibid., 356–59.

370. For Jesus as a prototype, Wedderburn cites Rom 8:11, 29; 1 Cor 15:20–23, 49.

371. Wedderburn, *Baptism and Resurrection*, 357–58.

372. Ibid., 358.

Building on Wedderburn's work, I would argue as follows:[373] First, there is, in the mystery religions, evidence of devotees identifying themselves with a deity. In the Eleusian mysteries, initiates mimic Demeter searching for her lost daughter, Persephone;[374] devotees of Dionysus mimic their god by drinking wine and performing acts of ecstasy;[375] those belonging to the cult of Attis mimic his frenzy and self-mutilation;[376] there is some indication from Plutarch and Firmicus Maternus that the rites of Isis led devotees to mimic some of her experiences;[377] and the annual festival for remembering the death of Adonis involves worshippers in a sharing of Aphrodite's grief.[378] In each of these cases devotees mimic the actions of a deity. It is difficult to demonstrate what this meant to people, but presumably they would have experienced a sense of sympathy and solidarity with the divine power. It is possible that another sense of identification—namely, deification—was experienced as part of the initiation rites in some mystery religions, but the paucity of evidence of these secret rites makes it impossible to say with certainty one way or the other.[379]

Second, mystery religions often tell the story of a deity who dies or goes to the place of the dead, but it is difficult to find a "dying and rising" pattern that could serve as a model for Christ's death and resurrection in Paul's gospel. Hades abducts Persephone and takes her to his domain, but there is no mention that she dies; later Zeus rescues her so that she can return to her mother, Demeter, but Hades tricks her so

373. Details of the myths and rites of the various mystery religions, as they relate to the following argument, can be found in Appendix C below.

374. Clement of Alexandria, *Protr.* 2.18 (cf. *Homeric Hymn to Demeter* 211); Arnobius, *Adv. nat.* 5.26; Ovid, *Fast.* 4.535–36; Wedderburn, *Baptism and Resurrection,* 315–16; Burkert, *Homo Necans,* 267–68.

375. Euripides, *Bacch.* 142–43, 274–84, 417–23, 707; Pausanias, *Descr.* 2.7.5; 6.26.1–2; Hesiod, *Op.* 609–14; Livy 39.8.5–6; 39.13.10–13; Plato, *Phaedr.* 265B; Homer, *Il.* 6.132; Herodotus, *Hist.* 4.79; see further, Harrison, *Prolegomena,* 425; Klauck, *Herrenmahl,* 107–9; Otto, *Dionysus,* 143–51.

376. Lucian, *Syr. d.* 15.

377. Plutarch, *Is. Os.* 27 [361D]; Firmicus Maternus, *Err. prof. rel.* 2.9; cf. Seneca, *Apol.* 13.

378. Ovid, *Metam.* 10.725–28; Aristophanes, *Lys.* 388–98; Ammianus Marcellinus 19.1.11; Plutarch, *Alc.* 18.3; *Nic.* 13.7.

379. Wedderburn, *Baptism and Resurrection,* 333, identifies three ways identification could be understood: (i) becoming identical with another, as in the process of deification; (ii) adopting the role of another, in the way an actor plays a role; and (iii) experiencing a sense of solidarity and sympathy.

that she has to spend a third of each year with him.[380] At the urging of Hera, the Titans murder Dionysus and tear his body apart; and there are various accounts of how he is rescued, but none of which seem to emphasize his death.[381] Some versions of the myth of Attis speak of him dying, but these do not speak of him coming back to life again;[382] the best one version can do is to describe how Zeus allows him to continue to move his little finger.[383] Also, the festival of Attis does not appear to have his resurrection in view.[384] Osiris is killed, or drowns, and later is raised up to become ruler of the underworld.[385] Adonis is killed by a wild boar, and there is no mention of him coming back to life;[386] the Gardens of Adonis do not appear to signify his resurrection.[387] In contrast to Paul's gospel, none of these deals with a historical incident, and none portrays anything equivalent to a resurrection as a victory over death: Persephone continues to move between the realm of life and the realm of the dead; Dionysus escapes death; neither Attis nor Adonis come back to life; and Osiris, although raised to rule, is confined to the realm of the dead.

Third, it appears that the experience of initiation was often described in terms of death. There are two clear indications of this. First, the priest of Isis speaks of Apuleius' initiation as a "voluntary death," and Apuleius describes his initiation as a journey in which he "came to the boundary of death."[388] And second, Plutarch likens physical death to the experience of initiation. Thus, he explains, "the verbs *teleutân* (die) and *teleisthai* (be initiated), and the actions they denote, have a

---

380. *Homeric Hymn to Demeter* 398–400, 445–47, 463–65.

381. Diodorus, *Bib. hist.* 3.62.6–7; Clement of Alexandria, *Protr.* 2.15; Plutarch, *De esu* 7 [996C]; Firmicus Maternus, *Err. prof. rel.* 6.2–4; see further Otto, *Dionysus*, 189–201.

382. Pausanias, *Descr.* 7.17.10–12; see further Wagner, *Pauline Baptism*, 217–18; Nilsson, *Geschichte*, 2:649–51.

383. See Wagner, *Pauline Baptism*, 218–19.

384. See ibid., 223–29.

385. See ibid., 117–20.

386. Firmicus Maternus, *Err. prof. rel.* 9.1; Athenaeus, *Deipn.* 2.69.b; Ovid, *Metam.* 10.708–39; cf. 10.542–44.

387. See Julian, *Caesars* 329D; Plato, *Phaedr.* 276B; Plutarch, *Sera* 17 [560B–C]; Theophrastus, *Caus. plant.* 1.12.2; see further Wagner, *Pauline Baptism*, 189–93.

388. Apuleius, *Metam.* 11.21, 23 (Hanson, LCL).

similarity."[389] This use of death language in connection with initiation should not, however, be surprising. Anthropologists and sociologists have demonstrated that the language of death and rebirth is fairly ubiquitous in cases of conversion and initiation. Mircea Eliade comments:

> The majority of initiatory ordeals more or less clearly imply a ritual death followed by resurrection or a new birth. The central moment of every initiation is represented by the ceremony symbolizing the death of the novice and his return to the fellowship of the living. But he returns to life a new man, assuming another mode of being. Initiatory death signifies an end at once of childhood, of ignorance, and of the profane condition.[390]

Fourth, there does not appear to be any clear first-century evidence of devotees identifying themselves with a deity in his or her death, at least not in the same sense that Paul does. As noted above, identification is typically with the saving deity rather than with the dying one, with Attis being the only possible exception. The death (or disappearance) of a deity is sometimes in view in the rites: the identification with Demeter has the disappearance of Persephone in view; the rites of Isis may have recalled her searching for her lost brother; and the devotees' grieving with Aphrodite have in view the death of Adonis. The evidence suggesting that the eating of raw flesh by devotees of Dionysus was, for them, an identification with the deity in his death, comes from well after the first century.[391] Some identified themselves with Attis by means of self-castration, but in the myth self-castration did not lead to the death of the deity.[392] The evidence for this as an act of imitation, however, comes from the second century CE,[393] and so we cannot be confident that this was the practice in Paul's day.

389. Plutarch, *Mor.* frg. 178 (Sandbach, LCL).

390. Eliade, *Rites and Symbols*, xii–xv, citation from p. xii; cf. pp. 13–14, 29, 34, 38, 73–76, 91, 108, 130, 135. Also, van Gennep, *Rites of Passage*, 110, argues that rites of passage contain "hypnosis, death, a transitional period, and resurrection"; La Fontaine, *Initiation*, 102, argues that both maturity rites (e.g., rites that mark initiation into adulthood) and rites that initiate one into a private society have in common "the symbolism of death and rebirth"; and Dowden, *Death and the Maiden*, 36, comments that "the motif of 'death of the initiate' in passage rites is common because it is part of a standard pattern."

391. Firmicus Maternus, *Err. prof. rel.* 6.5.

392. Pausanias, *Descr.* 7.17.10–12; Catullus 63; Julian, *Or.* 5.167C–169D; Minucius Felix, *Oct.* 22.4; Sallustius, *De diis et mundo* 4.

393. Lucian, *Syr. d.*, 15.

But even if it was first-century practice, there is no evidence that these devotees had an ongoing identification with Attis in his death like Paul had with Christ. The self-mutilation occurred on the "Day of Blood," part of the spring festival of Attis; but the following day was the "Day of Joy," marked by joyous celebration and suggesting that identification with the god in his death was a step to something else rather than a state to remain in.

And fifth, it is unlikely that the ritual baths of mystery religions informed Paul, to any significant extent, in his understanding of Christian baptism. A form of ritual washing was associated with the Eleusian mysteries, and in light of the general influence of these mysteries it would not be surprising to find such a ceremony in other mystery religions. But, as Wagner demonstrates, this was a preparatory bath for the purpose of ritual cleansing, and not part of the initiation itself.[394] Furthermore, since water rites are ubiquitous in religions,[395] the appearance of them in both mystery religions and Paul is no basis for an argument that one borrowed from the other; such an argument would need other evidence to support it which, as we have seen above, appears to be lacking. Finally, it is much more likely that Paul's understanding of baptism derives from the practice of the early church: the way he speaks of baptism suggests that he expects all believers to be baptized,[396] even those he has never met;[397] the testimony from the book of Acts not only confirms this but also shows that such practice went back to the beginning of the Christian movement;[398] and this consistent practice, together with the early Christians' memory of Jesus' own baptism,[399] suggests that Christian baptism was understood as a development from Jesus' baptism. It is difficult to imagine Paul

394. Wagner, *Pauline Baptism*, 71–73; cf. Wilckens, *Römer*, 2:57. Wagner (ibid., 100–103) argues similarly with regard to the ritual bathing in the cult of Isis and Osiris.

395. See, for example, the following articles in the *Encyclopedia of Religion*: Drijvers, "Ablutions," 1:9–13; Meslin, "Baptism," 2:779–83; Preston, "Purification: An Overview," 11:7503–11.

396. 1 Cor 12:13; Gal 3:27.

397. Rom 6:3–4.

398. Acts 2:38, 41, and passim.

399. We note the inclusion of the account of Jesus' baptism in each of the Gospels plus the references in Acts to the "beginning," meaning Jesus' baptism by John (Acts 1:22; 10:37).

deriving his understanding of baptism from another source without making a fundamental break with the early church—a break that would make it difficult to explain why he in other ways depends on early Christian tradition.

Conclusions and Consideration of Paul's Dependency on Jesus

What can we say, then, regarding the origin of Paul's "dying with Christ" language? The use of death imagery in connection with conversion and initiation is not exceptional or distinctive. Also, Paul's sense of identification with Jesus Christ—but not identification with him in his death—parallels what we find in mystery religions and may have derived from there, although another possible source would be Jewish mysticism. Indeed, his understanding of being "in Christ" may have its origin in his own mystical experiences. The Jewish sense of solidarity may have led Paul to understand believers to be, in some sense, participants in the salvation event that occurred in Jesus' death and resurrection. And his own experience of suffering, and the influence of the martyr tradition, may have nurtured an already existing identification with Christ in his death. But none of this clearly explains why Paul began to identify with him in his death.

We do, however, find in some of Jesus' sayings an explanation for some aspects of Paul's "dying with Christ" language. In particular: (i) Jesus speaks of losing life in order to find salvation, and he portrays this as an ongoing disposition rather than simply as a description of a conversion experience:

> For whoever would save his life will lose it; and whoever loses his life for my sake and the gospel's will save it. (Mark 8:35)

> If anyone would come after me, let him deny himself and take up his cross and follow me. (Mark 8:34[400])

Paul expresses a similar perspective when he speaks of "always carrying in the body the death of Jesus, so that the life of Jesus may also be manifested in our bodies"; when he uses the perfect tense in saying "I have been crucified with Christ"; when he uses the present participle to describe his goal—"becoming like him in his death"; and when

---

400. Modified from the RSV.

he describes the regular practice of the Lord's Supper as a κοινωνία in his body and blood.[401] But there is nothing in what we have seen elsewhere that speaks of an identification with death in the same way. Furthermore, (ii) Jesus tells his disciples that they would share his fate, and he does so—in addition to the inference in Mark 8:34—with reference to their sharing of a common cup. And likely at some later point, this saying was complemented with a parallel saying about sharing in Jesus' "baptism," probably in an attempt to adapt the saying for use either at the Lord's Supper or at a baptism:

> The cup that I drink you will drink; and with the baptism with which I am baptized, you will be baptized. (Mark 10:39)

The account of James and John asking for a seat on either side of Jesus in his kingdom, and of Jesus denying them and then instructing his disciples that greatness would be achieved only through servanthood, would have been appropriate teaching in any context, but with the mention of the cup and of baptism it would have been particularly apropos to recall this account and the imbedded saying in the contexts of the Lord's Supper and baptism where it would be natural to emphasize the importance of Christian commitment.

This suggests a context in which Paul could have learned of this saying of Jesus. And it suggests how he may have come to understand both baptism and the Lord's Supper as involving believers in a participation in the death of Christ. As noted above, religious initiation rites, generally speaking, which often include the use of water, are typically thought of in terms of a dying to an old way of life.[402] What is significant about Paul's understanding of baptism, however, is that it involves a dying *with Christ*. Furthermore, this is not the view of baptism that we find elsewhere in the New Testament. Luke, for example, connects Christian baptism with the forgiveness of sins and the gift of the Holy Spirit, and speaks of being baptized "into the name of Jesus,"[403] but there is no sense of sharing in Jesus' death. Similarly, the tradition that Paul received concerning the Last Supper[404] does not have the same dimension of participation in Jesus' death as when he speaks of the cup

---

401. 2 Cor 4:10; Gal 2:20; Phil 3:10; 1 Cor 10:16; cf. 2 Cor 13:4; Gal 6:17.

402. See the citation from Eliade above, p. 236.

403. Acts 2:38; 8:16; 10:47–48; 19:5; 22:16; cf. 1 Pet 3:21.

404. 1 Cor 11:23–26.

and the bread as being a κοινωνία in the death of Christ.[405] According to the tradition in 1 Cor 11:23–26, believers "participate" in the rite by eating the bread and drinking from the cup; and they "participate" in the salvation that the rite speaks of.[406] But it is not clear from this text that believers participate in the death of Christ in the same way that Paul speaks of in, for example, 1 Cor 10:16. This sense of participation in the death of Christ may have been Paul's own contribution to the rite. And, it is quite plausible that Paul came to this understanding of both baptism and the Lord's Supper via Jesus' saying regarding his followers drinking his cup (and being baptized with his baptism), which may very well have been transmitted, in connection with celebrations of the Lord's Supper and of baptism.[407] It is plausible that it was Paul

---

405. 1 Cor 10:16.

406. Hofius, "Lord's Supper," 98–99, comments: "The gift of which the word on the bread in 1 Cor 11:24b speaks is *a participation in the σῶμα of Jesus*. As in Romans 7:4, so here also . . . σῶμα means the body of Jesus Christ given over to death on the cross, and the prepositional attributive τὸ ὑπὲρ ὑμῶν specifies Jesus' self-surrender unto death as expiatory and reconciliatory event. To this event the word over the cup likewise refers, for αἷμα designates here . . . the expiatory blood of Jesus shed on the cross. The word on the bread (σῶμα) and the word on the cup (αἷμα) thus both speak of the *expiatory death* of Jesus Christ. . . . Whoever eats the eucharistic bread and drinks the eucharistic cup receives and so has *a share in the salvation* that has been settled by the expiatory death of Christ" (first and last emphasis mine). Here, what is meant by participation is a sharing in salvation made possible by Jesus' death, not a sharing in the death itself.

As a contemporary example for understanding the significance of the Lord's Supper, I note the Eucharistic Prayers in the Church of England's *The Order for the Celebration of Holy Communion*, which draw heavily upon the language of 1 Cor 11. The prayers, in various ways, speak of the worshippers receiving the body and blood of Christ when they receive the bread and the cup, of them remembering Jesus, receiving forgiveness and freedom, and of them offering a sacrifice of thanks and praise. They all adhere closely to the framework of understanding in which Jesus is the one who died *for us*, and that worshippers are invited to participate in the rite and thereby receive the many benefits that have resulted from Jesus' death. But nowhere is there any language to suggest that the worshippers have died with Christ—participation in that sense is not expressed here.

407. In this connection, it may be significant that, although Luke does not record the incident involving the request of James and John and of Jesus' saying regarding baptism and the cup, he does take from Mark the scene that immediately follows concerning Jesus' challenge to his disciples to be servants (Mark 10:42–44) and places it within the context of the Last Supper (Luke 22:24–27). In light of the fact that Paul was familiar with Luke's tradition of the Last Supper (see Fee, *1 Corinthians*, 546–47), if he also knew the account of the request of James and John, then this would support my suggestion that Paul may have heard in the context of the Lord's Supper the saying

who, within the context of these celebrations, saw the significance of Jesus' words to James and John, and developed the participatory understanding of those two rites. This perspective would only be further confirmed if Paul knew any of the other sayings we examined in the previous chapter.

Thus, even though there is no evidence of Paul citing these sayings of Jesus, I suggest the best explanation for Paul's connection of baptism with an identification with Jesus in his death, and for his understanding of this identification with Christ in his death as something that should continue to characterize believers through their lives, is that he is dependent on these sayings of Jesus. Other factors may very well have contributed to Paul's thought, but as we have seen above, none appears to be sufficient to explain Paul's "dying with Christ" language. The plausible hypothesis that Paul had in view specific sayings of Jesus provides this explanation.

---

of Jesus regarding his followers sharing in his cup. My thanks to John Nolland for this observation.

6

Jesus' Ministry in the Context of New Creation

THE PURPOSE OF THIS AND THE FOLLOWING CHAPTER IS TO EXPLORE
how lines of connection might be drawn between Jesus and Paul in
terms of eschatology. The onus of the present chapter will be to establish an eschatological perspective for Jesus, and this I will do by
demonstrating the new creation character of his ministry. The emphasis of the following chapter will be to argue that it is more plausible to
understand Paul's new creation focus as deriving from Jesus than from
any other source.

The Problem of Eschatology

Perhaps the easiest way to approach the issue of Jesus' stance vis-à-vis
the hope of Israel is to consider his teaching in connection with the
kingdom of God. It is widely agreed that one of the central images for
Jesus' understanding of God's activity in the world was the kingdom
of God. If we take the Gospel record at face value, we learn that Jesus
looked forward to the future establishment of the kingdom of God.
He taught his disciples to pray for God's kingdom to come[1]—an expectation that seems to have permeated his thinking and his hope;[2]
he instructed them as to the kind of behavior that would be rewarded
when the kingdom did come;[3] he depicted the establishment of God's

1. Matt 6:10//Luke 11:2: "Thy kingdom come" (pink). The colors in the following
footnotes indicate the ranking assigned by the Jesus Seminar.

2. Matt 26:29//Mark 14:25//Luke 22:18: "I shall not drink again of the fruit of the
vine until that day when I drink it new in the kingdom of God" (Mark; gray).

3. Matt 5:19–20: "unless your righteousness exceeds that of the scribes and
Pharisees, you will never enter the kingdom of heaven" (black); Matt 6:33//Luke
12:31: "seek his kingdom, and these things shall be yours as well" (Matt; black); Matt
18:1–5: "Whoever humbles himself like this child, he is the greatest in the kingdom

kingdom as a time when God would sort out those who belong and those who do not;[4] indeed, he declared that there would be a reversal of fortunes at that time: those presently excluded, specifically the poor, would inherit the kingdom, while many on the inside would be cast out.[5]

But, standing alongside this future expectation, Jesus also affirmed the present reality of that kingdom. In Mark's Gospel, Jesus begins his preaching by announcing the nearness of God's kingdom: "The time is fulfilled, and the kingdom of God is at hand."[6] And, even if this is Mark's creation, it is fitting in light of the similar pronouncement made by John the Baptist,[7] Jesus' commission to his disciples,[8] and his warning about the coming destruction of Jerusalem.[9] Indeed, he declared that some of his followers would live to see "the kingdom of God . . . come with power."[10] In other texts, however, the present reality of the kingdom is clear. Some of his parables depict the incipient nature of the kingdom: its present reality is likened to the planted seed which is tiny in comparison with what it will become,[11] but which inevitably will grow—albeit mysteriously[12] and albeit mixed with weeds[13]—until the final harvest. He told his disciples that they had

---

of heaven" (gray/black); Matt 18:23–35: parable of the unforgiving servant (pink); Matt 19:13–15//Mark 10:13–16//Luke 18:15–17 "Let the children come to me. . . ; for to such belongs the kingdom of God" (Mark; v. 14 pink, v. 15 gray); Matt 19:16–30//Mark 10:17–31//Luke 18:18–30: the rich young man and Jesus' teaching on wealth (gray); Matt 25:1–13: parable of the ten virgins (gray); Matt 25:14–30//Luke 19:11–27: parable of the talents (pink); Mark 9:43–48 (cf. Matt 18:8–9): "it is better for you to enter the kingdom of God with one eye than with two eyes to be thrown into hell" (gray); Luke 9:57–62 (cf. Matt 8:18–22): "Leave the dead to bury their own dead; but as for you, go and proclaim the kingdom of God" (pink, v. 62 black).

4. Matt 13:24–30 (gray), 47–50 (black).

5. Matt 5:3//Luke 6:20 (Lk: red); Matt 8:11–12//Luke 13:25–29 (black); Matt 7:21–23 (black); Matt 21:33–46//Mark 12:1–12//Luke 20:9–19 (Mk: vv. 1–8 gray, vv. 9–11 black); Matt 22:1–10//Luke 14:16–24 (pink); Matt 25:31–46 (black); Luke 22:28–30 (cf. Matt 19:28) (black).

6. Mark 1:15 par. (black).

7. Matt 3:2 (black).

8. Matt 10:7 (cf. Luke 9:2) (black); Luke 10:9, 11 (black).

9. Luke 21:31 (cf. Mark 13:29, "the end is near") (gray).

10. Mark 9:1, cf. Matt 16:28//Luke 9:27 (gray).

11. Matt 13:31–32//Mark 4:30–32 (pink); cf. Matt 13:33.

12. Mark 4:26–29 (pink).

13. Matt 13:24–30 (gray).

been given "the secret of the kingdom of God";[14] he claimed that his exorcisms were evidence that "the kingdom of God has come";[15] once, in response to the question from some Pharisees about when the kingdom would come, he said "the kingdom of God is among you";[16] he interpreted the positive response of various outcasts as evidence that they were entering the kingdom.[17] Jesus saw the time in which he lived as in some sense climactic with regard to the kingdom of God: ever since John the Baptist, the kingdom has been advancing;[18] now was a time for feasting rather than fasting.[19]

Thus, the Gospels' portrayal of Jesus' view of the kingdom is somewhat complex: it is something that will be fully established, presumably at the end of the age; it is something that was near; and it is something that can be experienced or entered into in the present, albeit in an incipient form.

The problem, however, is that the authenticity of several of the kingdom texts in the Gospels has been challenged. In particular, there are many who doubt that Jesus believed that the end of the age was near, and so they question the authenticity of those texts that speak of the kingdom being near or coming.[20] The Jesus Seminar, for example, takes the following view:

14. Matt 13:11//Mark 4:11//Luke 8:10 (black).

15. Matt 12:28//Luke 11:20 (pink).

16. Luke 17:20–21 (pink); on the rendering of ἐντὸς ὑμῶν ἐστιν as "among you" rather than "within you," see Nolland, *Luke* 2:853–54; Fitzmyer, *Luke*, 2:1161; Marshall, *Luke*, 655–56; Evans, *Luke*, 628–30.

17. Matt 21:28–32 (gray); Matt 22:1–10//Luke 14:16–24 (pink).

18. Matt 11:11–13//Luke 16:16 (gray). This text has been notorious to interpret. The choice between rendering βιάζεται in Matt 11:12 as passive or middle depends on whether one sees the two clauses of the verse as being complementary or contrastive. Assuming Matthew's version is original, Luke's use of εὐαγγελίζεται ("the good news of the kingdom of God is preached") shows that he took βιάζεται to be middle voice ("the kingdom of heaven advances forcefully") rather than passive ("the kingdom of heaven suffers violence"). In favor of this middle rendering are Nolland, *Matthew*, 457–58; Lenski, *Matthew*, 437; in favor of the passive rendering are Davies and Allison, *Matthew*, 2:254–56; Luz, *Matthew 8–20*, 140–42. Either way, however, the text still suggests that a new era began with John.

19. Matt 9:14–15//Mark 2:18–19//Luke 5:33–34 (pink); Matt 11:18–19//Luke 7:33–34 (gray).

20. Of the texts cited above, only the following were ranked red or pink by the Jesus Seminar: Matt 6:10//Luke 11:2 ("Thy kingdom come").

> Jesus conceived of God's rule as all around him but difficult to discern. God was so real for him that he could not distinguish God's present activity from any future activity. He had a poetic sense of time in which the future and the present merged, simply melted together, in the intensity of his vision.[21]

Indeed, there is at present a deep rift in New Testament scholarship over whether the eschatological language in the Gospels stems from Jesus or from the early church. Sanders is representative of those who, like Weiss and Schweitzer, interpret Jesus as an eschatological figure who expected the imminent end of the age.[22] To support this view Sanders argues as follows: (i) Jesus' overturning of the tables in the temple is best understood as a symbolic action, with reference not to the need for temple reform, but to the imminent destruction of the temple which would then be followed by God's provision of a new temple[23]—thereby fulfilling an aspect of Jewish expectation for the age to come.[24] Thus, Sanders describes Jesus' framework as "restoration eschatology." (ii) Jesus' close association with John the Baptist, on the one hand, whom the Gospels depict as "an eschatological prophet of repentance,"[25] and the early Christians' eschatological expectation, on the other hand, demonstrated by their anticipation of Jesus' soon return and by their mission to the Gentiles, taken together would make a non-eschatological Jesus a historical anomaly.[26] And (iii) Jesus' choice of twelve disciples[27] indicates, in light of Jewish eschatological expectation of the restoration of the twelve tribes of Israel,[28] that Jesus saw this restoration to be imminent.

Marcus Borg, on the other hand, is representative of those who see other aspects of Jesus' teaching—for example, his wisdom sayings, parables, threats regarding a historical Roman invasion—to be incompatible with an expectation that God was about to bring the present

---

21. Funk et al., *Five Gospels*, 137.

22. Sanders, *Jesus and Judaism*, chaps. 1–3. Cf. Allison, "Plea," 651–68.

23. Sanders, *Jesus and Judaism*, 61–76.

24. Ibid., 77–90.

25. Ibid., 92.

26. Ibid., 91–95. Sanders also cites Meyer, *Aims of Jesus*, 115–22.

27. Sanders, *Jesus and Judaism*, 98–106, admits there is difficulty in identifying with confidence the names of all twelve, but he argues that Jesus' use of the symbol of twelve disciples is historical.

28. Ibid., 95–98.

world to an end.[29] In response to Sanders he argues: (i) the fact that *some* Jews associated the eschaton with the establishment of a new temple does not necessarily mean that this is what *Jesus* intended to signify by his temple action; (ii) with regard to Jesus' association with John the Baptist, there are some who argue that John should be understood as a prophet warning of an impending *historical* judgment, but even if John were to be understood eschatologically, the Gospels also portray a contrast between John and Jesus; with regard to eschatological expectation in the early church, Borg notes that the expectation of Jesus' return is explained better with reference to the experience of the resurrection than to Jesus' own expectation, since, according to him, few scholars would argue that Jesus anticipated his own return; and (iii) even if the symbolic reference to twelve disciples does go back to Jesus, his intention may have been nothing more than to indicate that his mission had to do with all Israel.[30] Borg and others—particularly those associated with the Jesus Seminar—try to strengthen this case by arguing that the earliest sources we have of Jesus' teaching—supposedly the earliest layer of Q and the *Gospel of Thomas*—present Jesus as a sage teaching people how to live rather than as an apocalyptic prophet predicting the end of the world.[31] The eschatological language in the Gospels, therefore, they explain as having been created by the early Christians who, because of their experience of the resurrection, lived in expectation of the imminent end.

As a consequence, it is difficult from the outset to find common ground upon which to establish an eschatological perspective for Jesus. I do suggest, however, that a way forward can be found if we begin by making some careful distinctions with regard to what we mean by eschatology.

---

29. Borg, *Conflict*, chap. 8; idem., "Temperate Case," 47–68; idem., "Jesus and Eschatology," 69–96. Interestingly, in his first book Borg understood Jesus' eschatological language metaphorically, in similar fashion to Wright; in his later writings, however, he takes the eschatological language to be literal, in conflict with Jesus' wisdom sayings, and hence not authentic.

30. Borg, "Jesus and Eschatology," 75–80.

31. See Crossan, *Historical Jesus*.

The Language of Eschatology

The word "eschatology" is used in a variety of ways. In the context of New Testament studies, Wright demonstrates the problem by showing the range of ways eschatology is understood in current historical Jesus research:

1. Eschatology as the end of the world, i.e. the end of the space-time universe;

2. Eschatology as the climax of Israel's history, involving the end of the space-time universe;

3. Eschatology as the climax of Israel's history, involving events for which end-of-the-world language is the only set of metaphors adequate to express the significance of what will happen, but resulting in a new and quite different phase *within* space-time history;

4. Eschatology as major events, not specifically climactic within a particular story, for which end-of-the-world language functions as metaphor;

5. Eschatology as 'horizontal' language (i.e. *apparently* denoting movement forwards in time) whose *actual* referent is the possibility of moving 'upwards' spiritually into a new level of existence;

6. Eschatology as critique of the present world order, perhaps with proposals for a new order;

7. Eschatology as critique of the present socio-political scene, perhaps with proposals for adjustments.[32]

Wright aligns Schweitzer with (1),[33] himself with (3), Borg with (4), Bultmann with (5), and Crossan with (6) and (7). All of this is simply to illustrate that to claim that Jesus was "eschatological" means very little unless one clarifies further what one means by "eschatology."[34]

32. Wright, *Jesus*, 208, emphasis original.

33. Although he thinks Schweitzer himself would have chosen (2).

34. See also Caird, *Language and Imagery*, chap. 14. Caird distinguishes eight substantially different senses in which eschatology has been understood over the nineteenth and twentieth centuries: (i) eschatology as that branch of systematic theology concerned with the future of individuals: death, judgment, heaven, and hell; (ii) eschatology as the historical destiny of Israel and the nations; (iii) eschatology as the expectation of the imminent end of the world (see Matt 10:23; Mark 9:1)—

I take eschatology to be essentially the language of hope. It is the language Israel used when looking forward to God's salvation. Some careful distinctions, however, are in order. First, Israelite hope was diverse. Jewish writers could express their hope in terms of possession of the Promised Land, establishment of the nation, the rule of a Davidic king, the rebuilding of the temple in Jerusalem, or realization of the many blessings associated with the covenant—abundant harvests, prosperity, progeny, victory over enemies.[35] And some writers expressed hope for some of these but not for others.

Second, the expression of Israelite hope developed throughout its history. At a time when the country had fallen from its time of glory, Amos (or a later writer) looked for a restoration of David's kingdom.[36] When in exile, Second Isaiah raises hope for a return to the homeland,[37] while Ezekiel creates a vision of a restored temple.[38] After the return, Third Isaiah speaks of the nations bringing their wealth to Jerusalem,[39] and Zechariah looks forward to a time when "the LORD will become king over all the earth."[40] Focusing on the Second Temple period, Sanders identifies four lines of Jewish expectation prominent at that time: (i) the re-establishment of Israel as a unity of twelve tribes; (ii) the subjugation, destruction or conversion of the Gentiles; (iii) a rebuilt, renewed or purified temple and city of Jerusalem; and (iv) purity and righteousness in both worship and life.[41] And beginning probably in the second century BCE, in the face of the martyrdom of

---

so-called "consistent eschatology" (Weiss and Schweitzer); (iv) eschatology as what has been "realized" in the ministry of Jesus (see Luke 10:23–24; 11:20; Mark 1:15), that is the realization of what was expected in the eschaton (C. H. Dodd); (v) eschatology as what Jesus "inaugurated" during his ministry, to be completed at the last day (Jeremias); (vi) eschatology as language that needs to be interpreted existentially in order to speak of the imminence of God in our present situation (Bultmann); (vii) eschatology as the newness of what God is doing (Lindbolm); and (viii) eschatology as the purpose for which God had chosen Israel (Clements).

35. For the blessings of the covenant see Deut 28:1–14.

36. Amos 9:1–12.

37. Isa 45:13; 48:20; 49:8–12, 24–26; 51:11, 14.

38. Ezek 40–48.

39. Isa 60:1–14; 61:5–6.

40. Zech 14:9.

41. Sanders, *Practice and Belief*, chap. 14.

many godly people, hope for bodily resurrection grew.[42] Clearly the content of Israel's hope was not static.

Third, hope itself needs to be distinguished from the program designed to see the hope realized. Sanders notes that although most Jews living in first-century Palestine would have hoped for political independence, the means to achieve that independence varied markedly from one Jew to another: "Hope for the future ran the full gamut from plotting revolt and storing arms to praying quietly that God would do something to change things."[43] That is, some envisaged a historical process leading to the new situation, whereas others believed the new situation could be brought about only by a radical intervention by God.

Fourth, it is not always clear what relationship the writer sees, or later readers saw, between the present world and the world to come. In fact, the image we will be examining presently could be called either "new creation" or "renewed creation"; it is difficult to know in specific texts whether the prophet had in view the restoration of an idyllic past or the replacement of the present world with an entirely new one. The difficulty lies in the nature of the language itself, where imagination is often given to the use of metaphors and hyperbole. Given Jewish belief in God as creator and in God's commitment to his creation,[44] one suspects that *renewed* creation is what the seers had in mind, and it is in this way that we should probably understand the term "new creation"—a transformation of the present world in light of God's original purposes.

Fifth, the distinction between final consummation and hope realized prior to the final consummation is not always clear. Texts that speak of the resurrection of the dead, for example, seem to have in view a final consummation; but new creation also had in view healing, long life, abundant harvests, and peace, and these could be either part of a historical restoration or a final consummation. And sixth, where final consummation is in view, it is not always clear whether it involves a return to the original creation or a move to an even better world.[45]

---

42. See below, pp. 302–14.

43. Ibid., 280.

44. Gen 1–2; 9:12–16; Job 38–39; Pss 8; 19:1–6; 104; 146:6; 148:5.

45. Anderson, *Creation Versus Chaos*, 130–31, for example, argues that the Israelite prophets made the point that the end would be better than the beginning; but this is

In light of all of this, I suggest thinking of eschatology in connection with Jesus in terms of the *significance of the time* in which he lived, as opposed to the *actual time* with reference to a divine timeline. That is to say, it is a question of *kairos* rather than *chronos*. In Wright's typology, we would be thinking of eschatology according to either his third or fourth definition. If we can agree that Jesus understood his ministry in terms of the present reality of God's kingdom, I intend to show that he thought of this reality in terms of a realization of the hope of Israel—specifically in terms of the presence of new creation.

Jewish Hope and New Creation

The image of new creation is deeply rooted in Old Testament hope. David Petersen identifies three traditions that gave rise to expressions of hope in Israel: (i) the patriarchal promises of land and progeny; (ii) the David-Zion tradition that spoke of a Davidic descendant always reigning on the throne, a just Davidic king bringing blessing for the nation, and the city of David with its holy mount, Zion, being inviolable; and (iii) the Sinai covenant which held out blessings and curses for Israel depending on her compliance with the covenant requirements.[46] And underlying each of these traditions is the confidence that Israel's God, Yahweh, is the creator of the world and the Lord of history, and that he will one day establish his reign over all the earth.

The image of new creation is one of the many expressions of hope in Israel. Its origin is probably to be found in the ancient mythological view in which history, like the seasons of the year, was thought to be cyclical, and therefore future hope was described as a return to the primal past. Hermann Gunkel famously coined the phrase "Urzeit gleich Endzeit"—primal-time is the same as end-time.[47] The Israelite prophets used this image, but adapted it to a linear view of history having a beginning and an end: when Isaiah looks forward to when an ideal

---

not clear from the texts themselves. Anderson notes that some prophets affirm that the return from exile in Babylon will be more glorious that the exodus from Egypt (Isa 43:18–19; 48:6–7; Jer 23:7–8). But the point of the new creation language seems to be not that God will improve upon his original creation, but that he will resolve the current problems, create an idyllic situation, and make that situation permanent.

46. Petersen, "Eschatology," 576–77.

47. Gunkel, *Schöpfung und Chaos*. For a full discussion of the myth, see Eliade, *Cosmos and History*.

king will reign, he imagines a scene in which wild animals live together in peace;[48] Joel and Amos describe the restoration of Israel with images of fruitfulness and abundant harvests.[49] During the exile, Second Isaiah speaks of God *the Creator* about to do something radically *new* for his people,[50] and portrays their redemption with the image of God causing streams of water to flow into the desert to bring life, just as the rivers of Eden watered the garden.[51] Ezekiel brings together several images of renewal: God gathering his people from the nations, giving them a new heart and a new spirit so that they will keep his laws, making the crops abundant, restoring the land "like the garden of Eden,"[52] likening such restoration to dead bones being formed into bodies and reanimated,[53] and portraying the new temple as the source of rivers of water flowing out to make stagnant water fresh and to bring life to all kinds of trees.[54] And another exilic prophet speaks of Yahweh restoring his people to full health in preparation for their return to Zion through a desert made fertile by streams of water and made safe by the removal of wild animals.[55] Then, following the exile, Third Isaiah promises that if the people take care of the hungry and afflicted, they will be like "a watered garden";[56] and he describes the future restoration of Jerusalem

48. Isa 11:1–9; cf. 2:4; 9:7.

49. Joel 3:17–18; Amos 9:11–15.

50. Isa 43:15–21. Second Isaiah, more than any other prophet, combines together God's creative and salvific activity (Isa 42:5–6; 43:1; 44:24; 46:3–4; 51:9–11). He also emphasizes the *newness* of what God is about to do for Israel (Isa 42:9; 43:19; 48:6), suggesting that the return from Babylon be seen as a "new exodus." Anderson, *Creation Versus Chaos*, 129, writes: "Second Isaiah understands the 'New Exodus of salvation' to be a new creation, comparable to the event of the creation of Israel in the first Exodus. . . . The New Exodus will be the climax of Yahweh's work and, in a profound sense, something never heard of before."

51. Isa 41:17–19; 43:18–21; 44:3–4; 48:20–21; 49:8–10.

52. Ezek 11:19–20; 36:24–38; cf. 11:19–20; Isa 51:3. See also the theme of a "new covenant" both in Ezekiel (Ezek 16:60; 34:25; 37:26) and in Jeremiah (Jer 31:31–34).

53. Ezek 37:1–14.

54. Ezek 47:1–12; cf. Zech 14:8.

55. Isa 35:1–10. The mythological background of this new creation language can be seen in a number of texts where Yahweh is said to have defeated specific monsters, somewhat paralleling cosmic battles in other ancient Near Eastern texts. Thus, the psalmist celebrates God's victory over the watery forces of chaos (Pss 74:13–15; 89:9–10; 93:3–4; 104:6–9), and Second Isaiah appeals to Yahweh's victory over the dragon, Rahab, as justification for trusting in future deliverance (Isa 44:27; 51:9–11).

56. Isa 58:9–11.

in terms of joy, long life and possession of the land, and sets this vision within the context of God renewing creation—creating new heavens and a new earth with idyllic conditions.[57]

The unfulfilled hopes following the return from exile and the continuous domination of foreign rulers gave rise to new expressions of hope.[58] In Jewish apocalyptic literature the image of new creation served to depict the ideal age to come following the overthrow of the present evil age.[59] For example, the apocalypse of 1 Enoch likens the coming judgment of all sinners to the judgment of the Flood, a time when God will cleanse the earth from all injustice, to be followed by a time of permanent righteousness when people will live long lives in joy, harvests will be abundant, the nations will worship God, and peace and truth will reign.[60] Daniel looks forward to the establishment of God's everlasting kingdom with images of the taming of wild animals (whether the lions in the den or the beasts from the sea[61]) and the resurrection of the dead—some to life and others to shame and contempt.[62] The Sibylline Oracles describe the world, following the consummation, as a place of abundant crops and flocks, and of peace among nations.[63] The visionary of 4 Ezra looks forward to a time when God will "renew the creation."[64] And the author of 2 Baruch speaks of God renewing his creation and creating a new and incorruptible world in which the nations are subdued and Israel experiences joy, health, and peace—peace symbolized by wild animals serving men, and by snakes and dragons obeying children.[65] In several apocalyptic

---

57. Isa 65:17–25; cf. 66:22.

58. See Nickelsburg, "Eschatology," 579–94.

59. For expression of time being divided into two ages, see 2 Esd 7:50, 112–15; 8:1–3; 2 En. 66.6; 2 Bar. 15.7–8; 44.8–15. For the depiction of cosmic destruction, see 4 Ezra 6.20; 7.30–31; 2 En. 70.9–10; Apoc. Zeph. 12.5–8; Sib. Or. 3.75–92, 669–701; 7.118–49.

60. 1 En. 10–11; cf. 24.4–25.5: focus on the tree of life; 45.4–5: transformation of heaven and earth; 71.15: peace in the world that is to come; 72.1: new creation to abide forever; 91.15–16: a new and more glorious heaven.

61. Dan 6; 7:1–8.

62. Dan 12:2.

63. Sib. Or. 3.741–61.

64. 4 Ezra 7.75 (Metzger, OTP).

65. 2 Bar. 32.6; 44.8–15; 49.3; 57.2; 72–74.

writings, the destiny of the righteous is described as the Paradise of Eden returned.[66]

But during the Second Temple period the images of new creation are not limited to apocalyptic texts. When the author of *Jubilees*[67] looked into the future he saw a time when, after much evil, Israelites would return to the law and to righteousness, and conditions of long life, health, peace, and removal of all enemies (including Satan) would ensue[68]—a time he refers to as "new creation";[69] 2 Maccabees holds out the hope of resurrection "to an everlasting renewal of life" for those who die while remaining true to God's law;[70] *Pseudo-Philo* speaks of a consummation when God will raise the dead for judgment and will establish "another earth and another heaven, an everlasting dwelling place";[71] the *Rule of the Community* from Qumran tells of a new creation at "the appointed end" when God will purify the earth and endow the upright with insight, wisdom, and "all the glory of Adam";[72] and the *Hodayot* (*Hymns Scroll*) likens the future community of God's holy ones—redeemed humans and angels—to an everlasting tree whose branches cover the whole world which is watered by "the streams of Eden"[73]

66. *T. Levi* 18.10–11: "And he shall open the gates of paradise; he shall remove the sword that has threatened since Adam, and he will grant to the saints to eat of the tree of life" (Kee, *OTP*); *T. Dan* 5.12: "And the righteous shall refresh themselves in Eden; the righteous shall rejoice in the New Jerusalem, which shall be eternally for the glorification of God" (Kee, *OTP*); *1 En.* 25.4–5: "And as for this fragrant tree, . . . the elect will be presented with its fruit for life" (Kee, *OTP*); *4 Ezra* 8.52: "it is for you that Paradise is opened, the tree of life is planted, and the age to come is prepared, plenty is provided, a city is built, rest is appointed, goodness is established and wisdom perfected beforehand" (Metzger, *OTP*); cf. Rev 22:1–5. See further Jeremias, "παράδεισος," 767.

67. I have followed the classification in Charlesworth's *Old Testament Pseudepigrapha* in taking *Jubilees* as non-apocalyptic. While there is debate over this (see Wintermute, "Jubilees," 37, for a summary of the apocalyptic and non-apocalyptic features of *Jubilees*), the issue is not crucial for our purposes.

68. *Jub.* 23.26–31.

69. *Jub.* 1.29; 4.26. On new creation in *Jubilees*, see Hubbard, *New Creation*, 36–53.

70. 2 Macc 7:9; cf. v. 23.

71. *L.A.B.* 3.10 (Harrington, *OTP*); cf. 32.17 (the renewal of creation).

72. 1QS IV,22–25. 11QTemple XXIX,7–10 also refers to the "day of creation" when God will create his temple.

73. 1QH[a] XIV,12–17; cf. XVI,20. The reference to the creation of new things in 1QH[a] V,18 (formerly XIII,11–12) is often mentioned in this context; however, the sig-

Thus, new creation is an image that pervades Jewish hope. It is used by numerous writers in diverse genres over hundreds of years. It is also multi-faceted rather than singular, visionary rather than concrete, given to the language of poetry rather than prose. It served those trying to put into words that which had never been experienced and was difficult to imagine. The image of new creation can also be evoked in various ways—by reference, for example, to aspects of the creation story (e.g., Eden, Adam, animals under humanity's control) or to creative acts of God expected at the end of the age (e.g., resurrection, healing, granting everlasting life). It clearly has in view the idyllic conditions God has in store for his own people.

Healing on the Sabbath

We can begin to appreciate Jesus' new creation perspective by looking at his healing and exorcising activity, and in particular, his healing on the Sabbath. I wish to argue that his healings on the Sabbath in particular indicate that he saw this new activity of God within a new creation perspective. Jesus' reputation as a healer and an exorcist (here, taking exorcism to be a form of healing[74]) is widely attested.[75] Among the Gospel accounts, six locate Jesus' activity on the Sabbath,[76]

---

nificance of this text, with regard to future hope, is difficult to determine, due in part of the lacunae in the manuscript. The hymn seems to have in view beings (angels?) that God created in order to participate in his judgment of all creation (lines 14–19). These beings "recount your glory throughout all your dominion" (line 17); and God has shown them "what was there from of old and creating new things, demolishing ancient things and [erec]ting what would exist for ever" (lines 17–18). Then the writer asks, "[However, what is] the spirit of flesh to understand all these matters and to have insight in [your wondrous] and great counsel?" (lines 19–20), which seems to confirm that the beings mentioned earlier were not humans. In any case, it does not appear that the Jewish hope for new creation is in view here. On the angels involved in heavenly worship, see below, pp. 299–300. For further Jewish references to new creation, see Hubbard, *New Creation*, 35 n. 43.

74. See Vermes, *Jesus the Jew*, 61–65.

75. Blackburn, "Miracles of Jesus," 354–63, surveys the historical evidence for Jesus being an exorcist and healer noting (i) the early attestation in Mark and Q, (ii) multiple attestation in Q, Mark, M, L, and John, and in a variety of forms, (iii) the mention of healing and exorcisms in certain authentic sayings of Jesus, and (iv) mention in extra-biblical sources.

76. (i) Casting out an unclean spirit from a man in the Capernaum synagogue (Mark 1:21–28//Luke 4:31–37); (ii) healing a man with a withered hand in a synagogue, presumably also at Capernaum (Matt 12:9–14//Mark 3:1–6//Luke 6:6–11);

and on each occasion except for one[77] Jesus needs to defend his action against some who take offense. And alongside these there is one other Sabbath incident that causes offense—that of Jesus' disciples caught plucking grain.[78] What can we discern of Jesus' mindset from these actions? What did he intend?

Sabbath-keeping has always been one of the most distinctive of Jewish practices. In the Greco-Roman world it was a visible point of Jewish identity for it easily distinguished Jews from non-Jews.[79] Essentially Sabbath-keeping required rest from work on the seventh day of the week; this included everyone: men, women, children, servants, non-Israelites, and even animals.[80] Its importance is clear in

---

(iii) healing a crippled woman in a synagogue (Luke 13:10–17); (iv) healing a man with dropsy in a Pharisee's house (Luke 14:1–6); (v) healing a lame man by the Bethzatha Pool in Jerusalem (John 5:2–18); and (vi) healing a man born blind (John 9:1–41). According to Mark's narrative, we could conclude that the healing of Simon Peter's mother-in-law also took place on the Sabbath (Mark 1:29–31), but Mark does not draw attention to this fact, perhaps because this was a private healing and hence there was no reaction from Jesus' critics.

77. That Jesus did not offer a defense for his exorcising of the unclean spirit on the Sabbath is not surprising since he was responding to a verbal attack (Mark 1:21–28 par.). However, the action was probably questionable enough in the minds of those who took issue with Jesus to suggest to them that they should watch closely what he does on the Sabbath.

78. Mark 2:23–28 par. Sanders contends that this, and other accounts of Jesus' conflict with the Pharisees, "have more than a slight air of artificiality. . . . Pharisees did not organize themselves into groups to spend their Sabbaths in Galilean cornfields in the hope of catching someone transgressing" (Sanders, *Jesus and Judaism*, 265). The suggestion, therefore, is that this account was created by the early church in order to address the issue of Sabbath-keeping. Davies and Allison, however, defend the authenticity of the event by arguing: (i) Mark 2:23–24 does not necessarily imply that the Pharisees witnessed the event themselves; (ii) the Sabbath controversies are widely attested; (iii) the story coheres with the view of Jesus and his disciples being poor, itinerant preachers; (iv) although the account notes that only the disciples plucked grain, this does not need to be seen as evidence of an early church creation, since it is likely that Jesus would have been seen to have been responsible for their actions (cf. Mark 2:18; 7:5); (v) Jesus' use of a scriptural defense is consistent with his practice on other occasions (Mark 7:1–13; 12:18–27), and his use of 1 Sam 21 on this occasion is appropriate in light of the common issue of hunger, which was not an issue in the early church; and (vi) Jesus compares himself to David again in Mark 12:35–37. It may be, however, that one or the other of Jesus' responses to the Pharisees' question (vv. 25–26 or vv. 26–27) is secondary (see Marcus, *Mark 1–8*, 243).

79. Goldenberg, "Jewish Sabbath," 414–42.

80. Exod 20:10. Also, every seventh year the land was to be given a Sabbath rest (Lev 25:2–7).

that it is one of the Ten Commandments and its deliberate violation was punishable by death.[81] The rationale for the command is twofold according to the Old Testament: (i) it was a day to imitate God who rested on the seventh day of creation,[82] and (ii) it was a day to remember God's deliverance of the Israelites from slavery in Egypt.[83] Thus, although it was not technically a feast day in the Old Testament, it was fundamentally a day for celebration.[84] During the first century CE, Jews typically celebrated Sabbath by means of a special meal[85] and attendance at the synagogue where there would be prayer and study of the law.[86] But in a time when there was heightened awareness of the need to obey the law as carefully as possible, as was characteristic of Second Temple Judaism,[87] the need to define work became more urgent: In order to obey God's law, what specifically are Jews not permitted to do on the Sabbath? Attempts to answer this question can be found in the *Damascus Document*[88] and in the book of *Jubilees*,[89] but

81. Exod 31:14; Num 15:32–36. An inadvertent transgression of the Sabbath required a sin offering (Lev 4:27–35). The death penalty is upheld in *Jubliees* (*Jub.* 2.25–27), but interestingly not in the *Damascus Document* (CD XII,3–4) or in the Mishnah (*m. Šabb.* 7:1). On the importance of Sabbath, see also *y. Ber.* 1:4 (II.H).

82. Exod 20:11.

83. Deut 5:15.

84. Isa 58:13; *b. Šabb.* 119a, 137b; *b. Pesaḥ.* 68b; cf. Lohse, "σάββατον," 15–16. Also note that the Sabbath tractate in the Mishnah is included in the second order, *Mo'ed*, that deals with festival days.

85. Lohse, "σάββατον," 16, writes: "The day of rest was to be characterized by good eating, Jub. 2:21, 31; 50:9 f.; bShabb., 119a etc. Whereas two meals were normally eaten on weekdays, there were to be three on the Sabbath. To be able to enjoy the Sabbath properly at these meals it was advised that little should be eaten the day before and one should begin the Sabbath hungry, T. Ber., 5, 1. . . . On the Sabbath guests were often invited so that they could be entertained lavishly, Shab., 23, 2; T. Shabb., 17, 5 (137). Fasting on the Sabbath was not allowed lest the enjoyment of the feast be hampered, Jdt 8:6; bBer., 31b." See further: *y. Ber.* 3.1 (IV.C); Sanders, *Practice and Belief*, 210; idem., *Jewish Law*, 13.

86. Philo's common term for the synagogue was "house of prayer." For study of the law on the Sabbath in the synagogue see Philo, *Opif.* 128; Josephus, *Ag. Ap.* 2.175.

87. Note the actions of Nehemiah in the fifth century to enforce the observance of Sabbath (Neh 13:15–22). See Schmidt, "Sabbath Day," 127–30.

88. CD X,14–XII,5.

89. *Jub.* 50.6–13.

the most detailed instructions of work to be avoided on the Sabbath are in the rabbinic literature, particularly the Mishnah.[90]

The question of whether specific acts of exorcism, healing, and plucking grain on the Sabbath were breaches of the law would have been a matter for a judge to decide.[91] Individual Jews, or particular parties (like the Pharisees), might have had their own opinion, but these would be based on their own interpretation of the law and would not constitute an official ruling. For example, assuming for the sake of argument that the Mishnah's definition of work was accepted at the time of Jesus (an assumption that would be open to debate), Jesus' disciples could be judged by some to have broken the law by in essence reaping on the Sabbath;[92] however, if Jesus and his disciples were considered to be poor, they might have argued in their defense that the permission that people could prepare some food on the Sabbath provided a warrant for their action,[93] and that the importance of celebrating Sabbath and of not going hungry was of paramount value.[94]

In the case of healing, the general opinion was that the practice of medicine was work and should not be done on the Sabbath.[95] Exceptions were made, however, where there might be a threat to life. Rabbi Mattiah, in the early second century CE, articulated this principle: "any matter of doubt as to the danger to life overrides the prohibitions of the Sabbath."[96] In Jesus' Sabbath-healings it could be argued that since in none of the cases was there an obvious threat to life, he was there-

90. See, e.g., *m. Šabb.* 7:2, where thirty-nine forms of work are defined. On the variety of Sabbath traditions within different Jewish groups during the Second Temple period, see Rowland, "Sabbath Observance," 43–55; Yang, *Jesus and the Sabbath*, 53–99.

91. Josephus, *Ag. Ap.* 2.187, notes that priests acted as judges in legal cases.

92. Reaping is specifically prohibited in *m. Šabb.* 7.2. Exod 34:21 also prohibits work during ploughing and harvest season; cf. *Jub.* 50.12; Philo, *Mos.* 2.22; *y. Šabb.* 7:2 (IX.B); *t. Šabb.* 9:17.

93. See Nolland, *Matthew*, 482. Reaping in someone else's field was probably not the issue since the Torah permitted the poor to glean the corners of a farmer's field (Lev 19:9–10; 23:22; Deut 23:24–25).

94. Numerous explanations have been given for Jesus' rationale in defending his disciples' actions by appealing to the example of David: see Davies and Allison, *Matthew*, 2:310–11.

95. CD XI,9–18; *m. Šabb.* 14:3–4; *t. Šabb.* 12:8–14; cf. *b. Šabb.* 75b.

96. *m. Yoma* 8:6; cf. *t. Šabb.* 15:15–16. See further Schmidt, "Sabbath Day," 128–30; Str-B 1:623–29. More generally on the limits to infringement of the Sabbath law, see Abrahams, *Pharisaism*, 129–35.

fore guilty of breaking the Sabbath; one has to wonder, however, just how the Jewish legal system would have assessed a *miraculous* healing! What exactly did Jesus do that constituted work?[97] In any event, we note that Jesus was not arrested and charged, suggesting that while he may have offended some people by his Sabbath activity, his "offense" must not have been so clear-cut as to make a legal conviction probable.

In fact it is probably the case that those most opposed to Jesus were offended for other reasons than simply his Sabbath activity. Mark's account of Jesus healing the man with the withered hand in the synagogue states that there were some Pharisees there who "watched him, to see whether he would heal him on the sabbath, so that they might accuse him,"[98] implying that they had already been offended by Jesus and they were now looking for substantive legal evidence to bring charges against him. Similarly, the plucking grain incident also suggests some people were going out of their way to spy on Jesus on the Sabbath—why else would the observers be in the same grain field on the Sabbath?[99] That Jesus would have drawn the attention of those who cared about the piety of Israelites should be clear from the fact that he was a popular preacher, drawing crowds because of his distinctive teaching and his healings.[100] The source of the fundamental offense for those who opposed Jesus may have been a number of things: perhaps they were offended by his association with outsiders,[101] or perhaps they thought him pretentious because he identified his words and actions too easily with those of God,[102] or perhaps they feared that his charismatic gospel threatened to undermine the sacred institutions of Judaism,[103] or perhaps they were simply jealous of his success without having been properly trained. Whatever the cause, the two Markan accounts of plucking grain and healing in the synagogue suggest that

97. Nowhere is the dilemma raised for Jesus' opponents by such a charge better portrayed than in John's account of Jesus healing the man born blind (John 9).

98. Mark 3:2.

99. See above, p. 255 n. 78.

100. Jesus' popularity arising from his teaching and healing/exorcisms is recorded in several Gospel sources: Mark (1:32–34 par.; 3:7–10 par.; 6:54–56 par.), Q (Matt 14:14//Luke 9:11), M (Matt 15:30–31; 21:14), and John (2:23).

101. Mark 2:15–17 par.

102. A sentiment reflected, for example, in John 5:18. See Moule, "Gravamen against Jesus," 187–95.

103. See Freyne, "Jesus the Martyr," 54–57.

some had already taken offense, and thus their Sabbath investigations were an attempt to solidify their case against him.

Let us leave aside for the time being the questions of legality and of the motives of Jesus' opponents, and consider Jesus' own intentions. It appears that, although none of the Sabbath incidents was prearranged, on each occasion Jesus purposefully chose to act in the way he did, even though he could easily have found a way to avoid conflict. For example, in the five healing incidents, none of the cases was clearly life-threatening, so Jesus could easily have set up a meeting for the following day and no one would have been surprised; yet in each case Jesus took the initiative to heal, and to do so on the Sabbath.[104] Even in the case of the exorcism in the synagogue we could argue that Jesus took the initiative: presumably in the case of such an outburst the leader of the synagogue would be responsible for restoring order, and yet Jesus stepped forward to cast out the unclean spirit.[105] The point is that Jesus was not simply interested in healing, but on at least some occasions he purposefully healed *on the Sabbath*. Why was this?

In the incident concerning the plucking of grain on the Sabbath, Jesus makes the statement, "The sabbath was made for man, not man for the sabbath."[106] Here Jesus clearly is calling people back to God's original intention in creation, and he may implicitly be criticizing what he sees to be a skewed understanding of Sabbath.[107] Similarly, in the healing incidents, Jesus defends his actions by arguing that it is appropriate to do good on the Sabbath.[108]

But what exactly did Jesus intend with regard to the practice of Sabbath-keeping? Did he intend his healings to change how people observed Sabbath? Almost certainly he was not proposing an abolishment of Sabbath law. If he were it would be difficult to understand (i) why Jesus' followers continued to observe Sabbath: each of the Synoptic Gospels makes the point that between his death and resur-

---

104. Mark 3:3; Luke 13:11–12; John 5:6; 9:6. Jesus' initiative in the account of healing at the Pharisee's house is displayed by his raising of the question of whether it is right to heal on the Sabbath (Luke 14:3).

105. Mark 1:25.

106. Mark 2:27. The Jesus Seminar ranks this saying as pink (Funk et al., *Five Gospels*, 49). For a humanitarian concern connected with Sabbath, see Exod 23:12; Deut 5:14; for similar rabbinic expressions, see *Mek.* on Exod 31:14; *b. Yoma* 85b.

107. Collins, *Mark*, 203–4; Marcus, *Mark 1–8*, 245–46.

108. Mark 3:4 par.; Luke 13:15–16; 14:3–5.

rection, Jesus' followers took care to keep Sabbath;[109] (ii) why, in his Mount of Olives discourse, Jesus said "Pray that your flight may not be . . . on a sabbath";[110] (iii) why we find a saying of Jesus in *Gos. Thom.* 27:2—"If you do not observe the sabbath as a sabbath, you will not see the father"[111]—which, if authentic, may show Jesus to be supporting Sabbath-keeping;[112] and (iv) why there is no further indication in the Jesus tradition, outside of the incidents we have been discussing, that would suggest he taught otherwise.[113] Perhaps this last point is an argument from silence, but in light of how important Sabbath-keeping was in Jesus' day, it is a very loud silence.

Was he therefore proposing that *any* good deed should be permissible on the Sabbath? Arland Hultgren suggests that Jesus is again applying the *Qal wa-homer* principle: If it is permissible to save life on the Sabbath, then should it not also be permissible to do good deeds on the Sabbath?[114] While there may be some validity in this, what speaks against it is that, apart from the grain plucking incident, it is only healing which is at issue. We hear nothing of Jesus repairing his neighbor's door or lighting a fire for cooking or helping a friend with his crops on the Sabbath; for Jesus there seems to be a particular significance in the act of healing. Indeed, to allow all kinds of good deeds would seem to be tantamount to an abolishment of the Sabbath law. So, perhaps Jesus

109. Matt 28:1//Mark 16:1 assumes that readers would know why the women waited until the first day of the week to come to the tomb to anoint Jesus' body; Luke 23:56 explicitly mentions their Sabbath-keeping; see Weiss, "Sabbath," 16–17. Luke's description of the distance from Jerusalem to the Mount of Olives as "a sabbath day's journey" (Acts 1:12) probably suggests that Sabbath continued to be observed by early Christians. Indeed, one suspects that the break between Christianity and Judaism would have happened far earlier, and in Jerusalem, if the Jewish Christians had not kept Sabbath.

110. Matt 24:20. Even if this is not authentic, it still reflects Matthew's understanding that Jesus' followers were expected to keep Sabbath.

111. Plisch, *Gospel of Thomas*, 93, renders this as: "If you do not make the (entire) week into a Sabbath, you will not see the Father."

112. While the Jesus Seminar is probably correct in finding this saying not to be authentic (black ranking) because of its apparent support of asceticism (which *Thomas* advocates elsewhere) and its lack of any parallel to anything else in the Jesus tradition, it would be strange if such a saying in support of Sabbath-keeping had been created had Jesus been so clearly critical of Sabbath-keeping. See also Schmidt, "Sabbath Day," 126.

113. It may also be worth noting that there is no mention of the Sabbath in Q.

114. Hultgren, *Adversaries*, 83.

was saying more specifically that acts that bring health and wholeness to another person should be allowed on the Sabbath. Indeed, his defense of his healing of the crippled woman in the synagogue would suggest this: "Ought not this woman, a daughter of Abraham whom Satan bound for eighteen years, be loosed from this bond *on the sabbath day*?"[115] That is, what better day than the Sabbath—the day on which we celebrate God's creation and liberation—for someone to be released from suffering and made whole?[116] I suspect this does reflect Jesus' view. One wonders, however, just how he intended it to be applied for other people: not many had the ability to perform miraculous healings, and there is no other indication that Jesus was seeking to liberalize the law only for the sake of doctors!

Perhaps it should be noted at this point that it may very well be that the principal value of these stories of Jesus' Sabbath activity for the early church was their relevance to the question of whether or not Christians—particularly Gentile Christians—were required to keep Sabbath.[117] Almost certainly there would have been tension and confusion over this issue in the early church, particularly in the Gentile mission, especially given Paul's critical attitude toward the law,[118] and specifically given his argument that Gentiles need not be circumcised or observe Jewish food laws.[119] Paul's references to some people esteeming one day better than others may indeed reflect Sabbath controversy in his churches.[120] Also, *Barn.* 15.8–9 appears to be Christian polemic against Sabbath-keeping and in favor of an "eighth day" celebration, and *Diogn.* 4.3 specifically commends the doing of anything good on the Sabbath. That the stories of Jesus' Sabbath-healings may have been applied this way in the early church, however, does not necessarily mean that this is all that Jesus intended; much less does it mean that the early church created the stories: one suspects that early Christians could have devised much more apropos stories to address

---

115. Luke 13:16, emphasis added.
116. See Wright, *Jesus*, 394.
117. See Hultgren, *Adversaries*, 83–84.
118. See above, p. 126–27.
119. Rom 2:28–29; 14:14, 17; Gal 2:11–14; 5:2–6; Phil 3:2–3.
120. Rom 14:5–6; Gal 4:10; cf. Col 2:16.

their issue of Sabbath-keeping than incidents involving plucking grain and miraculous healing.[121]

I suggest a way forward at this point can be found by transposing the question and considering not how Jesus may have intended his healings to make a comment on Sabbath observance, but rather how the context of Sabbath may have had a bearing on the significance of his healings. Christian Dietzfelbinger emphasizes the importance of the significance both of Jesus' healings and of the Sabbath:

> Jesus . . . wanted to bring back the Sabbath to its original meaning. He wanted to have it be seen, therefore, as the day on which God should be experienced as the God who is bringing back people to their original humanity. . . . Jesus knew himself to be the one who was reaching people with the coming reign of God and who was displaying the coming reign of God in his behavior. But if the purpose of the Sabbath is that man should experience, in a decided manner, God's reign as a near, liberating and binding reign, then did not Jesus have to use precisely the Sabbath as the day on which, when the opportunity arises, he demonstrates the coming reign of God? Did he not have to give to the threatened and destroyed people the healing power of God precisely on the Sabbath?[122]

121. Nor does it necessarily follow that the early Christians misinterpreted or misused Jesus' words and actions in saying that Sabbath-keeping was not necessary for Christians, particularly Gentile Christians. They probably would have argued something like the following: Jesus' critique of Sabbath observance in his situation showed that God's true intention was for the well-being of all. This, together with additional revelation, debate, and observation of God at work among Gentiles, led (some) Christians to see that Sabbath-keeping was no longer necessary. An analogy might be seen in the case of Jewish food laws. In the controversy over hand-washing, Jesus asserts that "whatever goes into a man from outside cannot defile him," to which Mark comments, "Thus he declared all foods clean" (Mark 7:18–19). Many commentators argue, correctly in my view, that it was not Jesus' intention to nullify Jewish food laws, but rather to argue that the tradition of handwashing obscured the *true* source of defilement. But Mark's interpretation reflects the view that early Christians came to as a result of further reflection and revelation, particularly in the context of the Gentile mission (see Acts 10:1–11:18; Gal 2:11–16); quite possibly this may have involved taking a saying of Jesus that pertained to ritual purity and applying it to the issue of food laws. Such an interpretation helps to make sense of why Sabbath and food laws were issues of controversy within the early church. If Jesus had spoken clearly against them, it is difficult to understand why his followers were divided over the issue for many years to come. See Marcus, *Mark 1–8*, 457–58; Hooker, *Mark*, 178–80; Guelich, *Mark 1—8:26*, 374–79.

122. Dietzfelbinger, "Sabbatheilungen," 297 (my translation).

However, rather than arguing that Jesus wanted to change people's view of the Sabbath, I will argue that he wanted to use the significance of the Sabbath to inform people about the significance of his healings, and from that to say something about the activity of God in the present. Not only was Sabbath associated with both creation and liberation, but some rabbinic sayings associate Sabbath with new creation.[123] By considering some of Jesus' sayings made on other occasions regarding his healings and exorcisms, together with some sayings that reflect the climactic nature of the time in which Jesus saw himself to be living, I with to demonstrate that Jesus intended, by his healing on the Sabbath, to announce the inbreaking of new creation.

Jesus' Comment on His Healing Activity

On one occasion Jesus speaks to the significance of his healings in response to an inquiry from John the Baptist.[124] But before examining the account itself, it will be helpful to consider the nature of Jesus' relationship with John. Jesus' baptism by John is certainly historical, since it is very unlikely early Christians would have invented an account of Jesus submitting himself to a rite of repentance for the forgiveness of sins. Although the Synoptic accounts locate the beginning of Jesus' public ministry in Galilee shortly after his baptism, there are a number of indications that suggest that for some time prior to his ministry in Galilee he worked alongside John: (i) according to the Fourth Gospel, Jesus engaged in a ministry involving baptism in Judea prior to John's arrest, a ministry that was attracting more people than John was attracting;[125] (ii) again according to the Fourth Gospel, Jesus' first disciples were previously disciples of John;[126] (iii) Jesus and John were closely associated with each other in the popular opinion;[127] (iv) Jesus found it necessary later to distinguish himself from John;[128] and (v)

---

123. *Gen. Rab.* 17.5: "the incomplete form of the next world is the Sabbath" (cf. 44.17); *b. Ber.* 57b: "Three things are a reflex of the world to come: Sabbath, sunshine, and *tashmish* [footnote reads 'service']."

124. Matt 11:2–6//Luke 7:18–23.

125. John 3:22–26; 4:1–2. For a defense of the historicity of the portrayal of John the Baptist in the Fourth Gospel, see Dodd, *Fourth Gospel*, 248–312.

126. John 1:35–37.

127. Mark 6:14 par.; 8:27–28 par.

128. Mark 2:18–22 par.: an explanation of why John's disciples fast but not those of

much effort is spent in all the Gospels and in Acts to show that Jesus was superior to John, suggesting that this was not obvious to everyone at the time.[129] Presumably, therefore, Jesus preached a similar message to that of John.[130] All of this is best explained by the supposition that Jesus began as a disciple or co-worker of John.[131]

Each of the Gospels' depiction of Jesus in his own ministry, however, is very different from its depiction of John. Around the time of John's arrest, Jesus moves to Galilee,[132] does not baptize,[133] does not fast regularly[134] or lead an ascetic lifestyle,[135] associates with disreputable people, heals, exorcises, and preaches a different message from that of John who "warned people to flee from the wrath to come."[136] Indeed there appears to be a change in Jesus' perspective: the emphasis is not so much on the coming judgment as it was with John (although judgment is not lacking in Jesus' message), but rather on the good news of the coming of God's kingdom to restore his people. What happened to bring about such a change? No doubt Jesus' own baptism

---

Jesus; Matt 11:11//Luke 7:28: John was great, but all those in the kingdom are greater; Matt 11:18–19//Luke 7:33–35: Jesus was not an ascetic like John.

129. Luke 1:42: John jumps in the womb upon Mary's arrival; Mark 1:7–8 par.; Acts 1:5; 11:16: John baptizes with water, Jesus with the Holy Spirit; Matt 3:13–15: John is not worthy to baptize Jesus; John 1:6–8, 19–34; Acts 13:25: John denies he is the Christ and witnesses to Jesus as being the Lamb of God; John 3:27–30: John admits that he must give way to Jesus; Acts 18:24–19:7: the baptism of John is sub-Christian.

130. On the relationship between Jesus and John, see also Webb, "John the Baptist," 226–27; Meyer, *Aims of Jesus*, 122–28; Sanders, *Jesus and Judaism*, 91–93; Meier, *Marginal Jew*, 2:116–30.

131. While there are numerous texts indicating that John had disciples (Mark 2:18 par.; 6:29 par.; Luke 7:18–19 par.; 11:1; John 1:35, 37; 3:25), there is no indication that any of them other than Jesus baptized or engaged in a separate ministry prior to John's arrest. Luke's birth narrative suggests that Jesus and John were related (Luke 1:36), which might help to explain Jesus' special role as a co-worker; however, the word Luke uses to denote Elizabeth's relationship to Mary—ἡ συγγενίς σου—is not very specific and may indicate no more than that they were of the same tribe; see Michaelis, "συγγενής," 740.

132. In the Fourth Gospel Jesus moves between Galilee and Jerusalem.

133. Even the Fourth Gospel tries to disassociate Jesus from the act of baptizing (John 4:2).

134. Mark 2:18 par. A change in purification practices may also be implied from John 3:25.

135. Matt 11:18–19//Luke 7:33–35.

136. Matt 3:8//Luke 3:7.

had a profound effect on him, giving him a sense of call to mission;[137] but in view here seems to be a change subsequent to his baptism. John's arrest by itself does not appear to be a sufficient explanation. Paul Hollenbach has argued that this change in Jesus' activity is due to a conversion he had that grew out of his experience of God's power and grace demonstrated in his own healings and exorcisms.[138] Indeed, we can well imagine that such a discovery must have had a profound impact on Jesus. It must have led him to reflect on and reassess how he understood what God was doing and what it was that he himself was being called to. Hollenbach writes:

> [Jesus'] reasoning would have been something like the following: Why continue to baptize powerful people for repentance so they can escape God's wrath, when the sick are being visited directly with God's mercy without it? It is not a matter now of the powerful repenting for their oppressions but of God loving the oppressed. Why look any longer for someone to purify the repentant finally at a second baptism when people already now know the restoring and compelling power of God's love? Why fast and pray when people are no longer anticipating a final purification, but are already enjoying a gracious restoration of life? Why stay in the wilderness waiting for people to come to you, when there are so many more sick and oppressed in towns and countryside who are just waiting to receive the healing of their diseases, and to hear good news of liberation?[139]

137. See Marcus, "Vision," 512–21. Marcus goes on to locate the vision of Satan falling from heaven (Luke 10:18) at Jesus' own baptism, from which it would follow that his break with John stemmed directly from his baptismal experience. Marcus' argument for this, however, is not strong: if Jesus was a visionary, he could have had such a vision on any of numerous occasions, and it is just as likely to attach it to Jesus' exorcising activity as it is to John's baptism with its eschatological orientation.

138. Hollenbach, "Conversion of Jesus," 98–219. Hollenbach acknowledges Kraeling (*John the Baptist*) as the source of this view. See also Webb, "John the Baptist," 226–27.

139. Hollenbach, "Conversion of Jesus," 216–17. Meier, *Marginal Jew*, 2:124–27, challenges Hollenbach by arguing: (i) since the nature of the Gospels is such that we generally cannot with confidence determine the sequence of events, we therefore cannot tell whether his baptizing preceded his healings and exorcisms or not, and therefore we cannot draw a causal relationship between them; (ii) the Gospels do not give us information regarding how Jesus developed in his thought and strategy; and (iii) it is an argument from silence (no mention of baptizing in the Synoptics and no mention after 4:1 in John) to suggest that Jesus stopped baptizing at some point. I would respond by arguing: (a) according to each of the Gospels and Acts Jesus' ministry began with his own baptism; (b) if Jesus did practice baptism, it seems likely

But, while Jesus may have distinguished himself from John, he did not reject John and his ministry. In the context of criticizing his own generation for behaving like pouting children, Jesus contrasts the mode of his ministry from that of John—the one "eating and drinking," the other not—but at the same time he is not embarrassed to associate himself with John.[140] He would still speak of John as a prophet, and indeed as more than a prophet. In fact he would say, "among those born of women none is greater than John." And yet he would also make it clear that his own message was more important than that of John because "he who is least in the kingdom of God is greater than he."[141]

This helps to explain the incident involving John sending some of his disciples to Jesus to ask whether he was indeed "he who is to come."[142] While Q frames the disciples' question in Christological language, it would make sense, in light of the background given above, for John to inquire as to why Jesus had changed. And in response, Jesus focuses attention on his healing and preaching activity in language

---

that he would have begun this shortly after his own baptism, probably in association with John; (c) while we do not know when Jesus began healing and exorcising, it is plausible to suppose it was while he was still baptizing; (d) John's comment that it was his disciples, not Jesus himself, who baptized (John 4:2), together with the total silence of the Synoptics regarding baptizing (which is difficult to explain even if it was a less defining action for Jesus than it was for John), seems to be best explained by Jesus stopping the practice of baptism early in his ministry (How could the author of Acts fail to mention Jesus' baptizing activity if it had been part of his ongoing ministry?); and (e) while it is true that we need to move cautiously when proposing a line of development in Jesus' thinking, where appropriate evidence presents itself, such moves are warranted. And the evidence raises the question: How do we explain the change in Jesus who began with John but later engaged in a very different kind of ministry? It seems to me that Hollenbach's proposal is quite plausible: that through reflection on the significance of his own healings and exorcisms Jesus came to a new understanding of what God was calling him to do.

140. Matt 11:16–19//Luke 7:31–35. Although the Jesus Seminar ranks this pericope as gray, they also conclude that "Many of the Fellows thought the saying reflected accurate characterizations of John and Jesus" (Funk et al., *Five Gospels*, 180). The appearance of "son of man" weighed against authenticity for the Fellows.

141. Luke 7:28 par. in Matt 11:11; cf. *Gos. Thom.* 46:1–2. A split vote in the Jesus Seminar resulted in a gray ranking of this saying (Funk et al., *Five Gospels*, 178–79, 301–2, 498). Those who voted against authenticity assumed that any comment distinguishing Jesus and John must have come from the early church; if, however, as I am arguing, Jesus was first associated with John but later moved in a different direction, there is no reason why he would not have needed to explain the difference between himself and John.

142. Matt 11:2–6//Luke 7:18–23.

drawn from the book of Isaiah: "the blind receive their sight, the lame walk, lepers are cleansed, and the deaf hear, the dead are raised up, the poor have good news preached to them."[143]

The authenticity of this saying has been widely accepted[144] with some notable exceptions. The Jesus Seminar argues, "The basic list is . . . taken from scripture, which means that this response is a piece of Christian apologetic, designed to demonstrate that these activities fulfil ancient prophecies."[145] This is, however, a classic example of an invalid use of the criterion of dissimilarity: just because we know that early Christians reflected on Scripture in a particular way, does not mean that Jesus could not have done the same; indeed, it would make sense if Christians were following Jesus' example in this respect. John Kloppenborg thinks that the mention of cleansing the lepers, which does not appear in Isaiah, indicates that this saying "is a post-Easter interpretation of Jesus' deeds as evidence of the presence of the kingdom."[146] Reference to the lepers, however, would be just as curious if the saying came from the early church: if one is trying to show that Jesus fulfilled prophecy, why include something that was not part of Jewish expectation? More recently, the authenticity of the saying has been supported by the discovery of a similar pastiche of scriptural allusions at Qumran:

> (1) [for the heav]ens and the earth will listen to his anointed one. . . . (5) For the Lord will consider the pious, and call the righteous by name, (6) and his spirit will hover upon the poor, and he will renew the faithful with his strength. (7) For he will honour the pious upon the throne of an eternal kingdom, (8) freeing prisoners, giving sight to the blind, straightening out the twis[ted.] . . . (11) And the Lord will perform marvelous acts such as have not existed, just as he sa[id,] (12) [for] he will heal the badly wounded and will make the dead live, he will proclaim good news to the poor (13) and . . . he will lead the . . . and enrich the hungry. (4Q521 2ii1, 5–8, 11–13)

This fragment looks forward to a time when the Lord's "anointed one" will appear and when the Lord will reward the righteous with "an eternal kingdom" and will perform several "marvelous acts": note

143. Matt 11:5//Luke 7:22.

144. See, for example, Bultmann, *History*, 126, 128, 151.

145. Funk et al., *Five Gospels*, 177–78.

146. Kloppenborg, *Formation of Q*, 108.

specifically the mention of giving sight to the blind, straightening out the twisted (healing the lame?), healing the wounded, raising the dead, and proclaiming good news to the poor. The similarity with Jesus' saying strongly suggests that he may have drawn on a pre-existing collection of texts that would have been familiar to his hearers.[147]

There is wider debate on whether the setting of this incident is historical, many thinking that it makes better sense as an attempt to address the presumed ongoing rivalry in the first century between followers of John and followers of Jesus than it does as an incident in the life of Jesus. It should be noted, however, that Jesus' saying itself does not stand on its own but requires some kind of inquiry; the saying assumes that Jesus is responding to a question about who he is or what he is doing. Davies and Allison defend the authenticity of both the saying and its Q setting by pointing to evidence that speaks against this being a Christian composition. They highlight: (i) the lack of a clear Christological focus (even in light of John's question—"Are you he who is to come?"—Jesus' response focuses on what he is doing rather than on who he is); (ii) the lack of any Christological implication (the Messiah was not generally expected to be a miracle-worker[148]); and (iii) the lack of a concluding testimony on John's part (as we find, for example, in connection with Jesus' baptism).[149]

To appreciate the significance of Jesus' response, it is important to recognize that he is being allusive rather than direct. He is asked to explain himself, and he does so by referring to his actions in the language of certain Isaianic texts. Commentators generally agree that allusions are being made to Isa 26:19; 29:18–19; 35:5–6; 61:1; and possibly to Isa 42:6–7, 18.[150] What did Jesus mean to communicate? That he was alluding to texts from Isaiah was probably clear to his audience. But the connection that would almost certainly have been made, to those familiar with Isaiah, is that these were all from texts that spoke of God's

147. Kvalbein, "Wonders," 87–101, argues for a metaphorical understanding of the divine healing activities in the Qumran text. But even if he is correct, it does not mean that Jesus could not have used the same texts with a literal meaning.

148. See ibid., 101–6.

149. Davies and Allison, *Matthew*, 2:244–45; cf. Luz, *Matthew 8–20*, 131; Meier, *Marginal Jew*, 2:131–37, 833.

150. See Davies and Allison, *Matthew*, 2:242; Luz, *Matthew 8–20*, 134; Nolland, *Matthew*, 451; Fitzmyer, *Luke*, 1:662; Danker, *Jesus and the New Age*, 165; Bovon, *Luke 1:1–9:50*, 282.

promises for Israel's future: Isa 26:16–21 offers hope to Israelites who have suffered much by promising resurrection;[151] Isa 29:17–21 envisions a time when oppressors will be cut off and the meek will rejoice, and likens Israel to an abundantly fruitful Lebanon; Isa 42:1–9 speaks of the mission of the servant called to be "a light to the nations" (v. 6), through whom God will do "new things" (v. 9); Isa 42:18–25 is a call for blind Israel to open her eyes to her true condition so that God can restore her; and Isa 61:1–11 speaks of deliverance for God's people, the rebuilding of Jerusalem, and the submission of the nations, and it uses an image of an abundant garden to depict a world of righteousness and praise (v. 11). But Isa 35 is particularly significant: the context in which the prophet speaks of the blind seeing, the deaf hearing, and the lame leaping, is one of hope for return from exile, and the imagery throughout is strongly suggestive of new creation:

> The wilderness and the dry land shall be glad,
>   the desert shall rejoice and blossom;
> like the crocus it shall blossom abundantly,
>   and rejoice with joy and singing.
>   . . .
> Then the eyes of the blind shall be opened,
>   and the ears of the deaf unstopped;
> then shall the lame man leap like a hart,
>   and the tongue of the dumb sing for joy.
> For waters shall break forth in the wilderness,
>   and streams in the desert;
> the burning sand shall become a pool,
>   and the thirsty ground springs of water;
> the haunt of jackals shall become a swamp,
>   the grass shall become reeds and rushes. (Isa 35:1–2a, 5–7)

Supporting this conclusion that Jews read these Isaianic texts from an eschatological perspective is the Qumran manuscript that we cited above. While the role of the anointed one mentioned in this text is not clear in 4Q521, it is clear that the text expresses the future hope of God's restoration.[152] This eschatological perspective also seems to be

151. Cf. Ezek 37:1–14. Whether the prophet was speaking of resurrection literally or metaphorically is immaterial for our purpose. The point is that Jesus' saying alludes to this text.

152. Collins, "Pre-Christian Jewish Messianism," 15, suggests that the reference to the proclamation of good news probably has in view a messenger, which implies that the acts of the Lord here may be carried out by his "anointed one."

expressed in another fragment (unfortunately poorly preserved) from the same manuscript:

> (1) [. . .] see all th[at has made] (2) [the Lord: the ear]th and all that is in it, *Blank* the seas [and all] (3) [they contain,] and all the reservoirs of waters and torrents. *Blank* (4) [. . .] those who do the good before the Lor[d] (5) [. . .] like these, the accursed. And [they] shall b[e] for death, [. . .] (6) [. . .] he who gives life to the dead of his people. (4Q521 7+5ii1–6)

Working from the bottom up we find: (i) line 6 seems to have in view the resurrection of the righteous; (ii) lines 4–5 seem to refer to rewards for the righteous and the punishment of death for the wicked; and (iii) lines 1–3 seem to set what follows in the context of God and his creation, perhaps suggesting, in light of the eschatological events that do follow, that the overall perspective is one of new creation.

It seems likely then that by using these Isaianic allusions to refer to his healings and teaching, Jesus was implying that the salvation spoken of by the prophets was at hand. And a prominent image of that salvation was new creation—an image that his healing activity must have easily evoked, particularly when set against the context of a text like Isa 35[153]—and that therefore would have provided a framework for his preaching of the gospel to the poor—that is, for his message concerning the kingdom of God: it was a message about God acting to restore his creation in keeping with the hopes of Israel. Thus, it would be fair to say that new creation is the lens through which Jesus wants his audience to look in order to understand what he is saying.

Jesus' Comment on His Exorcising Activity

Jesus' reputation as an exorcist is also well attested. First, both Mark and Q record specific accounts of Jesus exorcising demons,[154] which would place him in company with other Jewish exorcists of whom we know.[155] Also, each of the Synoptics speaks of Jesus empowering

153. See also *Mek.* on Exod 15:26 which associates divine healing with the world to come.

154. Mark 1:23–28 par.; 5:1–20 par.; 7:24–30 par.; 9:14–29 par.; Matt 12:22–23// Luke 11:14–15 (cf. Matt 9:32–34 which appears to be the same incident as in 12:22–23); cf. Matt 12:43–45//Luke 11:24–26. See also summary statements in Mark 1:32–34, 39; 3:11; Luke 7:21; 13:32.

155. In defense against the charge that he cast out demons by an evil power, Jesus

his disciples also to cast out demons.[156] The historicity of this is made more certain by the fact that exorcism was apparently not a significant concern of the early church.[157] Second, there is a significant amount of evidence showing that Jesus was charged by both Jews and pagans with exorcising by means of an evil power—that is, that he was a magician or sorcerer.[158] Interestingly, his opponents do not suggest that the accounts of exorcism were false and that Jesus was a charlatan. In addition, sometimes this same accusation was leveled against Christians.[159] And third, it is significant that Jesus' name was used by others in performing exorcisms.[160]

The most significant account for our purposes is the one where Jesus' opponents accuse him of exorcising by means of the prince of demons, Beelzebul.[161] The composition of the account is somewhat complex being an instance of the so-called overlap between Mark and Q. The account consists of the following:

(a) an exorcism (Q):

> . . . when the demon had gone out, the dumb man spoke. (Luke 11:14, par. in Matt 9:33 and 12:22)

(b) an accusation that Jesus is possessed (Mark) and that he exorcises by means of an evil power (Mark and Q):

> He is possessed by Beelzebul, and by the prince of demons he casts out the demons. (Mark 3:22)

---

speaks of his opponents' "sons" as exorcists (Matt 12:27//Luke 11:19); and on one occasion the disciples refer to an unnamed exorcist casting out demons in Jesus' name (Mark 9:38–39//Luke 9:49–50); cf. Acts 19:11–17. For other Jewish and pagan references to exorcism, see Meier, *Marginal Jew*, 2:405–6.

156. Mark 3:14–15; Matt 10:1//Mark 6:7//Luke 9:1; Matt 10:8; Luke 10:17; although apparently the disciples were not always successful (Mark 9:18).

157. Only mentioned in Acts 8:7; 16:16–18.

158. Matt 12:24 (cf. 9:34)//Mark 3:22//Luke 11:15; cf. John 7:20; 8:48; 10:20. Justin, *Dial.* 69.7; cf. 17.1; 108.2. Origen, *Cels.* 1.68; 2.49; *b. Sanh.* 43a. For other possible references, see Smith, *Jesus the Magician*, 45–67.

159. Origen, *Cels.* 1.6.

160. By Jesus' disciples: Luke 10:17; Acts 16:18; Irenaeus, *Haer.* 2.32.5; by others: Matt 7:22; Mark 9:38; Acts 19:13; cf. *t. Ḥul.* 2:22. See also the mention of Jesus' name in some magical incantations: PGM 4:1233, 3020.

161. Matt 12:22–30//Mark 3:22–27//Luke 11:14–23.

> He casts out demons by Beelzebul, the prince of demons.
> (Luke 11:15, par. in Matt 12:24)

(c) a defense exposing the absurdity of Satan casting out himself (Mark and Q):

> How can Satan cast out Satan? If a kingdom is divided against itself, that kingdom cannot stand. And if a house is divided against itself, that house will not be able to stand. And if Satan has risen up against himself and is divided, he cannot stand, but is coming to an end. (Mark 3:23–26; cf. Matt 12:25–26// Luke 11:17–18)

(d) a defense based on the fact that since other respected Jews cast out demons, it cannot be concluded on the basis of his exorcisms alone that Jesus uses an evil power (Q):

> And if I cast out demons by Beelzebul, by whom do your sons cast them out? Therefore they shall be your judges. (Luke 11:19, par. in Matt 12:27)

(e) a saying connecting Jesus' exorcisms with the work of God and with the kingdom of God (Q):

> But if it is by the finger [Matt: "Spirit"] of God that I cast out demons, then the kingdom of God has come upon you. (Luke 11:20, par. in Matt 12:28)

(f) a parable about a strong man's house being plundered (Mark and Q):[162]

> But no one can enter a strong man's house and plunder his goods, unless he first binds the strong man; then indeed he may plunder his house. (Mark 3:27; cf. Matt 12:29)

> When a strong man, fully armed, guards his own palace, his goods are in peace; but when one stronger than he assails him and overcomes him, he takes away his armor in which he trusted, and divides his spoil. (Luke 11:21–22)

(g) a charge to people to decide for or against Jesus (Q).

> He who is not with me is against me, and he who does not gather with me scatters. (Matt 12:30//Luke 11:23)

---

162. Matthew follows Mark in this parable. Luke's version is significantly different and presumably closer to Q since Luke 11:21–22 does not have distinctively Lukan features. *Gos. Thom.* 35:1–2 has a version closer to Mark than to Luke.

Most commentators agree that there is a historical core here, although there is debate over the authenticity of specific elements, over which version of an element is more original, and over whether the sayings were given on the same occasion. We need not go into all the details. Most take Jesus' "finger/Spirit of God" saying (e) to be authentic,[163] although there is debate over whether "finger" or "Spirit" is original.[164] The accusation itself (b) is historically probable in light of the rarity of the name "Beelzebul" (it is not likely to have been introduced by Christians)[165] and in light of accusations in John and later Jewish literature of Jesus being a magician.[166] Finally, the parable of the strong man (f) has the marks of authenticity: the imagery is not otherwise found in early Christianity, however its message coheres well with Jesus' activity as an exorcist.[167] Commentators do not agree on whether Mark or Q (Luke) has the more original version of the parable; Mark's version appears to be more primitive,[168] but in this case there is no reason why Jesus could not have uttered both versions on different occasions.

The "finger/Spirit of God" saying (e) is particularly significant. Jesus points to his exorcisms as evidence of the presence of the kingdom of God.[169] In light of Jesus' acknowledgement in (d) to there be-

163. Often cited in support is Bultmann, *History*, 162. For full argumentation of historicity see Meier, *Marginal Jew*, 2:413–17. Dunn, "Matthew 12:28/Luke 11:20," 29–49, specifically challenges Sanders' skepticism on this point. The Jesus Seminar ranked this saying as pink (Funk et al., *Five Gospels*, 185–86, 329–30).

164. For a summary of the debate, see Davies and Allison, *Matthew*, 2:339–40; Nolland, *Luke*, 2:639–40. Also, due to the importance of this text with regard to the question of whether Jesus thought the kingdom was present or future, much discussion has focused on the sense of the verb, ἔφθασεν (Matt 12:28//Luke 11:20). For a defense of the traditional translation, "has come," see Meier, *Marginal Jew*, 2:412–13.

165. On Beelzebul see Davies and Allison, *Matthew*, 2:195–96.

166. See references above, p. 271 n. 158.

167. The Jesus Seminar ranked the saying as pink (Funk et al., *Five Gospels*, 51–52).

168. Mark has an anonymous plunderer whereas Luke speaks of "one stronger than he."

169. See Marcus, "Beelzebul Controversy," 247–77, for a hypothesis that Jesus' first defense (c), in the form of a *reductio ad absurdum* that Satan could not be casting himself out, which seems to assume that Satan's kingdom is still in fact standing, is authentic but comes from an earlier period in Jesus' ministry (Marcus thinks prior to his own baptism) before he came to believe that through his own ministry, and exorcisms in particular, Satan's kingdom was falling.

ing other Jewish exorcists at the time,[170] debate has focused on how Jesus concluded, on the basis of his own exorcisms, that the kingdom of God had come.[171] Davies and Allison insist that the issue for Jesus was his identity as Messiah: "Jesus accepts the miracles of others but holds his own to be of different import because of his identity."[172] The fact that Matthew sets this incident within the context of people asking, "Can this be the Son of David?"[173] suggests that he may share this view. It is possible, however, that the incident implies a difference in method between Jesus and other exorcists, the latter using elaborate rituals of various kinds while Jesus simply issues a command.[174] In any case, Jesus is not claiming that his exorcisms by themselves prove something about himself; rather, he is offering people an alternative explanation to that of the Pharisees, inviting them to see his exorcisms, and hence his whole ministry, as a demonstration of God winning a victory over the enemy, and indeed of the presence of the kingdom of God. And whether Jesus used the word "finger" or "Spirit," it is clear that he understood himself to be living at a climactic time in the history of Israel.[175]

The imagery of the parable of the strong man (f) is reminiscent of Isa 49:24–25 where the Israelites' return from exile is being likened to prey being taken from a strong man or captives rescued from a tyrant.[176] Another possible background is the common apocalyptic image of evil spiritual beings being bound and confined in a prison.[177] It is difficult to determine whether Jesus was consciously drawing on either of these images, but what the parable does clearly underline is that Jesus saw

170. Cf. Mark 9:38–39//Luke 9:49–50.

171. For a survey of the various solutions that have been proposed, see Davies and Allison, *Matthew*, 2:340–41.

172. Ibid., 2:341.

173. Matt 11:23.

174. Twelftree, *In the Name of Jesus*, 48–49. On methods of exorcism in antiquity, see ibid., 42–45; Vermes, *Jesus the Jew*, 63–69.

175. The word "finger" would allude back to Exod 8:19 and the account of the miracles performed before Pharaoh which led to the exodus; see Meier, *Marginal Jew*, 2:411. The word "Spirit" would evoke many instances of the activity of God's Spirit in the Old Testament, and perhaps would align Jesus with the Servant of Yahweh who was empowered by the Spirit; see Nolland, *Matthew*, 500.

176. Cf. *Pss. Sol.* 5.3.

177. Isa 24:21–22; Tob 3:17; 8:3; *1 En.* 10.4, 11–13; 13.1; 18.16; 21.6; 69.28; 90.23; *Jub.* 10.3–8; *T. Levi* 18.12; cf. 2 Pet 2:4; Jude 6; Rev 20:1–3.

his exorcisms as evidence of the overthrow of Satan and the liberation of those once held in his control.

Thus, we have in Jesus' defense of his exorcisms references to his winning the battle with Satan and to the presence of the kingdom of God, and possible allusions to the exodus from Egypt and the return from Babylon. And, we simply recall at this point that defeat of Israel's enemies, including Satan, the establishment of God's rule, and the restoration of God's people, often depicted with exodus language, were all part of the Jewish hope for new creation.

Other Indications of a New Creation Framework

Creation Standards

In one text Jesus makes a clear reference to creation as the standard for behavior.

> And Pharisees came up and in order to test him asked, "Is it lawful for a man to divorce his wife?" He answered them, "What did Moses command you?" They said, "Moses allowed a man to write a certificate of divorce, and to put her away." But Jesus said to them, "For your hardness of heart he wrote you this commandment. But from the beginning of creation, 'God made them male and female.' 'For this reason a man shall leave his father and mother and be joined to his wife, and the two shall become one flesh.' So they are no longer two but one flesh. What therefore God has joined together, let not man put asunder." (Mark 10:2–9, par. in Matt 19:3–8)

I leave aside the question of the historicity of the event itself which has often been challenged,[178] and focus instead on the authenticity of Jesus' reply. Jesus' prohibition of divorce is multiply attested.[179] Also, Matthew's qualification—"except for unchastity"[180]—is better explained in terms of embarrassment in the early church over Jesus' strict prohibition than supposing the church to have created a confusing tradition.[181] Furthermore, Bultmann argues that the way in which

---

178. Meier, *Marginal Jew*, 119–24.

179. Matt 5:32//Luke 16:18; Mark 10:11–12 (cf. Matt 19:9); 1 Cor 7:10–11.

180. Matt 19:9; cf. Matt 5:32.

181. Evans, *Mark 8:27—16:20*, 79–80.

Jesus set one text of Scripture against another without resolving the tension is dissimilar to Judaism in light of what we know of later rabbinic practice.[182] And finally, Jesus' conclusion (v. 9) is a pithy aphorism such as he is known to have spoken.

The arguments against the authenticity of Jesus' saying here presented by the Jesus Seminar are not sound: (i) the fact that there are variations in Jesus' teaching on this subject in the different sources is not necessarily due to the editorial activity of the early church but in fact may have been due to Jesus rephrasing and clarifying himself; and (ii) appeal to Scripture is not something that only the early church did.[183] Hultgren argues that the use of the Septuagint in Mark 10:7–8, together with the conclusion "So they are no longer two but one flesh," implies that the pericope was created in a Greek-speaking context (the LXX of Gen 2:24 reads "*the two* shall be one flesh," whereas the Hebrew has "*they* shall be one flesh").[184] While it certainly does appear that verse 8b was composed in light of the Septuagint, it seems quite plausible that in translating the incident into Greek, a Christian may have opted for the Septuagint version over the Hebrew and at the same time may have created verse 8b or possibly modified an original that read something like, "So they are now one flesh," to something that matched the Septuagint wording more closely.

Jesus' response is significant for our purpose in two ways: (i) he appeals to creation as a standard for behavior; and (ii) this creation standard now supersedes a concession given in the law. The latter is consistent with the intensification and refocus we observe in Jesus' teaching on the kind of behavior God now requires: Jesus calls for a level of righteousness higher than that of the scribes and Pharisees which he articulates in the antitheses in the Sermon on the Mount— "You have heard it said . . . but I say to you . . .";[185] to one person who had observed the law from his youth Jesus says: "You lack one thing; go, sell what you have, and give to the poor . . . and come, follow me";[186] and he calls on people to focus more on "the weightier matters of the law," meaning giving attention to issues such as justice, mercy, and

---

182. Bultmann, *History*, 49–50.

183. Funk et al., *Five Gospels*, 88–89; the Seminar ranked the saying as gray.

184. Hultgren, *Adversaries*, 121.

185. Matt 5:20–48.

186. Mark 10:21 par.

faith rather than tithing,[187] or giving attention to the thoughts of the heart rather than actions to maintain ritual purity.[188] But the fact that he points to the creation narrative to defend his high standard with regard to marriage is evidence of his new creation perspective.

The Newness of the Present

Recalling what we said above about Jesus distinguishing himself from John the Baptist, each of the Synoptics records an account of Jesus responding to a question of why John's disciples (and the Pharisees)[189] fast whereas his disciples do not.[190] In three parabolic sayings Jesus indicates the radical newness represented by his ministry.

(a) The inappropriateness of fasting at a wedding:

> Can the wedding guests fast while the bridegroom is with them? As long as they have the bridegroom with them, they cannot fast. The days will come, when the bridegroom is taken away from them, and then they will fast in that day.

(b) The inappropriateness of patching an old garment with a new piece of cloth:

> No one sews a piece of unshrunk cloth on an old garment; if he does, the patch tears away from it, the new from the old, and a worse tear is made.

---

187. Matt 23:23. Bultmann, *History*, 147, takes this to be authentic.

188. Matt 15:10–20//Mark 7:14–23. On the authenticity of Mark 7:15, see Booth, *Laws of Purity*, 205–15. Jesus demonstrates the greater importance he sees in the welfare of people over matters of purity by his willingness to touch unclean people (Mark 1:40–41 par.) and by his parable of the Good Samaritan (Luke 10:30–35).

189. The reference to the Pharisees (Matt 9:14) or their disciples (Mark 2:18 and Luke 5:33) seems somewhat peculiar here: Why would John's disciples be associated with the Pharisees? Marcus, *Mark 1–8*, 235, suggests that the Pharisees may have been added to the scene when it was combined with the account in Mark 2:13–17.

190. As their leader, Jesus was seen to have been responsible for the practices of his disciples. That Jesus himself did not fast regularly, in contrast to John, seems to be implied by Matt 11:18–19//Luke 7:33–34. Although, what seems to be in view here is the regular practice of fasting (twice a week for the Pharisees; cf. Luke 18:12; *Did.* 8.1) rather than the required annual fasts—especially that on the Day of Atonement (Lev 16:29–31; 23:26–29) and possibly fasts associated with the exile (Zech 8:19) and Purim (Esth 9:31)—or a special period of fasting, such as Jesus observed following his baptism (Matt 4:2//Luke 4:2).

(c) The inappropriateness of pouring new wine into old wineskins:

> And no one puts new wine into old wineskins; if he does, the wine will burst the skins, and the wine is lost, and so are the skins; but new wine is for fresh skins. (Mark 2:19–22, par. in Matt 9:15–17//Luke 5:34–39)

Apart from the last sentence in (a),[191] these parables are widely accepted to be authentic.[192] The metaphor of a marriage is used in the prophets to depict the relationship between God and Israel,[193] but most significant for this saying is Isa 62:5 where the prophet likens the future salvation and restoration of Israel to a wedding:[194] "For as a young man marries a virgin, so shall your sons marry you, and as the bridegroom rejoices over the bride, so shall your God rejoice over you." Thus, Jesus is implying that God's salvation is now at work, and that the most appropriate response is celebration, like at a wedding, not fasting.[195]

The two parables that follow, (b) and (c), underline the radical newness of what God is doing in the ministry of Jesus, and indeed warn of the destructive consequences of failing to recognize this. The underlying assumption of the first is that a patch of unshrunk cloth will shrink when washed, tear away, and further damage the garment; the point of the second is that new wine, which is still fermenting, will burst skins that have aged and become inflexible. In a similar way, those who experience the new work of God's salvation must have new

---

191. It is often suggested that the qualification regarding fasting being appropriate after the bridegroom has been removed reflects the situation of the early church and has its origin there (see Marcus, *Mark 1–8*, 237). One's judgment on this will depend in part on how one judges the authenticity of Matt 6:16–18 and the likelihood that Jesus would have prepared his followers for conditions following his own death. In any case, this part of the saying is not significant for our purposes.

192. The Jesus Seminar ranked Mark 2:19 as pink, v. 20 as black, v. 21 as gray, and v. 22 as pink (Funk et al., *Five Gospels*, 47–49).

193. Hos 2; Ezek 16; Jer 2:2; Isa 54:5. The writer of Ephesians likens the relationship between Christ and the church to a marriage (Eph 5:23–33).

194. The image of a wedding feast to depict the messianic age was popular in rabbinic literature; see Str-B 1:517–18; cf. Matt 25:1–13; Rev 19:7–9; 21:2, 9.

195. Jesus' hearers probably did not see in this saying a messianic claim by Jesus since the designation of the Messiah as a bridegroom was apparently not made prior to the Gospels; in Jewish literature it first appears in *Pesiq. Rab.* 37.2 (sixth-seventh cent.). France, however, thinks Jesus could be making "a veiled messianic claim" (France, *Mark*, 139).

forms of expression. While the theme of new creation is not explicit here, the images of a wedding and of wine—occasionally used as an image of the restoration of Israel[196]—are suggestive of the fulfillment of Israel's hopes, and thus these parables here are certainly supportive of a new creation perspective.

Conclusions

The evidence suggests that Jesus' mindset can appropriately be described in terms of new creation, understood in terms of God's work of transformation of this world. It is likely that in his healings and exorcisms Jesus saw God doing a new work of grace and restoration among his people, and that he connected this with the hope for new creation given in the Scriptures and other Jewish writings. One of the ways he demonstrated this connection was by healing on the Sabbath since the Sabbath was itself connected to the themes of creation and liberation. This is confirmed by Jesus' comments on both his healings and his exorcisms, by his comment on marriage and divorce, and by other parabolic sayings that imply that Jesus saw a radical newness at work in his ministry.

196. Joel 3:18; Amos 9:13–14.

7

Paul's New Creation Eschatology

THE PURPOSE OF THIS CHAPTER IS TO DETERMINE TO WHAT EXTENT
Paul was dependent on Jesus for his view of the present reality of new
creation. Paul's view of new creation will be explored in the context
of his eschatological perspective. The possibility that Paul's views can
be explained solely from his experience as a Christian or from certain
Jewish perspectives will be analyzed.

Paul's Reference to New Creation

Whereas in the previous chapter the case for a new creation perspective for Jesus was established to a large degree by inference, in the case
of Paul the evidence is much more explicit. Paul uses the term "new
creation" twice:

> Therefore, if any one is in Christ, he is a new creation; the old
> has passed away, behold, the new has come. (2 Cor 5:17)

> For neither circumcision counts for anything, nor uncircumci-
> sion, but a new creation. (Gal 6:15)

Unfortunately, Paul does not elaborate on what he means by new
creation in these texts. For most of the history of the church, it has
been assumed that here he has in view the transforming work of God
within believers.[1] In so doing, Christian interpreters mirrored a trend
in rabbinic thought which likened the forgiveness of sins and the conversion of a proselyte to a new creation.[2]

---

1. See sources in Hubbard, *New Creation*, 2 nn. 2–5.

2. On forgiveness as new creation, see *y. Roš Haš.* 4:8: "God said to them, since you
entered into judgment before me on the Holiday of the New Year, and you departed
in peace, I attribute it to you as if you were made as a new creature"; *Pesiq. Rab.* 40.5

In the twentieth century, with the discovery of the importance of Jewish apocalyptic for understanding Paul,[3] interpreters began to see a cosmic perspective in his reference to new creation. Commenting on the 2 Corinthians text, Strachan reflects this clearly when he writes: "The 'creature' is new, because the Creation, or world in which he now moves, is new."[4] Some commentators continue to defend the individual perspective;[5] others, however, while stressing the primary importance in these texts of personal transformation, set this within the broader cosmic perspective of new creation[6]—a perspective that Paul certainly shared.[7] Commenting on 2 Cor 5:17, Thrall writes:

> if anyone exists 'in Christ', that person is a newly-created being. In v. 17b the wider background is touched on, perhaps as providing the reason for v. 17a. In principle, through the Christ-event and in the person of Christ, the new world and the new age are already objective realities. Even so, the main emphasis

---

(on Num 29:2): "Remake yourselves by repentance during the ten days between New Year's Day and the Day of Atonement, and on the Day of Atonement I will hold you guiltless, regarding you as a newly made creature" (Braude, PR); *Midr. Ps.* 18.6 (69a): "R. Simon said: A man is not permitted to sing this song whenever he wishes to sing it. But when a miracle is done for him, he is permitted to sing this song; he may be sure that his sins will be forgiven him, and that he will be as if created anew" (Braude, MP). On conversion as new creation, see: *b. Yebam.* 48b: "R. Jose said: One who has become a proselyte is like a child newly born" (cf. 62a). See also other references that have an individual perspective of new creation in view: *Exod. Rab.* 3.15 (on Exod 4:12): "What is the meaning of 'And I will teach thee what thou shalt speak'? . . . R. Simeon said: I will create thee into a new being" (Lehrman, MR); *Gen. Rab.* 39.11 (on Gen 12:2): "R. Berekhiah said: It is not written, 'And I will give thee', or 'And I will set thee', but 'And I will make thee': i.e. after I have created thee as a new creation thou wilt be fruitful and multiply" (Freedman, MR); *Lev. Rab.* 30.3 (on Ps 102:19): "'And a people which shall be created shall praise the Lord' implies that the Holy One, blessed be He, will create them as a new being" (Slotki, MR; cf. *Midr. Ps.* 102.3). See further, Str-B 2:421–23.

3. Note, for example, Käsemann, "Apocalyptic," 108–37, who describes "apocalyptic as the mother of Christian theology" (137).

4. Strachan, *2 Corinthians*, 114; cf. Furnish, *2 Corinthians*, 333; Cousar, *Galatians*, 154–55; Dunn, *Galatians*, 343; Martyn, *Galatians*, 565; Caird, *New Testament Theology*, 161.

5. Harris, *2 Corinthians*, 432; Betz, *Galatians*, 319–20; Longenecker, *Galatians*, 296; and now esp. Hubbard, *New Creation*, 133–232.

6. Bruce, *Galatians*, 273; Bruce, *1 and 2 Corinthians*, 209; Kistemaker, *2 Corinthians*, 193; Matera, *2 Corinthians*, 137.

7. Rom 8:19–22.

must lie on the world of humanity: the transformation of the cosmos remains a hope for the future (Rom 8.19–22).[8]

I will return at the end of this chapter to suggest what grounds there might be for finding a family resemblance between Jesus' and Paul's understanding of the present reality of new creation. The onus of most of this chapter, however, will be to set new creation more generally within Paul's eschatological perspective, and to assess the role of other factors that are commonly thought to have shaped that perspective.

Paul's Eschatological Perspective

Paul reflects a Jewish perspective that conceives of history as being divided into two ages—"this age" and "the age to come."[9] This perspective first appears in apocalyptic writings where we read of the consummation of this age[10] and the dawning of the age to come;[11] but the appearance of this two-age perspective in rabbinic writings suggests its more general acceptance among Jews—and particularly important here are some rabbinic texts that appear to reflect traditions from the first century CE.[12] While Paul never actually uses the phrase "the age to come,"[13] he does speak of "this age" (ὁ αἰὼν οὗτος),[14] "this world" (ὁ κόσμος οὗτος),[15] and "the present time" (ὁ νῦν καιρός)[16] in such a way that another age, world, and time are implied; he describes the

8. Thrall, 2 Corinthians, 1:427.

9. See Sasse, "αἰών," 197–209; and texts cited above, p. 252 n. 59.

10. T. Levi 10.2; T. Ben. 11.3.

11. Some texts refer to "this age" (1 En. 48.7), others to "the age to come" (1 En. 71.15; 2 En. 43.3; 50.2; 61.2; 65.8), and some to both (2 En. 66.6(J); 4 Ezra 6.9; 7.112–13; 8.1 (cf. 7.47)).

12. Gen. Rab. 14.5 (on Gen 2:7) speaks of "creation in this world and creation in the world to come" (Neusner) in the context of a debate between the two houses of Shammai and Hillel concerning the order of human re-creation in the age to come; t. Pe'ah 4:18 cites King Monobazus, a mid-first century CE Jewish proselyte, as saying: "My ancestors stored up treasures in this world, but I have stored up treasures for myself in the world-to-come" (Neusner).

13. But see Eph 1:21; cf. Mark 10:30//Luke 18:30; Matt 12:32; Luke 20:34–35.

14. Rom 12:2; 1 Cor 1:20; 2:6 (twice), 8; 3:18; 2 Cor 4:4; cf. Luke 16:8. See also the use of "the present world" (ὁ νῦν αἰών) in 1 Tim 6:17; Titus 2:12; 2 Tim 4:10.

15. 1 Cor 3:19; 5:10; 7:31; cf. Eph 2:2.

16. Rom 3:26; 8:18; 11:5; 2 Cor 8:14.

present as an "evil age" from which God seeks to deliver people;[17] and he clearly has in view a time in the future, inaugurated by the parousia of Jesus Christ, when God's rule will be established.[18]

But Paul introduced a profound change into this Jewish eschatological framework.[19] While he believed that this age was evil and that in the age to come God would establish his rule, he also claimed that something of the reality of God's future reign had broken into this present age: he declares that "the form of this world is passing away,"[20] and he speaks of believers as those "upon whom the end of the ages has come."[21] While the new age has not come in its entirety, there is something profoundly new about the present: "Behold, now is the acceptable time; behold, now is the day of salvation."[22] Paul highlights this present newness by drawing a number of contrasts between life prior to Jesus and life now: previously we followed a written code but now we live by faith and are guided by the Spirit;[23] previously we were like slaves in the household but now we have been adopted as children;[24] previously a veil blocked people's vision, but now in Christ the veil is removed so that the greater glory of the new covenant can be seen.[25] And as a consequence, a new way of living is possible for believers.[26] Finally, that Paul continues to look forward to the full consummation of the age to come is evident not only from the texts cited above, but also from the sense of urgency with which he appeals to his readers: "it is full time now for you to wake from sleep. For salvation is nearer to us now than when we first believed; the night is far gone, the day is at hand."[27]

---

17. Gal 1:3–4.

18. Rom 6:8; 1 Cor 15:24–28; 1 Thess 4:13–18.

19. Dunn, *Theology*, 461–98; Vos, *Pauline Eschatology*, 1–61; Cullmann, *Christ and Time*, chap. 5; Beker, *Paul the Apostle*, 143–52; Furnish, *Theology and Ethics*, 115–35.

20. 1 Cor 7:31.

21. 1 Cor 10:11.

22. 2 Cor 6:2.

23. Gal 3:23–26; Rom 7:6; 2 Cor 3:6.

24. Gal 4:1–7.

25. 2 Cor 3:12–16.

26. Rom 6:4; 1 Cor 5:7–8.

27. Rom 13:11–12; cf. 1 Cor 7:29.

This new eschatological framework creates a tension for believers. Oscar Cullmann writes:

> The *new element* in the New Testament is not eschatology, but what I call the *tension* between the decisive 'already fulfilled' and the 'not yet completed,' between the present and the future.[28]

That Paul understood the Christian life in terms of tension is clear from what he says about the conflict between the flesh and the Spirit: these are both active within believers, pulling them in different directions, and Paul exhorts believers to choose the way of the Spirit.[29] That Paul understood the tension in the Christian life eschatologically—that is, that it was due to the experience in part, within this age, of a reality that will be experienced in full, in the age to come—is evident from a variety of ways in which he describes the Christian life. First, Paul can speak of salvation as a past event,[30] a present process,[31] and a future hope;[32] although he notes that believers have been "justified by faith," they also exercise "hope in sharing in the glory of God";[33] while Paul can speak of conversion as God shining into people's hearts "the light of the gospel of the glory of Christ, who is the likeness of God,"[34] the Christian life is one of "beholding the glory of the Lord" and thereby "being changed into his likeness from one degree of glory to another,"[35] until at last believers are "conformed to the image of [God's] Son";[36] and believers identify with Christ in his death now, but identification with him in his resurrection is still future.[37] Second, Paul uses several images to indicate that the believers' present experience is a foretaste of what is to come: the presence of the Spirit in the lives of believers is

---

28. Cullmann, *Salvation in History*, 172, emphasis original; cf. idem., *Christ and Time*, 145, 155.

29. Rom 8:1–17; Gal 5:16–25; see further Dunn, *Theology*, 477–82.

30. Rom 8:24; 1 Cor 15:2; cf. Eph 2:5, 8.

31. 1 Cor 1:18; 2 Cor 2:15.

32. Rom 5:9–10; 1 Cor 3:15; 5:5.

33. Rom 5:1–2.

34. 2 Cor 4:6.

35. 2 Cor 3:18.

36. Rom 8:29.

37. Rom 6:5.

the ἀρραβών[38] ("down payment") and the ἀπαρχή[39] ("first fruits"), both of which imply a fuller experience of the same reality in the future; similarly, Jesus' resurrection is the ἀπαρχή of believers who have died,[40] implying that a resurrection awaits all believers in the future; in being made children, believers are therefore now heirs[41] and hence awaiting their inheritance of the kingdom of God;[42] and, Paul uses the image of betrothal to depict the relationship between believers and Christ, which suggests a future wedding.[43]

The question for us is: *Why* does Paul conceive of the time in which he lives in this way? Why does he believe that there is a new dynamic in how God is at work in the world—a dynamic that can be described in terms of the present experience of new creation—and why does this lead him to adopt a modification of the standard Jewish eschatological framework so that he can now speak of a tension between the "already" and the "not yet"? In particular, is it reasonable to believe that the reason for this was the focus on new creation in Jesus' ministry?

In order to claim that Jesus' focus on new creation was influential in Paul's thinking, we need first to examine other possible sources, and in this case there are some clear candidates. With regard to why Paul thought something new was afoot, we should consider the likely effect on him of the resurrection of Jesus and of the common experience of the Spirit in the lives of believers. And, with regard to the modified eschatological framework—the "already" but "not yet" tension—we need to examine the possibility of a similar line of thought at Qumran. The question is, which is the more likely explanation: (i) Paul's belief in Jesus' resurrection and his experience of the Spirit led him to conclude that the reality of the age to come was breaking into this present age, which furthermore led him either to modify the typical Jewish eschatological expectation into an "already" but "not yet" pattern, or to adopt such a pattern that already existed among some Jews; or, (ii) Jesus, already during his ministry, taught his followers

38. 2 Cor 1:22; 5:5; cf. Eph 1:13–14.
39. Rom 8:23.
40. 1 Cor 15:20, 23.
41. Gal 4:1–7.
42. 1 Cor 6:9–10; 15:50; Gal 5:21; cf. Col 3:24; Eph 1:14, 18; 5:5.
43. 2 Cor 11:2; cf. Eph 5:25–27.

that Israel's hopes were about to be, or were in the process of being, fulfilled, and those same followers, and Paul afterwards, interpreted Jesus' resurrection and their experience of the Spirit, within that previously established eschatological framework, as evidence of the end of the ages coming upon them? Or, another way of asking the question: Is Paul's Jewish context sufficient to explain the significance he saw in Jesus' resurrection and in believers' experience of the Spirit, or do we need to assume a context established by Jesus' ministry in order to explain Paul's understanding? We will need to look carefully at the role that both resurrection and God's Spirit played within Jewish expectation, and at the nature of eschatological thinking at Qumran, in order to answer this question.

An Eschatological Tension at Qumran?

It is commonly argued that the community at Qumran expressed an eschatological tension similar to what Paul expressed. As early as 1961, Frank Moore Cross wrote:

> [T]he fully communal existence of the Essenes, as in the primitive Church, is a concomitant of an intense preoccupation with the qualities of life to be realized in the dawning New Age: unity (through the Spirit), brotherhood, love of one's fellow, the breakdown of the disparity between the (wicked) rich and the (oppressed) poor.[44]

> Both the Essenes and the primitive Church believed that the last age was imminent; indeed they were living in the last times; they were the last generation. In some sense the new age had dawned; at least its signs were discernible in the events of their day. History had reached its crisis.[45]

There is no question that the Qumran community lived in anticipation of the end of the age,[46] that they looked forward to God

---

44. Cross, *Library of Qumran*, 84.

45. Ibid., 216; cf. pp. 203–4.

46. See, for example, Collins, "Eschatology," 256–61; idem., "Expectation of the End," 74–90; Knibb, "Eschatology and Messianism," 379–82; Vermes, "Eschatological World View," 479–84; Deasley, *Qumran Theology*, 255–58; VanderKam and Flint, *Meaning*, 264–65, 303–6; Cross, *Library of Qumran*, 216–18; Ringgren, *Faith of Qumran*, 152–66.

renewing his creation,[47] and that they understood themselves as the community of the new covenant;[48] and in this sense they were certainly eschatologically oriented. But there is some question, I suggest, about whether it is appropriate to describe their experience of the reality of God in their midst in terms of a belief, in Cross's words, that "[i]n some sense the new age had dawned." If this were so, then it could be argued that Paul's eschatology was shaped not by Jesus but by the perspective we find at Qumran.[49] I will argue, however, that there is a significant difference between Qumran and Paul in how they each articulated the tension between the experience of the reality of God and the limitations of life in this present world.

George Nickelsburg and Heinz-Wolfgang Kuhn have provided the most substantial arguments to support the view that the Qumran community understood the blessings it was experiencing in terms of a prolepsis of the life of the age to come.[50] Central to their arguments are two hymns from the *Hodayot*—1QH[a] XI,19–36 and XIX,3–14;[51] Nickelsburg also makes use of a section from the *Manual of Discipline* commonly known as the Treatise of the Two Spirits.[52]

The crucial section of the first hymn reads as follows:

> (19) I thank you, Lord, because you saved my life from the pit, and from the Sheol of Abaddon (20) have lifted me up to an everlasting height, so that I can walk on a boundless plain. And I know that there is hope for someone (21) you fashioned out of dust for an everlasting community. The depraved spirit you have purified from great offence so that he can take a place with (22) the host of the holy ones, and can enter in communion with the congregation of the sons of heaven. You cast eternal destiny for man with the spirits of (23) knowledge, so that he praises your name in the community of jubilation, and tells of your wonders before all your creatures. But I, a creature of (24) clay, what am I? Mixed with water, as whom shall I

47. 11QTemple XXIX,9–10; 1QH[a] V,17–19; 1QS IV,25.

48. CD VI,19; XIX,33–34; see Talmon, "Community," 12–15.

49. For other points of similarity between Paul and Qumran, see Fitzmyer, "Paul," 2:599–621; Murphy-O'Connor, ed., *Paul and Qumran*.

50. Nickelsburg, *Resurrection*, 179–209, which is based on his doctoral dissertation submitted in 1967; Kuhn, *Enderwartung*; cf. Collins, "Patterns of Eschatology," 351–75.

51. Formerly 1QH[a] III,19–36 and 1QH[a] XI,3–14 respectively.

52. 1QS III,13–IV,26; also known as the Treatise of the Two Ways.

be considered? What is my strength? For I find myself at the
boundary of wickedness (25) and share the lot of the scoun-
drels. (1QHª XI,19–25)[53]

Nickelsburg notes that the author uses resurrection language to express his praise for God: he rescued him from Sheol and brought
him into fellowship with "the host of the holy ones" and "the sons of
heaven"—that is, with angels.[54] However, since there is no mention of
persecution against the author or of his death, Nickelsburg concludes
that the rescue here is not literal resurrection but rather incorporation into the community of the righteous.[55] That is, the author is using
eschatological language metaphorically to describe his present experience. The eschatological orientation of the hymn is evident, so it is
argued, from a number of factors: the two most significant are (i) the
fellowship of the author with the angels, and (ii) the reference to a person's גורל ("destiny") in line 22. Regarding the first, Nickelsburg refers
to an article by Jean van der Ploeg which demonstrates that association
with angels was, in several Second Temple texts, an element in Jewish
future hope;[56] regarding the second, he refers to Kuhn who writes:

53. Although Nickelsburg and Kuhn provide their own translations, I use, unless
otherwise indicated, translations from García Martínez and Tigchelaar, eds., *Dead Sea
Scrolls*. Also, for the designation of texts from the Dead Sea Scrolls, I have adopted the
format used in Abegg et al., *Dead Sea Scrolls Concordance*, 1:xiv.

54. Lines 19–22. On the angels, see below, pp. 296–300; cf. Kuhn, *Enderwartung*,
66–70.

55. Nickelsburg, *Resurrection*, 189–90.

56. Van der Ploeg, "Immortality," 118–24. In addition to the Qumran texts under discussion here, the most significant other Second Temple texts he points to are:
1 En. 51.1–5: at the time of the resurrection of the dead, "he [the Elect One?] shall
choose the righteous and the holy from among (the risen dead)" (v. 2), and "the faces
of all the angels in heaven shall glow with joy" (v. 4; Isaac, *OTP*); 104.2–6: on the day
of judgment, the righteous will "shine as the lights of heaven" (v. 2), they will "have
great joy as the angels of heaven" (v. 4), and they will "become companions of the
hosts of heaven" (v. 6; Charles, *APOT*—note that there is a dispute on the text of v.
6: Nickelsburg, *1 Enoch 1*, 512, concurs with Charles, but E. Isaac, "1 Enoch," 85, has
that they will be "partners with the good-hearted people of heaven"); *As. Mos.* 10.9:
when God's kingdom appears, "God will raise you to the heights. Yea, he will fix you
firmly in the heaven of the stars" (Priest, *OTP*); *2 Bar.* 51.5, 10: the righteous will be
changed "into the splendor of angels" and "will be like the angels and be equal to the
stars" (Klijn, *OTP*); *4 Ezra* 7.75–101: after death the souls of the righteous return to
God: they behold his glory, and they themselves are glorified so that their faces shine
like the sun and they are made like the stars.

> In 1QH 3,22f [now, XI,22-23] one will find the concept of
> community with the angels as a participation in an 'eternal
> lot'. Considering the background of terminology and thought
> of late Judaism, there is almost no other way to think of this
> concept (of community with angels) other than in the sense
> of possessing eschatological salvation. Thus there is present
> here not only a spreading of priestly self-image to the whole
> community, but also, through the term 'eternal lot', a state-
> ment that is directed to the eschatological. As distinct from
> the usual late-Jewish eschatology, then, in this passage the fu-
> ture salvation would already be taken into the present of the
> community.[57]

From the end of line 23 to the beginning of line 25, however, we learn
that the author still sees himself as a creature with limitations living
in a world of wickedness. Thus, Nickelsburg concludes, "[t]here is a
tension between the now and the not yet. The full consummation of
salvation belongs to the future."[58]

The second hymn in which Nickelsburg and Kuhn find an eschatological tension is from column XIX:

> (3) I give you thanks, my God, because you have done won-
> ders with dust; with the creature of mud you have acted in a
> very, /very/ powerful way. And I, what am I that (4) you have
> [ta]ught me the basis of your truth, and have instructed me
> in your wonderful works? You have put thanksgiving into my
> mouth, praise on my tongue, (5) the utterance of my lips in
> a place of jubilation. . . . (8) . . . In your wrath are all pun-
> ishing judgments, (9) but in your goodness, abundance of
> forgiveness; and your compassion for all the sons of your
> approval, for you have taught them the basis of your truth,
> (10) and have instructed them in your wonderful myster-
> ies. *Blank* For the sake of your glory, you have purified man
> from offence, so that he can make himself holy (11) for you
> from every impure abominations and guilt of unfaithfulness,
> to become united wi[th] the sons of your truth and in the
> lot with (12) your holy ones, to raise the worms of the dead
> from the dust, to an ever[lasting] community and from a de-

---

57. Kuhn, *Enderwartung*, 47 (my translation). Kuhn (pp. 73–75) notes texts from
the Apocrypha and Pseudepigrapha where (i) "lot" has a spatial aspect (*1 En.* 39.8;
71.16; *2 En.* 9; 10.6; 55.2; *4 Ezra* 7.9; 17; *Pss. Sol.* 14.9); (ii) "lot" serves as a sign of
future salvation or destruction (Wis 3:14; *1 En.* 37.4; 48.7; *Pss. Sol.* 14.9; 15.10; *L.A.B.*
23.13); and (iii) "lot" signifies eschatological destiny (Wis 5:5; *1 En.* 58.2; 103.2–3).

58. Nickelsburg, *Resurrection*, 191.

> praved spirit, to [your] knowledge, (13) so that he can take his
> place in your presence with the perpetual host and the spirits
> [. . .], to renew him with everything (14) that will exist, and
> with those who know in a community of jubilation. (1QH^a
> XIX,3–5, 8–14[59])

The focus of attention is on the phrase in line 12 beginning with "to
raise the worms of the dead," which is the third of five subordinate
clauses following the main sentence in line 10. While line 12 appears
to use resurrection language, Nickelsburg gives two reasons for interpreting it metaphorically:[60] (i) the word "dust" is parallel to "depraved
spirit" here, and is used earlier in the same hymn (line 3) in parallel
with "creature of clay," suggesting that the reference to raising "the
worms of the dead from the dust" in line 12 should be interpreted as
a metaphorical raising of people above the limitation and depravity
of their human existence; and (ii) line 12 states that the resurrection
is not to life, but to knowledge, something that the author previously
claimed (lines 4, 9–10) was already the possession of his community.[61]
In light of this metaphorical reading of line 12, Nickelsburg suggests
that the eschatological language of the following two clauses should
also be taken metaphorically as referring to the author's present situation: "Already he stands in the ranks of the angelic chorus. Even now
the renewal of creation has begun."[62]

Nickelsburg argues that an eschatological tension is also evident
in the Treatise of the Two Spirits.[63] Here the writer describes how from
the time of creation God placed within humankind two spirits—a

59. Note that the hash marks (as in, e.g., "/very/") indicate text inserted between
the lines by the copyist.

60. Ibid., 192.

61. The argument of Nickelsburg and Kuhn is somewhat weakened by the uncertainty of the text in line 12: they both follow Dupont-Sommer in reading the Hebrew
as לסוד [אמתכה] (ibid., 182 n. 18; Kuhn, *Enderwartung*, 79 n. 2), which is perhaps suggested by the appearance of לבינת[ה]כ[ה] ("to [your] understanding") in the parallel line
to follow: hence, Nickelsburg's translation, "to the secret [of your truth]" (cf. Vermes
and Dupont-Sommer). García Martínez and Tigchelaar, however, read the Hebrew as
לסוד ע[ולם] and translate it accordingly as "to an ever[lasting] community," and this
seems to be the majority opinion at present (see Lohse, ed., *Texte aus Qumran*, 154;
Kittel, *Hymns of Qumran*, 110; Mansoor, *Thanksgiving Hymns*, 169; Parry and Tov,
eds., *Poetic and Liturgical Texts*, 52; Holm-Nielsen, *Hodayot*, 187. Note that according
to *HALOT*, סוד can mean either council or counsel (or secret counsel).

62. Nickelsburg, *Resurrection*, 193.

63. 1QS III,13–IV,26.

spirit of truth and a spirit of deceit—and how these vie for control, the former leading people towards righteousness and the latter leading them to wickedness.[64] Those who follow the former are "in the hand of the Prince of Lights," and those who follow the latter are "in the hand of the Angel of Darkness."[65] God established this arrangement at creation, and it will continue until God's "visitation" in the "last time" when he will destroy all injustice and will purify humanity.[66] Then the righteous will be rewarded with healing, peace, fruitfulness, eternal blessings, and endless life,[67] but the wicked will be punished with eternal damnation, terror, and shame without end.[68]

Nickelsburg suggests that the description of the conflict here, between the Prince of Lights and the Angel of Darkness, resembles the "end of the age" battle that we find in apocalyptic literature.[69] Both have in view God's final destruction of all wickedness, but in the Treatise of the Two Spirits we do not need to wait until the end of the age for the spiritual battle to take place—it is happening now within people's hearts.[70] It is significant, argues Nickelsburg, that although this text depicts the final judgment and the ultimate destiny of both the righteous and the wicked, there is no mention of death or of resurrection.[71] The reason, he suggests, is that unlike in apocalyptic where the problem was the injustice of the death of the righteous—a problem whose solution was resurrection—in the *Manual of Discipline* the problem is an evil spirit tempting the righteous—a problem whose solution was the final destruction of that spirit.[72] This use of eschatological language to depict the present reality, and the lack of any mention of

64. 1QS III,17–19; IV,23.

65. 1QS III,20–21. For the identity of the Prince of Lights, see Yadin, *Scroll of the War*, 235–36.

66. 1QS IV,16–21.

67. 1QS IV,6–8.

68. 1QS IV,11–12.

69. Nickelsburg, *Resurrection*, 196; see Dan 12:1; *T. Mos.* 10.2. Other texts that describe the end of the age speak of the destruction of evil, but do not specifically mention a battle (*Jub.* 23.29; *T. Jud.* 25.3 (but cf. 20.1); cf. Rev 12:7–9).

70. 1QS IV,23.

71. Nickelsburg, *Resurrection*, 197–204, surveys other literature (esp. *Mandates of Hermas*, *Testament of Asher* and Wisdom of Solomon 1–5) that propounds the "two ways" to show that this lack of any mention of a resurrection is not an anomaly.

72. Ibid., 196–97.

death or resurrection, even in a context of the last judgment, suggests to Nickelsburg that here, as in the *Hodayot*, we have an eschatological tension where the righteous enjoy the reality of the age to come while still living in a world of wickedness and frailty.[73]

Although they bear many valuable insights, the arguments of Nickelsburg and Kuhn, I suggest, should not go unchallenged. I grant that they have established that these documents depict a tension between life as it is and life as it ought to be. My question, however, is whether it is appropriate to describe this tension as *eschatological*; it is a realization of salvation, but is it appropriate to call it a "realized eschatology"? In light of the strong eschatological consciousness evident in many of the Scrolls it might seem natural to suppose that they would have understood the tension between what is and what ought to be in eschatological terms—that is, that they were experiencing now in part what they will experience fully in the near future. But I suggest that, based on the texts themselves, the tension is better described as cosmological rather than eschatological—that is, it is a tension due to a spatial dislocation rather than a temporal one: the experience of the Qumran community involved tasting the blessings of the world above while living in the world below, rather than tasting of the age to come while living in the present age. At least I will argue that this was the dominant mode at Qumran.

Taking first Nickelsburg's discussion of the Treatise of the Two Spirits, the references to the destruction of wickedness at the end of the age, the reward for the righteous and the punishment for the wicked, and the establishment of a new creation all provide a strong eschatological perspective. There is nothing particularly eschatological, however, about the spiritual battle taking place within human hearts. The text is clear that this battle is a constituent part of creation: from the beginning God established two spirits/angels to watch over two groups of humanity, and this has resulted in a "feud in the heart of man."[74] Other Jewish texts depict the same spiritual struggle without any sense that the language is eschatological.[75] Furthermore, for our

73. Ibid., 204–5.

74. 1QS IV,23.

75. *T. Ash.* 1.3–9 speaks of God having established "two dispositions" (v. 5) within people for them to choose between good and evil and, when they choose evil, they are overmastered by Beliar. *T. Jud.* 20.1–5 speaks of there being two spirits—the "spirit of truth" and the "spirit of error"—that try to influence human decisions; only later,

purposes it is significant to note that new creation is explicitly mentioned in this text, and that it is definitely something expected at "the
appointed end," not before.[76]

It may be that one *could* think of this battle within the human
heart as a metaphorical application of the literal battle anticipated in
apocalyptic literature at the end of the age—in which case it would be
an *eschatological* tension. But I suggest that, since the battle has been
waged since the creation of humanity, it is better to see this battle as
a *cosmological* tension that will come to a climax at the end of the age
when the Angel of Darkness will be destroyed—thus, the final battle is
a climax of the present reality, rather than the present reality being a
prolepsis of the final battle. In this way the final battle is not lost sight
of by means of metaphorical interpretation.[77]

Paul's perspective is different: (i) the eschatological tension, according to Paul, relates not to the human condition, but rather to the
condition of those who have joined the eschatological community—
a community recently formed by means of an eschatological event (the
resurrection)—and it is not based on vying good and evil spirits, but
on a conflict between the Spirit of God and the "flesh";[78] and (ii) for
Paul, the present experience of the eschatological reality does not lose
sight of the literal future occurrence of the same reality: Jesus' resurrection does not lose sight of the future resurrection of believers, and
the experience of the Spirit does not lose sight of the full blessing of the
Spirit in the age to come.[79]

Moving to the two hymns from the *Hodayot*, I grant, with Kuhn
and Nickelsburg, that neither hymn is speaking of a bodily resurrection.[80] However, I question, first, whether "resurrection" is the best

when the writer describes the end of the age, do we read that "Beliar's spirit of error
. . . will be thrown into eternal fire" (25.3; Kee, *OTP*).

76. 1QS IV,25: "For God has sorted them into equal parts until the appointed end
and the new creation."

77. Contra, e.g., Bultmann's mythological interpretation of eschatological language in the New Testament.

78. Rom 8:2–14; Gal 5:16–23.

79. A more plausible case can be made for finding a common perspective between
the Treatise of the Two Spirits and the Gospel of John; see Charlesworth, "Dualism,"
389–418.

80. Nickelsburg argues that the sectarian documents of the Dead Sea Scrolls show
little interest in death or in bodily resurrection. In several hymns he notes that even
though the context is often one of persecution—which in apocalyptic literature often

adjective to describe the language being used in these hymns, even if it is understood metaphorically. In the first hymn, the reference to being lifted up from the "pit" and the "Sheol of Abaddon" *could* reflect the imagery of resurrection, but it need not. Similar language of rescue from Sheol or from the pit is found in other hymns, both in the *Hodayot*[81] and the Psalms,[82] where there is no eschatological connotation.[83] Also, a very similar scenario to that of these two hymns is found in the *Rule of the Community* with no sense of an eschatologi-

---

led the writer to speak about resurrection as God's solution in bringing justice to the righteous—the author often thanks God for having already delivered him from persecution (1QH[a] X,20–30, 31–37; XI,19, 37–38; XIII,5–6; XV,6–9), and although judgment of the wicked is still awaited (1QH[a] XII,18–20, 26–27; XIV,29–34), there is no clear reference to resurrection (contra Puech; see also Collins, Review of *La croyance des Esséniens*, 246–53). For example, in one place where the author looks forward to the coming judgment of the wicked, instead of reminding the righteous that resurrection awaits them, we read: "and they who are according to your soul will stand before you forever; and they who walk in the way of your heart stand fast eternally" (1QH[a] XII,21–22).

With regard to 1QH[a] XIV—which, it is sometimes claimed, refers to resurrection—Nickelsburg (186–88) argues (i) that "all the sons of his t[ru]th will awaken, to destroy [the sons of] wickedness" (lines 29–30) refers not to resurrection but to arousing people for battle, and (ii) that "Those who lie in the dust will hoist the flag, and the worm of the dead will raise the banner" (line 34) is at best ambiguous concerning whether it refers to a literal or a metaphorical resurrection.

81. 1QH[a] X,21: "[you] have protected me from all the traps of the pit, for vicious men have sought my soul"; XIII,5–6, 11–12: "you did not desert me when I stayed among a sovr[eign] people . . . but you saved my life from the pit. . . . For you, my God, hid me from the sons of Adam."

82. Pss 18:5, 19: "the cords of Sheol entangled me, the snares of death confronted me. . . . He brought me forth into a broad place; he delivered me, because he delighted in me"; 30:3: "O LORD, thou hast brought up my soul from Sheol, restored me to life from among those gone down to the Pit"; 86:13: "thou hast delivered my soul from the depths of Sheol"; 103:4: "Bless the LORD, O my soul, . . . who redeems your life from the Pit, who crowns you with steadfast love and mercy . . . so that your youth is renewed like the eagle's"; 116:3: "The snares of death encompassed me; the pangs of Sheol laid hold on me; I suffered distress and anguish. . . . For thou hast delivered my soul from death, my eyes from tears, my feet from stumbling."

83. 1QH[a] X,20–30 and XIII,5–19 are hymns of thanksgiving for deliverance from wicked men; Ps 18 is a psalm of thanksgiving for victory in battle; Pss 30, 103, and 116 are psalms of thanksgiving for healing; and Ps 86 is a prayer for deliverance. Laurin, "Immorality," 346, writes: "Neither the Psalmist nor the author of 1QH meant anything 'eschatological' by what he said. . . . It is simply an expression of praise to God for his protecting care amid the heavy persecutions that we know were heaped upon the sect."

cal context.[84] Furthermore, the description of the destination—"to an everlasting height [לרום עולם]" in order to "walk on a boundless plain [מישור לאין חפר]"—may suggest that something more akin to exaltation is in view here.[85] Holm-Nielsen suggests that this language points to "a characteristic of the community that man's expectation of heavenly glory is realized in the existence of the community."[86] This seems to be confirmed in the second hymn where the verb רום is used to denote the raising of "the worms of the dead" (line 12)—a word that *can* be used in the sense of raising something up, but that typically has the sense of exaltation[87]—a sense well-established in the other occurrences of the verb in the *Hodayot*.[88] And the point is, exaltation to heavenly glory *could* be conceived of eschatologically, but it need not be.

Second, it is true, as Kuhn shows, that the idea of one's lot sometimes appears in an eschatological context in Second Temple literature, and we might add that the word גורל, which is used in 1QH[a] XI,22,[89] can also bear an eschatological significance.[90] But גורל does not *necessarily* imply an eschatological perspective. Commonly in the Dead Sea Scrolls גורל is used in the sense of "one's portion in life" without any eschatological connotation.[91] Etymologically, גורל referred to a means of decision-making ("casting lots"),[92] and by extension a parcel of land allotted by means of the גורל could itself be called a גורל ("lot").[93] In

84. 1QS XI,7–9.

85. Both phrases are unique, but the sense of being set free from the confines of the underworld seems to be clear enough.

86. Holm–Nielsen, *Hodayot*, 67 n. 3; cf. Laurin, "Immortality," 344 n.3–4.

87. See Dahmen, "רום." 402–12.

88. 1QH[a] XIV,8: "shortly you will raise a survivor among your people, a remnant in your inheritance"; XV,22: "You have exalted my horn above all those who denounce me"; XVIII,25: "The strength of heroes lies in the abundance of luxuries...; they take pride [רום] in their belongings and possessions"; XIX,15: "I give you thanks, my God, I exalt you, my rock."

89. See a similar usage in 1QS XI,7–8: "To those whom God has selected he has given them [wisdom, knowledge, fount of justice, well of strength, and spring of glory] as everlasting possession; and he has given them an inheritance in the lot of the holy ones."

90. Cf. 1QS IV,26; XI,7.

91. See Dommershausen, "גורל," 455–56.

92. Ibid., 2:450–55.

93. See Josh 15:1; 16:1; 17:1, 14, 17; Ps 125:3; Mic 2:5.

a similar way, when it is God who is making the decision about the well-being of people, the outcome of that decision—one's portion in life or one's destiny—can also be called a גורל.[94] Even God has a גורל, in this sense, which consists of those who belong to him,[95] in contrast to those who belong to the גורל of Belial.[96] In several cases, the גורל of those in the Qumran community is simply their membership in that community[97] or their rank within the community.[98] Thus, from the perspective of the Qumran community, one's גורל is commonly thought of as something one has at present—one's lot in life—and not necessarily the destiny that one looks forward to. Thus, the mention of the גורל by itself does not provide the eschatological perspective to the hymn that Kuhn claims it does.

Third, the fellowship with the angels, in both hymns, does not provide that eschatological tenor either. The thrust of van der Ploeg's argument, to which Nickelsburg refers, is that the Qumran community believed in the immortality of the soul rather than the resurrection of the body;[99] and in arguing this, he notes that the fellowship with the angels, described in the *Hodayot* and other Qumran documents, mirrors a description of the deceased righteous living with the angels or being transformed into an angel. In fact, the texts that van der Ploeg cites speak of the righteous being transformed after death to become

94. See Ps 16:5–6.

95. 1QS II,2; 1QM I,5; XIII,5; XV,1; XVII,7. These are also referred to as the גורל of light (1QM I,13; XIII,9), the גורל of truth (1QM XIII,12), and the גורל of God's covenant (1QM XVII,6).

96. 1QS II,5, 17; 1QM I,5; IV,2. These are also referred to as the גורל of darkness (1QM I,1, 11; XIII,5) and the גורל of injustice (1QS IV,24). Note also reference to the spirits of his גורל (1QS III,24; 1QM XIII,2, 4, 12).

97. CD XIII,12: "everyone who joins his congregation he should examine. . . ; and they shall inscribe him in his place according to his inheritance in the lot of light"; 1QSa I,9: When someone reaches the age of twenty, he will "enter the lot amongst his fam[il]y and join the holy commun[ity]"; 1QSa I,19–20: "No man who is a simpleton shall enter the lot to hold office in the congregation of Israel"; cf. CD XX,3–4: "he shall be expelled from the congregation, like one whose lot did not fall among the disciples of God"; 1QHᵃ XV,34: "you did not /make/ my lot /fall/ in the congregation of deceit."

98. 1QS I,10: the Teacher is to love all the sons of light "according to his lot in God's plan"; 1QS II,23: "no-one shall move down from his rank or move up from the place of his lot."

99. In addition to the texts cited above (see p. 288 n. 56), van der Ploeg also mentions Josephus' description of the Essenes as people who believed in the immortality of the soul (*Ant.* 18.14, 18).

like the angels, but there is very little evidence to support the view
that the hope for the righteous included fellowship *with* the angels;
regardless of whether such fellowship makes logical sense in light of
the transformation involved, the fact is that fellowship with angels was
not a prominent focus in texts that described life after death.[100] If, for
the sake of argument, we assume that the Qumran community believed in the immortality of the soul rather than the resurrection of the
body, then we have a very real difference between the eschatological
expectation at Qumran and what we find in Paul, and hence it would
be difficult to argue for the latter's dependence on the former.

But regardless of the view the Qumran community had of life
after death, this theme of fellowship with angels in the hymns is better
understood, I suggest, from a cosmological, rather than eschatological,
perspective. The divine rescue is described in connection with being
incorporated into a community. In the first hymn the author speaks of
taking "a place with the host of the holy ones [צבא קודשים]," entering
"in communion with the congregation of the sons of heaven [שמים
עדת בני]," and praising God's "name in the community of jubilation
[יחד רנה]."[101] There may be an intentional double meaning in these
terms: within the Dead Sea Scrolls, the term "holy ones" can denote
either the Qumran community[102] or the angels,[103] and in some places
the author seems to intend both senses;[104] similarly, the word "host"
can mean either a human army or a group of angels, although in the
Hodayot, the latter usage predominates;[105] the term "sons of heaven"
occurs several times in the Dead Sea Scrolls, although it is not always

100. Of the texts van der Ploeg cites (see p. 288 n. 56), only *1 En.* 104.6 explicitly
speaks of fellowship with the angels, and that reading is a matter of dispute. Van der
Ploeg, "Immortality," 120, also thinks that *1 En.* 51.4 states that "the risen ones shall
be angels in heaven," but it does not.

101. 1QHᵃ XI,21–23.

102. 1QM X,10; 1QS VIII,11; 1QSb III,2.

103. 1QS XI,7–8; 1QHᵃ V,14; XVIII,34–35.

104. 1QM X,10–12; XII,1–7.

105. 1QHᵃ V,14–15: "together with the host of your spirits and the assembly of
[your holy ones, wi]th your holy vault and [al]l its hosts"; XI,34–35: "For God will
thunder with the roar of his strength, . . . and the host of the heavens adds to their
noise"; XV,28–29: "Who is like you, Lord, among the gods? . . . No spirit can reply to
your reproach, no /host/ can stand up against your anger"; and probably XVIII,34–35:
"I was appalled to hear your verdict against the powerful heroes, your trial against the
host of your holy ones."

clear whether humans or angels are in view;[106] and the term "community of jubilation" occurs in both hymns[107] without clear indication of whether humans or angels are in view.[108] In commenting on this hymn, Holm-Nielsen concludes that this language has in view "the membership of the community, which is expressed as a fellowship with God and His angels."[109] This dual focus on being incorporated into both an earthly and a heavenly community seems to be expressed again in the second hymn: "to raise the worms of the dead from the dust, to an ever[lasting] community..., so that he can take his place in [God's] presence with the perpetual host and the spirits."[110]

This reference to fellowship with angels is significant because it reflects a perspective that we find in several Qumran documents. From the *War Scroll* we learn that in the final battle the angels will fight alongside the children of light.[111] But elsewhere we read that the community at present enjoys fellowship with the angels,[112] as is evident in the following hymn:

> For you have brought [your truth and] your [glo]ry (13) to all the men of your council and in the lot, together with the angels of the face, without there being a mediator between [your holy ones]. . . . (14) . . . They will respond to your glorious commands, and they will be your princes in the lo[t of your holy ones]. (1QH[a] XIV,12–14)

106. A reference to angels is certain in 1QS IV,22; XI,8; but the reference in 4Q418 69ii13 could be read either as humans or as angels. The other instances of "sons of heaven" lack sufficient context to determine the referent with confidence.

107. See also 1QH[a] XIX,14.

108. Interestingly, the phrase בקול רנה ("with a voice of jubilation") occurs more frequently in the Dead Sea Scrolls, sometimes where it is people who are expressing jubilation (1QM XII,15; XIX,7; 4Q492 1,7), once where it is angels (4Q405 23i6–8), and once where the subject appears to be all God's creatures (1QH[a] XIX,26).

109. Holm-Nielsen, *Hodayot*, 68 n. 11.

110. 1QH[a] XIX,12–13; the reference to the earthly community is dependent on the reading of ע[ול]ם in line 12 (see above, p. 290 n. 61).

111. 1QM I,10–11; VII,4–6; XII,1–9; cf. 1QSb IV,24–28; 4Q491 1–3,3, 10.

112. 1QS XI,7–8; 1QSa(=1Q28a) II,8–9; 1QM X,8–11; 4Q181 1ii3–6; cf. 4Q369 1i9. Davidson, *Angels at Qumran*, 319, concludes that the fellowship with angels at Qumran indicates a "partially realized or inaugurated eschatology," and yet he also admits that "there is no further development of the concept of fellowship with angels expressed as expectation of life in heaven in the future." See further, Laurin, "Immortality," 347–53; Ringgren, *Faith of Qumran*, 84–87; Mach, "Angels," 26.

Another indication that fellowship with the angels is the proper context in which to read these two hymns is their concern for purity. Not only do both hymns describe God's salvation in terms of purification, but they also note that the purpose of purification was so that one can join the company of angels:

> The depraved spirit you have purified from great offence so that he can take a place with the host of the holy ones, and can enter in communion with the congregation of the sons of heaven. (1QH^a XI,21–22)

> For the sake of your glory, you have purified man from offence, so that he can make himself holy for you from every impure abominations and guilt of unfaithfulness, to become united wi[th] the sons of your truth and in the lot with your holy ones. (1QH^a XIX,10–12)

This concern for purity in connection with the angels is also reflected in the *War Scroll* where we read that no impure person would be permitted in the camp because of the presence of angels.[113]

The fundamental importance of the fellowship with angels is indicated by the sectarians' understanding of worship. According to the first hymn above, the purpose of joining the fellowship of angels was to engage in praise,[114] something that the angels do continuously.[115] The *Songs of the Sabbath Sacrifice*[116] reveal how important angelic worship was to the community.[117] Composed to be sung each Sabbath,[118] possibly in connection with the Sabbath sacrifice,[119] these songs, focusing on worship in the heavenly temple, summon the angels to praise.[120] Carol Newsom describes these songs as

---

113. 1QM VII,6; cf. CD XV,15–17; 4Q266 8i6–9; 4Q491 1–3,10.

114. 1QH^a XI,23; cf. 1QM XII,1–2.

115. 1QM XII,1–2.

116. 4Q400–407; 11Q17; these texts are also known as the *Angelic Liturgy*.

117. For an introduction to these texts, see Collins, *Apocalypticism*, 136–43.

118. The thirteen songs are dated for the first thirteen Sabbaths of the year. It is debated whether or not they were repeated in the following three quarters of the year: in favor is Maier, "Shîrê 'Ôlat hash-Shabbat," 544; opposed is Newsom, *Songs of the Sabbath*, 19.

119. But see Newsom, *Songs of the Sabbath*, 18–19.

120. See 4Q400 1i1–2; 2,1–5; 4Q403 1i31–46; 1ii18–19; 4Q404 4,6–10; 4Q405 4+5+69+6+58+77,4–5, 7–14; 8–9,2; 14–15i2–7; 19,2; 20–22,7–9; 23i6–8. For a description of the contents of the songs, see Newsom, "Priesthood," 101–13; full commentary in Newsom, *Songs of the Sabbath*.

a quasi-mystical liturgy designed to evoke a sense of being present in the heavenly temple. . . . [T]he hypnotic quality of the language and the vividness of the description of the celestial temple cause even the modern reader of these fragments to feel the power of the language to creating a sense of the presence of the heavenly temple.[121]

It is helpful to recall in this connection that, according to *Jubilees*, the angels were keeping Sabbath even before the command was given to Israel; and, as the angel explains it to Moses, God gave the command only to Israel so that "they might keep the sabbath *with us*."[122] To the Qumran community, therefore, worship appears to have involved a merging of the earthly and the heavenly communities.[123]

Significantly, the *Songs of the Sabbath Sacrifice* are arranged according to the 364-day calendar used at Qumran, in contrast to the 354-day calendar apparently used in Jerusalem.[124] The purpose of their calendar was to schedule worship properly—in particular, to determine the correct days for festivals.[125] The crucial importance of the calendar is indicated by the strict commands given to keep it, together with indications that this was probably a significant point of contention between the Qumran community and the Jewish lead-

---

121. Newsom, *Songs of the Sabbath*, 59, 72; cf. Strugnell, "Angelic Liturgy," 320, who writes: "This is . . . a *Maśkîl's* composition for an earthly liturgy in which the presence of the angels is in a sense invoked and in which . . . the Heavenly Temple is portrayed on the model of the earthly one and in some way its service is considered the pattern of what is being done below."

122. *Jub.* 2.17–21, 30, citation from v. 21; emphasis added.

123. Rietz, "Jesus' Eschatology," 197–98. See also Nitzan, "Covenantal Ceremony," 487–506, who argues that the angels attended the annual liturgy of the renewal of the covenant.

124. Evidence for the Qumran community using a 364-day calendar can be found in (i) the *Calendrical Documents* (4Q320–330) and 4QOtot (4Q259+319) which lay out a six-year cycle of temple service for the twenty-four priestly courses in which each course serves for thirteen weeks, implying that the years must be fifty-two weeks in length (i.e., 364 days); (ii) 11QPsᵃ(=11Q5) XXVII,2–7; the *Songs of the Sabbath Sacrifice* (4Q400–407) which, in dating the songs for each Sabbath, assume a 364-day calendar; (iii) 4Q252 II,2–3; and (iv) 4QMMTᵃ(=4Q394) 3–7i2–3. For an examination of the issues involved in the calendrical system at Qumran, see Glessmer, "Calendars," 2:213–78; VanderKam, *Calendars*.

125. One of the advantages of the 364-day calendar was that holy days never landed on a Sabbath, and so there was never a conflict over how the day was to be celebrated.

ers in Jerusalem.[126] This strong insistence on the 364-day calendar is more explicable when seen in light of the community's conviction that earthly worship needed to be synchronized with heavenly worship.

I conclude, therefore, that the tension between life as it is and life as it ought to be at Qumran had an important cosmological dimension that is lacking in Paul. The Treatise of the Two Spirits speaks of a tension within the created order, and the *Hodayot* speak of tasting of the worship of heaven while still dwelling on earth. It is not entirely clear how this cosmological perspective related to the community's strong eschatological expectation. Perhaps they believed that if they were going to be like angels one day that they could also experience fellowship with those who are angels now. Or, it may be, if they believed in the immortality of the soul rather than the resurrection of the body, that while the establishment of God's reign on earth would be important for future generations, the destiny of individuals after death was still to live on a spiritual plane with God and his angels. Or, perhaps they did not integrate the two, but merely saw them as complementary perspectives. In any case, in light of the tension being expressed cosmologically at Qumran but eschatologically in Paul, it is unlikely that Qumran thought served as a source for Paul's in this area.[127]

---

126. See 1QS I,8–9, 13–15; X,3–8; CD III,12–16; VI,18–19; XII,3–6; XVI,2–4; 1QH[a] XX,4–9; 4QMMT[d] (=4Q397) 14–21,7–8; cf. *1 En.* 75.1–3; 79.1–2; 82.4–6; *Jub.* 6.32–38 (note the important reference to Enoch in 4Q227 2,1–6). For discussion, see Talmon, "Calendars and Mishmarot," 112–16; VanderKam, *Calendars*, 45–51. Talmon, "Yom Hakkippurim," 549–63, argues, based on 1QpHab XI,4–8, where we read of the Wicked Priest pursuing the Teacher of Righteousness on the Day of Atonement, that the two must have been using different calendars since such a pursuit would be a violation of the law concerning that day; see also idem., "Calendar Controversy," 379–95. VanderKam, *Calendars*, 113–16, suggests that the Qumran community may have originated out of a conflict, following the Maccabean restoration of the Temple, when the high priest—known to us as the Teacher of Righteousness—tried to reinstate the 364-day calendar which had been replaced by the Syrians (note the texts that could refer to calendrical changes: Dan 7:25; 1 Macc 1:45; 2 Macc 6:6–7).

127. It is worth noting that the cosmological tension does surface in the deutero–Pauline literature, where the eschatological tension is not as prominent. In both Ephesians and Colossians we read that believers have already been raised with Christ (Eph 2:6; Col 2:12; 3:1)—a metaphor we do not find in the primary Pauline literature; and we find in these two books a focus on heaven: believers are located in "heavenly places" (Eph 1:3; 2:6) and are enjoined to set their minds "on things that are above" (Col 3:1–2). These themes, however, have not entirely replaced a hope for the future (Eph 1:12, 14, 21; 2:7; Col 1:27; 3:4, 24), even if the eschatological urgency is not as sharply felt here as in the primary letters. Interestingly, both of these perspectives

Hope for Resurrection

We now need to consider whether Paul's eschatology can be adequately explained with reference to Jesus' resurrection. There is no doubt that Paul's encounter with the risen Lord revolutionized his thinking. And in particular, it appears from 1 Cor 15 that he connected Jesus' resurrection not only with the eschatological expectation of a general resurrection, but also specifically with the idea of new creation: in the context of emphasizing the significance and the importance of Jesus' resurrection, Paul describes Christ as the "first fruits" of believers who have died and as the "last Adam."[128] Furthermore, while he refers to Jesus' resurrection on numerous occasions, he does not refer to Jesus' healings which we saw to be so important in the previous chapter. The question remains, however: How likely is it that Paul (and other early Christians) would have interpreted what happened to Jesus after his death as an eschatological event without any reference to the ministry of Jesus? It would be understandable if Paul saw the resurrection as the supreme evidence that God had vindicated Jesus and that God was powerfully at work among his people, but is it likely that Paul would have taken it, *by itself,* as grounds for revising the Jewish eschatological framework into an "already" but "not yet" tension? Or, in a word, was Jesus' resurrection self-explanatory? I will argue that there is good reason to doubt this and that it is much better to place Jesus' resurrection within the context of his own eschatological perspective in order to explain how Paul understood the resurrection and from it developed his own eschatological views.

The word "resurrection" (ἀνάστασις) has to do not simply with "life after death," but specifically with a restored *bodily* "life after death."

---

come together in Eph 2:6–7: God "raised us up with him, and made us sit with him in the heavenly places in Christ Jesus, that in the coming ages he might show the immeasurable riches of his grace in kindness toward us in Christ Jesus"; and in Col 3:1–4: "If then you have been raised with Christ, seek the things that are above, where Christ is, seated at the right hand of God. Set your minds on things that are above, not on things that are on earth. For you have died, and your life is hid with Christ in God. When Christ who is our life appears, then you also will appear with him in glory." Furthermore, this latter text, which expresses both the cosmological and the eschatological perspectives, leads immediately into an appeal for godly living—that is, it addresses the tension between life as it is and life as it ought to be. Presumably, therefore, both the writer and the readers saw these two perspectives as complementary.

128. 1 Cor 15:20, 23, 45.

Hellenistic culture contained two main views of human destiny: the first—going back at least to Homer and finding expression in Hesiod, in the Athenian dramatists, Aeschylus, Sophocles, and Euripides, and, albeit in different ways, in Stoicism and Epicureanism—affirms that human life is limited to life in this world; the souls of all who die are consigned to Hades forever where they appear as a shadow of their former selves, typically unconscious. The second view of human destiny is found firstly in the philosophical tradition of Socrates and Plato who spoke of the immortality of the soul and the transmigration of souls, and secondly in the mystery religions which offered hope for escape from Hades and from the continuous cycle of death and rebirth.[129] But both traditions agreed that people did not rise from the dead[130]—even if some isolated miraculous instances were acknowledged.[131]

Belief in resurrection did take root in Israel, but not until the Second Temple period. Although some ancient cultures did take an interest in life after death, ancient Israel did not. The dominant view in the Old Testament is that there was no life after death.[132] When people died they went to Sheol, the place of the dead, where, while continuing to exist, they did so only as a shadow of their former selves, separated from the land of the living and from God,[133] and from there there was no hope of return.[134] When we read of Job and some psalmists praying for God to save them from Sheol, or thanking God for having saved them,[135] we should probably understand this in terms of a rescue from the threat of death.[136] There are three psalms that may express a glim-

129. Brandon, *Man and His Destiny*, 153–90.

130. Homer, *Il.* 24.549–51; Herodotus, *Hist.* 3.62; Aeschylus, *Ag.* 1360–61; *Eum.* 647–48; Sophocles, *El.* 137–43.

131. Plato, *Symp.* 179c; Lucian, *Salt.* 45; Xenophon, *Cyn.* 1.6; Pausanias, *Descr.* 2.26.5; Philostratus, *Vit. Apoll.* 4.45.1.

132. For discussions of death in the Old Testament, see Wright, *Resurrection*, 87–93; Johnston, *Shades of Sheol*; Preuss, *Old Testament Theology*, 261–63; Wolff, *Anthropology*, 99–118; Eichrodt, *Theology*, 2:210–23; Martin-Achard, *Death to Life*, 16–51.

133. Gen 3:19; 2 Sam 14:14; Job 3:13–14, 17–19; Pss 6:5; 30:9; 88:3–7, 10–12; 115:17; Eccl 9:5–6, 10; Isa 14:9–11, 18–19; 38:10–11, 18–19; Sir 14:16–17.

134. Job 7:7–10; 14:1–2, 7–14; 16:22; Ps 39:13; Eccl 3:19–21; Jer 51:39, 57.

135. Job 33:15–30; Pss 6:5; 16:8–11; 18:4–6, 16–17; 28:1; 30:2–3, 8–10; 86:12–13; 88:1–18; 103:2–5; 116:2–4; 143:7.

136. On the notoriously difficult text in Job 19:26, see Clines, *Job* 1–20, 433–34, 461–66.

mer of hope for a rescue after death,[137] but this interpretation is much debated.[138] Ezekiel uses the image of resurrection metaphorically to speak of the restoration of the nation.[139] And although some rabbis, and indeed even Jesus, maintained that belief in resurrection was implicitly supported by the Torah,[140] the explicit expression of this hope probably does not appear until the second century BCE.

The Old Testament gives a few exceptions to the rule that death is the final end for all. Three apparently miraculous resurrections occur in connection with the prophets Elijah and Elisha;[141] King Saul, unable to elicit divine counsel concerning his campaign with the Philistines, engages the services of a medium to summon Samuel back from the dead;[142] and some key figures ascend to be with God without dying— Enoch and Elijah, according to the Old Testament and Second Temple

---

137. See Pss 16:10-11: "For thou dost not give me up to Sheol, or let thy godly one see the Pit. Thou dost show me the path of life; in thy presence there is fullness of joy, in thy right hand are pleasures for evermore"; 49:15: "God will ransom my soul from the power of Sheol, for he will receive me"; 73:24: "afterward thou wilt receive me to glory." Dahood, *Psalms*, 1:302, 2:195, suggests in each case that the psalmist is asking for the same privilege as that granted to Enoch and Elijah. See further, Wright, *Resurrection*, 105–7.

138. Among modern interpreters, those in favor of finding a reference to life after death in these psalms include: Dahood, *Psalms*, 1:91, 301; 2:195; Weiser, *Psalms*, 176–78, 389–90, 514–15; cf. Rowley, *Faith of Israel*, 175 n. 2, who describes the psalmists as having "an incipient faith," "a glimpse, rather than a firm faith" in life after death. Those partially in favor include: Briggs and Briggs, *Psalms*, 1:121–22, 410–11; 2:147 (Pss 16:10 and 73:24 only); Kraus, *Psalms 1–59*, 239–40, 483–84, and idem., *Psalms 60–150*, 90–91 (Pss 49:15 and 73:24 only); those opposed include: Kirkpatrick, *Psalms*, 77–78, 273–74, 437–38; Gunkel, *What Remains*, 105; Craigie, *Psalms 1–50*, 158, 357, 360 (comments only on Pss 16:10 and 49:15).

139. Ezek 37:1–14. Given Ezekiel's historical situation and the explanation of the vision (vv. 11–14) it is clear that the reference is to the restoration of Jews to Palestine; however, given the imagery used of people being brought up from their graves (vv. 12–13), it is understandable why early Christian writers saw here a prediction of resurrection (Irenaeus, *Haer.* 5.15.1; Tertullian, *Res.* 30; see further, Stevenson and Glerup, eds., *Ezekiel, Daniel*, 120–24).

140. *m. Sanh.* 10:1; *b. Sanh.* 92a; *Sipre Deut* §329 (on Deut 32:39); Matt 22:31–32//Mark 12:26–27//Luke 20:37–38.

141. 1 Kgs 17:17–24; 2 Kgs 4:32–37; 13:20–21.

142. 1 Sam 28:3–19. Legislation and prophetic warnings against contacting the dead (e.g., Lev 19:31; 20:6, 27; Deut 18:10–11; Isa 8:19–22) suggest that necromancy may have been practiced in Israel from time to time.

literature,[143] and Moses, according to later traditions.[144] But these are all exceptions to the dominant view that all people died and remained dead.

During the Second Temple period we find a diversity of views being expressed regarding the dead.[145] The Sadducees represented the ancient Israelite perspective, denying any form of life after death.[146] Philo and other Jews, under the influence of Hellenistic philosophy, believed in the immortality of the soul, that is, that individuals would survive death, but in a non-bodily form.[147] But a growing number of Jews looked forward to a bodily resurrection at the end of the age.[148] We need not be concerned as to *why* this view appears during this time,[149] but in looking forward to Paul and the early Christians, it will be helpful to know exactly how Jews expressed this hope and what role it played in the overall expectation of the future.

One of the earliest pieces of evidence of an interest in resurrection during the Second Temple period is the Septuagint.[150] Certain

143. Enoch: Gen 5:24; cf. Sir 44:15; *1 En.* 14.9–18; 87.3–4; *Jub.* 4.23. Elijah: 2 Kgs 2:11; cf. Sir 48:12; 1 Macc 2:58.

144. Although Moses' death is recorded in Deut 34:5–8, later tradition speaks of his ascension to heaven: Josephus, *Ant.* 4.323–26, describes Moses' death as a disappearance in similar fashion, according to Thackeray (note b to the above text in the LCL volume), to how Dionysius of Halicarnassus describes the passing away of Aeneas and of Romulus in terms of an ascension to the gods (*Ant. rom.* 1.64.4; 2.56.2); Philo, *Mos.* 2.288, speaks of Moses' "pilgrimage from earth to heaven" when God "resolved his twofold nature of soul and body into a single unity, transforming his whole being into mind, pure as the sunlight" (Colson, LCL)); *Sipre Deut* §357 (on Deut 34:5); *b. Soṭah* 13b. Bryan, "Jewish Background," 168, argues, based on *1 En.* 89.1, 9 and parallels with other Mesopotamian flood heroes, that Noah was also considered by some Jews to have ascended directly to God.

145. See Wright, *Resurrection*, 129–206 (but also see the constructive critique of Wright in Bryan, "Jewish Background," 155–69); Segal, "Life after Death," 102–6.

146. Matt 21:23//Mark 12:18//Luke 20:27; Acts 23:8; Josephus, *J.W.* 2.165; *Ant.* 18.16; *m. Sanh.* 10:1 (assuming that "Epicurean" here is a derogatory reference to Sadducees); *b. Sanh* 90b; cf. Sir 11:26–28; 14:16–19; 17:27–28; 38:21–23; 41:4; 1 Macc 2:49–70; Bar 2:17.

147. See above, pp. 225–26; Wis 3:1–4; *Ps.-Phoc.* 105–15; *T. Ab.* 20.14 [rec. A]; *1 En.* 103.3–8; 4 Macc 9:21–22; 13:13–17; 14:5; 17:12; 18:23–24.

148. For treatments of the development of belief in resurrection, see Nickelsburg, *Resurrection*; Wright, *Resurrection*, 146–200; Segal, "Life after Death," 90–125.

149. On this, see Ollenburger, "If Mortals Die," 29–44; Greenspoon, "Resurrection," 247–322.

150. The Septuagint was probably produced over several generations from the third to the second century BCE.

texts have been translated so that a reference to resurrection is made more explicit than the original Hebrew warranted. For example, the questions in Hos 13:14, to which from the context we would expect a negative answer, appear in the Septuagint as affirmative statements that God will indeed raise his people from the dead:

> MT: Shall I ransom them from the power of Sheol? Shall I redeem them from Death?

> LXX: I will rescue them from the hand of Hades, and I will redeem them from death.[151]

Two texts in the Hebrew Scriptures speak clearly of the hope for resurrection.[152] The Apocalypse of Isaiah (Isa 24–27)[153] holds out hope for the righteous dead:[154]

> Thy dead shall live, their bodies shall rise.
> O dwellers in the dust, awake and sing for joy! (Isa 26:19)

Daniel appears to echo this language[155] when he writes:

> And many of those who sleep in the dust of the earth shall awake, some to everlasting life, and some to shame and everlasting contempt. And those who are wise shall shine like the brightness of the firmament; and those who turn many to righteousness, like the stars for ever and ever. (Dan 12:2–3)

An important difference, however, appears in these two texts which can be traced right through into rabbinic literature: the Isaiah text

151. Compare also the MT and LXX on Deut 32:29; Pss 1:5; 21:30(22:30); Job 14:14; 19:26; cf. Job 42:17 (LXX). See Cavallin, *Life after Death*, 103–11; Wright, *Resurrection*, 147–50.

152. A reference to a general resurrection in Hos 6:1–3 is debatable: in favor are Andersen and Freedman, *Hosea*, 419–21; Martin-Achard, *Death to Life*, 74–86; opposed are Wolff, *Hosea*, 117–19; Brown and Coenen, "Resurrection," 267–68, who interpret the text in terms of God's healing of a sick nation. In either case, this is a view that is rejected by the prophet (vv. 4–6).

153. The Apocalypse of Isaiah is difficult to date. The majority of scholars assign it to the post-exilic period, although opinions vary from the fifth down to the second century BCE: see Eissfeldt, *Old Testament*, 323–27; Driver, *Old Testament*, 219–23; Gray, *Isaiah*, 1:397–401; Kaiser, *Isaiah 13–39*, 173–79. Conservative commentators continue to defend it as the work of Isaiah: see Keil and Delitzsch, *Isaiah*, 421–24.

154. On the debate over this difficult text, see Motyer, *Prophecy of Isaiah*, 218–20; Kaiser, *Isaiah 13–39*, 215–20.

155. Collins, *Daniel*, 392.

envisions the resurrection of only the righteous, whereas Daniel's "many"—while possibly not including everyone—involves both righteous and wicked people. Assumed in the latter is a final judgment.

The book of *1 Enoch* is important for tracing the development of the hope for resurrection in Judaism. This is generally recognized as a composite work written, for the most part, during the second century BCE; it is debated when the section known as the Similitudes (chs. 37–71) was written, especially since these chapters were not found at Qumran along with the other sections of *1 Enoch*.[156] The beginning of the Book of Watchers (chs. 1–36) introduces the theme that pervades most of *1 Enoch*—a future judgment in which all people will be judged, with the wicked being destroyed and the righteous being blessed with peace and prosperity.[157] Later we read, in God's instructions to Michael, of all injustice being removed from the earth and of the righteous enjoying life to its full—receiving abundant harvests and long life lived in peace on the earth:

> Destroy injustice from the face of the earth. And every iniquitous deed will end, and the plant of righteousness and truth will appear forever and he will plant joy. And then all the righteous ones will escape; and become the living ones until they multiply and become tens of hundreds; and all the days of their youth and the years of their retirement they will complete in peace. And in those days the whole earth will be worked in righteousness, all of her planted with trees, and will find blessing. And they shall plant pleasant trees upon her—vines. And he who plants a vine upon her will produce wine for plenti-

---

156. There has been a diversity of opinion regarding the dating and provenance of the Similitudes. Early in the twentieth century, Charles, "Introduction," 171, suggested a pre-Roman date (between 94 and 64 BCE). At the other end of the spectrum, Milik, "Problèmes," 373–78, went so far as to argue that the Similitudes were a third century CE Christian composition. While some scholars continue to defend a pre-Roman date (e.g., Bampfylde, "Similitudes of Henoch," 9–31), the majority of scholars now tend to avoid both extremes: most take them to be Jewish and date them sometime between the latter part of the first century BCE and the end of the first century CE. Charlesworth, "Date of the Parables," 450–68, dates the Similitudes during the reign of Herod the Great; Greenfield and Stone, "Enochic Pentateuch," 51–65, favor a dating close to the turn of the millennium (cf. Hannah, "Book of Noah," 469–77); Mearns, "Dating the Similitudes," 360–69, suggests a date during the 40s; Suter, "Enoch in Sheol," 415–43, locates the Similitudes within the Hekhalot movement prior to the fall of Jerusalem; and Knibb, "Parables of Enoch," 345–59, argues (tentatively) for a date around the end of the century.

157. *1 En.* 1.1–2, 7–9.

tude. And every seed that is sown on her, one measure will
yield a thousand (measures) and one measure of olives will
yield ten measures of presses of oil. And you cleanse the earth
from all injustice, and from all defilement, and from all oppression, and from all sins, and from all iniquity which is being
done on earth; remove them from the earth. And all the children of the people will become righteous, and all nations shall
worship and bless me; and they will all prostrate themselves
to me. . . .

And in those days I shall open the storerooms of blessing
which are in the heavens, so that I shall send them down upon
the earth, over the work and the toil of the children of man.
And peace and truth shall become partners together in all
the days of the world, and in all the generations of the world.
(1 *En.* 10.16–11.2; Isaac, *OTP*)[158]

This is reminiscent of the new creation vision we saw above in the
prophets.[159] There is no explicit reference to resurrection here, although in one text Enoch tells of seeing specially prepared places for
"the spirits of the souls of the dead" to wait "until the day of their
judgment,"[160] which implies some kind of future for the dead; the souls
of the wicked, however, will not rise on the day of judgment.[161]

This perspective is expressed variously in later sections of
1 *Enoch.* The Similitudes of Enoch (chs. 37–71) also speak of a present resting place "underneath the wings of the Lord of the spirits"[162]
where the souls of the righteous dead await the day when they will
rise from Sheol to dwell upon the earth wearing "garments of glory"
that will never wear out.[163] The Book of Dreams (chs. 83–90) develops
an allegorical vision of the messianic kingdom in which all of God's
people, represented here by sheep, are gathered, including "[a]ll those
which have been destroyed and dispersed."[164] The Epistle of Enoch
(chs. 91–107) speaks of a day of judgment when "the righteous shall
arise from their sleep, and wisdom shall arise and be given to them."[165]

158. Cf. 1 *En.* 5.7, 10; 25.4–7.

159. See above, pp. 250–52.

160. 1 *En.* 22.3–4 (Isaac, *OTP*).

161. 1 *En.* 22.14.

162. 1 *En.* 39.7 (Isaac, *OTP*).

163. 1 *En.* 51.1–2, 5; 62.13–15, citation from v. 15 (Isaac, *OTP*).

164. 1 *En.* 90.33 (Isaac, *OTP*).

165. 1 *En.* 91.10 (Charles, *APOT*). Charles translates "the righteous" correctly, in

The righteous are encouraged to have hope, firstly because the wicked who have oppressed them will be judged, and secondly because they themselves will be rewarded.[166] Similarly, the souls of the righteous dead are given hope that they will "live and rejoice"[167] and that they will "shine like the lights of heaven."[168] That they will be re-embodied is suggested by the prophecy that the earth will one day be restored: in a future generation "sin shall disappear from upon the earth, and every good thing shall come upon her."[169]

Thus, while a day of resurrection is explicitly expressed only in the Similitudes,[170] the idea is implied in various places. The central concern of *1 Enoch* is judgment: one day God will judge and remove the wicked and restore and bless the righteous with prosperity and peace. And in this the righteous can take hope—this promise will be fulfilled even if they die while wickedness still reigns. The implication is, therefore, that they must rise from the dead.

The book of 2 Maccabees, probably dating from the first century BCE,[171] explicitly expresses the hope for the bodily resurrection of the righteous.[172] God "will raise . . . up to an everlasting renewal of life" those who are martyred for their faithfulness to the law—both ordinary people who are tortured to death for their refusal to eat pork, and militants who lose their lives in the struggle to preserve Israel's laws.[173] Furthermore, it is clearly implied that this resurrection will entail a re-embodiment,[174] and it is stated that there will be no resurrection for the wicked but rather judgment.[175] Thus, the same narrative seems to

---

my opinion, as a singular used collectively (contra Issac's translation: "the righteous one shall arise")—similarly, in 92.3. Verses 12–13 clearly have a collective sense of the righteous in view: "sinners shall be delivered into the hands of the righteous" and "they shall acquire great things through their righteousness." It would follow, therefore, that vv. 10–11 have to do not with the actions of a righteous Messiah, but with the righteous community eradicating wickedness; see Nickelsburg, *1 Enoch 1*, 415.

166. *1 En.* 96.1–8.
167. *1 En.* 103.3–4, citation from v. 4 (Isaac, *OTP*).
168. *1 En.* 104.2 (Isaac, *OTP*).
169. *1 En.* 107.1 (Isaac, *OTP*); cf. 108.11–15.
170. *1 En.* 51.1.
171. See Goldstein, *2 Maccabees*, 71–83.
172. See Wright, *Resurrection*, 150–53.
173. 2 Macc 7:9; cf. 7:23, 29; 12:43–45.
174. 2 Macc 7:11; 14:45–46.
175. 2 Macc 7:14, 31–36.

be at work here as in *1 Enoch*: there is coming a day of judgment when God will separate the wicked from the righteous and will restore the righteous to life on earth.

Evidence from the *Testament of the Twelve Patriarchs* is often cited in this context.[176] It is well known, however, that the extant manuscripts contain many Christian interpolations, and David Bryan has demonstrated the likelihood of Christian influence precisely in the texts that speak of resurrection,[177] making their status as Jewish evidence suspect.[178]

An assortment of other Jewish texts, dating prior to the first century CE, also witness to the hope for resurrection. The *Psalms of Solomon* speak of judgment which will result in sinners being destroyed and the righteous rising and living forever:[179]

> The destruction of the sinner is forever,
> and he will not be remembered when (God) looks after the righteous.
> This is the share of sinners forever,
> but those who fear the Lord shall rise up to eternal life,
> and their life shall be in the Lord's light, and it shall never end.
> (*Pss. Sol.* 3.11–12; Wright, *OTP*)

Debate rages over whether the Qumran community believed in the resurrection of the dead.[180] The most likely example of a reference

176. See esp. *T. Jud.* 25.1–4; *T. Zeb.* 10.1–4; *T. Ben.* 10.6–11.

177. Bryan, "Jewish Background," 163–64.

178. Similarly for *T. Job* 4.9.

179. Cf. *Pss. Sol.* 13.11.

180. Puech, *La croyance des Esséniens*, is the most optimistic in finding references to resurrection in the Dead Sea Scrolls; others see few or no references. A helpful approach is that of Charlesworth, "Resurrection Texts," 237–38; see also the literature cited there. If we assume that the Qumranites were Essenes, then this debate can be traced back to a confusion in ancient sources: Josephus (*J.W.* 2.154) ascribes to the Essenes a belief in the immortality of the soul, whereas Hippolytus (*Haer.* IX,27) says that they believed in both immortality of the soul and resurrection of the body. Two key issues shape this debate. The first concerns the extent to which the Dead Sea Scrolls reflect the beliefs of the Qumran community. Care clearly needs to be taken here since some of the scrolls were authored elsewhere. Charlesworth, "Introduction," xvi–xviii, for example, argues that the most important scrolls for determining the perspectives of the community are the *Rule of the Community* (1QS), the *Rule of the Congregation* (1QSa = 1Q28a), the *Rule of Benedictions* (1QSb = 1Q28b), the *War Scroll* (1QM), the *Hodayot* (1QHª), the *Songs of the Sabbath Sacrifice* (4QShirShabba-h = 4Q400–407), and the pesherim to Habakkuk (1QpHab), Nahum (4QpNah = 4Q169), and Psalms (1QpPs 68). On the other hand, one could argue that

to resurrection among the Dead Sea Scrolls is in 4Q521. In fragment 2 of this manuscript[181] we notice that one of the "marvelous acts" that the Lord will perform for his people is to "make the dead live"—an allusion back to Isa 26:19.[182] We also noted above that fragments 5 and 7 seem to have in view the resurrection of the righteous, possibly set within the context of new creation.[183]

Other Qumran texts may have bodily resurrection in view, but they are often ambiguous and could instead be referring to some other form of restoration or future hope.[184]

---

the community valued all of the scrolls to some extent, otherwise they would not have been included in its library. The key phrase here, however, is "to some extent"; as in all libraries, some works are highly valued because they express the fundamental commitments of the community, whereas other works may be thought to be important but not as central as the former group. That said, it is generally agreed that the quest for the core beliefs of the Qumran community ought to begin with the works that Charlesworth lists.

The second issue concerns whether resurrection language is to be taken literally or metaphorically. Charlesworth, "Resurrection Texts," 237–64, offers a helpful set of categories that provides a range of possible meanings that resurrection language can be used to convey.

181. See above, p. 267, for the quoted text.

182. 4Q521 2ii12.

183. 4Q521 7+5ii1–6; see above, p. 270, for the quoted text.

184. Charlesworth, "Resurrection Texts," 256–57, also thinks that 4Q416 contains a reference to resurrection. He translates the phrase ואחריתכה תנחל שמחה as "and finally ([in] your future) you will inherit joy." It is problematic, however, that Charlesworth has to provide the preposition ב ("in") which does not appear in the text; furthermore, אחרית typically refers (with reference to a person) to the end of one's life or to one's posterity (see *HALOT*). Noting that the verb, תנחל, could also be construed as third person feminine, the translation of Vermes seems more natural: "and your posterity will inherit joy" (cf. García Martínez and Tigchelaar). Thus, a post-mortem life is not necessarily in view here.

Another possible reference to bodily resurrection is in 4Q385 2,8–9 which includes a reflection on Ezekiel's vision of the dry bones (Ezek 37). Puech, *Résurrection*, 614, argues that the questions in the fragment asking God about when and how the just will be rewarded "have changed the character of the national restoration of Ezek 37, made explicit in vv. 11–13 but of which there is no longer a question here, into an image of promise of individual resurrection at the end of the time of distress" (my translation). It is not obvious, however, that these questions of "when" and "how" *necessarily* change the focus of Ezekiel's vision from national restoration to individual resurrection. It is quite possible that in his reflection on Ezek 37, the writer still thinks metaphorically in terms of the restoration of the nation.

Numerous texts from the first and second centuries CE continue to express hope for resurrection.[185] The *Apocalypse of Moses*[186] speaks of a general resurrection of all people with sinners being transformed by being given, in place of their evil heart, "a heart that understands the good and worships God alone."[187] The fourth book of the *Sibylline Oracles*[188] envisions a conflagration in which God will destroy the whole world with fire, after which "he will raise up mortals again as they were before," judging sinners by sending them back under the earth to Tartarus and Gehenna, and restoring the pious to "live on earth again."[189] Similarly, the *Fourth Book of Ezra*[190] tells of the world returning to "primeval silence," and then all people being raised up for judgment.[191] And *2 Baruch*[192] describes a general resurrection of all people who will be judged and then transformed—the righteous into "the splendor of angels" and the wicked into "startling visions and horrible shapes."[193] The second benediction of the early Jewish prayer known as the *Shemoneh Esre*, or the Eighteen Benedictions,[194] which probably dates from the first century CE,[195] blesses God for "resurrecting the dead."[196] Josephus speaks of the souls of the righteous dead waiting for "the revolution of the ages" when they will "return to find

---

185. For references to resurrection in later rabbinic literature see, for example, *m. Sanh.* 10:1; *m. Soṭah* 9:15; *Gen. Rab.* 14:5 (on Gen 2:7); *Lev. Rab.* 14:9; *b. Sanh.* 90–92; see further, Str-B 4.2:1172–98.

186. Johnson, "Life of Adam and Eve," 252, locates this work between 100 BCE and 200 CE, "more probably toward the end of the first Christian century."

187. *Apoc. Mos.* 13.3–5 (Johnson, *OTP*); cf. 28.3–4; 41.3; 43.2.

188. Collins, "Sibylline Oracles," 381–82, places the final redaction in the late first century CE, but notes that some of the material is much older.

189. *Sib. Or.* 4.179–92 (Collins, *OTP*).

190. Metzger, "Fourth Book of Ezra," 520, dates this work ca. 100 CE.

191. *4 Ezra* 7.30–35 (Metzger, *OTP*).

192. Klijn, "2 (Syriac Apocalypse of) Baruch," 616–17, dates this work in the first twenty years of the second century CE.

193. *2 Bar.* 50.2–51.6 (Klijn, *OTP*); cf. 30.1–2.

194. The prayer is also known as the *Tefillah* ("Prayer") or the *Amidah* ("Standing [Prayer]").

195. Heinemann, *Prayer in the Talmud*, 21–23, argues that this prayer pre-dated the fall of Jerusalem; Zahavy, "Politics of Piety," 55–62, however, argues that it was developed later by the sages at Yavneh.

196. Heinemann, *Prayer*, 26 n. 16; cf. Wright, *Resurrection*, 146–47.

in chaste bodies a new habitation."[197] And Pseudo-Philo[198] foresees when God will "bring the dead to life and raise up those who are sleeping in the earth" so that he "may render to each according to his works. . . . And there will be another earth and another heaven, an everlasting dwelling place."[199]

A variety of perspectives and emphases is represented in this literature, but the underlying narrative is the same: at the end of the age God will sit in judgment over all people; the wicked will be punished for their deeds and sent away, while the righteous will be restored to a bountiful life on earth. Within this framework a number of variations can be found, the most significant one being that some texts speak of all the dead being raised for judgment,[200] while others foresee only the righteous being raised.[201] Naturally, different texts will place emphasis differently—some on the present state of the dead, others on the ultimate end of the wicked, and still others on the nature of life in store for the righteous. But the narrative framework is consistent.

Given this background we may now ask our critical question: Is it likely that Paul's experience of having seen the risen Jesus, and his acceptance of the early church's tradition that Jesus had risen and had appeared to the apostles and to others, would have led him to conclude that (i) what had happened to Jesus was an "end of the age" event, and (ii) the reality of the "age to come" was breaking into this world now? Clearly, Jesus' resurrection was revolutionary. Paul's own encounter with the risen Jesus changed him from being a persecutor of the church to being one of its chief promoters. The one whom he thought to be a deceiver, he now believed to be Israel's Messiah. But was the nature of the resurrection, in and of itself, such that it would have led Paul, not simply to believe that the end was near, but that the framework of eschatological expectation itself had changed?

---

197. Josephus, *J. W.* 3.374–75 (Thackeray, LCL); cf. *Ag. Ap.* 2.217–18.

198. Harrington, "Pseudo-Philo," 299, notes the difficulty in dating this work. It could conceivably have been written any time between 135 BCE and the end of the first century CE.

199. *L.A.B.* 3.10 (Harrington, *OTP*); cf. 19.12–13.

200. Dan 12:2; *Apoc. Mos.* 13.2–5; 41.3; *Sib. Or.* 4.179–92; Str-B 4.2:1174–82. Note that John seems to ascribe both views to Jesus within the same context (John 5:25–29).

201. Isa 26:19; *Pss. Sol.* 3.10–12; *1 En.* 91.10; 92.3; 100.5; *2 Bar.* 30.1–5; Str-B 4.2:1182–98.

Although an affirmative answer to this question is widely assumed, I suggest that there are significant reasons to doubt this. First,
the Jewish expectation of the end of the age was for a general resurrection—either of all people or of all the righteous—not of only one
person. And where there were individual resurrections, even those
within the Jesus tradition,[202] there is no indication that people saw this
as a sign of the end of the age.[203] Second, there is no obvious judgment
associated with Jesus' resurrection such as there was associated with
the expectation of a general resurrection: the wicked continue to op-
press the righteous. And third, and perhaps most importantly, Jesus
is no longer physically present. The dominant expectation for the age
to come was for a long and prosperous life on earth. It may be that
Paul accepted the tradition that Jesus had been exalted to heaven[204]—
perhaps like Enoch, Elijah and Moses—but an ascension is not evidence of the end of the age. The absence of Jesus would seem to be
significant counter-evidence to the view that Jesus' resurrection was
an "end of the age" event. The point is, that unless Paul (and the early
Christians) already had reason to think that the age to come was
breaking into the present—for example, from Jesus himself—it is not
obvious that his experience of Jesus' resurrection by itself would have
given rise to such a view.

Hope for the Spirit of God

Having considered the likely effect of Jesus' resurrection on the shape
of Paul's eschatological perspective, we now consider the effect of his
conviction regarding the present activity of the Spirit of God. In fact,
while we may treat these topics separately, they are clearly not independent in Paul's thought: according to him, it was by the Spirit that

202. The raising of a widow's son from Nain (Luke 7:11–17); the raising of Jairus'
daughter who was presumed dead (Mark 5:35–43//Luke 8:49–56); the raising of
Lazarus from after his burial (John 11:1–44).

203. The account of the raising of Lazarus (John 11:1–44) is not a counter example: it is Jesus who suggests that resurrection could be a reality now, not just in the
future (vv. 23–26); furthermore, the problem created by the raising of Lazarus was not
that people were now accepting a heterodox eschatology, but rather than they were
believing in Jesus (12:10–11). Thus the account of Lazarus points to the inbreaking of
the age to come only in light of Jesus' ministry.

204. Phil 2:9.

Jesus was raised from the dead[205] and it is the Spirit who will enliven the bodies of believers.[206] And significantly for our purpose, in the context of speaking of the latter, Paul goes on to discuss not only the untimate renewal of believers, but the renewal of all creation,[207] suggesting that he drew a connection between the role of the Spirit and the emergence of new creation. So, it is almost certain that Paul saw resurrection, the work of the Spirit, and new creation as all interrelated in the same nexus of thought; however, for the sake of argument, we shall consider Paul's statements about the Spirit separately, as we did with Jesus' resurrection, to see what grounds there might be here for *why* Paul developed his eschatological perspective in the way that he did. Clearly Paul understood God to be at work among his people in a radically new way, and perhaps the main way he expressed this was with reference to the Spirit of God. Our question, however, is this: Is it likely that the behavior that Paul saw among believers and that he interpreted as the activity of the Spirit would, *in itself*, have led Paul to revise the framework of his eschatology? Here again I will argue that there is good reason to doubt an affirmative answer and that the rationale for Paul's thinking becomes clearer if we assume that Jesus' own eschatological perspective was influential in shaping early Christian thought, including that of Paul.

In the Hebrew Scriptures, רוּחַ is frequently associated with acts of salvation and with prophecy.[208] The empowerment by the Spirit of Yahweh is essential for those exercising leadership or seeking justice for people—generally for judges,[209] kings[210] and governors,[211] and specifically for the ideal Davidic king who will judge the poor with righteousness,[212] for the Servant of Yahweh who brings justice to the

---

205. Rom 1:4; cf. 1 Tim 3:16.

206. Rom 8:11. See further, Hamilton, *Holy Spirit*, 17–21. It is also significant that rabbinic writings draw a connection between the Spirit and the resurrection of the dead: *m. Soṭah* 9:15: "the Holy Spirit leads to the resurrection of the dead" (Neusner); *b. ʿAbod. Zar.* 20b: "the holy spirit leads to life eternal [lit. 'resurrection of the dead']."

207. Rom 8:18–25.

208. For a full discussion of רוּחַ, see Tengström and Fabry, "רוּחַ," 365–402; Kleinknecht et al., "πνεῦμα," 359–89.

209. Jud 3:10; 6:34; 11:29; 13:25; 14:6, 19; 15:14.

210. 1 Sam 16:13–14.

211. Hag 2:5; Zech 4:6.

212. Isa 11:1–5.

nations,[213] and for the prophet who comforts those who mourn and proclaims liberty to the captives.[214] Perhaps important in this connection is the role of the רוּחַ in the account of the Exodus: God sent a mighty רוּחַ to make a way for his people to escape through the sea;[215] this would later be remembered as a time when God put his Spirit in the midst of his people.[216] Also, it is often noted that those who spoke words of prophecy did so by means of God's רוּחַ,[217] and prophecy typically had to do with judgment or salvation. It is not surprising, therefore, to find God's רוּחַ in texts that speak of the hope of salvation. During the exile, the pouring out of God's רוּחַ was indicative of the restoration of God's people[218]—a restoration likened to the appearance of new growth in the desert,[219] to the exchange of a heart of stone for a heart of flesh,[220] or to the re-animation of dry bones.[221] The tangible effect of this restoration that the outpouring of God's רוּחַ brings is expressed variously: the most common effect is the return of Israel to her homeland;[222] but one prophet also speaks of the establishment of justice, righteousness, and peace,[223] Ezekiel looks forward to the people keeping God's laws and of God providing abundant harvests,[224] and Joel describes the effect in terms of all the people prophesying.[225]

213. Isa 42:1–4.

214. Isa 61:1–4.

215. Exod 14:21; 15:8, 10.

216. Isa 63:11–14. Tengström and Fabry, "רוּחַ," 381–82, note numerous places where "*rûah* in the sense of 'wind' is associated directly with God's active intervention" (382).

217. Moses and the seventy elders (Num 11:16–17, 25–26, 29); Balaam (Num 24:2); Saul (1 Sam 10:6, 10; 19:23–24); Saul's messengers (1 Sam 19:20–21); David (2 Sam 23:2); Ezekiel (Ezek 2:2; 3:12, 14, 24; 11:1, 5, 24; 37:1; 43:5); Micah (Mic 3:8); Jehaziel (2 Chron 20:14); Zechariah (2 Chron 24:20); unnamed prophets (Isa 61:1; Zech 7:12; Neh 9:20, 30). Note also the role of the divine Spirit in connection with the interpretation of dreams (Gen 41:38; Dan 4:8–9, 18; 5:11–12, 14).

218. Isa 59:21; Ezek 39:29.

219. Isa 32:15; 44:3.

220. Ezek 11:19–20; 36:26–27.

221. Ezek 37:4–10, 14.

222. Isa 44:3 (prominent in Second Isaiah is the theme of return from exile); Ezek 36:28; 37:12–14.

223. Isa 32:15–18.

224. Ezek 11:19–20; 36:26–30; 39:25–29; cf. Jer 31:31–34. Rabbinic literature also closely related the Spirit with a life of obedience; see Kleinknecht et al., "πνεῦμα," 383.

225. Joel 2:28–29.

In spite of the widespread belief that with the end of the classical prophets God's Spirit was no longer present in Israel,[226] Palestinian Judaism continued to show some interest in the Spirit.[227] Wisdom literature speaks of God's Spirit being everywhere,[228] and of the present possibility of receiving a spirit from God.[229] Apocalyptic writers testify to being inspired by a spirit[230] and portray historical people as being given a spirit from God.[231] In several places we read that the Messiah will be endowed with the Spirit,[232] and in two places this endowment is shared among God's people.[233]

The Dead Sea Scrolls stand out among Second Temple literature for their interest in the Spirit of God, in addition to a focus on good and evil spirits and on the human spirit.[234] Here we learn that it is by his Spirit that God atones for his people's sins,[235] cleanses them,[236] and teaches them, either directly[237] or by way of the prophets.[238] In addi-

---

226. *t. Soṭah* 13:2–3; Str-B 1:127.

227. Isaacs, *Concept of Spirit*, 82, observes that Hellenistic Jewish literature as a whole shows little interest in eschatology. The only text that connects spirit with future hope is *Sib. Or.* 4.45–46, 188–89, which states that in the last judgment God will give the pious "spirit and life and favor" (Collins, *OTP*).

228. Wis 1:7; 12:1.

229. Wis 7:7 ("the spirit of wisdom"); 9:17 ("thy holy Spirit"); Sir 39:6 ("the spirit of understanding").

230. *1 En.* 91.1 ("the spirit"); *2 Esd* 5:22 ("the spirit of understanding"); 14:22 ("the Holy Spirit"); *T. Levi* 2.3 ("a spirit of understanding").

231. *T. Ab.* 4.8 (God's "holy spirit"); 18.11 ("a spirit of life"); *T. Sim.* 4.4 ("the spirit of God"); *Jos. Asen.* 16.14 (the "spirit of life").

232. *Pss. Sol.* 17.37; cf. 18.7. *1 Enoch* (49.3; 62.2) depicts the "Elect One" as a messianic figure who possesses the divine spirit. The *Testament of Judah* (24.1–6) tells of the "Star from Jacob" who is showered with the spirit and who brings salvation (cf. *T. Levi* 18.7). *Tg. Isa* 42:1–7 makes the spirit-anointed Servant of Yahweh into a messianic figure (cf. *Tg. Isa* 11:1–2).

233. *T. Levi* 18.11; *T. Jud.* 24.3.

234. Of the 442 Hebrew references and the 54 Aramaic references to רוח in Abegg et al., *DSS Concordance*, I count 34 clear references to the Spirit of God, at least 90 references to good and evil spirits, and about 85 references to the human spirit (this is in addition to numerous references to רוח as wind, breath or side/face, and many fragmentary references).

235. 1QS III,6, 8.

236. 1QS III,7; 1QHᵃ VIII,20; 4Q255 2,1–2.

237. CD II,12; 1QHᵃ V,25; VI,25; XX,11–12; 4Q444 1,1, 3.

238. 1QS VIII,16; 4Q381 69,4.

tion, we often find, particularly in the *Hodayot*, expressions of thanks for the presence of God's Spirit with members of the community.[239] H.-J. Fabry comments that "[t]he holy spirit is the gift of God to the elect of the Qumran community, a power given to each member when he enters the community . . . which works within him for his salvation."[240] Thus, there is clearly a present experience of God's Spirit.[241]

Some have argued that there is also at Qumran, like in Paul, an eschatological expectation of God's Spirit. In his study of the Spirit of God in Second Temple Judaism, Werner Foerster concludes that "[t]he sending of the Holy Spirit is for Qumran . . . an eschatological event."[242] Somewhat more nuanced is J. Coppens: "We are, therefore, well authorized, apparently, to affirm that the sect of Qumran did not believe that the great eschatological out-pouring of the Holy Spirit had already been realized, but we must accord to its members the belief in a certain anticipation of the gift of the Spirit."[243] Such a perspective would not be surprising in light of the community's understanding that the end of the age was near.[244] Marie Isaacs tries to demonstrate this eschatological perspective by noting the spiritual conflict described both in the *War Scroll* and in the *Rule of the Community*. In the former we read of the final battle in which the sons of light will battle the sons of darkness, with each side joined by their respective spirits—the angels of God and the spirits of Beliar.[245] It is assumed that this battle is imminent.[246] In the latter document we read of two spirits at war within

---

239. 1QH^a IV,26; V,25; VI,13, 25; VIII,14–15; XV,7; XVII,32; XX,11–12; cf. 1Q34bis 3ii6–7; 4Q504 4,5. Note also references to a particular type of spirit—e.g., the "spirit of your compassion" (1QH^a VIII,17) or the "spirit of salvation" (4Q438 4ii3)—which appear to be ways of speaking of God acting by his Spirit.

240. Tengström and Fabry, "רוּחַ," 399.

241. Fabry (ibid., 400) is probably correct to conclude that "the Qumran Essences did not think of the holy spirit as a person, since it is never assigned personal independence." Reference to God's רוּחַ is a means of speaking of the activity and presence of God.

242. Foerster, "Heilige Geist," 134 (my translation).

243. Coppens, "Don de l'Esprit," 217 (my translation).

244. See above, p. 286 n. 46.

245. 1QM I,10–11; VII,4–6; XII,1–9; cf. 1QSb IV,24–28; 4Q491 1–3,3, 10.

246. The text Issacs gives to indicate the imminence of the battle (1QM XVII,6–8) in fact says nothing about imminence; it merely speaks of Michael's role in the battle. But in light of the community's eschatological self-understanding, it seems safe to assume that they thought the battle was imminent.

each person, engaged in a battle that began with creation and that will ultimately be resolved in the eschatological battle.[247] Thus, Isaacs concludes that for the Qumran community, "the spirit was both a present possession and a future gift."[248] It should be noted, however, that none of the texts here speak of the Spirit *of God*, and indeed nowhere in the Dead Sea Scrolls do we find it explicitly stated that the life of the age to come would be characterized by a further bestowal of God's Spirit. The claim of Foerster, Coppens, and Isaacs regarding the future expectation of God's Spirit is based on a particular understanding of the eschatological perspective at Qumran (which we examined above), and either a confusion between angelic spirits and God's Spirit, or an assumption that current blessings will be multiplied in the future. In any case, it is not based on exegesis of texts that specifically speak of the Spirit of God.

It is clear that Paul believed that the Spirit of God was at work among believers. From his perspective, the presence of the Spirit was so fundamental for Christian existence[249] that he could refer to the time in which he was living as the "dispensation of the Spirit."[250] Paul does not, however, tell us explicitly what evidence led him to this conviction. A number of factors may have played a role. The connection he made between the Spirit and resurrection, as we noted above,[251] could easily have led him to the conclusion that since Jesus had been raised from the dead, the Spirit of God was at work in a new way among God's people, in which case the real question would be how Jesus' resurrection served as grounds for Paul's thought, as we discussed in the previous section. But Paul also connects other tangible evidence with the work of the Spirit: he points to his own preaching as an example, not characterized by good rhetoric, but by a "demonstration of the Spirit and power" which was at times accompanied by the performance of "signs and wonders";[252] he also identifies various "gifts" within the Christian community which demonstrate the presence of

247. 1QS III,18–IV,26; see above, pp. 290–92.

248. Isaacs, *Concept of Spirit*, 86.

249. Rom 8:9, 14, 23; 1 Cor 3:16; 6:19; 12:13; 2 Cor 1:22; 5:5; Gal 3:2–3; 1 Thess 4:8; cf. Eph 1:13; 4:30; 2 Tim 1:14.

250. 2 Cor 3:8.

251. See above, pp. 314–15.

252. 1 Cor 2:4; 2 Cor 11:6; 1 Thess 1:5; Rom 15:19; Gal 3:5.

the Spirit—abilities given to people for the purpose of strengthening the community;[253] and he refers to character qualities that the Spirit produces in people, qualities that include righteousness, peace, joy, hope, freedom, and others that he could collectively call the "fruit of the Spirit."[254] Some of these qualities, while clearly having an outward manifestation, stem from a subjective experience, which Paul points to in other contexts as evidence of the Spirit's presence. Specifically, Paul speaks of the following as being due to the presence of the Spirit within believers: the experience of God's love,[255] the sense of being adopted as God's children,[256] the conviction of the truth of genuine preaching and prophecy,[257] and the reality of empowerment[258] and guidance for life.[259]

In various ways, therefore, Paul describes the work of the Spirit in ways that reflect various lines of expectation from the Old Testament. Of particular importance for Paul were the prophecies of Ezekiel. When Paul speaks of the believers at Corinth being a letter written "with the Spirit of the living God, not on tablets of stone but on tablets of human hearts,"[260] he draws directly on the imagery Ezekiel used when he prophesied that God would put "a new spirit" within his people in exchange for their "heart of stone."[261] At least this is the clearest allusion Paul makes to a text that expresses an expectation of the Spirit. And so, it would follow that Paul would probably have understood the transformation in believers, that he spoke of in various ways, in line with the consequence to this inner exchange that Ezekiel draws, namely that the people would "walk in my statutes and keep my

---

253. 1 Cor 12:3–11; cf. Eph 4:1–16, where gifts are mentioned in the context of the presence of the Spirit.

254. Rom 12:11; 14:17; 15:13; Gal 5:5; 5:22–23; 2 Cor 3:17; 1 Thess 1:6.

255. Rom 5:5; 15:30.

256. Rom 8:15–16; Gal 4:6.

257. 1 Cor 2:10–13; 1 Thess 5:19–20; cf. Eph 3:5; 1 Tim 4:1.

258. Rom 8:13: "by the Spirit of God you put to death the deeds of the body"; 8:26: "the Spirit helps us in our weakness"; 2 Cor 3:6: "the Spirit gives life"; 3:18: "we all . . . are being changed into his likeness" by "the Lord who is the Spirit"; cf. Eph 3:16; 5:18.

259. Paul speaks of the Spirit serving as a standard in contrast to the law (Rom 7:6; Gal 5:18) and shaping the lives of believers (2 Cor 3:3; Phil 1:19); and of believers living "according to the Spirit" (Rom 8:4–6; Gal 5:16, 25), being "led by the Spirit" (Rom 8:14), and enjoying the "fellowship of the Spirit" (2 Cor 13:14; Phil 2:1).

260. 2 Cor 3:3; cf. 1 Thess 4:8.

261. Ezek 11:19–20; 36:26–27; cf. *Apoc. Mos.* 13.3–5. See further, Thrall, *2 Corinthians*, 1:226; Furnish, *2 Corinthians*, 183; Martin, *2 Corinthians*, 52.

ordinances and obey them."[262] Granted, Paul might not have expressed the transformation in terms of keeping the law, but he certainly would have affirmed the idea of believers now living according to God's will.

The curious thing is, however, that regardless of how much evidence Paul had that suggested the presence of the Spirit, there was also plenty of counter-evidence. Even leaving aside Ezekiel's prophecy of Israel dwelling in the land of their fathers and enjoying abundant harvests, Paul's letters themselves suggest many ways in which believers were not living according to God's will. Believers—in whom, according to Paul, the Spirit resides—could be factious, immoral, self-serving, inconsiderate, and led astray by charlatans, to name some of the common vices Paul addresses. The question then arises, why would Paul's experience—experience that included both the transformation of believers and their ongoing sinfulness—and that experience on its own, have led him to conclude that the reality of the age to come was breaking into this age? At best the evidence was ambiguous. It would be quite understandable if he concluded that God, by his Spirit, was at work among his people in a new way—what church historians might refer to as a "movement of the Spirit." But unless he already had in place a revised eschatological framework that saw a tension between the "already" and the "not yet," it is not clear that his experience of the Spirit likely would have led him to adopt such a framework.

Christianity as a Messianic Movement

It might be argued at this point that reference to early Christianity as a messianic movement would be sufficient to explain the eschatological perspective of Paul and others. Given the close connection in Jewish thought between messianism and eschatology, would it not follow that if early Christians believed that theirs was a messianic movement, they would then also think in terms of eschatological fulfillment and the beginning of a new age? Hence, we would not need recourse to the teaching of Jesus in order to explain Paul's eschatological perspective. Due to the limits of space we cannot develop an exhaustive understanding of Jewish messianism, but we do need to examine this question carefully before we draw our conclusions.

262. Ezek 11:20; cf. 36:27.

A close connection between messianism and eschatology is evident in some Jewish texts.[263] In Second Temple literature, the expression of messianic expectation is in fact quite sparse. However, where it does appear, it typically goes together with an eschatological expectation of the establishment of ideal conditions. The author of *Pss. Sol.* 17 prays for the coming of the "son of David" who will destroy Israel's enemies, will gather Israel back to her land, and will reign with righteousness, wisdom, and power.[264] Texts from Qumran confirm this expectation for a warrior-Messiah who will drive out the Gentiles.[265] Several Qumran texts speak of two Messiahs being expected—one a royal figure and the other priestly;[266] but the coming of these Messiahs will be marked by the establishment of a new order: note in particular the scene of the messianic banquet in 1QSa and the association of the "anointed one" with the Lord's acts of healing, liberation, and proclamation in 4Q521.[267] And we note that in the Jewish revolt of 132–135 CE, Rabbi Akiba ascribed the title "Bar Kokhba" ("Son of the

263. See, for example, Amos 9:11–12; Isa 11:1–9; Mic 5:2; Jer 23:5–6; 33:14–18; Ezek 37:24–25; Sir 45:24–25; 47:22. Some texts look forward to a new priest: *T. Levi* 18.2–14;

264. *Pss. Sol.* 17.21–46.

265. 4Q252 V,1–4: "The sceptre shall [no]t depart from the tribe of Judah. While Israel has the dominion, there [will not] be cut off someone who sits on the throne of David. For «the staff» is the covenant of royalty, [and the thou]-sands of Israel are «the standards». Blank Until the messiah of righteousness comes, the branch of David. For to him and to his descendants has been given the covenant of the kingship of his people for everlasting generations. . . ." See also texts that refer to Messiah as the "Branch of David": 1QSb V,20–25: "To bless the prince of the congregation, who [. . .] And he will renew the covenant of the [Com]munity for him, to establish the kingdom of his people for eve[r, to judge the poor with justice,] to reproach the [hu]mble of the earth with upri[ghtness,] to walk in perfection before him. . . . With your sceptre may you lay waste the earth. With the breath of your lips may you kill the wicked" (cf. 4Q285 where the "prince of the con-gregation" is identified as the "branch of David"); 4Q161(Isaiah Pesher A) 8–10,3.11–25: "[*Isa 11:1–5* . . . The interpretation of the word concerns the shoot] of David which will sprout in the fi[nal days, since with the breath of his lips he will execute] his [ene]-my and God will support him with [the spirit of c]ourage. . . . He will rule over all the pe[ople]s. . .". cf. 4Q174(Florilegium) 1i. For discussion of these texts, see Fuller, "Davidic Messiah," 73–83; Collins, "Pre-Christian Jewish Messianism," 8–11.

266. 1QS IX,11; CD XII,21–XIII,1; XIV,19; XIX,10–11; XX,1. This dual role mes-siahship is probably modelled after the partnerships of Moses and Aaron, and of Joshua and Zerubbael; see Schürer, *History*, 2.551.

267. 1QSa II,11–22; on 4Q521 see above, pp. 267–68.

Star")[268] to Simon, the leader of the revolt, explicitly heralding him as the Messiah;[269] and coins discovered from the period, bearing the words "Year I of the Liberation of Israel" or "Year II of the Freedom of Israel," show that Jews believed that a new era had begun.[270] It is not true that eschatological expectation always included a messianic figure: there are numerous Jewish texts that speak of hope for the future without mentioning a Messiah.[271] The converse, however, probably is true: the presence of a Messiah would have entailed an eschatological perspective of some kind.

Early Christianity was clearly both eschatological and messianic. But what is the likelihood that it was first messianic, and that its eschatological perspective followed from this? In particular, with reference to Paul, what is the likelihood that he became convinced that Jesus was the Messiah based on his own conversion experience and the testimony of other Christians, and then deduced from this that the end of the ages had come? Two texts might be thought to lend support for this likelihood: On the day of Pentecost, Peter announces, "This Jesus God raised up. . . . Let all the house of Israel therefore know assuredly that God has made him both Lord and Christ, this Jesus whom you crucified."[272] And in a text possibly drawn from early Christian tradition, Paul writes that Jesus was "designated Son of God in power . . . by his resurrection from the dead."[273] Does this not suggest that it was the resurrection that was all important for the development of early Christology? And, if so, and if there was a close connection between messianism and eschatology, do we need to look to anything but the resurrection in order to explain the eschatological perspective of the early church and of Paul?

I draw attention at this point to the argument of A. E. Harvey against the view that the resurrection is sufficient, in and of itself, to

---

268. The allusion is to Num 24:17 ("A star shall go forth from Jacob") which was understood as a messianic reference.

269. *y. Ta'an.* 4:5 (X.G–H).

270. Schürer, *History*, 1:543–45.

271. See, for example, Isa 2:2–4; 26:1–4; 35:1–10; 65:17–25; Mic 2:12; 4:2–4; Zeph 3:19–20; Jer 31:31–33; Ezek 34:11–12; Dan 7:13–14; Sir 36:1–22; Bar 4:36–5:9; *Jub.* 23.29–30; *T. Sim.* 6.2–5; *T. Jud.* 25.3–5; *As. Mos.* 10.1–10; *2 Bar.* 44.12; 48.53–4; 73.1–74.4.

272. Acts 2:32–36.

273. Rom 1:4; see above, p. 124 n. 304.

explain why early Christians came to regard Jesus as the Messiah. He argues, first, that given a context in which people's concept of a Messiah—that is, the concept of those who thought about a Messiah at all—was one of a victorious warrior who would defeat Israel's enemies and re-establish the nation of Israel, it is highly unlikely that anyone would have been persuaded, simply on the basis of the resurrection, that Jesus was the Messiah.[274] And thus it would be highly unlikely that Christians would have, from the beginning, placed at the center of their message the claim that Jesus was the Messiah. It may be that Christians re-interpreted messianic expectation not only in light of texts that speak of a Messiah, but also in light of those that have in view a righteous sufferer; but Harvey notes that this process would have taken some time to develop. But prior to this re-interpretation, there would have been too much of an incompatibility between the account of Jesus' death and resurrection and the common expectation surrounding the Messiah for the claim "Jesus is the Messiah" to make any sense. And yet, all the evidence we have suggests that the proclamation that Jesus was the Messiah characterized the Christian movement from the very beginning.[275]

Second, Harvey argues that it is not obvious why even Jesus' followers, if they had not already identified Jesus as the Messiah during his ministry, would have done so solely on the basis of the resurrection.[276] The immediate effect of the resurrection was no doubt one of vindication:[277] Jesus' followers would have been convinced that he had been vindicated by God, that during his ministry he truly had been empowered by God, and that he had been an authentic spokesperson for God; and they would have begun to ponder the significance of this Jesus. Harvey suggests it would have been understandable for them to think of Jesus in terms of the Jewish figures "Son of Man" or "Son of God"; but unless there had already been an identification of Jesus as the Messiah *in some fashion* during his ministry, it is not clear why his followers would have made such an identification simply on the basis of the resurrection. Contrary to common messianic expectation, Jesus had not restored political independence to Israel, and in fact had died

---

274. Harvey, *Constraints*, 137–38.

275. Rom 1:4; 1 Cor 15:3; Acts 2:36, passim.

276. Harvey, *Constraints*, 138; cf. Hengel, *Atonement*, 48–49.

277. Harvey notes the emphasis on Jesus being "just" in Acts 3:14; 7:52; 22:14.

at the hands of Israel's enemies; furthermore, there was no expectation that Messiah would be raised from the dead.

And third, Harvey argues that Paul's regular use of "Christ" as a name rather than as a title[278] makes better sense if Jesus had been called "Messiah" during his lifetime than if his followers had only begun to call him "the Messiah" following his resurrection. He gives evidence from the Gospels that suggest that Jesus may have been called "Messiah" during his lifetime:[279] Matthew's qualification of Jesus' name with the phrase "who is called Christ"[280] may be an indication that "Messiah" was something of a nickname for Jesus during his ministry, in the same way that "Peter" was for Simon,[281] "Twin" was for Thomas,[282] and "Justus" was for Paul's co-worker, Jesus;[283] and, it may have been a means of distinguishing Jesus from others of the same name,[284] as perhaps is indicated in Matt 27:16 where Jesus occurs alongside Jesus Barabbas.[285] Furthermore, if the title "Messiah" was in fact ambiguous in Jesus' time, or at least ambiguous as it was applied to Jesus, this would raise the need for qualifying phrases—such as "the Son of the living God,"[286] "the Son of God,"[287] "the Son of the Blessed,"[288] or "of God, his Chosen One"[289]—even during Jesus' lifetime. Thus, Harvey concludes, if Jesus had, for whatever reason, been identified with the name "Messiah" during his ministry, this would help explain Paul's use of "Christ" as a name for Jesus. This does not necessarily mean that

278. Wright, "ΧΡΙΣΤΟΣ as "Messiah,"" 41–55, argues that Paul did, in fact, have in view the titular significance when he spoke of Χριστός. Even if we grant this, however, it is clear that in virtually every instance, Paul *uses* the word Χριστός as though it were a proper name. For example, he writes Ἰησοῦς Χριστός rather than Ἰησοῦς ὁ Χριστός.

279. Harvey, *Constraints*, 80–81.

280. Ἰησοῦς ὁ λεγόμενος χριστός; Matt 1:16; 27:17, 22.

281. Σίμων ὁ λεγόμενος Πέτρος; Matt 10:2.

282. Θωμᾶς . . . ὁ λεγόμενος Δίδυμος; John 20:24; 21:2.

283. Ἰησοῦς ὁ λεγόμενος Ἰοῦστος; Col 4:11.

284. Harvey, *Constraints*, 80, notes that "Jesus" was a common name: Josephus mentions twenty-one people named Jesus, sixteen during the first century CE.

285. The reading Ἰησοῦν τὸν βαραββᾶν in Matt 27:16 and 17 is slightly to be preferred over βαραββᾶν; see Metzger, *Textual Commentary*, 56; Davies and Allison, *Matthew*, 3:584–85.

286. Matt 16:16.

287. Matt 26:63.

288. Mark 14:61.

289. Luke 23:35.

Paul did not reflect on the significance of Jesus as the Messiah of Israel; only that he and later writers (such as the Evangelists) used the word Χριστός as though it were a name for Jesus.

These three arguments suggest that there was at least some kind of messianic awareness prior to Jesus' death. Much more could be said about how Jesus conceived of his own role vis-à-vis Jewish messianic expectation. But what we have established is enough to come to a conclusion similar to what we arrived at above:[290] just as the resurrection by itself is not sufficient to explain the shape of early Christian eschatology, so also the resurrection is not sufficient to explain Jesus' identification as Messiah by his followers. The best way to understand both of these early Christian convictions is to see the resurrection as vindicating, and perhaps leading to a further development of, a prior understanding that originated during Jesus' ministry. If Harvey is correct in arguing that Jesus was dubbed "Messiah" during his ministry, and if Jesus did not have aspirations of leading a military campaign, as seems to be the case, it would have made sense for him to have taken steps to clarify how he understood his "messianic" role, particularly in light of other popular movements in which leaders claimed royal titles for themselves. Josephus tells of several of these: Judas, son of Ezekias, after raiding the palace in Sepphoris for its arms, led a campaign "of terror" in which he pursued his "ambition for royal rank";[291] Simon, a servant of Herod, looted and set fire to several royal residences and, being "bold enough to place the diadem on his head," he was "proclaimed king" by his followers;[292] and Athronges, a shepherd, who led a band of guerrillas who attacked both Roman and Herodian troops, also "put on the diadem" and "had the title of king."[293] Josephus also mentions that one of the factors leading to the outbreak of war in 66 CE was an "ambiguous oracle" stating that "one from their country would become ruler of the world," which most understood to be a Jew, but which Josephus took to be Vespasian who was proclaimed emperor while in Judea.[294] Josephus' brief and clearly hostile treatment of such Jewish groups makes it virtually impossible for us to know

---

290. See above, p. 314.

291. Josephus, *Ant.* 17.271–72, citations from 272 (Marcus, LCL).

292. Josephus, *Ant.* 17.273–76, citations from 273–74 (Marcus, LCL).

293. Josephus, *Ant.* 17.278–84, citations from 280 and 281 (Marcus, LCL).

294. Josephus, *J.W.* 6.312–13 (Thackerary, LCL).

whether they were motivated by any messianic, let alone eschatological, convictions, or, if they were, what form these convictions took. What is clear, however, is that as a leader of a popular movement, Jesus would have needed to have distinguished himself from other movements with royal claimants—especially so, if he was known in some sense as Messiah.

It could be argued at this point that, if the recognition of Jesus as the Messiah began (at least in some sense) during his ministry, as opposed to after his resurrection, then it could still be that Paul developed his eschatological perspective from this messianic awareness. And I will admit this is a possibility. However, if the argument I gave in the previous chapter is sound—that Jesus believed that new creation was breaking into the world during his ministry—then, given the close relationship between eschatology and messianism that we noted above, it would be highly likely that the ideas about Jesus as Messiah and the ideas about the reality of new creation developed together. That is, the same evidence that gave rise to one would have given rise to the other. Or, to put it another way, the idea of new creation most likely qualified what was meant by Jesus' messiahship as we see, for example, in Matt 11:2–6//Luke 7:18–23 where, in response to the question, "Are you he who is to come. . . ?" Jesus points to evidence of new creation in his ministry.

All things considered, therefore, it is probably not the case that the eschatological perspective of Paul and other early Christians was derived simply from their awareness of being part of a messianic movement which in turn was a product solely of their conviction that Jesus had been raised from the dead. It is much more likely that both of these have their roots in the ministry of Jesus, and that they developed together. Certainly the resurrection gave Jesus' followers a new perspective, but it was a new perspective on something that already existed. As Sanders concludes more generally with regard to Jesus' preaching about the kingdom of God:

> We have every reason to think that Jesus had led [his disciples] to expect a dramatic event which would establish the kingdom. The death and resurrection required them to adjust their expectation, but did not create a new one out of nothing.[295]

---

295. Sanders, *Jesus and Judaism*, 320.

The same can be said with regard to their understanding of who Jesus was and of the nature of the time in which they lived.

Conclusions and Consideration of Paul's Dependency on Jesus

Clearly Paul's understanding both of Jesus' resurrection and of the Spirit fit his "already" but "not yet" eschatological framework. The question is, were either or both of these the cause of that framework? Or, were there other things in the Christian tradition that Paul received that led to such a framework, such that he then understood Jesus' resurrection and the activity of the Spirit in terms of that framework? It is almost a "chicken and the egg question," but some things can be said in favor of the latter view, and hence in favor of the possibility that Jesus' emphasis on new creation may have been formative for Paul.

Admittedly it is difficult to say with certainty how a unique event like Jesus' resurrection, or the intensely personal and transformative experience of the Spirit, would have, or would not have, affected someone like Paul. Not having the effects from other resurrections to study, we need to be careful what we claim. I have given evidence, however, that suggests there is some reason to doubt the common assumption that Jesus' resurrection and the coming of the Spirit alone are sufficient to explain Paul's eschatological perspective. Furthermore, I have argued that the Qumran community did not—again, contrary to popular assumption—express an eschatological tension like Paul did, and therefore cannot be seen as Paul's source for this line of thought.

Returning to the more specific topic of new creation, is there any evidence to suggest Paul's view shared a family resemblance with that of Jesus? It is possible that Paul was aware of Jesus' teaching on divorce, which we argued above was an indication of a new creation perspective.[296] Paul explicitly draws on Jesus in support of his instruction on divorce,[297] although his citation is not exact and it is not clear from this alone that he has in view Jesus' appeal to the story of creation as his rationale for denying divorce. A few verses earlier in 1 Corinthians, however, Paul uses the same Genesis text that Jesus cited—"the two shall become one flesh"—to explain why having sexual relations with

---

296. See above, pp. 275–77.

297. 1 Cor 7:10–11.

a prostitute was wrong.[298] Putting this together, then, we may have a connection between Jesus and Paul that has to do with the reality of new creation.[299] Beyond this, however, since Paul does not elaborate on what exactly he understands by new creation, it is difficult to make a strong case for there being a family resemblance with Jesus, beyond the facts that some of Jesus' words and deeds are characterized by a new creation perspective and that Paul specifically refers to the present reality of new creation.

It may, however, be possible to detect one other line of connection. We mentioned above that the rabbis understood new creation in terms of proselyte conversion.[300] Moyer Hubbard argues that new creation language is also used in the Jewish novel, *Joseph and Aseneth*,[301] to describe proselyte conversion.[302] In the key text Joseph prays for his Egyptian fiancée, Aseneth:

> Lord God of my father Israel,
> the Most High, the Powerful One of Jacob,
> who gave life to all (things)
> and called (them) from the darkness to the light,
> and from the error to the truth,
> and from the death to the life;
> you Lord, bless this virgin,
> and renew her by your spirit,
> and form her anew by your hidden hand,
> and make her live again by your life,
> and let her eat your bread of life,
> and drink your cup of blessing,
> and number her among your people
> that you have chosen before all (things) came into being,
> and let her enter your rest
> which you have prepared for your chosen ones,
> and live in your eternal life for ever (and) ever.
> (*Jos. Asen.* 8.9; Burchard, *OTP*)

298. 1 Cor 6:16.

299. See Wenham, *Paul*, 245.

300. See above, p. 280.

301. *Joseph and Aseneth* is difficult to date with precision; Burchard, "Joseph and Aseneth," 187, suggests a date anywhere between 100 BCE and the early second century CE.

302. Hubbard, *New Creation*, 54–75.

Although the term "new creation" does not appear, the idea seems to be clearly present given the depiction of God as Creator ("who gave life to all") and the nature of the transformation being requested ("renew her," "form her anew," "make her live again").

In Gal 6:15 Paul contrasts new creation with circumcision, making the point that the former is far more important than the latter. Elsewhere, Paul contrasts circumcision of the flesh with circumcision of the heart.[303] It is suggestive, therefore, that Paul thought of new creation—at least with regard to its present realization—and of circumcision of the heart as pointing to the same reality. Support for this can be found by noting, on the one hand, that Paul understood circumcision of the heart to be an act of the Spirit,[304] and on the other hand that Joseph, in using new creation language in his prayer above, asks for God to "renew her by your spirit"—that is, both new creation and circumcision of the heart are acts of God's Spirit. Furthermore, according to the Scriptures, circumcision of the heart had to do with restoring people to proper relationship with God—to a relationship characterized by love and humility.[305] So, in the same way that Jesus drew on the significance of Sabbath in order to indicate that his ministry was about the restoration of people at a fundamental level, Paul drew on the significance of circumcision to speak of human restoration, and both had the concept of new creation in view. Granted, this is not a strong argument, but it does suggest a possible line of connection between Jesus and Paul which is made more likely when the weaknesses of alternative suggestions for Paul's new creation perspective are considered.

It may also be that the renewal and creation language that we find in the deutero-Pauline literature is a development of the new creation theme, extending a trajectory that began with Jesus and was built on by Paul. In Colossians we read of Christ being intimately involved in creation—"in him all things were created. . . ; all things were created

---

303. Rom 2:29; cf. Phil 3:3.

304. The similar contrast between πνεῦμα and γράμμα in Rom 7:6 and 2 Cor 3:6, where it is clear that Paul has in view the Spirit of God, suggests that ἐν πνεύματι here in Rom 2:29 should also be understood as "by the Spirit," rather than seeing it as a reference to the human spirit or a spiritual quality; see Cranfield, *Romans*, 1:175 n. 3; Dunn, *Romans*, 1:124; Moo, *Romans*, 174–75.

305. Lev 26:41; Deut 10:16; 30:6; Jer 4:4; cf. 1QpHab XI,13–14; 1QS V,5.

through him and for him. . . . in him all things hold together"[306]—and we read of believers "being renewed in knowledge after the image of [their] creator."[307] Then in Ephesians we read of God creating one new humanity by means of the cross.[308] While these expressions are clearly different from what we find in the Gospels or in Paul, it is conceivable that they are a further development, building on Paul, of the theme of Jesus effecting new creation in people's lives.

I conclude, therefore, that it is reasonable to understand Paul's eschatological perspective to have been profoundly shaped by Jesus' conviction regarding the present reality of new creation. Since Jesus' communication of this conviction was both cryptic and diverse, it is understandable that in speaking of the manifestation of new creation, Paul focuses on Jesus' resurrection and the work of the Spirit—two events that gave identity to the early Christians, and two topics that could easily be connected to the Jewish hope for new creation—rather than on the specific acts and sayings of Jesus himself. Without the latter, however, it is questionable whether Paul in the first place would have formulated the eschatological tension as he did or made reference to new creation.

306. Col 1:16–17.
307. Col 3:10.
308. Eph 2:15–16.

8

Conclusions

I HAVE ARGUED IN THREE WAYS THAT PAUL WAS FUNDAMENTALLY shaped by perspectives of Jesus and shared areas of core commitment with him, each of which was distinctive within the Jewish and Greco-Roman milieux. The findings in each case supported the thesis that Paul was dependent on the historical Jesus, even if the evidence available did not yield the same strength of conclusion in each case.

First, I argued that the perspective Jesus demonstrated by associating with tax collectors and sinners was expressed first by the Christian Hellenists, and later by Paul, in welcoming Gentiles into fellowship. Although the evidence suggests that Jesus held high moral standards, he was also known to have caused offense by associating with disreputable people. He was charged with associating with tax collectors—a stereotype of sinful people—apparently because one of his followers had been a tax collector and because on at least one occasion he ate with some tax collectors. From here I built on the work of Wedderburn and Simmons who argued that the Hellenists modeled Jesus' practice of welcoming the marginalized by welcoming Gentiles into their fellowship. After the Hellenists established a church in Antioch, they served as a bridge between Jesus and Paul by providing the context for Paul to work out his own calling as apostle to the Gentiles. I nuanced the argument somewhat differently than did both Wedderburn and Simmons. I agreed with both by positing that the Hellenists' fellowship with Gentile believers lay behind the persecution particularly of that wing of the church. However, in contrast to Wedderburn, I did not find it necessary to assume that the Hellenist Christians in Jerusalem were proposing that Gentiles be admitted to the temple; rather, their mere fellowship with Gentiles, in the context of general opposition against Christians, would have been sufficient to explain the charges brought against the Hellenists in connection with the temple and the law. And, in contrast to Simmons, I argued that it was primarily the practice of having table fellowship with Gentiles that offended Jews in Jerusalem, rather than a supposed waiving of the requirement of circumcision, the latter being a unique contribution that Paul would later bring to the church. I maintain that this hypothesis that Gentiles were welcomed by the Hellenists into fellowship while still in Jerusalem explains both the criticism (they spoke against the temple and the law) and the persecution brought against the Hellenists better than alternative hypotheses do.

Second, I looked in particular at Jesus' sayings that challenged his followers to sacrifice their lives for his cause or that implied that they would in some way share in his own fate. I found it to be historically probable that Jesus would have anticipated his own death, if not all the details of it, and that this provided a plausible context for his predictions that his followers would, in one way or another, share in that experience. I then examined Paul's participatory language with regard to Jesus' death on the cross, and found that while a number of sources may have helped to shape Paul's thinking in this regard, none of them adequately explains why Paul spoke of an identification with Jesus in his death. I disputed with Campbell about the cause and effect relationship between Paul's own suffering and his sense of sharing in the death of Christ, arguing that the way Paul speaks of baptism and the Lord's Supper—both being points of identification with Christ—fail to focus on suffering. Drawing on the works of Morray-Jones and Segal, I noted the likely effect of mysticism on Paul's thought, agreeing that his concept of believers being "in Christ" may find its origin there; however, I disagreed, with Segal in particular, that Paul's involvement in Jewish mysticism would adequately explain believers' identification with the death of Christ. I assessed Wedderburn's proposal that the Jewish sense of solidarity provided a sufficient reason for this identification, but ultimately found that it came short owing to Jewish solidarity having in view those being saved rather than the savior. I critiqued Seeley's argument that set Paul's understanding of the significance of Jesus' death against the backdrop of the tradition of the martyrs, and concluded that while there are some similarities between Paul's thought and that of 2 and 4 Maccabees, the key issue of why Jesus' death, for Paul, is not simply a source of inspiration for believers, but is in fact an event they identify with, is still left unexplained. Building on the work of Wagner and Wedderburn, I re-examined the evidence behind the history of religions' assertion that mystery religions had provided the conceptual framework for Paul's concept of dying with Christ. I suggested that while the mystery religions are not irrelevant for understanding Paul (e.g., the experience of identifying with a deity), there is no pertinent evidence that would explain the element of dying with Christ in Paul's thought. A better explanation, I argued, was to be found in the assumption that Paul was dependent on the sayings of Jesus that referred to his followers sharing in his death or to the irony that life was to be found by means of dying. This would explain the common perspective in both Jesus and Paul that the dying being commended was to be an ongoing disposition, rather than simply a description of a conversion experience. Furthermore, I proposed the possibility of a line of connection between Jesus and Paul by way of the celebration of the Lord's Supper, noting the appropriateness of Jesus' saying—"The cup that I drink you will drink"—and the participatory language Paul uses in connection with both of these rites.

And third, I suggested that "new creation" would be an appropriate description of how Jesus understood God's activity being expressed through his own ministry. The evidence suggests that he understood his healings and exorcisms within a new creation perspective, and that he expressed this by means of healing on the Sabbath, by describing his exorcising activity with reference to the overthrow of Israel's enemy and the establishment of God's kingdom, and by making other statements that spoke of a radical newness being expressed in his ministry. Paul also believed that aspects of new creation were breaking into the world. I challenged the view of Nickelsburg and Kuhn, who argue that Paul may have adopted his eschatological dualism—a "now" but "not yet" framework—from Qumran, by arguing that the Qumran perspective is better described as a cosmological dualism—an experience of heaven while still on earth—rather than an eschatological one. I also raised some questions for the common assumptions that Paul's eschatological perspective was based on the resurrection of Jesus and the common Christian experience of the Spirit: Jesus being no longer physically present, and the clear failure of many believers to live according to God's will consistently would be obvious pieces of counter-evidence for this hypothesis, suggesting that these two profoundly important aspects of Paul's thought required an interpretive framework for them to be seen as eschatological events—a framework, I argued, such as what Jesus had provided in his ministry. Furthermore, I have suggested that if Paul connected new creation with circumcision of the heart—an image that spoke of restoration—then we could conclude that he thought of new creation in ways similar to that of Jesus who saw people being restored through his ministry. And finally, once the resurrection of Jesus had been interpreted by Paul and other Christians as an eschatological event—a prolepsis of many more resurrections to follow at the end of the age—given the new creation framework that had been established by Jesus, it is understandable why Paul would focus on the resurrection, in contrast to say Jesus' miracles, as the primary evidence of the in-breaking of the life of the age to come into this world, simply given the magnitude of that event in the life of the church. But, had the new creation context not been previously established by Jesus, it is uncertain how Paul and other Christians would have understood Jesus' resurrection.

These conclusions best fit within the "continuity with development" model, first championed by von Harnack, but of course along very different lines than he was advocating. In the case of Paul's mission to the Gentiles, he was emulating the perspective that Jesus exhibited by having table fellowship with the marginalized and the wicked; in the case of the participation language of Paul, he appears to have taken Jesus' teaching that challenged his followers that they would in some sense share in his fate, and has developed the view that believers die with Christ; and it is probable that the new creation framework provided by Jesus was directly responsible for Paul's interpretation of Jesus' resurrection and the common experience of the Spirit as eschatological realities. In each case there is a seed planted by Jesus that develops in new ways in Paul: there are clear lines of family resemblance in each case; in the first case we can actually trace the historical development, whereas in the latter two we can propose plausible lines of connection between Jesus and Paul; but in all cases Paul expresses the reality we saw in Jesus' ministry in new and creative ways.

The project as a whole has been an attempt to move the Jesus-Paul debate forward (i) by taking into account new developments in the study of Jesus and Paul, particularly the renewed confidence in historical Jesus research, and the so-called new perspective in Pauline studies; (ii) by focusing on matters that would have been of fundamental importance for both Jesus and Paul; and (iii) by avoiding major fault lines in New Testament scholarship so that we can engage with a wider audience—in particular, an audience of those who generally are not persuaded that Paul was dependent on Jesus of Nazareth. Evidence of (i) can be found throughout the work, although I have tried not to assume a priori a particular historical Jesus construction or a particular scholar's view on Paul. With regard to defending the authenticity of various sayings of Jesus, I sometimes take issue with the more skeptical views of the Jesus Seminar, and tend towards the views of scholars such as Davies and Allison. And with regard to Paul, I share a view similar to that of Dunn, although my own lines of inquiry lead me in specific directions to distinctive conclusions. Aims (ii) and (iii) were somewhat in tension: scholarly fault lines lie not far from most matters of fundamental importance. I do not think there is any question that the three lines of inquiry I have pursued do in fact focus on matters that were fundamentally important to both Jesus and Paul. While it will be for others to assess, and while I certainly make historical judgments here and there that others may take issue with, for the most part I have tried to avoid areas of scholarly entrenchment. Only briefly did I need to deal with Christology; while I discussed Jesus' expectation of his own death, I stayed away from exploring whether or not, or in what way, he saw his death as part of his vocation; and while my portrayal of Jesus within a new creation framework may be at odds with those who see Jesus primarily as a teacher of wisdom, I have tried to anticipate this by focusing on eschatology in terms of the kind of time rather than the calendrical time.

I have argued that the strategy of looking for Paul's dependence on *perspectives* of Jesus is both complementary to and an advance upon the attempt to find verbal echoes of the life and teaching of Jesus in Paul's letters, as pursued by Allison, Dunn, Furnish, and most extensively by Wenham and Thompson. While the latter enterprise is of value for finding similarities between Jesus and Paul, it is limited by the reality that Paul rarely cites the Jesus tradition explicitly *as Jesus tradition*. In fact, on only one occasion does Paul explicitly cite a saying of Jesus in order to support his argument.[1] If Paul had known a large amount of Jesus tradition, we are left wondering why he did not cite it more, particularly in contexts where it could only have helped his argument: for example, when encouraging the church at Corinth to give generously,[2] would it not have helped to refer to Jesus' teaching on wealth, poverty, and true riches? When criticizing the "super-apostles" who had belittled Paul to the Corinthians because of his poor rhetorical skills and humble conditions,[3] would it not have helped to have appealed to Jesus' teaching on servanthood? When instructing the Galatians to restore a fellow believer who has sinned,[4] would it not have helped to refer to Jesus' teaching about rebuking another disciple who sins and forgiving those who repent? This lack of clear citation in Paul of the Jesus tradition, together with the general paucity of evidence relating to the development of Christianity from the beginning through to the time of Paul, are clear limitations to any attempt to relate Paul to Jesus.

While explanations of why Paul explicitly cites Jesus tradition very little will be speculative, I suggest there are at least three that are plausible. First, it may be that, because he faced opposition from a segment of the church in Jerusalem—that is, from people who could claim authoritatively to know the Jesus tradition—Paul felt that strategically, in order to be most effective, he needed to show how his gospel was consistent with Scripture more than how it was consistent with the Jesus tradition. There are two issues here: (i) his opponents, being from Jerusalem, could claim (perhaps with some legitimacy) to know the Jesus tradition better than Paul did; and (ii) Paul may have believed that the most important strategy for defending his gospel was not to show how it related to the teaching of Jesus, but to show how it was supported by the Scriptures. Thus, in focusing on Scripture, Paul not only plays to his strengths, but he also ensures that the Christian movement does not lose its roots in the story of Israel. Second, it is possible that Paul's knowledge of the Jesus tradition—at least knowl-

---

1. 1 Cor 7:10. When Paul cites Jesus in 1 Cor 9:14, he actually goes on to explain why he does *not* use Jesus' instruction, with regard to earning one's living by the gospel, with regard to himself!

2. 2 Cor 8–9.

3. 2 Cor 10–11.

4. Gal 6:1–2.

edge specific enough to enable him to cite Jesus—was limited. Clearly he reflects some of Jesus' teaching here and there in his letters, but much of this could be due to him becoming familiar with the language of the church in Antioch. While Dodd is certainly correct in supposing that during the fortnight Paul was with Peter in Jerusalem they spoke about more than just the weather,[5] it may be helpful to speculate on what their conversation might have been.[6] I suggest it is more likely that these apostles focused on the *significance* of Jesus for understanding the movement of God that was taking place than on memorizing specific sayings of Jesus. No doubt there was frequent reference to the life of Jesus, but I suspect the goal was not one of passing on the tradition (the early church does not bear the marks of a rabbinic school) so much as it was one of reflecting on the significance of Jesus' life, death, and resurrection for the life and mission of the Christian movement. And third, we should bear in mind that Paul's first-hand encounter with Jesus was with him as the risen Lord, and understandably he spoke out of the experience that had transformed his own life. This is not to say that he therefore did not value the tradition of Jesus of Nazareth, but rather that his conviction of the truth of the gospel and of his calling as an apostle lay in his own experience of God having revealed his Son to him, and it would be surprising then if the emphasis in his writings was not first on Jesus as the risen Lord.

It may be appropriate at this point to suggest further areas of investigation that could build on this study. First, lines of connection between Jesus and Paul could be investigated in more areas that explore the perspectives of them both. I suspect fruitful examinations could be made with regard to the nature of the commitment Jesus and Paul were calling people to—commitment in terms of how one understood God and what God was doing in the world, and how one was to live in light of the traditions of Israel—taking into consideration, for example, Torah, but moving beyond the somewhat simplistic choice of being either pro or con. Some questions arise naturally from this study: while we found an aspect of inclusivity in both Jesus and Paul, it would be fair to ask how they each understood the boundaries of fel-

---

5. Dodd, *Apostolic Preaching*, 16.

6. Presumably, Paul would have had further opportunity to learn of the Jesus tradition through his contact with Barnabas, who appears to have been a key figure in the Jerusalem church and who formed a close association with Paul (Acts 4:36; 9:27; 11:22, 25, 30; 12:25).

lowship, since they both clearly believed some people were excluded; also, it would be good to explore further *how* Jesus and Paul understood the image of the cross was to shape the lives of the faithful—how it affected the values and priorities of the faithful; and finally, further detail with regard to the eschatological expectations of Jesus and Paul, set particularly within the context of the hope of Israel, would help to clarify Paul's dependence on Jesus. Second, as Furnish commented back in the 1960s, explanation needs to be given as to why Paul sounds so different in comparison to Jesus.[7] While I have demonstrated some similarities between Jesus and Paul, I have not focused on their differences. Assuming that Paul was dependent on Jesus, how is it to be explained that he does not act like a typical Jewish disciple passing on his rabbi's teaching? I have suggested some factors involving the difference in their respective contexts, but the question warrants a full-scale study. It would be interesting to consider the implications of how Paul expressed his gospel, in light of the message of Jesus, for the expression of Christianity in different contexts today. And third, a reconsideration of the orientation in Pauline studies is in order. In the twentieth century, debate has focused on whether to read Paul against his Jewish background or within the Greco-Roman context, and indeed against which stream within those broad contexts. Now the question is raised, in what ways should he be understood with reference to the historical Jesus?

---

7. See above, pp. 10–11.

Appendix A

Dating of Ancient Sources

THE DATES OF MANY ANCIENT WRITERS AND THEIR WRITINGS ARE DISputed and the following is meant to serve only as a guide to determine the relevance of a work with respect to the interpretation of the New Testament. Only those cited in this study have been included. Sources used for the dates include the following: Craig A. Evans, *Noncanonical Writings and New Testament Interpretation* (Peabody, MA: Hendrickson, 1992); James H. Charlesworth, ed., *The Old Testament Pseudepigrapha* (Garden City, NY: 1983–1985); the Loeb Classical Library series; and Hubert Cancik and Helmuth Schneider, eds. *Brill's New Pauly Encyclopaedia of the Ancient World: Antiquity* (Leiden/Boston: Brill, 2002–). All dates are CE unless otherwise indicated.

Jewish Sources

Jewish Writers

Josephus	ca. 37–after 97
Jewish historian and apologist	
Philo	ca. 20 BCE–50 CE
Hellenisitic Jewish philosopher	

Apocrypha

Baruch	ca. 100 BCE
1 Esdras	2nd cent. BCE
2 Esdras	1st–3rd cent.
Judith	2nd cent. BCE
Letter of Jeremiah	ca. 300 BCE
1 Maccabees	late 2nd cent. BCE

2 Maccabees	1st cent. BCE
3 Maccabees	1st cent. BCE
4 Maccabees	1st cent. BCE[1]
Tobit	2nd cent. BCE
Wisdom of Ben Sira	ca. 180 BCE
Wisdom of Solomon	1st cent. BCE

Pseudepigrapha

Apocalypse of Abraham	1st–2nd cent.
Aristobulus	2nd cent. BCE
2 Baruch	early 2nd cent.
Biblical Antiquities (Pseudo-Philo)	1st cent. BCE–1st cent. CE
1 Enoch	200 BCE–50 CE
Ezekiel the Tragedian	2nd cent. BCE
The Fourth Book of Ezra	late 1st cent.
Joseph and Aseneth	1st cent. BCE–early 2nd cent. CE
Jubilees	135–105 BCE
Letter of Aristeas	130–70 BCE
Life of Adam and Eve	1st cent. BCE–1st cent. CE
Martyrdom and Ascension of Isaiah	2nd cent. BCE
(Christian additions	4th cent. CE)
Odes of Solomon	late 1st cent.–early 2nd cent.
Psalms of Solomon	ca. 50 BCE
Pseudo-Philo	135 BCE–100 CE
The Sentences of the Syriac Menander	3rd cent.
Sibylline Oracles	2nd cent. BCE–7th cent. CE
Testament (Assumption) of Moses	1st cent.
Testament of Abraham	1st cent.
Testament of the Twelve Patriarchs	109–106 BCE

1. See above, p. 99 n. 183.

Rabbinic Writings

Tannaitic Period:

Mishnah	200–220
Tosephta	220–230
Halakhic Midrashim	
Mekhilta of Rabbi Ishmael	mid–late 4th cent.
Sipre on Deuteronomy	350–400

Amoraic Period:

Jerusalem/Palestinian Talmud	400–425
Babylonian Talmud	500–550
Midrash Rabbah	
Genesis	425–450
Exodus	ca. 1000
Leviticus	ca. 550
Song of Songs	600–650
Pesiqta Rabbati	550–650
Midrash Tanhuma	ca. 800

Christian Sources

Arnobius *Christian apologist*	d. ca. 330
Augustine *Latin Church father*	354–430
Clement of Alexandria *Greek Church father and theologian*	ca. 150–215
Eusebius *Church historian and apologist*	ca. 260–340
Firmicus Maternus *Christian apologist*	4th cent.

Hippolytus   ca. 170–236
   Christian writer and martyr

Irenaeus   2nd cent.
   Church father and Christian apologist

Jerome   ca. 347–420
   Christian theologian

Justin Martyr   103–165
   Christian apologist

Minucius Felix   2nd/3rd cent.
   Christian apologist

Origen   ca. 185–254
   Christian theologian

Tertullian   ca. 150–222
   Christian apologist

Classical Sources

Aeschines   ca. 395–319 BCE
   Greek orator and statesman

Aeschylus   525–456 BCE
   Greek tragic dramatist

Ammianus Marcellinus   ca. 330–400
   Roman soldier and historian

Apollodorus   ca. 180–110 BCE
   Greek historian and Homer scholar

Apuleius   ca. 125–after 170
   Latin philosopher and orator

Aristides   ca. 117–182
   Athenian statesman

Aristophanes of Athens   ca. 446–386 BCE
   Greek comic dramatist

Aristotle   384–322 BCE
Greek philosopher

Arrian   early 2nd cent.
Roman military and political leader

Athenaeus   2nd–3rd cent.
Greek rhetorician and grammarian

Cassius Dio   ca. 155–229
Roman consul and historian

Catullus   84–54 BCE
Roman poet

Celsus   2nd cent.
Anti-Christian philosopher

Cicero   106–43 BCE
Roman statesman, orator, and philosopher

Demosthenes   384–322 BCE
Greek statesman and orator

Dio Chrysostom   ca. 40–120
Stoic orator, philosopher, and historian

Diodorus   ca. 80–20 BCE
Greek historian

Diogenes Laertius   3rd cent.
Biographer of Greek philosophers

Diogenes of Sinope   ca. 408–322 BCE
Greek Cynic philosopher

Dionysius of Halicarnassus   ca. 60–after 7 BCE
Greek historian and rhetorician

Epictetus   ca. 50–125
Greek Stoic philosopher

Erotianus   1st cent.
Greek grammarian

Euripides   ca. 480–406 BCE
    Greek tragedian

Herodas   3rd cent. BCE
    Greek poet and playwright

Herodotus   ca. 48–424 BCE
    Greek historian

Heraclitus   1st cent.
    Greek grammarian and rhetorician

Hesiod   8th cent. BCE
    Greek poet

Homer   8th cent. BCE
    Greek epic poet (Iliad, Odyssey)

Horace   65–8 BCE
    Roman lyric poet and satirist

Hyginus   ca. 64 BCE–17 CE
    Latin philologist

Hyperides   ca. 390–322 BCE
    Greek orator and speech writer

Isocrates   436–338 BCE
    Greek rhetorician

Julian   331/2–363
    Roman emperor

Julius Pollux   2nd cent.
    Greek or Egyptian grammarian and sophist

Juvenal   ca. 55–127
    Roman satirical poet

Livy   ca. 59 BCE–17
    Roman historian

Lucian   ca. 120–190
    Greek rhetorical-satirical writer

Martial	ca. 40–103
Roman poet	
Ovid	43 BCE–17
Roman poet	
Pausanias	ca. 120–180
Greek historian and geographer	
Persius	34–62
Roman poet and satirist	
Petronius	ca. 27–66
Roman satirical novelist and poet	
Panyassis	5th cent. BCE
Greek epic poet	
Philostratus	ca. 172–250
Biographer	
Plato	ca. 427–347 BCE
Greek philosopher	
Plautus	254–184 BCE
Roman writer of comedies	
Plutarch	ca. 45–120
Greek philosopher, historian, and essayist	
Pompeius Trogus	1st cent. BCE
Roman historian	
Porphyry	3rd cent.
Greek philosopher	
Procopius	late 5th–mid 6th cent.
Byzantine historian	
Sallustius	4th cent.
Roman philosopher	
Seneca	ca. 4 BCE–65 CE
Roman philosopher and rhetorician	

Sextus Empiricus   ca. 160–210
Greek physician and philosopher

Sophocles   497/6–406 BCE
Greek tragedian

Statius   ca. 45–96
Roman poet

Strabo   ca. 64 BCE–25 CE
Greek historian and geographer

Suetonius   ca. 69–after 122
Roman historian and biographer

Tacitus   ca. 56–117
Roman senator and historian

Theocritus   ca. 310–250 BCE
Greek poet

Theophrastus   ca. 371–287 BCE
Greek philosopher and naturalist

Thucydides   ca 471–395 BCE
Greek historian

Varro   116–27 BCE
Roman scholar and soldier

Xenophon   ca. 430–354 BCE
Greek historian and soldier

Appendix B

Description of the Pharisees

Since the Gospels portray the Pharisees as the chief opponents of Jesus—at least prior to his last week in Jerusalem—it would be helpful to understand their perspective as accurately as possible. Unfortunately, our sources have limited information regarding Pharisees, are in some cases far removed historically from the first half of the first century CE, and are sometimes colored by their own perspectives. The only writings we have from a self-professing Pharisee prior to 70 CE are those of Paul, but Pharisees would hardly consider him or the Gospel writers to be sympathetic witnesses. The Gospels speak often of the Pharisees, but in light of the post-70 dating of at least three of the Gospels (according to the majority opinion) and the sympathetic view of the rabbis toward the Pharisees, we need to consider the possibility that some of the Gospel texts may reflect the Christian-Jewish conflict in the latter part of the first century. Josephus, who identifies himself as a Pharisee, gives us more information, but his apologetic concerns in commending the Jews to a Roman audience and the Romans to a Jewish one must be kept in mind when assessing his work. And rabbinic sources, the Mishnah and the Talmuds, are notoriously difficult to assess both because of their historical distance from the first century and the way the rabbis shaped the tradition in light of their understanding of themselves in relation to the Pharisees. With these cautions in mind, then, we can now turn to the sources themselves.[1]

1. Omitted from this discussion is any reference to Qumran literature. While it is a matter of debate whether the Dead Sea Scrolls make some reference to Pharisees (e.g., the "seekers after smooth things"), the language is so polemical that its historical value for describing the Pharisees is questionable beyond making very broad strokes. We can safely assume that the sectarians disagreed strongly with the Pharisees, but it is difficult to know what to infer from this concerning the Pharisees themselves.

Josephus

On three occasions Josephus describes the Pharisees in terms of a "philosophy"—alongside those of the Sadducees and the Essenes[2]—and mentions some of its general characteristics. From these descriptions we learn: (i) Pharisees were known for their skill in interpreting the law,[3] (ii) they believed in both divine providence and human freedom, and (iii) they believed that the human soul survived after death and would be rewarded or punished according to deeds done in this life.[4] These may all very well be true, but they clearly fall short of defining the distinctives of a movement. It would appear that Josephus is describing the Pharisees so as to commend them as a legitimate school of philosophical thought, similar to those with which his Greco-Roman readers would be familiar.[5]

Josephus does not mention the Pharisees often in his historical accounts, but the few references we have are significant. Pharisees appear in connection with the reign of John Hyrcanus (134–104 BCE) because they apparently had significant influence over him.[6] He is described as one of their disciples (at least at first) who desired to be righteous and to please God in everything he does, and the Pharisees are described as having great influence over the people.[7] Judging from the fact that after they had a falling out Hyrcanus abolished certain decrees, it appears that the Pharisees had previously persuaded Hyrcanus to enact legislation having to do with the observance of certain tradi-

2. *J.W.* 2.119; *Ant.* 13.171; 18.11. In *Ant.* 18.23 Josephus adds a fourth philosophy, the movement begun by Judas the Galilean, often identified with the revolutionary Zealots.

3. Josephus repeatedly uses the word ἀκρίβεια in connection with the Pharisees' interpretation of the law (*J.W.* 1.110; 2.162; *Ant.* 17.41; *Life* 191; cf. Acts 22:3; 26:5) implying, as Dunn, "Pharisees," 67, notes, "that they were well known as those who interpreted the law with scrupulous exactness and strictness in detail."

4. *J.W.* 2.162–63; *Ant.* 13.172; 18.12–15.

5. Saldarini, "Pharisees," 294, suggests that Josephus' use of the word αἵρεσις ("sect") to describe the Pharisees should be understood in the sense of "school of thought" rather than "separatist movement." Cf. Acts 15:5; 26:5.

6. *Ant.* 13.288–98.

7. *Ant.* 13.288–89. Of the Pharisees Josephus writes: "so great is their influence with the masses that even when they speak against a king or high priest, they immediately gain credence" (13.288; Marcus, LCL). Later he notes that "all prayers and sacred rites of divine worship are performed according to their exposition" (18.15; Feldman, LCL).

tions which had been passed on from their ancestors but which were not written in the law of Moses.[8] Observance of such traditions was a fundamental difference between the Pharisees and the Sadducees, the latter insisting that only what was written in the law (Torah) should be required.[9]

The Pharisees appear again in Alexandra's reign (76–67 BCE). While on his deathbed, her husband, Alexander Jannaeus, advised her that in order to secure her rule she should share some of her authority with the Pharisees because they "had so much influence with their fellow-Jews."[10] This she did, and she also restored those practices that Hyrcanus had abolished.[11] In appreciation, the Pharisees, although previously enemies of Alexander, proclaimed him among the people as a "righteous king" and persuaded them to honor him with an elaborate funeral.[12] And, although Josephus does not say as much, they may have done much to establish Alexandra's rule, for her husband was resented by many for the barbarous acts he committed against his own people.[13]

At the end of Herod's reign the Pharisees appear in the context of some court intrigue. Here again they are described as a group of Jews "priding itself on its adherence to ancestral custom and claiming to observe the laws of which the Deity approves."[14] The details of the intrigue are not important, but it is significant that they were involved in a political plot to see Herod's son, Antipater, succeed him as king.[15] At this time Josephus estimates their number to be six thousand.[16]

And finally, Josephus mentions two more incidents: in 6 CE a Pharisee named Sadduc joined with Judas the Galilean to lead a revolt against the new taxation;[17] and on the eve of the revolution in 66

8. *Ant.* 13.296–97.

9. *Ant.* 13.297–98. These two groups also differed in that the Pharisees were respected by the populace whereas the Sadducees were popular only among the wealthy.

10. *Ant.* 13.401 (Marcus, LCL).

11. *Ant.* 13.408.

12. *Ant.* 13.406.

13. *Ant.* 13.379–80.

14. *Ant.* 17.41 (Marcus & Wikgren, LCL).

15. *Ant.* 17.32–45; cf. *J.W.* 1.567–71.

16. *Ant.* 17.42.

17. *Ant.* 18.4.

CE, Josephus himself, together with the high priests and the leading Pharisees in Jerusalem, tried to prevent the war.[18]

From these incidents we can conclude the following about the Pharisees: (i) they were known for their strict interpretation of the law; (ii) they observed certain traditions that were not written in the law; (iii) at times they had political influence because of their popularity with the people and their ability to persuade the people,[19] which also implies that they had a mechanism to communicate their message;[20] and (iv) they used political influence where they could to shape the life of the nation, probably by enforcing some of their traditions.

Paul

In the one text where Paul mentions that he had been a Pharisee, he warns the believers in Philippi about those who insist that Gentile Christians must be circumcised in order to be part of the people of God, because in his view such an act would demonstrate one's "confidence in the flesh" rather than true faith in Christ Jesus.[21] Then, in order to convince his readers that he knows what he is talking about, he lists his Jewish credentials—which were presumably as good as, if not better than, those of his opponents:

> circumcised on the eighth day, of the people of Israel, of the tribe of Benjamin, a Hebrew born of Hebrews; as to the law a Pharisee, as to zeal a persecutor of the church, as to righteousness under the law blameless. (Phil 3:5–6)

From this we can conclude that: (i) Pharisees were known well enough that Paul could expect a passing reference to them to be understood by people living in Philippi; (ii) Pharisees were well respected, otherwise Paul would not have claimed this as a credential; (iii) Pharisees were distinctive in the way in which they followed the law—meaning either their particular interpretation of the law or their diligence in keeping

---

18. *J.W.* 2.411; *Life* 21.

19. See also *Ant.* 18.15.

20. See Dunn, "Pharisees," 65–66, for a defense of the historicity of the view of the Pharisees in *The Jewish Antiquities* in light of far fewer references to them in *The Jewish War*.

21. Phil 3:2–6; cf. Acts 23:6; 26:5.

the law, or perhaps both;[22] and (iv) being zealous to the point of persecuting opponents was consistent with Pharisaism.

In one other text Paul speaks of his pre-Christian experience:

> For you have heard of my former life in Judaism, how I persecuted the church of God violently and tried to destroy it; and I advanced in Judaism beyond many of my own age among my people, so extremely zealous was I for the traditions of my fathers. (Gal 1:13–14)

Although Paul does not specifically mention Pharisaism here, he is speaking, as in the Philippians text, about his pre-Christian life in which he persecuted the church. Thus, when he speaks about being zealous for the traditions of the fathers, we should probably understand this as an expression of his commitments as a Pharisee. Paul's former persecution of the church should be read in light of the classic examples of zeal in the Old Testament and Jewish literature.[23]

Paul confirms Josephus' view that the Pharisees were known for their interpretation of the law and for their adherence to other ancestral traditions. Whereas Josephus depicts the Pharisees to be at times involved politically, Paul speaks of his own active opposition against the church. Underlying these two, however, may be a similar motivation: the Pharisees in Josephus use political means when possible to shape the life of the nation in accordance with their own understanding of the law and the ancestral traditions, and Paul tries to preserve the life of the nation by removing what he perceives to be a threat.[24]

---

22. Luke's account of Pharisaic Christians at the Jerusalem Council is consistent with this. They insisted that Gentile believers must be circumcised and must keep the law of Moses (Acts 15:5).

23. See above, pp. 110–11.

24. The situation that Paul faced in Galatia may be instructive here. Jewett, "Agitators," 198–212, argues that Paul's opponents were Jewish Christians who, by insisting that Gentile Christians must be circumcised, were trying to avoid persecution from Jewish nationalists who were insisting on strict observance of Jewish identity markers and strict separation from Gentiles. It is plausible that Paul himself could have been motivated by a similar nationalist agenda in the 30s.

The Gospels

It is clear that some of the references to Pharisees in the Gospels are redactional[25] and should thus be read in light of the conflict between Christians and Jews later in the first century who were Pharisaic in orientation.[26] James Dunn, however, offers good reasons to see the controversies in Mark 2:15–28 and 7:1–5 as being authentic.[27] He argues: (i) even if Mark was written shortly *after* the fall of Jerusalem (the minority view), it is not likely that the rabbinic school at Yavneh had by that time developed to the point where it could pressure the Christian community and thereby influence Christians to shape its tradition accordingly; (ii) both of these texts have indications of subsequent editing,[28] implying the traditions are pre-Markan; (iii) the disputes in these texts are inter-Jewish by nature rather than Christian-Jewish— a question of *how*, not *whether*, Sabbath is to be observed, and a question of eating with "defiled"[29] hands, a term that apparently needed to be explained for non-Jewish readers as "unwashed" hands;[30] and (iv) we know from elsewhere that prior to 70 there was concern among Jews for the proper keeping of Sabbath[31] and maintenance of food laws.[32] Dunn concludes:

> Pharisees [appear] as a sufficiently clearly defined group . . . whose most characteristic concern was to observe the law and ancestral traditions with scrupulous care, with a deep desire to maintain Israel's identity as the people of the law, as expressed

25. Some clear examples of redactional insertion of "Pharisee(s)" are: Matt 3:7 (cf. Luke 3:7); Matt 9:34 (cf. Mark 3:22); Matt 12:24 (cf. Mark 3:22); Matt 15:12 (cf. Mark 7:17); Matt 21:45 (cf. Mark 12:12//Luke 20:19); Matt 22:34 (cf. Mark 12:28//Luke 10:25); Matt 22:41 (cf. Mark 12:35//Luke 20:41); Luke 5:17, 21 (cf. Mark 2:2, 6).

26. See, for example, Hultgren, *Adversaries*, 86–87.

27. Dunn, "Pharisees," 69–71.

28. E.g., Mark 2:20; 7:3–4.

29. The word κοινός is used to denote Jewish ritual impurity (Acts 10:14–15, 28; 11:8–9; 21:28; Rom 14:14; Heb 9:13; 10:29).

30. Mark 7:2.

31. 1 Macc 2:29–41; 2 Macc 6:1–6; 8:27; 12:38; 15:3–4; *Jub.* 2.29–30; 50.6–13; CD X,14–XI,18.

32. Josephus, *Ant.* 11.346–47; *Let. Aris.* 128–71; Dan 1:3–17, esp. v. 8; 1 Macc 1:62–63; 2 Macc 11:30–31; 4 Macc 5:1–38, esp. v. 25; 6:18–19; 8:12; Acts 10:14; Gal 2:11–14.

not least in developing *halakoth* regarding the sabbath and particularly ritual purity.[33]

Rabbinic Literature

In developing a critical methodology for reading rabbinic writings for information about the Pharisees, Jacob Neusner argues that consideration should be given only to those traditions that are attached to houses known to exist (Hillel or Shammai), or to sages known to live, prior to 70.[34] From examining the materials in this way, he concludes that the majority of the laws that are contained in such traditions have to do with issues of food, festivals, and Sabbath. He writes:

> Approximately 67% of all legal pericopae deal with dietary laws: ritual purity or meals and agricultural rules governing the fitness of food for Pharisaic consumption. Observance of Sabbaths and festivals is a distant third.[35]

The primary issue of rules governing food fit for consumption is that of tithing. In Jewish law this was the responsibility of the farmer;[36] but from the consumer's perspective, if one sees tithing as being vital and if one does not trust that all farmers tithe properly, then the only way to ensure that all food is tithed is to tithe oneself what one purchases at the market. Regarding issues of purity,[37] Neusner suggests that the goal

33. Dunn, "Pharisees," 71.

34. Neusner, *Pharisees*, 3:301–3. Sanders, *Jesus and Judaism*, 388 n. 59, criticizes Neusner for disregarding the large body of anonymous traditions "which probably represent *common* belief and practice, including large bodies of law on civil matters, worship, feasts, and the temple cult" (emphasis original). But Dunn, "Pharisees," 64–65, notes in response that while no doubt some of the anonymous traditions in the rabbinical writings do pre-date the fall of Jerusalem, it is significant that those traditions that can be specifically attributed to pre-70 Pharisees have largely to do with ritual purity. He writes, "It strongly suggests that these rulings were sensitive matters or matters of dispute among the predecessors of the rabbis, so that relevant rulings were remembered by the post-70 dominant party by their attribution to leading figures of the past or as part of the houses' disputes. The clear implication is that the purity of table-fellowship was thus remembered as a matter of great importance with pre-70 Pharisaic circles or by a group or faction of Pharisees."

35. Neusner, *Pharisees*, 3:304; cf. idem., *Evidence of the Mishnah*, 45–75.

36. Deut 14:22–24.

37. For a summary of biblical purity laws see Neusner, *Idea of Purity*, chap.1; Sanders, *Jesus and Judaism*, 182–87.

of this legislation was to apply at large the purity laws that pertained only to the priests in the temple.[38] And, since the Pharisees, according to the Gospels, opposed Jesus over matters of food, purity, and Sabbath, and since Jesus criticized Pharisees over the matter of tithing, it is often concluded that it was the Pharisees who were responsible for this body of rabbinic legislation.[39] Such a conclusion is partially confirmed by some rabbinic texts that depict the Pharisees as being concerned with ritual purity[40] and others that restrict the Pharisees from eating with or exchanging food with the עַמֵּי הָאָרֶץ.[41]

Neusner also concludes from his study, however, that Pharisees were solely an inwardly focused group: "The rabbinic traditions about the Pharisees as a whole may be characterized as self-centered, the internal records of a party concerning its own life, its own laws, and its own partisan conflicts."[42] He finds no record, for example, of conflicts with non-Pharisees or of political issues, and thus concludes that they appear to be truly sectarian. This conclusion, however, stands at odds with what we saw of the Pharisees in Josephus—apart from his general statement that they kept the traditions of the fathers. Neusner, in fact, admits this.[43] Consequently, he suggests that the Pharisees, under the influence of Hillel, changed their focus from politics to piety.[44]

Such a fundamental change, however, seems implausible for a number of reasons. First, we note that according to Josephus,

38. Neusner, *Politics to Piety*, 81–96, esp. p. 83; idem., *Evidence of the Mishnah*, 50–51.

39. Saldarini, "Pharisees," 5:299. It is sometimes objected that the concern of Pharisees for ritual purity is not in Josephus. His silence on this issue, however, is not surprising in light of Roman association of food laws with strange cults. See Seneca, *Ep.* 108.22: "Some foreign rites were at that time being inaugurated, and abstinence from certain kinds of animal food was set down as a proof of interest in the strange cult" (Gummere, LCL); Cicero, *Flac.* 28.67: Judaism is referred to as "this barbarous superstition" (Lord, LCL); Tacitus, *Ann.* 2.85.4: Jewish rites are referred to as "that superstition" (Jackson, LCL).

40. *m. Ḥag.* 2:7; *m. Yad.* 4:6–7; *m. Nid.* 4:3; *t. Šabb.* 1:15; *t. Ḥag.* 3:35.

41. *m. Demai* 2:2–3; *m. Ḥag.* 2:7. It is possible, albeit disputed, that the word "Pharisee" derives from the root פרש meaning "to separate" or "to interpret," the understanding being that they had separated themselves from the rest of Jewish society for the purpose of rigorous observance of the law. Others think the name relates more to the Pharisees' skill in interpreting the law.

42. Neusner, *Pharisees*, 3:304.

43. Ibid., 304–5.

44. Neusner, *Politics to Piety*.

Pharisees were politically active at the end of Herod's reign, in the revolt over taxation in 6 CE, and again just prior to the Jewish War in 66.[45] Second, the respective purposes of Josephus and of the rabbis need to be considered. Josephus was interested in Jewish political history; he probably considered elements such as food laws to be either irrelevant to his purpose or liable to be misunderstood by his Roman readers. Rabbis, on the other hand, were concerned with the continuing practice of the Jewish faith in the absence of the temple. Historical developments were not important to them, nor were the contents of almost all Jewish literature; what mattered were the legal traditions upon which halakhah could be developed.[46] And third, Anthony Saldarini notes that the emphasis on purity issues as a means of creating social boundaries "is typical of minority groups who are striving to keep their identity and bring about change in a strong society."[47] These were laws that a people subject to a foreign power could still observe and thereby maintain their distinctiveness. Thus, purity and politics are not necessarily mutually exclusive goals.

Synthesis

From these three sources—the New Testament, Josephus, and rabbinic literature—it seems safe to conclude that the Pharisees in Jesus' day were a group of Jews committed to a strict adherence of the law and to certain traditions not written in the law that, at least for some, became expressed in concern over matters of food, ritual purity, Sabbath-keeping, and festival observance. Furthermore, although they did not have political power, they used their position of influence (whatever that happened to be at the time) to try to get other Jews to do the same. From their perspective, the distinctiveness of Israel was at stake. Some Pharisees would even go out of their way to oppose those whom they considered a threat to their program.

45. See above, p. 350–52.
46. Neale, *None but the Sinners*, 36–38.
47. Saldarini, *Pharisees, Scribes and Sadducees*, 286.

Appendix C

Identification with Deities
in the Mystery Religions

IN AN ATTEMPT TO DISCOVER THE NATURE AND EXTENT OF IDENTI-
fication between devotee and divine being in the mystery religions, I
have in what follows given a brief description of both the myth and the
rites of several religions in an attempt to find points of contact—the
idea being that a measure of identification could be assumed if the
devotees re-enacted aspects of their respective myth. The focus has
been narrowed, for the purpose of this study, to aspects that deal with
death. The religions I have selected are those that (i) appear to have
been active in the Hellenistic world during the first century CE, and
(ii) have something to do with death in their myth or rites.[1] I should
add that the relationship between myth and rite in ancient religions
is a complicated one, and I make no assumptions about which is primary—for example, whether the rite is an expression of the myth or
whether the myth is a development from the rite. I give evidence that
there were interactions between the two, and that is enough for the
argument here.[2]

The Cult of Eleusis

The home of the cult of the Eleusian mysteries was the town of Eleusis,
located about twenty kilometers north-west of Athens,[3] but they
were also celebrated elsewhere and their influence was widespread.

---

1. A third criterion might be, those of which we have sufficient information in
order to meet points (i) and (ii).

2. See further, Burkert, *Homo Necans*, 29–34.

3. Klauck, *Religious Context*, 91.

Indeed, this was the most influential and popular of all the mystery religions, due in part, no doubt, to its connection with Athens:[4] Cicero speaks of the "awe-inspiring sanctuary of Eleusis, 'Where tribes from the earth's remotest confines seek Initiation'";[5] and Aristides writes: "the Eleusinian mysteries are superior on every count."[6] The religion promised prosperity in this life and immortality after death.

The foundational myth is recorded in the *Homeric Hymn to Demeter*, an anonymous hymn written ca. 650 BCE in the style of Homer. It tells the tale of Demeter, the goddess of agriculture and fertility, looking for her lost daughter Persephone (or Kore) who had been stolen away by her uncle Hades, the god of the underworld. When Demeter learns what has happened, she leaves the realm of the gods, disguises herself as a woman and comes to Eleusis where she is welcomed by the queen, Metaneira. In humility she declines to sit on the seat of honor, but accepts the offer from the maid, Iambe, of a fleece-covered stool. She sits there in silence with a veil over her face, not eating or drinking, until Iambe revives her spirits by telling jokes. Declining the offer of a cup of wine, Demeter suggests instead a concoction (κυκεών) of barley, water, and mint which she drinks, the poet says, "for the sake of the rite [ὁσίης ἕνεκεν]."[7] After some time, still not having found her daughter, Demeter causes a great famine, and since this has the consequence of fewer sacrifices being offered, it gets Zeus' attention. He agrees to arrange for Persephone's freedom, but just as she is leaving the underworld, Hades tricks her with magic, such that while she is allowed to return to her mother, she must spend one-third of every year back in the underworld with Hades.[8]

From ancient times, this myth has often been interpreted as a representation of the agricultural cycle: Persephone's pattern of alternating between the world of the gods and the underworld is reflected in the annual seasons that allow crops to grow for part of the year, but not for the rest.[9] Burkert notes, however, that such an interpretation is

---

4. Wedderburn, *Baptism and Resurrection*, 148; Burkert, *Homo Necans*, 248, 255; Meyer, ed., *Ancient Mysteries*, 17; Butterworth, "Greek Mysteries," 380–81.

5. Cicero, *Nat. d.* 1.42 (Rackham, LCL); the source of Cicero's quote is unknown.

6. Aristides, *Pan. Or.* 373 [311D] (Behr, LCL).

7. *Homeric Hymn to Demeter* 211.

8. Ibid., 398–400, 445–47, 463–65.

9. Augustine, *Civ.* 7.20 citing Varro; Plutarch, *Is. Os.* 66 [377D]; cf. 69 [378F]; Cicero, *Nat. d.* 2.66; Aristophanes, *Vesp.* 1438; Eusebius, *Praep. ev.* 3.11.9, citing Porphyry; Arnobius, *Adv. nat.* 5.32, 43.

complicated by the facts that nowhere around the Mediterranean does seed stay in the ground for four months before sprouting, and that the Eleusian mysteries were celebrated neither at the time of sowing nor at the time of harvest.[10] Thus, while there may have been a connection with the rhythm of the seasons, the connection was a loose one. Burkett suggests instead that "[t]he myth is shaped not by natural phenomena but by purely human themes: marriage and death, grief and anger, and final reconciliation."[11]

When we turn to the Eleusian rites, we find a correspondence with the myth, as we might have expected from the phrase "for the sake of the rite" cited above. According to Clement of Alexandria, initiates fasted and drank a mixed drink (κυκεών) similar to what Demeter drank.[12] Ovid draws a connection between the myth and the rites when he writes: "because she [Demeter] broke her fast at nightfall, the initiates time their meal by the appearance of the stars."[13] Pictorial evidence from the sarcophagus at Torre Nova and from the Lovatelli urn depict the use of the stool, the fleece and the veil in initiation or preparatory rites, implying, as Wedderburn observes, that "the initiates' posture reflects that of the mourning Demeter."[14]

As the goddess of agriculture and fertility, and as the one who found a way to rescue her daughter from the underworld (albeit temporarily), it is understandable why devotees would look to Demeter for salvation, in terms of both prosperity and immortality.[15] And while

10. Burkert, *Homo Necans*, 260.

11. Ibid., 261.

12. Clement of Alexandria, *Protr.* 2.18: "And the formula of the Eleusinian mysteries is as follows: 'I fasted; I drank the draught [κυκεών]; I took from the chest; having done my task, I placed in the basket, and from the basket into the chest'" (Butterworth, LCL); cf. Arnobius, *Adv. nat.* 5.26. For a discussion of the κυκεών, see Richardson, *Hymn to Demeter*, 344–48; Klauck, *Religious Context*, 96–97. It is peculiar, however, that just prior to this, Clement (*Protr.* 2.17) explains that initiates were forbidden to display grief at a well where Demeter had sat and grieved her lost daughter "lest the worshippers should seem to imitate the goddess in her sorrow" (Butterworth, LCL). Assuming Clement is correct in his observation of their behavior, this would not invalidate the conclusion that in other ways the initiates imitated Demeter.

13. Ovid, *Fast.* 4.535–36 (Frazer, LCL). For a thorough discussion of the appearance of elements from lines 192–211 of the *Homeric Hymn to Demeter* in the Eleusian ritual, see Richardson, *Hymn to Demeter*, 211–17.

14. Wedderburn, *Baptism and Resurrection*, 315–16, citation from p. 316; cf. Burkert, *Homo Necans*, 267–68.

15. Plato, *Phaed.* 69C: the initiated will "dwell with the gods" (Fowler, LCL); *Resp.*

it is true, as Wagner points out, that there are also differences between the myth and the rite,[16] the similarities that do exist certainly give the impression that devotees understood themselves to be participating in the story. Yet it is significant for our purpose to notice that their identification is not with Persephone, who alternates between the place of the dead and the world of the living, but with Demeter. There is no indication that devotees thought that their fate was bound up with that of Persephone.

The Cult of Dionysus

The popularity of the myth and cult of Dionysus, prior to the beginning of Christianity, is clearly widespread as evidenced from the numerous temples and burial inscriptions found throughout the Mediterranean world.[17] Furthermore, in contrast to other mysteries, those of Dionysus were not limited to a specific location and priesthood; they were practiced wherever there were adherents.[18]

A description of the myth of Dionysus (known to the Romans as Bacchus) is complicated not only by the variety of names he is known by,[19] but by the diversity of accounts involving a god by this name: Plutarch says "Dionysus they depict in many guises and forms; and they attribute . . . to Dionysus a certain variability combined with play-

---

363C–D: the gods treat the righteous to a sumptuous feast; Diogenes Laertius, *Vit. phil.* 6.39: the initiated "enjoy a special privilege" in the other world (Hicks, LCL); Plutarch, *Mor.* frg. 178: in the other world the initiated enjoy a land of joy, freedom, and perfection; Isocrates 4.28: initiates enjoy "sweeter hopes regarding both the end of life and all eternity" (Norlin, LCL); cf. Cicero, *Leg.* 2.36: "we have learned from [the initiations] the beginnings of life, and have gained the power not only to live happily, but also to die with a better hope" (Keyes, LCL); Sophocles, frg. 837: "thrice fortunate are those among mortals who have seen these rites before going to Hades; for they alone have life there, while others have every kind of misery" (Lloyd-Jones, LCL).

16. Wagner, *Pauline Baptism*, 75–79.

17. We also recall the attempts to compel Jews in Judea and in Alexandria to participate in Dionysiac practices (2 Macc 6:7; 3 Macc 2:27–30), and the action taken by the Roman Senate in 186 BCE to curb the practice of the cult (Livy 39.14.7–10), all illustrating the wide geographical range of the Dionysian cult.

18. Burkert, *Greek Religion*, 291; Schlesier, "Dionysus," 502.

19. Harrison, *Prolegomena*, 413, lists the following proper names used for Dionysus: "Bacchos, Baccheus, Iacchos, Bassareus, Bromios, Euios, Sabazios, Zagreus, Thyoneus, Lenaios, Eleuthereus," some being local names, others being descriptive titles that became proper names.

fulness, wantonness, seriousness, and frenzy";[20] Cicero lists five different Dionysi, each with different parentage, stories, and cults;[21] Klauck
calls him the most "polymorphous" of the gods.[22] This complexity is
also reflected in the cult: Guthrie identifies several contradictions in
the worship of Dionysus: joy versus gruesomeness, stillness versus
mad frenzy, Dionysus as the giver of good gifts versus Dionysus as the
eater of raw flesh.[23]

The elements of the mythology of Dionysus that are relevant for
our purposes begin with the account of his birth to Zeus, king of the
gods, and Semele, the (human) princess of Thebes. When Hera, the
queen of the gods, hears of Semele's pregnancy and of her relationship
with Zeus, she becomes jealous and cunningly tricks Zeus into killing
Semele before she gives birth. But Zeus rescues the child and sews
him into his own thigh until he is ready to be born.[24] For this reason,
Dionysus is called "twice-born."[25] Now, when Hera learns of his birth,
she orders the Titans to kill him: while he is playing with his toys,
they catch him, tear him to shreds, and boil him in a cauldron. There
are numerous versions of what happens next: according to Diodorus,
Demeter gathers the parts of his body together and causes him to have
another new birth;[26] according to Clement of Alexandria, Athena rescues his heart and so preserves his life, and Apollo gathers his corpse
and buries it;[27] according to Plutarch, while the Titans are destroyed
by a thunderbolt for having tasted the blood of Dionysus, the meaning
of the myth has to do with "rebirth [παλιγγενεσία]";[28] and according to
Firmicus Maternus the Titans also feasted on the child's limbs.[29] One

20. Plutarch, *E Delph.* 9 [389B].

21. Cicero, *Nat. d.* 3.58.

22. Klauck, *Religious Context*, 107.

23. Guthrie, *Greeks*, 145–46.

24. Apollodorus, *Bib.* 3.4.3; Euripides, *Bacch.* 88–104.

25. Diodorus, *Bib. hist.* 3.62.5, 10 (Oldfather, LCL).

26. Diodorus, *Bib. hist.* 3.62.6–7.

27. Clement of Alexandria, *Protr.* 2.15.

28. Plutarch, *De esu* 7 [996C] (Cherniss & Helmbold, LCL).

29. Firmicus Maternus, *Err. prof. rel.* 6.2–4. Cf. Arnobius, *Adv. nat.* 5.19, who
describes the event but mentions nothing of the Titans feasting on Dionysus or of
his coming to life again. On the death and rebirth of Dionysus, see further Otto,
Dionysus, 189–201.

other aspect of the mythology of Dionysus that is worth noting concerns his journey to the underworld to rescue his mother Semele.[30]

There are numerous ways in which the worship of Dionysus reflects its mythology, suggesting that to some extent his devotees identified themselves with the deity. Following the pattern of numerous accounts of Dionysus,[31] Dionysiac celebrations typically involved the consumption of copious amounts of wine.[32] Similarly, celebrations were marked by expressions of ecstasy (not necessarily as a result of drunkenness), as were the accounts of Dionysus:[33] Plato ascribes "mystic madness" to Dionysus.[34] Burkert writes: "One must surrender to the madness and allow oneself to be seized by the god in order to become free and well, not only for the present but for all the future."[35] Not infrequently, the ecstasy took the form of a wild frenzy,[36] again mimicking Dionysus.[37] On two occasions Euripides describes the bacchic women tearing apart an animal or a person with their bare hands and scattering the pieces in a way that recalls the account of the Titans tearing Dionysus apart.[38]

There are indications that the cult of Dionysus involved mysteries: Euripedes includes a benediction on the man who serves Dionysus by performing "the sacred mysteries of Mother Cybele of the mountains,"[39] and he speaks of rites that may not be disclosed to the

30. Apollodorus, *Bib.* 3.5.3; Diodorus, *Bib. hist.* 4.25.4; Pausanias, *Descr.* 2.31.2.

31. Euripides, *Bacch.* 142–43, 274–84, 374–85, 417–23, 651, 707, 769–72; Pausanias, *Descr.* 6.26.1–2; Hesiod, *Op.* 609–14. Harrison, *Prolegomena*, 425, writes: "Intoxication is of the essence of the god Dionysus, it is the element that marks him out from other gods, it is the secret of his missionary impulse"; cf. Klauck, *Herrenmahl*, 107–9.

32. Livy, 39.8.5–6; see also Otto, *Dionysus*, 143–51.

33. Schlesier, "Dionysus," 4.498–502.

34. Plato, *Phaedr.* 265B (Fowler, LCL).

35. Burkert, *Greek Religion*, 292.

36. Livy 39.13.10–13, perhaps reflects the perspective of Romans concerned with order and moral standards when he describes the Dionysiac celebrations as a frenzied orgy of debauchery and crime, even including murder (human sacrifice?): "To consider nothing wrong," he writes, "was the highest form of religious devotion among them." (Sage, LCL).

37. Homer, *Il.* 6.132, in the oldest literary reference to Dionysus, describes him with the adjective "raging" [μαινόμενος]; cf. Pausanias, *Descr.* 2.7.5; Herodotus, *Hist.* 4.79.

38. Euripides, *Bacch.* 734–47, 1043–1152.

39. Euripides, *Bacch.* 72–82 (Kovacs, LCL).

uninitiated.[40] Burkert suggests that the forms of initiation may have varied from group to group and from time to time, some being more sublime, others very wild.[41] Regarding the latter kind we have evidence of the eating of raw flesh (ὠμοφαγία),[42] which is also a distinctive trait of Dionysus.[43]

To what extent does the cult reflect the accounts of the death and rebirth of Dionysus, thereby suggesting an identification with the deity in his death? There are indications that the cult of Dionysus gave its devotees hope for an afterlife: In a letter written on the occasion of the death of their child, Plutarch tries to console his wife—both of whom were initiates of Dionysus—by saying that the soul released from the body is in a better place.[44] In his work, *Isis and Osiris*, he notes that at Delphi they perform rites which recall the account of the Titans tearing Dionysus to pieces, and which are analogous to rites of Osiris in that they deal with the issues of resurrection and regeneration.[45] This relates to his discussion later where he likens Dionysus to nature deities who disappear and reappear again with the passing of the seasons.[46]

40. Euripides, *Bacch.* 470–72.

41. Burkert, *Greek Religion*, 292.

42. Euripides, *Cretans* frg. 472.9–15; Plutarch, *Def. orac.* 14 [417C], is not willing to speak of "rites of the Mysteries," but he notes that the festivals and sacrifices include "eating of raw flesh, rending of victims, fasting, and beating of breasts," and he goes on to say that "these acts are not performed for any god, but are soothing and appeasing rites for the averting of evil spirits" (Babbitt, LCL); Arnobius, *Adv. nat.* 5.19: "We shall also pass by the wild Bacchanalia bearing in Greek the name of Omophagia in which with pretended frenzy and with sanity of mind set aside, you bind around you snakes, and to show yourselves full of the divinity and majesty of the god, tear asunder with gory jaws the flesh of loudly-bleating goats" (McCracken, ACW); Firmicus Maternus, *Err. prof. rel.* 6.5: describes the biannual rite performed by the Cretans: "They tear a live bull with their teeth, representing the cruel banquet with this regular commemoration; and amid the forest fastness they howl with dissonant outcries, feigning the insanity of madmen to create the belief that the crime was not done in treachery but in madness" (McCracken, ACW).

43. Euripides, *Bacch.* 135–40.

44. Plutarch, *Cons. ux.* 10 [611D–F].

45. Plutarch, *Is. Os.* 35 [364F]: "the tales regarding the Titans and the rites celebrated by night agree with the accounts of the dismemberment of Osiris and his revivifaction and regenesis" (Babbitt, LCL).

46. Plutarch, *Is. Os.* 69 [378F]: "The Phrygians, believing that the god is asleep in the winter and awake in the summer, sing lullabies for him in the winter and in the summer chants to arouse him, after the manner of bacchic worshippers" (Babbitt, LCL).

Further evidence of hope for an afterlife can be found in the existence of funerary gifts discovered in people's graves,[47] some gold-leaf inscriptions that have been found in tombs giving instructions to guide the deceased in his or her life in the underworld,[48] and burial inscriptions that speak of the practice of dressing statues of a dead person so that they look like Dionysus.[49] Susan Cole observes: "Dionysus was a god whose myths about a double birth, death and rebirth, and a journey to the underworld made him a figure attractive to those who wished to find a way to escape the anxieties of death."[50] She goes on to note, however, that there is not consistent evidence of a confident hope for the afterlife among devotees of Dionysus. From a study of inscriptions from tombs of followers of Dionysus throughout the Mediterranean world, Cole concludes that:

> Dionysus is not a savior who promises to his worshipers regeneration, but with the stories of his own rebirth and rejuvenation, he is one who makes this life more sweet and the next one, perhaps, only a little less harsh.[51]

Beyond the hope for an afterlife, is there any other evidence of an identification with Dionysus in his death? There does seem to be an identification with Dionysus on a general level in the drinking of wine and the experience of ecstasy. Guthrie comments that "[t]he Dionysiac worshipper, at the height of his ecstasy, was one with his god. Divinity had entered into him, he was *entheos*, and the one name Bacchos covered both deity and devotee."[52]

---

47. Burkert, *Greek Religion*, 294–95.

48. Graf, "Dionysian and Orphic Eschatology," 239–47; Cole, "New Evidence," 223–38; Burkert, *Greek Religion*, 293–94.

49. Cole, "Voices," 279–80.

50. Ibid., 179–80.

51. Ibid., 295.

52. Guthrie, *Greeks*, 174; similarly Burkert, *Homo Necans*, 225: "the drinker of the wine would be drinking the god himself." See Euripides, *Bacch.* 284: after mentioning Demeter who gives food he writes: "But he who came next, the son of Semele, discovered as its counterpart the drink that flows from the grape cluster and introduced it to mortals. It is this that frees trouble-laden mortals from their pain—when they fill themselves with the juice of the vine—this that gives sleep to make one forget the day's troubles: there is no other treatment for misery. Himself a god, he is poured out in libations to the gods, and so it is because of him that men win blessings from them" (Kovacs, LCL); *Cycl.* 519–28.

It is, however, difficult to argue that the practice of eating raw flesh was an identification with Dionysus in his death and rebirth at the hands of the Titans. It is not until at least the third century, possibly the fourth, that we read of the Titans feasting on Dionysus and of the Cretans re-enacting this feast;[53] according to Clement, they tore him to pieces, boiled him and stuck his body parts on spits;[54] according to Plutarch, they only tasted his blood.[55] Furthermore, it would seem to be odd for devotees of Dionysus to be imitating those who killed him and who were punished for doing so. It is interesting that Dionysus adopts a practice that seems to mirror the way he died at the hands of the Titans, but the significance of this is never developed; the eating of raw flesh appears to be simply an act of wild frenzy, and the devotees seem to be imitating their god in this respect.[56]

Otto argues that followers of Dionysus imitated the actions of those in the myths who were also devotees. And these stories often include accounts of persecution—persecution directed against Dionysus, but which his followers share. Thus, Otto concludes: Dionysus was "the persecuted god, the suffering and dying god, and all whom he loved, all who attended him, had to share his tragic fate." Yet Wedderburn counters this by noting that in the stories, Dionysus does not die, but typically escapes. He writes: "Dionysus is one who brings death to his followers, but almost all the stories just mentioned show him escaping."[57] Thus, while there is evidence that devotees identified themselves with Dionysus, there is no evidence that they thought of themselves as sharing in his death.

53. Firmicus Maternus, *Err. prof. rel.* 6.5; cf. Stählin, ed., *Clemens Alexandrinus*, 1:318 lines 5–7, who cites a scholiast on Clement of Alexandria, *Protr.* 2.119.1: "ὠμὰ γὰρ ἤσθιον κρέα οἱ μυούμενοι Διονύσῳ, δεῖγμα τοῦτο τελούμενοι τοῦ σπαραγμοῦ, ὃν ὑπέστη Δόνυσος ὑπὸ τῶν Μαινάδων [For the Dionysiac initiates ate raw flesh, performing this as an example of the mangling which Dionysus suffered from the Maenads]."

54. Clement of Alexandria, *Protr.* 2.15.

55. See Wedderburn, *Baptism and Resurrection*, 323–24, for a refutation of Klauck's argument that the eating of raw flesh constituted an eating of the deity.

56. Ibid., 320–21.

57. Ibid., 326.

The Cult of Attis

The homeland of the Attis cult was Phrygia, and even though there was significant resistance to it due to its orgiastic character, it did become widespread after the sixth century BCE.[58] A number of variants of the myth involving Attis exist. In the Lydian version, which is probably the oldest, Attis provokes Zeus' anger by promoting the cult of the Mother Goddess, and so Zeus sends a wild boar to kill him while hunting. In the Phrygian version, which became more popular, Attis suffers as a result of the jealousy of an admirer: according to Pausanias,[59] a wild creature, Agdistis, in a fit of rage causes Attis to go mad so that he castrates himself and dies;[60] according to Ovid[61] it is the goddess Cybele who in jealousy makes him go mad so that he castrates himself and runs away, but does not die.[62] It should also be noted that none of the variants that depict Attis' death speak of him coming to life again.[63] In one version Agdistis repents and Zeus grants that the body of Attis will not decay; in another version Jupiter (the Roman counterpart to Zeus) grants that his hair will continue to grow and that his little finger will still move.[64]

It has often been argued, from the events in the spring festival of Attis, that a resurrection was celebrated. The "Day of Blood," March 24, was a day of mourning for Attis and was marked by frenzied dancing in which some went so far as to inflict wounds on themselves, some even to the point of self-castration, and in so doing are said to "imitate Attis" (Αττεα μιμέονται).[65] The following day, the "Day of Joy," was marked by joyous celebration. Some have suggested that this implies a belief that Attis was resurrected. Wagner, however, points out

---

58. Wagner, *Pauline Baptism*, 208–13.

59. Pausanias, *Descr.* 7.17.10–12.

60. The death of Attis is not specifically mentioned, but it can probably be safely assumed from Agdistis' prayer to Zeus that he grant that the body of Attis not decay.

61. Ovid, *Fast.* 4.221–46.

62. Several ancient writers speak of Attis' castration without any mention of his death: Catullus 63; Julian, *Or.* 5.167C–169D; Minucius Felix, *Oct.* 22.4; Sallustius, *De diis et mundo* 4.

63. Wagner, *Pauline Baptism*, 217–18, notes a number of accounts of the myth that do not mention Attis' death; cf. Nilsson, *Geschichte*, 2:649–51.

64. Wagner, *Pauline Baptism*, 218–19.

65. Lucian, *Syr. d.*, 15.

a number of problems with this view: (i) it appears that the Day of Joy was a later addition to a festival of mourning, the earliest evidence of it being from the early third century CE;[66] and (ii) there is no explicit evidence of resurrection being associated with the Day of Joy, which is remarkable if in fact that was the significance of the day.[67]

Wagner suggests that the self-castration was "not a genuine, deliberate *imitatio* of Attis, its object is rather assimilation to the goddess."[68] That is, the focus was on becoming like Cybele, not like Attis. However, it cannot be denied that both the ecstasy and the self-castration do mimic Attis. Ovid writes: Attis' "madness set an example, and still his unmanly ministers cut their vile members."[69] The fact that priests were often given the name "Attis," even if it does reflect a common practice in ancient religions, does imply that "his was an example that was not regarded as abhorrent or as something to be avoided, but rather as endowed with honour and prestige."[70] There is no evidence that devotees saw any saving significance in the death of Attis itself. Wedderburn suggests that the hope of salvation rested either on the power of Attis or the power of Cybele to rescue people's souls.[71] But there does appear to be in the annual festival an attempt to identify with Attis in his madness, if not in his death.

One aspect of the cult of Attis that has received much attention is the taurobolium—a rite, apparently not held in conjunction with the spring festival,[72] involving the slaughtering of a bull whose blood is allowed to rain down on a person standing in a pit underneath. It is thought that the person's descent into the pit is like a death, and their re-emergence like a rebirth.[73] This view is, however, plagued with numerous problems: (i) there is no evidence that the descent into the pit

66. Wagner, *Pauline Baptism*, 223–25.

67. Ibid., 225–29.

68. Ibid., 266; cf. pp. 238–39.

69. Ovid, *Fast.* 4.243–44 (Frazer, LCL).

70. Wedderburn, *Baptism and Resurrection*, 330. Wagner, *Pauline Baptism*, 236, argues that it does not follow from this practice that the priest "was deified, or that the destiny of Attis was simply transferred to him." According to Julian, *Or.* 5.167C, the significance of the castration of Attis is found in "the checking of the unlimited" (Wright, LCL).

71. Wedderburn, *Baptism and Resurrection*, 327.

72. Wagner, *Pauline Baptism*, 234.

73. Klauck, *Religious Context*, 127–28.

was thought of as a death—it may just have been a practical means of standing beneath the bull; (ii) none of the ancient texts speak of the taurobolium as a dying and rising again; and (iii) the earliest the taurobolium can be traced within the cult of Attis is to 160 CE.[74]

There is some evidence of a meal in connection with the Attis cult,[75] but, apart from the evidence being late, there is no indication that it involved an identification with Attis.[76]

The Cult of Isis and Osiris

Worship of Isis and her consort Osiris (sometimes identified as Serapis) can be located in Egypt back to the third millennium BCE, and evidence shows that cults devoted to them existed in Italy and Greece several hundred years prior to the rise of Christianity.[77] The myth describing the activities of the deities can be pieced together from the Egyptian Pyramid Texts, although a full account can also be found in Plutarch's essay, *Isis and Osiris*.

The account of the death of Osiris has two versions. The first tells of Osiris' brother Seth, the god of chaos, murdering him, dismembering his body and scattering the pieces abroad. In the second, Osiris dies by drowning in the Nile. In Plutarch's account the two versions are combined. Isis then finds the body, gathers the pieces, mourns over the corpse and buries it properly. Following this there are various accounts of Osiris being resuscitated and raised up to become ruler over the world of the dead.[78]

According to Plutarch, Isis "intermingled in the most holy rites portrayals and suggestions and representations of her experiences," which included "the contests and struggles which she had endured

74. Wagner, *Pauline Baptism*, 244–54.

75. Clement of Alexandria, *Protr.* 2.14: "I ate from the drum; I drank from the cymbal; I carried the sacred dish; I stole into the bridal chamber" (Butterworth, LCL); Firmicus Maternus, *Err. prof. rel.* 18.1: "I have eaten from the tambourine, I have drunk from the cymbal, and I have mastered the secrets of religion" (Forbes, LCL), the last word being a translation of Ἄττεως.

76. Wagner, *Pauline Baptism*, 239–42, argues that the connection that Firmicus Maternus makes between the cup and death (*Err. prof. rel.* 18.2, 8) is due to his belief that such pagan rites lead to death rather than to the devotees' belief that they were identifying with Attis.

77. Ibid., 90–91; Klauck, *Religious Context*, 132–33.

78. See Wagner, *Pauline Baptism*, 117–20.

... [and] her own wanderings,"[79] suggesting there was some correspondence between the myth and the cult. Firmicus Maternus also refers to her devotees searching for an idol, probably in imitation of Isis searching for Osiris.[80] But was the death of Osiris part of this initiation experience such that initiates came to identify themselves with him?[81]

Our main source of information about the initiation rite of Isis in the Hellenistic world is the eleventh book of Apuleius' *Metamorphoses*.[82] It concerns the experiences of one Lucius who is transformed from an ass back into a man at a procession in honor of Isis. Isis appears to him and identifies herself as sovereign:

> the mother of the universe, mistress of all the elements, and first offspring of the ages; mightiest of deities, queen of the dead, and foremost of heavenly beings; my one person manifests the aspect of all gods and goddesses. With my nod I rule the starry heights of heaven, the health-giving breezes of the sea, and the plaintive silences of the underworld. My divinity is one, worshipped by all the world under different forms, with various rites, and by manifold names.[83]

She then instructs him regarding his initiation into her mysteries. In return for his devotion she promises him happiness and security throughout life; if he is especially diligent, she will prolong his life; and when he at last dies and goes to the place of the dead, he will continue to experience her presence.[84] After waiting many days in strict discipline, the time finally comes for his initiation. After a bath

79. Plutarch, *Is. Os.* 27 [361D] (Babbitt, LCL).

80. Firmicus Maternus, *Err. prof. rel.* 2.9; cf. Seneca, *Apol.* 13.

81. See esp. Wedderburn, *Baptism and Resurrection*, 300–315; Wagner, *Pauline Baptism*, 104–14.

82. In the mid-second century CE, Apuleius testifies to his personal involvement with mystery religions in his formal defense against the charge of sorcery: "I have been initiated into many mystery cults in Greece. . . . I have learned numerous cults, manifold rites, and various ceremonies in my ardour for truth and my sense of duty towards the gods" (*Apol.* 55; Hunink).

83. Apuleius, *Metam.* 11.5 (Hanson, LCL). Later a priest states that "both the gates of death and the guardianship of life were in the goddess's hands" (11.21; Hanson, LCL); and after his initiation Lucius prays to Isis as the "holy and eternal saviour of mankind" (11.25; Hanson, LCL).

84. Apuleius, *Metam.* 11.6.

and a purifying sprinkling,[85] the priest takes him into the temple and gives him "certain instructions too holy for utterance" and tells him to fast for ten days.[86] After this, on the day he describes as "appointed for my appearance before the gods,"[87] the priest takes him into "the innermost part of the sanctuary"[88] and he experiences something that the priest calls a "voluntary death":[89]

> I came to the boundary of death and, having trodden the threshold of Proserpina,[90] I travelled through all the elements and returned. In the middle of the night I saw the sun flashing with bright light. I came face to face with the gods below and the gods above and paid reverence to them from close at hand.[91]

On the following day Lucius is elaborately dressed with special garments, given a torch to hold in one hand, and adorned with a crown of shining leaves on his head; he describes it as having "been decorated in the likeness of the Sun and set up in the guise of a statue."[92]

One year later, after his return to Rome, Isis again speaks to Lucius in a dream and instructs him to be initiated into the mysteries of Osiris for, he learns, "[A]lthough the nature of his deity and cult was connected, even unified, with that of Isis, there was still a very great distinction in the rites of initiation."[93] In fact, he undergoes this initiation twice. However, he gives no specific description of his experience.

It is significant to note that, in Lucius' initiation into the Isis mysteries, Osiris is not mentioned at all. Even though he describes some kind of journey to death and back, it is difficult to interpret any of this

---

85. See Wagner, *Pauline Baptism*, 127–35.

86. Apuleius, *Metam.* 11.23 (Hanson, LCL).

87. Apuleius, *Metam.* 11.23 (Hanson, LCL).

88. Apuleius, *Metam.* 11.23 (Hanson, LCL).

89. Apuleius, *Metam.* 11.21, relates the counsel from the high priest: "both the gates of death and the guardianship of life were in the goddess's hands, and the act of initiation was performed in the manner of voluntary death and salvation obtained by favour" (Hanson, LCL).

90. Proserpina is the queen of the dead. Earlier, when Isis first appeared to Lucius, he speculates on her identity, suggesting several names, including the "dreaded Proserpina of the nocturnal howls" (Apuleius, *Metam.* 11.2 (Hanson, LCL)).

91. Apuleius, *Metam.* 11.23 (Hanson, LCL).

92. Apuleius, *Metam.* 11.24 (Hanson, LCL).

93. Apuleius, *Metam.* 11.27 (Hanson, LCL).

as an identification with Osiris in his death. His appearance on the following day "in the likeness of the Sun" could suggest an identification with Horus, the sun-god, but not with Osiris.[94] In any case he seems to be totally taken up with the sovereign power and goodness of Isis.[95]

And when Lucius is initiated into the mysteries of Osiris, there is no mention of Osiris even being in the underworld; he is simply referred to, on the first occasion, as "the great god and supreme parent of the gods, Osiris the unconquered"[96] and, on the second occasion, as "he that is mightiest of the great gods, the highest of the mightiest, the loftiest of the highest, and the sovereign of the loftiest."[97] Not only is there no mention of identification with Osiris in his death, but Lucius does not appear to be aware that Osiris is confined to the underworld. Wedderburn appropriately concludes:

> [T]he complex evidence of the Egyptian cults shows us clearly the initiate and the goddess Isis entering into a relationship in which the initiate throws himself upon the sovereign power of Isis to protect him in this world and the next. . . . [B]ut there is no hint in Lucius' initiation into the rites of Isis that he was identified with Osiris or re-enacted Osiris' sufferings.[98]

Attempts have been made to demonstrate identification with Osiris from Egyptian funerary rites, such as those found in the Pyramid Texts. Rituals were performed on behalf of a deceased person, originally the king, so that he might share the fate of Osiris.[99] One text, for example, speaks of King Unis:

> Atum, this Osiris here is your son, whom you have made
>   revive and live:
> he will live and this Unis will live, he will not die and this Unis
>   will not die,
> he will not perish and this Unis will not perish;
> he will not be taken away and this Unis will not be taken away:
> he will be taken away should this Unis be taken away.[100]

---

94. Wedderburn, *Baptism and Resurrection*, 309–10.

95. Ibid., 302.

96. Apuleius, *Metam.* 11.27 (Hanson, LCL).

97. Apuleius, *Metam.* 11.30 (Hanson, LCL).

98. Wedderburn, *Baptism and Resurrection*, 314.

99. See Wagner, *Pauline Baptism*, 122–27; Brandon, *History*, 21.

100. PT 219 = W 152.

The text goes on to address numerous other Egyptian deities, including Isis, followed by the same last four lines. Thus, just as Osiris was revived in the underworld, so would be King Unis.[101] Wagner notes that after the Eighteenth Dynasty (1550–1292 BCE), such rites were applied to all who died.[102] However, apart from it not being clear that an identification between the person and Osiris is in view,[103] it is significant for our purpose to note that the person in question is already dead. We are not dealing here with living people identifying themselves with a deity in his death.[104]

The Cult of Adonis

The center of the Adonis cult was the city of Byblus in Phoenicia, but there is evidence of its practice in Alexandria, Cyprus, Greece, and Italy several hundred years before the Christian era.[105] According to Pseudo-Apollodorus (who in turn says he is drawing on Panyasis (usually spelled Panyassis)), Adonis, from his infancy, was shared between two goddesses, Persephone and Aphrodite: part of each year he spent with one, and the rest of the year with the other.[106] Although the same writer knows that Persephone spent part of each year in the underworld,[107] in this context no mention is made of Adonis spending part of his year in the underworld:[108] Wagner describes this alternation between gods as "merely a matter of change of address which implies no idea of death and 'resurrection.'"[109] This conclusion seems to be sup-

101. Griffiths, *Origins of Osiris*, 64, notes that these texts represent "the earliest expression in literature of a belief in life after death."

102. Wagner, *Pauline Baptism*, 123.

103. Wedderburn, *Baptism and Resurrection*, 305–6, mentions the possibility that the human may be merely following the pattern of Osiris, like an actor playing a role.

104. The Sed, or Thirty-year Festival—a magical ceremony held every three or four years in which the king identifies himself with Osiris for the purpose of re-establishing his own authority—is not relevant here since it was only for the king. See Wagner, *Pauline Baptism*, 121.

105. Ibid., 173–78.

106. Apollodorus, *Bib.* 3.14.4.

107. Apollodorus, *Bib.* 1.5.3.

108. Hyginus, *Fab.* 251, lists Adonis as one of those who was permitted to return from the underworld.

109. Wagner, *Pauline Baptism*, 181. On the difficulty in seeing Adonis as a "dying and rising god," see ibid., 178–201; Wedderburn, *Baptism and Resurrection*, 201–3.

ported by the fact that at the end of his report Apollodorus mentions that Adonis was killed by a boar while hunting.[110] This latter account is elaborated by Ovid:[111] when news of Adonis' death reached Aphrodite (here called Cytherea), she tore her clothes and her hair, beat her breasts, and spoke words mourning his death. She then took some of his blood and sprinkled it, mixed with nectar, on the ground, whereupon a flower soon sprang up, but because of its frailty it was quickly killed by the wind.

According to Ovid, Aphrodite predicted that the event of Adonis' death would be remembered every year: "My grief, Adonis, shall have an enduring monument, and each passing year in memory of your death shall give an imitation of my grief."[112] Interestingly, however, it is her grief rather than his death that is said to be the focus of attention. And this seems to be born out in what we know of the annual summer festival, Adonia, in which devotees mourned the death of Adonis.[113] According to Plutarch this involved laying out images of Adonis for burial and women mimicking burial rites, beating their breasts, wailing, and singing dirges;[114] Theocritus recites a dirge which concluded with a supplication to Adonis for grace for another year.[115] The Gardens of Adonis were planted around this time, in which plants were made to grow rapidly; but rather than symbolizing the resurrection of Adonis, as was argued at one time,[116] these gardens are more likely an image of the transience of life.[117]

110. Cf. Firmicus Maternus, *Err. prof. rel.* 9.1; Athenaeus, *Deipn.* 2.69.b; Ovid, *Metam.* 10.708–16; cf. 10.542–44.

111. Ovid, *Metam.* 10.708–39; cf. 10.542–44.

112. Ovid, *Metam.* 10.725–28 (Miller, LCL).

113. Aristophanes, *Lys.* 388–98; Ammianus Marcellinus 19.1.11.

114. Plutarch, *Alc.* 18.3; *Nic.* 13.7. Elsewhere he (*Quaest. conv.* 4.5.3 [671B]) likens the festivals of Adonis to those of Dionysus.

115. Theocritus 15.100–144.

116. Frazer, *Golden Bough*, 341–47.

117. Julian, *Caesars* 329D: "They bloom for a little space and fade forthwith" (Wright, LCL); Plato, *Phaedr.* 276B: the Gardens of Adonis are used as an example of poor husbandry; Plutarch, *Sera* 17 [560C]: the Gardens of Adonis are given as an example of something that withers quickly; Theophrastus, *Caus. plant.* 1.12.2: the Gardens of Adonis are likened to "cuttings that run up at once [but that] turn out weak in the end and bear no fruit" (Einarson & Link, LCL). See Wagner, *Pauline Baptism*, 189–93.

In all of this, if there is any identification between the devotees and the deity, it is with the grieving Aphrodite rather than with the dead Adonis. Wagner argues that there is no evidence, prior to the second century CE, of any kind of identification with Adonis as there typically was in mystery religions. He denies that Adonis shares his life with his adherents,[118] that followers believed in a personal resurrection,[119] that they shared a mystical union with Adonis,[120] or that their destiny was dependent on that of Adonis.[121] The significance of Adonis' death seems to be that it speaks of the transience and tragedy of life—not something to be identified with, but rather something to be mourned.

The Cult of Mithras

Study of the cult of Mithras must proceed differently from study of other cults due to differing kinds of evidence: in contrast to other mystery religions, we have almost no literary descriptions of the cult of Mithras, but we have an abundance of structural, iconographic, and epigraphic evidence. Consequently, it is not possible for us to compare the myth with the ritual, as we have with the other cults. From what we do know of the cult, however, we can draw some conclusions regarding the likelihood that it served as a source for Paul's thought.

What do we know about Mithraism?[122] We know that it flourished more in the Latin-speaking west than in the Greek-speaking east, that all the members were male, with a large proportion being soldiers, officials in the empire's organizational structures, or from wealthy families. Roger Beck concludes that this was not so much a religion as it was a collegium, and that it was "a cult for loyalists and conformists that replicated within the sacred sphere the systems and values of the secular. It was not a religion for failures, the disaffected, social

118. Ibid., 201–2.

119. Ibid., 202–3.

120. Ibid., 203–4.

121. Ibid., 204–5.

122. For a survey of research on the cult of Mithras, see Beck, "Mithraism since Cumont," 2002–2115; idem., "Mithraism, 1984–2003," 3–23.

outsiders or the unworldly."[123] Reinhold Merkelbach has labeled it "the Religion of loyalty";[124] Walter Burkert likens it to the Freemasons.[125]

Regarding the practices of the cult, we know that members met in cave-like structures called Mithraea where they performed initiations and ate sacred meals;[126] there is no evidence that sacrifices were offered either within the Mithraea or elsewhere.[127] Furthermore, there is no evidence that there was a public aspect to the cult, as there was with other mystery religions; everything seems to have occurred within the Mithraea, and recruitment was conducted simply by word of mouth. According to Porphyry, the initiation involves "explaining to [the candidate] the downward journey of souls and their subsequent return"[128]—that is, they involved some kind of soul-journey.[129] The most important iconographic image for the cult—prominent in almost all of the Mithraea that have been discovered—involves a portrayal of Mithras slaying a bull (a tauroctony)[130] which was in some sense interpreted salvifically: an inscription from the Mithraeum under the Church of Santa Prisca in Rome reads, "you have saved us after having shed the eternal blood."[131] The second most important iconographic image shows Mithras and Sol celebrating a banquet together on the hide of the slain bull, suggesting that the meal shared in the Mithraea had sacramental significance to them.

123. Beck, "Mysteries of Mithras," 177–78, citation from p. 178.

124. Merkelbach, *Mithras*, 153–88 (my translation).

125. Burkert, *Mystery Cults*, 41.

126. On the Mithraea, see Beck, "Mithraism since Cumont," 2090; Lease, "Mithraism and Christianity," 1321.

127. Beck, "Mysteries of Mithras," 182–83.

128. Porphyry, *Antr. nymph.*, 6 (Lamberton); cf. Beck, *Mithras Cult*, 41–42.

129. There were seven grades in the cult, each involving initiation: see Beck, "Mysteries of Mithras," 180–82; idem., "Mithraism since Cumont," 2090–93.

130. Vermaseren, *Mithras*, 67, describes the iconographic convention in the following way: "the god, young and supple, strong as Herakles himself, forces down the heavy animal with his knee and, holding up its head by one horn or the nostrils, thrusts his dagger deep into the bull's heart."

131. Vermaseren and van Essen, *Excavations*, 217. These authors comment: "[Mithras] has saved his faithful followers by killing the bull, and in each of his sanctuaries therefore this representation is present. In the S. Prisca grotto this scene is conceived in a very original and beautiful way. In some representations the blood of the bull immediately changes into ears of corn, and ears of corn sometimes spring out from the bull's tail in the moment that the animal dies" (218).

There is some evidence to suggest that the cult of Mithras existed as early as the first century CE. According to Plutarch, pirates from Cilicia "offered strange sacrifices of their own at Olympus, and celebrated there certain secret rites, among which those of Mithras continue to the present time, having been first instituted by them."[132] If he is correct, this would place the cult in Lycia-Pamphylia as early as 67 BCE. A comment by Statius (ca. 40–79) may connect Mithras with a tauroctony,[133] although this is debated.[134] And Dio Cassius tells of one Tiridates revering Nero with the words, "I have come to thee, my god, to worship thee as I do Mithras."[135] The difficulty with these statements, however, is that archaeological evidence for the cult does not appear until the beginning of the second century CE, and when it does appear, it does so in a number of diverse sites at the same time.[136] No satisfying explanation has been given to resolve this discrepancy.

Assuming the cult of Mithras did exist during the first century CE, is there any evidence to suggest that Paul may have been influenced by it? That there were similarities between Mithraism and Christianity is evident from the comments of Christian apologists who saw the two as rivals: in the second century, both Justin Martyr and Tertullian charged that the cult of Mithras was a demonic imitation and corruption of Christian practices.[137] The history of religions school, however, from the beginning of the twentieth century, sought to explain the similarity in terms of borrowing in the opposite direction, namely that Paul was shaped by Mithraism. Thus Bultmann, to take one example, commenting on the Lord's Supper as a sacramental meal, writes: "in the mysteries . . . it is communion with a once dead and risen deity, in

132. Plutarch, *Pomp.* 24.5 (Perrin, LCL).

133. Statius, *Theb.* 1.719–20: "Mithras, that beneath the rocky Persean cave strains at the reluctant-following horns" (Mozley, LCL).

134. Beck, "Mithraism since Cumont," 2073, notes that the iconography does not depict Mithras taking hold of the bulls' horns as indicated in Statius' saying.

135. Cassius Dio, 62.5.2 (Cary, LCL).

136. Gordon, "Mithraism," 6089.

137. Justin, *Dial.* 70, 78; 1 *Apol.* 66; Tertullian, *Bapt.* 5; *Cor.* 15; *Praescr.* 40; cf. Origen, *Cels.* 6.22; Jerome, *Epist.* 107.2. While now generally considered to be an exaggeration, in 1882 Renan, *Marc-Aurèle*, 579, went so far as to say, "If Christianity had been stopped in its growth by some mortal illness, the world would have been Mithraic" (my translation).

whose fate the partaker receives a share through the sacramental meal, as we know from the mysteries of Attis and Mithra."[138]

Providing a basis for this view was the work of Franz Cumont whose interpretation of Mithraism dominated the field from the beginning of the twentieth century through to the 1970s.[139] He argued that Mithras was the Latin and Greek form of the Persian god, Mithra, and that the cult of Mithras was essentially a transplant of a Persian religion. This was the needed key to understanding Mithraism: the elements of the cult were interpreted in light of supposed Persian parallels. Of particular importance was the (supposed) association of Mithra with an Iranian myth involving the slaying of the cosmic bull which resulted in bringing life to the world.[140] In fact, there is no evidence of an Iranian myth in which Mithra slays a bull. There is, however, a myth in a ninth-century CE Zoroastrian text, the Bundahishn ("Original Creation"), which tells of Ahura Mazda—the supremely good god who was an ally of Mithra—creating a bull, and of Ahriman—the evil god—killing it, but with the result that all kinds of life flowed out from the body of the bull. Based on this myth, Cumont then hypothesized that a variant form of the myth had developed with Mithra as the bull-slayer.[141] Vermaseren even goes so far as to query, "Is it then possible that Mithras, personified in the bull, was thought of as killing himself only to be resurrected?"[142] But now we are truly into flights of fancy: there is no evidence, Iranian or Roman, of Mithra/Mithras being identified with the bull or of the bull rising from the dead.

In the latter half of the twentieth century, however, Cumont's dominance began to be undermined as numerous scholars challenged his hypothesis. The net effect of this challenge was the breaking of the interpretive link with Persian sources. It was still acknowledged that there were some Persian connections—the name Mithras implies as much; but what was questioned was whether the elements of the cult of Mithras bore the same significance as elements from Persian religions.[143] Perhaps the most significant development that arose was the

---

138. Bultmann, *Theology*, 1:148.

139. Cumont, *Textes et monuments*.

140. Cumont, *Mysteries of Mithra*, 135–37.

141. Vermaseren, *Mithras*, 68–69; Ulansey, *Origins*, 8–9.

142. Vermaseren, *Mithras*, 68.

143. Ulansey, *Origins*, 3–24; Gordon, "Mithraism," 6088–89.

astrological interpretation of the tauroctony. No longer was the image of Mithras slaying the bull seen as a mythic death that brought life; rather, it was now being read as a star map. David Ulansey, for example, argues that Mithras represents Perseus, the constellation that appears directly above Taurus (the bull) in the sky.[144] He argues that the cult of Mithras began among Stoic intellectuals in Tarsus who, in learning of Hipparchus' discovery of the precession of the earth sometime in the second century BCE, identified the locally popular god, Perseus, as the one responsible for this phenomenon. But, in an effort to maintain the secrecy of the cult, they called the god Mithras, drawing on the long-standing Persian influence in that city.[145] What developed was a cult that addressed "the widespread longing in the Graeco-Roman world for a connection to a power capable of overcoming the forces of the cosmos which, according to astrological doctrine, were in control of human destiny."[146]

The significance of this change in the understanding of the Mithras cult, for our purposes, is that there appear to be no grounds whatsoever for seeing in this cult an identification with a deity, let alone identification with one who dies. The evidence for drawing such a connection with Paul's thought is entirely lacking. And as for similarities between Christianity and Mithraism, these can be explained in terms of two contemporary religions sharing the same culture and addressing the same needs. Gary Lease comments:

> Christianity . . . drank deeply at the same wells from which all other Hellenistic religions of late antiquity were drinking for the very simple reason that it was competing for the same people and striving to meet their demands and needs. Thus it is not at all surprising . . . that Christianity appeared to share, and in fact in many cases did share, many of the same conceptions, beliefs, hopes and practices of the Mediterranean Basin's widely varied populations and cultures.[147]

144. Ulansey, *Origins*, 25–39.

145. Ibid., 67–94.

146. Ibid., 86.

147. Lease, "Mithraism and Christianity," 1328; cf. Beck, "Mithraism since Cumont," 2096.

Non-Specific References

There are two more relevant texts that speak of death in the context of mystery religions, but which are not explicit with regard to which religion is in view. Writing in the second century CE, Plutarch draws an analogy between literal death and initiation experiences:

> In this world it [the soul] is without knowledge, except when it is already at the point of death; but when that time comes, it has an experience like that of men who are undergoing initiation into great mysteries; and so the verbs *teleutân* (die) and *teleisthai* (be initiated), and the actions they denote, have a similarity. In the beginning there is straying and wandering, the weariness of running this way and that, and nervous journeys through darkness that reach no goal, and then immediately before the consummation every possible terror, shivering and trembling and sweating and amazement. But after this a marvellous light meets the wanderer, and open country and meadow lands welcome him; and in that place there are voices and dancing and the solemn majesty of sacred music and holy visions. And amidst these, he walks at large in new freedom, now perfect and fully initiated, celebrating the sacred rites, a garland upon his head, and converses with pure and holy men; he surveys the uninitiated, unpurified mob here on earth, the mob of living men who, herded together in mirk and deep mire, trample one another down and in their fear of death cling to their ills, since they disbelieve in the blessings of the other world. For the soul's entanglement with the body and confinement in it are against nature, as you may discern from this.[148]

This does suggest that the initiation experience can be described as a kind of death, but there is no suggestion here of an identification with a deity who has died. The fourth-century Christian apologist, Julius Firmicus Maternus, described part of a mystery celebration in the following way:

> On a certain night a statue is laid flat on its back on a bier, where it is bemoaned in cadenced plaints. Then when the worshipers have had their fill of feigned lamentation, a light is brought in. Next a priest anoints the throats of all who were mourning, and once that is done he whispers in a low murmur:

148. Plutarch, *Mor.* frg. 178 (Sandbach, LCL).

Θαρρεῖτε μύσται τοῦ θεοῦ σεσωσμένου ·
ἔσται γὰρ ἡμῖν ἐκ πόνων σωτηρία.

("Rejoice, O mystai! Lo, our god appears as saved!
And we shall find salvation, springing from our woes.")[149]

This cult, according to Firmicus Maternus, is a parody of Christianity. But unlike Christianity, while the death of their god is apparent, there is no mention, let alone evidence, of his resurrection.[150] And when he goes on to say, "So you should die as he dies, and you should live as he lives,"[151] Firmicus Maternus is speaking ironically meaning that the fate of the devotees is as doomed as their lifeless stone idol. It is difficult to conclude from this parody that, although there is clearly a change of mood from sorrow to joy at the mention of the salvation of their god, there is an identification with this god.[152]

Conclusions

Based on this survey we can draw the following conclusions: (i) devotees of mystery religions did appear to identify themselves with a deity; (ii) mystery religions often tell of a deity who dies or who goes to the place of the dead, but it is difficult to find anything akin to a resurrection of such a deity; (iii) the experience of initiation was often described in terms of death; but (iv) there is little evidence to show that devotees identified themselves with a deity in his or her death, and the evidence we do have is later than the first century CE.

---

149. Firmicus Maternus, *Err. prof. rel.* 22.1 (Forbes, ACW). Note that the Greek text might also be translated: "Rejoice, O mystai of the god who has been saved; for salvation from sorrows is ours."

150. Firmicus Maternus, *Err. prof. rel.* 22.2.

151. Firmicus Maternus, *Err. prof. rel.* 22.3 (Forbes, ACW).

152. Wedderburn, *Baptism and Resurrection*, 330.

Bibliography

Primary Sources

Jewish Sources

The Apocrypha and Pseudepigrapha of the Old Testament in English with Introductions and Critical and Explanatory Notes to the Several Books. Edited by R. H. Charles. 2 vols. Oxford: Clarendon, 1913.

The Aramaic Bible. Vol. 5A: *Targum Neofiti 1: Deuteronomy: Translated, with Apparatus and Notes.* Translated by Martin McNamara. Edinburgh: T. & T. Clark, 1997.

———. Vol. 5B: *The Targum Pseudo-Jonathan: Deuteronomy: Translated, with Apparatus and Notes.* Translated by Ernest G. Clarke. Edinburgh: T. & T. Clark, 1998.

———. Vol. 8: *The Targum Onqelos to Leviticus and the Targum Onqelos to Numbers: Translated, with Apparatus and Notes.* Translated by Bernard Grossfeld. Edinburgh: T. & T. Clark, 1988.

———. Vol. 9: *The Targum Onqelos to Deuteronomy: Translated, with Apparatus, and Notes.* Translated by Bernard Grossfeld. Edinburgh: T. & T. Clark, 1988.

———. Vol. 11: *The Isaiah Targum: Introduction, Translation, Apparatus and Notes.* Translated by Bruce D. Chilton. Wilmington, DE: Michael Glazier, 1987.

———. Vol. 14: *The Targum of the Minor Prophets: Translated, with a Critical Introduction, Apparatus, and Notes.* Translated by Kevin J. Cathcart and Robert P. Gordon. Wilmington, DE: Michael Glazier, 1989.

———. Vol. 19: *The Targum of Ruth: Translated, with Apparatus and Notes.* Translated by D. R. G. Beattie. Edinburgh: T. & T. Clark, 1994.

The Babylonian Talmud. Edited by Isidore Epstein. 18 vols. London: Soncino, 1978.

The Complete Dead Sea Scrolls in English. Edited by Geza Vermes. New York: Allen Lane/Penguin, 1997.

The Dead Sea Scrolls: A New Translation. Edited by Michael Wise, Martin Abegg, and Edward Cook. San Francisco: HarperSanFrancisco, 1996.

The Dead Sea Scrolls: Hebrew, Aramaic, and Greek Texts with English Translations. Vol. 4B: *Angelic Liturgy: Songs of the Sabbath Sacrifice.* Translated by James H. Charlesworth and Carol A. Newsom. Louisville, KY: Westminster John Knox, 1999.

García Martínez, Florentino, and Eibert J. C. Tigchelaar, eds. *The Dead Sea Scrolls: Study Edition.* 2 vols. Leiden: Brill, 1997.

The Gospel of Thomas: The Hidden Sayings of Jesus. Translated by Marvin Meyer. San Francisco: HarperSanFrancisco, 1992.

Hebrew-English Edition of the Babylonian Talmud. Edited by Isidore Epstein. 30 vols. London: Soncino, 1984–1990.

The Holy Bible from Ancient Eastern Manuscripts Containing the Old and New Testaments Translated from the Peshitta, the Authorized Bible of the Church of the East. Translated by George M. Lamsa. Philadelphia: Holman, 1957.

Josephus. Translated by H. St. J. Thackeray, et al. 9 vols. LCL. London: Heinemann, 1926–1965.

Mekilta of Rabbi Ishamel. Translated by Jacob Z. Lauterbach. 3 vols. Philadelphia: Jewish Publication Society of America, 1933.

The Midrash on the Psalms. Translated by William G. Braude. 2 vols. YJS. New Haven, CT: Yale University Press, 1959.

The Midrash Rabbah. Translated by H. Freedman, S. M. Lehrman, J. Israelstam, Judah J. Slotki, J. Rabinowitz, A. Cohen, L Rabinowitz, and Maurice Simon. Edited by H. Freedman and Maurice Simon. Compact ed. 5 vols. London: Soncino, 1977.

Midrash Tanhuma: Translated into English with Introduction, Indices, and Brief Notes. Edited by John T. Townsend. 3 vols. Jersey City, NJ: KTAV, 1989–2003.

The Mishnah: A New Translation. Edited by Jacob Neusner. New Haven, CT: Yale University Press, 1988.

The Mishnah: Translated from the Hebrew with Introduction and Brief Explanatory Notes. Translated by Herbert Danby. Oxford: Oxford University Press, 1933.

The Old Testament Pseudepigrapha. Edited by James H. Charlesworth. 2 vols. Garden City, NY: Doubleday, 1983–1985.

Pesikta Rabbati: Discourses for Feasts, Fasts, and Special Sabbaths. Translated by William G. Braude. 2 vols. YJS. New Haven, CT: Yale University Press, 1968.

Philo of Alexandria. Translated by F. H. Colson, G. H. Whitaker, and Ralph Marcus. 10 vols. LCL. Cambridge, MA: Harvard University Press, 1929–1962.

Septuaginta: Id est Vetus Testamentum graece iuxta LXX interpretes. Edited by Alfred Rahlfs. 2 vols. Stuttgart: Württembergisch Bibelanstalt, 1935.

Sifre: A Tannaitic Commentary on the Book of Deuteronomy. Translated by Reuven Hammer. YJS. New Haven, CT: Yale University Press, 1986.

The Talmud of the Land of Israel. Translated by Jacob Neusner, et al. Edited by Jacob Neusner. 35 vols. Chicago: University of Chicago Press, 1982–1994.

Die Texte aus Qumran: Hebräisch und Deutsch: Mit masoretischer Punktation. Edited by Eduard Lohse. Darmstadt: Wissenschaftliche Buchgesellschaft, 1986.

The Tosefta: Translated from the Hebrew with a New Introduction. Translated by Jacob Neusner. 2 vols. Peabody, MA: Hendrickson, 2002.

Christian Sources

The Ante-Nicene Fathers: Translations of the Writings of the Fathers Down to A.D. 325. Edited by Alexander Roberts and James Donaldson. 10 vols. 1885–1887. Reprint, Grand Rapids, MI: Eerdmans, 1956.

Arnobius of Sicca. *The Case against the Pagans.* Translated by George E. McCracken. ACW 7–8. Ramsey, NJ: Newman, 1949.

Clement of Alexandria. *Exhortation to the Greeks; The Rich Man's Salvation; To the Newly Baptized.* Translated by G. W. Butterworth. LCL. Cambridge, MA: Harvard University Press, 1919.

Eusebius. *Ecclesiastical History.* Translated by Kirsopp Lake and J. E. L. Oulton. 2 vols. LCL. London: Heinemann, 1926–1932.

Firmicus Maternus, Julius. *The Error of the Pagan Religions.* Translated by Clarence A. Forbes. ACW 37. New York: Newman, 1970.

Hippolytus. *Refutatio Omnium Haeresium.* Edited by Miroslav Marcovich. New York: de Gruyter, 1986.

Horsley, G. H. R. *A Review of the Greek Inscriptions and Papyri Published in 1978.* Vol. 3 of *New Documents Illustrating Early Christianity.* North Ryde, Australia: The Ancient History Documentary Research Centre, Macquarie University, 1983.

Minucius Felix, Marcus. *Octavius.* Translated by G. W. Clarke. ACW 39. New York: Newman, 1974.

Origen. *Contra Celsum.* Translated by Henry Chadwick. Cambridge: Cambridge University Press, 1980.

Stählin, Otto, ed. *Clemens Alexandrinus.* 4 vols. Leipzig: Hinrichs, 1905–1936.

Greek, Roman, and Egyptian Sources

Aeschylus. Translated by Herbert Weir Smyth. 2 vols. LCL. Cambridge, MA: Harvard University Press, 1926.

Ammianus Marcellinus. Translated by John C. Rolfe. 3 vols. LCL. Cambridge, MA: Harvard University Press, 1935–1939.

The Ancient Egyptian Pyramid Texts. Translated by James P. Allen, SBLWAW. Leiden: Brill, 2005.

Apollodorus. *The Library.* Translated by James George Frazer. 2 vols. LCL. Cambridge, MA: Harvard University Press, 1921.

Apuleius. *Metamorphoses.* Translated by J. Arthur Hanson. 2 vols. LCL. Cambridge, MA: Harvard University Press, 1989.

———. "Apology." In *Apuleius: Rhetorical Works*, edited by Stephen Harrison, translated by Vincent Hunink, 11–121. Oxford: Oxford University Press, 2001.

Aristides. Translated by C. A. Behr. 4 vols. LCL. Cambridge, MA: Harvard University Press, 1973.

Aristophanes. Translated by Jeffrey Henderson. 5 vols. LCL. Cambridge, MA: Harvard University Press, 1998–2007.

Aristotle. *The Nicomachean Ethics.* Translated by H. Rackham. Rev. ed. LCL. Cambridge, MA: Harvard University Press, 1934.

Athenaeus. *The Deipnosophists.* Translated by Charles Burton Gulick. 7 vols. LCL. Cambridge, MA: Harvard University Press/London: Heinmann, 1927–1941.

Barrett, C. K., ed. *The New Testament Background: Selected Documents.* New York: Harper & Row, 1956.

Betz, Hans Dieter. *The Greek Magical Papyri in Translation, Including the Demonic Spells.* 2nd ed. Chicago: Chicago University Press, 1996.

Cantarella, R. *Eripide: 1 Cretesi. Classici greci e latini.* Milano: Instituto editorial italiano, 1964.

Cassius Dio. *Dio's Roman History.* Translated by Earnest Cary. 9 vols. Cambridge, MA: Harvard University Press/London, Eng.: Heinemann, 1914–1927.

Cicero. *De officiis.* Translated by Walter Miller. LCL. London: Heinemann/New York: Macmillan, 1913.

———. *De re publica; De legibus.* Translated by Clinton Walker Keyes. LCL. Cambridge, MA: Harvard University Press, 1928.

———. *De natura deorum; Academica.* Translated by H. Rackham. LCL. Cambridge, MA: Harvard University Press, 1933.

Demosthenes. *Funeral Speech; Erotic Essay 60, 61; Exordia and Letters.* Translated by Norman W. DeWitt and Norman J. DeWitt. 7 vols. LCL. Cambridge, MA: Harvard University Press, 1949.

Dio Chrysostom. Translated by J. W. Cohoon and H. Lamar Crosby. 5 vols. LCL. Cambridge, MA: Harvard University Press, 1932–1946.

Diodorus of Sicily. *The Library of History.* Translated by C. H. Oldfather, Charles L. Sherman, C. Bradford Welles, R. M. Geer, and Francis R. Walton. 12 vols. LCL. Cambridge, MA: Harvard University Press, 1933–1967.

Diogenes Laertius. *Lives of Eminent Philosophers.* Translated by R. D. Hicks. 2 vols. LCL. New York: Putnam, 1925.

Dionysius of Halicarnassus. *The Roman Antiquities.* Translated by Earnest Cary. 7 vols. LCL. Cambridge, MA: Harvard University Press, 1937–1950.

———. *The Critical Essays.* Translated by Stephen Usher. 2 vols. LCL. Cambridge, MA: Harvard University Press, 1974–1975.

Epictetus. *The Discourses as Reported by Arrian; Fragments; Encheiridion.* Translated by W. A. Oldfather. 2 vols. LCL. Cambridge, MA: Harvard University Press, 1925–1928.

Euripides. Translated by David Kovacs, Christopher Collard, and Martin Cropp. 7 vols. LCL. Cambridge, MA: Harvard University Press, 1994–.

Herodas. *The Mimes and Fragments.* Translated by Walter Headlam. Cambridge: Cambridge University Press, 1922.

Herodotus. Translated by A. D. Godley. 4 vols. LCL. Cambridge, MA: Harvard University Press, 1926.

Hesiod. *Theogony; Works and Days; Testimonia.* Translated by Glenn W. Most. LCL. Cambridge, MA: Harvard University Press, 2006.

Hippocrates. Translated by W. H. S. Jones, et al. 8 vols. LCL. Cambridge, MA: Harvard University Press, 1939.

Homer. *Iliad.* Translated by A. T. Murray and William F. Wyatt, 2 vols. LCL. Cambridge, MA: Harvard University Press, 1999.

The Homeric Hymn to Demeter: Translation, Commentary, and Interpretive Essays. Edited and translated by Helene P. Foley. Princeton: Princeton University Press, 1994.

Hyperides. In *Minor Attic Orators,* 2:363–605. Translated by J. O. Burtt. Cambridge, MA: Harvard University Press, 1954.

Isocrates. Translated by George Norlin and La Rue Van Hook. 3 vols. LCL. Cambridge, MA: Harvard University Press, 1928–1945.

Julian. *The Works of the Emperor Julian.* Translated by Wilmer Cave Wright. 3 vols. LCL. Cambridge, MA: Harvard University Press, 1969–1990.

Lamberton, Robert. *On the Cave of the Nymphs/Porphyry: Translation and Introductory Essay.* Barrytown, NY: Station Hill Press, 1983.

Livy. *History of Rome.* Translated by B. O. Foster, et al. 14 vols. LCL. Cambridge, MA: Harvard University Press, 1919–1959.

Lucian. Translated by A. M. Harmon, et al. 8 vols. LCL. New York: Putnam, 1913–1967.

Malherbe, Abraham J., ed. *The Cynic Epistles: A Study Edition.* Missoula, MT: Scholars, 1977.

Ovid. Translated by Grant Showerman, J. H. Mozley, Frank Justus Miller, and James George Frazer. 6 vols. LCL. Cambridge, MA: Harvard University Press, 1976–1984.

Pausanias. *Description of Greece.* Translated by W. H. S. Jones and H. A. Ormerod. 5 vols. LCL. Cambridge, MA: Harvard University Press, 1918–1935.

Philostratus. Translated by F. C. Conybeare. LCL. Cambridge, MA: Harvard University Press, 1950.

————. Translated by Christopher P. Jones. 3 vols. LCL. Cambridge, MA: Harvard University Press, 2005.

Plato. Translated by Paul Shorey, W. R. M. Lamb, Harold North Fowler, and R. G. Bury. 12 vols. LCL. Cambridge, MA: Harvard University Press, 1930–2003.

Plautus. Translated by Paul Nixon. 5 vols. LCL. Cambridge, MA: Harvard University Press, 1979–1984.

Pliny. *Letters.* Translated by William Melmoth. 2 vols. LCL. New York: Putnam, 1927.

Plutarch. *Lives.* Translated by Bernadotte Perrin. 11 vols. LCL. New York: Putnam, 1914–1926.

————. *Moralia.* Translated by F. C. Babbitt, William C. Helmbold, Phillip H. de Lacy, Benedict Einarson, Paul Clement, Herbert B. Hoffleit, Edwin L. Minar, F. H. Sandbach, Harold North Fowler, F. H. Pearson, and Harold Cherniss. 16 vols. LCL. Cambridge, MA: Harvard University Press, 1927–1969.

Preisendanz, Karl, ed. *Papyri graecae magicae: Die griechischen Zauberpapyri.* Translated by Karl Preisendanz. 2 vols. Leipzig/Berlin: Teubner, 1928.

Sallustius, *Concerning the Gods and the Universe.* Edited with Prolegomena and Translation by Arthur Darby Nock. Hildesheim: Georg Olms Verlagsbuchhandlung, 1966.

Seneca. Translated by John W. Basore, R. M. Gummere, T. H. Corcoran, and Frank Justus Miller. 10 vols. LCL. Cambridge, MA: Harvard University Press, 1917–1979.

————. *Four Dialogues: De vita beata, De tranquillitate animi, De constantia sapientis, Ad Helviam matrem de consolatione.* Translated by C. D. N. Costa. Warminster: Aris & Phillips, 1994.

Sextus-Empiricus. Translated by R. G. Bury. 4 vols. LCL. Cambridge, MA: Harvard University Press, 1968–1983.

Sophocles. Translated by Hugh Lloyd-Jones. 3 vols. LCL. Cambridge, MA: Harvard University Press, 1994–1996.

Statius. Translated by J. H. Mozley. 2 vols. LCL. Cambridge, MA: Harvard University Press, 1928.

————. Translated by D. R. Shackleton Bailey. 3 vols. LCL. Cambridge, MA: Harvard University Press, 2003.

Strabo. *The Geography.* Translated by Horace Leonard Jones. 8 vols. LCL. New York: Putnam, 1930.

Tacitus. Translated by M Hutton, W. Peterson, Clifford H. Moore, and John Jackson. 5 vols. LCL. Cambridge, MA: Harvard University Press, 1914–1937.

Theocritus. In *The Greek Bucolic Poets*. Translated by J. M. Edmonds. Cambridge, MA: Harvard University Press, 1928.

Theophrastus. *De causis plantarum*. Translated by Benedict Einarson and George K. K. Link. 3 vols. LCL. Cambridge, MA: Harvard University Press, 1976–1990.

Thucydides. *History of the Peloponnesian War*. Translated by Charles Foster Smith. 4 vols. LCL. New York: Putnam, 1919–1923.

Xenophon. *Anabasis*. Translated by Carleton L. Brownson. LCL. Cambridge, MA: Harvard University Press, 1998.

Secondary Sources

Reference Tools

Abegg, Martin G., James E. Bowley, and Edward M. Cook. *The Dead Sea Scrolls Concordance*. 2 vols. Leiden: Brill, 2003.

Alexander, Patrick H., John F. Kutsko, James D. Ernest, Shirley A. Decker-Lucke, and David L. Petersen, eds. *The SBL Handbook of Style for Ancient Near Eastern, Biblical, and Early Christian Studies*. Peabody, MA: Hendrickson, 1999.

Botterweck, G. Johannes, Helmer Ringgren, and Heinz-Josef Fabry, eds. *Theological Dictionary of the Old Testament*. Translated by John T. Willis, Geoffrey W. Bromiley, David E. Green, and Douglas W. Scott. 15 vols. Grand Rapids, MI: Eerdmans, 1974–2006. [*TDOT*]

Cancik, Hubert, and Helmuth Schneider, eds. *Brill's New Pauly Encyclopaedia of the Ancient World: Antiquity*. 15 vols. Leiden: Brill, 2002–. [*BNP*]

The Compact Edition of the Oxford English Dictionary: Complete Text Reproduced Micrographically. 2 vols. Oxford: Oxford University Press, 1971. [*OED*]

Danker, Frederick W., ed. *A Greek-English Lexicon of the New Testament and Other Early Christian Literature*. Translated by William F. Arndt and F. Wilbur Gingrich. 3rd ed. Based on Walter Bauer's Griechisch-deutsches Wörterbuch zu den Schriften des Neuen Testaments und der frühchristlichen Literatur, 6th ed. Chicago: University of Chicago Press, 2000. [*BDAG*]

Denis, Albert-Marie. *Concordance grecque des Pseudépigraphes d'Ancien Testament: Concordance, corpus des textes, indices*. Louvain-la-Neuve: Université Catholique de Louvain, 1987.

Freedman, David Noel, ed. *The Anchor Bible Dictionary*. 6 vols. New York: Doubleday, 1992. [*ABD*]

Funk, Robert W., Roy W. Hoover, and the Jesus Seminar. *The Five Gospels: The Search for the Authentic Words of Jesus*. San Francisco: HarperSanFrancisco, 1993.

Green, Joel B., Scot McKnight, and I. Howard Marshall, eds. *Dictionary of Jesus and the Gospels*. Downers Grove, IL: InterVaristy 1992. [*DJG*]

Hatch, Edwin, and Henry A. Redpath. *A Concordance to the Septuagint and the Other Greek Versions of the Old Testament (Including the Apocryphal Books)*. Graz, Austria: Akademische Druck- U. Verlagsanstalt, 1954.

Hawthorne, G. F., R. P. Martin, and D. G. Reid, eds. *Dictionary of Paul and His Letters*. Grand Rapids, MI: InterVarsity, 1993. [*DPL*]

Jones, Lindsay, ed. *Encyclopedia of Religion*. 2nd ed., 15 vols. Detroit: Macmillan, 2005. [*ER*]

Kittel, Gerhard, and Gerhard Friedrich, eds. *Theological Dictionary of the New Testament*. Translated by Geoffrey W. Bromiley. 10 vols. Grand Rapids, MI: Eerdmans, 1964–1976. [*TDNT*]

Koehler, Ludwig, Walter Baumgartner, and Johann Jakob Stamm. *The Hebrew and Aramaic Lexicon of the Old Testament*. Translated by M. E. J. Richardson. 4 vols. Leiden: Brill, 1994–1999. [*HALOT*]

Schiffman, Lawrence H., and James C. Vanderkam, eds. *Encyclopedia of the Dead Sea Scrolls*. 2 vols. Oxford: Oxford University Press, 2000. [*EDSS*]

Strack, Hermann L., and Paul Billerbeck. *Kommentar zum Neuen Testament aus Talmud und Midrasch*. 6 vols. Munich: C. H. Beck'she Verlagsbuchhandlung, 1922–1961. [Str-B]

Books and Articles

Abrahams, I. *Studies in Pharisaism and the Gospels*. LBS. New York: KTAV 1967 [1917].

Allen, Leslie C. *Ezekiel 20–48*. WBC 29. Dallas: Word, 1990.

Allison, Dale C. *The Historical Christ and the Theological Jesus*. Grand Rapids, MI: Eerdmans, 2009.

———. "The Pauline Epistles and the Synoptic Gospels: The Pattern of the Parallels." *NTS* 28 (1982) 1–32.

———. "A Plea for Thoroughgoing Eschatology." *JBL* 113 (1994) 651–68.

Andersen, Francis I., and David Noel Freedman. *Hosea: A New Translation with Introduction and Commentary*. AB 24. Garden City, NY: Doubleday, 1980.

Anderson, Bernhard W. *Creation Versus Chaos: The Reinterpretation of Mythical Symbolism in the Bible*. Philadelphia: Fortress, 1987.

Anderson, Hugh. "Maccabees, Books of (Fourth Maccabees)." In *ABD* 4:452–54.

Arnold, J. P. "The Relationship of Paul to Jesus." In *Hillel and Jesus: Comparative Studies of Two Major Religious Leaders*, edited by James H. Charlesworth and Loren L. Johns, 256–88. Minneapolis: Fortress, 1997.

Aune, D. E. "Jesus and Cynics in First-Century Palestine: Some Critical Considerations." In *Hillel and Jesus: Comparative Studies of Two Major Religious Leaders*, edited by James H. Charlesworth and Loren L. Johns, 176–92. Minneapolis: Fortress, 1997.

Baird, William. "Visions, Revelation, and Ministry: Reflections on 2 Cor 12:1–5 and Gal 1:11–17." *JBL* 104 (1985) 651–62.

———. "What Is the Kerygma? A Study of 1 Cor. 15:3–8 and Gal. 1:11–17." *JBL* 76 (1957) 181–91.

Balla, Peter. "What Did Jesus Think about His Approaching Death?" In *Jesus, Mark and Q: The Teaching of Jesus and Its Earliest Records*, edited by Michael Labahn and Andreas Schmidt, 239–58. Sheffield: Sheffield Academic, 2001.

Bampfylde, G. "The Similitudes of Henoch: Historical Illusions." *JSJ* 15 (1984) 9–31.

Barclay, John M. G. "Jesus and Paul." In *Dictionary of Paul and His Letters*, edited by Gerald F. Hawthorne and Ralph P. Martin, 492–503. Downers Grove, IL: InterVarsity, 1993.

———. "'Offensive and Uncanny': Jesus and Paul on the Caustic Grace of God." In *Jesus and Paul Reconnected: Fresh Pathways into an Old Debate*, edited by Todd D. Still, 1–17. Grand Rapids, MI: Eerdmans, 2007.

Barrett, C. K. *A Commentary on the First Epistle to the Corinthians*. 2nd ed. BNTC. London: Black, 1971.

———. *A Critical and Exegetical Commentary on the Acts of the Apostles*. 2 vols. ICC 34. Edinburgh: T. & T. Clark, 1994–1998.

———. *The Epistle to the Romans*. 2nd ed. BNTC. London: Black, 1991.

Bartchy, S. Scott. "Table Fellowship." In *Dictionary of Jesus and the Gospels*, edited by Joel B. Green, Scot McKnight and, I. Howard Marshall, 796–800. Downers Grove, IL: InterVarsity, 1992.

———. "Who Should Be Called Father? Paul of Tarsus between the Jesus Tradition and Patria Potestas." *BTB* 33 (2003) 35–47.

Barth, Karl. *Church Dogmatics*. Translated by G. W. Bromiley, et al. 14 vols. Edinburgh: T. & T. Clark, 1936–1977.

Bauckham, Richard. *Jesus and the Eyewitnesses: The Gospels as Eyewitness Testimony*. Grand Rapids, MI: Eerdmans, 2006.

———. "Kingdom and Church according to Jesus and Paul." *HBT* 18 (1996) 1–26.

Baur, Ferdinand Christian. "Die Christuspartei in der korinthischen Gemeinde, der Gegensatz des petrinischen und paulinischen Christenthums in der ältesten Kirche, der Apostel Petrus in Rom." *TZTh* 4 (1831) 61–206.

———. *Vorlesungen über neutestamentliche Theologie*. Leipzig: Fues's (L. W. Reisland), 1864.

Beck, Roger. "Mithraism after 'Mithraism since Franz Cumont', 1984–2003." In *Beck on Mithraism: Collected Works with New Essays*, 3–23. Aldershot, Eng./Burlington, VT: Ashgate, 2004.

———. "Mithraism since Franz Cumont." In *ANRW*, edited by Wolfgang Haase, 17.4: 2002–2115. New York: de Gruyter, 1984.

———. "The Mysteries of Mithras." In *Voluntary Associations in the Graeco-Roman World*, edited by John S. Kloppenborg and Stephen G. Wilson, 176–85. New York: Routledge, 1996.

———. *The Religion of the Mithras Cult in the Roman Empire: Mysteries of the Unconquered Sun*. Oxford: Oxford University Press, 2006.

Beckwith, Roger T. "The Qumran Calendar and the Sacrifices of the Essenes." *RevQ* 7 (1969–1971) 587–91.

Beker, J. Christiaan. *Paul the Apostle: The Triumph of God in Life and Thought*. Edinburgh: T. & T. Clark, 1980.

Bernstein, Moshe J. "כי קללת אלהים תלוי (Deut. 21:23) A Study in Early Jewish Exegesis." *JQR* 74 (1983) 21–45.

Best, Ernest. "The Revelation to Evangelize the Gentiles." *JTS* ns. 35 (1984) 1–30.

Betz, Hans Dieter. *Galatians: A Commentary on Paul's Letter to the Churches in Galatia*. Hermeneia. Philadelphia: Fortress, 1979.

———. "Jesus and the Cynics: Survey and Analysis of a Hypothesis." *JR* 74 (1994) 453–75.

Betz, Otto. "φωνή, κτλ." In *TDNT* 9:278–309.

Bianchi, Ugo. *The Greek Mysteries*. Leiden: Brill, 1976.

Bickermann, E. J. "The Date of Fourth Maccabees." In *Studies in Jewish and Christian History*, 275–81. Leiden: Brill, 1976.

Blackburn, Barry L. "The Miracles of Jesus." In *Studying the Historical Jesus: Evaluations of the State of Current Research*, edited by Bruce Chilton and Craig A. Evans, 353–94. Leiden: Brill, 1998.

Blatz, Beate. "Introduction to 'The Coptic Gospel of Thomas.'" In *New Testament Apocrypha*, edited by Wilhelm Schneemelcher, translated by R. McL. Wilson, 110–16. Louisville, KY: Westminster John Knox, 2003.

Blomberg, Craig L. *Contagious Holiness: Jesus' Meals with Sinners*. NSBT 19. Downers Grove, IL: InterVarsity, 2005.

Bockmuehl, Markus. *The Epistle to the Philippians*, BNTC 11. London: Black, 1998.

———. *Jewish Law in Gentile Churches: Halakah and the Beginning of Christian Public Ethics*. Edinburgh: T. & T. Clark, 2000.

Booth, Roger P. *Jesus and the Laws of Purity: Tradition History and Legal History in Mark 7*. JSNTSup 13. Sheffield: JSOT Press, 1986.

Borg, Marcus J. *Conflict, Holiness, and Politics in the Teachings of Jesus*. Harrisburg, PA: Trinity, 1998 [1984].

———. "The Currency of the Term 'Zealot.'" *JTS* 22 (1971) 504–12.

———. *Jesus: A New Vision: Spirit, Culture, and the Life of Discipleship*. San Francisco: HarperSanFrancisco, 1987.

———. "Jesus and Eschatology: Current Reflections." In *Jesus in Contemporary Scholarship*, 69–96. Harrisburg, PA: Trinity, 1994.

———. "A Temperate Case for a Non-Eschatological Jesus." In *Jesus in Contemporary Scholarship*, 47–68. Harrisburg, PA: Trinity, 1994.

Borg, Marcus J., and John Dominic Crossan. *The First Paul: Reclaiming the Radical Visionary behind the Church's Conservative Icon*. London: SPCK, 2009.

Borgen, Peder. "The Early Church and the Hellenistic Synagogue." *ST* 37 (1983) 55–78.

Bornkamm, Günther. "μυστήριον, κτλ." In *TDNT* 4:802–28.

Bousset, Wilhelm. *Kyrios Christos: A History of the Belief in Christ from the Beginnings of Christianity to Irenaeus*. Translated by John E. Steely. Nashville/New York: Abingdon, 1970 [1913].

Bovon, François. *A Commentary on the Gospel of Luke 1:1–9:50*. Translated by Christine M. Thomas. Hermeneia. Minneapolis: Fortress, 2002.

Bowker, J. W. "'Merkabah' Visions and the Visions of Paul." *JSS* 16 (1971) 157–73.

Brandon, S. G. F. *History, Time and Deity: A Historical and Comparative Study of the Conception of Time in Religious Thought and Practice*. Manchester: Manchester University Press, 1965.

———. *Man and His Destiny in the Great Religions*. Toronto: University of Toronto Press, 1962.

Braun, Herbert. "Das 'Stirb und Werde' in der Antike und im Neuen Testament." In *Gesammelte Studien zum Neuen Testament und seiner Umwelt*, 136–58. Tübingen: Mohr (Siebeck), 1962.

Briggs, Charles Augustus, and Emilie Grace Briggs. *A Critical and Exegetical Commentary on the Book of Psalms*. 2 vols. ICC. Edinburgh: T. & T. Clark, 1906–1907.

Brondos, David A. *Paul on the Cross: Reconstructing the Apostle's Story of Redemption*. Minneapolis: Fortress, 2006.

Brown, Colin, and Lothar Coenen. "Resurrection." In *NIDNTT* 3:259–309.

Brown, Raymond E. *The Gospel according to John: Introduction, Translation, and Notes*. 2 vols. AB 29–29A. New York: Doubleday, 1966–1970.

———. *An Introduction to the New Testament*. ABRL. New York: Doubleday, 1997.

Bruce, F. F. *1 and 2 Corinthians*. NCB. Greenwood, SC: Attic, 1971.

―――. *The Acts of the Apostles: The Greek Text with Introduction and Commentary.* 3rd ed. Grand Rapids, MI: Eerdmans, 1990.

―――. "The Curse of the Law." In *Paul and Paulinism: Essays in Honour of C. K. Barrett*, edited by M. D. Hooker and S. G. Wilson, 27–36. London: SPCK, 1982.

―――. *The Epistle to the Galatians: A Commentary on the Greek Text.* NIGTC. Grand Rapids, MI: Eerdmans, 1982.

―――. *New Testament History.* New York: Doubleday, 1969.

―――. *Paul and Jesus.* Grand Rapids, MI: Baker, 1974.

―――. *Paul: Apostle of the Heart Set Free.* Grand Rapids, MI: Eerdmans, 1977.

Bryan, David J. "The Jewish Background to 'The Resurrection of the Son of God' by N. T. Wright." *JSHJ* 3 (2005) 155–69.

Bultmann, Rudolf. *The History of the Synoptic Tradition.* Rev. ed. Translated by John Marsh. Peabody, MA: Hendrickson, 1963.

―――. "Jesus and Paul." In *Existence and Faith: Shorter Writings of Rudolf Bultmann*, edited and translated by Schubert M. Ogden, 183–201. London: Hodder & Stoughton, 1960 [1936].

―――. "The Significance of the Historical Jesus for the Theology of Paul." In *Faith and Understanding*, edited by Robert W. Funk, translated by Louise Pettibone Smith, 220–46. London: SCM, 1966 [1929].

―――. *Theology of the New Testament.* Translated by Kendrick Grobel. 2 vols. London: SCM, 1952.

Burchard, C. "Joseph and Aseneth: A New Translation and Introduction." In *OTP* 2:177–247.

Burkert, Walter. *Ancient Mystery Cults.* Cambridge, MA: Harvard University Press, 1987.

―――. *Greek Religion.* Translated by John Raffan. Cambridge, MA: Harvard University Press, 1985.

―――. *Homo Necans: The Anthropology of Ancient Greek Sacrificial Ritual and Myth.* Translated by Peter Bing. Berkeley: University of California Press, 1983.

Burridge, Richard A. *Imitating Jesus: An Inclusive Approach to New Testament Ethics.* Grand Rapids, MI: Eerdmans, 2007.

Burton, Ernest DeWitt. *A Critical and Exegetical Commentary on the Epistle to the Galatians.* ICC 35. Edinburgh: T. & T. Clark, 1921.

Butterworth, G. W. "The Greek Mysteries." In *Clement of Alexandria: Exhortation to the Greeks; The Rich Man's Salvation; To the Newly Baptized*, edited by G. W. Butterworth, 379–90. Cambridge, MA: Harvard University Press, 1919.

Caird, G. B. *The Language and Imagery of the Bible.* Philadelphia: Westminster, 1980.

―――. *New Testament Theology.* Edited by L. D. Hurst. Oxford: Clarendon 1994.

Campbell, Alastair. "Dying with Christ: The Origins of a Metaphor?" In *Baptism, the New Testament and the Church: Historical and Contemporary Studies in Honour of R.E.O. White*, edited by Stanley E. Porter and Anthony R. Cross, JSNTSup 171, 273–93. Sheffield: Sheffield Academic, 1999.

Carson, D. A., Peter T. O'Brien, and Mark A. Seifrid, eds. *Justification and Variegated Nomism.* 2 vols. WUNT 140. Tübingen: Mohr Siebeck, 2001.

Casey, Maurice. *Aramaic Sources of Mark's Gospel.* SNTSMS 102. Cambridge: Cambridge University Press, 1998.

Cavallin, Hans Clemens Caesarius. *Life after Death: Paul's Argument for the Resurrection of the Dead in 1 Cor 15.* ConBNT 7. Lund: Gleerup, 1974.

Chamblin, Knox. "Revelation and Tradition in the Pauline *Euangelion*." *WTJ* 48 (1986) 1–16.

Charles, R. H. "Book of Enoch: Introduction." In *APOT* 2:163–87.

Charlesworth, James H. "Can We Discern the Composition Date of the Parables of Enoch?" In *Enoch and the Messiah Son of Man: Revisiting the Book of Parables*, edited by Gabriele Boccaccini, 450–68. Grand Rapids, MI: Eerdmans, 2007.

———. "A Critical Comparison of the Dualism in 1QS III, 13–IV, 26 and the 'Dualism' Contained in the Gospel of John." *NTS* 15 (1968–1969) 389–418.

———. "Introduction to the Expanded Edition: The Theologies of the Dead Sea Scrolls." In *The Faith of Qumran: Theology of the Dead Sea Scrolls,* by Helmer Ringgren, xv–xxi. New York: Crossroad, 1995.

———. "Prolegomenous Reflections Towards a Taxonomy of Resurrection Texts (1QHᵃ, 1 *En*, 4Q521, Paul, Luke, the Fourth Gospel, and Psalm 30)." In *The Changing Face of Judaism, Christianity, and Other Greco-Roman Religions in Antiquity*, edited by Ian H. Henderson and Gerbern S. Oegema, SJSHRZ, 237–64. Gütersloh: Gütersloher Verlagshaus, 2006.

Charlesworth, James H., and Craig A. Evans. "Jesus in the Agrapha and Apocryphal Gospels." In *Studying the Historical Jesus: Evaluations of the State of Current Research*, edited by Bruce Chilton and Craig A. Evans, 479–534. Leiden: Brill, 1994.

Chilton, Bruce. "Jesus and the Repentance of Sanders." *TynBul* 39 (1988) 1–18.

———. "The Kingdom of God in Recent Discussion." In *Studying the Historical Jesus: Evaluations of the State of Current Research*, edited by Bruce Chilton and Craig A. Evans, 255–80. Leiden: Brill, 1994.

———. "The Purity of the Kingdom as Conveyed in Jesus' Meals." *SBLSP* 31 (1992) 473–88.

Chilton, Bruce, and Craig A. Evans, eds. *Authenticating the Words of Jesus*. Leiden: Brill, 2002.

———. "Jesus and Israel's Scriptures." In *Studying the Historical Jesus: Evaluations of the State of Current Research*, edited by Bruce Chilton and Craig A. Evans, 281–335. Leiden: Brill, 1994.

Clements, R. E. "Isaiah 53 and the Restoration of Israel." In *Jesus and the Suffering Servant: Isaiah 53 and Christian Origins*, edited by William H. Bellinger and William R. Farmer, 39–54. Harrisburg, PA: Trinity, 1998.

Clines, David J. A. *Job 1–20*. WBC 17. Dallas: Word, 1989.

Cohen, Shaye J. D. "Crossing the Boundary and Becoming a Jew." *HTR* 82 (1989) 13–33.

Cole, Susan Guettel. "New Evidence for the Mysteries of Dionysus." *GRBS* 21 (1980) 223–38.

———. "Voices from Beyond the Grave: Dionysus and the Dead." In *Masks of Dionysus*, edited by Thomas H. Carpenter and Christopher A. Faraone, 276–95. Ithaca: Cornell University Press, 1993.

Collins, Adela Yarbro. "From Noble Death to Crucified Messiah." *NTS* 40 (1994) 481–503.

———. *Mark: A Commentary*. Hermeneia. Minneapolis: Augsburg Fortress, 2007.

———. "The Seven Heavens in Jewish and Christian Apocalypses." In *Death, Ecstasy, and Other Worldly Journeys*, edited by John J. Collins and Michael Fishbane, 59–93. New York: State University of New York Press, 1995.

Collins, John J. *Apocalypticism in the Dead Sea Scrolls*. LDSS. New York: Routledge, 1997.

———. *Daniel: A Commentary on the Book of Daniel*. Hermeneia. Minneapolis: Fortress, 1993.

———. "Eschatology." In *EDSS* 1:256–61.

———. "The Expectation of the End in the Dead Sea Scrolls." In *Eschatology, Messianism, and the Dead Sea Scrolls*, edited by Craig A. Evans and Peter W. Flint, 74–90. Grand Rapids, MI: Eerdmans, 1997.

———. "Patterns of Eschatology at Qumran." In *Traditions in Transformation: Turning Points in Biblical Faith*, edited by Baruch Halpern and Jon D. Levenson, 351–75. Winona Lake, IN: Eisenbrauns, 1981.

———. "Powers in Heaven: God, Gods, and Angels in the Dead Sea Scrolls." In *Religion in the Dead Sea Scrolls*, edited by John J. Collins and Robert A. Kugler, 9–28. Grand Rapids, MI: Eerdmans, 2000.

———. "Pre-Christian Jewish Messianism: An Overview." In *The Messiah in Early Judaism and Christianity*, edited by Magnus Zetterholm, 1–20. Minneapolis: Fortress, 2007.

———. Review of Émile Puech, *La croyance des Esséniens en la vie future: Immortalité, résurrection, vie éternelle? Histoire d'une croyance dans le Judaïsme ancien*. *DSD* 1 (1994) 246–53.

———. "Sibylline Oracles: A New Translation and Introduction." In *OTP* 1:317–472.

Conzelmann, Hans. 1 *Corinthians: A Commentary on the First Epistle to the Corinthians*. Translated by James W. Leitch. Hermeneia. Philadelphia: Fortress, 1975.

———. *Acts of the Apostles*. Translated by James Limburg, A. Thomas Kraabel, and Donald H. Juel. Hermeneia. Philadelphia: Fortress, 1987.

Cooke, G. A. *A Critical and Exegetical Commentary on the Book of Ezekiel*. ICC 21. Edinburgh: T. & T. Clark, 1936.

Coppens, J. "Le don de l'esprit d'après les textes de Qumran et le Quatrième Evangile." In *L'Évangile de Jean: Études et problémes*, edited by M. É. Boismard, et al., RechBib 3, 209–23. Bruges: Brower, 1958.

Corley, Kathleen E. "Jesus' Table Practice: Dining with 'Tax Collectors and Sinners,' Including Women." *SBLSP* 32 (1993) 444–59.

———. *Private Women, Public Meals: Social Conflict in the Synoptic Tradition*. Peabody, MA: Hendrickson, 1993.

Court, John M. "Mithraism among the Mysteries." In *Religious Diversity in the Graeco-Roman World: A Survey of Recent Scholarship*, edited by Cohn-Sherbok and John M. Court, 182–95. Sheffield: Sheffield Academic, 2001.

Cousar, Charles B. *Galatians*. IBC. Atlanta: John Knox, 1982.

Craffert, Pieter F. "Paul's Damascus Experience as Reflected in Galatians 1: Call or Conversion." *Scriptura* 29 (1989) 36–47.

Craigie, Peter C. *Psalms 1–50*. WBC 19. Waco, TX: Word, 1983.

Cranfield, C. E. B. *A Critical and Exegetical Commentary on the Epistle to the Romans*. 2 vols. ICC 32. Edinburgh: T. & T. Clark, 1975.

———. *The Gospel according to Saint Mark*. London: Macmillan, 1953.

———. "A Response to Professor Richard B. Hays' *The Moral Vision of the New Testament*." In *On Romans and Other New Testament Essays*, 167–75. Edinburgh: T. & T. Clark, 1998.

Cross, Frank Moore. *The Ancient Library of Qumran and Modern Biblical Studies.* Rev. ed. Garden City, NY: Doubleday, 1961.

Crossan, John Dominic. *The Birth of Christianity: Discovering What Happened in the Years Immediately after the Execution of Jesus.* San Francisco: HarperSanFrancisco, 1998.

———. *The Historical Jesus: The Life of a Mediterranean Jewish Peasant.* San Francisco: HarperSanFrancisco, 1991.

———. "Open Healing and Open Eating: Jesus as a Jewish Cynic?" *BR* 36 (1991) 6–18.

Crossan, John Dominic, and Jonathan L. Reed. *In Search of Paul: How Jesus's Apostle Opposed Rome's Empire with God's Kingdom: A New Vision of Paul's Words and World.* San Francisco: HarperSanFrancisco, 2004.

Cullmann, Oscar. *Christ and Time: The Primitive Christian Conception of Time and History.* Translated by Floyd V. Filson. London: SCM, 1951.

———. *Early Christian Worship.* Translated by A. Stewart Todd and James B. Torrance. SBT 10. London: SCM, 1953.

———. *Salvation in History.* Translated by Sidney G. Sowers. NTL. London: SCM, 1967.

———. "The Tradition." In *The Early Church*, edited and translated by A. J. B. Higgins, 55–99. London: SCM, 1956.

Cummins, Stephen Anthony. *Paul and the Crucified Christ in Antioch: Maccabean Martyrdom and Galatians 1 and 2.* SNTSMS 114. Cambridge: Cambridge University Press, 2001.

Cumont, Franz. *The Mysteries of Mithra.* Translated by Thomas J. McCormack. New York: Dover, 1956.

Dahmen, "דור." In *TDOT* 13:402–12.

Dahms, John V. "Dying with Christ." *JETS* 36 (1993) 15–23.

Dahood, Mitchell. *Psalms.* 3 vols. AB 16–17A. Garden City, NY: Doubleday, 1966–1970.

Daly, Robert J., "The Soteriological Significance of the Sacrifice of Isaac." *CBQ* 39 (1977) 45–75.

Danker, Frederick W. *Jesus and the New Age: A Commentary on St. Luke's Gospel.* Revised and Exp. ed. Philadelphia: Fortress, 1988.

Davidson, Maxwell J. *Angels at Qumran: A Comparative Study of 1 Enoch 1–36, 72–108 and Sectarian Writings from Qumran.* JSPSup 11. Sheffield: JSOT Press, 1992.

Davies, Philip R. "Eschatology at Qumran." *JBL* 104 (1985) 39–55.

Davies, Philip R., and Bruce D. Chilton. "The Aqedah: A Revised Tradition History." *CBQ* 40 (1978) 514–46.

Davies, W. D. *Invitation to the New Testament: A Guide to Its Main Witnesses.* London: Darton, Longman & Todd, 1967.

———. *Paul and Rabbinic Judaism: Some Rabbinic Elements in Pauline Theology.* 4th ed. Philadelphia: Fortress, 1980 [1948].

Davies, W. D., and Dale C. Allison. *A Critical and Exegetical Commentary on the Gospel according to Saint Matthew.* 3 vols. ICC. Edinburgh: T. & T. Clark, 1988–1997.

Davila, James R. "Heavenly Ascents in the Dead Sea Scrolls." In *The Dead Sea Scrolls after Fifty Years: A Comprehensive Assessment*, edited by Peter W. Flint and James C. VanderKam, 2:461–85. Leiden: Brill, 1999.

———. "The *Hoydayot* Hymnist and the Four Who Entered Paradise." *RevQ* 17 (1996) 457–78.

Deasley, Alex R. G. *The Shape of Qumran Theology*. Carlisle, UK: Paternoster, 2000.

Deines, Roland. "The Pharisees between 'Judaisms' and 'Common Judaism.'" In *The Complexities of Second Temple Judaism*. Vol. 1 of *Justification and Variegated Nomism*, edited by D. A. Carson, Peter T. O'Brien, and Mark A. Seifrid, WUNT 140, 443–504. Tübingen: Mohr Siebeck, 2001.

Deissmann, Adolf. *Paul: A Study in Social and Religious History*. Translated by William E. Wilson. 2nd ed. New York: Harper, 1957 [1927].

Delling, Gerhard. "Zur Taufe von 'Häusern' im Urchristentum." In *Studien zum Neuen Testament und zum hellinistischen Judentum*, edited by Ferdinand Hahn, Traugott Holtz, and Nikolaus Walter, 288–310. Göttingen: Vandenhoeck & Ruprecht, 1970.

Derrett, J. Duncan M. "New Creation: Qumran, Paul, the Church, and Jesus." *RevQ* 13 (1988) 597–608.

deSilva, David A. *4 Maccabees*. GAP. Sheffield: Sheffield Academic, 1998.

Dibelius, Martin. *Paul*. Translated by Frank Clarke. London: Longmans, Green, 1953.

———. "The Speeches in Acts and Ancient Historiography." In *Studies in the Acts of the Apostles*, edited by Heinrich Greevan, translated by Mary Ling, 138–85. London: SCM, 1956.

Dietzfelbinger, Christian. *Die Berufung des Paulus als Ursprung seiner Theologie*. Neukirchen-Vluyn: Neukirchener Verlag, 1985.

———. "Vom Sinn der Sabbatheilungen Jesu." *EvT* 38 (1978) 281–98.

Dodd, C. H. *According to the Scriptures: The Sub-Structure of New Testament Theology*. London: Nisbet, 1952.

———. *The Apostolic Preaching and Its Developments*. New York: Harper, 1962.

———. *Historical Tradition in the Fourth Gospel*. Cambridge: Cambridge University Press, 1963.

Dommershausen, W. "גּוֹרָל." In *TDOT* 2:450–56.

Donahue, John R. "Tax Collectors and Sinners: An Attempt at Identification." *CBQ* 33 (1971) 39–61.

Donaldson, Terence L. "The 'Curse of the Law' and the Inclusion of the Gentiles: Galatians 3:13–14." *NTS* 32 (1986) 94–112.

———. "Israelite, Convert, Apostle to the Gentiles: The Origin of Paul's Gentile Mission." In *The Road from Damascus: The Impact of Paul's Conversion on His Life, Thought, and Ministry*, edited by Richard N. Longenecker, 62–84. Grand Rapids, MI: Eerdmans, 1997.

———. *Paul and the Gentiles: Remapping the Apostle's Convictional World*. Minneapolis: Fortress, 1997.

———. "Proselytes or Righteous Gentiles? The Status of Gentiles in Eschatological Pilgrimage Patterns of Thought." *JSP* 7 (1990) 3–27.

———. "Zealot and Convert: The Origin of Paul's Christ-Torah Antithesis." *CBQ* 51 (1989) 655–82.

Donfried, Karl P. "Chronology: New Testament." In *ABD* 1:1011–22.

Douglas, Mary. "Deciphering a Meal." In *Implicit Meanings: Essays in Anthropology*, 249–75. London: Routledge & Keegan Paul, 1975.

Dowden, Ken. *Death and the Maiden: Girls' Initiation Rites in Greek Mythology*. New York: Routledge, 1989.

Downing, F. Gerald. *Christ and the Cynics: Jesus and Other Radical Preachers in First-Century Tradition*. Sheffield: Sheffield Academic, 1988.

———. *Cynics and Christian Origins*. Edinburgh: T. & T. Clark, 1992.

———. "Cynics and Early Christianity." In *Le Cynisme ancien et les prolongements*, edited by Marie-Oldie Goulet-Cazé and Richard Goulet, 281–304. Paris: Presses Universitaires de France, 1993.

———. "Deeper Reflections on the Jewish Cynic Jesus." *JBL* 117 (1998) 97–104.

———. "The Jewish Cynic Jesus." In *Jesus, Mark and Q: The Teaching of Jesus and Its Earliest Records*, edited by Michael Labahn and Andreas Schmidt, 184–214. Sheffield: Sheffield Academic, 2001.

Downing, John. "Jesus and Martyrdom." *JTS* 14 (1963) 279–93.

Drijvers, Han J. W. "Ablutions." In *ER* 1:9–13.

Driver, S. R. *An Introduction to the Literature of the Old Testament*. 9th ed. Edinburgh: T. & T. Clark, 1913.

Droge, Arthur J., and James D. Tabor. *A Noble Death: Suicide and Martyrdom among Christians and Jews in Antiquity*. San Francisco: HarperSanFrancisco, 1992.

Dungan, David L. *The Sayings of Jesus in the Churches of Paul: The Use of the Synoptic Tradition in the Regulation of Early Church Life*. Oxford: Blackwell, 1971.

Dunn, James D. G. *The Epistle to the Galatians*. BNTC. Peabody, MA: Hendrickson, 1993.

———. "The Incident at Antioch (Gal. 2.11–18) (with Additional Note)." In *Jesus, Paul, and the Law: Studies in Mark and Galatians*, 129–82. Louisville, KY: Westminster John Knox, 1990.

———. "Jesus and Ritual Purity: A Study of the Tradition-History of Mark 7.15 (with Additional Note)." In *Jesus, Paul, and the Law: Studies in Mark and Galatians*, 37–60. Louisville, KY: Westminster John Knox, 1990.

———. *Jesus and the Spirit: A Study of the Religious and Charismatic Experience of Jesus and the First Christians as Reflected in the New Testament*. Philadelphia: Westminster, 1975.

———. "Jesus Tradition in Paul." In *Studying the Historical Jesus: Evaluations of the State of Current Research*, edited by Bruce Chilton and Craig A. Evans, 155–78. Leiden: Brill, 1994.

———. "'A Light to the Gentiles', or 'The End of the Law'? The Significance of the Damascus Road Christophany for Paul (with Additional Note)." In *Jesus, Paul, and the Law: Studies in Mark and Galatians*, 89–107. Louisville, KY: Westminster John Knox, 1990.

———. "Mark 2.1–3.6: A Bridge between Jesus and Paul on the Question of the Law (with Additional Note)." In *Jesus, Paul, and the Law: Studies in Mark and Galatians*, 10–36. Louisville, KY: Westminster John Knox, 1990.

———. "Matthew 12:28/Luke 11:20: A Word of Jesus?" In *Eschatology and the New Testament: Essays in Honor of George Raymond Beasley-Murray*, edited by W. Hulitt Gloer, 29–49. Peabody, MA: Hendrickson, 1988.

———. "The New Perspective on Paul: Whence, What and Whither?" In *The New Perspective on Paul*, 1–98. Grand Rapids, MI: Eerdmans, 2008.

————. *The Partings of the Ways: Between Christianity and Judaism and Their Significance for the Character of Christianity.* London: SCM/Philadelphia: Trinity, 1991.

————. "Paul and Justification by Faith." In *The Road from Damascus: The Impact of Paul's Conversion on His Life, Thought, and Ministry,* edited by Richard N. Longenecker, 85–101. Grand Rapids, MI: Eerdmans, 1997.

————. "Paul's Conversion: A Light to Twentieth Century Disputes." In *Evangelium, Schriftauslegung, Kirche: Festschrift für Peter Stuhlmacher,* edited by Jostein Ådna, Scott J. Hafemann, Otfried Hofius, and Gerlinde Feine, 77–93. Göttingen: Vandenhoeck & Ruprecht, 2002.

————. "Pharisees, Sinners, and Jesus (with Additional Note)." In *Jesus, Paul, and the Law: Studies in Mark and Galatians,* 61–88. Louisville, KY: Westminster John Knox, 1990.

————. *Romans.* 2 vols. WBC 38A–38B. Dallas: Word, 1988.

————. *The Theology of Paul the Apostle.* Grand Rapids, MI: Eerdmans, 1998.

————. *Unity and Diversity in the New Testament: An Inquiry into the Character of Earliest Christianity.* 2nd ed. London: SCM/Philadelphia: Trinity, 1990.

————. "What Was the Issue between Paul and 'Those of the Circumcision'?" In *Paulus und das antike Judentum,* edited by Martin Hengel and U. Heckel, 295–317. Tübingen: Mohr Siebeck, 1991.

————. "Works of the Law and the Curse of the Law (Gal. 3.10–14) (with Additional Note)." In *Jesus, Paul, and the Law: Studies in Mark and Galatians,* 215–41. Louisville, KY: Westminster John Knox, 1990.

Dupont, Jacques. "The Conversion of Paul, and Its Influence on His Understanding of Salvation by Faith." In *Apostolic History and the Gospel: Biblical and Historical Essays Presented to F. F. Bruce on His 60th Birthday,* edited by W. Ward Gasque and Ralph. P. Martin, translated by Ralph P. Martin, 176–94. Grand Rapids, MI: Eerdmans, 1970.

Eddy, Paul R. "Jesus as Diogenes? Reflections on the Cynic Jesus Thesis." *JBL* 115 (1996) 449–69.

Eichrodt, Walther. *Theology of the Old Testament.* Translated by J. A. Baker. 2 vols. OTL. Philadelphia: Westminster, 1961–1967.

Eissfeldt, Otto. *The Old Testament: An Introduction Including the Apocrypha and Pseudepigrapha, and Also the Works of Similar Type from Qumran.* Translated by Peter R. Ackroyd. New York: Harper & Row, 1965.

Eliade, Mircea. *Rites and Symbols of Initiation: The Mysteries of Birth and Rebirth.* Translated by Willard R. Trask. New York: Harper & Row, 1958.

Ellis, Earle E. "Traditions in 1 Corinthians." *NTS* 32 (1986) 481–502.

Eriksson, W. "Maranatha in the Letter's *Peroratio.*" In *Traditions as Rhetorical Proof: Pauline Argumentation in 1 Corinthians,* 279–98. Stockholm: Almqvist & Wiksell, 1998.

Esler, Philip Francis. *Community and Gospel in Luke-Acts: The Social and Political Motivations of Lucan Theology.* SNTSMS 57. Cambridge: Cambridge University Press, 1987.

Evans, Craig A. "Authenticating the Words of Jesus." In *Authenticating the Words of Jesus,* edited by Bruce Chilton and Craig A. Evans, 6–10. Leiden: Brill, 2002.

———. "Did Jesus Predict His Death and Resurrection?" In *Resurrection*, edited by Stanley E. Porter, Michael A. Hayes, and David Tombs, 82–97. Sheffield: Sheffield Academic, 1999.

———. "Jesus' Actions in the Temple: Cleansing or Portent of Destruction?" *CBQ* 51 (1989) 237–70.

———. "Jesus' Exorcisms and Proclamation of the Kingdom of God in the Light of the Testaments." In *The Changing Face of Judaism, Christianity, and Other Greco-Roman Religions in Antiquity*, edited by Ian H. Henderson and Gerbern S. Oegema, 210–33. Gütersloh: Gütersloher Verlagshaus, 2006.

———. "Jesus in Non-Christian Sources." In *Studying the Historical Jesus: Evaluations of the State of Current Research*, edited by Bruce Chilton and Craig A. Evans, 443–78. Leiden: Brill, 1994.

———. *Mark 8:27–16:20*. WBC 34B. Nashville: Thomas Nelson, 2001.

———. *Noncanonical Writings and New Testament Interpretation*. Peabody, MA: Hendrickson, 1992.

Evans, C. F. *Saint Luke*. TPINTC. London: SCM/Philadelphia: Trinity, 1990.

Fallon, F. T., and R. Cameron. "The Gospel of Thomas: A *Forschungsbericht* and Analysis." In *ANRW*, edited by Wolfgang Haase and H. Temporini, 25.6:4195–4251. New York: de Gruyter, 1988.

Farmer, William Reuben. *Maccabees, Zealots, and Josephus: An Inquiry into Jewish Nationalism in the Greco-Roman Period*. New York: Columbia University Press, 1956.

———. "Who Are the 'Tax Collectors and Sinners' in the Synoptic Tradition?" In *From Faith to Faith: Essays in Honor of Donald G. Miller on His 70th Birthday*, edited by Dikran Y. Hadidian, 167–74. Pittsburgh: Pickwick, 1979.

Fee, Gordon D. *The First Epistle to the Corinthians*. NICNT. Grand Rapids, MI: Eerdmans, 1987.

———. "Paul's Conversion as Key to His Understanding of the Spirit." In *The Road from Damascus: The Impact of Paul's Conversion on His Life, Thought, and Ministry*, edited by Richard N. Longenecker, 166–83. Grand Rapids, MI: Eerdmans, 1997.

———. *Paul's Letter to the Philippians*. NICNT. Grand Rapids, MI: Eerdmans, 1995.

Feeley-Harnik, Gillian. *The Lord's Table: The Meaning of Food in Early Judaism and Christianity*. Washington: Smithsonian, 1994.

Fitzmyer, Joseph A. *The Acts of the Apostles: A New Translation with Introduction and Commentary*. AB 31. New York: Doubleday, 1998.

———. "Crucifixion in Ancient Palestine, Qumran Literature, and the New Testament." *CBQ* 40 (1978) 493–513.

———. *First Corinthians: A New Translation with Introduction and Commentary*. AYB 32. New Haven, CT: Yale University Press, 2008.

———. *The Gospel according to Luke: Introduction, Translation, and Notes*. 2 vols. AB 28–28A. Garden City, NY: Doubleday, 1981–1985.

———. "Paul and the Dead Sea Scrolls." In *The Dead Sea Scrolls after Fifty Years: A Comprehensive Assessment*, edited by Peter W. Flint and James C. VanderKam, 2:599–621. Leiden: Brill, 1999.

———. *Romans: A New Translation with Introduction and Commentary*. AB 33. New York: Doubleday, 1993.

Fjärstedt, Biörn. *Synoptic Tradition in 1 Corinthians: Themes and Clusters of Theme Words in 1 Corinthians 1–4 and 9*. Uppsala: Theologiska Institutionen, 1974.

Foakes Jackson, F. J., and Kirsopp Lake, eds. *The Beginnings of Christianity: Part I: The Acts of the Apostles*. 5 vols. London: Macmillan, 1920–1933.

Foerster, Werner. "Der Heilige Geist im Spätjudentum." *NTS* 8 (1961–1962) 117–34.

———. "σῴζω, κτλ." In *TDNT* 7:965–1024.

Forbes, Christopher. "Comparison, Self-Praise and Irony: Paul's Boasting and the Conventions of Hellenistic Rhetoric." *NTS* 32 (1986) 1–30.

France, R. T. *The Gospel of Mark: A Commentary on the Greek Text*. NIGTC. Grand Rapids, MI: Eerdmans, 2002.

Fraser, John W. *Jesus and Paul: Paul as Interpreter of Jesus from Harnack to Kümmel*. Abingdon: Marcham Manor, 1974.

Frazer, James George. *The Golden Bough: A Study in Magic and Religion*. Abridged ed. New York: Macmillan, 1943.

Freyne, Seán. "Jesus the Martyr." In *Rethinking Martyrdom*, edited by Teresa Okure, Jon Sobrino, and Felix Wilfred, 49–58. London: SCM, 2003.

———. "The Jesus-Paul Debate Revisited and Re-Imaging Christian Origins." In *Christian Origins: Worship, Belief and Society: The Milltown Institute and the Irish Biblical Association Millennium Conference*, edited by Kieran J. O'Mahony, 143–63. New York: Sheffield Academic, 2003.

Fridrichsen, Anton. "The Apostle and His Message." *UUA* (1947) 3:1–23.

Fuchs, Ernst. *Zur Frage nach dem historischen Jesus*. Tübingen: Mohr, 1960.

Fuller, Michael E. "The Davidic Messiah in Early Jewish Literature." In *The Spirit and the Mind: Essays in Informed Pentecostalism*, edited by Terry L. Cross and Emerson B. Powery, 65–86. Lanham, MD: University Press of America, 2000.

Fung, Ronald Y. K. "Revelation and Tradition: The Origins of Paul's Gospel." *EvQ* 57 (1985) 23–41.

Funk, Robert W., and the Jesus Seminar. *The Acts of Jesus: The Search for the Authentic Deeds of Jesus*. San Francisco: HarperSanFrancisco, 1998.

Furnish, Victor Paul. *II Corinthians: Translated with Introduction, Notes, and Commentary*. AB 32A. Garden City, NY: Doubleday, 1984.

———. *Jesus according to Paul*. UJT. Cambridge: Cambridge University Press, 1993.

———. "The Jesus-Paul Debate: From Baur to Bultmann." In *Paul and Jesus: Collected Essays*, edited by A. J. M. Wedderburn, 17–50. Sheffield: JSOT Press, 1989.

———. *Theology and Ethics in Paul*. Nashville/New York: Abingdon, 1968.

Gasque, W. Ward. *The History of the Criticism of the Acts of the Apostles*. Grand Rapids, MI: Eerdmans, 1975.

Gaventa, Beverly Roberts. *From Darkness to Light: Aspects of Conversion in the New Testament*. OBT 20. Philadelphia: Fortress, 1986.

Gempf, Conrad. "Public Speaking and Published Accounts." In *The Book of Acts in Its Ancient Literary Setting*, edited by Bruce W. Winter and Andrew D. Clarke, BAFCS 1, 259–303. Grand Rapids, MI: Eerdmans/Carlisle, UK: Paternoster, 1993.

Gennep, Arnold van. *The Rites of Passage*. Translated by Monika B. Vizedom and Gabrielle L. Caffee. London: Routledge & Kegan Paul, 1960.

Gibson, J. "HOI TELŌNAI KAI HAI PORNAI." *JTS* ns. 32 (1981) 429–33.

Glasson, T. Francis. "The Speeches in Acts and Thucydides." *ExpT* 76 (1964–1965) 165.

Glessmer, Uwe. "Calendars in the Qumran Scrolls." In *The Dead Sea Scrolls after Fifty Years: A Comprehensive Assessment*, edited by Peter W. Flint and James C. VanderKam, 2:213–78. Leiden: Brill, 1999.

Goldenberg, Roberg. "The Jewish Sabbath in the Roman World up to the Time of Constantine the Great." In *ANRW*, edited by Wolfgang Haase, 19.1:414–47. New York: de Gruyter, 1979.

Goldstein, Jonathan A. *II Maccabees: A New Translation with Introduction and Commentary*. AB 41A. New York: Doubleday, 1983.

Goppelt, L. "ποτήριον." In *TDNT* 6:148–58.

Gordon, Richard. "Mithraism." In *ER* 9:6088–93.

Graf, Fritz. "Dionysian and Orphic Eschatology: New Texts and Old Questions." In *Masks of Dionysus*, edited by Thomas H. Carpenter and Christopher A. Faraone, 239–58. Ithaca: Cornell University Press, 1993.

Gray, George Buchanan. *A Critical and Exegetical Commentary on the Book of Isaiah*. 2 vols. ICC 18. Edinburgh: T. & T. Clark, 1912.

Greenberg, Moshe. *Ezekiel 21–37: A New Translation with Introduction and Commentary*. AB 22A. New York: Doubleday, 1997.

Greenfield, Jonas C., and Michael E. Stone. "The Enochic Pentateuch and the Date of the Similitudes." *HTR* 70 (1977) 51–65.

Greenspoon, Leonard J. "The Origin of the Idea of Resurrection." In *Traditions in Transformation: Turning Points in Biblical Faith*, edited by Baruch Halpern and Jon D. Levenson, 247–322. Winona Lake, IN: Eisenbrauns, 1981.

Griffiths, J. Gwyn. *The Origins of Osiris and His Cult*. SHR 40. Leiden: Brill, 1980.

Gruenwald, Ithamar. *Apocalyptic and Merkabah Mysticism*. AGJU 14. Leiden: Brill, 1980.

Guelich, Robert A. *Mark 1–8:26*. WBC 34A. Nashville: Thomas Nelson, 1989.

Gunkel, Hermann. *Schöpfung und Chaos in Urzeit und Endzeit: Eine religions-geschichtliche Untersuchung über Gen. 1 und Ap. Joh. 12*. Göttingen: Vandenhoeck & Ruprecht, 1895.

———. *What Remains of the Old Testament and Other Essays*. Translated by A. K. Dallas. New York: Macmillan, 1928.

Guthrie, W. K. C. *The Greeks and Their Gods*. London: Methuen, 1950.

Haenchen, Ernst. *The Acts of the Apostles: A Commentary*. Translated by R. McL. Wilson. Philadelphia: Westminster, 1971.

Halperin, David J. *The Merkabah in Rabbinic Literature*. New Haven, CT: American Oriental Society, 1980.

Hamilton, Neill Q. *The Holy Spirit and Eschatology in Paul*. SJT Occasional Papers. Edinburgh: Oliver & Boyd, 1957.

Hannah, Darrell D. "The Book of Noah, the Death of Herod the Great, and the Date of the Parables of Enoch." In *Enoch and the Messiah Son of Man: Revisiting the Book of Parables*, edited by Gabriele Boaccaccini, 469–77. Grand Rapids, MI: Eerdmans, 2007.

Harnack, Adolf von. *What Is Christianity?* Translated by T. B. Saunders. London: Williams & Norgate, 1901.

Harrington, D. J. "Pseudo-Philo: A New Translation and Introduction." In *OTP* 2:298–377.

Harris, Murray J. *The Second Epistle to the Corinthians: A Commentary on the Greek Text*. NIGTC. Grand Rapids, MI: Eerdmans, 2005.

Harrison, Jane Ellen. *Prolegomena to the Study of Greek Religion*. New York: Arno 1975.

Harvey, A. E. *Jesus and the Constraints of History*. Philadelphia: Westminster, 1982.

Hauck, F. "μαμωνᾶς." In *TDNT* 4:388–90.

Hawthorne, Gerald F., and Ralph P. Martin. *Philippians*. Rev. ed. WBC 43. Nashville: Nelson, 2004.

Hays, Richard B. "Crucified with Christ: A Synthesis of the Theology of 1 and 2 Thessalonians, Philemon, Philippians, and Galatians." In *Thessalonians, Philippians, Galatians, Philemon*. Vol. 1 of *Pauline Theology*, edited by Jouette M. Bassler, 227–46. Minneapolis: Fortress, 1991.

———. *The Faith of Jesus Christ: The Narrative Substructure of Galatians 3:1–4:11*. 2nd ed. BRS. Grand Rapids, MI: Eerdmans, 2002.

———. *The Moral Vision of the New Testament: Community, Cross, New Creation: A Contemporary Introduction to New Testament Ethics*. San Francisco: HarperSanFrancisco, 1996.

Hedrick, C. W. "Thomas and the Synoptics: Aiming at a Consensus." *SecCent* 7 (1989–1990) 39–56.

Heinemann, Joseph. *Prayer in the Talmud: Forms and Patterns*. Translated by Richard S. Sarason. New York: de Gruyter, 1977.

Heitmüller, Wilhelm. "Zum Problem Paulus und Jesus." *ZNW* 13 (1912) 320–37.

Hengel, Martin. *The Atonement: A Study of the Origins of the Doctrine in the New Testament*. Translated by John Bowden. London: SCM, 1981.

———. "Between Jesus and Paul." In *Between Jesus and Paul: Studies in the Earliest History of Christianity*, translated by John Bowden, 1–29. London: SCM, 1983.

———. *The Charismatic Leader and His Followers*. Translated by James C. G. Greig. Edinburgh: T. & T. Clark, 1981.

———. "'Christos' in Paul." In *Between Jesus and Paul: Studies in the Earliest History of Christianity*, translated by John Bowden, 65–77. London: SCM, 1983.

———. *Crucifixion in the Ancient World and the Folly of the Message of the Cross*. Translated by John Bowden. London: SCM, 1977.

———. "The Stance of the Apostle Paul toward the Law in the Unknown Years between Damascus and Antioch." In *The Paradoxes of Paul*. Vol. 2 of *Justification and Variegated Nomism*, edited by D. A. Carson, Peter T. O'Brien, and Mark A. Seifrid, WUNT 140, 75–103. Tübingen: Mohr Siebeck, 2004.

———. *The Zealots: Investigations into the Jewish Freedom Movement in the Period from Herod I until 70 A.D.* Translated by David Smith. Edinburgh: T. & T. Clark, 1989.

Henten, Jan Willem van. "Datierung und Herkunft des Vierten Makkabäerbuches." In *Tradition and Re-Interpretation in Jewish and Early Christian Literature*, edited by Jan Willem van Henten and H. J. de Jonge, 136–49. Leiden: Brill, 1986.

Henten, Jan Willem van, and Friedrich Avemarie. *Martyrdom and Noble Death: Selected Texts from Graeco-Roman, Jewish and Christian Antiquity*. New York: Routledge, 2002.

Hill, Craig C. *Hellenists and Hebrews: Reappraising Division within the Earliest Church*. Minneapolis: Fortress, 1992.

Himmelfarb, Martha. *Ascent to Heaven in Jewish and Christian Apocalypses.* Oxford: Oxford University Press, 1993.

Hodgson, Robert. "Paul the Apostle and First Century Tribulation Lists." *ZNW* 74 (1983) 59–80.

Hofius, Otfried. "The Lord's Supper and the Lord's Tradition: Reflections on 1 Corinthians 11:23b–25." In *One Loaf, One Cup: Ecumenical Studies of 1 Cor and Other Eucharistic Texts*, edited by Ben F. Meyer, 75–115. NGS 6. Macon, GA: Mercer University Press, 1993.

Hollenbach, Paul W. "The Conversion of Jesus: From Jesus the Baptizer to Jesus the Healer." In *ANRW*, edited by Hildegard Temporini and Wolfgang Haase, 25.1: 196–219. New York: De Gruyter, 1982.

Holm-Nielsen, Svend. *Hodayot: Psalms from Qumran.* ATDan 2. Aarhus: Universitets-forlaget, 1960.

Hooker, Morna D. *The Gospel according to Saint Mark.* BNTC 2. Peabody, MA: Hendrickson, 1991.

———. "Traditions about the Temple in the Sayings of Jesus." *BJRL* 70.1 (1988) 7–19.

Horsley, Richard A. *Jesus and the Spiral of Violence.* Minneapolis: Fortress, 1987. Reprint, Minneapolis: Fortress, 1993.

———. "Jesus: Itinerant Cynic or Israelite Prophet?" In *Images of Jesus Today*, edited by James H. Charlesworth and Walter P. Weaver, FCS 3, 68–97. Valley Forge, PA: Trinity, 1994.

———. "*Logoi Prophētōn?* Reflections on the Genre of Q." In *The Future of Early Christianity*, ed. Birger A. Pearson, 195–209. Minneapolis: Fortress, 1991.

Hubbard, Moyer V. *New Creation in Paul's Letters and Thought.* SNTSMS 119. Cambridge: Cambridge University Press, 2002.

Hultgren, Arland J. "Paul's Pre-Christian Persecutions of the Church: Their Purpose, Locale, and Nature." *JBL* 95 (1976) 97–111.

———. *Jesus and His Adversaries: The Form and Function of the Conflict Stories in the Synoptic Tradition.* Minneapolis: Augsburg, 1979.

Hurtado, Larry W. "Convert, Apostate or Apostle to the Nations: The 'Conversion' of Paul in Recent Scholarship." *SR* 22 (1993) 273–84.

———. "Jesus as Lordly Example in Phil 2:5–11." In *From Jesus to Paul: Studies in Honour of Francis Wright Beare*, edited by Peter Richardson and John C. Hurd, 113–26. Waterloo, ON: Wilfrid Laurier University Press, 1984.

———. "Jesus' Death as Paradigmatic in the New Testament." *SJT* 57 (2004) 413–33.

———. *Lord Jesus Christ: Devotion to Jesus in Earliest Christianity.* Grand Rapids, MI: Eerdmans, 2003.

Isaac, E. "1 (Ethiopic Apocalypse of) Enoch: A New Translation and Introduction." In *OTP* 1:5–89.

Isaacs, Marie E. *The Concept of Spirit: A Study of Pneuma in Hellenistic Judaism and Its Bearing on the New Testament.* HeyM. London: Heythrop College, 1976.

Jeremias, Joachim. *The Eucharistic Words of Jesus.* Oxford: Blackwell, 1955.

———. *Jerusalem in the Time of Jesus: An Investigation into Economic and Social Conditions During the New Testament Period.* Translated by F. H. Cave, C. H. Cave, and M. E. Dahl. Philadelphia: Fortress, 1969.

———. *New Testament Theology 1: The Proclamation of Jesus*. Translated by John Bowdon. London: SCM, 1971.

———. "παράδεισος." In *TDNT* 5:765–73.

Jewett, Robert. *Romans: A Commentary*, Hermeneia. Minneapolis: Fortress, 2007.

———. "The Agitators and the Galatian Congregation." *NTS* 17 (1970–1971) 198–212.

Johnson, Luke Timothy. *The Writings of the New Testament: An Interpretation*. Philadelphia: Fortress, 1986.

Johnson, M. D. "Life of Adam and Eve: A New Translation and Introduction." In *OTP* 2:249–95.

Johnston, Philip S. *Shades of Sheol: Death and Afterlife in the Old Testament*. Downers Grove, IL: InterVarsity, 2002.

Jonge, M. de "Jesus' Death for Others and the Death of the Maccabean Martyrs." In *Text and Testimony: Essays on New Testament and Apocryphal Literature in Honour of A. F. J. Klijn*, edited by T. Baarda, A. Hilhorst, G. P. Luttikhuizen, and A. S. van der Woude, 142–51. Kampen: Kok, 1988.

Jüngel, Eberhard. *Paulus und Jesus: Eine Untersuchung zur Präzisierung der Frage nach dem Ursprung der Christologie*. Tübingen: Mohr (Siebeck), 1964.

Kaiser, Otto. *Isaiah 13–39: A Commentary*. Translated by R. A. Wilson. OTL. Philadelphia: Westminster, 1974.

Karr, Don. "Notes on the Study of *Merkabah* Mysticism and *Hekhalot* Literature in English, with an Appendix on Jewish Magic." Cited 9 December 2009. Online: http://www.digital-brilliance.com/kab/karr/mmhie.pdf.

Käsemann, Ernst. "Primitive Christian Apocalyptic." In *New Testament Questions of Today*, translated by W. J. Montague, 108–37. Philadelphia: Fortress, 1969.

Kee, Howard Clark. "Jesus: A Glutton and a Drunkard." *NTS* 42 (1996) 374–93.

Keegan, Terence J. "Paul and the Historical Jesus." *Ang* 52 (1975) 450–84.

Keil, C. F., and F. Delitzsch. *Isaiah*. Vol. 7 of *Commentary on the Old Testament*. Translated by James Martin. Grand Rapids, MI: Eerdmans, 1978.

Kennedy, H. A. A. *St. Paul and the Mystery-Religions*. London: Hodder & Stoughton, 1913.

Kim, Seyoon. "Jesus, Sayings of." In *Dictionary of Paul and His Letters*, edited by Gerald F. Hawthorne and Ralph P. Martin, 474–92. Downers Grove, IL: InterVarsity, 1993.

———. *The Origin of Paul's Gospel*. 2nd ed. Tübingen: Mohr Siebeck, 1984.

———. *Paul and the New Perspective: Second Thoughts on the Origin of Paul's Gospel*. Grand Rapids, MI: Eerdmans, 2002.

Kirkpatrick, A. F. *The Book of Psalms*. CBC. Cambridge: Cambridge University Press, 1906.

Kistemaker, Simon J. *Exposition of the Second Epistle to the Corinthians*. NTC. Grand Rapids, MI: Baker, 1997.

Kittel, Bonnie Pedrotti. *The Hymns of Qumran: Translation and Commentary*. SBLDS. Chico, CA: Scholars, 1981.

Klauck, Hans-Josef. *Herrenmahl und hellenistischer Kult: Eine religionsgeschichtliche Untersuchung zum Ersten Korintherbrief*. Münster: Aschendorff, 1982.

———. *The Religious Context of Early Christianity: A Guide to Graeco-Roman Religions*. Translated by Brian McNeil. SNTW. Edinburgh: T. & T. Clark, 2000.

Klausner, Joseph. *From Jesus to Paul*. Translated by W. F. Stinespring. London: Allen & Unwin, 1942.

Kleinknecht, Hermann, Friedrich Baumgärtel, Werner Bieder, Erik Sjöberg, and Eduard Schweizer. "πνεῦμα, κτλ." In *TDNT* 6:332–455.

Klijn, A. F. "2 (Syriac Apocalypse of) Baruch: A New Translation and Introduction." In *OTP* 1:615–52.

Kloppenborg, John. *The Formation of Q: Trajectories in Ancient Wisdom Collections.* Philadelphia: Fortress, 1987.

Knibb, Michael A. "The Date of the Parables of Enoch: A Critical Review." *NTS* 25 (1979) 345–59.

———. "Eschatology and Messianism in the Dead Sea Scrolls." In *The Dead Sea Scrolls after Fifty Years: A Comprehensive Assessment*, edited by Peter W. Flint and James C. VanderKam, 379–402. Leiden: Brill, 1999.

Koch, Dietrich-Alex. "Crossing the Border: The 'Hellenists' and Their Way to the Gentiles." *Neot* 39 (2005) 289–312.

Koester, Helmut. *Ancient Christian Gospels: Their History and Development.* London: SCM, 1990.

Kramer, Werner. *Christ, Lord, Son of God.* Translated by Brian Hardy. SBT 50. London: SCM, 1966.

Kraus, Hans-Joachim. *Psalms 1–59.* Translated by Hilton C. Oswald. Minneapolis: Augsburg, 1988.

———. *Psalms 60–150.* Translated by Hilton C. Oswald. Minneapolis: Augsburg, 1989.

Kuhn, Heinz-Wolfgang. *Enderwartung und gegenwärtiges Heil: Untersuchungen zu den Gemeindeliedern von Qumran mit einem Anhang über Eschatologie und Gegenwart in der Verkündigung Jesu.* Göttingen: Vandenhoeck & Ruprecht, 1966.

Kümmel, Werner Georg. *Introduction to the New Testament.* Translated by Howard Clark Kee. Rev. ed. Nashville: Abingdon, 1975.

———. *The New Testament: The History of the Investigation of Its Problems.* Translated by S. McLean Gilmour and Howard Clark Kee. London: SCM, 1973.

———. *The Theology of the New Testament according to Its Major Witnesses: Jesus—Paul—John.* Translated by John E. Steely. London: SCM, 1973.

Kvalbein, Hans. "The Wonders of the End-Time Metaphoric Language in 4Q521 and the Interpretation of Matthew 11.5 par." *JSP* 18 (1998) 87–110.

Ladd, G. E. "Revelation and Tradition in Paul." In *Apostolic History and the Gospel: Biblical and Historical Essays Presented to F. F. Bruce on His 60th Birthday*, edited by W. Ward Gasque and Ralph P. Martin, 223–30. Grand Rapids, MI: Eerdmans, 1970.

Laenen, J. H. *Jewish Mysticism: An Introduction.* Translated by David E. Orton. Louisville, KY: Westminster John Knox, 2001.

La Fontaine, J. S. *Initiation.* TSA. Manchester: Manchester University Press, 1986.

Laurin, Robert B. "The Question of Immorality in the Qumran 'Hodayot.'" *JSS* 3 (1958) 344–55.

Lease, Gary. "Mithraism and Christianity: Borrowings and Transformations." In *ANRW*, edited by H. Temporini and Wolfgang Haase, 23.2:1306–32. New York: de Gruyter, 1980.

Lenski, R. C. H. *The Interpretation of St. Matthew's Gospel.* Minneapolis: Augsburg, 1943.

Leon-Dufour, Xavier. "To Lose One's Life." *Cross Currents* 38 (1988) 340–51.

Lietzmann, Hans. *Mass and Lord's Supper: A Study in the History of the Liturgy.* Translated by Dorothea H. G. Reeve. Leiden: Brill, 1979.

Lightfoot, J. B. "Discoveries Illustrating the Acts of the Apostles." In *Essays on the Work Entitled Supernatural Religion*, 291–302. London: Macmillan, 1889.

Loisy, Alfred. *Les Actes des Apotres.* Paris: E. Nourry, 1920.

Longenecker, Bruce. "Good News to the Poor: Jesus, Paul, and Jerusalem." In *Jesus and Paul Reconnected: Fresh Pathways into an Old Debate*, edited by Todd D. Still, 37–65. Grand Rapids, MI: Eerdmans, 2007.

Longenecker, Richard N. "A Realized Hope, a New Commitment, and a Developed Proclamation: Paul and Jesus." In *The Road from Damascus: The Impact of Paul's Conversion on His Life, Thought, and Ministry*, edited by Richard N. Longenecker, 18–42. Grand Rapids, MI: Eerdmans, 1997.

———. *Galatians.* WBC 41. Dallas: Word, 1990.

Lohse, E. "σάββατον, κτλ." In *TDNT* 7:1–35.

Love, Stuart L. "Women and Men at Hellenistic Symposia Meals in Luke." In *Modelling Early Christianity: Social-Scientific Studies of the New Testament in Its Context*, edited by Philip F. Esler, 198–210. New York: Routledge, 1995.

Luz, Ulrich. *Matthew 1–7: A Commentary.* Translated by Wilhelm C. Linss. Minneapolis: Augsburg, 1989.

———. *Matthew 8–20.* Translated by James E. Crouch, Hermeneia. Minneapolis: Fortress, 2001.

Maccoby, Hyam. "How Unclean Were Tax-Collectors?" *BTB* 31 (2001) 60–63.

Mach, Michael. "Angels." In *EDSS* 1:24–27.

———. "From Apocalypticism to Early Jewish Mysticism?" In *The Origins of Apocalypticism in Judaism and Christianity.* Vol. 1 of *The Encyclopedia of Apocalypticism*, edited by John J. Collins, 229–64. New York: Continuum, 1998.

Mack, Burton L. *The Lost Gospel: The Book of Q and Christian Origins.* San Francisco: HarperSanFrancisco, 1993.

———. *A Myth of Innocence: Mark and Christian Origins.* Philadelphia: Fortress, 1988.

———. "Q and a Cynic-Like Jesus." In *Whose Historical Jesus?* edited by William E. Arnal and Michel Desjardins, 25–36. Waterloo, ON: Wilfrid Laurier University Press, 1997.

Maier, J. "Shîrê 'Ôlat Hash-Shabbat: Some Observations on Their Calendric Implications and on Their Style." In *The Madrid Qumran Congress: Proceedings of the International Congress on the Dead Sea Scrolls, Madrid, 18–21 March, 1991*, edited by Julio Trebolle Barrera and Luis Vegas Montaner, 2:543–60. Leiden: Brill, 1992.

Malherbe, Abraham J., ed. *The Cynic Epistles: A Study Edition.* Missoula, MT: Scholars, 1977.

Mansoor, Menahem. *The Thanksgiving Hymns: Translated and Annotated with an Introduction.* STDJ 3. Leiden: Brill, 1961.

Marcus, Joel. "The Beelzebul Controversy and the Eschatologies of Jesus." In *Authenticating the Activities of Jesus*, edited by Bruce Chilton and Craig A. Evans, NTTS 28, 247–77. Leiden: Brill, 2002.

———. "Jesus' Baptismal Vision." *NTS* 41 (1995) 512–21.

————. *Mark 1–8: A New Translation with Introduction and Commentary.* AB 27. New York: Doubleday, 2000.

Marrou, Henri-Irénée. "The Conditions and Means of Comprehension." In *The Meaning of History*, translated by Robert J. Olsen, 103–30. Montreal: Palm, 1966.

Marshall, Christopher. "Paul and Jesus: Continuity or Discontinuity." *Stimulus* 5 (1997) 32–42.

Marshall, I. Howard. *Acts: An Introduction and Commentary.* TNTC. Norton Street, Eng./Downers Grove, IL: InterVarsity, 1980.

————. *The Gospel of Luke: A Commentary on the Greek Text.* NIGTC. Grand Rapids, MI: Eerdmans, 1978.

Martin, Luther H. "Roman Mithraism and Christianity." *Numen* 36 (1989) 2–15.

Martin, Ralph. P. *2 Corinthians.* WBC 40. Waco, TX: Word, 1986.

Martin-Achard, Robert. *From Death to Life: A Study of the Development of the Doctrine of the Resurrection in the Old Testament.* Translated by John Peney Smith. Edinburgh/London: Oliver & Boyd, 1960.

Martyn, J. Louis. *Galatians: A New Translation with Introduction and Commentary.* AB 33A. New York: Doubleday, 1997.

Matera, Frank J. *II Corinthians: A Commentary.* NTL. Louisville, KY: Westminster John Knox, 2003.

Mattila, Sharon Lea. "Two Contrasting Eschatologies at Qumran (4Q246 vs 1QM)." *Biblica* 75 (1994) 518–38.

McEleney, N. J. "Conversion, Circumcision and the Law." *NTS* 20 (1974) 319–41.

Mearns, Christopher L. "Dating the Similitudes of Enoch." *NTS* 25 (1979) 360–69.

Meeks, Wayne A. *The First Urban Christians: The Social World of the Apostle Paul.* New Haven, CT: Yale University Press, 1983.

Meier, John P. *A Marginal Jew: Rethinking the Historical Jesus.* 4 vols. ABRL. New York: Doubleday, 1991–2009.

Menoud, Philippe H. "Revelation and Tradition: The Influence of Paul's Conversion on His Theology." *Int* 7 (1953) 131–41.

Merkelbach, Reinhold. *Mithras.* Königstein: Hain, 1984.

Meslin, Michel. "Baptism." In *ER* 2:779–83.

Mettinger, Tryggve N. D. *The Riddle of Resurrection: 'Dying and Rising Gods' in the Ancient near East.* ConBOT 50. Stockholm: Almqvist & Wiksell, 2001.

Metzger, Bruce M. "The Fourth Book of Ezra with the Four Additional Chapters: A New Translation and Introduction." In *OTP* 1:517–59.

————. *A Textual Commentary on the Greek New Testament.* 2nd ed. Stuttgart: Deutsche Bibelgesellschaft/United Bible Societies, 1994.

Meyer, Arnold. *Jesus or Paul?* Translated by J. R. Wilkinson. London: Harper, 1909.

Meyer, Ben F. *The Aims of Jesus.* PTMS 48. San Jose, CA: Pickwick, 2002 [1979].

Meyer, Marvin W., ed. *The Ancient Mysteries: A Sourcebook: Sacred Texts of the Mystery Religions of the Ancient Mediterranean World.* San Francisco: HarperSanFrancisco, 1987.

Michaelis, Wilhelm. "συγγενής, συγγένεια." In *TDNT* 7:736–42.

Michel, Otto. "τελώνης." In *TDNT* 8:88–105.

Milik, J. T. "Problèmes de la littérature hènochique à la lumière des fragments araméens de Qumrân." *HTR* 64 (1971) 333–78.

Moo, Douglas J. *The Epistle to the Romans.* NICNT. Grand Rapids, MI: Eerdmans, 1996.

Morray-Jones, C. R. A. "Paradise Revisited (2 Cor 12:1–12) The Jewish Mystical Background of Paul's Apostolate." *HTR* 86 (1993) 177–217, 265–92.

———. "Transformational Mysticism in the Apocalyptic-Merkabah Tradition." *JJS* 43 (1992) 1–31.

Motyer, J. Alec. *The Prophecy of Isaiah: An Introduction and Commentary.* Downers Grove, IL: InterVarsity, 1993.

Motyer, Stephen. "Always Being Given up to Death." *Chm* 95 (1981) 294–305.

Moule, C. F. D. "The Gravamen against Jesus." In *Jesus, the Gospels, and the Church: Essays in Honor of William R. Farmer,* edited by E. P. Sanders, 177–95. Macon, GA: Mercer University Press, 1987.

———. "Once More: Who Were the Hellenists?" *ExpT* 70 (1958–1959) 100–102.

———. "A Reconsideration of the Context of Maranatha." *NTS* 6 (1959–1960) 307–10.

Murphy-O'Connor, Jerome. "'Even Death on a Cross': Crucifixion in the Pauline Letters." In *Cross in Christian Tradition: From Paul to Bonaventure,* edited by Elizabeth Dreyer, 21–50. New York: Paulist, 2000.

———, ed. *Paul and Qumran: Studies in New Testament Exegesis.* London: Chapman, 1968.

Neale, David A. *None but the Sinners: Religious Categories in the Gospel of Luke.* JSNTSup 58. Sheffield: JSOT Press, 1991.

Neirynck, Frans. "Jesus and the Sabbath: Some Observations on Mark II, 27." In *Jésus aux Origines de la Christologie,* edited by Jacques Dupont, 227–270. Leuven: Leuven University Press, 1989.

———. "Paul and the Sayings of Jesus." In *L'apôtre Paul: Personalité, style et conception du ministére,* edited by A. Vanhoye, 265–321. Leuven: Leuven University Press, 1986.

Neufeld, Dietmar. "Jesus' Eating Transgressions and Social Impropriety in the Gospel of Mark: A Social Scientific Approach." *BTB* 30 (2000) 15–26.

Neufeld, Vernon H. *The Earliest Christian Confessions.* NTTS 5. Leiden: Brill, 1963.

Neusner, Jacob. *From Politics to Piety: The Emergence of Pharisaic Judaism.* Englewood Cliffs, NJ: Prentice-Hall, 1973.

———. *The Idea of Purity in Ancient Judaism.* Leiden: Brill, 1973.

———. *Judaism: The Evidence of the Mishnah.* 2nd ed. BJS 129. Atlanta, GA: Scholars, 1988.

———. *The Rabbinic Traditions about the Pharisees before 70.* 3 vols. Leiden: Brill, 1971.

Neusner, Jacob, and Bruce D. Chilton, eds. *In Quest of the Historical Pharisees.* Waco, TX: Baylor University Press, 2007.

Newman, Carey C. *Paul's Glory-Christology: Tradition and Rhetoric.* NovTSup 69. Leiden: Brill, 1992.

———. "Transforming Images of Paul: A Review Essay of Alan Segal, *Paul the Convert.*" *EQ* 64 (1992) 61–74.

Newsom, Carol. "'He Has Established for Himself Priests': Human and Angelic Priesthood in the Qumran Sabbath Shirot." In *Archaeology and History in the Dead Sea Scrolls: The New York University Conference in Memory of Yigael Yadin,* edited by Lawrence H. Schiffman, 101–20. Sheffield: JSOT Press, 1990.

—————. *Songs of the Sabbath Sacrifice: A Critical Edition.* HSS. Atlanta: Scholars, 1985.

Neyrey, Jerome H. "Meals, Food, and Table Fellowship." In *The Social Sciences and New Testament Interpretation,* edited by Richard Rohrbaugh, 159–82. Peabody, MA: Hendrickson, 1996.

Nickelsburg, George W. E. *1 Enoch 1: A Commentary on the Book of 1 Enoch, Chapters 1–36; 81–108.* Hermeneia. Minneapolis: Fortress, 2001.

—————. "Eschatology (Early Jewish Literature)." In *ABD* 2:579–94.

—————. "Resurrection (Early Judaism and Christianity)." In *ABD* 5:684–91.

—————. *Resurrection, Immortality, and Eternal Life in Intertestamental Judaism and Early Christianity.* Exp. ed. HTS 56. Cambridge, MA: Harvard University Press, 2006.

Nietzsche, Friedrich. *The Anti-Christ, Ecce Homo, Twilight of the Idols, and Other Writings.* Translated by Judith Norman. CTHP. Cambridge: Cambridge University Press, 2005.

Nilsson, Martin P. *Geschichte der griechischen Religion.* 2 vols. Munich: Beck, 1961–1967.

Nitzan, Bilhah. "4QBerakhota-e (4Q286–290) A Covenantal Ceremony in the Light of Related Texts." *RevQ* 16 (1995) 487–506.

Nock, Arthur Darby. "The Vocabulary of the New Testament." *JBL* 52 (1933) 131–39.

Nolland, John. *The Gospel of Matthew: A Commentary on the Greek Text.* NIGTC. Grand Rapids, MI: Eerdmans/Bletchley, Eng.: Paternoster, 2005.

—————. *Luke.* 3 vols. WBC 35A–35C. Dallas: Word, 1989–1993.

—————. "Luke's Readers: A Study of Luke 4.22–8; Acts 13.46; 18.6; 28.28 and Luke 21.5–36." PhD diss., University of Cambridge, 1977.

—————. "Uncircumcised Proselytes?" *JSJ* 12 (1981) 173–94.

Novakovic, Lidija. "4Q521: The Works of the Messiah or the Signs of the Messianic Time?" In *Qumran Studies: New Approaches, New Questions,* edited by Michael T. Davis, B. A. Strawn, and J. A. Sanders, 208–31. Grand Rapids, MI: Eerdmans, 2007.

O'Brien, Kelli S. "The Curse of the Law (Galatians 3.13) Crucifixion, Persecution, and Deuteronomy 21.22–23." *JSNT* 29 (2006) 55–76.

O'Brien, Peter T. "Was Paul Converted?" In *The Paradoxes of Paul.* Vol. 2 of *Justification and Variegated Nomism,* edited by D. A. Carson, Peter T. O'Brien, and Mark A. Seifrid, WUNT 140, 361–91. Tübingen: Mohr Siebeck, 2004.

O'Collins, Gerald G. "Crucifixion." In *ABD* 1:1207–10.

O'Neill, J. C. "Did Jesus Teach That His Death Would Be Vicarious as Well as Typical?" In *Suffering and Martyrdom in the New Testament: Studies Presented to G. M. Styler by the Cambridge New Testament Seminar,* edited by William Horbury and Brian McNeil, 9–27. Cambridge: Cambridge University Press, 1981.

Ollenburger, Ben C. "If Mortals Die, Will They Live Again?" *Ex Auditu* 9 (1993) 29–44.

The Order for the Celebration of Holy Communion, also Called the Eucharist and the Lord's Supper. London: Church House, 2000.

Orr, William F., and James Arthur Walther. *1 Corinthians: A New Translation.* AB 32. Garden City, NY: Doubleday, 1976.

Otto, Walter F. *Dionysus: Myth and Cult.* Translated by Robert B. Palmer. Bloomington: Indiana University Press, 1965.

Parrish, John W. "It's All in the Definition: The Problem with 'Dying and Rising Gods.'" *CSSR* 35 (2006) 71–75.

Parry, Donald W., and Emanuel Tov, eds. *Poetic and Liturgical Texts.* DSSR 5. Leiden: Brill, 2005.

Patterson, Stephen J. "Consider Yourself Dead: On the Martyrological Understanding of Jesus' Death." In *Once and Future Faith,* edited by Karen Armstrong, et al., 161–87. Santa Rosa, CA: Polebridge, 2001.

———. "The Gospel of Thomas: Introduction." In *Q-Thomas Reader,* edited by John S. Kloppenborg, M. W. Meyer, Stephen J. Patterson, and M. G. Steinhauser, 86–88. Sonoma, CA: Polebridge, 1990.

———. "Paul and the Jesus Tradition: It Is Time for Another Look." *HTR* 84 (1991) 23–41.

Pelser, Gert M. M. "Could the 'Formulas' *Dying* and *Rising with Christ* Be Expressions of Pauline Mysticism?" *Neot* 32 (1998) 115–34.

Perrin, Norman. *Rediscovering the Teaching of Jesus.* London: SCM, 1967.

Pervo, Richard I. *Acts: A Commentary.* Hermeneia. Minneapolis: Fortress, 2009.

Pesch, Rudolf. *Das Markusevangelium.* 2 vols. HTKNT 2. Basel: Herder, 1976–1977.

Petersen, David L. "Eschatology (Old Testament)." In *ABD* 2:575–79.

Plisch, Uwe-Karsten. *The Gospel of Thomas: Original Text with Commentary.* Translated by Gesine Schenke Robinson. Stuttgart: Deutsche Bibelgesellschaft, 2008.

Ploeg, Jean van der. "The Belief in Immortality in the Writings of Qumran." *BO* 18 (1961) 118–24.

Porter, J. R. "The Legal Aspects of the Concept of 'Corporate Personality' in the Old Testament." *VT* 15 (1965) 361–68.

Porter, Stanley E. "Two Myths: Corporate Personality and Language/Mentality Determinism." *SJT* 43 (1990) 289–307.

Preston, James J. "Purification: An Overview." In *ER* 11:7503–11.

Pretorius, Mark. "The Key to the Present Fulfilment of the Eschatological Inclusion of the Gentiles into the People of God." *HvTSt* 61 (2005) 1339–52.

Preuss, Horst Dietrich. *Old Testament Theology.* Translated by Leo G. Perdue. 2 vols. OTL. Louisville, KY: Westminster John Knox, 1995.

Price, Robert M. "Punished in Paradise: An Exegetical Theory on II Corinthians 12:1–10." *JSNT* 7 (1980) 33–40.

Provan, Iain W. "Knowing and Believing: Faith in the Past." In *'Behind' the Text: History and Biblical Interpretation,* edited by Craig Bartholomew, E. Stephen Evans, Mary Healy, and Murray Rae, 229–66. Grand Rapids, MI: Zondervan, 2003.

Puech, Émile. *La croyance des Esséniens en la vie future: Immortalité, résurrection, vie éternelle? Histoire d'une croyance dans le Judaïsme ancien.* 2 vols. Paris: Librairie Lecoffre, 1993.

———. "Messianism, Resurrection, and Eschatology at Qumran and in the New Testament." In *The Community of the Renewed Covenant: The Notre Dame Symposium on the Dead Sea Scrolls,* edited by Eugene Ulrich and James VanderKam, 235–56. Notre Dame, IN: University of Notre Dame Press, 1994.

————. "Some Remarks on 4Q246 and 4Q521 and Qumran Messianism." In *The Provo International Conference on the Dead Sea Scrolls: Technological Innovations, New Texts, and Reformulated Issues*, edited by Donald W. Parry and Eugene Ulrich, 545–65. Leiden: Brill, 1999.

Quispel, Gilles. "Ezekiel 1:26 in Jewish Mysticism and Gnosis." *VC* 34 (1980) 1–13.

Räisänen, Heikki. "The 'Hellenists': A Bridge between Jesus and Paul?" In *Jesus, Paul and Torah: Collected Essays*, translated by David E. Orton, 149–202. Sheffield, JSOT Press, 1992.

————. *Paul and the Law*, WUNT 29. Tübingen: Mohr Siebeck, 1983.

————. "Paul's Call Experience and His Later View of the Law." In *Jesus, Paul and Torah: Collected Essays*, translated by David E. Orton, 15–47. Sheffield: JSOT Press, 1992.

————. "Paul's Conversion and the Development of His View of the Law." *NTS* 33 (1987) 404–19.

Reiser, Marius. "Eschatology in the Proclamation of Jesus." In *Jesus, Mark and Q: The Teaching of Jesus and Its Earliest Records*, edited by Michael Labahn and Andreas Schmidt, translated by Linda M. Maloney, 216–38. Sheffield: Sheffield Academic, 2001.

Reitzenstein, Richard. *Hellenistic Mystery-Religions: Their Basic Ideas and Significance*. Translated by John E. Steely. Pittsburgh: Pickwick, 1978 [1927].

Renan, Ernest. *Marc-Aurèle et la fin du monde antique*. Paris: Calmann-Lévy, 1923.

Rengstorf, Karl Heinrich. "ἁμαρτωλός, κτλ." In *TDNT* 1:317–35.

Resch, D. Alfred. *Der Paulinismus und die Logia Jesu in ihrem gegenseitigen Verhältnis*. Leipzig: Hinrichs, 1904.

Reumann, J. "The Gospel of the Righteousness of God: Pauline Reinterpretation in Romans 3:21–31." *Int* 20 (1966) 432–52.

Reventlow, Henning Graf. "Basic Issues in the Interpretation of Isaiah 53." In *Jesus and the Suffering Servant: Isaiah 53 and Christian Origins*, edited by William H. Bellinger and William R. Farmer, 23–38. Harrisburg, PA: Trinity, 1998.

Rhoads, David. "Zealots." In *ABD* 6:1043–54.

Richardson, N. J. *The Homeric Hymn to Demeter*. Oxford: Clarendon 1974.

Richardson, Peter, and John C. Hurd, eds. *From Jesus to Paul: Studies in Honour of Francis Wright Beare*. Waterloo, ON: Wilfrid Laurier University Press, 1984.

Riesner, Rainer. "Paulus und die Jesus-Uberlieferung." In *Evangelium, Schriftauslegung, Kirche*, edited by Jostein Ådna, Scott J. Hafemann, and Otfried Hofius, 347–65. Gottingen: Vandenhoeck & Ruprecht, 1997.

Rietz, Henry W. M. "Reflections on Jesus' Eschatology in Light of Qumran." In *Jesus and Archaeology*, edited by James H. Charlesworth, 186–205. Grand Rapids, MI: Eerdmans, 2006.

Ringgren, Helmer. *The Faith of Qumran: Theology of the Dead Sea Scrolls*. Translated by Emilie T. Sander. Exp. ed. New York: Crossroad, 1995.

Robinson, H. Wheeler. *The Christian Doctrine of Man*. 3rd ed. Edinburgh: T. & T. Clark, 1926.

————. *Corporate Personality in Ancient Israel*. Philadelphia: Fortress, 1964.

Robinson, J. A. T. "Traces of a Liturgical Sequence in 1 Cor. 16:20–24." *JTS* 4 (1953) 38–41.

Rogerson, J. W. *Anthropology and the Old Testament*. Atlanta: John Knox, 1979.

———. "The Hebrew Conception of Corporate Personality: A Re-Examination." *JTS* 21 (1970) 1–16.

Rosner, Brian. *Paul, Scripture, and Ethics: A Study of 1 Corinthians 5–7*. BSL. Grand Rapids, MI: Baker, 1994.

Rowland, Christopher. *The Open Heaven: A Study of Apocalyptic in Judaism and Early Christianity*. New York: Crossroad, 1982.

———. "A Summary of Sabbath Observance in Judaism at the Beginning of the Christian Era." In *From Sabbath to Lord's Day: A Biblical, Historical, and Theological Investigation*, edited by D. A. Carson, 43–55. Grand Rapids, MI: Zondervan, 1982.

Rowley, H. H. *The Faith of Israel*. London: SCM, 1956.

———. "The Herodians in the Gospels." *JTS* 41 (1940) 14–27.

Rudolph, Kurt. "Mystery Religions." In *ER* 9:6326–34, translated by Matthew J. O'Connell.

Saldarini, Anthony J. "Pharisees." In *ABD* 5:289–303.

———. *Pharisees, Scribes and Sadducees in Palestinian Society: A Sociological Approach*. Wilmington, DE: Michael Glazier, 1988.

———. "Scribes." In *ABD* 5:1012–16.

Salvesen, Alison. *Symmachus in the Pentateuch*. JSS Monograph. Manchester: University of Manchester, 1991.

Sanders, E. P. *Jesus and Judaism*. Minneapolis: Fortress, 1985.

———. "Jewish Association with Gentiles and Galatians 2:11–14." In *The Conversation Continues: Studies in Paul and John in Honor of J. Louis Martyn*, edited by Robert T. Fortna and Beverly R. Gaventa, 170–88. Nashville: Abingdon, 1990.

———. *Jewish Law from Jesus to the Mishnah: Five Studies*. Philadelphia: Trinity, 1990.

———. *Judaism: Practice and Belief 63 BCE–66 CE*. Philadelphia: Trinity, 1992.

———. *Paul and Palestinian Judaism: A Comparison of Patterns of Religion*. Minneapolis: Fortress, 1977.

———. *Paul, the Law, and the Jewish People*. Minneapolis: Fortress, 1983.

Sanders, E. P., and Margaret Davies. *Studying the Synoptic Gospels*. Philadelphia: Trinity, 1989.

Sanders, Jack T. "Paul's 'Autobiographical' Statements in Galatians 1–2." *JBL* 85 (1966) 335–43.

Sandmel, Samuel. *Judaism and Christian Beginnings*. New York: Oxford University Press, 1978.

———. "Parallelomania." *JBL* 81 (1962) 1–13.

Sänger, Dieter. "'Verflucht ist Jeder, der am Holze hängt' (Gal 3,13b) Zur Rezeption einer frühen antichristlichen Polemik." *ZNW* 85 (1994) 279–85.

Sasse, Hermann. "αἰών, αἰώνιος." In *TDNT* 1:197–209.

Schäfer, Peter. "New Testament and Hekhalot Literature: The Journey into Heaven in Paul and in Merkavah Mysticism." *JJS* 35 (1984) 19–35.

Schlesier, Renate. "Dionysus." In *BNP* 4:496–508.

Schmidt, Daryl D. "The Sabbath Day: To Heal or Not to Heal." *Dialogue* 27 (1994) 124–47.

Schnabel, Eckhard J. "Jesus and the Beginnings of the Mission to the Gentiles." In *Jesus of Nazareth*, edited by Joel B. Green and Max Turner, 37–58. Grand Rapids, MI: Eerdmans, 1994.

Schnackenburg, Rudolf. *The Gospel according to St. John.* Translated by Cecily Hastings, Francis McDonagh, David Smith, and Richard Foley. 3 vols. London: Burns & Oates, 1980.

Schneider, Johannes. "σταυρός, κτλ." In *TDNT* 7:572–84.

Schoeps, H. J. *Paul: The Theology of the Apostle in the Light of Jewish Religious History.* Translated by Harold Knight. London: Lutterworth, 1961.

Scholem, Gershom G. *Jewish Gnosticism, Merkabah Mysticism, and Talmudic Tradition.* 2nd ed. New York: The Jewish Theological Seminary of America, 1965.

———. *Major Trends in Jewish Mysticism.* New York: Schocken, 1995 [1946].

Schürer, Emil. *The History of the Jewish People in the Age of Jesus Christ (175 B.C.– A.D. 135).* Edited by Geza Vermes, Fergus Millar, Martin Goodman, and Matthew Black. Rev. ed. 3 vols. Edinburgh: T. & T. Clark, 1973–1987.

Schweitzer, Albert. *The Mysticism of Paul the Apostle.* Translated by William Montgomery. 2nd ed. London: A & C Black, 1953 [1930].

———. *Paul and His Interpreters: A Critical History.* Translated by W. Montgomery. London: Black, 1912.

Schweizer, Eduard. "Dying and Rising with Christ." *NTS* 14 (1967) 1–14.

Scobie, Charles H. H. "Jesus or Paul: The Origin of the Universal Mission of the Christian Church." In *From Jesus to Paul: Studies in Honour of Francis Wright Beare,* edited by Peter Richardson and John C. Hurd, 47–60. Waterloo, ON: Wilfrid Laurier, 1984.

Scott, James M. "Throne-Chariot Mysticism in Qumran and in Paul." In *Eschatology, Messianism, and the Dead Sea Scrolls,* edited by Craig A. Evans and Peter W. Flint, 101–19. Grand Rapids, MI: Eerdmans, 1997.

———. "The Triumph of God in 2 Cor 2.14: Additional Evidence of Merkabah Mysticism in Paul." *NTS* 42 (1996) 260–81.

Scroggs, Robin. "The Earliest Christian Communities as Sectarian Movement." In *Early Christianity.* Vol. 2 of *Christianity, Judaism and Other Greco-Roman Cults: Studies for Morton Smith at Sixty,* edited by Jacob Neusner, 1–23. Leiden: Brill, 1975.

Seccombe, David. "The Story of Jesus and the Missionary Strategy of Paul." In *Gospel to the Nations: Perspectives on Paul's Mission: In Honour of Peter T. O'Brien,* edited by Peter Bolt and Mark Thompson, 115–29. Downers Grove, IL: InterVarsity, 2000.

———. "Take up Your Cross." In *God Who Is Rich in Mercy: Essays Presented to Dr. D. B. Knox,* edited by Peter T. O'Brien and David G. Peterson, 139–51. Homebush, Australia: Lancer, 1986.

Seeley, David. "Jesus and the Cynics Revisited." *JBL* 116 (1997) 704–12.

———. "Jesus' Death in Q." *NTS* 38 (1992) 222–34.

———. *The Noble Death: Graeco-Roman Martyrology and Paul's Concept of Salvation.* JSNTSup 2. Sheffield: JSOT Press, 1990.

Segal, Alan F. "Life after Death: The Social Sources." In *The Resurrection: An Interdisciplinary Symposium on the Resurrection of Jesus,* edited by Stephen T. Davis, Daniel Kendall, and Gerald O'Collins, 90–125. Oxford: Oxford University Press, 1997.

———. "Paul and the Beginning of Jewish Mysticism." In *Death, Ecstasy, and Other Worldly Journeys*, edited by John J. Collins and Michael Fishbane, 95–122. Albany, NY: State University of New York Press, 1995.

———. *Paul the Convert: The Apostolate and Apostasy of Saul the Pharisee*. New Haven, CT: Yale University Press, 1990.

Setzer, Claudia. *Jewish Responses to Early Christians: History and Polemics, 30–150 C.E.* Minneapolis: Fortress, 1994.

———. "'You Invent a Christ!': Christological Claims as Points of Jewish-Christian Dispute." *USQR* 44 (1991) 315–28.

Sherwin-White, A. N. *Roman Society and Roman Law in the New Testament*. Oxford: Oxford University Press, 1963.

Simmons, William A. *A Theology of Inclusion in Jesus and Paul: The God of Outcasts and Sinners*. MBP 39. Lewiston, NY: Mellen, 1996.

Simon, Marcel. "The *Religionsgeschichtliche Schule*: Fifty Years Later." *Rel Stud* 11 (1975) 135–44.

Smith, Dennis E. *From Symposium to Eucharist: The Banquet in the Early Christian World*. Minneapolis: Fortress, 2003.

———. "The Historical Jesus at Table." *SBLSP* 28 (1989) 466–86.

———. "Table Fellowship." In *ABD* 6:302–4.

Smith, Jonathan Z. "Dying and Rising Gods." In *ER* 4:2535–40.

Smith, Morton. *Jesus the Magician*. San Francisco: Harper & Row, 1978.

Snodgrass, K. R. "The Gospel of Thomas: A Secondary Gospel." *SecCent* 7 (1989–1990) 19–38.

Stanton, Graham N. "Jesus of Nazareth: A Magician and a False Prophet Who Deceived God's People?" In *Jesus of Nazareth: Lord and Christ: Essays on the Historical Jesus and New Testament Christology*, edited by Joel B. Green and Max Turner, 164–80. Grand Rapids, MI: Eerdmans, 1994.

Stegemann, Hartmut. "Some Aspects of Eschatology in Texts from the Qumran Community and in the Teachings of Jesus." In *Biblical Archaeology Today: Proceedings of the International Congress on Biblical Archaeology Held in Jerusalem April 1984*, 408–26. Jerusalem: Israel Exploration Society, 1985.

Stendahl, Krister. "The Apostle Paul and the Introspective Conscience of the West." *HTR* 56 (1963) 199–215.

———. "Paul among Jews and Gentiles." In *Paul among Jews and Gentiles and Other Essays*, 1–77. Philadelphia: Fortress, 1976.

Stern, Menahem. *Greek and Latin Authors on Jews and Judaism*. 3 vols. Jerusalem: Israel Academy of Sciences and Humanities, 1976.

Stevenson, Kenneth, and Michael Glerup, eds. *Ezekiel, Daniel*. ACCS 13. Downers Grove, IL: InterVarsity, 2008.

Still, Todd D., ed. *Jesus and Paul Reconnected: Fresh Pathways into an Old Debate*. Grand Rapids, MI: Eerdmans, 2007.

Stone, Michael E., ed. *Jewish Writings of the Second Temple Period: Apocrypha, Pseudepigrapha, Qumran Sectarian Writings, Philo, Josephus*. CRINT. Philadelphia: Fortress, 1984.

Strachan, R. H. *The Second Epistle of Paul to the Corinthians*. MNTC. London: Hodder and Stoughton, 1935.

Strugnell, J. "The Angelic Liturgy at Qumrân: 4Q Serek Šîrôt 'Olat Haššabāt." In *Congress Volume: Oxford 1959*. VTSup 7, 318–45. Leiden: Brill, 1960.

Suter, David W. "Enoch in Sheol: Updating the Dating of the Book of Parables." In *Enoch and the Messiah Son of Man: Revisiting the Book of Parables*, edited by Gabriele Boccaccini, 415–43. Grand Rapids, MI: Eerdmans, 2007.

Tabor, James D. *Things Unutterable: Paul's Ascent to Paradise in Its Greco-Roman, Judaic, and Early Christian Contexts*. Lanham, MD: University Press of America, 1986.

Tabor, James D., and Michael O. Wise. "4Q521 'on Resurrection' and the Synoptic Gospel Tradition: A Preliminary Study." *JSP* 10 (1992) 149–62.

Talmon, Shemaryahu. "Calendar Controversy in Ancient Judaism: The Case of the 'Community of the Renewed Covenant." In *The Provo International Conference on the Dead Sea Scrolls: Technological Innovations, New Texts, and Reformulated Issues*, edited by Donald W. Parry and Eugene Ulrich, STDJ 30, 379–95. Leiden: Brill, 1999.

———. "Calendars and Mishmarot." In *EDSS* 1:108–17.

———. "The Community of the Renewed Covenant: Between Judaism and Christianity." In *The Community of the Renewed Covenant: The Notre Dame Symposium on the Dead Sea Scrolls*, edited by Eugene Ulrich and James VanderKam, 3–24. Notre Dame, IN: University of Notre Dame Press, 1994.

———. "Yom Hakkippurim in the Habakkuk Scroll." *Biblica* 32 (1951) 549–63.

Tannehill, Robert C. *Dying and Rising with Christ: A Study in Pauline Theology*. Berlin: Töpelmann, 1967.

Taylor, Vincent. *The Formation of the Gospel Tradition*. London: Macmillan, 1953.

———. *The Gospel according to St. Mark: The Greek Text with Introduction, Notes, and Indexes*. London: Macmillan, 1952.

Tengström, Sven and Heinz-Josef Fabry. "רוּחַ." In *TDOT* 13:365–402.

Theissen, Gerd. *Sociology of Early Palestinian Christianity*. Translated by John Bowden. Philadelphia: Fortress, 1978.

Theissen, Gerd, and Dagmar Winter. *The Quest for the Plausible Jesus: The Question of Criteria*. Translated by M. Eugene Boring. Louisville, KY: Westminster John Knox, 2002.

Thiselton, Anthony C. *The First Epistle to the Corinthians: A Commentary on the Greek Text*. NIGTC. Grand Rapids, MI: Eerdmans, 2000.

Thompson, Michael. *Clothed with Christ: The Example and Teaching of Jesus in Romans 12.1–15.13*. JSNTSup 59. Sheffield: JSOT Press, 1991.

Thrall, Margaret E. *A Critical and Exegetical Commentary on The Second Epistle to the Corinthians*. 2 vols. ICC 65. Edinburgh: T. & T. Clark, 1994–2000.

———. "Paul's Journey to Paradise: Some Exegetical Issues in 2 Cor 12, 2–4." In *The Corinthian Correspondence*, edited by R. Bieringer, 347–63. Leuven: Leuven University Press, 1996.

Tomson, Peter J. *Paul and the Jewish Law: Halakha in the Letters of the Apostle to the Gentiles*. Minneapolis: Fortress, 1990.

Tuckett, Christopher M. "A Cynic Q?" *Bib* 70 (1989) 349–76.

———. "Deuteronomy 21,23 and Paul's Conversion." In *L'apôtre Paul: Personalité, style et conception du ministère*, edited by A. Vanhoye, 345–50. Leuven: Leuven University Press, 1986.

———. "Paul and the Synoptic Mission Discourse?" *ETL* 60 (1984) 376–81.

———. "Paul, Tradition and Freedom." *TZ* 47 (1991) 307–25.

———. "Synoptic Tradition in 1 Thessalonians." In *The Thessalonian Correspondence*, edited by Raymond R. Collins, BETL 87, 160–82. Leuven: Leuven University Press, 1990.

———. "Thomas and the Synoptics." *NovT* 30 (1988) 132–57.

Twelftree, Graham H. *In the Name of Jesus: Exorcism among Early Christians*. Grand Rapids, MI: Baker, 2007.

Ulansey, David. *The Origins of the Mithraic Mysteries: Cosmology and Salvation in the Ancient World*. New York/Oxford: Oxford University Press, 1989.

VanderKam, James C. *Calendars in the Dead Sea Scrolls: Measuring Time*. LDSS. New York: Routledge, 1998.

VanderKam, James, and Peter Flint. *The Meaning of the Dead Sea Scrolls: Their Significance for Understanding the Bible, Judaism, Jesus, and Christianity*. San Francisco: HarperSanFrancisco, 2002.

Vansina, Jan. *Oral Tradition as History*. Madison: University of Wisconsin Press, 1985.

Vermaseren, M. J. *Mithras: The Secret God*. Translated by Therese Megaw and Vincent Megaw. New York: Barnes & Noble, 1963.

Vermaseren, M. J., and C. C. van Essen. *The Excavations in the Mithraeum of the Church of Santa Prisca in Rome*. Leiden: Brill, 1965.

Vermes, Geza. "Eschatological World View in the Dead Sea Scrolls and in the New Testament." In *Emanuel: Studies in Hebrew Bible, Septuagint and Dead Sea Scrolls in Honor of Emanuel Tov*, edited by Shalom M. Paul, Robert A. Kraft, Lawrence H. Schiffman, and Weston W. Fields, 479–94. Leiden: Brill, 2003.

———. *Jesus the Jew: A Historian's Reading of the Gospels*. Philadelphia: Fortress, 1973.

Vos, Geerhardus. *The Pauline Eschatology*. Princeton: Princeton University Press, 1930. Reprint, Grand Rapids, MI: Baker, 1979.

Wagner, Günter. *Pauline Baptism and the Pagan Mysteries: The Problem of the Pauline Doctrine of Baptism in Romans VI. 1–11, in the Light of Its Religio-Historical 'Parallels'*. Translated by J. P. Smith. London: Oliver & Boyd, 1967.

Walker, W. O. "Jesus and the Tax Collectors." *JBL* 97 (1978) 221–38.

Walsh, Brian J., and J. Richard Middleton. *The Transforming Vision: Shaping a Christian World View*. Downers Grove, IL: InterVarsity, 1984.

Walter, Nikolaus. "Paul and the Early Christian Jesus-Tradition." In *Paul and Jesus: Collected Essays*, edited by A. J. M. Wedderburn, 51–80. Sheffield: JSOT Press, 1989.

Watson, Francis. *Paul, Judaism and the Gentiles: A Sociological Approach*. SNTSMS 56. Cambridge: Cambridge University Press, 1986.

Webb, Robert L. "John the Baptist and His Relationship to Jesus." In *Studying the Historical Jesus: Evaluations of the State of Current Research*, edited by Bruce Chilton and Craig A. Evans, 179–230. Leiden: Brill, 1994.

Wedderburn, A. J. M. *Baptism and Resurrection: Studies in Pauline Theology against Its Greco-Roman Background*. Tübingen: Mohr, 1987.

———. *A History of the First Christians*. New York: T. & T. Clark, 2004.

———. "Paul and Jesus: Similarity and Continuity." In *Paul and Jesus: Collected Essays*, edited by A. J. M. Wedderburn, 117–43. Sheffield: JSOT Press, 1989.

———. "Paul and the Story of Jesus." In *Paul and Jesus: Collected Essays*, edited by A. J. M. Wedderburn, 161–89. Sheffield: JSOT Press, 1989.

Weiser, Artur. *The Psalms: A Commentary.* Translated by Herbert Hartwell. OTL. Philadelphia: Westminster, 1962.

Weiss, Herold. "The Sabbath in the Synoptic Gospels." *JSNT* 38 (1990) 13–27.

Weiss, Johannes. *Paul and Jesus.* Translated by H. J. Chaytor. New York: Harper, 1909.

Wendt, Hans Hinrich. "Die Lehre des Paulus verglichen mit der Lehre Jesu." *ZTK* 4 (1894) 1–78.

Wenham, David. *Paul: Follower of Jesus or Founder of Christianity?* Grand Rapids, MI: Eerdmans, 1995.

———. "The Story of Jesus Known to Paul." In *Jesus of Nazareth: Lord and Christ: Essays on the Historical Jesus and New Testament Christology,* edited by Joel B. Green and Max Turner, 297–311. Grand Rapids, MI: Eerdmans, 1994.

Westerholm, Stephen. *Jesus and Scribal Authority.* Lund: CWK Gleerup, 1978.

———. "Law and Gospel in Jesus and Paul." In *Jesus and Paul Reconnected: Fresh Pathways into an Old Debate,* edited by Todd D. Still, 19–36. Grand Rapids, MI: Eerdmans, 2007.

———. "The 'New Perspective' at Twenty-Five." In *The Paradoxes of Paul.* Vol. 2 of *Justification and Variegated Nomism,* edited by D. A. Carson, Peter T. O'Brien, and Mark A. Seifrid, WUNT 140, 1–38. Tübingen: Mohr Siebeck, 2004.

Whiteley, D. E. H. *The Theology of St. Paul.* 2nd ed. Oxford: Blackwell, 1974.

Wiens, D. "Mystery Concepts in Primitive Christianity and Its Environment." In *ANRW,* edited by H. Temporini and Wolfgang Haase, 23.2:1248–84. New York: de Gruyter, 1980.

Wilckens, Ulrich. *Der Brief an die Römer.* 3 vols. Zürich: Benziger, 1978.

Wilcox, Max. "Upon the Tree: Deut 21:22–23 in the New Testament." *JBL* 9 (1977) 85–99.

Williams, S. K. *Jesus' Death as Saving Event: The Background and Origin of a Concept.* HDR 2. Missoula, MT: Scholars, 1975.

Windisch, H. "Ἕλλην, κτλ." In *TDNT* 2:504–16.

Winger, Michael. "Tradition, Revelation and Gospel: A Study in Galatians." *JSNT* 53 (1994) 65–86.

Wintermute, O. S. "Jubilees: A New Translation and Introduction." In *OTP* 2:35–142.

Wolff, Christian. "Humility and Self-Denial in Jesus' Life and Message and in the Apostolic Existence of Paul." In *Paul and Jesus: Collected Essays,* edited by A. J. M. Wedderburn, 145–60. Sheffield: JSOT Press, 1989.

Wolff, Hans Walter. *Anthropology of the Old Testament.* Translated by Margaret Kohl. Philadelphia: Fortress, 1974.

———. *Hosea: A Commentary on the Book of the Prophet Hosea.* Translated by Gary Stansell. Hermeneia. Philadelphia: Fortress, 1974.

Wood, H. G. "The Conversion of Paul: Its Nature, Antecedents and Consequences." *NTS* 1 (1954–1955) 276–82.

Wrede, William. *The Messianic Secret.* Translated by J. C. G. Greig. London: James Clarke, 1971.

———. *Paul.* Translated by Edward Lummis. London: Philip Green, 1907 [1904].

Wright, N. T. "ΧΡΙΣΤΟΣ as 'Messiah' in Paul: Philemon 6." In *The Climax of the Covenant: Christ and the Law in Pauline Theology,* 41–55. Minneapolis: Fortress, 1992.

————. *Jesus and the Victory of God*. Minneapolis: Fortress, 1996.

————. *The New Testament and the People of God*. Minneapolis: Fortress, 1992.

————. "Putting Paul Together Again: Toward a Synthesis of Pauline Theology (1 and 2 Thessalonians, Philippians, and Philemon)." In *Thessalonians, Philippians, Galatians, Philemon*. Vol. 1 of *Pauline Theology*, edited by Jouette M. Bassler, 183–211. Minneapolis: Fortress, 1991.

————. *The Resurrection of the Son of God*. Minneapolis: Fortress, 2003.

Wright, R. B. "Psalms of Solomon: A New Translation and Introduction." In *OTP* 2:639–70.

Yadin, Yigael. *The Scroll of the War of the Sons of Light against the Sons of Darkness*. Translated by Batya Rabin and Chaim Rabin. Oxford: Oxford University Press, 1962.

Yang, Yong-Eui. *Jesus and the Sabbath in Matthew's Gospel*. JSNTSup 139. Sheffield: Sheffield Academic, 1997.

Yeung, Maureen W. *Faith in Jesus and Paul: A Comparison with Special Reference to 'Faith That Can Remove Mountains' and 'Your Faith Has Healed/Saved You'*. Tübingen: Mohr Siebeck, 2002.

Young, Norman H. "'Jesus and the Sinners': Some Queries." *JSNT* 24 (1985) 73–75.

Zahavy, Tzvee. "The Politics of Piety: Social Conflict and the Emergence of Rabbinic Liturgy." In *The Making of Jewish and Christian Worship*, edited by Paul F. Bradshaw and Lawrence A. Hoffman, 42–68. Notre Dame: University of Notre Dame Press, 1991.

Ziesler, John. *The Epistle to the Galatians*. London: Epworth, 1992.

————. *Paul's Letter to the Romans*. TPINTC. Philadelphia: Trinity, 1989.

Zimmerli, Walther. *Ezekiel: A Commentary on the Book of the Prophet Ezekiel Chapters 25–48*. Translated by James D. Martin. Edited by Paul D. Hanson. Hermeneia. Philadelphia: Fortress, 1983.

Ancient Documents Index

∿

Apocrypha

∼

Pseudepigrapha

~

New Testament

Matthew

Romans (*cont.*)

15:13	320n254
15:15–16	118n276
15:18	213n244, 216n268
15:19	319n252
15:20	212n234
15:30–31	74n52
15:30	213n248, 320n255
16:2	179n39
16:3	179n38
16:7	179n38
16:8	179n39
16:9	179n38
16:10	179n38
16:11	179n39
16:12	179n39
16:13	179n39
16:18	213n248
16:19	216n268
16:20	213n248
16:22	179n39
16:25–26	118n276
16:25	122n298
16:26	216n268

1 Corinthians

1:2–3	213n248
1:2	179n38
1:4	179n41
1:7–10	213n248
1:13	173n6
1:16	103n197
1:18–25	80n79
1:18	121n294, 148n80, 173n14, 173n16, 185n71, 221n295, 284n31
1:20	282n14
1:23	148n80, 149n88, 173n15
1:25–30	212n238
1:26–31	132n361
1:26–30	173n14
1:30	174n20, 179n38

2:1–2	148n80
2:2	173n15
2:4	319n252
2:6	282n14
2:7	204n184
2:8	203n177, 213n248, 282n14
2:10–13	320n257
2:10	122n298
3:15	284n32
3:16	96n170, 116n267, 319n249
3:18	282n14
3:19	282n15
4:9	192n103
4:10–13	192n102
4:10	179n38
4:12	74n52
4:17	179n39
4:21	79n78
5:1–2	128n333
5:4	213n248
5:5	284n32
5:7–8	283n26
5:9–13	128n333
5:10	282n15
6:1–11	128n333
6:9–10	285n42
6:11	174n19, 213n248
6:13–18	185
6:14	124n308, 212n234, 213n248, 219n287
6:16	329n298
6:18	97n176
6:19	96n170, 116n267, 319n249
6:20	196n121
7:10–11	11n62, 275n179, 328n297
7:10	337n1
7:18	71n45
7:19	116n267, 128n342
7:23	196n121
7:25	11n63
7:29–31	5n17

~

DEAD SEA SCROLLS

1QH[a] (*Hodayot or Thanksgiving Scroll*)

~

Rabbinic Writings

Modern Authors Index

Subject Index

Adam, 174, 179, 193, 202–4,
209–11, 233, 253–54,
294n81, 302
Angels
connection with worship,
299–300
evil angel, 291, 293
fellowship with, 253, 288–90,
296–301
heavenly army, 291, 298,
318–19
heavenly guardians, 201, 292
heavenly messenger, 210
Jacob's encounter with,
198n133
people transformed into,
202–4, 296–97, 301, 312; cf.
200, 207, 305n144
relationship with God, 201–2,
226
Satan, 201, 253, 261, 265n137,
272, 273n169, 275
Antioch
church in Antioch, 64, 68, 71,
73, 84, 109, 114, 117–20,
135–36, 332, 338
incident with Paul and Peter,
102, 106
Jewish community, 112–13,
176n29, 192, 195
within the Holy Land, 76

Banquets
Greco-Roman, 43, 56–58,
364n42, 376
Jews and Gentiles, 104n207
in the life of Jesus, 59–61, 171

messianic, 18n90, 38, 322
Baptism
baptismal liturgy, 124
baptized in/into the name,
195n120, 239
derived from Jesus, 240–41
entering a new reality, 181,
184n66
initiation rite, 5, 183, 194–95,
205–7
Jesus practicing baptism, 263,
265n139, 264–65
Jesus' baptism, 237, 263–65,
268, 273n169, 277n190
John practicing baptism, 60
metaphorical usage, 163–64
mystery religions, 233, 237
participation with Christ, 175,
177, 182–83, 190, 215, 222,
239
Paul's understanding of, 237,
240–41, 333
water rites, 164, 237, 239
Barnabas, 116, 119, 135, 338n6

Calendars, 54, 300–301
Charismatic Activity, 85–86,
168n187, 258
Christianity as a Jewish Sect,
77–78
Circumcision
dispute over, 65n2, 72, 116,
353n22, 353n24
Hellenists' view, 9, 66, 68,
71–72, 102, 108, 114–17,
135, 333